Business Leader Profiles
for Students

Business Leader Profiles
for Students

Volume 2

Jaime E. Noce, Project Editor

Detroit • New York • San Diego • San Francisco
Boston • New Haven, Conn. • Waterville, Maine
London • Munich

Business Leader Profiles
for Students

Staff

Editorial: Jaime E. Noce, *Project Editor*. Erin B. Braun, *Managing Editor, Content*. Jacqueline K. Mueckenheim, *Managing Editor, Product*. Jason B. Baldwin, Eric Hoss, Kathleen E. Maki Potts, Rebecca Marlow-Ferguson, *Contributors*. Synapse, the Knowledge Link Corporation, *Indexer*. Paul Lewon, *Technical Training Specialist*.

Imaging and Multimedia Content: Barbara J. Yarrow, *Manager*. Robyn V. Young, *Project Manager*. David G. Oblender, *Image Cataloger*. Lezlie Light, *Imaging Coordinator*. Randy Bassett, *Imaging Supervisor*. Robert Duncan, *Senior Imaging Specialist*.

Permissions: Maria L. Franklin, *Manager*. Margaret A. Chamberlain, *Permissions Specialist*.

Product Design: Cynthia Baldwin, *Manager*. Pamela A.E. Galbreath, *Senior Art Director*.

Manufacturing and Composition: Mary Beth Trimper, *Manager, Composition and Electronic Prepress*. Evi Seoud, *Assistant Manager, Composition and Electronic Prepress*. Rhonda Williams, *Buyer*

Copyright Notice

Table of Contents

S

T

W

Y

Z

Advisors and Contributors

Advisors

For this second volume of *Business Leader Profiles for Students (BLS)*, the editors worked in conjunction with Bob Kirsch, Librarian, Lake Forest High School, Lake Forest, Illinois. Mr. Kirsch served as one of the five original advisors to *BLS*, and he offered invaluable assistance and subject expertise in the development of the content for this volume.

Contributors

The following writers contributed to the text of *Business Leader Profiles for Students, Volume 2*:

Don Amerman

Kari Bethel

Lauri R. Harding

Daniel J. Harvey

Hilary White

Introduction

Business Leader Profiles for Students (BLS) provides readers with a comprehensive resource of business biographies that focus on the world's leading corporate founders, officers, directors, and innovators. As part of Gale's successful line of business products for students, *BLS* profiles prominent individuals who have made significant contributions to business and industry. Focusing on present, as well as past, leaders, *BLS* is specifically designed to meet the curricular needs of high school and undergraduate college students and their teachers, as well as the interests of general readers and researchers studying business.

With this second volume of *Business Leader Profiles for Students*, 100 new biographies were developed, and the scope for inclusion was expanded to give greater attention to women and minority business leaders, as well as to individuals associated with organizations/institutions that greatly impact business. Some of the individuals profiled include:

- **Hector Barreto, Jr.,** Administrator, U.S. Small Business Administration—one of the most influential leaders in business, he is the first Hispanic to ever hold this position.

- **Linda Chavez-Thompson,** Executive Vice President, AFL-CIO—highest rank ever held by a woman in the history of the organization.

- **Carly Fiorina,** President & CEO, Hewlett-Packard—the highest-ranking female executive in the United States.

- **Alan Greenspan,** Chairman, Federal Reserve Board—by controlling interest rates and monitoring the growth of the U.S. economy, the Chair position wields crucial influence over business and industry.

- **Robert L. Johnson,** Founder, Chairman, and CEO, Black Entertainment Television—established the first and only cable network with programming designed by and developed for African-Americans.

- **Richard Rivera,** President, Red Lobster—one of the highest-ranking minorities in the restaurant industry.

- **Muriel Siebert,** Founder & President, Muriel Siebert & Company—the first woman to own a seat on the New York Stock Exchange.

- **Pamela Thomas-Graham,** President & CEO, CNBC, and Executive Vice President, NBC—the highest-ranking woman executive to ever head a division at NBC.

In addition, 25 biographies from *BLS, Volume 1* were updated in order to provide more current information for business leaders who had experienced a significant and/or interesting change in either their professional and/or personal lives since the first volume was published. Updated profiles are included for the following individuals:

- **Jeff Bezos,** Amazon.com
- **Warren Buffett,** Berkshire Hathaway
- **Steve Case,** AOL Time Warner
- **Jim Clark,** myCFO, Inc.
- **Bennett R. Cohen,** Ben & Jerry's Homemade
- **Scott Cook,** Intuit
- **Jenny Craig,** Jenny Craig, Inc.
- **Michael Eisner,** Walt Disney Co.
- **Roger Enrico,** PepsiCo
- **Bill Gates,** Microsoft

- **Ellen Gordon,** Tootsie Roll Industries
- **Berry Gordy, Jr.,** Motown Records
- **Katharine Graham,** Washington Post
- **Tommy Hilfiger,** Tommy Hilfiger Corp.
- **Steve Jobs,** Apple Computer
- **Michael Jordan**
- **Calvin Klein,** Calvin Klein, Inc.
- **Scott McNealy,** Sun Microsystems
- **Rupert Murdoch,** The News Corp.
- **Howard Schulz,** Starbucks
- **Steven Spielberg,** Amblin Entertainment/Dream Works
- **Martha Stewart,** Martha Stewart Living
- **Ted Turner,** Turner Broadcasting
- **Jack Welch,** General Electric
- **Oprah Winfrey,** Harpo Inc.

Each entry in *Business Leader Profiles for Students* includes an overview of the person's greatest accomplishments, information on his/her personal life, career details, and a section on how the person influenced society and the economy. The reader will also learn about the person's education, management style, and business philosophy. To aid the reader, a chronology is provided in each entry, detailing key dates in the person's life, and interesting and important facts about the leader's life and career.

The topic list of both historical and contemporary business leaders for this volume was selected by surveying many sources on business, economics, and history and also by analyzing course curricula for various school districts.

While *BLS* focuses on individuals—their lives, careers, and impact—Gale's *Company Profiles for Students (CPS)* offers a comprehensive collection of essays on the world's top corporations, many of which are discussed within the *BLS* biographies. A collection that includes both *BLS* and *CPS* is sure to offer students and other patrons a comprehensive resource for vital information about the world's top individuals, corporations, and institutions in business and industry.

How Each Entry Is Organized

The chapters in *BLS* are organized alphabetically by last name. Each profile focuses on one business leader and begins with the person's name, date of birth, and the person's company/organization affiliation or occupation. The following elements are contained in each entry.

- **Overview:** this section provides a summary of the person's most important contributions to business, industry, and society. This paragraph will give interesting information on the person's greatest achievements.

- **Personal Life:** this section includes a detailed description of the person's life, circumstances of birth and childhood, family life, influential friends or relatives, experiences that may have affected the person later in life, marriage, religion, and circumstances around his/her death (if applicable). This section also includes information on the person's education, business or personal memberships, affiliations, or awards the person has won.

- **Career Details:** discusses significant factors about the career of the individual, especially when the greatest successes were achieved. It focuses on highlights of the person's career including details about what the person may have invented or innovations and new practices that have impacted business and industry. This section may also include information on how the individual tailored the product or service to compete successfully in the marketplace. It may detail the past and current strategies of the person's professional career or management style.

- **Social and Economic Impact:** this section discusses what effect the individual or the product or service has had on industry or on society in general.

- **Chronology:** the element featured in an easy-to-read box lists dates of major events or achievements highlighting the individual's personal and professional life.

- **Sources of Information:** lists contact information, including address, phone, and/or web site when available to help the reader with further research.

- **Bibliography:** provides user with suggested further reading on the business leader. These sources, also used to compile the essays, are publicly accessible materials such as magazines, general and academic periodicals, books, and online databases.

Comments and Suggestions

Gale welcomes your comments and ideas pertaining to *Business Leader Profiles for Students*. Readers who wish to suggest business leader names for inclusion in future volumes, who have other suggestions, and/or who are interested in further information on any of Gale's business products "for students", are encouraged to contact the Managing Editor:

Managing Editor, *Business Leader Profiles for Students*
Gale Group, Inc.
27500 Drake Rd.
Farmington Hills, MI 48331-3535
Telephone: (248)677-4253
Toll-Free (800)347-GALE
E-mail: BusinessProducts@gale.com

Raul Alarcon, Jr.

Overview

Raul Alarcon Jr. is the president and chief executive officer (CEO) of Spanish Broadcasting System, which owns and operates 26 Spanish–language radio stations across the United States.

Personal Life

Raul Alarcon Jr. was born in Camaguey, Cuba, in 1956 and moved to New York with his family as political refugees in 1960. His father, who started the first radio network in Camaguey, later worked as a disc jockey at WBNX–AM, a Spanish–language station in the Bronx, often bringing home stacks of cassette tapes. Even as a young boy, Alarcon would spend hours listening to and reviewing the music and giving his father advice on which songs should get air time.

Although Alarcon's parents started with very little, his father managed to fulfill his dream of buying his own radio station in 1983 when he purchased WSKO–AM in New York for $3.25 million. Thus began the family business of Spanish Broadcasting System (SBS). Alarcon admired his parents' hard work and determination, later saying, according to *Hispanic* magazine, "It is important to have a dream and hold it no matter what....If you can endure and persevere, you can achieve anything." In 1999 Alarcon was the recipient of the Governor's Award for Excellence, given by New York governor George Pataki.

Chronology:

Raul Alarcon, Jr.

1956: Born.

1960: Immigrated from Cuba to New York.

1983: Alarcon's father purchased first radio station and formed Spanish Broadcasting System (SBS).

1986: Became SBS's president and chief executive officer.

1998: New York SBS station WSKQ–FM topped charts for the first time, beating out longtime leader WLTW–FM.

1999: Completed initial public offering.

1999: Received Governor's Award for Excellence from New York Governor George Pataki.

1999: Purchased LaMusica.com.

2000: Purchased group of eight radio stations in Puerto Rico.

2001: New York SBS–owned station WPAT–FM knocked off air by September 11 terrorist attack on World Trade Center.

Career Details

Working with his father to develop SBS, Alarcon took over as the company's chief executive officer and president in 1986, positions he continues to maintain. Alarcon, Sr., serves as the chairman of the board of directors. Over the first several years of the life of SBS, Alarcon and his father purchased five more stations, covering Hispanic markets in New York, Florida, and Los Angeles. In the fall of 1988, Alarcon spent $55.5 million to buy WSKQ–FM in New York, promoted as "Mega 97.9." The station, originally purchased from the *Jewish Daily Forward* newspaper, was reformatted to provide salsa and merengue music, targeting an audience of 18– to 34–year–olds. *Fortune* reported the acquisition, noting that Alarcon was not afraid of paying high prices and quoting Alarcon as saying, "Some people call me a crazy Cuban, but if you don't take calculated risks, you can't make huge gains." It appears that this risk, anyway, was a profitable one. In the summer of 1998, Mega 97.9 passed long–time market leader WLTW–FM, a light rock station, to become the leading station in metropolitan New York.

From the start, Alarcon sought numerous opportunities to expand his company; by 1998 SBS owned a dozen stations. In a 1998 interview with the *New York Times*, Alarcon said, "I am continuing to buy stations. We have built up a tremendous amount of equity." Sales for 1998 totaled $85 million, an increase of 27 percent from the previous year's $66.7 million. Profits were also up 16 percent to $39 million.

True to his word, Alarcon added significantly to the number of stations under the SBS umbrella. In 1999 SBS acquired three more stations, bringing the number up to fifteen, making it the second largest Hispanic–owned radio broadcasting company behind number one Hispanic Broadcasting Corporation. Also in 1999, Alarcon was in the middle of negotiations to purchase a group of eight radio stations in Puerto Rico at the same time that SBS completed an initial public offering (IPO). The transaction, in which 21.8 million shares were sold to the public, was the second largest such offering in the history of the radio broadcasting industry. The funds generated by the IPO—approximately $435 million—gave Alarcon the chance to push down some of the substantial high–cost debt SBS had acquired due to its rapid expansion into new markets and to provide cash to finance further expansion. Initially, the IPO was expected to raise $280 million, but the stock rose from $20 to $28, thus generating an additional $155 million.

Just weeks after the IPO was finalized, Alarcon talked about the experience with Stephen Lacey in an *IPO Reporter* article, "It's exhilarating and draining at the same time. Obviously it's a matter of great pride to complete the IPO." Alarcon's positive vision of SBS's future was clear: "We're looking very expectantly to what we can do in the future. Now my stock is desirable to many people that we have been talking to for years." According to Lacey, "Because of Spanish Broadcasting's strategically clustered stations, which reach 51 percent of the Hispanic population in the United States, there was strong investor appetite for both the company's stock and note offerings."

By the end of 1999, SBS had thirteen of its radio stations in five of the nation's largest centers of Hispanic population: Los Angeles, New York, Miami, Chicago, and San Antonio. During 1999, SBS also purchased an 80 percent stake in JuJu Media, which operates LaMusica.com, a bilingual Spanish–English web site that provides coverage of current trends and issues in Latin music, culture, entertainment, and news. On January 14, 2000, Alarcon announced the completion of the acquisition Primedia Broadcast Group, a subsidiary of AMFM Operating, Inc., which held rights to eight Puerto Rican radio stations. The deal was valued at $90.3 million; SBS financed the expansion venture with cash on hand. The transaction made SBS the largest Hispanic–owned radio broadcasting company in the United States.

In February 2000, SBS released financial statements that reflected a healthy 18.9 percent increase in net revenues in the first quarter of the fiscal year 2000. The profits reflected an increase of $4.6 million to $28.9 million compared to the same quarter of 1999, which showed a net profit of $24.3 million. Cash flow also increased by nearly 25 percent. In a company press release picked up by *PR Newswire*, Alarcon noted, "This quarter's results reflect our continued success in identifying and exploiting the revenue potential of major FM radio outlets in the largest U.S. Hispanic markets. Our management team continues to effectively translate overall Hispanic market growth into increased, sustainable operating profits." At the end of fiscal year 2000, SBS had 568 employees; the nearly 42 percent increase in numbers reflected the ongoing and substantial acquisition of new radio stations.

In November 2000, SBS reached an agreement with the International Church of the Foursquare Gospel to purchase KXOL–FM (formerly KFSG–FM). This addition gave SBS two major stations in the Los Angeles area—newly acquired KXOL–FM and already established KLAX–FM. KXOL–FM, dubbed "El Sol 96.3," kicked off with a sensational promotion of a summer of commercial–free broadcasting of music—a total of 50,000 songs in a row, completely uninterrupted. With its 50,000–watts of power, KXOL became the strongest radio signal in the market. Upon the announcement of the completion of the purchase deal, Alarcon declared in a press release carried by *PR Newswire*, "I am confident of the strategic role KXOL will play in the future growth of SBS and I very much look forward to delivering Los Angeles listeners and advertisers the very best that Spanish radio has to offer."

By mid–2001 SBS owned and operated 26 stations (a number that includes pending acquisitions) and had expanded into new Hispanic market arenas in San Francisco and Dallas. Also, SBS's Chicago station WLEY–FM was quickly becoming a major station. Acquired in 1997 and known as "La Ley 107.9," WLEY was dominating the Hispanic market in the Windy City within two years. It ranked first across all major demographics in both 2000 and 2001, and it placed sixth on the list of all Chicago radio stations regardless of format or language.

Despite all the positive forces working in his favor, Alarcon is not without challenges. According to Geraldine Fabrikant of the *New York Times*, SBS faces three significant obstacles: increased competition, lower than average advertising profits, and heavy debt. First, there has been a significant increase in competition, in part due to the Federal Communication Commission's deregulation of the radio industry that permitted companies to own multiple stations (up to eight) within a single market. In 1993 there were 365 radio stations with a Spanish–language format; by 1998 that number had grown to 454. As a result of more choices on the air, KLAX, SBS's older station in Los Angeles, went from being ranked first in 1994 for that market's segment to being rated eleventh in 1998.

The second obstacle—and perhaps more significant to the overall durability of the company—is the stature of Hispanic radio stations as second–rate citizens among advertisers. For example, in 1997 the premiere New York SBS station "Mega 97.9" placed third in terms of listeners but just thirteenth in terms of advertising revenues. Advertisers tend to prefer more mainstream audiences; however, the rapidly growing Hispanic population may push reluctant advertisers to reconsider.

Finally, due to Alarcon's strong commitment to growth and his willingness to take calculated risks, SBS incurred a significant level of debt, which places a constant drain on profits. In the early 1990s, SBS took on $175 million in high–cost debt and another $175 million in private stock that paid shareholders 14.25 percent in additional shares annually. By 1998 Alarcon was considering his options for addressing his company's debt load—bring in a financially valuable partner, go public (IPO), or sell outright. Although Alarcon hinted that he had received a $1 billion offer to purchase the company, instead he chose to complete the IPO. Even after the public offering, Alarcon continues to own approximately 41 percent of shares and retains 83 percent of the voting power, placing him firmly in charge of his company's future.

Social and Economic Impact

In his ongoing drive to build his company, Alarcon has taken advantage of a growing Hispanic population in the United States and the corresponding increase in Hispanic listeners. The Hispanic radio audience grew from 5 percent to 6.5 percent of the overall radio listening ratings. Considering the U.S. Hispanic population is growing at four times the rate of the general population and is expected to become the largest U.S. minority group by 2005, numbers of Spanish–speaking listeners are expected to continue to rise.

Alarcon has also made a concerted effort to raise the nation's level of awareness of the significance of the growing Hispanic population. In 1999 SBS joined in partnership with National Puerto Rican Day Parade, Inc., to broadcast what is traditionally known as the nation's largest parade. In a *PR Newswire* release, Alarcon stated, "We are truly honored to be able to form this strategic alliance with the National Puerto Rican Day Parade—the first national media partnership for the parade. SBS has supported the New York Puerto Rican Day Parade for the last decade, and is now proud to use its national chain to promote the organization's efforts on a national basis.'

Alarcon's company was affected by the terrorist attacks against the World Trade Center in New York on September 11, 2001. WPAT–FM, an SBS–owned station, sent its signal from a transmitter facility on the north tower of the World Trade Center. Soon after the first airplane crashed into the tower, the station was knocked off the air. Alarcon worked quickly with officials of the Federal Emergency Management Association and had the station back on the air in just 59 hours. Prior to reestablishing the transmission, WPAT announcers joined sister station WSKQ–FM staff, which operates from the Empire State Building. According to a *PR Newswire* report, Alarcon said, "Amid this national tragedy, it is vitally important to clearly signal to listeners our unwavering determination and steadfast commitment to serving them and our city."

Sources of Information

Contact at: Spanish Broadcasting System, Inc.
    3191 Coral Way
    Miami, FL 33145
    Business Phone: (305) 441–6901
    URL: http://www.spanishbroadcasting.com

Bibliography

Broadcasting & Cable, 1 November 1999.

Davenport, Carol. "Raul Alarcon Jr., 33 (On the Rise)." *Fortune*, 3 July 1998.

Fabrikant, Geraldine. "Spanish Broadcasting Builds on Growing Radio Audience." *New York Times*, 14 December 1998.

Lacy, Stephen. "Loan Helps Position Spanish Broadcasting for IPO." *Bank Loan Report*, 22 November 1999.

Lacy, Stephen. "Road Warrior Spanish Broadcasting Markets IPO, Debt Offering and Credit Facility." *The IPO Reporter*, 22 November 1999.

Muto, Henry. "Programming Pioneers." *Hispanic*, September 1995.

"National Puerto Rican Parade, Inc. and Spanish Broadcasting System Announce First National Partnership for the Nation's Largest Parade." *PR Newswire*, 10 March 1999.

"SBS Announces Ratings Gains at WLEY Chicago." *PR Newswire*, 25 July 2001.

"Spanish Broadcasting System Clarifies Report: Chairman Still Holds More Than 70 Percent of the Voting Power of the Company." *PR Newswire*, 2 December 1999.

"Spanish Broadcasting System Debuts New Spanish FM KXOL in Los Angeles." *PR Newswire*, 30 April 2001.

"Spanish Broadcasting System Finalizes Puerto Rico Acquisitions." *PR Newswire*, 14 January 2000.

"Spanish Broadcasting System, Inc. Reports Record First Quarter Fiscal Year 2000 Results." *PR Newswire*, 7 February 2000.

Torpey–Kemph. "SBS Teams With LaMusica.com." *MediaWeek*, 10 May 1999.

"WPAT–FM in New York City Returns to the Air." *PR Newswire*, 17 September 2001.

Madame Beatrice Alexander Behrman

(1895-1990)
Alexander Doll Company

Overview

Madame Beatrice Alexander Behrman, often referred to simply as "Madame Alexander," became known as the First Lady of dollmaking of the twentieth century. Her innovative, high quality dolls were first introduced in the 1920s, and over the next 65 years, Alexander designed a wide array of highly popular dolls that remain valuable collectors' items.

Personal Life

Beatrice Alexander Behrman was born on March 9, 1895, in Brooklyn, New York, as Bertha Alexander—a name she later changed because she thought Beatrice sounded more sophisticated. Her mother, Hannah Pepper, was born in Austria and lived in Russia for a time before immigrating to the United States as a young woman to escape Jewish persecution. Two stories circulate among Alexander's descendents regarding her mother's early life. Some relatives testify that Alexander's mother was pregnant with Beatrice when she arrived in the United States, having lost her first husband and other children to the violent Jewish persecution. Other descendents suggest that the couple arrived in the United States together, and Alexander's father died when Alexander was approximately a year and a half old. Regardless, it is certain that Alexander's mother was widowed and married again shortly after arriving in the United States. Maurice Alexander, another young Russian immigrant, became Alexander's much–adored stepfather and the man she always considered her father. The family, including Alexander's three sisters, Rose, Flo-

Chronology:

Madame Beatrice Alexander Behrman

1895: Born.

1912: Married Philip Behrman.

1923: Established Alexander Doll Company.

1936: Created the Scarlet O'Hara doll.

1951: Won the first of four consecutive Fashion Academy Gold Medals for design.

1953: Developed a 36–doll series to honor the coronation of Queen Elizabeth II.

1955: Introduced Cissy, the first full–figured 21–inch doll.

1957: Introduced Cissette, a 10–inch version of the popular Cissy doll.

1988: Officially retired and sold Alexander Doll Company.

1990: Died.

---

rence, and Jean, grew up in the center of New York's thriving immigrant community of the Lower East Side on Grand Street.

Alexander was introduced to the world of dolls in infancy. In the same year as her birth, her stepfather opened the first doll hospital in the United States. At the turn of the century, dolls were made of porcelain, a very fragile, breakable substance. In the doll hospital, Alexander's father repaired the beloved dolls of innumerous grateful children. Before they were repaired, Alexander and her sisters often played with the broken dolls. Thus, Alexander's upbringing exposed her not only to the overwhelming poverty of the Lower End Side but also to the wealth and affluence of many of her father's customers. By the time she was eleven years old, Alexander knew she wanted to enjoy the finer things in life, often dreaming of riding in a carriage wearing a hat with ostrich feathers.

Shortly after graduating from high school as valedictorian on June 30, 1912, Alexander married Philip Behrman. She then completed a six–month accounting course and secured a position as a bookkeeper at the Irving Hat Stores. Behrman worked in the personnel department of a hat manufacturer. In 1915 the couple's daughter, Mildred, was born. Alexander's life was dis-

rupted by the onset U.S. involvement in World War I. Although her family remained physically safe, the economic impact was devastating. Because most dolls (and doll parts) were manufactured in Europe (primarily Germany and France), the source of dolls dried up as did the market for doll repair. With the future of the doll hospital, and her parents' financial well–being, highly uncertain, Alexander became determined to keep the family business open.

Soliciting the help of her three sisters, Alexander began sewing cloth dolls to sell in her father's shop. The dolls, made of inexpensive cloth rather than expensive and often unavailable china, were a great success and provided enough additional income to keep the doll shop open during the war years. The first doll designed by Alexander was based on a Red Cross nurse, thus drawing on the common national interest in the war effort, and foreshadowed Alexander's life–long ability to select models for her dolls that appealed to the general public. After the war ended, Alexander and her sisters continued to gather around their parents' kitchen table to manufacture dolls. Devastated by the war, Europe could not yet provide an adequate number of dolls to the United States, and, having decided she enjoyed the doll business, Alexander moved to expand her efforts into a permanent venture. The work also provided an effective distraction to Alexander's grief over the death of her second daughter in infancy during an outbreak of Spanish flu in the early 1920s. In 1923 Alexander secured a $1,600 loan and established the Alexander Doll Company. Thus she began her career as the world's leading lady of dollmaking.

Over the next 60 years, Alexander Doll Company grew from four sisters sewing around the kitchen table to a multi–million dollar business, the largest American doll company and the largest employer on the Lower East Side. Alexander's husband eventually quit his job at the hat company on the insistence of his wife to join the family business, working alongside his wife until his death in 1966. Led by Alexander's high standards for quality, artistic skill in fashion design, and efficient management abilities, her dolls became not just high quality toys for children but also collectors' items of great value; the Madame Alexander Doll Club was formed in 1961, with membership growing to over 12,000 by the early 1990s. At some point, probably during the 1920s, an advertising executive who thought Alexander looked French dubbed her "Madame Alexander," a name of honor that remained throughout her lifetime.

Alexander won numerous awards during her lifetime for her fine craftsmanship and innovation in dollmaking. In 1951 she was honored with the Fashion Academy Gold Metal Award, winning again in 1952, 1953, and 1954. On United Nations Day, October 22, 1965, the United Nations honored her at New York's City Hall with a full display of her 42 authentically dressed international dolls. In 1981 the Anti–Defamation League bestowed on her the Distinguished Public Service Award, and in 1986 she received the first Doll Reader Magazine Lifetime

Patti Lewis, current CEO, holding the Alexander Doll Company's Cissy doll. (AP/Wide World Photos.)

Achievement Award. FAO Schwartz, a high–end toy store, also bestowed on her a Lifetime Achievement Award, naming her the "First Lady of Dolls." She held a lifetime membership in the Brooklyn Institute of Arts and Sciences, and her dolls have been on display around the world, including the Brooklyn Children's Museum of New York, the Congressional Club and the Smithsonian Institute, both in Washington, D.C., and the Children's Trust Museum in New Delhi, India. In February 2000, she was inducted into the American Toymakers Hall of Fame, and in 2001 the Jewish Women's Archives announced Alexander as one of three winners of the Women of Valor award.

Alexander remained actively involved in her company into her early nineties. However, during the 1970s, she gradually turned over daily operations to her son–in–law, Richard Birnbaum, and grandson, William Birnbaum. She spent more and more time at her second home in Palm Beach, Florida, making rare public appearances on the company's behalf. At the age of 93, Alexander sold her company to private investors, and she officially retired, although she did maintain a primarily honorary position as design consultant. Two years later, on October 3, 1990, Alexander died in her sleep at her home in Palm Beach; she was 95 years old.

Career Details

After establishing the Alexander Doll Company, Alexander increased production by hiring 16 people from her neighborhood to sew dolls at her kitchen table in the evenings after work. She was soon able to afford the $40 a month rent to move her business to a small shop down the street. The first doll produced by the new company was based on Alice in Wonderland; it first sold for $14.40 a dozen wholesale, but after complaints by the shopkeepers who would stop by the house to carry off baskets of dolls to stock their shelves, Alexander lowered the price to $13.50 a dozen. Barely staying afloat, Alexander's company hit several roadblocks in its infancy. First, in the late 1920s, a burst water tower flooded the shop; all the dolls and clothing had to be carefully dried and sold at cut–rate prices. Then, in the early 1930s the Great Depression hit. Unexpectedly, however, the business survived the economically difficult times, probably because Alexander's lifelike dolls provided people a pleasant escape from the harsh realities of their lives.

Many of Alexander's early doll designs were based on popular literary characters: Alice in Wonderland, Little Dorrit, Tiny Tim, the Three Little Pigs, and Jo, Beth, Meg, and Amy, the four sisters from the classic *Little Women*. The *Little Women* series tied in with the release of the movie, thus adding to the dolls' popularity and introducing a marketing ploy Alexander would use again. Not only did the dollmaker work hard to identify models for her dolls that would appeal to the public, she also developed innovative design features that transformed the traditional flat–faced dolls into more lifelike creations. Even before switching from cloth to a moldable composite material made up of saw dust, resin, and paper–mache to create the dolls' heads, Alexander added three–dimensional characteristics to her cloth dolls' faces by devising new techniques of sculpting the cloth into noses, eyes, and cheeks. According to the Jewish Women's Archives, Alexander was ever attentive to the minutest details of her dolls' features: "I didn't want to make just ordinary dolls with unmeaning, empty smiles on their painted lips and a squeaky way of saying 'mama' after you pinched. I wanted to do dolls with souls. You have no idea how I labored over noses and mouths so that they would look real and individual." Alexander also introduced the use of rooted hair, sleep eyes, and walking dolls.

The Alexander Doll Company came to fame 1935 when Alexander announced that she had secured the right to produce a series of dolls based on the Dionne children, the world's first surviving quintuplets. The popular dolls were followed by the production of an entire line of clothing for the quintuplet dolls. Alexander also obtained the patent on a Scarlet O'Hara design based on the novel *Gone With the Wind*. She also developed dolls based on Walt Disney's "Snow White" and on England's Princess Elizabeth. By 1936, just 13 years after the creation of the company, *Fortune* magazine named Alexander Doll Company as one of the United States's three largest doll manufacturers.

In the early 1940s Alexander was once again leading the field in innovation as she was one of the first to begin using the revolutionary substance of plastic to manufacture dolls. Finally able to make the unbreakable doll, Alexander continued to focus on developing high quality artistic designs for her dolls and their clothing. For many of her creations, including the doll based on child star Margaret O'Brien, Alexander provided custom–made costume sets of clothing that modeled some of the most popular designs of the day. Alexander took the designing of her doll clothes very seriously, noting often that her dolls were merely mannequins so that she could display her design talents. In 1952 the department store Abraham and Straus commissioned Alexander to design a series of dolls based on the coronation of Queen Elizabeth II. After considerable research to ensure that her dolls and costumes were historically accurate, Alexander produced a 36–doll set that, along with the queen, included honor guards, choir boys, maids of honors, and the royal family. Alexander even purchased the fabric for the doll outfits at the same mill used by the queen herself. The doll set was priced at $25,000 in 1953.

Alexander made headlines again in 1955 when she introduced the world to the 20–inch Cissy doll, the first full–figured, high–fashion doll, complete with high heels and lacy undergarments. Cissy, on the market four years before Barbie, caused a stir and became an overwhelming success. Cissy was followed two years later by a 10–inch version, named Cissette. According to *Doll Reader*, Alexander boasted in a promotional brochure, "Cissette is jointed at the knee, hips, shoulder, and neck, and is so exquisitely modeled that she looks like a real person, tiny and perfect." The dolls, considered the hallmarks of the Alexander Doll Company, had their own catalog that offered innumerable accessories, including a complete wardrobe from hats and shoes to lingerie, casual wear to formal wear, and brass furnishings such as a bed, dining table and chairs, and a tea set.

Continuing to develop dolls based on literary, film, or real–life women over the next several decades, Alexander's creations included a 21–inch Jacqueline and a 15–inch Caroline doll, modeled after the presidential family, a 12–inch Nancy Drew doll, a series of dolls based on the film *The Sound of Music*, and a series of "First Ladies", commissioned to celebrate the United State's bicentennial. Despite the wide array of characters created by Alexander, each doll was produced carefully with the highest regard for quality. This often led to a much grander demand than supply; people would wait in line for hours simply to purchase an Alexander doll. But Alexander would never allow consumerism to thwart her commitment to excellence. She told *Play things* magazine in a 1984 interview, "We cannot supply the demand for our dolls. I do not permit cutting corners that would diminish the quality. My slogan is: 'American dolls for American children.'" Along with her desire to bring high quality toys to American children, Alexander was also pleased by the collectors' desire for her work, telling *Playthings*, "Doll collectors are highly cultured people who have the capacity to appreciate my work."

Social and Economic Impact

Alexander had a complex relationship with her social and business surroundings. On one hand, she was a great woman entrepreneur during a time when the business world was unaccustomed to female competitors. Rather than marrying rich—the only way her mother envisioned the fulfillment of Alexander's dreams of wealth—Alexander built her doll company into a multi–million dollar business. Until her retirement, Alexander ran her company with an unfailing sense of style, business sense, and independence. On the other hand, even though she was a pioneer for women's place in industry, her products often left her at odds with the growing feminist movement, who viewed the pretty dolls as a step back for women's rights and self–worth. Alexander argued strongly that the dolls provided positive role models for girls, teaching them how to love others and themselves. Nonetheless, her love of high fashion and pretty hats with ostrich feathers did little to endear her to the feminist movement.

At its peak, the Alexander Doll Company employed some 1,500 people at numerous factories and produced over a million dolls annually, with annual sales topping $20 million by the mid–1980s. The company, having suffered some financial setbacks after Alexander sold it in 1988, was acquired by another group of investors. The company maintains a factory in Harlem, which employs 600 people, making it the area's largest private employer; the company continues to produce high quality dolls for high–end toy dealers and collectors. Original "Madame Alexander" dolls are often priced high at the auction block. For example, a mid–1950s Lucille Ball doll, originally priced at $49.95, sold at auction for $4,000. Since her death, the famous doll maker has been memorialized with the creation of a "Madame Alexander" doll that celebrates her incredible life.

Sources of Information

Bibliography

Alexander Doll Company. Available at http://www.alexanderdoll.com.

Ellias, Marian. "Madame Alexander: 'American Dolls for American Children.'" *Playthings*, July 1984.

Healy, Kathleen. "A Doll's House." *Forbes*, 28 December 1987.

"Madame Alexander." *Jewish Women's Archives.* Available at http://www.jwa.org.

"Madame Alexander, Legendary Dollmaker, Dead at 95." *Playthings*, November 1990.

"Madame Alexander Wins Lifetime Award." *Playthings*, 6 May 1986.

Schwartz, Benita. "The Little Debutante ... Madame Alexander's Cissette." *Doll Reader*, September 2000.

Shaw, Gayle, and Milton Shaw. "History of Madame Alexander and Alexander Doll Company." *Treasures and Dolls.* Available at http://www.alexanderdolls.com.

Walter Hubert Annenberg

(1908-)
Annenberg Foundation

Overview

Walter Annenberg is well known as a publisher, philanthropist, and art lover. Heir to one of America's largest publishing empires, he managed to build his inheritance into an even greater force through his uncanny ability to predict the country's changing tastes and demands. Triangle Publications, under Annenberg's direction, developed and debuted *Seventeen* and *TV Guide*, two of America's most successful magazines. Annenberg's years as a publisher, however, were not without bitter criticism from those who charged him with using Triangle's *Philadelphia Inquirer* as a vehicle for his personal vendettas against members of the Philadelphia establishment who had steadfastly refused to admit him into their ranks. In the years since he sold off Triangle in 1988, Annenberg has further established himself as a philanthropist of extraordinary generosity. His Annenberg Foundation, founded in 1989, has distributed millions to educational institutions and most recently has focused on reforming pre–collegiate public school education.

Personal Life

Annenberg lives in suburban Philadelphia with his second wife, Lenore (Lee) Cohn Annenberg. He has a daughter, Wallis, from his first marriage to Veronica Dunkelman. That marriage ended in divorce and also produced a son, Roger, who committed suicide in 1962. Apart from managing his extensive philanthropic enterprises, he focuses much of his time on his vast collections of fine art.

Annenberg was born on March 13, 1908, in Milwaukee, Wisconsin, the only son of publisher Moses Louis Annenberg and Sadie Cecilia Friedman Annenberg. Moses Annenberg, a Russian Jew, came to this country from Russia at the age of eight in 1885. Tobias Annenberg, Moses' father, had shepherded Moses and his seven siblings from their native village of Kalvishken because of increasing persecution under the anti–Semitic regime of Czar Alexander III.

Walter Annenberg through much of his life has been inspired and challenged by his father's meteoric rise through the ranks of the publishing business. When he was old enough to work, Moses hooked up with the Hearst newspaper chain in Chicago, handling distribution chores. Moses proved willing to resort to some extreme measures to get the job done. When Hearst decided to launch the *Chicago American* in 1900, Moses and his staff used strong–arm tactics to ensure the paper got distributed. These tactics included assaulting rival distributors with baseball bats.

Moses moved his family to Milwaukee, where Walter was born in 1908. In 1922, Moses purchased the *Daily Racing Form*, the most popular horseracing publication in America. Shortly thereafter he founded Nationwide News Service, a wire service designed to disseminate racing results quickly and in detailed form. Before long, Moses added the *Morning Telegraph* to his stable of racing publications, now operating under the name of Triangle Publications. The older Annenberg next acquired the *Philadelphia Inquirer*, a purchase that soon got him and his son into hot water with the federal government. Moses unashamedly used his latest purchase as a vehicle to advance his political and ideological philosophy, which was deeply conservative and staunchly opposed to the liberal policies of the Democratic presidential administration of Franklin D. Roosevelt.

Young Walter attended the prestigious Peddie School in Hightstown, New Jersey, and in 1927 graduated from the University of Pennsylvania's Wharton School with a degree in business.

Career Details

Shortly after his graduation from the Wharton School in 1927, Walter joined the family business, eventually rising through the ranks to the position of vice president by 1939. That year, both Moses and Walter, as well as three Annenberg associates, were indicted on charges of tax evasion. The senior Annenberg, in April 1940, pleaded guilty to one count of evading taxes in return for the government's dropping all other charges against him, his son, and his associates. Moses was sentenced to three years in prison, and his companies were ordered to pay nearly $10 million in penalties. Moses was released from prison in June 1942 after he was diagnosed with a massive brain tumor. He died a month later. On the day of

Chronology:
Walter Hubert Annenberg

1908: Born.

1927: Graduated with business degree from Wharton School.

1936: Father acquired *Philadelphia Inquirer*.

1939: Indicted, with father, on tax evasion charges.

1942: Father died, leaving Walter in charge of Triangle Publications.

1944: *Seventeen* launched by Triangle.

1953: Triangle began publishing *TV Guide*.

1969: *Inquirer* and sister newspaper sold for $55 million.

1969: Appointed ambassador to England by Nixon.

1988: Sold Triangle Publications for $3.2 billion.

1989: Established Annenberg Foundation.

his death, according to biographer John Cooney, author of *The Annenbergs: The Salvaging of a Tainted Dynasty*, Moses told his son: "You know, Walter, who knows what is the scheme of things? My suffering is all for the purpose of making a man out of you."

Before his death, Moses had often confided in friends his profound doubts about Walter's readiness to take on the management of a major publishing chain. The challenge facing Walter was made all the more burdensome by the massive debt overhanging the company, much of it back taxes and penalties owed to the federal government. The family's humiliation over this widely publicized scandal and his subsequent efforts to repay the debt proved traumatic for Walter. In 1946, he told his fiancée that the whole affair had left him fearful of "getting enmeshed with federal trade authorities, Treasury snoopers, agents, immigration officials, Customs officers, and various and sundry other official (and officious) individuals who have and still would like to make life miserable for me."

However, when it came to managing Triangle, Walter proved himself more than equal to the task. Only two years after his father's death, Annenberg created a magazine for teenage girls, a market he believed was woefully underserved. That magazine, *Seventeen*, proved immensely popular right from the start and remains one of

Walter Annenberg speaking at the White House. (AP/Wide World Photos.)

the best–selling publications in America. Annenberg's next brainchild proved even more inspired. Seeking to provide TV viewers around the country with an accurate guide to programming, Triangle, in 1953, launched *TV Guide*, a venture that many in the business felt sure was bound to fail, largely because it involved the publication of multiple regional editions. Although the guide got off to a somewhat slow start, it eventually grew into one of the top–selling magazines in the country, a position it continues to enjoy.

Like his father, Walter came under fire from critics who charged that he used his Philadelphia newspapers, particularly the *Inquirer*, as a weapon against some of his enemies as well as those in Philadelphia society who

had rebuffed his efforts to join their ranks. Politicians opposed by Annenberg were often denied coverage in the newspaper altogether or subjected to vitriolic attacks on its editorial page.

Criticism of Walter's management of the *Inquirer* and its sister publication, the *Philadelphia Daily News*, came to an abrupt end in 1969, when Annenberg sold both Philadelphia newspapers for a reported total of $55 million.

That same year, Annenberg was nominated to be U.S. ambassador to the Court of St. James in England—one of the most coveted diplomatic positions available—by President Richard Nixon, a close personal friend of the publisher. It was not a job that Annenberg jumped at, fearing he might bring dishonor upon Nixon and his country through his lack of diplomatic experience. In the end, he was convinced by Nixon to take the post and underwent a trying Senate hearing, during which his family's past entanglements with the law were thoroughly dissected. Despite this humiliating ordeal, Annenberg's nomination was approved. Both Annenberg and his wife, Lee, were met with a somewhat subdued reception by the British, particularly in the press where he was characterized as a wealthy American businessman who had bought the ambassador's job. However, Annenberg worked hard to master his new job and to learn more about the British people and their ways. Helping to win him acceptance among the British were a number of business deals between U.S. and British interests that Annenberg took steps to facilitate. By the end of his years in England, he had made close alliances with many in London, including the Queen Mother. He returned to the United States in 1974.

Throughout his lengthy publishing career and beyond, Annenberg developed and maintained strong ties with the nation's political leaders, particularly those in the Republican Party. In addition to his close relationship with Richard Nixon, Annenberg was good friends of Ronald Reagan, long before the latter was elected to the White House. In fact, in 1975 Annenberg introduced Reagan to Margaret Thatcher, whom Annenberg knew well from his days as ambassador to England. Reagan and Thatcher would later develop an extraordinarily close relationship themselves.

The collection of fine art—a passion of Annenberg's since the 1940s—occupied an increasing segment of his time after his return from London. A fancier of impressionist and post–impressionist art, he assembled one of the largest private collections of paintings from those periods. A strong believer in the importance of making great art accessible to all Americans, he unveiled a plan to create a fine arts center at New York's Metropolitan Museum of Art. Annenberg's vision called for a center that employed a wide variety of media to teach the public about both the nature and history of art. When Met and city officials balked at Annenberg's plan, he abruptly withdrew his offer, which would have involved a grant of $40 million. In 1991 he once again demonstrated his belief in the role of the Met as America's premier art museum when he announced his intention to leave his beloved art collection to the prestigious New York museum upon his death.

In 1988, Annenberg sold Triangle Publications to Australia–born media giant Rupert Murdoch for $3.2 billion. The following year he founded the Annenberg Foundation, which today enjoys an endowment of more than $3 billion, making it the twelfth largest foundation in the country. From its inception, the focus of the foundation has been on improving the quality of pre–college education in this country. This is perhaps best exemplified by Annenberg's best–known grant—a total of $500 million pledged in 1993 towards school reform. Ap-

proximately 10 percent of the grant was earmarked for the National Institute of School Reform, based at Brown University, with most of the rest being distributed to bureaucrats, consultants, researchers, and study groups who specialize in school reform.

Social and Economic Impact

Annenberg built Triangle Publications—heavily burdened by debt when he inherited it in 1942—into a media giant of enormous influence. Most significantly, he developed and launched two of America's most successful magazines, *TV Guide* and *Seventeen*. In 1988, seeing no successor within his family to continue to lead Triangle, Annenberg sold his publishing empire to Rupert Murdoch for $3.2 billion. Perhaps even more important are Annenberg's contributions to his country as a philanthropist. Much of his generosity has been funneled through the Annenberg Foundation, which he founded in 1989 and which focuses largely on improving the quality of pre–college education in this country. Other recipients of Annenberg's beneficence have been art museums throughout the country.

Annenberg's generosity to educational institutions is legendary. He gave the University of Pennsylvania a grant of $239 million to set up the Annenberg School of Communications and later provided $177 million to the University of Southern California to set up a similar school there. He has added more than $130 million to the endowment fund of the Peddie School, the prep school he attended as a youth, and also made generous grants to the United Negro College Fund and Harvard University. Annenberg, in 1997, was described as "the most beneficent philanthropist in the history of the world" in a survey conducted by *American Benefactor*, a magazine that ceased publication in 1998.

Sources of Information

Contact at: Annenberg Foundation
    St. David's Center, Ste. A–200, 150 Radnor–Chester Road
    St. David's, PA 19087
    Business Phone: (610) 341–9066
    URL: http://www.whannenberg.org

Bibliography

The Complete Marquis Who's Who. New Providence, NJ: Marquis Who's Who, 2001.

Cooney, John. *The Annenbergs: The Salvaging of a Tainted Dynasty.* New York: Simon & Schuster, 1982.

Grossman, Jennifer A. "Philanthropy Is Revolutionizing Education." *USA Today,* 9 May 2000.

Ogden, Christopher. *Legacy: A Biography of Moses and Walter Annenberg.* New York: Little, Brown, & Co., 1999.

"Philadelphia Museum of Art's $200 Million Capital Campaign Passes $125 Million Mark." *PR Newswire,* 7 September 2001.

C. Michael Armstrong

(1938-)

AT&T Corporation

Overview

C. Michael Armstrong is the chief executive officer (CEO) and chair of the board of the AT&T Corporation. Since joining AT&T in 1997, he has invested over $10 billion in developing technology and expanding the company's infrastructure. His goal is to remake the company, which had been floundering in the declining long distance business, into a state–of–the–art high tech communications provider.

Personal Life

Armstrong was born on October 18, 1938, in Detroit, Michigan. He graduated from the University of Miami of Ohio in 1961 with a Bachelor of Science degree in business and economics. Fifteen years later, in 1976, he completed coursework in advanced management at Dartmouth Institute. He received honorary Doctor of Law degrees from Pepperdine University and Loyola Marymount in 1997 and 1998, respectively.

Actively involved in numerous organizations, Armstrong serves as a trustee of Johns Hopkins University and is a member of the advisory board of Yale's School of Management. He is a director of Citicorp, Inc., a member of the board of directors of Travelers Corporation, and a supervisory board member of the Thyssen–Bormemisza Group and the National Cable Television Association. He is chairman of the President's Export Council, which serves in an advisory capacity to the President and Secretary of Commerce on matters of international trade. He also chairs the Federal Communications

Commission's Network Reliability and Interoperability Council. Other positions include a seat on the Council on Foreign Relations, the National Security Telecommunications Advisory Committee, and the Defense Policy Advisory Committee on Trade.

Known for his energetic optimism, his hands–on approach to management, and his courage to take on risks, the 6–foot 2–inch, 210–pound Armstrong has built a strong reputation in the business community for his accomplishments. Armstrong enjoys riding his collection of Harley Davidson motorcycles, skiing, and spending as much time with his family as possible. Ranking 29th on Worth.com's 1999 list of top corporate leaders and moving up to 25th place in 2000, Armstrong told Worth.com that his mother is his personal hero because she "believed in my brothers and me, and gave us the confidence to believe we could do anything we set our minds to—if we worked at it hard and long enough."

Career Details

Armstrong spent the first 30 years of his career with IBM. Starting out as a systems engineer, over the next three decades he moved his way up the corporate ladder to attain the position of senior vice president and chairman of the board of IBM World Trade Corporation. In 1991, having decided that he had reached a plateau within IBM, Armstrong resigned to become chairman of the board and chief executive officer of General Motors–owned Hughes Electronics. During his six–year tenure at Hughes, Armstrong moved the giant aerospace company away from primarily defense, specializing in governmental contract in space and communications technology, to become a diversified enterprise that refocused on the public sector, including development of DirecTV, the company's notable entry into the satellite television business.

However, Armstrong stirred controversy in 1993 when, as Hughes's CEO, he aggressively lobbied Congress and President Clinton to ease restrictions on the exportation of technology to China so that he could complete a $240 million deal with Beijing involving two Hughes–made satellites. The State Department had banned sales of all satellites to China for two years upon learning that China had been selling the technology to Pakistan and was strongly opposed to easing the sanctions. As a Republican, Armstrong held little personal sway with the Democratic White House, so he hired two high–powered Democratic lobbyists to pitch his case. The results were swift; within weeks the regulation of satellites was transferred from the Department of State to the Department of Commerce, creating a loophole that allowed Armstrong to deal with China. In 1997 Armstrong was called before a Senate investigation panel to testify, at which time he strongly maintained the legality of his actions, noting that no sensitive technology that

Chronology:
C. Michael Armstrong

1938: Born.

1961: Began 30–year career with IBM.

1991: Appointed chairman and chief executive officer (CEO) of Hughes Electronics.

1993: Controversy arose over Hughes' lobbying practices.

1995: AT&T announced plans to restructure.

1997: Selected as chairman and CEO of AT&T.

1998: Purchased Tele–Communications, Inc. and MediaOne Group.

1999: AT&T stock prices rose 60 percent in value during first 18 months as CEO.

2000: Announced second restructuring of company; stock prices plummeted.

2001: AT&T Wireless completed split with parent company.

could be useful to hostile militaries was attached to the satellites involved in the transactions.

In 1996 Armstrong met with an AT&T executive recruiter; however, when he discovered that he was being approached for the position of chief operations officer rather than CEO, he politely declined any interest in the position. AT&T hired John Walter to fill the company's top spot, but to the company's embarrassment, the relationship failed quickly, and Walters tendered his resignation soon after he was appointed. With the chairmanship of the company open once again, this time AT&T called Armstrong back to the table to offer him the job he wanted. In November 1997, AT&T named Armstrong the new chairman of the board and CEO; Armstrong received nearly $15 million in restricted stock awards for accepting the position.

When Armstrong came on board AT&T, the giant communications company was struggling to come to terms with its future. In September 1995, the company announced it was restructuring into three separate, publicly traded entities. The systems and equipment division became Lucent Technologies; the computer segment split off as NCR; and all the communication services remained as AT&T. It constituted the largest voluntary break–up

C. Michael Armstrong. (AP/Wide World Photos/Marty Lederhandler.)

From a company that handles mostly voice calls to a company that connects you to information in any form that is useful to you—voice, data, and video. From a primarily domestic company to a truly global company." Armstrong wanted to move AT&T from simply a long–distance provider to a company equipped to provide full–scale communication services.

Within the first two years, Armstrong shelled out over $100 billion for expansion. In June 1998 he purchased Tele–Communications, Inc. (TCI) for $48 billion, followed by the purchase of cable provider MediaOne Group, a $58 billion acquisition. He also formed a $10 billion venture with British Telecom, called Global Ventures, to move into the international markets. Other purchases included TCG, a provider of local telephone service to businesses and IBM Global Network, a data networking service. Armstrong's vision was to provide a complete line of communications produced from one place, so–called "one-stop shopping." If the future evolved as Armstrong planned, customers would be able to make local and long distance calls, access the Internet, get cable and pay–per–view television, plus wireless and data communication services—all from AT&T.

Armstrong's bold vision ignited new energy within the company, among shareholders, and on Wall Street. In May 1999, *Newsweek*'s Allan Sloan called Armstrong "AT&T's Golden Boy," noting, "he's earned a glittering reputation on Wall Street, which loves his dramatic multi–billion–dollar deals, the huge fees they generate and the attention he devotes to the care and feeding of the investment bankers and analysts." Armstrong's popularity extended to shareholders, too; stocks rose 60 percent in the first 18 months after his appointment as head of the company. By mid–2000 AT&T was working to expand three networks—broadband, wireless, and data— and the company operated four quasi–independent businesses: cable, wireless, business, and consumer.

The only problem with Armstrong's grand plan was that life very rarely comes out the way it is planned. The hope was that AT&T's expanded cable services would boost profits enough to make up for the downfall of its consumer (i.e., long distance) division, thus providing Armstrong enough time to grow his other new ventures. However, AT&T Broadband, its cable division, proved to be the least profitable of its four segments, posting a loss of $5.4 billion dollars in 2000, primarily because broadband Internet access and cable–network local telephone service did not grow as fast as expected. Also, the necessary time and expense to expand the infrastructure to realize Armstrong's vision cost much more in time and financial resources than first assumed. Shortly after the announced AT&T–TCI merger, *Business Week*'s Peter Elstrom noted, "Think of it this way: AT&T has bought the dirt road that leads to American homes. Now it must grade it and pave it to carry all the new traffic." Early excitement turned into concern as AT&T failed to show the quick results expected by investors. As a result, shareholders began dumping their stock *en masse*, causing the price to plummet.

of a private company in American history. The problem faced by Armstrong when he came to AT&T—which maintains over 80 million customers, 163,000 employees, and in excess of $62 billion in revenues—was simple to understand, but more challenging to solve. In 1997 over 80 percent of AT&T's business was long distance; however, the consumer long distance market and profitability was disappearing rapidly. Armstrong felt it was imperative to act quickly and decisively. To remake the corporation into a viable business for the next century, Armstrong took aggressive, sometimes risky, steps to set AT&T on a new path. "We are transforming AT&T," he wrote in the company's 1998 Annual Report, "from a long distance company to an 'any–distance' company.

By October 2000, stocks had fallen to $24 a share, some 20 percent less than when Armstrong was hired three years before. In another bold attempt to salvage the value of stock, Armstrong announced on October 25, 2000, that AT&T would once again undergo restructuring. By breaking up the company into four separate businesses—wireless, cable television, consumer, and business services—each with separate management organizations and shareholders, Armstrong hoped to isolate the weaker divisions from those with the most growth potential. *Business Week* reported that Armstrong noted, 'The creation of these four companies is the foundation for a path to value creation. The journey hasn't been simple, but I believe it will be successful." Despite Armstrong's optimism, investors were not completely convinced, and some were outright hostile to the idea, believing that Armstrong had abandoned his foundational concept of "one-stop" communications shopping.

Armstrong maintained his optimism and defended his actions. Expanding at the price of bottom–line profits for the first three years, Armstrong decided that the new separated structure would best serve the needs of the customers and the shareholders as well as providing new motivation for employees. In a February 2001 interview with *Business Week*'s Steve Rosenbush, Armstrong explained, "Shareowners had been very patient while we made those investments....And would shareholders have the patience to wait much longer [to see a return on their investments]? I judged not. It was time for the currencies, the equities, and the shareholder value to come through. I couldn't make it happen any other way." Rejecting the idea that the devaluation of AT&T stock was due to the restructuring plan, Armstrong asserted that the drop in value was a result of the industry–wide destabilization of the basic long distance service. He also reminded his critics that in three years, AT&T had come a long way, from simply being a long distance provider to a company prepared to meet the challenges of the next century of high tech global communication demands.

Social and Economic Impact

The final verdict is still out on what the total impact of Armstrong's aggressive strategies will be on AT&T in particular and the communications industry in general. To no one's surprise AT&T Consumer is expected to continue to operate with a negative profit margin. Some analysts speculate that this weak link in the AT&T structure may likely be sold off in the future. Although Business AT&T was negatively affected by a restructuring of the sales force early in 2000 that resulted in poor customer service and the loss of several large accounts, some analysts believe it has the potential eventually to show significant revenue growth. AT&T Wireless is the hands–down favorite to be the most successful product line offered by the AT&T family. With over 11 million customers, it is the third largest wireless provider in the

United States. By selling stock in 2000, the company raised $10 billion, which can be used to purchase technology and upgrade its services. With strong investor support of some $42 billion, in July 2001 AT&T Wireless completed its split with AT&T. Armstrong began to come under pressure from investors in 2001 to merge AT&T Broadband with an outside company. Armstrong is unwilling to consider selling unless an ideal offer comes his way. Instead, he continues to preach patience to shareholders who have yet to see a return on their investments.

"What I started out to do was to re–create AT&T and in doing that, I set out against time, which was my enemy," Armstrong told the *Wall Street Journal* in July 2001. "Certainly some wonder whether we'll deliver the value of this strategy. The first legacy of that strategy is wireless. Business services, consumer and broadband will fulfill the same potential." Armstrong has hinted that he may retire in 2004 when he turns 65. Until then, he continues working to ensure that he leaves behind a healthier, more productive, and more profitable AT&T.

Sources of Information

Contact at: AT&T Corporation
32 Avenue of the Americas
New York, NY 10013–2412
Business Phone: (212)387–5400
URL: http://www.att.com

Bibliography

"Armstrong on the Record." *Business Week Online*, 5 February 2001. Available at http://www.businessweek.com.

"AT&T–TCI: Telecom Unbound." *Business Week*, 6 July 1998. Available at http://www.businessweek.com.

"Biography of Michael Armstrong." International Trade Administration, U.S. Department of Commerce, 2001. Available at http://www.ita.doc.gov/td/pec/bioarmst.html.

Elstrom, Peter. "AT&T: Breaking Up is Still Hard to Do." *Business Week*, 6 November 2000.

"50 Best CEOs." *Worth*, 2000. Available at http://www.worth.com.

Hochheiser, Sheldon. "History of AT&T." AT&T, Inc., May 2001. Available at http://www.att.com.

"Q & A: A Frank Talk with Mike Armstrong." *Business Week*, 23 July 2001.

Sloan, Allan. "AT&T's Golden Boy." *Newsweek*, 10 May 1999.

Solomon, Deborah, and Nikhil Deogun. "For AT&T's Armstrong, Comcast Bid Validates His Vision—Sort Of." *Wall Street Journal*, 13 July 2001.

"Webcast With C. Michael Armstrong." National Press Club, National Public adio, 7 February 2001. Available at http://www.npr.org.

Hector V. Barreto, Jr.

(1961-)

U.S. Small Business Administration

Overview

In July 2001, Hector Barreto Jr. was confirmed by the U.S. Senate as the 21st Administrator of the U.S. Small Business Administration (SBA) in Washington, D.C. His organization has 2,800 employees, 70 district offices nationwide, a 2001 budget of $900 million, and a loan portfolio of $45 billion. In 2001 there were an estimated 25 million small businesses in the United States. At the time of Barreto's appointment, he was just 39 years old.

Personal Life

Barreto grew up in Kansas City, Kansas. His father, Hector Sr., had come to the United States from Guadalajara, Mexico, in 1958 and started out by picking potatoes for 50 cents an hour. Barreto adored his father, and he credits his family upbringing with the business and personal success he now enjoys.

As a nine–year–old boy, Barreto waited on tables in his father's Independence, Missouri, restaurant, "Mexico Lindo," which became a big success. His family eventually opened up two other restaurants in Kansas City, and lived out what they always spoke of, "the American Dream." Barreto's father became a well–known Kansas City businessman, president of Sol International, Inc., and co–founder of the U.S. Hispanic Chamber of Commerce in 1979. In 1986 the senior Barreto was a presidential appointee to the delegation of the National White House Conference on Small Business.

Barreto later worked in some of his father's other businesses, including an import–export company and a

construction company. On one such job, Barreto actually laid marble tile that was imported from Mexico to use in construction. The laborious work proved a factor in shaping his desire to work with his mind, not his physical strength. He decided to pursue a career in management.

Barreta attended Kansas City's Rockhurst University and graduated with a degree in business administration and management and in Spanish. His close friends described him as "polished and driven" for a 2001 article in *Hispanic* magazine. Barreto told the magazine's interviewers that, while he never dreamed he would end up as the head of the SBA, he always had "ganas" to do something big. Translated loosely, *ganas* means "an unrelenting desire to accomplish a great goal." Barreto is quoted in the magazine's article as stating, "This isn't just a job for me. It's something I consider a higher purpose."

Barreto often refers to the influence his parents have had upon his own life and purpose. According to him, their *ganas* to achieve the "American Dream" affected him so much that he made particular mention of it during the Senate confirmation hearings. Barreto is quoted in the *Hispanic* magazine article as having said, "My father is a hero to me, he is my role model. He has been a trailblazer all his life, always a visionary leader. This is an immigrant who came to the United States with no money or contacts and he really built a life. To see in one generation his son obtain such a position was a culmination of a dream for him."

Barreto had already amassed an impressive portfolio of awards and honors even before his presidential appointment. For his previous work in promoting diversity and improving race relations, he was awarded the Gold Medal of Honor by the Multicultural Institute of Leadership. He also has received recognition from the U.S. Congress, the California State Senate and Assembly, and the County of Los Angeles for his contributions to the business community and professional relations. In 1999 *Hispanic* magazine named him one of America's "100 Most Influential Hispanics."

Barreto and his father share a love for politics and are both active members of the Republican Party. Barreto Jr. served as co–chairman of the Bush–Cheney campaign in California during the 2000 campaign. He is married to Robin and has two daughters, Avrial and Tahlia.

Career Details

Shortly after graduation from college in 1982, Barreto and a friend left Kansas City and went to work together as merchandisers for the Miller Brewing Company. Their jobs took Barreto to Texas as an area manager, and his friend to Atlanta. Four years later, in 1986, Barreto moved to Southern California to start his own company, Barreto Insurance and Financial Services,

Chronology:
Hector V. Barreto, Jr.

1961: Born in Kansas City.

1982: Earned B.S.B.A. at Rockhurst University.

1982: Became Area Manager for the Miller Brewery Inc.

1986: Launched Barreto Insurance and Financial Services in Los Angeles.

1997: Named chairman of the Latin Business Association.

1999: Named as one of 100 Most Influential Hispanics in *Hispanic* magazine.

2000: Served as vice chairman of Bush Campaign in California.

2000: Named vice chairman of the U.S. Hispanic Chamber of Commerce.

2001: Appointed to head the SBA.

in Los Angeles. His clear intention was to serve the undertapped market in the region's large Hispanic communities. By appealing to this niche population while forming strategic alliances in the local business community, Barreto was able to increase his revenues from approximately $65,000 in the first year to $3 million in 2000. Primarily an employee benefits firm, the company has ten employees and continues to serve local interests. Barreto has said that he wants the business to continue growing so that he can pass it on to his children one day. He also started a securities broker–dealer firm, Telacu/Barreto Financial Services, that specialized in retirement planning.

Appointed in 1997 to head the Latin Business Association (LBA) in Los Angeles, Barreto was credited with doubling revenues and membership during his two–year appointment that ended in 1999. He also created the Latino Business Expo, an event that focuses on procurement opportunities, corporate exhibitions, and business education. During his tenure with LBA, Barreto founded the Latin Business Association Institute (LBAI), an extension of LBA that provides technical assistance, education, and business development opportunities for its members.

In 2000 Barreto was appointed vice chairman of the U.S. Hispanic Chamber of Commerce, co–founded by his father. The organization represents approximately 1.5 million Latino businesses in the United States and is the largest Latino business organization in the country. The appointment to vice chair gave Barreto the visibility he needed in Washington. President Bush nominated Barreto to the SBA position in February 2001, but his confirmation hearing was delayed over the summer by (among other things) the shift in power within the Senate from Republican to Democrat. Once the hearings began, he sailed through the process (the Senate Committee on Small Business and Entrepreneurship voted an uncontested 19–0 for his confirmation)—having already been endorsed by 149 groups and business leaders. Several senators spoke in favor of his candidacy as well, praising his lengthy experience as an entrepreneur and his involvement in business groups that extended opportunities to minority business owners. He is the first administrator from the West Coast.

While there was some concern among those in Washington that his lack of experience working in a federal bureaucracy might inhibit his ability to make an impact, Barreto's longtime friend Manuel Rosales told *Hispanic* magazine interviewers that skeptics would be pleasantly surprised with Barreto's abilities. "It's been a long time since the SBA has had a head who was actually a small businessman," Rosales stated. "He understands the complexities of running a small business on a shoestring." Another interviewee in the same article, Richard Amador, president and chief executive of CHARO Community Development Corporation (which also serves small businesses in Los Angeles) described Barreto as "having the qualities of a leader, but above all of that, he's *buena gente* (good people)." He stated that Barreto possessed "the human spirit" that was often found lacking in leaders and executives.

Moreover, the financial services business that he runs with his wife has led to an expanding number of small business enterprises among minorities, especially women of color. Barreto hopes to carry that initiative and experience into the SBA's list of priorities. SBA's charter stipulates that it will ensure small businesses a "fair proportion" of government contracts and sales of surplus property. And within that "fair proportion" that is slated for small businesses, Barreto intends to make sure that there is also a "fair proportion" of minority–run small businesses represented as well.

In his new $133,700 position, Barreto will oversee a portfolio of direct and guaranteed business loans and disaster loans worth more than $45 billion. He also will direct financial and business development plans to the nation's entrepreneurs. According to the SBA's organizational chart found on its Web site, Barreto has an executive deputy–administrator under him to help in overseeing the massive agency. Associate deputy–administrators head up the areas of Capital Access, Entrepreneurial Development, Government Contracting and Business Development, and general Management & Administration. Reporting directly (through his deputy administrator) are the Offices of Field Operations, General Counsel, Disaster Assistance, Hearings and Appeals, Congressional and Legislative Affairs, Veterans Business Development, EEO and Civil Rights Compliance, and the Chief Financial Officer.

Prior to Barreto's appointment, the SBA had taken some heat from Capitol Hill for not better informing fledgling small businesses of the services available—from start–up loans to technical assistance. Critics of the SBA, created in 1953 to "aid, counsel, assist and protect. . . the interests of small business concerns." complain that the agency helps only about one percent of its target market each year—or about 250,000 businesses. But Barreto is committed to making the SBA more user–friendly (with such things as extended office hours and upgrades to its Web site) and plans to reach out to business owners across the country through advocacy and entrepreneurial development. In fact, outreach effort is one of the top priorities Barreto identified for SBA, and in an interview with the *Los Angeles Times*, he stated that he planned to "have a top–down review of the agency and get a handle on the programs that are working well." For those that were not, he planned to demand a full accounting

Barreto stated in a *Los Angeles Times* article that he saw untapped potential in the SBA's venture capital program, in which SBA–guaranteed funds supplement the money already committed by private venture capital firms to create privately owned and managed investment firms. As his friend from his Miller Brewing Company days told Kevin Murphy in the *Kansas City Star*, "He has a passion for business, a passion for bringing ideas and people together."

Social and Economic Impact

Barreto believes he brings a fresh perspective to Washington. As he stated in *Hispanic* magazine, "I think anytime a new leader comes into a position like this, they will bring their enthusiasm and excitement and vision for the future. I think that's positive." He went on to add, "I don't feel pressure that I'm coming from California and am new to the agency. We've got a lot of talented people in this agency, people with lots of experience who truly care about small business. You are as strong as your people and we've got a lot of good people. We are going to be able to do a lot of things to empower small business in the future."

Barreto was interviewed by Jan Norman of the *Orange County Register* in August 2001 about his plans for the SBA. When asked what he brought with him to the SBA leadership, he responded, "First of all, relatability. I've had to make a payroll. I've had to raise money to start a business. I've had to market my business, adjust to changes in the marketplace, deal with employees. I learned to listen to customers. We want the SBA to be customer–friendly. If we listen, they will tell us what we need to do."

Sources of Information

Contact at: U.S. Small Business Administration
    Washington, DC
    URL: http://www.sba.com.

Bibliography

Brown, Ann. "Friend or Foe?" *Black Enterprise*, November 2001.

Brunning, S. "In at SBA." *Money*, 26 July 2001. Available at http://money.com/2001/07/26/sbrunning/barreto.

Hernandez, Greg. "Con Ganas!" *Hispanic*, September 2001.

Murphy, Kevin. "U.S. Small Business Administrator Learned from Parents' Persistence." *The Kansas City Star*, 1 August 2001.

Norman, Jan. "New Chief of U.S. Small Business Administration Plans Changes for Agency." *The Orange County Register*, 7 August 2001.

Robinson–Jacobs, Karen. "SBA Nominee Has High Hopes, Uncertain Budget." *The Los Angeles Times*, 23 July 2001.

Craig R. Barrett

(1939-)
Intel Corporation

Overview

A recruit from academia nearly four decades ago, Craig Barrett has never really been able to shake his nickname of "the professor" at Intel Corporation's headquarters in Santa Clara, California. As Intel's president since 1997 and chief executive officer since 1998, the tall, scholarly–looking Barrett saw the company's stock soar in value to record highs in the late summer of 2000, only to see it plunge precipitously in the months that followed as the American technology sector suffered through an agonizing shakeout. Outside observers who had long credited Barrett for Intel's impressive technological and manufacturing advances of the 1980s and 1990s began to wonder whether Barrett had what it took to lead the company into the twenty-first century. After all, Barrett's predecessor as CEO, Andrew Grove, had achieved near legendary status during his years at the helm of Intel. Closer analysis of the company's reversal of fortune in 2001 revealed that much of Intel's problems could be traced to flawed decisions and misguided strategizing, a fair amount of which had occurred before Barrett ever took command. Magnifying the drop in Intel's stock price was the general plunge in tech sector equities that followed the bursting of the dot.com bubble. Grove himself suggested that part of Intel's problem in recent years has been the absence of Barrett's input as chief operating officer since he'd been kicked upstairs to CEO. For his part, Barrett expressed confidence that Intel could fight its way back to the top by slashing its profit margins in an effort to regain some of the market share it had lost in the company's most recent downturn. Barrett also made it clear that Intel was determined to stay on track in terms of technology development. The CEO does his best to monitor the product development

progress throughout the company, meeting occasionally with engineering groups he fears may be falling behind. He told Brett Schlender of *Fortune:* "If you or anyone at Intel asks me what keeps me awake at night, I'll say the same thing I've been saying for more than ten years: I worry about the internal execution of our product road maps. If we do that, we win. If we stumble there, we give the competition a chance."

Personal Life

Barrett and his wife, Barbara, an attorney, live in Paradise Valley, Arizona, outside Phoenix. Barrett commutes between there and Intel headquarters in Santa Clara, California. The couple also owns Triple Creek Ranch in Darby, Montana, in the southwestern part of the state. The 333–acre Montana property, purchased by the Barretts in 1993, is a widely popular guest ranch with 18 cabins that can accommodate up to 42 adults. When the Barretts decide to spend some time at the ranch, they book their stay there just like the resort's paying guests, who pay all–inclusive nightly rates of $510 and up. When they can fit it in, the Barretts enjoy entertaining friends and family at the ranch, in the heart of the Bitterroot Mountains. Family includes Barrett's two grown children—Scott and Dawn—from his first marriage.

Barrett's wife, Barbara, serves as president and CEO of Triple Creek Ranch. She previously served as an executive with the Greyhound Corporation and in the early 1980s was named vice chairman of the Civil Aeronautics Board by President Ronald Reagan. She later served as deputy administrator of the Federal Aviation Administrator, the first woman ever to have served in that post. The couple met in 1980 after they had hiked separately to the top of 6,167–foot Squaw Peak near Phoenix. They were married in 1985. Barbara Barrett earned her bachelor's, master's, and law degrees from Arizona State University. In 2001, she completed a two–year term as president of the International Women's Forum, a global organization made up of women of high achievement.

One of three children in a lower–middle–class family, Barrett was born in San Francisco on August 29, 1939. After graduation from high school in 1957, he spent the next seven years at Stanford University in nearby Palo Alto. There he earned his bachelor's, master's, and doctoral degrees in materials science. Academia in general—and Stanford in particular—obviously appealed to him, because after winning his doctorate in 1964, Barrett signed on as a professor at Stanford, teaching there for most of the next decade. In 1969, Barrett, a member of National Academy of Engineering, was honored with the Hardy Gold Medal from the American Institute of Mining and Metallurgical Engineers. In 1973 he took a one–year leave to work for Intel, which was then a small start–up company developing memory chips for use in personal computers. He found the transition from the rel-

Chronology:
Craig R. Barrett

1939: Born.

1961: Earned B.S. degree in materials science at Stanford University.

1964: Earned Ph.D. degree in materials science at Stanford and joined faculty.

1974: Joined staff of Intel Corporation as manager of technology development.

1984: Named a vice president at Intel.

1990: Promoted to executive vice president at Intel.

1992: Elected to Intel's board of directors.

1993: Named chief operating officer of Intel.

1997: Named president of Intel.

1998: Given added responsibility of CEO.

ative calm of academia to the hectic pace of the business world somewhat unsettling and happily returned to Stanford after his year at Intel was completed. However, within six months, Barrett had to admit he'd been bitten by the business bug, and in 1974 he returned to Intel as technology development manager.

Away from Intel's corporate headquarters, Barrett spends much of his free time engaged in outdoor sports, including hiking, cycling, skiing, horse riding, golfing, and snowmobiling. His greatest love of all among the outdoor sports is flyfishing, a pastime he enjoys particularly when he and his wife spend time in Montana. In addition to serving on Intel's board of directors, Barrett sits on the boards of SEMATECH, Qwest Communications, the Semiconductor Industry Association, and the National Forest Foundation.

Career Details

At Intel, one of Barrett's early mentors was the company's future CEO, Andrew Grove, who helped the former professor to learn about the various processes of chip manufacture. Only three years earlier, in 1971, Intel had invented dynamic random–access memory chips, known as DRAMs, but the company had been surpassed in the chip market by Japanese manufacturers who produced a

Craig R. Barrett. (AP/Wide World Photos.)

much faster, more efficient chip. Barrett worked tirelessly to find out what it was that made the Japanese memory chips superior, visiting the U.S. manufacturers of equipment used to manufacture chips and questioning them about how their products differed, if at all, from those of their foreign competitors. He inspected the manufacturing facilities of Intel's Japanese partners and pored over published information about the design and operation of chipmaking equipment, all to no avail. In the end, Intel discontinued production of DRAMs in the mid–1980s, forcing a layoff of about one–third of the company's workforce.

After phasing out its production of memory chips, Intel began concentrating more heavily on the manufacture of microprocessors, which are computer processors on microchips, each of which can run a personal computer. The company had landed a big contract from IBM to produce microprocessors for Big Blue's line of personal computers. These tiny engines, which are capable of running arithmetical and logical calculations, drive the operation of a computer, and the mid–1980s saw a frenzied race to turn out ever faster microprocessors that could be used to produce faster computers.

Intel's microprocessor chips were each assigned a number to indicate its generation. The earliest Intel chip, introduced in 1971, was the 4004, followed shortly thereafter by the 8008. By the early 1980s, the Intel family of microprocessors had grown to include the 8–bit 8088 and the 16–bit 8086. Subsequent generations of Intel chips were known as the 80286, 80386, and 80486, or the 286,

386, and 486 for short. With its production of reliable, efficient microprocessors, Intel made a major name for itself. The 80486 chip was followed by Intel's Pentium microprocessors, including the Pentium II, III, and IV.

One of Barrett's most significant contributions at Intel was his introduction of the "Copy Exactly" production system. The system mandated that each Intel manufacturing facility use the same equipment and production standards in an effort to maintain high quality standards and eliminate product variations. Barrett was promoted to vice president in 1984. The following year, he embarked on a campaign to double Intel's production of microprocessors by 1988, a goal he far exceeded. As Intel's production continued to climb, Barrett climbed the ladder within the company's management structure, becoming a senior vice president in 1987, executive vice president in 1990, and president and chief operating officer in 1993. By 1996 the company's output of microprocessors had increased sevenfold.

Ever watchful against inroads made by its competitors—both at home and abroad—Intel adopted a tougher management style. In an interview, Barrett told *Christian Science Monitor,* "We accept that people are coming after us. That just permeates our entire management style. Only the paranoid survive." The mid–1990s brought booming business for Intel, a period of unparalleled growth overseen by Barrett as chief operating officer. The company captured more than 90 percent of the microprocessor market, and sales rocketed from about $8.8 billion in 1993 to nearly $20 billion in 1996. All was not rosy, however. Intel suffered an embarrassing setback in 1994 when reports surfaced that its new Pentium microchip had difficulties correctly processing certain complex mathematical calculations. Barrett campaigned to have the chips recalled, while CEO Andy Grove argued that the chip's flaw was so narrow in scope that it was unlikely to affect many customers. In the end, Barrett's argument prevailed.

Although the mid–1990s witnessed a surge in business for Intel, it also saw a sharp rise in competition from Advanced Micro Devices (AMD) and Cyrix. In 1995, Barrett helped to head off a lawsuit by AMD, which wanted to begin marketing chips comparable to Intel's 80386 microprocessors. He also kept close tabs on Intel's growing international operations, making frequent inspection tours of overseas manufacturing facilities.

In March of 1998, Intel announced that Barrett would succeed Grove as the company's CEO. Grove, however, would remain Intel's chairman. Although the company continued to dominate the microprocessor market, price pressure began to gnaw into its profits. Barrett moved aggressively to diversify, engineering a number of acquisitions in the telecommunications and networking fields. Analysts later questioned the wisdom of these acquisitions when the new companies failed to contribute as much to Intel's bottom line as had been anticipated.

Social and Economic Impact

Although the timing of Barrett's accession to the helm at Intel hasn't been the greatest, given the plummeting fortunes of the tech sector in the early years of the new millennium, "the professor" seems confident that the good times will return—and hopefully sooner rather than later. Barrett has an ambitious, long–term plan to make Intel's microprocessors as indispensable in other high–tech products as they already are in personal computers.

Barrett's vision calls for reducing Intel's vulnerability to the sudden ups and downs in the personal computer market by getting Intel's chips into a wide variety of other products, including mainframe computers, hand–held computers and personal digital assistants (PDAs) like the Palm, cell phones, and data networking equipment. In order for Barrett's plan to work, Intel will need to make a lot of changes, but the overall benefits should prove worthwhile. New classes of microprocessors and hardware architectures will have to be invented, and Intel will undoubtedly need to make some big acquisitions.

It's an ambitious plan to reinvigorate Intel's business, and it will take a lot of work and a lot of time, but given Barrett's track record, companies in the businesses Intel is eyeballing would do well to watch the company's moves closely. In the meantime, Barrett is expected to keep paring profit margins on the company's core product in order to win back market share in microprocessors.

Sources of Information

Contact at: Intel Corporation
2200 Mission College Blvd.
Santa Clara, CA 95052–8119
Business Phone: (408) 765–8080
URL: http://www.intel.com

Bibliography

"Barbara Barrett," Network of Executive Women in Hospitality. Available at http://www.newh.org/Barrett.htm (29 November 2001).

"Craig R. Barrett." *Newsmakers*, Issue 4. Farmington Hills, MI: Gale Group, 1999.

"Craig's Biography," Intel Corporation. Available at http://www.intel.com/craigbarrett/bio.htm (28 November 2001).

"Craig's Profile." Intel Corporation. Available at http://www.intel.com/craigbarrett/profile.htm (28 November 2001).

DeTar, Jim. "Barrett Takes Helm at Intel." *Electronic News*, 30 March 1998.

Forgrieve, Janet. "Ray of Hope: Intel CEO Craig Barrett Sees Positive Signs for PC Market." *Denver Rocky Mountain News*, 6 August 2001.

Roth, Daniel. "Craig Barrett Inside." *Fortune*, 18 December 2000.

Schlender, Brent. "Intel Unleashes Its Inner Attila." *Fortune*, 15 October 2001.

Schlender, Brent. "Techno File/Infotech: The New Man Inside Intel." *Fortune*, 11 May 1998.

Spang, Kelly. "20 to Watch: Craig Barrett: Intel." *Computer Reseller News*, 10 November 1997.

Richard N. Barton

(1968-)
Expedia, Inc.

Richard Barton is one of Microsoft's golden boys who created the idea for what was to become Expedia and then was offered the opportunity to spin off from Microsoft and run with it on his own. He made the most of that opportunity: Expedia users may book vacation and golf packages as well as airline flights, make hotel reservations, and secure car rentals from one online Web site. In addition to the United States, Expedia has Web sites in Canada, Germany, Italy, the Netherlands, and the United Kingdom. The company produces the "Expedia Radio Show" and publishes *Expedia Travels* magazine. Microsoft still owned 70 percent of Expedia in 2001 but had agreed to sell its stake to USA Networks in 2002.

Personal Life

Born in 1968, Barton admits to being a "closet geek" as a youngster. He once told an *Advertising Age* interviewer that he was one of the first kids in the neighborhood to own a Radio Shack TRS 80—an early personal computer (PC). He graduated from Stanford University in 1989 with a degree in industrial engineering. He is an avid outdoorsman and fly fisherman.

Barton told *Fortune*'s Nina Munk that "Work is not work. It's a hobby that you get paid for." He personifies the X–generation's "gold–collar" workers who believe they should be working in jobs that are fun and which provide self–satisfaction more than pay the rent. He runs his business by making sure that his employees love travel and share his philosophy. Barton also serves as a director of Atom, Inc.

Career Details

After graduating from Stanford, Barton worked for two years with Boston–based Alliance Consulting Group as a strategy consultant. Alliance is an information technologies consulting and education company. It also specializes in turning larger companies into e–businesses. Some of the company's previous clients have included Disney, Coca–Cola, and Visa. In an *Advertising Age* interview, Barton referred to his two years at Alliance as a "business boot camp," eliminating the need for him to go to business school.

Apparently feeling unfulfilled, Barton next tried to incorporate his love of the outdoors into his employment. He interviewed with Patagonia, the outdoor clothing maker, and the fly fishing gear retailer, Orvis Co. Ultimately, he chose instead to go with Microsoft in Redmond, Washington, eventually being placed in various product management positions involving Windows and MS–DOS. These included projects on Windows 95, Windows 3.1, MS–DOS 6, and MS–DOS 5 operating systems.

When Microsoft named Barton a unit manager for its growing travel business, things began to heat up. He originally was assigned to develop a line of CD–ROM travel guides for Microsoft. But the same intuition that made him get a Radio Shack PC before anyone else also made him become enthusiastic about an online travel agency service. Instead of CD–ROM viewing, Barton envisioned a bigger opportunity with interactive travel arrangements through e–commerce. He correctly presumed that people would be more interested in having some input and control in their travel arrangements. During his first review on the CD–ROM product with CEO Bill Gates in 1994, Barton suggested to move online.

True, Microsoft and Barton did not invent the concept of online travel arrangements. Sabre Group's EasySabre had been selling tickets on Prodigy since the 1980s. (Expedia would later compete with Sabre Group's online Travelocity, as well as the America Online–Preview Travel Web site.) Barton believed that the Microsoft name and reach would help beat out rivals and build trust in targeting consumers. Gates was receptive, and Barton began working out the details of his new brainchild.

In 1996, Microsoft announced plans to launch its new Expedia travel service online. It spent $1 million on advertising for the new service and teamed up with other travel–related partners to help get the site off the ground. It arranged for joint promotions with Doubletree Hotels, National car rental, and American, Continental, and Northwest airlines. The coordinated advertising was needed: at that time, there were already some 2,000 sites on the Internet promoting individual brands, destinations, and booking services. American Express and Preview Travel were planning online and mass media campaigns of their own. But Barton and his team retained the advertising firm of Anderson & Lembke in San Francisco

Chronology:
Richard N. Barton

1968: Born.

1989: Graduated from Stanford University.

1991: Joined Microsoft.

1994: Created Expedia

1996: Expedia.com website was launched.

1999: Expedia became an independent, publicly traded entity.

1999: Became Expedia's first president, director, and CEO.

2001: Expedia sold to USA Networks Inc.

to create a campaign that offered a free vacation, courtesy of Expedia, Doubletree, and National, to kick off the new web site. Expedia offered bonus miles on Continental, American, and Northwest to those who booked flights through the website. From the start, Expedia began to create website links to other "content sites" for travelers such as weather services, theater and museum sites, city news, and traveling–consumer favorites such as the bookseller Amazon.com and 1–800–FLOWERS.

By 1997, Barton had been promoted to general manager of Microsoft's traveler business unit, which included the Expedia group. Expedia was holding its own, with about two million Web visitors a month, and the site had sales of more than $4 million a week. But it was not yet making money. Barton came up with more ideas. The Microsoft name had provided the name–recognition security to draw customers, but it was the software behind Expedia that he was relying on to move ahead from there. "Brand is very important," Barton said in a 1998 *Advertising Age* article. "But the very greatest brands in the world are built on the best products in the world. You can't have one without the other." He believed he had the very best product in Expedia. He envisioned Expedia becoming an on–demand, interactive, multimedia experience similar to an online TV. He was merely waiting for bandwidth and technology to take Expedia to the next level.

That opportunity came the following year. In late 1999, Microsoft scheduled its first public offering (IPO) as its own company, independent of Microsoft. A letter dated October 25, 1999, and signed by Greg Maffei, Pres-

Richard and Sarah Barton holding their newborn son William Marcus. *(AP/Wide World Photos/*
Greg Gilbert.)

ident of Expedia Inc., offered Barton the position of chief executive officer (CEO) of the new company, conditioned upon the execution of the IPO, among other things. The letter further went on to state that if an IPO did not take place by June 30, 2000, the offer of employment was void. However, the letter continued, "Microsoft informs us that, in that event, in lieu of becoming employed by Expedia, Inc., you will have the opportunity to continue your employment with Microsoft Corporation." The IPO occurred as planned and Barton became Expedia's first president, CEO, and director in late 1999. Barton had realized his dream to have his own business.

Since the spin–off from Microsoft, Barton worked toward supremacy in the online travel agency business.

According to Internet research and rankings firm, Gomez Advisors, in the third quarter of Expedia's first fiscal year, Barton had brought the company into the number one spot overall, also taking the first spot in business travel, the bargain travel profiles, and the "ease–of–use" category.

Initially, Expedia suffered the same redundancy as the traditional travel agencies: it had focused mainly on selling airline tickets for its "bread and butter" income. As airlines continued to reduce commissions to sellers and agencies, Expedia, along with the others, began to suffer revenue shortcomings. But once again, Barton was ahead of the pack. Expedia began to shift its focus on more profitable lodging and vacation package transactions. "Don't just travel, travel right," became Expedia's motto.

In March 2000, Barton was able to secure the acquisition of Las Vegas–based Travelscape.com and Seattle–based VacationSpot.com for $177 million—two other Internet sites that could pull consumers away from Expedia. Expedia then developed new services for consumers such as hotel price matches, flight price matches, and a fare calendar that allows users to see when airlines are offering the best rates or deals. All this led to a glowing report from Gomez Advisers in mid–2000, noting "these cool new features produce positive, easy–to–use results."

The purchase of the two other web sites and the development of its own unique product of synchronized travel arrangements and packages helped Expedia to tap into the growing worldwide lodging market by providing bookings for more than 65,000 lodging properties in 240 cities. VacationSpot had the properties that Expedia wanted on its web site, and Travelscape had the best prices, plus a desirable cruise product. Expedia also started to shift its business from airline ticket sales to cruise and vacation packages. By mid–2000, the sale of airline tickets represented less than 30 percent of company revenues.

Further, in February 2000, Expedia opened its golf travel section in conjunction with TheGolfer.com, an online tee–time booking service. The new product offered reservations at more than 11,000 golf courses and provided golf destination information, golf news, and special golf vacation package deals. The Course of the Week feature provided photographs and course details of its subject golf course, and Golf Travel Deals linked customers to a variety of golf products and supplies, schools and clinics, and complete golf getaways. There was also a community "chat" area for golfers to exchange vacation stories and tips, along with Expedia.com's acclaimed Airport Survival Guide. Last but not least, Expedia launched into the communications networks to reach new customers not otherwise visiting its website. Expedia Radio, offered in 90 markets and on the Web, was distributed through CBS and reached 2.5 million viewers. In the fall of 2000, the company launched its own magazine, *Expedia Travels*, in conjunction with Ziff Davis Publishing, originally published bi–monthly but with plans to publish monthly in fall 2001.

In October 2000, Barton was a guest speaker on the *Mark Holland Show* on the IT Radio Network. He told listeners that he saw himself as an "intrapreneur," starting up a little start–up inside a big company. The main difference, according to Barton, was not the amount of autonomy but, instead, the line of command. Barton told his audience that he now reports to the general public. "You're my new bosses," he stated, "[now] I have thousands of new bosses to answer to and these new bosses are very demanding." Barton and Holland both agreed that it was a "customer economy" in the Web World, and that in order to be successful, employees needed to re-

spect and love their customers, who were only "one click away" from going to a competitor. Barton also said that a prerequisite for employment at Expedia was a love of travel, which was "not a hard task luckily."

Anecdotally, Barton also told Holland and his listeners that his young age (32 at the time) gave him an advantage, because he was raised "in a very technology engineering oriented environment," which helped him to appreciate how technology could change a business. But, he admitted, it also gave him a lack of experience. He agreed that Bill Gates had a "tremendous influence" on his management style and the way he thinks about business. Gate's optimistic outlook and ability to foresee how technology could change people and industries—long before the change occurred—was something that Barton relished. He also told listeners that working for Steve Balmer at Microsoft taught him how to motivate and lead large groups of people. By taking the best from both of these leaders, Barton was able to take his group at Microsoft's Expedia to the top and then spin off on its own.

In July 2001, USA Networks Inc. agreed to acquire Microsoft's stock interest in Expedia. USA Networks, which owns the Home Shopping Network (HSN), planned to combine Internet (Expedia) with cable TV (HSN) for retail travel sales. USA projected that within two years it would have 20 million subscribers to its cable channel—many of whom would be directed to its Expedia web site. Expedia's fiscal year sales ending in June 2001 were $222 million, representing a one–year sales growth of 64.7 percent.

Social and Economic Impact

Barton is the quintessential X–generation business leader. He does not try to capitalize on existing markets but rather tries to foresee the future trends of a sometimes finicky public and develop a new market to accommodate that need. Most of all, he wants to have fun doing it, which is a motivator for both him and his staff. A background expertise in state–of–the–art technology, coupled with the ability to gauge the pulse of would–be travelers, has changed not only Barton's career, but also the way consumers arrange and purchase their travel plans. Everyone has benefited, but mostly consumers (Barton's "new bosses"), who can often save money and time by visiting Expedia.com online.

Sources of Information

Contact at: Expedia, Inc.
    13810 SE Eastgate Way, Ste. 400
    Bellevue, WA 98005
    Business Phone: (425) 564&–7200
    URL: http://www.expedia.com

Bibliography

"30 Seconds or Less." *Computer Reseller News*, 31 July 2000.

Anderson, Karen. "Life After Microsoft." *Travel Agent*, 15 May 2000.

"Employment Agreement Between Expedia and R. Barton." Available at http://techdeals.biz.findlaw.com/agreements/expedia/expediaemployagt.html.

"Expedia, Inc. Capsule." Available at http://www.hoovers.com/co/capsule/8/0,2163,61378,00.html.001.

"Expedia Posts Better–than–expected Q1 Results." *News Bytes News Network*, 22 October 2001.

Ferguson, Kevin. "Expedia–Travelscape Deal Makes Finding Dream Vacation Easier." *Las Vegas Business Press*, 12 June 2000.

Johnson, Bradley. Z. "Microsoft Expedia." *Advertising Age*, 26 June 1998.

"Management Biography." Available at http://investor.expedia.com/iredge.

Munk, Nina. "The New Organization Man." *Fortune*, 16 March 1998.

"Richard Barton, President and CEO—Expedia.com." *IT Radio Network*, 12 October 2000. Available at http://www.itradionetwork.com/scripts/bartonr.html.

Schaal, Dennis. "Cable Firm to Buy Expedia." *Travel Weekly*, 19 July 2001.

Torres, Giselle. "Allied Consulting Group." *Caribbean Business*, 23 October 1997.

Underwood, Elaine. "Microsoft Loads Up Big Cybersplash in Travel." *Brandweek*, 21 October 1996.

Waltner, Charles. "Richard Barton." *Advertising Age*, 14 July 1997.

Burton Baskin & Irvine Robbins

(1913-1967)
(1917-)
Baskin–Robbins Ice Cream

Overview

Baskin–Robbins is the world's largest ice cream specialty store, operating more than 5,000 retail stores in more than 50 countries around the globe. The founding of the company represents an all–American success story, and Baskin–Robbins ice cream has grown up with many families as an icon of Americana, just as much as *Leave It to Beaver* and Beatlemania. A trip to Baskin–Robbins was the perfect way to end the day. It still is, more than 50 years later.

Personal Life

Burton Baskin was born in Chicago, Illinois, in 1913; his future brother–in–law, Irvine "Irv" Robbins, was born in Tacoma, Washington, four years later, in 1917. Their success story started during the depression years. As a teenager in the 1930s, Robbins managed a small ice cream parlor in his father's dairy store in Tacoma. He hated the drudgery of the "vanilla, chocolate, strawberry" routine, day after day and started staying up late at night concocting his own combinations by adding fresh fruit and candies to the standard flavors. Then he started giving exotic names to his concoctions. He also noticed that people entering the shop were coming not only for ice cream but also to take a break from the hustle and bustle of everyday life. That perception stayed with him and helped him formulate the type of ambiance he wanted to create for his own ice cream business in the future. Meanwhile, he tried out some of his newly created flavors in local grocery stores, hoping to eventually sell to them in bulk. However, other vendors

Chronology:

Burton Baskin and Irvine Robbins

1913: Baskin born in Chicago.

1917: Robbins born in Tacoma.

1945: Robbins opened "Snowbird" ice cream store.

1946: Baskin joined Robbins to form Baskin–Robbins.

1948: Baskin–Robbins created the industry's first franchise ice cream store.

1953: "31 Flavors" made its debut.

1967: Baskin died at age 54.

1973: J. Lyons & Co. of London purchased Baskin–Robbins.

1974: Baskin–Robbins went international.

1978: Robbins retired as chairman.

1986: Baskin–Robbins Incorporated was formed.

1996: Baskin–Robbins celebrated 50th anniversary.

regularly removed his signs, making his initial venture only moderately successful. Then World War II broke out and postponed his dream.

Career Details

On the other side of the world, Baskin had learned the art of making ice cream while serving as a PX operator with the U.S. Navy in New Hebredes, South Pacific. (PXs, or post exchanges, are military retail establishments.) At that time, Baskin had obtained a freezer from an aircraft carrier supply officer and began concocting his own creamy treats for his fellow servicemen, using local tropical fruits found on the islands. During World War II, he met and married Shirley Robbins, who happened to be Irv Robbins's sister. They settled in Pasadena, California, where Baskin opened his own ice cream shop called "Burton's," and was enjoying his own entrepreneurial success.

When Robbins was discharged from the U.S. Army in 1945, he needed to consider whether an ice cream venture could support a wife and child. He had decided during his own military tour that offering his product through grocery retail stores was not really what he had envi-

sioned in the long run. He remembered that people had come into his father's shop wanting more than just to purchase a product; rather, the ice cream shop itself appeared to be a treat for them, making them forget their daily cares. So he decided to open his own special parlor. During a vacation trip to Los Angeles, he spotted a store for rent in the suburb of Glendale. The setting appeared ideal for an ice cream shop. Robbins took $3000 savings and $3000 from an insurance policy to come up with the necessary $6000 investment. He named his new parlor "Snowbird" and opened for business on December 7, 1945. Sporting a crisp white uniform shirt and a colorful bow tie, he greeted excited customers and tempted them with his new dessert creations. Inside his shop, they could forget about the world outside and simply enjoy the moment's pleasure of an exotic ice cream flavor, often with a humorous name. Robbins eventually offered 21 different flavors to his clientele.

When the war ended, Robbins was about to open his fourth store. He was having so much fun and doing so well that he had convinced Baskin, now his brother–in–law, to join him in a partnership. They agreed, in theory, but continued running their respective shops separately for the first year on the advice of Robbins' father, who counseled them not to compromise their individual ideas out of respect for each other or in an effort to get along. Ultimately, the two men agreed to combine their talents and successes. They flipped a coin to see whose name would get top billing; Baskin won. "Baskin and Robbins" ice cream was born in 1946. In the next two years, the two entrepreneurs opened five additional ice cream stores in order to keep up with demand.

Initially, the men kept low expectations for themselves; after all, they were selling ice cream cones, not automobiles. "We just wanted to make $75 a week. And we wanted to enjoy ourselves doing it," Robbins is quoted as saying in Thaddeus Wawro's *Radicals and Visionaries: Entrepreneurs who Revolutionized the 20th Century.* "Of course, when we reached that goal, we upped it to $100, then $125 and so on."

Both men realized all too well the hard work and personal commitment needed to be successful. They also knew that the proper care needed to run a store required a manager who had a vested interest in the operation. Moreover, managing their six existing stores proved exhausting. It also removed them from their first love, which was creating new and fun ice cream flavors and catchy names for them. Thus, in 1948, they decided to license out the operations of future Baskin–Robbins stores, thereby creating the concept of "franchising" in the ice cream industry. (Their former malt–machine salesman, Ray Kroc, later applied this same strategy to his fast–food restaurant chain, McDonald's.)

Clearly, the signature selling point at Baskin–Robbins was the tempting array of ever–changing flavors of ice cream to choose from. In 1953 the big "31" sign made its debut at all Baskin–Robbins store. The two entrepreneurs chose that number to capitalize on the idea that customers could get a new flavor for every day of the month. Many of those flavors became classics, including "Pralines 'n Cream" and "Jamoca Almond Fudge" and the ever–popular "Rocky Road," with its chunks of nuts, marshmallow, and chocolate. There were a few failures along the way as well. For example, "Goody Goody Gumdrop" was recalled to avoid the potential of customers chipping their teeth on the frozen gumdrops.

In 1957, when the Brooklyn Dodgers baseball team moved to Los Angeles, Baskin–Robbins was there to greet them with its specially made "Baseball Nut" flavor—complete with a raspberry for the umpire. This started a new, and important, selling trend for the company: acknowledging special events, times, or persons with an ice cream flavor. A few of the best–remembered ones include 1964's "Beatle Nut," singing the praises of Beatlemania, and 1965's "0031 Secret Bonded Flavor" for James Bond. Down the road, there would be 1968's "Here Comes the Fudge" as Americans tuned into television's *Laugh–In* and 1969's "Lunar Cheesecake" to commemorate Neil Armstrong's historic step on the moon.

The first Baskin–Robbins ice cream store outside of California opened in Phoenix, Arizona, in 1959. This was the beginning of what was to be a rapid–growth period for the next two decades. Unfortunately, however, Burt Baskins died unexpectedly eight years later at the age of 54. Meanwhile, John Robbins, Irv's only son and heir apparent, became a health food advocate and rejected both his father's product and his inheritance of the business. Father and son Robbins sank into an icy relationship that would last for years, and Baskin–Robbins was sold for an estimated $12 million (but officially an undisclosed amount) to United Fruit Company. At the time of the purchase in 1968, Baskin–Robbins controlled 476 outlets in 31 states and had 57 more stores under construction.

A few years later, in 1973, Baskin–Robbins was purchased by the London–based J. Lyons & Co., Ltd. Robbins, 55 years old at the time, stayed on as chairman of the board. During the 1970s, Baskin–Robbins experienced rapid domestic franchise growth, but in 1974 it began international expansion with the opening of its first store in Brussels, Belgium.

In 1976 Baskin–Robbins specialty stores around the country celebrated the chain's 31st birthday with special events and treats for their customers. Two years later, Irv Robbins retired as chairman, and another London entity, Allied Brewery, bought the company from J. Lyons.

Under its new owner, Baskin–Robbins Incorporated was formed in 1986 and then created two new subsidiaries, Baskin–Robbins USA Co. and Baskin–Robbins International. Although *Dairy Foods* magazine named Baskin–Robbins "Ice Cream Retailer of the Year" in 1987, and Irv Robbins received the International Franchise Association's Hall of Fame Award in 1988, the

company had not done as well in the 1980s as it had previously. Baskin–Robbins' parlors became simply "dated" rather than "retro," while new upstarts like Ben & Jerry's and Haegen–Dazs began to tug at customers with a new super–fat creamy ice cream. However, Baskin–Robbins began to bounce back near the end of the 1990s, introducing an all–natural line of low–fat and non–fat frozen yogurts. In 1989 it became the first ice cream specialty store to introduce a no–sugar–added frozen dairy product. This was followed in 1991 with the introduction of the first fat–free frozen dairy dessert.

In 1993 Baskin–Robbins was named "America's Favorite Sweets Chain" for the tenth time in *Restaurants and Institutions* magazine's prestigious national survey. The following year, Baskin–Robbins' parent company, Allied Lyons, merged with Pedro Domecq to form Allied–Domecq PLC, one of the world's largest spirits and quick service restaurant companies. Baskin–Robbins thus acquired new corporate siblings as well: sister companies Dunkin' Donuts and Togo's.

Baskin–Robbins celebrated 50 years in business in 1996. Since that time, it has continued to create innovative flavor campaigns and add new products—not as easy as it once was. In 1997 the company added its ice cream "Smoothie" and in 2000 introduced the "Freeze Frame" cake program in which a favorite color or black and white photograph could be scanned and printed with edible ink and paper on the top of an ice cream cake.

In late 2000, the company launched a multi–million–dollar renovation project to give its parlors a new look. However, its greatest hope for the future appeared to be in overseas franchising, where Baskin–Robbins has remained an icon of Americana, particularly in areas such as Japan and Korea.

Anecdotally, the requirements for being considered for a Baskin–Robbins franchise store in 2001 included an investment of $179,000, a franchise fee of $30,000, a net worth of $300,000, and a cash liquidity of $200,000. U.S. franchises have dropped approximately 500 since 1997. Notwithstanding, U.S. stores serve approximately 150 million ice cream cones each year (not counting sundaes, shakes, smoothies, etc.). The company also boasts an archive list of 1,000 different ice cream flavors, but the top–selling flavors continue to be old standbys such as Vanilla, Chocolate, Mint Chocolate Chip, and Pralines 'n Cream.

Social and Economic Impact

In his 1997 book, *The Food Revolution*, John Robbins remarked that he was "born into ice cream." He recalled growing up in affluence in the family's Encino, California, mansion. The back yard of the Robbins' home that he shared with two sisters and full–time homemaker mother, Irma, as well as his famous father, had an ice–cream–cone–shaped swimming pool. He remembered sometimes eating ice cream for breakfast. Sadly, he also remembered that several members of his family suffered with weight problems and were more often sick than not, including him. Uncle Burt (Baskin) had died of a heart attack in his early fifties (which John blamed at least in part on ice cream), and John's own father, Irvine, suffered from high blood pressure and diabetes. Back in 1968, "low–fat" ice cream was a nonentity; frozen yogurt was years away from development. It seemed the Great American Success Story of Baskin–Robbins had a downside.

But ingenuity and creativity came to the rescue—and prevailed. Staying one step ahead of health–conscious Americans, Baskin–Robbins was able to induce them to have their cake and eat it too: with nonfat, low–fat, non–dairy, no–sugar, and frozen yogurt products to satisfy every sweet tooth. And more recent studies have indicated that ice cream is fine—in moderation. In other words, eating it for breakfast is not recommended. Accordingly, today's customers may choose their ice cream desserts according to their own particular health needs or desires.

Irv Robbins once said, "You look at any giant corporation, and I mean the biggies, and they all started with a guy with an idea, doing it well." (He and his vegetarian son have since mended their relationship, and he often adopts his son's health alternatives and dietary advice.) John told a *People* magazine interviewer in 1997, "I think he's quite proud of me now. He said to me recently, 'Thank God, you had the courage to follow your own star.'"

Sources of Information

Contact at: Baskin–Robbins Ice Cream
　　　　　14 Pacella Park Dr.
　　　　　Randolph, MA 02368
　　　　　Business Phone: (800)777–9983
　　　　　URL: http://www.baskinrobbins.com/

Bibliography

"Baskin–Robbins." Available at http://www.baskinrobbins.com/about/history.shtml.

"Baskin–Robbins USA Co." Available at http://www.entrepreneur.com/Franchise_Zone/FZ_Franchise.

Carlin, Peter Ames, and Johnny Dodd. "Quitting Cold." *People*, 25 August 1997.

Gajilan, Arlyn Thomas. "Burt and Irv's Place." *FSB: Fortune Small Business*, July/August 2000.

"Quotes on Ideas." Available from http://www.cyberquotations.com/sorted/qIdeas.htm.

Robbins, John. *The Food Revolution.* Berkeley, CA: Conari Press, 2001. Book review available from http://wholisticresearch.com/info/artshow.

"Saluting Franchising's Best and Brightest." *Franchising World*, January/February 2001.

"Side Dishes." *Nation's Restaurant News*, 12 May 1997.

Wawro, Thaddeus. *Radicals and Visionaries: Entrepreneurs Who Revolutionized the 20th Century.* Irvine: Entrepreneur Media, 2000.

Robert Behar

(1949-)
GlobeCast America

Overview

Techno–wizard Robert Behar created a multi–billion dollar state–of–the–art telecommunications giant out of a backyard hobby. He started building a satellite behind his Miami, Florida, home in the 1970s, in order to watch the locally non–televised soccer playoffs for the World Cup. It took him four months, and he missed the Cup results. But he had successfully built one of the first home satellites and realized he was on the verge of something very big. He began building systems in the local Miami market and grew into an $18 million business. In 1998, he merged with the giant GlobeCast and became president/CEO of North American operations. The company reported 2000 revenues over $100 million. Now he has a new hobby: boating. He can watch all the soccer games he wants—from virtually anywhere on the globe, right from the berth of his yacht's cabin.

Personal Life

Havana–born Behar is the son of Enrique and Reina, who came to the U.S. from Cuba in 1960 and settled in the Miami, Florida, area. Behar was 11 years old at the time. His father ran a construction business in Florida, and his mother had a garment factory. Behar, who had always dreamed of getting into the television industry, dropped out of Miami–Dade Junior College in 1970, just three credit hours short of a degree. The reason was to take a job as a master control operator at Miami's WCKT–TV (now WSVN).

In 2000 Behar was named Executive of the Year and a recipient of the Teleport Award for Excellence in Wash-

Chronology:

Robert Behar

1949: Born in Havana, Cuba.

1960: Behar family immigrated to the U.S.

1974: Started AB Electronics & Communications.

1979: AB Electronics & Communications became Hero Communications.

1985: Started Omni Video Productions.

1998: Hero Communications merged with GlobeCast; Behar became president and CEO.

2000: Named Executive of the Year and received Teleport Award of Excellence.

---

ington, D.C. The awards are presented to companies and individuals who have dramatically demonstrated excellence in the field of teleport operations. He is married to Estrella (*nee* Mitrani) and has three children.

Career Details

From 1970 to 1974, Behar worked at several Miami–area television stations in various capacities, including WAJA–TV (later WLTV), where he was assistant chief engineer, and CBS Miami affiliate WTVJ–TV, where he was an editor/engineer. In 1974 he and a coworker started their own business, AB Electronics & Communications, in CB radio sales and installation. (He continued dual employment with WTVJ until 1979.) "I have always been an entrepreneur at heart," Behar told a *Hispanic* magazine interviewer many years later. In any event, with only $500 in capital, the two men did not see any return on their investment for a few years.

Then in 1976, the small company was awarded a contract by the Venezuelan government to install a radio system for the World Cup games from nearby Buenos Aires, Argentina. Behar got hooked on watching the games and the competition while performing on his contract. He and his workers finished the contract prior to the end of the World Cup and returned to Florida. At that time, not all Floridians shared the same enthusiasm for soccer as did, for example, Europeans and South Americans, and the games were not televised in Behar's com-

munity. Behar felt lost, unable to watch the remaining games. As the old maxim goes, "necessity is the mother of invention"; Behar decided to construct his own satellite system in his backyard to catch the final games. "I realized that this was a business and decided that I would change the focus of the company to building satellite antennas," Behar later said in an interview for *Broadcasting & Cable* magazine.

The company also changed its name to Hero Communications—a story in and of itself. While Behar was doing an installation in Saudi Arabia, a member of the king's court remarked, "You are going to be heroes in bringing the world together." Behar knew he was on to something big. He left his job with WTVJ late in 1979 to focus full–time on his new company. He became heavily involved with the satellite trade association SPACE (now the Satellite Broadcasting & Communications Association of America, or SBCA). In 1982, as founder and president of Hero Communications, he traveled to Washington to lobby Congress for the use of home satellites. During the lobbying rally, Behar organized a three–hour satellite broadcast, but it turned into a twelve–hour marathon of one–upsmanship as companies like HBO and Showtime scrambled his signals to avoid competition from small–timers like his company. The experience left him disappointed with the industry, and Behar decided to return to TV.

Behar then purchased a used production truck from his old station WTVJ and started his third company, Omni Video Productions, in 1985. Soon thereafter, the Hispanic Broadcasting Company retained him to produce a regular half–hour newscast for the Spanish–language broadcasting company Telemundo Productions. By 1997 Telemundo had offered to buy him out. As part of the deal, Behar was named senior vice president and chief operating officer (COO) of Telemundo Productions. But when Behar sensed operational troubles within the company, he jumped ship in 1992. (The following year, Telemundo filed for Chapter 11 bankruptcy.) Ultimately, the efforts of Behar and others led Congress to pass the Satellite Home Viewers Act, which prohibited the monopolizing of signals by large companies and mandated that they sell to the "backyard industry."

Behar returned to what he knew and loved best. He organized Hero Productions, a "one–stop–shopping" teleport and television production facility. The company grew from a 3,000 square foot garage to a 60,000 square foot building. It also added post–production capability and translation services to its business. By 1997 the company posted revenues of $18 million and caught the eye of GlobeCast, the giant satellite company. GlobeCast was impressed with Behar's experience in both North American and Latin American markets. Moreover, Behar was heavily experienced in both television and satellite industries as well. Although GlobeCast, which had wanted to expand, was interested in Behar's business, it was also interested in the man. Said Michel Combes, GlobeCast's CEO at the time, in *Broadcasting & Cable* magazine,

"We were very happy with his main skills, which in my mind are in leadership; he's a very dynamic guy, and he knows how to run a business." In 1998 the two companies merged, with Behar assuming the position of president and CEO of the surviving company, GlobeCast North America (a subsidiary of France Telecom). When re–interviewed six months later, Combs added, "I am more than happy with our decision. He has done a tremendous job with this company."

As far as Behar's comments on the merger, he later remarked in *Hispanic* magazine, "You look at a deal and if it makes sense, you do it, and if not, you walk away from it." He saw huge potential in joining GlobeCast. "I knew that if I wanted to see programming from the world, other people wanted programming from the U.S.," he continued. Knowing Congress had mandated that television become digital by 2001, Behar wanted to seize the opportunity to start producing programming for that pipeline.

At GlobeCast, Behar was running one of the most important satellite–transmission and production–services companies of all. GlobeCast supplied end–to–end video and audio production and transmission services for programmers such as MetroGoldwyn–Mayer and Hallmark Entertainment Networks. Speaking with *Television Broadcast* interviewers in 1999, Behar noted, "The digitizing of signals and the digitization of the industry is full speed ahead as of right now. . . . It's an exciting time in the teleport industry right now." Interestingly, he projected that ten years out, the technology would literally reach people's back yards. "I think the infrastructure will develop for news organizations and all broadcasters to have their own capacity because the digital onslaught will make that capacity fairly economical. People will own their own slots and will be doing their own traffic," he continued, "so [our role] will be more of the permanent service."

In 2000, GlobeCast remained the largest network origination provider in North and Latin America. Due mostly to Behar's influence, the company offered a full spectrum of technology–driven, end–to–end solutions for every segment of the global satellite broadcasting industry. This included channel distribution, multimedia and IP multicasting, Internet backbone services, global sports and special events coverage, newsgathering, business television, digital and HDTV transmission, and translation services for global programming. Behar was able to predict a growing need to provide live news coverage for news organizations; consequently, the company created its Newsforce subsidiary. Additionally, Behar continued to steer his company toward IP (Internet provider) webcasting and multicasting services, using MPEG–1 and MPEG–4 technologies to deliver high quality, full motion video and sound. GlobeCast's IP gateway on the Telstar satellite allowed the company to offer live and on–demand video and audio streaming, high speed file transfer, and webcasting in a high bandwidth, secure environment.

But that "secure" bandwidth environment was not without compromise. In 2000 one of GlobeCast's international television clients, National Iranian Television (NITV, not affiliated with any political or government organization) suffered blocked broadcast signals from a surreptitious rogue unknown party. When GlobeCast tried to send up NITV's signal, it was blocked and returned to Globecast with Eutelsat orders to stop the transmission.

A growing market that Behar predicted years ago is that of "niche content." As more people leave their native countries, the demand for esoteric broadcasts in native languages has nearly outgrown the capability. GlobeCast has maintained itself on the forefront of the market. For some companies, programming that is so specific to such a small group of people is not economical. But state–of–the–art DT (digital transmission) transponders with steerable spotbeams on specific satellites, such as that maintained by GlobeCast, enables the company to make use of a satellite already in use for other purposes. This means a separate DTH satellite does not have to be launched in order to provide niche content services. As of 2001, GlobeCast had access to 60 satellites on 15 systems. It was broadcasting 27 niche channels, of which 21 could be viewed at no cost to a subscriber with Globe-Cast equipment. Behar anticipated this growing market and prepared the company to be available for such services. Incidentally, Behar is also the founder and chairman of HTV, the first 24–hour, all–Spanish–language television music network, which was sold to Cisneros Television Group in 1999.

In May 2000, Behar authored an article for *Digital TV*, entitled "There's No Shortage of Bandwidth." The article offers reassurance that there was not, and would not be, a shortage of satellite capability to handle increasing demand. Part of the speculative concern was that the Internet was taking up more and more bandwidth, creating more traffic and demanding service. Behar reminded the reader, "[Y]ou only have to look at the America Online/Time Warner merger to see where alternate supply options are opening up. The merger of these two media giants will produce high–speed, high–bandwidth Internet delivery against the background of a growing wire infrastructure." Behar did acknowledge that the conversion of full–time analog to digital signals will require a great deal of duplicate capacity through 2001.

Of more concern to Behar was the international marketplace, where fewer fiber interconnects existed between international destinations. He predicted that within the next few years, new fiber would be deployed throughout the world to meet the demand. Additionally, new satellites were being designed and built to meet the anticipated need of Internet services between Latin America and Europe, as well as in Africa and Asia. Finally, Behar informed readers that GlobeCast was adding new satellite–based services but had no need to add any new capacity to its current inventory of more than 25 transponders to service the Americas. Instead, the company would focus on developing new digital services to multiply existing capacity.

An independent report released in November 2001 by Northern Sky Research concluded that, despite current difficulties, it expected a positive long–term market for consumer broadband satellite services worldwide. The report, "Consumer Broadband Satellite Services: A Global Analysis of Key Players and Market Opportunities," included GlobeCast as one of the profiled companies. The company noted that "future Ka–band services have the potential to ignite growth by offering a faster performing service at a lower price point and bandwidth on par with terrestrial offerings." GlobeCast was already making use of some of that technology in preparing for the Winter Olympics in Salt Lake City, Utah, 2002. In October 2001, it announced its availability to provide broadcasters with transmission and production services at its owned–and–operated technical operations center in Salt Lake City.

Social and Economic Impact

Robert Behar possesses not only the creative ability to visualize the future but also the technical capability to make the vision a reality. His uncanny ability to forecast technological needs and markets has kept him on the top of a list of telecommunications gurus who come with crystal balls. There is always a certain excitement that attaches to his predictions as well; perhaps it is because

the industry trusts him and his opinions. With Behar at the helm of GlobeCast, no doubt technology will go as far as it can to meet the needs of a global community still maturing in its vision of worldwide "live" communications.

Sources of Information

Bibliography

Anderson, Karen. "GlobeCast Leader Stays Grounded." *Broadcasting & Cable*, 21 September 1998.

Behar, Robert. "There's No Shortage of Bandwidth." *Digital TV*, 19 May 2000. Available at http://www.technologyage.co,/tvb2000/0519/0519.5.htm.

Calvo, Lisa. "A Backyard Hobby's Giant Step." *Hispanic*, May 2001.

"Economic and Technical Issues to Affect Short–Term Consumer Broadband Satellite Market Growth. . . ." *Business Newswire*, 7 November 2001.

"GlobeCast in Winter 2002." *TVB Europe*, October 2001.

Jakel, Peter. "Demanding Niche." *Satellite Broadband: The Cutting Edge of Satellite Communications*, September 2001.

"Teleport Awards of Excellence." Undated. Available at http://www.worldteleport.org/AwardsSponsors/Teleawards.html.

Webb, Jessica. "Casting a Global Net." *Technology Age*, 27 November 2000.

Webb, Jessica. "The Great Satellite Shift." *Technology Age*, 15 October 1999.

Jeff Bezos

(1964-)
Amazon.com, Inc.

Overview

Pioneer retailer on the World Wide Web, Jeff Bezos has proven that a fortune can be made by convincing people to rethink the way they shop. With Amazon.com, Bezos has created the world's largest bookstore of available titles with virtually no inventory or property costs. Browsing for a book will never be quite the same again with the online ease and convenience that Amazon provides.

Personal Life

Jeff Bezos was born in Albuquerque, New Mexico, in 1964. His father is an Exxon executive, and Bezos was brought up in affluence and privilege. Until he was 16, Bezos spent his summers rounding up herds and fixing windmills on his grandfather's ranch in tiny Cotulla, Texas. Although he did not pursue a career as a cowboy, there is something about the lure of the frontier that caught Bezos's imagination and spurred his interest in the untapped potential of the Internet. From an early age, Bezos wanted to be an entrepreneur.

He attended Princeton University, where he graduated in 1986 with a Bachelor of Science degree in electrical engineering and computer science (*summa cum laude* and a member of Phi Beta Kappa). He is married to MacKensie, an aspiring novelist, and has a Labrador retriever named Kamala after a minor *Star Trek* character. Relocating from New York City to Seattle to create Amazon.com, Bezos set out to found a company that could take advantage of the 230 percent annual growth in Internet usage. When the company went public in 1996, his net worth

Chronology:

Jeff Bezos

1964: Born.

1986: Graduated from Princeton University.

1986: Hired by Fitel.

1988: Hired by Bankers Trust Co.

1990: Promoted to vice president.

1990: Hired by D. E. Shaw & Co.

1992: Promoted to senior vice president.

1995: Founded Amazon.com.

1997: Amazon.com went public.

1998: Amazon.com sold its millionth book.

1998: Amazon.com began trend of offering products other than books, starting with compact discs.

1998: Stepped down as president and chief operating office; remained CEO and chairman.

1999: Named *Time* magazine's Person of the Year.

2001: Placed fifth on *Fortune* magazine's list of the Forty Richest Americans Under Forty.

---

was valued at more than $500 million. By 2001, with a net worth of $1.23 billion, *Fortune* magazine named Bezos number five on its list of America's Forty Richest Under Forty. For a time, Amazon grew at a rate of 3,000 percent a year; by mid–2001, the company had sold some $5.9 billion in products to over 32 million customers. When Amazon sold its millionth book, Bezos fulfilled his promise to personally deliver it: a Princess Diana biography to Tokyo. Bezos works in a somewhat rundown section of Seattle, Washington, in a small office with a desk he made of a door nailed to two–by–fours as legs; he built all his company's desks according to this model in Amazon's early days. As he proudly declares, "We spend money only in areas where it matters to our customers." Analytical and methodical, Bezos is also enthusiastic and tireless in promoting his company and the potential of the Internet to change the way people buy. Ironically, however, Bezos confessed to buying about half of his books in regular stores where the browsing helps fulfill a social function. Bezos was named Person of the Year by *Time* magazine in 1999. In the fall of 2001, he appeared in a Taco Bell commercial promoting the "hand–held" quesadilla, donating his pay to the Special Olympics.

Career Details

When Bezos graduated from Princeton, he headed to Wall Street. Interested in a job with a high–tech start–up company, he joined Fitel, a new company that coupled high tech with high finance by creating software for tracking international stock trades. Under the management of David Shaw, whom Bezos credits for teaching him a great deal about becoming a good manager, Fitel had only 11 employees when Bezos joined the firm. In 1988 Fitel was sold to a Japanese firm, and Bezos joined the Bankers Trust Company, which leads the development of computer systems that helped manage more than $250 billion in assets. In 1990 Bezos moved to D. E. Shaw & Co. where he helped build one of the most successful and technically sophisticated quantitative hedge funds on Wall Street, becoming the company's youngest vice president in 1992.

The genesis for the creation of Amazon.com began in the spring of 1994 when Bezos was struck by the amazing annual growth of Internet usage. Nothing was growing as quickly, and Bezos began to explore the idea of creating a business that would tap into that growth. He decided on Internet retailing and methodically prepared a ranked list of the leading products that could best be sold over the Internet. Books led the list because there are so many items and no existing traditional bookstore could possibly offer 2.5 million titles, as Amazon.com does. The largest bookstore carries fewer than 200,000 titles. Settling on his product, he next considered a location for his business. Bezos carefully and methodically examined his options. He needed a location near a major book wholesaler, within reach of a pool of high–tech talent to make online sales work, and in a small–population state, to avoid sales tax when products were shipped across state lines. Narrowing it down to the western United States, Bezos eventually chose Seattle, Washington. In choosing a name for his company, Bezos was equally precise and analytical. He wanted a name that started with the letter *A* to head any alphabetical list, would be short and easy to spell, would be internationally recognizable, and most important, would convey a sense of size that his company would offer as the largest bookstore in the world. He finally settled on Amazon.com, after the largest river in the world. Bezos launched Amazon.com in June 1995. Early investors who put up $30,000 in 1994 would be holding Amazon stock worth $4.5 million at the end of 1997. By the end of 1998, the company had revenues of $610 billion. By late 1999, the company holdings were estimated at $8 billion.

Bezos's company was able to grow quickly by ordering the vast majority of Amazon.com books from book wholesalers' warehouses, allowing Bezos to start his company with little capital and relatively no investments in real estate or inventory.

Despite his company's successful growth, analysts predicted that Amazon.com could not survive once the other bookstore giants such as Barnes & Noble and Borders copied Bezos's simple idea. But Bezos claimed that many competing e–commerce sites focused too much effort on marketing mediocre products and creating an attractive–looking Web site, rather than focusing on logistics and customer service. Bezos also brought innovative features to Amazon.com that were soundly and technologically based, such as one–click shopping, forums that allowed readers to post and read both positive and negative reviews of a product, and links to other books by the same author or related topics. Bezos insisted that kind of information offered on the Web site (even negative reviews) was crucial for customers, since "Amazon's business is not selling things; our business is helping customers make purchasing decisions." Bezos also introduced a means of customer analysis that tracks purchases online and later suggests related products that the customer might be interested in purchasing. Although this strategy earned a reprimand for Bezos from the IBM chairman when Bezos identified online what IBM employees were buying, the strategy has reaped rewards for Bezos. Almost 70 percent of the company's revenues in 1999 originated from returning customers.

By 1998 Bezos began a strategy that would eventually serve the company very well; he began offering CD products in addition to books. By September 1999 Bezos announced, "Tomorrow, Amazon.com will be a place where you can find anything." True to his word, Bezos had already been building toward this initiative in 1999. By 2001, Amazon.com had established a formal relationship with the retail stores Toys "R" Us, Circuit City, and Target. Other items were also made available, including music, pet supplies, household goods, electronics, software, an auction service for customers, used items, and a service called "zshops" that searched for hard–to–find items. In 2001 the company also negotiated a deal with Borders to take over the latter's online bookselling operation. Bezos' purpose and aim for the company was to provide online customers with "earth's biggest river, earth's biggest selection." The new partnership with Circuit City allowed Amazon.com to greatly expand its consumer electronic selection, a department that has seen rapid expansion in sales.

Bezos is confident that his company has an advantage over the others because Amazon.com is technologically based and focused exclusively online. Other companies that are real estate based, he predicts, will have a harder time successfully accomplishing both Internet and traditional retailing. Success will depend, according to Bezos, on customer satisfaction and ease of service, which Amazon.com is determined to provide. Although Amazon.com has achieved remarkable success in dominating the online book market, the company has never shown a profit on its books and has accumulated losses of $2.7 billion. His personal wealth of $1.23 billion in 2001 was down from $4.05 billion in 2000. But Bezos insisted that he would continue to grow the company by returning any profits to the company. Bezos has invested in expanding his business rather than increasing the profit

Jeff Bezos. (AP/Wide World Photos.)

margin, following the principle of GBF: "Get Big Fast." Long–term success, according to Bezos, will depend on becoming one of the few "brands that matter." As he has said, "There are always two or three or four brands that matter. With the lead we have today, we should be the number one player."

Jeff Bezos is a pioneer in online retailing who has played an important role in helping to transform the way people shop today. Although skeptics have dismissed the financial viability of conducting large businesses on the Internet, Bezos has shown how it can be done by anticipating what consumers want and skillfully using the best technology to re–imagine the book business. Bezos realized that the Web could offer what a traditional bookstore could never deliver: a "stock" of more than 2.5 million titles. Customers can sample reviews and follow links to other books by the same author or to other books on comparable subjects. Convenience and service, the Amazon.com specialties, are factors that could substantially alter retailing.

Social and Economic Impact

Bezos, in creating a business plan and implementing it with Amazon.com, showed how an upstart company can quickly become an industry leader in the high–tech age. Without the need for great initial investment or inventory but with considerable focus on his market and the demands of online retailing, Bezos almost immediately challenged the largest bookstore giants. Information is the Internet's greatest attribute, and Bezos has shown how his customers' desire for books and other products can be satisfied in a radically different way.

Amazon.com has also established new benchmarks in the publishing industry while raising the level of customer service. Amazon has caused publishers to lower inventory and centralized distribution. The industry can also advance order certain books and pre–sell some titles by getting feedback from readers about what their favorite authors should publish. Through Amazon.com, Bezos has cut prices for the customer up to 40 percent on specially featured books, customized book selections, created reader forums, and provided interactivity between readers and authors. In response to changes in book retailing, traditional bookstores have also changed what they sell, stressing more reasons to visit their stores, such as coffee and pastries, poetry readings, and book signings. Bezos' inclusion of a wide array of products (in addition to books) at Amazon.com has created innumerable possibilities for customers to buy a variety of products online in a speedy fashion, without ever leaving their computers.

By 2001, Amazon.com had, for many, come to represent the best and the most reliable of Internet shopping experiences. But the company had very few friends on Wall Street. In September 2001 the company's per–share stock value had fallen from its peak value of $92 in January 1999 to less than $9. Many considered this to be an ominous sign for other Internet retailers: after all, they argued, if Amazon.com can't succeed, then who can?

In mid–2001 the good news for the company included its outstanding visibility and high volume of Web site traffic, its rising sales (projected to be $4 billion for the year), and its familiarity with the tastes of online shoppers. But the company was still struggling with profitability—it had lost almost $90 million on $1 billion in sales in a recent quarter and laid off 15 percent of its staff in mid–2001. It was also hampered by a marketing plan that failed to explain how it could make money shipping marginal items to customers with three–day deliveries. Finally, there was concern among some investors about the way the company assembled its profit–and–loss columns. While some financial analysts foresee eventual bankruptcy, a majority of advisors continue to hold back doomsday predictions, citing Amazon.com's growth into new areas, especially consumer electronics, as holding out promise for the company's future.

Sources of Information

Contact at: Amazon.com, Inc.
   PO Box 80387
   Seattle, WA 98108–0387
   Business Phone: (206)346–2992
   URL: http://www.amazon.com

Bibliography

Business Week, 27 September 1999.

Content Factory, 28 June 1999.

Daily Telegraph, 14 May 2001.

DSN Retailing Today, 3 September 2001.

eWeek, 16 April 2001.

Fortune, 8 November 1999.

Fortune, 4 September 2001.

Gentlemen's Quarterly, March 1998.

Money, 1 May 2001.

Publisher's Weekly, 5 January 1998.

Publisher's Weekly, 30 July 2001.

St. Louis Post–Dispatch, 7 October 1999.

Seattle Post, 20 September 2001.

U.S. News & World Report, 11 October 1999.

Newsweek International, 11 October 1999.

Clarence Birdseye

(1886-1956)
General Seafood Corporation

Overview

Billionaire scientist and inventor Clarence Birdseye was not the first person to preserve fresh food by freezing it for later consumption; in the early seventeenth century, English philosopher–statesman Francis Bacon had experimented with stuffing chickens with snow. As early as 1908, West Coast growers routinely froze their fruits, using what was known as a "cold–pack" process (freezing drums of sugared fruit and berries in an ice–salt mixture), to preserve them for storing and shipping (mostly by rail) to distant markets. During the same period, East Coast users of the cold–pack process included ice cream manufacturers and "New York dressed" (cold storage) chicken and fish wholesalers.

Yet it is Birdseye who is considered the father of frozen foods, and his Birds Eye Frosted Foods Company—along with the discovery of household refrigeration—changed the world's food industry forever. Birdseye's personal contributions to the industry were two–fold. First, he perfected a rapid method for freezing foods that preserved their cellular structure and composition, thus retaining their freshness, taste, and vitamin content. Second, he was the first to package frozen foods to be sold directly to the end–user, or consumer market.

Personal Life

Birdseye was born in Brooklyn, New York, the son of Clarence Frank Birdseye, lawyer and legal scholar, and Ada Underwood. As a young boy, Birdseye already

Clarence Birdseye. *(The Library of Congress.)*

lege expenses included the sale of frogs to the Bronx Zoo for snake food and the live trapping of 135 specimens of the comparatively rare black rat for a Columbia University professor's breeding experiments.

From 1910 to 1912, Birdseye was a field naturalist for the Biological Survey of the United States Department of Agriculture, work that led to his publication of a short monograph entitled "Some Common Mammals of Western Montana in Relation to Agriculture and Spotted Fever" (1912). A successful venture in marketing western furs during this period took him in 1912 to Labrador, Newfoundland, where he was associated for a time with the medical missionary Sir Wilfred Grenfell. Birdseye traded in furs in Labrador for the next five years.

During a visit to the United States, Birdseye married Eleanor Gannett on August 21, 1915; the couple had four children. In 1916 he returned to Labrador with his wife and their infant son. His changed domestic circumstances drew Birdseye's attention to the problems of food preservation. An avid fisherman, Birdseye preserved his catches in snow in the sub–zero winds. Impressed with the flavor and freshness of his frozen fish upon thawing them out—as though they had just been caught—Birdseye started to experiment with other indigenous species such as caribou and rabbit. He discovered that the meat from these animals, if frozen quickly and deeply, also retained its freshness and flavor until thawed out weeks later.

After perfecting a mechanical quick–freeze method for preserving food that would simulate the natural sub–zero climate he found in Labrador, Birdseye started his own company in New York in 1922, freezing fish fillets. Over the next several decades, his name and the Birds Eye logo became synonymous with retail frozen foods, in much the same way as the word "Kleenex" was used to indicate facial tissues.

Although his process ultimately made Birdseye very wealthy, he continued to work for his entire life. His last project (1953–1955) took him to Peru on an assignment to develop a new method of making paper stock from bagasse (crushed sugarcane stalks). While there, he suffered a heart attack that he attributed to the high altitude. He never fully recovered and died the following year in New York City.

Birdseye was a hands–on inventor and experimenter in the tradition of Benjamin Franklin and Thomas Edison. He was an original thinker and investigator, gifted with keen powers of observation and an enormous curiosity. He was also a capable businessman who held some 300 American and foreign patents. His early interest in the natural world never carried over into the business world but became a lifelong avocation nonetheless. Near the end of his life, he was coauthor with his wife of *Growing Woodland Plants* (1951).

had developed a keen interest in natural history. At the age of five, Birdseye gave his mother a mouse skin that he had dressed. Before he reached his teens, his proficiency in taxidermy led him to insert an advertisement in a sporting magazine offering instruction in the art, under the auspices of the American School of Taxidermy. At Montclair, New Jersey, where he attended high school, his other enduring interest, food preparation, came to light when he enrolled in the cooking class.

Following a family tradition, Birdseye entered Amherst College with the class of 1910 (majoring in biology), but financial difficulties adversely affected his attendance, and he did not graduate. Nonetheless, during his tenure there, his imaginative schemes for meeting col-

Career Details

World War I had interrupted Birdseye's search for a commercial application of his findings. After returning to the United States, he became the purchasing agent for the United States Housing Corporation (1917–1919) and assistant to the president of the United States Fisheries Association (1920–1922). In 1922 he resumed his experiments with quick–freezing, establishing himself in the corner of an icehouse in New Jersey. Encouraged, he formed Birdseye Seafoods, Inc., in New York, with a $20,000 stock subscription. His own capital investment consisted of $7 for an electric fan, buckets of brine, and cakes of ice. The first successful product was dressed fillets of haddock, frozen brick–hard in square containers made from old candy boxes. However, the general public proved disinterested, confusing his product with regular "cold storage" fish. Families were disinclined to know the detailed effects of scientific freezing upon the microscopic cellular composition of fish tissue and the benefits thereof, and soon his new company went bankrupt.

Undaunted, Birdseye started a new company, General Seafoods Corporation, with a $60,000 stock exchange in 1924. Located near a reliable source of fresh fish in Gloucester, Massachusetts, the company also housed laboratories for research and development. With a small group of associates, Birdseye perfected his novel process for quick–freezing, which consisted of packing dressed fish in cartons, then freezing the contents between two refrigerated surfaces under pressure (the "double–belt freezer," which later used refrigerated metal plates) that allowed the heat exchange to be accomplished directly and evenly upon the foods. By 1928 he was able to apply the technique to meat, poultry, fish, and shellfish in commercial quantities. He coined the word "quick–freeze," and referred to his products as "frosted foods." The missing element, public acceptance, appeared after 1929. In that year the Postum Company, skilled in the distribution of consumer food products, together with the Goldman Sachs Trading Corporation, acquired all patents and assets of Birdseye's company for a reported $22 million ($20 million for the patents and $2 million for the assets). Subsequently, the Postum Company purchased the Goldman Sachs interest and adopted the name General Foods.

In the 1940s, Birdseye invented a machine capable of quick–freezing loose vegetables individually and a process for preserving foods by quick–drying that he called the "anhydrous method." Neither was developed commercially. He also invented a reflector, an infrared heat lamp and a recoilless harpoon gun.

Social and Economic Impact

The scientific principle of freezing foods was already known when Birdseye began his first experiments.

Chronology:
Clarence Birdseye

1886: Born in Brooklyn, New York.

1910: Attended Amherst College.

1912: Traded furs in Labrador, Newfoundland.

1922: Founded Birdseye Seafood Inc.

1924: Developed quick–freeze process for freezing food; founded General Seafood Corporation.

1928: Developed the double–belt freezer.

1929: Sold patents and assets and became the frozen food division of General Foods Corporation.

1930: Birds Eye Frosted Foods appeared in retail markets, creating the birth of the retail frozen food industry.

1934: Birds Eye Frosted Food contracted with American Radiator Corporation to provide retail frozen food display cases.

1956: Died in New York City.

However, he was able to perfect and then apply this principle to consumer needs, thus bringing about the birth of the retail frozen food industry. Timing was perfect: his "frosted foods" market coincided with both the development of home refrigeration and freezing units, as well as with the onset of the Great Depression (1929), during which time the preservation of food for future use became of paramount importance. Of additional importance was the new availability of frozen fruits and vegetables on a year–round basis nationwide—previously available only during the harvesting season (with the exception of states where year–round growing occurred, such as in California) unless canned or bottled for later use.

Parallel in time, during the 1920s, farmers represented 27 percent of the population, and hydroponics (the growing of plants in water) had been invented. The U.S. Department of Agriculture created the Bureaus of Home Economics and Dairying during these years. Interest in the preservation of surplus crops and meats heightened on a commercial level but had not yet trickled down to the end–users, or consumers. Families began purchasing refrigerators during the 1920s, just as facilities for transporting, storing, and displaying the frozen foods were being developed. An article appearing in the September 1929 issue of the *Ladies' Home Journal*, entitled "A New Food Vision," featured a photograph of Birdseye's belt freezer and speculated what the food stores of the future would look like.

With the onset of the depression later in 1929, Birds Eye eased the burden and kept the growth trend continuing by contracting with a commercial credit company to finance retailer display cases, allowing grocers to make monthly installments on the equipment. In 1934, Birds Eye contracted with the American Radiator Corporation to manufacture cost–effective freezer display cases for local grocery markets and leased them to retailers for approximately eight dollars a month. Articles and recipes devoted to the new trend in frozen foods began to appear regularly in *The Times* and other publications. By 1943 food writer Clementine Paddleford described the variety of quick–frozen, box–packed meals as "wartime savers of storage and shipping space." For those who could not afford free–standing home freezers (old–fashioned ice-boxes were still common through the 1940s), another article promoted the rental of neighborhood frozen–food lockers for storing freezer foods. (The mass production of free–standing home freezers was put on hold during World War II but resumed on a large scale in the 1950s, coinciding with the introduction of frozen "TV dinners.")

The new technology created a competitive market, and, according to Paddleford, 60 varieties of frozen food were available to the public in 1943, packed by 140 companies and sold under 72 brands in 30,000 stores across 48 states. Advertisements from that period show that Penguin brand "frozen–fresh" peas sold for 21 cents, while Birds Eye brand frozen cherries sold for 30 cents. Exulted Paddleford in a 1943 *Times* article, "cardboard and plastic film are all it takes," to package one million pounds of frozen peas, whereas "some 269,196 pounds of steel and tin" were required to store the same amount of peas in cans. These were important considerations during the wartime years, not to mention the improved taste and freshness of the frozen foods, compared to the canned ones. In 1944, Birds Eye had leased the first insulated railroad cars designed to transport food nationwide. The refrigerated shipping industry was thus born. Within a few years, quick–frozen foods had revolutionized food distribution and had brought about sweeping changes in national eating habits. Additionally, it had effected fundamental improvements in American agriculture through stimulating the seed industry to refine varieties for quick–frozen products, introducing quality controls in field production and stabilizing prices which brought millions of acres of farmland into more profitable use.

Although Birdseye died in 1956, he lived long enough to appreciate the thriving success of his revolutionary ideas. His company remained at the forefront of frozen food technology, being the first to offer foil over-wraps on boxed vegetables, which held moisture ten times better than waxed paper, and also was the first to introduce vegetables and sauces to which meat was added, for the health–conscious consumers. Since the mid–1990s, Birds Eye has introduced 57 new items on the frozen food market, and the familiar 'Birds Eye" logo remains prominent in both small groceries and supermarkets worldwide.

Sources of Information

Bibliography

"A Man Named Birdseye." 23 November 2001. Available at http://www.birdseye.com.

Bernstein, Leilah. "Times Past." *Los Angeles Times*, 24 January 2001.

Flatow, Ira. "Analysis: History and properties of absolute zero; experiments and discoveries relating to the science of cold and freezing." *Talk of the Nation/Science Friday (NPR)*, 14 January 2000.

Hoffman, Gene. "Visit with Clarence Spurs Insights into Frozens' Future." *Frozen Food Age*, October 1999.

"In the Beginning." *Frozen Food Age*, August 1997.

Stelljes, Kathryn Barry. "Timeline: A Legacy of Research." *Agricultural Research*, December 1999.

Carole Lynn Black

(1944-)
Lifetime Entertainment Services

Overview

Carole Black is widely regarded as one of the most influential women in the entertainment business industry. As president and CEO of Lifetime Entertainment Services, a joint venture of the Hearst Corporation and the Walt Disney Company, Black heads a company that includes Lifetime Television, the Lifetime Movie Network, Lifetime Real Women, and Lifetime Online. The Lifetime channel alone reaches 80 million households in the country. With no prior broadcasting industry experience, Black became the first woman ever to head a network owned–and–operated station in a major market in her position as president and general manager of KNBC–TV, Los Angeles. She went on to lead the station to become the number one in its market. Before that, Black had a very successful ten–year history as an executive at the Walt Disney Company.

Personal Life

Black divides her time between her two–bedroom apartment in Manhattan, New York, and a house in Beverly Hills, California. She is divorced and has one son, Eric, a television producer.

She serves on the board of the Hollywood Radio and Television Society (HRTS), the National Association of Television Programming Executives (NATPE), American Women in Radio and Television (AWRT), the Walter Kaitz Foundation, Cable Positive, and Cable in the Classroom. She is a member of the Cable Television Administration and Marketing Society, Inc. (CTAM), the Inter-

Carole Lynn Black. *(Hulton/Archive.)*

national Radio & Television Society Foundation, Inc. (IRTS), New York Women in Communications, New York Women in Film, Women in Cable & Telecommunications, and the Women's Sports Foundation. Black was named one of America's 100 Most Important Women by *Ladies' Home Journal* in 1999 and listed as one of New York's 100 Most Influential Women in Business by *Crain's New York Business*. In 2001, Black was ranked 18 among *CableFAX Magazine's* Top 100, and *The Hollywood Reporter* has repeatedly named her as one of the Top Women in Entertainment. She received the Media Leader of the Year Award from the National Association of Women Business Owners of Los Angeles in 2001.

Black was born July 18, 1944, and raised in Cincinnati, Ohio. She was brought up by her grandparents, who

were Armenian, after her parents divorced when she was very young. She gives credit to her grandmother, who, she told *People*, "made me feel I could do everything in life" and named both grandparents as her mentors in *CableFAX Magazine*. She received a Bachelor of Art's degree in English literature from Ohio State University in 1966.

After graduation, Black began as an assistant brand manager at Procter & Gamble in her hometown of Cincinnati, Ohio. She helped develop campaigns for Gleem and Crest toothpastes and Head & Shoulders shampoo, among others. She told *Broadcasting & Cable* years later, "My experience at Procter & Gamble taught me that branding is about finding the uniqueness in two very similar products, presenting that positive uniqueness to the consumer and driving that message home constantly." She stayed with the company for three years, until 1969.

After the birth of her son that year, Black became a freelance writer and marketing consultant in order to work out of her home. In 1972 she became a writer for TransAmerican Press, a group of magazines that covered the transportation industry. Black was named executive vice president of the company in 1981 and moved to Los Angeles to run TransAmerican, which later folded.

Black then joined advertising agency DDB Needham in Chicago, Illinois, in 1983 as an account supervisor. She stayed with the firm until 1986, eventually becoming senior vice president, management representative.

Career Details

It was that year she decided to jump into the entertainment industry, taking an executive position at the Walt Disney Company. As vice president, worldwide marketing home video, she was credited with initiating brand management and the flourishing sell–through business of Disney–branded films. Under her guidance, the domestic video division, as well as the Disney brand itself, became the leader worldwide. In 1988, Black was promoted to senior vice president of marketing and television at Disney, where she developed and launched the successful children's programming franchise with *The Disney Afternoon*, as well as leading one of the most profitable syndication deals ever with *Home Improvement*.

In 1994, Black left Disney to accept the position of president and general manager of KNBC–TV and became the first woman to head a network owned–and–operated station in a major market. Although well respected in her field, Black lacked any broadcast experience, causing her appointment to shock some industry insiders. She quickly caught on, however, and used her marketing background to promote the Los Angeles television station as a brand and highlight its high–quality programs among viewers. She boosted the number of female viewers by the addition of lifestyle segments and positive human interest features. Under her guidance, the network rose from second to become the leader in its marketplace in less than two years. In 1998 the station became the first to win seven out of seven weekday and weekend news races during the sweeps period, beating its own previous record of six out of seven in 1996 and 1997.

Black was named president and CEO of Lifetime Entertainment Services in February of 1999, replacing former president Doug McCormick. As soon as Black assumed the post on March 22 of the same year, she began making some important changes. Launched in 1984 and designated as "Television for Women" in 1994, the network easily leads the female demographic in cable, though many female cable subscribers weren't familiar with it. Feeling that the network had become lax due to a lack of strong competition, Black brought a new team of executives to the marketing department and gave it more money in order to raise the station's profile and gain greater awareness among consumers. Brand recognition, Black knows, is key, as competition in the field has recently sprung up with Oxygen Media, partly owned by Oprah Winfrey, with Turner Broadcasting System now in the mix.

About half of the programming on Lifetime is supplied by the broadcast networks. Shows including *Golden Girls* and *Designing Women* are run every day. The ex–Fox series purchased by Lifetime, *Party of Five*, airs five days a week, while *Chicago Hope* runs four. The network also runs games of the Women's National Basketball Association (WNBA) that, though not big ratings–getters, improve the network's image, according to Black. Black also has plans to beef up Lifetime's original programming line–up as well, launching several prime time series and a daily live information show produced by ABC News. Black has also built on the success of such popular Lifetime fare as *Intimate Portrait* and the acclaimed series *Any Day Now* and plans to expand its Internet presence through its Lifetime Online unit. Black's initiatives yielded results as early as October 1999, when Lifetime became number one among basic cable viewers in the total day in all women's demographics, including women in the 18–34 and 25–54 categories. Continuing its momentum, Lifetime snagged the number two position in both prime time and total day household ratings in January 2000 after Black had been on the job less than a year. The network also continues its dominance in the female demographic. When asked of her five–year plan, Black told *Crain's New York Business*, "Professionally, to continue to make Lifetime the leading source of entertainment, information and support for women."

Black is also committed to making the network even more socially active and, in return, the network has been recognized by such leading women's groups and organizations as the National Women's Political Caucus, the

Chronology:
Carole Lynn Black

1944: Born.

1966: Received a Bachelor of Arts degree in English literature from Ohio State University.

1966: Began as an assistant brand manager at Procter & Gamble.

1972: Started as a writer for TransAmerican Press.

1983: Joined DDB Needham advertising agency as an account supervisor.

1986: Became vice president, worldwide marketing home video of The Walt Disney Company.

1988: Promoted to senior vice president, marketing, television at Disney.

1994: Accepted the position of president and general manager of KNBC–TV.

1996: KNBC became the leader in its marketplace.

1999: Named president and CEO of Lifetime Entertainment Services.

National Multiple Sclerosis Society, the Susan G. Komen Foundation, Women in Communications, the New York Women's Agenda, and Women in Cable & Telecommunications, among others. Lifetime's initiative for breast cancer awareness garnered them the 1996 Golden CableACE award, the cable industry's highest honor. Black led Lifetime's public service campaign begun in 1999, Caring for Kids: Our Lifetime Commitment, advocating innovations in childcare. In her testimony to the Senate Help Committee on the initiative, Black said, "It's a subject close to my heart both personally and professionally. Having been a single working mother, I know first–hand how challenging childcare can be." Black and Lifetime have also been promoting the involvement of women in politics and have teamed up with the National Organization for Women (NOW) seeking to advocate on behalf of women worldwide with a campaign tentatively called "Standup Against Violence."

Social and Economic Impact

Black has charted new territory for women throughout her illustrious career, which is littered with achievements and awards. With the female market always in mind, Black spoke to women early in her career, helping launch the "softer side of Sears" campaign when she worked at an advertising agency. When she was vice president at Disney, Black was credited with boosting home video sales and creating a branding strategy that targeted working mothers. At KNBC, she was the first female to head a commercial television station in a major market and brought more female viewers to the network by the addition of lifestyle segments and positive human interest features that women wanted to see. Along the way, she helped build brand identity and build sales with better ratings and more viewers. At Lifetime, she continues to develop programming and entertainment designed specifically for women. She is credited with bringing newer, fresher programming to the station as well as enhancing its image with her savvy marketing maneuvers.

In a position to provide more than just entertainment for women, Black has also been a staunch advocate for a number of women's issues that she has brought to public attention through the company she heads. As part of Lifetime's childcare initiative, Black even expanded part of the company's website to help families with child care problems contact elected officials to share their stories with them. Committed to such causes as child care and breast cancer awareness, Black and Lifetime have been recognized for their efforts by several prestigious nonprofit organizations and leading women's groups.

Sources of Information

Contact at: Lifetime Entertainment Services
309 W. 49th St.
New York, NY 10019
Business Phone: (212)957–4610
URL: http://www.lifetimetv.com

Bibliography

"About Lifetime." *Lifetime Entertainment Services*, 2001. Available at http://www.lifetimetv.com.

American Women in Radio and Television, 2001. Available at http://www.awrtla.org.

"Black is Golden." *Broadcasting & Cable*, 19 March 2001.

"Building a Better Brand in L.A." *Broadcasting & Cable*, 3 June 1996.

CableFAX Magazine. 6 October 2001. Available at http://cabletoday.com.

"Careers of Humanities Graduates." *Ohio State University*, 2001. Available at http://www.cohums.ohio–state.edu.

"Carole Black." *People Weekly*, 14 May 2001.

"Femmes Fence for Cable Auds." *Variety*, 6 December 1999.

"Lifetime Entertainment Services." *Hoover's*. November 2001. Available at http://www.hoovers.com.

"Lifetime Entertainment Services." *The Industry Standard*. November 2001. Available at http://www.thestandard.com.

"New York's 100 Most Influential Women in Business." *Crain's New York Business*. Available at http://www.crainsny.com.

"Opportunity of a Lifetime." *Broadcasting & Cable*, 18 October 1999.

Arthur M. Blank

(1942-)
The Home Depot, Inc.

Overview

Arthur M. Blank, with partner Bernard Marcus, founded The Home Depot, Inc., the largest home improvement chain in the world. With more than 1,200 stores and 227,000 employees, the company offers everything for do–it–yourselfers from lumber and plumbing supplies to paint and wall coverings. Each store, which is approximately 130,000 square feet, stocks 40,000 to 50,000 different products. Stores are located in 48 states in the United States, seven Canadian provinces, Chile, Puerto Rico, and Argentina. Home Depot also owns 30 EXPO Design Centers, with high quality products and custom showrooms, found throughout the United States.

Personal Life

Blank is married and has four children. With three children from a previous marriage, he lives with wife, Stephanie, and son, Joshua, in Atlanta, Georgia. The couple were also expecting twins in the summer of 2001. An avid runner, he logs about 20 miles a week and has run in several marathons, including the New York marathon. He also regularly participates in the six–mile Peachtree Road Race held each July in Atlanta, Georgia. He has been described as the quieter partner to Marcus' showman–like personality.

He serves on the board of trustees of the Carter Center, Emory University, the National Conference of Christians and Jews, the Georgia Council of the Arts, and the North Carolina Outward Bound School, among others. He is chairman–elect of the Atlanta Chamber of Com-

Arthur M. Blank. *(AP/Wide World Photos/Alan Mothner.)*

merce. Blank is a member of Babson College's Entre-preneurship Advisory Board and Academy of Distin-guished Entrepreneurs. He established the Home Depot Entrepreneurial Scholarship program for undergraduates, as well as the Arthur M. Blank Family Foundation. Blank was inducted into the Babson College Academy of Dis-tinguished Entrepreneurs and has received several awards, including the Brotherhood/Sisterhood Award (1994) from the National Conference of Christians and Jews, the Selig Distinguished Service Award (1996) from the American Jewish Committee, an honorary doctor of law degree from Babson College (1998), named *Geor-gia Trend's* Most Respected CEO for the year 2000 and ranked eighth on *Worth* magazine's list of the 50 Best;

co–author of the book, *Built from Scratch: How a Cou-ple of Regular Guys Grew the Home Depot from Noth-ing to $30 Billion*, which is about the founding of Home Depot.

He was born September 27, 1942, in Queens, New York. The family—including Blank, his parents, and his brother—lived in a series of one–bedroom apartments in Sunnyside, then Flushing, New York. In high school, Blank played football and baseball and ran on the track team. His father, a talented runner, quit running after col-lege and died of a heart attack when Blank was 15. When Blank ran the New York Marathon in 1986, he honored his father and recognized their mutual love of running by wearing a shirt that said "For Pop."

In 1963 he received a Bachelor of Science degree in business administration from Babson College in Wellesley, Massachusetts. He worked as an accountant and later joined a small pharmaceutical company that his father, a pharmacist, had started. The company was bought by Daylin, Inc., so Blank took an executive position at one of Daylin's drugstores. Daylin also owned Handy Dan Home Improvement Centers, where Blank then took a position and where he met future partner, Bernard Marcus. Blank worked his way up from corporate controller to vice president of finance, and Marcus served as Handy Dan's CFO. Blank and Marcus were later fired from Handy Dan by a corporate raider in 1978. Both were completely distraught. Blank considered suing the company for wrongful termination but was advised by a friend to forget it and get on with his life.

Career Details

Blank and Marcus did get on with their lives and with a little money set out to open their own chain of home improvement centers. The two founders met over coffee to develop their plans. As the two fielded offers for seed money to open the stores, instinct played a big part in whether or not they accepted the money. One early prospective investor was billionaire Ross Perot, who offered $25 million for a controlling stake in the company but insisted the employees drive only Chevrolets. Blank and Marcus turned him down.

They gathered enough money to open the first three stores in Atlanta, Georgia, in 1979 under the name the Home Depot. The first few stores were attached to Treasure Island stores and stocked around 25,000 products. Blank and Marcus relate in their book, that the managers of the first stores, in preparation for the grand opening, got the store all tidied up, not realizing the partners wanted it to look like a warehouse. "We wanted sawdust. We wanted skid marks on the floor," they recalled. After a night appropriately "dressing down" the place, the Home Depot was ready to open. The company had 200 employees and $7 million in sales but sustained a loss of nearly $1 million that year. By 1980, however, the stores were turning a profit and the company went public the next year. The initial public offering (IPO) raised more than $4 million dollars for the company. The company cartoon mascot, Homer D. Poe, appeared in the company's advertising for the first time in 1981, and their first Florida store opened. At the end of 1981, the company had grown to eight stores, 700 employees, and sales of $51 million. They were also named by *Management Horizons* as High Growth Retailer.

The company opened its first stores in Arizona and Louisiana in 1983 and computerized checkout systems were then installed. The next year, Home Depot's stock was listed on the New York Stock Exchange. That year, the company acquired Bowater Home Centers, with

Chronology:
Arthur M. Blank

1942: Born.

1979: Opened first Home Depot stores.

1981: Home Depot went public.

1986: Sales topped $1 billion; first super–sized store of 140,000 square feet opened.

1991: Opened first EXPO Design Center.

1996: Home Depot celebrated 40 quarters, or ten years, of consecutive record financial results.

1999: First Villager's Hardware opened.

1997: Named CEO.

2000: Stepped down as CEO.

2001: Stepped down as co–chairman.

stores in Dallas, Shreveport, Baton Rouge, and Mobile. The company made its expansion into California in 1985, establishing a West Coast division. By then, Home Depot was comprised of 50 stores and 5,400 associates and was selling $700 million in products. Sales topped $1 billion in 1986 as the company opened its first supersized store of 140,000 square feet. Two years later, the company began building stores in the Northeast and continued to receive honors, including Retailer of the Year from *Management Horizons*. In 1989 the company opened its Northeast Division and also began its community service programs for affordable housing and at–risk youth and built their first Habitat for Humanity homes in Atlanta, Dallas, Tampa, and Miami.

The 1990s were a time of continuing growth for Home Depot. The first EXPO Design Center was opened in 1991 in San Diego, California. The stores featured upscale home appliances and other products shown in their custom showrooms. The year 1993 saw Home Depot stores open in the Pacific Northwest. The next year, its Midwest Division was established after expanding into the Detroit and Chicago markets. The company had by then made considerable charitable contributions, including raising $7 million for City of Hope Medical Research Center and sponsoring the 1996 Paralympic Games. *Fortune* magazine named Home Depot the Most Admired Specialty Retailer in 1994 and again in 1995, which by then had 423 stores and sales of $15.5 billion. With charitable contributions of more than $8 million, the company began collecting several awards for its social consciousness, including the President's National Community Service Award, and the Robinson Humphrey Alexander Award for Corporate Citizenship, both in 1995. The company celebrated 40 quarters, or ten years, of consecutive record financial results in 1996. It had over 500 stores that year, nearly 100,000 employees, and $19.5 billion in sales.

Although Blank ran the company for years as president and chief operating officer with Marcus, Marcus had served as the company's CEO since its inception. Blank was officially elected to the position of CEO and president in 1997 after Marcus stepped into the chairman role. The growth continued with the launch of Load 'N Go, the company's truck rental service, and the purchase of National Blinds & Wallpaper Factory, a telephone mail order company. Home Depot announced a new convenience store format called Villager's Hardware in 1999. Blank told *Your Company* the new stores were designed for those who just want to "park their car right in front, go in, buy a can of paint or a hammer, walk out and be done." That year, they partnered with Emerson Electric to create an exclusive line of tools. They also announced a partnership with NASCAR's Joe Gibbs Racing.

In 1998, Home Depot branched out, opening stores in Puerto Rico and Chile. The company opened its first store in Argentina in August 2000, furthering the company's goal of operating more that 2,300 stores by the end of 2004. Blank and Marcus' book was published in 1999, the same year the store launched its internal Home Depot University and launched the new customer–driven website. Home Depot stock also was added to the Dow Jones Industrial Average. Blank's foundation, the Arthur M. Blank Family Foundation, and Home Depot contributed $1 million to Zoo Atlanta for a home for Chinese pandas Lun Lun and Yang Yang. The Legend Museum also opened that year, which was dedicated to the history and values of the Home Depot and located at the Atlanta Store Support Center. The museum is for the education and benefit of employees, their families, vendors, stockholders, and other interested parties. The company was named *Fortune* magazine's Most Admired Specialty Retailer for the sixth consecutive year in 1999.

In 2000, Blank announced he would step down as the company's CEO, making room for successor Robert L. Nardelli, the first person to run the company other than Blank and Marcus. The year Blank retired, *Fortune* named it the ninth Most Admired Company in America and again listed the company as the Most Admired Specialty Retailer for the ninth year in a row. The company expanded its international reach, opening stores in Argentina and Quebec. The first e–commerce online store was offered to customers in Las Vegas, and the Home Depot Floor Store was launched in Plano, Texas. The company continued to expand its online ordering service, with customers able to order about 20,000 of the company's roughly 50,000 in–store items online as of early 2001 and grew to nearly 100,000 items by late 2001.

In February 2001, Blank announced he would step down as co–chairman of the company, effective May 30, 2001. His plans included focusing on the work of the Arthur M. Blank Family Foundation and becoming more active in nonprofit and business communities in his hometown of Atlanta. He also wanted to spend more time with his family. Blank left Home Depot with 34.8 million shares in the company—its seventh largest individual stockholder. Marcus also decided to step down as chairman by the end of 2001.

Social and Economic Impact

Blank redefined retailing with the $46 billion home–improvement giant he founded. Not only did Home Depot become the leader in its field but it spawned retailers in a variety of other sectors to utilize a similar format that they perfected, consisting of a no–frills warehouse store filled with tens of thousands of products with low prices and highly trained employees. The company has been recognized eight years in a row by *Fortune* magazine as America's Most Admired Specialty Retailer and is instantly recognizable to customers familiar with the bright orange aprons of its employees. Additionally, the company is the second largest retailer in the country, behind Wal–Mart.

The company, which had a philanthropic budget of more than $25 million in 2000, gives back to the community with donations to at–risk youths and the environment and work aimed at providing affordable housing. The company's Team Depot, a volunteer program organized in 1992, encourages employees to contribute to local causes. Home Depot has been the recipient of numerous philanthropic awards over the years. In addition to making philanthropy part of Home Depot's corporate culture, his own Arthur M. Blank Family Foundation has also provided millions of dollars to a variety of causes over the years. Blank has planned to donate 75 percent of his wealth to the foundation after his death.

Sources of Information

Contact at: The Home Depot, Inc.
2455 Paces Ferry Rd.
Atlanta, GA 30339–4024
Business Phone: (770)433–8211
URL: http://www.homedepot.com

Bibliography
"About Us." *The Home Depot, Inc.*, November 2001. Available at http://www.homedepot.com.

"Arthur Blank." *Chain Store Age Executive With Shopping Center Age*, September 1997.

"Chairman of the Boards: Arthur Blank Corporate Executive." *Runner's World*, March 1995.

"Co–founder Trade Depot's Orange Apron for Family and Community." *National Home Center News*, 5 March 2001.

"Exit the Builder, Enter The Repairman." *Fortune*, 19 March 2001.

"The 50 Best CEOs." *Worth*, 1999–2001. Available at http://www.worth.com.

"The Handyman." *Business Week*, 10 January 2000. Available at http://www.businessweek.com.

"Home Depot Builds Up Its Web Presence." *The Industry Standard*, 26 April 2001. Available at http://www.thestandard.com.

"The Home Depot Builds Online Success with Broadvision One–to–One Enterprise 6.0–World's Largest Home Improvement Retailer Enhances Sites with Broadvision's J2ee–Enabled Applications." *Business Wire*, 20 August 2001.

"Home Depot Founder Blank Quits Board to Clear Path for Current CEO Nardelli." *Wall Street Journal*, 22 February 2001.

"Home Depot,"14 August 2001. Available at http://www.forbes.com.

"The Home Depot, Inc." *Hoover's*, November 2001. Available at http://www.hoovers.com.

"Home Depot Looks to Fill in Blank." *Home Textiles Today*, 26 February 2001.

"Home Depot: Now It Can Be Told." *Your Company*, 1 May 1999.

"Home Is Castle." *Georgia Trend*, May 2000.

"Stories of Entrepreneurs." *National Commission on Entrepreneurship*, 2001. Available at http://www.ncoe.org.

"There's No Place Like Home Depot." *Nation's Business*, February 1992.

Bobbi Brown

(1957-)
Bobbi Brown Cosmetics

Overview

For many little girls, playing with their mothers' cosmetics is just part of the fun of growing up. For Bobbi Brown, it turned into a $50 million line of exclusive cosmetics bearing her name. Estee Lauder acquired her company in 1995, but Brown remained as CEO, retaining full creative control over the product line. Brown's exclusive products grace the faces of Hollywood's most glamorous—and for good reason. She seems to have captured the true essence of natural color—so natural in fact that Oprah Winfrey once asked, "How does a white girl get these colors so perfect for us girls?" Princess Diana and the Spice Girls were also big fans. Brown, a career mom, has also published several bestseller books on beauty and the art of makeup. She is the exclusive beauty editor of the NBC "Today" show. Her product line, Bobbi Brown Essentials, is distributed in 170 exclusive stores in the U.S. and 16 countries worldwide.

Personal Life

The eldest of three children, Brown started playing with her mother's old makeup at an early age. She was wholly captivated with her mother's glamour and beauty rituals. She used her mother's old lipsticks as though they were crayons or markers, and proceeded to bring out the best look in her dolls—as well as her sister Linda. Brown credits her mother, Sandra, a homemaker, with teaching her at an early age to pursue whatever she loved most to do. The angst of adolescence and career indecision that plagued many young adults did not visit Brown: she knew what she wanted and didn't need to think about it.

She loved cosmetics. Even her father James, a lawyer, agreed in a *People Weekly* story featuring his daughter that "it was something she always had on her mind." Brown related to interviewers for that article that during a vacation in Florida as a teenager, she covered herself with layers of baby oil and iodine. But coming home on the plane, she wanted to look even more bronzed, so she slipped into the plane's bathroom and covered herself with dark foundation. When everyone remarked about her deep tan, she kept her makeup secret to herself.

Brown was unhappy and unfulfilled in college. In 1976, she dropped out of the University of Arizona, and at her mother's suggestion, enrolled at Emerson College in Boston, a liberal arts school that allowed her to create a major in theatrical makeup. She graduated in 1979 and ultimately found employment as an assistant to a New York City makeup artist. Her salary was meager, but her father sent monthly rent money to help her along. Eventually, she made a name for herself, went solo as a makeup artist working on top models, and developed her own line of products after tiring of the limited colors and textures commercially available to her at the time.

Brown received the Cosmetic Executive Women's "Achievement Award" in 1998, and *Glamour* magazine's "Women of the Year Award" in 1997. She has two *New York Times* best–selling books, *Bobbi Brown Beauty* (1997), and *Bobbi Brown Teenage Beauty* (1998). She offers beauty advice columns in *Seventeen* and *Allure* magazines, and has appeared on "Oprah," "Entertainment Tonight," and "E! TV's" Style channel. Brown's charitable interests include running Image workshops for the Family Respite Center, fund–raising for The Breast Cancer Research Foundation, the Fresh Air Fund, and Dress for Success.

Today, Brown works mostly out of her house in Montclair, New Jersey. She is married to Steven Plofker, a lawyer and real estate developer, and has three sons, Dylan, Dakota, and Duke. She told *People Weekly* interviewers that career moms who carry some recognition among the general public do not always have it so easy. She recalled a recent trip to the grocery store, when another shopper asked whether she was Bobbi Brown? "I said yes," she lamented, "but was embarrassed because I looked like a schlump." Brown is a down–to–earth mother who on most days wears a ponytail and very little makeup. She hates travel and loves spectator basketball, particularly if her sons are playing—or the New Jersey Nets.

Career Details

Brown's modest internship as an assistant to a makeup artist eventually panned out, but it took several years. As her reputation grew, she began a solo career working on top models from *Glamour* and *Vogue,* and other "A–list" fashion designers and photographers. One

Bobbi Brown. *(Hulton/Archive/Diane Cohen.)*

of her early high–visibility jobs was a magazine cover for *Vogue.* The more experience she developed, the more disappointed she became with the available makeup she was forced to work with. She particularly disliked the unflattering colors and poor consistency of many of the products. There was a conspicuous absence of shades that complimented a large bandwidth of skin tones along the color spectrum. Her early motivation to create her own colors stemmed from a desire to simplify her life and work, allowing her to find just the right color for a model without having to play around for hours mixing up several other colors. Often, to find just the right color she wanted, she would mix eye pencil, blush, gloss, theatre cosmetics, or makeup from overseas.

Chronology:
Bobbi Brown

1957: Born.

1976: Dropped out of University of Arizona and enrolled at Emerson College.

1979: Graduated from Emerson College with major in theatrical makeup.

1990: With friend Rosalind Landis, marketed her own product at Bergdorf Goodman.

1995: Sold her line to Estee Lauder, but remained as CEO.

At this turning point, Brown, already married and the mother of her first son, was asked to participate in a photo shoot for a Ralph Lauren ad campaign. She really wanted the job, which represented what she had always worked toward, but it required a two–week absence from her family. After much deliberation, she turned it down.

However, her frustration over the limited choice of product colors she had to work with stirred an entrepreneurial interest in her. Her personal goal was to develop a lipstick that would look more natural than any product commercially available at that time. With the help of an independent chemist she had found in New York, Brown decided to come up with her own lipstick product and colors. First, she created a brown–toned lipstick for herself. The chemist was able to develop just the perfect color she had envisioned, but the final result lacked the texture and consistency she wanted. Since the chemist was a man, he wouldn't try the product on his lips, but his female assistant worked with Brown to help communicate to the chemist just exactly what Brown was looking for. They worked and worked and finally got it right. Brown had a few tubes made up for her. When it drew raves from friends and models, who wanted to purchase them, she knew she was onto something good.

She decided to create ten basic lipstick colors. From the beginning, Brown had a distinct philosophy about makeup that later turned into her signature approach to fashion: she did not want her products to mask or disguise a woman's own natural good looks. As she later told *Your Company*'s Susan Caminiti, "Beauty to me is about being yourself, and makeup should be used as a tool to enable every woman to feel good about herself."

Brown's friend, Rosalind Landis, was a publicist at Cairns and Associates in New York. She was so impressed with the colors that in 1990, she and Brown decided to market them. ("Roz" Landis is now the company president, alongside her CEO friend.) Landis agreed to write a few press releases about the lipstick. They placed an ad in *Glamour*, which identified Brown, the creator of the product, as a professional makeup artist. Her phone began ringing with orders. Meanwhile, Landis had referred Brown to one of her friends who was a cosmetics buyer at Bergdorf Goodman in Manhattan. The friend thought it was a great idea to market a makeup artist's own line of makeup. She agreed to give Brown and Landis some display space at Bergdorf's and to carry the product. In a competitive field already filled with more cosmetic brands than any woman could ever use in a lifetime, this was a major step for them.

In February 1991, Brown and Landis marched into Bergdorf Goodman and set up their little display on a table that held makeup bags and which had been partially cleared off for them. Their entire inventory was about 500 tubes, estimated to sell at approximately 100 tubes a month. They sold 100 tubes the first day. During the first week, men would come in to buy all ten lipstick shades in one shot. "I learned the importance of 'buzz,'" Brown remarked in the *Los Angeles Times* article. "Many of those lipsticks were sold to men in suits from other cosmetic companies. They wanted to see what I was up to."

While Brown was still marketing her lipsticks at Bergdorf's, her freelance customers and the beauty editors of women's magazines like *Vogue* and *Harper's Bazaar* began asking for lip pencils to go with the lipsticks. Brown decided to make that her next product. Needless to say, Brown's calendar began to fill up. She was still working as a freelance makeup artist, she had a husband and son, and she had her contract with Bergdorf's. After about six months, the women knew they had to find some office space to keep up with the demand. At that time, the two friends decided to make the plunge. Each committed $10,000 from her savings, and Landis quit her full–time job. "For us, it was a huge amount of money at the time," Brown told Susan Vaughn of the *Los Angeles Times*. "My husband was in law school, and we'd just had our first kid." The women opened up a small office at 505 Park Avenue, but had very little overhead beyond the rent. But they never had to take out a loan. Orders kept coming in, and the business was profitable the first year. They did no advertising, and their business was built upon word of mouth. The buzz from their sales at Bergdorf's attracted Neiman Marcus, then Henri Bendel, then Saks, and so on. Soon, stores from overseas began calling. Brown realized that her two–person operation might be grossly inadequate for the demand her products created. Another turning point in her career was at hand.

In 1995, Brown received a telephone call from an investment banker asking if she would be interested in having dinner with Estee Lauder CEO, Leonard Lauder.

Brown and Landis accepted the invitation. Over a wonderful dinner on his veranda overlooking Central Park, Lauder informed the women that he was enamored with their company, that their products were outselling his, and that he wanted to buy them out. Brown demurely replied that the company was not for sale, but agreed to think about it. She thought about it for six minutes. She knew before she left that evening that she wanted the deal to happen. She considered Lauder the best of the best, and if she were ever going to sell, she would hope it would be to Lauder.

Many meetings followed. Later, Brown told *Your Company*'s Susan Caminiti, "[T]he best advice I can give entrepreneurs [is that]...if you sell your company and want a working relationship with the new owners, you'd better be honest about your needs and goals. Otherwise you have an arrangement that's bound to fail." As for Lauder, he told *Los Angeles Times* interviewers, "There was nothing we wanted to change. I was extremely impressed with her quiet ambition and her almost religious desire to make women look pretty. It was very obvious that she had what women wanted."

The deal closed for a reported $100 million. Importantly, Brown retained her position at the head of new firm and could now concentrate more on the things she knew and loved best: product development and advertising. It was a win–win situation.

Social and Economic Impact

Bobbi Brown has made nonmodels feel (and look) like models; average looking women feel beautiful. But her message in not about painted ladies. Brown has pro-moted products that intertwine with her philosophy of beauty coming from within, not from the surface. She strove to make products that would bring out the best in any person's natural looks, rather than try to conceal, disguise, or mask the looks. As a result, "little" has become "more" when it comes to makeup, and women can enjoy a polished appearance that looks more natural and becoming of their own personal features. For her efforts, Brown has amassed a personal fortune and a popularity that she has deserved, because she is always willing to pass her secrets on to her fans.

Sources of Information

Contact at: Bobbi Brown Cosmetics
767 Fifth Ave., 43rd Fl.
New York, NY 10153
URL: http://www.bobbibrowncosmetics.com

Bibliography

"Bobbi Up Close." Available at http://www. bobbibrowncosmetics.com/bobbi/index.html.

Camaniti, Susan. "The Makeover Artist." *Your Company,* April 1999.

Gregory, Sophronia Scott. "Powder Broker: Cosmetic Queen Bobbi Brown's Success is More Than Skin Deep." *People Weekly,* 14 July 1997.

Vaughn, Susan. "Making It." *Los Angeles Times,* 10 September 2000.

"Virtual Runway's Shining Stars." Available at http:// www.virtualrunway.com/shining/stars_brown01.htm.

Wheeler, Carol. "The New American Heroines." *Executive Female,* March/April 1997.

Warren Buffett

(1930-)
Berkshire Hathaway Inc.

Overview

Warren Buffett is regarded as one of America's most brilliant investors and was one of its richest men in the late twentieth century. Though he rarely grants interviews, there are scores of books, articles, and websites devoted to his investment strategies. His own insights are revealed in his annual shareholder's letter and meeting of Berkshire–Hathaway, where he is chairman and CEO. The subject of a cult of personality among satisfied investors, Buffett has been variously dubbed "St. Warren," the "Oracle of Omaha," and the "Corn–Fed Capitalist" among other nicknames. Despite his vast fortune, he's remained somewhat of a midwestern folk hero, lunching on hamburgers, wearing rumpled suits, and living in the same house in Omaha, Nebraska, that he bought in 1958 for $31,500. Outside his business concerns, Buffett has professed interest in funding a foundation devoted to halting population growth worldwide and to reduce nuclear proliferation.

Personal Life

Warren Edward Buffett was born in Omaha, Nebraska, on August 30, 1930, the son of Howard Homan and Leila (Stahl) Buffett. His father was a stockbroker who was later elected to the U.S. House of Representatives. Buffett, quoted in a 1995 *Time* article, said he had always "wanted to be very, very rich." As a boy, he was often taken by his father to his workplace where he had an opportunity to learn the stock market business at a very early age. Before he was even a teenager, Buffett was doing such routine duties at his father's office as

Warren Buffett. (AP/Wide World Photos.)

chalking in stock prices on the main blackboard and charting the performance of various stocks. In 1942, when Buffett was 12 years old, he and his parents moved to Fredericksburg, Virginia, where they lived while his father served in Congress.

By the age of 16, Buffett was clearly a prodigy in the area of mathematics and statistics. He enrolled at the University of Pennsylvania, where he focused on mathematics and statistics and then moved to the University of Nebraska to finish his degree. He graduated at age 20 with a bachelor's degree and then entered Columbia University's graduate school of business, where he obtained a master's degree in business.

Buffett, who was once described by *New York Times* writer David Barboza as "a kind of Will Rogers character with John D. Rockefeller's bank account," lives a relatively unassuming life. He separated from his wife, Susan, in 1977 but maintains an amicable relationship with her and has no plans for a divorce. He is a good friend of Bill Gates, whose personal fortune is the only one in the world exceeding Buffett's own.

Buffett lives in Omaha with his girlfriend and former housekeeper, Astrid Menks. Though Buffett rarely gives interviews, he enjoys hosting an annual Berkshire Hathaway investors' meeting in his hometown. His wife lives in California, but as the second largest shareholder of Berkshire Hathaway, she may maintain control of the business if Buffett predeceases her.

Career Details

Buffett has claimed that his career started when his father exposed him to the stock market business as a child and taught him the basics of investing. He has declared that the great turning point in his life and career came when he met his mentor in business, Benjamin Graham. In 1954, after having worked at his father's brokerage business in Omaha, Buffett joined Graham's Wall Street investment firm, Graham–Newman Corporation. Buffett was already a genius at mathematics and statistical analysis when he met Graham, but Graham had a theory about the investment market that Buffett has used during most of his career. The Graham theory involved what Graham called "value investing." The core idea was that people picking stocks to invest in should buy shares of stock that are valued cheaper than the company's worth on paper, in conventional auditing terms.

It was a simple theory, but it required diligence and ambition to practice. Buffett's mathematical and statistical talent plus ambition enabled him to excel at finding out what companies were undervalued. He had to ignore everything published about a company, including its annual reports, go back to the "raw data" of the company, and make his own patient analysis, starting from scratch. Buffett personally analyzed every stock in which he invested and has consistently avoided markets he did not understand or knew little about.

During this period, Buffett married Susan Thompson, fathered two of his three children, and earned

Chronology:
Warren Buffett

1930: Born.

1950: Received B.A. in math and statistics from University of Pennsylvania.

1952: Obtained M.B.A. at Columbia University.

1952: Apprenticed at his father's brokerage in Omaha.

1954: Joined Benjamin Graham's investment firm on Wall Street.

1956: Established Buffett Partnership Ltd. in Omaha.

1965: Gained control of Berkshire Hathaway Company.

1969: Dissolved successful partnership.

1991: Became interim chairman of Salomon Brothers brokerage firm.

2001: Net worth estimated at $32.3 billion.

$140,000 in New York before he was 25. In 1956, when Graham shut down his firm on Wall Street, Buffett left New York, returned to Omaha, raised $105,000, and started an investment partnership. By the time Buffett ended the partnership in 1969, it had grown at an annual compounded rate of 29.5 percent and had a value of $105 million.

Buffett next turned his focus to Berkshire Hathaway, a struggling textile mill in Massachusetts, and bought several additional companies. Although he closed the textile manufacturing business in the mid–1980s, Buffett kept the name for his holding company, and he continued to head the company into the early twenty–first century. During the 1980s, Buffet also developed what became known as the "white knight" strategy of investing, by which he saved certain businesses from being bought out by competitors. He would infuse the company with the money it needed to fend off takeovers but allowed its existing management to continue running the business. Buffett demanded in return that his investment pay off well. He arranged to get a preferred stock that always carried a healthy dividend, whether the company did well or not. Though Buffett took the rather old–fashioned approach of investing in companies associated with everyday products, such as Coca–Cola, Gillette, and See's Candy, his conservative strategy made him exceptionally wealthy.

One of Buffett's most dramatic successes was his brief stint as chairman of the investment firm Salomon Inc., one of the world's largest investment services. Through Berkshire he had acquired a 12 percent minority interest in the firm in 1987—one of his white knight investments. In 1991 it was revealed that senior staff had engaged in illegal trading of government securities, and there was an apparent attempt to cover up the scandal once Salomon management learned of t. In addition, it grew evident that the company's finances were perilously dependent on a heavy debt load.

The resulting management shake–up brought in Buffett, already a director at Salomon, as the firm's chairman. Simultaneously, Salomon was on the brink of bankruptcy because the U.S. Treasury Department penalized it with a ban on participating in federal securities auctions. The same day the crippling ban was announced, Buffett pleaded successfully with authorities at the Treasury and the Federal Reserve to reverse the ban. This critical victory saved Salomon from financial collapse; and both Buffett's management decisions and his high esteem in the investment world quickly stabilized Salomon's market position, which was heading into a free fall until he stepped in. Though he withdrew as chairman less than a year later, Buffett reduced Salomon's debt and, more important, helped restore confidence in Salomon. His investment in Salomon paid off in 1997 when the firm was sold to the Travelers Group for $9 billion. Of that amount, Berkshire Hathaway's share was worth about $1.9 billion, more than twice his initial investment a decade earlier.

Since about the mid–1990s, Buffett has concentrated on the reinsurance business. His single biggest purchase came in 1998, when Berkshire spent $22 billion to acquire General Re Corporation, a company providing reinsurance for catastrophes such as earthquakes, floods, and hurricanes. This move, according to industry analysts, basically transformed Berkshire from a closed–end fund to a real holding company. Between 1996 and 1999, Berkshire's assets increased four–fold, from $29.9 billion to $124 billion.

Another change in focus for Buffett was real estate investment trusts (REITs), publicly traded companies that own properties like shopping malls and apartment complexes. In 1999 he disclosed expenditures of $50 million for shares in four REITs. Much of this sum came from Buffett's personal funds. In addition, however, he continues to look for big acquisitions for Berkshire. *Business Week* has reported that Buffett would like to find a $10 to $15 billion acquisition for the company.

Buffett's emphasis on value investing has proved immensely profitable. By 1999, class A shares of Berkshire Hathaway were priced at $77,000 per share, and class B shares sold for about $2,500 per share. Buffett's personal worth in 1999 was estimated at $36 billion.

In November 2001, Buffett's Berkshire–Hathaway was nearing a deal with creditors of Fruit of the Loom to buy the apparel maker out of bankruptcy for about $840 million. Fruit of the Loom, a 130–year–old Chicago company known for its namesake underwear, filed for Chapter 11 protection in December 1999 hampered by heavy debt and manufacturing and inventory problems. Berkshire has been negotiating to buy the apparel giant which, at the time of bankruptcy filing, claimed one–third of the U.S. market for men and boys underwear.

Social and Economic Impact

Warren Buffett's investments have held significant sway over a number of large U.S. companies and even whole industries. He has built up a major position in the insurance industry, which accounted for about two–thirds of Berkshire's 1997 revenues, by purchasing such companies as GEICO Corporation and General Re. Other fully owned subsidiaries include the H. H. Brown Shoe Company, International Dairy Queen, and See's Candies. Buffett has also purchased long–standing minority stakes in American Express, Coca–Cola, the Washington Post, and Gillette. In a surprise 1998 move, however, Buffett invested heavily in silver—capturing over a third of the world market—because he thought it was undervalued. This was an uncharacteristic choice for Buffett because commodity investments are usually regarded as more speculative and short–lived than his conservative long–term approach deems appropriate.

At the close of the twentieth century, Buffett was well known as a billionaire capitalist who made his own fortune. He is famous for such eccentricities as wearing rumpled suits and drinking five Cherry Cokes a day. He has declared himself an agnostic and has arranged that after his death his money will endow the Buffett Foundation, which he established in the mid 1960s and which is managed by Buffett's former son–in–law, Allen Greenberg. The foundation disbursed about $11 to $12 million annually in the late 1990s for programs oriented to halting population growth worldwide and fighting nuclear proliferation. Analysts believe that, when the foundation receives its full endowment after Buffett's death, it will be the largest philanthropy in the world.

Buffett has said, in the entrepreneurial spirit, that he intends to leave his three children just $5 million apiece out of his more than $36 billion. He explained this decision in a 1988 interview with *Esquire*: "I think kids should have enough money to be able to do what they want to do, to learn what they want to do, but not enough money to do nothing."

In Berkshire Hathaway's 1989 annual report, Buffett wrote: "We do not wish to join with managers who lack admirable qualities, no matter how attractive the prospects of their business. We've never succeeded in making a good deal with a bad person." In applying the investment strategy he developed with Graham, Buffett has always done his own company analyses. He is known

by this hands–on style, and is perhaps the only billionaire who has always figured his own income taxes.

As Buffett put it in a *Business Week* article in 1999, "Berkshire is my painting, so it should look the way I want it to when it's done . . . Berkshire is the company I wanted to create. It's not the company Alfred P. Sloan wanted to create. It fits me. I run it with our investors and managers in mind, but it is designed to fit me."

According to financial advisor Tom Wolf, Buffett once told Berkshire Hathaway shareholders that if he were teaching a class on security analysis, he might ask his students to determine a value for Internet stocks that had no earnings but sold at high price–to–earnings ratios. And if any of the students did, he would fail them.

While tech issues continued to plummet in 2001 to new lows, Berkshire's stock was setting a series of new highs. That year, Berkshire was comfortably cushioned from short–term pressures by its insurance businesses, which accounted for roughly half of its profits. That year, Buffett reportedly sent a newsletter to shareholders stating, "We have embraced the twenty–first century by entering such cutting–edge industries as brick, carpet, insulation and paint. Try to control your excitement."

Buffett has been one of the most successful capitalists of the twentieth century. Using his analytical skills, he has invested in other people's ideas, inventions, and organizations, and through them has amassed great personal wealth. In 1991 a *Wall Street Journal* reporter described Buffett as "a standard bearer for long–term investing, the perfect antidote to the get–rich–quick schemers of Wall Street."

Sources of Information

Contact at: Berkshire Hathaway Inc.
    1440 Kiewit Plz.
    Omaha, NE 68131
    Business Phone: (402)346–1400
    URL: http://www.berkshirehathaway.com

Bibliography

Barboza, David. "A Capitalist Hero Keeps on Pitching: The Corny Charm of Buffettpalooza." *New York Times*, 29 May 1999.

"Berkshire Nears Deal on Fruit of the Loom." *The Wall Street Journal*, 2 November 2001.

"Brilliant Careers." *Salon.com*, 31 August 1999.

"Charity, the Buffett Way." *Business Week*, 25 October 1999.

"The Charts Have Been Turned Upside Down." *123Jump*, May 17, 2001.

"Chasing Warren Buffett Via the Web." *The Street.com*, 5 May 2001.

Marsh, Virginia. "Business Leaders: Entrepreneurs Win High Admiration." *The Financial Times*. 7 December 1999.

Oppel, Richard A. "The Markets: Market Place; Investors Show More Interest in REIT Stocks." *New York Times*, 30 April 1999.

"The Oracle Strikes Back." *The Economist (US)*, 17 March 2001.

Setton, Dolly, and Robert Lenzner. "The Berkshire Bunch." *Forbes*, 12 October 1998.

Silverman, Gary, and Andrew Osterland. "Buffett's $22 Billion Hedge." *Business Week*, 6 July 1998.

"Warren Buffett." *CyberInvestment.com*, 2001.

"Warren the Buffett You Don't Know." *Business Week*, 5 July 1999.

Wolf, Tom. "Wolf On Equities." *FWN Select*, 8 June 2001.

Mark Burnett

(1960-)
Survivor and Eco–Challenge

Overview

Mark Burnett is the British–born athlete–turned–producer of the wildly popular reality–TV program, *Survivor*, along with his other productions that include Discovery Channel's popular *Eco–Challenge* (originally cast on MTV). Burnett's adventure series have been captivating audiences worldwide since the mid–1990s, and there is no end in sight. To the contrary, there are thousands of would–be contestants who would rather earn their million contriving and surviving out in the wilderness than sitting in a television studio guessing at multiple–choice answers. Burnett is singularly responsible for popularizing what is known as "adventure racing" in the United States and has greatly enhanced the prevalence of "extremesports" in general. Equal to that, he has shrewdly created a television spectator audience that can't seem to get enough of the thrilling competition (albeit vicariously)—or for that matter, stop talking about it on the telephone, at the water fountain, or on the Internet.

Personal Life

There really is little to say about Mark Burnett's personal life; he is what he does. A superb athlete, the British–born adventurer was a competitor and team leader in the world's oldest adventure race, the French–sponsored Raid Gauloises (Race of the Warriors) when he dreamed up his own race event. Wanting to start a business that would be both highly profitable and fun as well, Burnett formed Eco–Challenge Lifestyles, Inc. in 1992. His idea was based on the success of multi–

Mark Burnett (left) and "Survivor" host Jeff Probst holding Emmy Award statues for Outstanding Non-Fiction Program. (Corbis Corporation.)

discipline adventure racing such as he had seen in New Zealand and elsewhere. He had also spent some time conducting market research prior to forming his company, intended to gauge the profit potential for his idea. His research taught him that successful and smart business acumen in the 1990s was centered on health and fitness, ecology, and personal growth. Proposing a business plan that incorporated responsible and recreational use of back country terrain—while promoting environmental awareness—Burnett believed he had discovered a business "gold mine." When he added the competition element to

his plan, thus engaging the "personal growth and enrichment" factor, he started cashing in on the gold.

Burnett started a human skill and endurance snowball that has not yet stopped rolling—across deserts, down canyons, through waterfalls, around predators, and into the very heart of man and his most primal need: survival. His hugely successful Eco–Challenge Expedition Competitions led to the founding of the Eco–Challenge Adventure School (motto: "A Taste of the Race") for would–be contestants to the competitions. From there came the founding of the Eco–Challenge Travel agency and the Eco–Challenge Lifestyles Web site. But his biggest home run yet has been the *Survivor* series. In 2001 Burnett revealed future plans to create a new groundbreaking reality drama series that will select one American to travel to Russia's Mir Space Station.

Burnett is a certified scuba diver, whitewater guide, skydiver, and wilderness first aid expert. If he had been born 200 years ago, he told online interviewer Susan Johnston, he would have been an explorer. "I'm an entertainer," he continued, "[b]ut personally, I'm interested in the sociological." He also is the author of several books, among them, *The Survival Manual: Based on U.S. Armed Forces Survival Techniques* (2001), *Survivor II: The Field Guide* (2001), *Survivor III: The Diary* (2001), and *Dare to Succeed: How to Survive and Thrive in the Game of Life* (2001). Burnett resides in California and is married and the father of two children.

Career Details

The Raid Gauloises have been held in various locations around the world since 1989. A regular contestant in those races—and a member of the first American team to compete in the Raid—was the highly competitive and ambitious Burnett. He captained the Team American Pride in the 1992 ten–day Raid endurance race in the Sultanate of Oman, which included running, hiking, horseback riding, camel riding, climbing, sea kayaking, and orienteering. Regrettably, the team suffered a mutiny by one of its members and finished in 39th place. The following year in Madagascar, Burnett again captained the Team American Pride on a five–sport race, this time finishing in 9th place. The 1994 race in Borneo was a disaster: the five–member team consisting of captain Burnett, three Navy SEALs, and one woman, all managed to get lost on the first day and subsequently dropped out. It was time for Burnett to move on.

In 1995, under the auspices of his new company, Burnett staged the first U.S. Eco–Challenge race in Utah for cable channel MTV. (The show later moved to USA Networks.) He also contracted to produce the New England Eco–Challenge at the 1995 Extreme Games for cable sports channel ESPN. To create viewer interest, the Eco–Challenge was billed as "the toughest race in the world." It attracted entrants ranging from U.S. Navy

SEALs to a 72–year–old great–grandmother. Most participants were in between—fitness experts, marathoners, adventurers—and Burnett had no problem filling the field with contestants. In the inaugural running, 50 five–person teams (one woman per team) raced 24 hours a day for seven days over 370 miles of remote terrain in southern Utah. The first event was a marathon–length horseback segment in which team members took turns riding the horse or running alongside for 26 miles. Next, the teams sloshed through water–filled canyons, sometimes having to swim in the 50–degree water with backpacks, and then hiked more than 100 miles across vast stretches of waterless desert. After negotiating 1,200–foot cliff faces with ropes, the teams had to raft the rapids along Colorado River (class IV advanced rafting). In the final stretch, the teams had to complete a 50–mile, 12–hour canoe paddle across Lake Powell. Fewer than half finished the race, but the genie of thrills had been let out of the bottle. Even some who had to be "chopped out" said they would definitely be back the next year.

Why would anyone in his or her right mind pay a $7,500 entrance fee and invite those hardships into his or her life, knowing full well that the chance of failure was greater than 50 percent? "Only by taking people to their lowest low do they learn something about themselves," explained Burnett in a 1996 article for *Boys Life*. Likewise, the intent of the Eco–Challenge School was to strip away preconceptions or misconceptions about participants and then teach outdoor skills under stress. That way, Burnett told a *Men's Health* magazine interviewer, "you never, ever, forget them."

In 1996 Burnett signed a multi–year agreement with Discovery Channel to produce an annual Eco–Challenge expedition competition as well as a television documentary covering the event. But the wildly successful event was not without controversy. Following the 1995 competition, the Utah office of the U.S. Bureau of Land Management (BLM) cited Burnett's company for environmental damage. According to BLM reports, several participants either got lost or cheated; either way, they wandered off the approved courses and created new trails in sensitive areas. Moreover, several participants left human waste behind in "catholes," and support personnel and spectators trampled vegetation and left litter. Burnett's company was cited again when the East Coast race along the Appalachian Trail in the Bigelow Mountain Preserve brought in helicopters, despite an agreement that there would be none. Camera crews were also larger than promised, with their attendant excess burden on the fragile environment. Environmental protesters waved angry signs in front of television camera crews at the starting line, and race organizers promised more trail–planning and enforcement in the future.

Within two years of the first U.S. Eco–Challenge competition, Burnett had drawn millions of dollars in entry fees and major sponsorship from Subaru and Columbia Sportswear. An estimated seven million viewers watched the final five hours on television. But Burnett

Chronology:
Mark Burnett

1960: Born in London, England.

1992: Formed Eco–Challenges Lifestyles, Inc.

1995: First U.S. Eco–Challenge race in Utah.

1996: Signed multi–year contract with Discovery Channel for annual races.

2000: *Survivor* debuts.

grew restless with his success. Admitting to a fascination with competitor alliances under stressful circumstances, Burnett envisioned more "reality–soap" adventures. When asked what gave him the inspiration for *Survivor*, he told *USA Today*'s online participants, "My other TV show, *Eco–Challenge*, proved to me that the communication within groups was much more a factor in an expedition success than technical or physical attributes. And that's what attracted me to *Survivor*." He also confessed that the original idea for *Survivor* was not his own but had come ten years earlier from Charlie Parsons, a prolific British producer.

But the game rules are Burnett's. In what he calls "social Darwinism," a group of contestants compete for a $1 million prize by participating in challenges and voting off one fellow survivor at a time by secret ballot. The first event drew over 6,000 applicants. The first broadcast was in mid 2000. According to *Associated Press Online*, Burnett had remarked, "*Survivor* isn't reality. It's contrived. The outcome and the emotions and the storytelling are not contrived, but we put real people in a contrived situation and then watch real emotions." He told the interviewers, "Everything I do relates to adventure and psychology. The group dynamic against nature." He also stated that before he started *Survivor I*, he had sold a TV book exploring the philosophy that mean people couldn't win. He laughed, "How wrong was I?!"

The immediate success of the 39–day series, filmed in Borneo, led Burnett to cautiously prepare his next series. As he told *Entertainment Tonight*, "I think one of the secrets of anyone's longevity is never overdo it, always leave people at the end of the TV hour wishing it didn't finish, and over–saturation could kill the golden goose." He went on to explain the differences between his first love, the Eco–Challenge events, and his big hit, *Survivor*. According to Burnett, one is a race, the other about "surviving on an island or in the Outback with politics over tribal live." But both were rooted in the human condition, one that recognized that people are at the mercy of nature. Burnett mused at the irony of the Eco–Challenge being the purer and the harder of the two but that the *Survivor* participant got the $1 million.

Of course, the success of *Survivor* spawned a slew of imitators. One such contender was *The Beast 2000*, which Burnett was accused of squashing. The grueling show covering a proposed 12–day slog through the Alaskan wilderness was cancelled by producer Don Mann, who complained that Burnett warned participants that they had to choose between the *Beast* and an upcoming Eco–Challenge. Burnett denied the charge, stating that prospective teams may have misconstrued his medical director's ruling that competitors must choose one or the other, for medical and legal reasons. However, Burnett threw in free airfare for those choosing his race, and the *Beast* disappeared. While many thought it was unfair, Burnett commented in an *Outside* magazine online article that "there is a shakeout going on, just like the dotcom business."

Social and Economic Impact

What was life like before *Survivor*? Does anyone even remember what he or she watched? The amazing thing about Mark Burnett's program is that it draws audiences across the board—from all ages, backgrounds, personalities, and skill levels. As many couch potatoes watch "Survivor" as do those of superior candidate potential. Perhaps, as Kelly Kahl, CBS's senior vice president of program planning and scheduling, told *Broadcasting & Cable*'s Joe Schlosser, "Part of the success of the show will depend on making. . . viewers feel like survivors as well."

The show's official Web site (http://survivor.cbs.com) explains that in selecting contestants, casting personnel look for strong–willed, outgoing, adventurous, physically and mentally adept, adaptable people. Is it simply the vicarious adventure that draws so many fol-

lowers? Said Burnett to *Adventure* magazine's Gretchen Reynolds, "As I see it, it's what people are looking for these days. And there's lots of money in that market, mate." Reynolds put it differently. In her article, "Master of the Ego Challenge," she mused that ". . . 'Survivor' may represent the zenith of manipulated, televised adventuring, a kind of *Swiss Family Robinson* as rejiggered by Machiavelli and MTV."

Sources of Information

Bibliography

Bane, Michael. "Between a Rock and a Hard Place." *Men's Health*, March 1997.

Barcot, Bruce. "The Ultimate Survivor." *Outside*, October 2000. Available at http://www.hp.com/outsidemag.com/magazine/200010.

Boga, Steve. "Challenge of a Lifetime." *Boys' Life*, August 1996.

Hamilton, Kendall, and Susan Miller. "Outer Limits." *Newsweek*, 19 June 1995.

"Interview: Mark Burnett." 28 March 2001. Available at http://www.etonline.com/television/a2231.html

Johnson, Susan. "Watch Out. More Rats Ahead." February 2001. Available at http://www.findarticles.com.

Lee, Janet. "And What Did You do on Your Vacation?" *Women's Sports & Fitness*, March 1995.

"Mark Burnett Wins With 'Survivor.'" Available at http://www.jsonline.com/enter/tvradio/ap/jan01.

Motavalli, Jim. "The Eco–Challenge Gets Challenged." *E Magazine*, July/August 1995.

"The Mountain Zone Interviews Eco–Challenge Founder, Mark Burnett." 1998. Available at http://classic.mountainzone.com/features/ecochallenge98/burnett.html.

Reynolds, Gretchen. "Master of the Ego Challenge." *Adventure*, July/August 2000.

Schlosser, Joe. "Who Wants to be a Castaway?" *Broadcasting & Cable*, 11 October 1999.

"Survivor: Mark Burnett." 19 July 2000. Available at http://www.usatoday.com/community/chat/0719burne t.html.

Robin Burns

(1953-)
Intimate Brands, Inc.

Overview

A major figure in the beauty business for more than 25 years, Robin Burns is president and chief executive officer (CEO) of Intimate Beauty Corporation, a subsidiary of Intimate Brands, Inc., and Victoria's Secret Beauty Company. She leads the development and building of a portfolio of distinctive beauty brands, including the Victoria's Secret Beauty Company. Often demonstrating a "golden touch," Burns has a track record of success in the industry that is almost incomparable.

Personal Life

Robin Burns was born in 1953, the only child of divorced parents, in the small mining town of Cripple Creek, Colorado. She was raised by her mother, Bettina Jones, a very independent woman who taught her daughter to stand on her own two feet. Because she adopted her mother's values (and grew up in the wide–open spaces of the American West), Burns has often been called a "frontier girl." Turning out to be as self–reliant as her mother, she first went to work when she was only 13 years old and would later earn a scholarship to Syracuse University in New York.

After graduating from Syracuse in 1974, Burns considered a teaching career, but she found the red tape of the educational system too restrictive. Instead, she went to New York City to find work. In 1974 she accepted a position in Bloomingdale's executive training program. The regimen at the world–famous department store proved grueling. Burns worked 10 hours a day, seven

Robin Burns. (AP/Wide World Photos/Kathy Willens.)

days a week. But she persevered and would later become one of the city's most powerful businesswomen.

Upon completing the program, Burns worked for Bloomingdale's in home furnishings and later in cosmetics. She followed that by making several career moves that eventually would take her to the top of the cosmetic industry. In 1982 she joined Calvin Klein. In 1990 she was appointed president and CEO of Estee Lauder. In July 1998 she joined The Limited, Inc.

Observers say that major contributing factors to her success are her limitless energy and a passion for the business.

Career Details

From Bloomingdale's executive training program, Burns gained her entrance in the department store world. She started out in home furnishings first involved with window coverings and then pillows and lamps. Bloomingdale's then wanted her to become more involved with imports. So, when she was only in her early twenties, she found herself making eight–week trips to Europe, India, and Japan. Burns felt as if she were on top of the world. However, she would soon gain a promotion that would keep her stateside and profoundly alter the direction of her career. Bloomingdale's management had always liked the way Burns was able to interact easily with people who were older and more sophisticated than she was, so they promoted her into cosmetics. She first worked in the retailing end, buying men's fragrances. Eventually, she became the head of the beauty department, where she would learn the fundamentals of the cosmetics industry.

Burns left Bloomingdale's in 1983 to take a position in the Calvin Klein marketing department. However, as she did at Bloomingdale's, Burns would soon move on to bigger and better things within the organization. By the time she turned 30, she had become president of Calvin Klein cosmetics. At the time, the company's cosmetics line was struggling. With Burns on board, the line performed a remarkable turnaround. In her seven years in the position, she steered the company through a period of tremendous growth. When she assumed the position, the brand was taking in $6 million a year in sales. By the end of Burn's tenure, it was taking in $600 million. During her seven years, she oversaw the launches of the Calvin Klein Obsession and Eternity fragrances. While at Calvin Klein, Burns learned even more about the cosmetics business, and she applied that knowledge to effective marketing strategies, particularly for the Obsession and Eternity perfumes. For those two products, she produced an innovative ad campaign designed to be openly sexy.

Later, Burns would say that working at Calvin Klein was like earning her Ph.D. It was an appropriate analogy, as each job move in her career turned out to be an educational experience. At Bloomingdale's, Burns learned the fundamentals of the cosmetics industry from Mike Blumenfield, who was then the store's beauty chief. At Calvin Klein, she learned a great deal about business operations, and Calvin Klein himself taught her about marketing. Burns has always been quick to credit people she considered her mentors. These included Blumenfield, Marvin Traub, and Lester Gribetz at Bloomingdale's; Klein and Robert Taylor at Calvin Klein; Leonard and Estee Lauder at Estee Lauder, and Leslie Wexner at Intimate Brands.

In 1989 the Calvin Klein company was sold to Unilever Group. At the same time, Burns was fielding offers by Leonard Lauder, who was the president of the Estee Lauder cosmetics firm, which had been established by his mother 44 years earlier. Lauder was persistent in recruiting efforts, and Burns found herself more and more interested in his offers. Finally, in 1990, she agreed to join Lauder, and she became CEO and president of Estee Lauder USA and Canada. She saw the opportunity as something too good to refuse. For one thing, she realized she would be running a company that many considered to be the greatest and largest in the prestige–cosmetics industry. For another, she would be earning an annual salary of $1.5 million, which, at that time, would make her one of the highest–paid woman executives in the United States. It would also provide her with the kind of professional challenge she relished. Her mission, as she perceived it, was to get the business in shape so that the company could go public. As a result, she would change the internal management and the creative personnel.

At Estee Lauder, Burns learned how to run a huge, complex business. She managed the domestic business of the Lauder brand, which was then ranked number one with $700 million in wholesale volume. She also learned how to manage makeup and treatment at different levels including product development, merchandising, education, and retail. Later, Leonard Lauder would say that he never disagreed with Burns about anything she wanted to do. Products that Burns helped launch included Fruition and Estee Lauder Pleasures, which became the company's first global women's fragrance best seller.

By 1998 the Limited, Inc., the company headed by Wexner, was very interested in acquiring Burn's talents. Wexner wanted Burns to become part of their Intimate Brands, Inc. The company began to actively recruit her, enticing her with the opportunity to build her own brands and develop new retail concepts. Burns joined the company in July of that year. Once there, she created Intimate Beauty Corp. as a subsidiary of Intimate Brands Inc. Essentially, she built the subsidiary from the ground up.

One of her primary goals was to overhaul Victoria's Secret Beauty, which sold mostly low–cost scented creams and body gels. This included developing a line of upscale perfumes, lotions, and makeup. The new line would target women who usually buy their beauty products in department stores. As part of this overhaul, she moved Victoria's Secret Beauty from Ohio to New York, where it became Intimate Beauty's first division, and began transforming the lingerie chain into a more sophisticated retailer. In recent years, Victoria's Secret has become more focused on keeping up with fashion trends. It also reduced the number of discounts offered and raised prices to attract upscale customers.

The Dream Angels Heavenly line was the first collection under the new Victoria's Secret Beauty brand to reach the stores. It includes creams, perfume, mist, and body wash. It proved to be a success, and it showed Burns the power of the Victoria's Secret brand. The next fragrance in the line that was launched, Halo, was another success. Sales were strong in stores and through the Victoria's Secret catalogue and web site. Burns also

Chronology:
Robin Burns

1953: Born.

1974: Graduated from Syracuse University and went to work for Bloomingdale's.

1983: Hired at Calvin Klein.

1990: Became CEO and president of Estee Lauder USA and Canada.

1995: Launched Obsession with innovative ad campaign.

1998: Joined The Limited Ltd., and created Intimate Brands, Inc.

launched a laundry collection that included high–priced detergents and softeners packaged in pink candy–striped containers.

Burns also started building freestanding Victoria's Secret Beauty stores, designed with chrome fixtures and soft lighting. She is using the same look to renovate areas within the lingerie stores that will be dedicated to beauty products. Part of her plan includes educating salespeople on how to sell beauty products.

In 2001, Intimate Beauty Corporation announced the formation of a joint venture with Shiseido Co., Ltd. to develop, market, and sell new lines of prestige beauty products that will be offered for sale in the Shisheido free–standing stores. Shiseido, which was founded in 1872, is the leading cosmetics manufacturer in Japan. The collaboration is a coup for Burns, as Shiseido sells its cosmetics for men and women in approximately 60 countries. Wexner felt that alliance would allow his company to leverage Shiseido's global expertise in product and package research and development, and he felt the Japanese company would benefit from Intimate Brand's expertise in retailing and brand development. He added that both companies anticipated building a billion–dollar worldwide brand. Burns would function as the CEO of the joint venture.

Social and Economic Impact

Robin Burns is highly regarded as a savvy businesswoman and powerful player in the beauty industry.

Through her career, she was such an eager and receptive student of the beauty business that she has become one of its masters. She has been behind some of the best–known name brands in the industry including Calvin Klein Eternity and Obsession fragrances and Estee Lauder cosmetics. She's also known as an innovator who is not afraid to break or bend the rules of established marketing strategies. It was her groundbreaking tactics that turned Calvin Klein Cosmetics from a faltering concern into one of the giants of the fragrance industry. Wexner has said that Burns has the ability to spot trends and predict scale and timing. She has proved that designer–priced fragrances can be sold outside department stores in a vertical specialty store format.

At Calvin Klein, Burns came in and developed a marketing strategy at a company in which there was no marketing strategy. Under her leadership, the marketing team became enthusiastic and devoted. Burns would later say that the Obsession launch in 1995 was the high point of her professional life and her most innovative act. She said she modeled her strategy on ideas she gained from Gloria Vanderbilt, Giorgio Beverly Hills, and Yves Saint Laurent's Opium. The Launch involved a saturation advertising campaign that cost $14 million. In the process, she changed the way fragrances are launched.

Burns turned Intimate Brands, Inc. into a leading specialty retailer of intimate apparel, beauty and personal care products through Victoria's Secret, Bath and Body Works, and Intimate Beauty Corporation. By July 2001, Victoria's Secret products were available through 887 lingerie and 471 beauty stores, the Victoria's Secret Catalogue, and online. The company also offered a selection of personal care, home fragrance, and decor products through 1,481 Bath and Body Works and 129 White Barn Candle Company stores.

Sources of Information

Contact at: Intimate Brands, Inc.
    3 Limited Parkway
    Columbus, Ohio 43230
    Business Phone: (614) 415–7546

Bibliography

"Intimate Brands Establishes Beauty Company in New York City: Robin Burns Named President," *Intimate Brands IBI Exclusives*, 1998. Available at http://www.intimatebrands.com/press/1998/1208b.asp.

"Featured Woman: Robin Burns," *The Strait Times Interactive*, July 2000. Available at http://straitstimes.asia1.com.sg/mnt/html/women/archive/featured1.html.

Born, Peter. "The Burns Equation." *Beauty Biz WWD*, June 2001.

LicensingWorld.com. "Intimate Brands,Inc. and Shiseido Sign Joint Venture Agreement." *Licensing Resource Center*, 14 September 2001. Available at http://www.licensingworld.com/news/html/0914001.html.

Hoovers.com. "Intimate Brands." *Hoover's Online*, 2001. Available at http://www.hoovers.com.

Chester F. Carlson

(1906-1968)
Xerox Photocopier

Overview

Chester F. Carlson's invention of the copying process now known as xerography transformed the way business is done in this country and around the world. As a young man, Carlson worked as a patent analyzer for a manufacturer of electrical components. As part of his job, Carlson was responsible for preparing the documentation that had to be submitted to the patent office. This involved producing multiple copies of the invention's specifications and drawings, all of which had to be duplicated by hand, a long and tedious process. Carlson was convinced there had to be a better way and, over time, developed the basic process that we all use today to quickly and accurately reproduce important documents. In 1937, Carlson first was granted a patent to protect his idea for electrophotography. Just over a year later, with the assistance of physicist Otto Kornei, Carlson successfully produced copies using the principles of electrophotography. It was another 10 years before the process was sufficiently refined to attract the interest of a major company, namely Haloid Company. Finally, in 1950 the first commercial xerographic equipment was marketed by Haloid, which later changed its name to Xerox.

Personal Life

He was born Chester Floyd Carlson in Seattle, Washington, on February 8, 1906, son of Olaf and Ellen Carlson. His forebears on both sides had come to the United States from Sweden about a century earlier, drawn to this country by the promise of freedom of religion. Settling first in Minnesota, they had gradually moved west.

Chester F. Carlson and the first Xerox copier. (Corbis-Bettmann.)

Carlson's childhood was not an easy one. About a year after his birth, Carlson's father, an itinerant barber, was stricken with a severe case of tuberculosis. 'As if that were not enough," Carlson later recalled, "he also developed arthritis of the spine, the two together rapidly reducing him to a bent, emaciated wreck of a man who was to spend the greater part of each day for the next 26 years lying flat on his back, wracked by coughing spells and defeated by the world. This, plus the resulting poverty and isolation, was to have a profound effect on my development."

The Carlson family left Seattle shortly after Carlson's birth and for a few years endured a fairly nomadic

existence, residing briefly in a number of cities in California, Arizona, and Mexico before finally settling down in San Bernadino, California. It was in San Bernadino that Carlson attended grammar school and high school. By the time he was 14, he had become the primary support of his family, working before and after school and on the weekends as well. Two of his after–school jobs—working as a janitor in a newspaper office and setting type for a small printing business—left him with a lifelong interest in "the difficult problem of getting words onto paper or into print." His mother always frail, died of tuberculosis when he was only 17. After graduating from high school in 1924, he worked for a year and then joined a cooperative education program at Riverside Junior College for three years. Under the program, Carlson attended class half of the time and worked outside the classroom the other half of the time. Later, Carlson transferred to the California Institute of Technology, where he earned his B.S. degree in physics in 1930.

Fresh out of college, Carlson landed a job in New York with Bell Telephone Laboratories. He found his position as research engineer to be boring and not at all stimulating, so he asked to be transferred to the company's patent department, hoping that the flow of information about new products and processes would be more interesting. Carlson was made assistant to a patent attorney in the Bell Lab's patent department, a position he held until 1933 when he was laid off.

It was the depths of the Great Depression, and Carlson found himself on the streets with countless other men and women who'd lost their jobs. Looking back on that experience, he later told biographer Alfred Dinsdale: "So then I walked the streets for a while . . . and finally landed a job in a patent attorney's office down near Wall Street, working on patent applications. I served my apprenticeship, ended up my clerkship there, thus enabling me to be registered as a patent attorney. I still didn't have any law training." In the early 1930s, it was not necessary to have any formal law training to be registered as a patent attorney.

In 1934, Carlson landed a higher–paying job as a patent attorney in the patent department of P.R. Mallory Company, an electrical equipment manufacturer based in New York City. In 1936 he began attending night classes at New York Law School to earn his law degree (which he received in 1939), but during the day he labored in Mallory's patent department. His responsibilities at Mallory involved the evaluation of new products and processes developed by company researchers and engineers and the preparation of the documentation necessary to apply for patents on these products and process. Applications to the U.S. Patent Office required the preparation of multiple copies of certain specifications and product drawings, work that for the most part had to be done either by hand or by the typing pool using messy carbon paper. Carlson was convinced there had to be a better way.

Career Details

Carlson's frustration with the lack of any quick and easy way in which to reproduce documents sent him on a voyage of discovery that began to occupy most of his time away from work. In the late 1930s, documents could be duplicated by mimeograph or by offset printing, but these processes required a specially prepared stencil or mat and were impractical unless hundreds of copies were needed. Carlson pored over scientific books and journals in the reading room of the New York Public Library, searching for the key to an alternative technology.

During his research, Carlson became interested in photoconductors, materials whose conductivity is altered when exposed to light. With the scientific knowledge he'd picked up in his reading, Carlson began experimenting with various processes and chemicals in his apartment. He drew the protests of neighbors when he experimented with sulfur, which created unpleasant odors and occasionally burst into flame when it was melted.

Much to his neighbors' relief, Carlson finally decided to set up a small laboratory away from his home. He rented a room above a bar in Astoria, Queens. To assist him in his experiments, Carlson hired German physicist Otto Kornei, who had recently arrived in the United States as a refugee from Germany. A breakthrough finally came on October 22, 1938. Carlson later recounted to biographer Dinsdale what happened on that fateful day: "I went to the lab . . . and Otto had a freshly prepared sulphur coating on a zinc plate. We tried to see what we could do toward making a visible image. Otto took a glass microscope slide and printed on it in India ink the notation '10–22–38 ASTORIA.' We pulled down the shade to make the room as dark as possible, then he rubbed the sulphur surface vigorously with a handkerchief to apply an electrostatic charge, laid the slide on the surface and placed the combination under a bright incandescent lamp for a few seconds.

"The slide was then removed and lycopodium powder was sprinkled on the sulphur surface. By gently blowing on the surface, all the loose power was removed and there was left on the surface a near–perfect duplicate in powder of the notation which had been printed on the glass slide. Both of us repeated the experiment several times to convince ourselves that it was true, then we made some permanent copies by transferring the powder images to wax paper and heating the sheets to melt the wax. Then we went out to lunch and to celebrate."

Carlson lacked the financing to commercialize the process, but he quickly applied for patents on his electrostatic copying process. His experience as a patent attorney enabled him to draw up patents that were tight and comprehensive and still considered classics to this day. However, he had a hard time finding any company interested in backing his invention. Among the big corporations he courted were Eastman Kodak, IBM, RCA,

Chronology:
Chester F. Carlson

1906: Born.

1930: Graduated from California Institute of Technology with B.S. in physics.

1933: Laid off from job in Bell Lab's patent department.

1934: Converted kitchen of his New York City apartment into a laboratory.

1937: Filed preliminary patent application for concept of electrophotography (xerography).

1938: Made first electrophotographic copy.

1939: Graduated from New York Law School with LLB degree.

1940: First basic patent for process issued.

1944: Signed agreement with Battelle Development Corp. to sponsor the new invention.

1948: Battelle and Haloid (later Xerox) publicly announce copying process.

1968: Died.

and Remington Rand. His presentations of the new technology were met "with an enthusiastic lack of interest," he later recalled. The process was still relatively unsophisticated and the images it produced were fuzzy and imprecise.

In 1944, the patent department of P.R. Mallory was visited by a representative of Battelle Memorial Institute, an industrial research organization based in Columbus, Ohio. Intrigued by Carlson's invention, Battelle offered to spend $3,000 of its money to further refine Carlson's technology in return for 60 percent of any royalties that might be earned in the future. Carlson accepted Battelle's offer. One of Battelle's first suggestions involved changing the name of the process that Carlson had discovered. Carlson's "electrophotography" didn't appeal to Battelle officials, who suggested he change the name to "xerography," a combination of the Greek words for "dry" and "writing." More importantly, Battelle's research revealed that amorphous selenium was a far more effective photoconductor than either the sulfur or anthracene that Carlson and Kornei had used in their experiments.

Haloid Company, based in Rochester, New York, in 1946 expressed an interest in Carlson's copying process and agreed to sponsor research work at Battelle, beginning in January 1947. A little more than 18 months later, Haloid and Battelle jointly announced the development of the xerography process. The first xerographic copier manufactured by Haloid hit the market in 1950. Nicknamed the "Ox Box" by insiders at Haloid, the copier was cumbersome, difficult to operate, and slow, taking two to three minutes to produce a single copy. The public was unimpressed, and few of these early copiers were sold. However, Haloid continued to refine and improve its copiers, spending nearly $90 million in the process. By 1959, the company, which had since changed its name to Haloid–Xerox, finally had a product it felt confident would attract more interest than its earlier copiers. The public found the company's latest copier too expensive and too big. Demand never exceeded 5,000 machines.

Haloid–Xerox finally hit on the right combination in 1960, when it rolled out its Model 914. Although it was still big and expensive, the 914 quickly produced excellent copies on ordinary paper. Demand soared, and by 1962, more than 19,000 of the copiers were in use.

Carlson, who had retired from Mallory in 1945 and moved to Rochester, New York in 1948, sold full title to his xerography patents to Haloid in 1955 for 50,000 shares of stock plus royalties. Now a multimillionaire, he devoted much of his energies in later years to philanthropic endeavors, donating more than $150 million to worthy causes. He died on September 19, 1968, after suffering a heart attack in a New York City movie theater. He was survived by his wife, Doris, and a daughter, Catherine.

Social and Economic Impact

Against great odds, Chester F. Carlson came up with the idea for a process that transformed the way business is done in this country and around the world. His childhood was one of great difficulty, and in his early teens he found himself the sole support of his family. Despite these obstacles, Carlson managed to get the education he needed to make something of his life. Even more remarkably, he took a problem he found in the working world and dedicated his life to finding a practical solution.

As a young man, Carlson began working behind the scenes in the preparation of patent applications, an ex-

perience he found frustrating because of the difficulty in duplicating documentation required by the U.S. Patent Office. Convinced that there had to be a practical alternative to hand–copying the diagrams and schematics, multiple copies of which had to be submitted with a patent application, he began researching the problem in his spare time. Early in his research, he began considering the possibility that a solution might lie in the science of photoconductivity. Carlson had learned that the electrical conductivity of a photoconductive material is increased when it is exposed to light and in some cases for a short time thereafter. He moved his research from the library to the laboratory and began experimenting with photoconductivity. When he had proved to himself that the process he called electrophotography could provide a way to readily copy documents, he applied for a preliminary patent to protect his idea.

In 1938 Carlson, working with German physicist Otto Kornei, his assistant, successfully copied an image, and the science of electrophotography—later known as xerography—was born. It took years and significant outside support to refine the process so that it was commercially practical, but in 1948 Haloid Company announced to the world the imminent debut of this exciting new technology.

Carlson was generous with the millions he earned from his discovery of xerography, donating more than $150 million to worthy causes before his sudden death in 1968.

Sources of Information

Bibliography

"50 anos de Xeroxcopias." http://www.rm.es/eutsum/escuela/Apuntes_Informatica/Divulgacion/Informatica/Xerografia.html (November 17, 2001).

"Chester F. Carlson: The Photocopier." The Lemuelson–MIT Prize Program. http://web.mit.edu/invent/www/investorsA-H/Carlson.html (November 17, 2001).

Dinsdale, Alfred. "Chester F. Carlson, Inventor of Xerography." *Photographic Science and Engineering,* Vol. 7, 1963.

Hall, Dennis G., and Rita Hall. "Chester F. Carlson: A Man to Remember." *Optics & Photonics News, September 2000.*

Encyclopedia of World Biography, 2nd ed. 17 Vols. Detroit: Gale Research, 1998.

World of Invention, 2nd ed. Farmington Hills. MI: Gale Group, 1999.

Frank Carney

(1938-)
Houston Pizza Venture

Overview

A giant in the pizza industry, Frank Carney, along with older brother, Dan, founded the Pizza Hut chain in Wichita, Kansas, in 1958. Although neither brother knew anything about making pizza, they acted on the suggestion of a local real estate agent who convinced them pizza was going to be the next big thing in the restaurant business. The Carney brothers managed to find someone to teach them how to make pizza only two weeks before their first store opened. Despite their lack of basic knowledge about pizza and business in general, Frank and Dan Carney by 1977 had molded their business into an empire of more 4,000 outlets with annual sales in the billions. Pizza Hut was sold in 1977 to PepsiCo Inc. for more than $300 billion, although Frank stayed on as Pizza Hut president and a member of the PepsiCo board until 1980. After more than 20 years in the pizza business, Frank Carney was glad to turn his attention to new possibilities, determined never to return to pizza. He turned down numerous pleas to lend his support to fledgling pizza ventures, but when a good friend prevailed upon him to sample the product being turned out by John Schnatter, founder of Papa John's International, Carney couldn't refuse. Very much impressed with the Papa John's product, Carney threw his very considerable weight behind the young company's promotional campaign and signed on as a franchisee. Today, under the umbrella of four different companies—Houston Pizza Venture, Devlin Partners LLC, P.J. Wichita LLC, and P.J. Nor–Cal LLC—Carney operates a franchise chain of more than 120 Papa John's outlets. Not surprisingly, his shift in allegiances in the pizza business brought him into sharp conflict with the current owners of Pizza Hut.

Frank Carney. *(AP/Wide World Photos/Monty Davis.)*

Personal Life

Frank Carney was raised in a large, close family with six sisters and brothers. He must have decided early on that there was something special about growing up with plenty of company, because he and wife Zenda have eight children of their own. Today, with most of the children grown and on their own, the Carneys maintain a long–distance relationship as Frank travels frequently between his scores of Papa John's franchise operations, while wife Zenda, an associate producer of television specials, lives and works in Santa Monica, California.

Carney was born in Wichita, Kansas, on April 26, 1938. One of seven children, he attended local schools

and helped out in the family grocery business after school and on the weekends. When Frank was only 10, his father died, but before his death Carney's mother promised her husband that she would see that all of their children got a college education. After completing high school in 1956, Frank began attending classes at the University of Wichita, which has since changed its name to Wichita State University. A couple of years later, Frank and older brother Dan, also a student at the University of Wichita, became involved in a business venture that took so much of Frank's time that he eventually dropped out of college.

Carney's family never really let him forget his mother's promise to his father that all the Carney kids

Chronology:
Frank Carney

1938: Born.

1956: Entered University of Wichita (later called Wichita State University).

1958: Opened, with brother Dan, first Pizza Hut store.

1961: Dropped out of college.

1969: Named president of Pizza Hut.

1973: Given added responsibilities of chairman and CEO at Pizza Hut.

1977: Carney brothers sold Pizza Hut to PepsiCo for $320 million.

1980: Stepped down as Pizza Hut president.

1994: Joined franchise family of Papa John's International.

2000: Earned bachelor's degree from Wichita State University.

---

would finish college. All his sisters and brothers had earned their college degrees, leaving Frank the only one who'd not yet fulfilled their mother's vow. In 1997, when he accepted Wichita State University's Board of Trustees Award, he mentioned his mother's pledge and said he hoped she'd be proud of his accomplishments even though he'd never finished college. Shortly thereafter, a college official got in touch with Carney and urged him to finish work toward his bachelor's degree. Before long he was back in the classroom, at work on the 33 credit hours he needed to complete his degree. About half of the classes were taken by telecourse, which allow the student to view most of the lectures and receive assignments on videotape, with occasional on–campus meetings. In December 2000, Carney received his bachelor's degree in general studies.

Career Details

The business venture that eventually forced Carney out of college was the launch in 1958 of a little pizza business Frank and Dan Carney called Pizza Hut. A local real estate agent, who'd read in the New York City press of pizza's growing popularity along the East Coast, convinced the Carneys that they might make a fortune in pizza if they hopped on the bandwagon early. At that time, few in Wichita, Kansas, knew much about pizza. Borrowing $600 from their mother, the Carney brothers located a vacant store, not far from the family's grocery business. Neither Frank nor Dan knew anything about making pizza, but "two weeks before we opened, we found someone to teach us how to make it," Carney later told *Nation's Restaurant News*. As for the company name—Pizza Hut—that now can be found on the chain's more than 10,000 stores worldwide, that was the inspiration of Dan's wife, Beverly. The sign above the Carney's first hut–shaped building could not accommodate any more than eight characters, so Beverly decided that "Pizza Hut" was a good fit for the venture, in more ways than one.

Wichita quickly embraced Pizza Hut, and long lines formed outside the Carney's first outlet. Perhaps because the local Kansas market had never really seen pizza like the Carneys were selling, with fresh toppings and plenty of herbs, the business took off quickly, allowing Frank and Dan to open five more outlets by the end of their first year. The first store was pulling in weekly sales of about $1,500, a lot of money in the late 1950s.

Despite the enormous success of Pizza Hut in Wichita, it was difficult for Carney and his brother to expand their business beyond the metropolitan area of the Kansas City where they opened their first stores. The brothers' idea of franchising the operation won little sympathy from Wichita bankers, who doubted the profitability of such a concept. But the Carneys were not dissuaded. Eventually they began franchising the Pizza Hut

name for an initial fee of $100 and a monthly royalty of $100. Some of the college friends who had helped out in the first of the Carney's Pizza Hut outlets later decided to become franchisees themselves. At the end of Pizza Hut's first decade in business, the chain had grown to 310 locations, serving more than a million people weekly. "We never had a reason to stop growing," Carney later told *Your Company*. In 1969, Pizza hut went public, and two years later it became the undisputed leader in the pizza business worldwide.

Nearly two decades after the Carney brothers launched the first Pizza Hut in Wichita, PepsiCo Inc. in 1977 acquired the empire it had become for $320 million in stock paid to Pizza Hut shareholders. The Carneys, who owned 10 percent of the company's stock, pocketed a cool $32 million. Frank was asked by PepsiCo to remain as Pizza Hut's president and to serve on PepsiCo's board of directors as well. Carney did so until 1980, when he left both posts and the pizza business for good. Or at least that's what he thought at the time.

For the next eight years, Carney was involved in a number of enterprises, none of which had anything to do with pizza. He made some investments in real estate, oil and gas exploration, as well as the automotive, rental, recreation, and food service businesses. In 1988 he was persuaded to join Western Sizzlin' Inc. as chairman, and from 1991 to 1993, he served as that low–cost steak restaurant chain's chief executive officer. In 1994 he was named vice chairman of TurboChef Inc., a company involved in the design, development, and manufacture of high–speed cooking systems for the food service industry.

After leaving Pizza Hut in 1980, Carney consciously avoided anything to do with the pizza business, turning down a number of offers from pizza companies that sought to involve him once again in the business. In a 1998 interview with *Nation's Restaurant News,* Carney said: "I had no desire to get back into the pizza business. I never saw anything that was compelling enough to get back in. . . ." However, when close friend Martin Hart asked Carney to join him and former Hardee's Chairman Jack Laughery in a franchise venture with Papa John's International, Carney decided to at least give the fledgling pizza company a taste test. He sampled the Papa John's product and liked what he tasted so well that he decided to go ahead with the proposed franchising venture. He bought into his first Papa John's franchise in 1994.

In addition to his belief in the Papa John's product, part of the new pizza company's appeal to Carney probably lay in the similarities between its beginnings and his launch of Pizza Hut with brother Dan in the late 1950s. John Schnatter, chairman and CEO of Papa John's International, launched his company in the broom closet of his family's tavern in Jeffersonville, Indiana. As Carney's stake in the Papa John's business grew, it began to make sense for him to throw his weight into the company's promotional efforts, which he did with a bang in 1997. In Papa John's first major national TV ad campaign, Carney appeared at a fictional meeting of Pizza Hut franchise holders and announced, "Sorry, guys, I found a better pizza." The folks back at Pizza Hut were understandably unhappy about Carney's outspoken switch in loyalties. The ruffled feathers at Pizza Hut headquarters were not smoothed down at all by Carney's criticism of the operation's product. He told *Nation's Restaurant News*: 'Pizza Hut has great marketers, but customers are telling them that they don't have great pizza. They have to fix that. In my opinion, they are better marketers than operators. They need to take a lot more care . . . that each element is superior, use better ingredients and make better pizza.' Pizza Hut's corporate spokesman, Jay Allison, begged to differ, arguing, "We go out of our way to give the customers what they want and what they ask for." Tensions between the two pizza purveyors were further exacerbated by Papa John's use of the tagline "Better Ingredients, Better Pizza" in its advertising.

By the middle of 2001, Carney had shares in nearly 130 Papa John's stores through the four holding companies—Houston Pizza Venture, Devlin Partners LLC, P.J. Wichita LLL, and P.J. Nor-Cal LLC—he'd created for that purpose. Carney is president and a partner in all four

companies. He announced that his companies planned to take shares in 53 more Papa John's franchises over the next five years.

Social and Economic Impact

Despite some of the controversy accompanying his return to the pizza business, Carney is enjoying his life immensely. "I'm probably having more fun now that ever before," he told *Nation's Restaurant News*. "It's more fun than anything I've ever done. It's kind of like a replay. The difference is like being a parent and a grandparent. The first time everything was new. This time I'm more experienced, more relaxed."

Carney's brother Dan, his partner in the original Pizza Hut venture, has gone on to become a venture capitalist, but Frank is happy to be doing what he's doing, much to his own surprise, considering that he fought a return to the pizza business for almost a decade and a half. In 1998, he told an interviewer for *Your Company*: "I wanted to relive the best time of my life—growing Pizza Hut. I'm lucky to ride two horses like this in a lifetime."

When he isn't on the road, checking out one of his Papa John's franchises, Carney enjoys spending time with wife Zenda, his eight children, and many grandchildren. He serves on the boards of directors of Intrust Financial Corporation and Intrust Bank N.A. Previously he served on the boards of Southland Corporation, Chi-Chi's Inc., Scandia Down Inc., Safelight Glass Company Inc., Rent–a–Center Inc., National Recovery Systems Inc., and Steamboat Springs Ski Corporation. Carney is a past president of the International Franchise Association, as well as the Wichita Chamber of Commerce. In 1974, he was named Man of the Year by the Multi–Unit Foodservice Organization, which in 1986 honored him with its Pioneer of the Year Award. In 1991 he received the Hall of Fame Award of the International Franchise Association.

Sources of Information

Contact at: Houston Pizza Venture
        8312 Louetta Rd.
        Spring, TX 77379-6734
        Business Phone: (281) 251-8855

Bibliography

Conkling, Judith. "Pizza Magnate Returns to WSU to Complete His Degree." *Wichita Business Journal,* 30 April 1999.

Elan, Elissa. "P.J. Wichita LLC: Pizza Hut's Founder Says He's Found a Better Pie at Papa John's." *Nation's Restaurant News,* January 1998.

Geiszler–Jones, Amy. "Pizza Magnate Has Success, Now a Sheepskin." *InsideWSU*, 18 January 2001.

Greenwald, John. "Business: Slice, Dice, and Devour: Papa John's Uses Sweet–Tasting Sauce and Tangy Ads to Win Market Share in the Pizza Wars. Can Anyone Stoppa the Papa?" *Time*, 26 October 1998.

Nance–Nash, Sheryl. "A Look Back/Pizza Hut: How Two Brothers from Wichita Created the World's Largest Pizza Chain with $600 and a Little Basil." *Your Company*, 1 February 1998.

Sarnoff, Nancy. "Papa John's Suffers Costly Defeat in Pizza War." *Houston Business Journal*, 28 January 2000.

Zimmerman, Malia. "New Guy in Town Knows How to Make a Pizza and a Profit." *Pacific Business News*, 14 May 1999.

Steve Case

(1958-)
AOL Time Warner, Inc.

Overview

Steve Case is chairman of AOL Time Warner. Prior to the its merger with Time Warner, Case served as chairman and chief executive officer (CEO) of America Online, a company he founded that became the world's largest Internet service provider. More than any other business leader he has made the Internet accessible to the masses. Through his market–leading AOL, he was actively involved in the transformation of dial–up computer networking services from obscurity to a mass–market, multi–billion–dollar industry. By the end of 2000, America Online had 24.6 million subscribers, and the company was connecting more than 11 percent of the U.S. population to the Internet.

Personal Life

Case was born on August 21, 1958, in Honolulu, Hawaii. His father was a corporate lawyer, and his mother was a teacher. He has three siblings: an older brother, Dan, an older sister, Carin, and a younger brother, Jeff.

Case was an enterprising boy and was involved in a number of ventures with his younger brother throughout the boys' childhood. When Case was six years old, the two opened a juice stand charging customers $.02 a cup; many gave them a nickel and told the boys they could keep the change. For Case, it was an early lesson in high margins in business. Later, the brothers opened a company to sell products through a catalog and door–to–door. The two also shared a newspaper route.

While Case was a student at the Punau School, a private college–preparatory school in Honolulu, he wrote album reviews for the school newspaper. Although the position didn't pay, it did get Case on the mailing lists of several different record companies. He began receiving free concert tickets and promotional albums.

Case then attended Williams College in Williamstown, Massachusetts, where he was a political science major. While in school, Case ran the student entertainment committee, which organized campus concerts and produced an album of some of the best musical offerings. He also became the lead singer in two rock bands, both musically fashioned after two relatively obscure new wave groups, one being The Knack.

In 1980 Case graduated with a B.A. from Williams and went to work in the marketing department of Procter & Gamble. He left the company after two years, having realized he was not comfortable working for such a well–established corporation.

Case lives in Fairfax, Virginia, and is divorced from his wife, Joanne, to whom he was married for 11 years. They have three children. He enjoys reading social history and political science.

Career Details

It was in his next job with the Pizza Hut arm of PepsiCo that Case first began to explore the personal computer. He was hired to work in new pizza development, which entailed traveling the country in search of innovative pizza toppings. He devoted his nights on the road to learning about the portable computer. He had bought a Kaypro CP/M personal computer and subscribed to The Source, one of the earliest online services. He was especially intrigued by the chance to talk with people around the world, which the service provided. Case's fascination with the world accessible by computer was the first step in what would become his lifelong passion. Regarding the pizza company position, however, Case once said in an interview with the *Washington Post*, "I learned a lot about the big corporation experience, and that was good. But a lot of it was about leveraging business and not about innovating. . . . It was all incremental rather than breaking new ground."

In 1983 Case's older brother, Dan, introduced him to the start–up business Control Video Corporation at an electronics show in Las Vegas. Dan, an investment banker, was excited about the company's first product, a service that delivered Atari video games to personal computers. Case was offered the job of marketing assistant, only realizing later that he had entered the company as the video gaming industry was dying. Control Video let most of its employees go but retained Jim Kimsey as chief executive officer. Kimsey, a former venture capitalist, retained Case to help him develop new capital.

Chronology:
Steve Case

1958: Born.

1980: Graduated with B.A. from Williams College.

1985: Co–founded Quantum Computer Services, Inc. with Jim Kimsey.

1991: Quantum renamed America Online.

1992: Became AOL's CEO.

1994: Acquired Booklink Technologies.

1994: AOL subscriber count surpassed 1 million.

1995: AOL became a publicly traded company.

1997: AOL gained 2.6 million subscribers from CompuServe.

1997: AOL subscriber count surpassed 10 million.

1998: Stepped down as AOL president while remaining chairman and CEO.

1999: AOL acquired Netscape Communications for $4.2 billion.

2000: AOL announced it would acquire Time Warner Inc. to form AOL Time Warner, with Steve Case as chairman of the new company.

2000: Received the Millennium Award from Columbia Business School.

2001: AOL Time Warner, valued at $219 billion, looked for ways to increase its overseas revenue.

2001: AOL had an estimated 31 million subscribers; announced expansion of cable services to China.

In 1985 Case and Kimsey began a new company, Quantum Computer Services, Inc., which provided on-line services for users of Commodore computers, then a leading brand of home computers. Quantum quickly grew, and two years after the company was started, Case worked out an arrangement with Apple Computer, Inc. to provide his online service for Apple's operating system and developing software for both the Macintosh and the Apple II. Soon, Quantum was signing similar deals with other companies, including Tandy Corporation and IBM, which was then the industry leader. Although this was undoubtedly progress, the company's overhead costs were prohibitively high, eating through the $5 million capital the company had received. In 1991 Quantum was

Steve Case. *(Archive Photos Inc.)*

renamed America Online (AOL), and Case was appointed chief executive officer, replacing Kimsey, who then became company chairman. AOL stock went public in March 1992, at $1.64 a share. The stock offering garnered $66 million for the company.

Case then focused his energies and the increased company revenues on usurping the two established leaders of online services—Prodigy and CompuServe. He developed a strategy for market dominance that included alliances with companies that would benefit AOL, dropping membership prices below those of the major competitors and shipping out huge quantities of diskettes to potential clients, offering them a free trial period for the service. Membership began to grow, jumping apprecia-

bly each month until the end of 1993, by which time it had surpassed the 600,000 mark. The company had a difficult time keeping up with such rapid growth, foreshadowing the service problems that would plague it for the next few years.

That same year, Case warded off two attempted buyout offers—the first from Microsoft cofounder Paul Allen. Allen, who had already left Microsoft, had purchased a 24.9 interest in AOL and had attempted to secure a seat on its board of directors. The second buyout offer came from Microsoft head, Bill Gates, who would subsequently go on to develop his own online service, bundling it with his company's other popular software titles.

Case continued to explore new marketing strategies and either purchased or forged alliances with companies that would further its foothold in the online services marketplace. These included content agreements with the *New York Times*, *Time*, and the National Broadcasting Corporation (NBC). He also developed a distinctive, user–friendly framework for his service, which was both intuitive and graphics intensive. By the fall of 1994, Case was beginning to establish a way to link his service with the World Wide Web, an increasingly popular arm of the Internet. Until then, AOL was essentially a closed network, meaning that subscribers could only interact with content provided by AOL, its vendors, or other AOL subscribers rather than the provider–independent content associated with the Internet. The company first bought Advanced Network Services, Inc., which was experienced in building the fiber optic support needed to access the Internet. The December 1994 acquisition of BookLink Technologies and the following purchase of Global Network Navigator provided the means for AOL customers to browse the Internet with graphic browsing software from BookLink, which competed with Netscape's Navigator browser.

As fierce competition heated up between the two leading web browser vendors, Microsoft and Netscape, Case came under significant pressure to choose one of the independent browsers for use on AOL. Until that point AOL subscribers were mostly restricted to using AOL's proprietary software from BookLink, which lacked the performance and features of the leading browsers. Whereas Microsoft had made heavy overtures to AOL, Netscape, which many inside AOL management favored, had given AOL a chilly reception. Presiding over the largest single base of web users, Case was especially wary of signing an agreement with Microsoft, which had recently debuted its Microsoft Network, a competitor to AOL. Thus, in 1996 he pulled off a pair of stunning and controversial deals, in which he formed a nonexclusive alliance with Netscape to use its browser but made Microsoft's Internet Explorer the primary one used with AOL services. Although some Netscape executives characterized these actions as "slimy," these agreements proved favorable to AOL.

During this period, AOL continued to grow at an unprecedented rate, outpacing all its competitors in the number of new users. By 1994, AOL had more than 600,000 members; by March of the next year, membership exceeded 2 million and continued to rise meteorically until, by August 1996, it tripled to more than 6 million. Two months later, Case announced that AOL would begin to charge a flat monthly rate of $19.95 for unlimited access to its service. Prior to the institution of this system, customers were billed a monthly charge of $9.95 for their first five hours, plus $2.95 for every additional hour spent online. Customers complained, however, that under the original rate system, the company was rounding online usage time up to the next minute, rather than basing billing calculations on a per–hour monthly rate. In addition to changing the rate structure, Case offered AOL users a free hour of online time to compensate for the perceived unfairness.

To manage AOL's sprawling services, in 1996 Case brought in Bob Pittman, founder of MTV and reputed as a successful brand manager, to improve the company's customer service and better establish AOL as a consumer brand. This decision was seen as a partial retreat by Case on some of his earlier strategies. Pittman succeeded in stabilizing AOL by reducing subscriber growth to sustainable levels and improving AOL's customer service reputation. For his efforts, Case rewarded Pittman in 1998 with a promotion to president and chief operating officer of AOL. Under this arrangement Case relinquished his title as president while remaining chairman and CEO.

In 1997, AOL gained nearly 3 million subscribers from CompuServe, which had been acquired by WorldCom from H. & R. Block. WorldCom traded CompuServe's subscriber base to AOL in exchange for AOL's network integration division. The deal also gave AOL access to about 100,000 more modems and discounts from WorldCom. AOL continued to operate CompuServe as a separate business. The acquisition raised AOL's subscriber base to 11.6 million.

During 1998, AOL's stock increased in value by 600 percent and even more in 1999. This greatly increased the market capitalization of the company and gave it the power to make more and bigger acquisitions. In November 1998, AOL announced it would acquire Netscape Communications for $4.2 billion in stock, about 10 percent of AOL's market value. Among the assets AOL acquired were Netscape's Netcenter, a leading Web portal, and its browser. As part of the deal AOL formed an alliance with Sun Microsystems to provide support for e–commerce ventures. By March 1999, AOL, Netscape, and Sun had formed an independent division, the Netscape Enterprise Group, to focus on building Internet–commerce applications.

Among AOL's acquisitions in 1999 were two Internet–related music companies, Spinner.com and Nullsoft, for about $400 million in stock. Spinner.com was a streaming audio site, and Nullsoft was an MP3 software company. Analysts believed that the Internet music market would explode, once broadband access to the Internet through cable modems became more widespread.

In January 2000, AOL announced it would acquire Time Warner Inc. for approximately $165 billion in stock, with the exact value to be determined by the stock prices of both firms. The new company, called AOL Time Warner, positioned Case as chairman. Case became the new company's chairman, Time Warner's chairman Gerald Levin became the new CEO, and Turner Broadcasting System's Ted Turner, who had sold TBS to Time Warner in 1996, filled the vice chairman spot. The merger gave AOL access to 20 million homes connected to Time Warner's cable lines and 300,000 cable modems already installed in Time Warner's Road Runner network. As a result, AOL started to deliver its content through high–speed cable access as well as telephone lines.

On July 27, 2000, Case and Time Warner chairman Gerald Levin defended their plan to federal regulators in the face of accusations by competitors and consumers that the massive deal could stifle customer choice. The two men argued before the Federal Trade Commission in Washington that the merger would be good for consumers and serve as a catalyst to speed availability of high–speed Internet and cable access.

The acquisition was eventually approved, and by 2001, Case was looking at ways to transform his media giant into a truly global enterprise by significantly increasing its revenues from outside the United States. Speaking at a JP Morgan technology conference that year, Case told the audience, "I really do think that in the next 5 to ten years you will see that we are really serious about becoming a truly global company. You are going to see more aggressive investments and acquisitions," adding that AOL Time Warner expected to get half of its sales in the next 10 years from international markets. To that end, at the end of October 2001, AOL Time Warner announced that it had gained cable rights to provide service in China, making it the first foreign provider of cable programming to the country.

Social and Economic Impact

Case's important contribution to the information age was his vision of a mass–market online service, a vision that was translated into reality within a decade. Case understood—perhaps better than any of his counterparts at other online service vendors—how to obtain and market unique content that was broadly popular and accessible. His aggressive marketing strategies of mailing out millions of free disks and CDs to consumers and offering free introductory service helped create the largest service of its kind. More important, Case was an adaptive leader in the rapidly changing online services business; he was able to embrace new technologies and new business models as they presented a competitive advantage. The result was a multi–billion–dollar powerhouse, headed by a man who just turned 40 in 1998, in the still young online services industry.

While the impact of the merger between AOL and Time Warner has yet to be played out completely, clearly Case has once again foreseen the future of the Internet as connected to high–speed delivery of Internet content via cable modems. Time Warner had already converted 85 percent of its cable infrastructure to Internet–capable high–speed networks. Its Road Runner network had installed 300,000 cable modems, about one–sixth of all cable modems in the United States. As a result, the merger made AOL the biggest provider of cable Internet access in North America.

The merger of AOL and Time Warner also combined the power of mass media, represented by Time Warner's popular magazines (*Time, People, Sports Illustrated*, and others) and cable television service, with two–way interactive communication over the Internet. That gave the new company the opportunity to combine powerful commercial messages with online purchases and boost revenue through advertising and e–commerce.

Delivering AOL content through cable modems is part of Case's "AOL Anywhere" strategy that aims to provide content "anywhere, anytime, on any kind of device." Prior to the Time Warner acquisition, AOL announced it would invest $1.5 billion in Hughes Electronics Corporation, a subsidiary of General Motors and the parent of satellite television provider DirectTV. The investment would facilitate delivering AOL content to subscribers through high–speed broadband channels via satellite. Other plans called for delivering content outside the home on portable devices.

Sources of Information

Contact at: AOL Time Warner, Inc.
22000 AOL Way
Dulles, VA 20166
Business Phone: (703) 448–8700
URL: http://www.aol.com

Bibliography

"AOL Time Warner." *Hoover's Online,* 2001. Available at http://www.hoovers.com.

"AOL TW plans world domination." *CableFAX's Pay–TV Today*, 8 May 2001.

Fick, Jeffrey A. "Case Paid Nearly $270 Million." *USA Today*, 28 March 2001.

Follett, Hagendorf. "Readers' Choice: Steve Case, America Online." *Computer Reseller News*, 13 November 2000.

Krantz, Michael. "America Online is All Set to Devour an Internet Giant, but How Will it Feel the Next Morning?" *Time*, 7 December 1998.

Landler, Mark. "AOL Gains Cable Rights in China by Omitting News, Sex and Violence." *New York Times*, 29 October 2001. Available at http://www.nytimes.com.

Ledbetter, James. "AOL–Time Warner Make it Big." *Yahoo! News*, 11 January 2000. Available at http://www.dailynews.yahoo.com.

Lemos, Robert. "Blockbuster Merger to Boost Broadband." *Yahoo! News*, 11 January 2000. Available at http://dailynews.yahoo.com.

Luh, James C. "AOL Goes Shopping to Build its Base among Music Fans." *Internet World*, 7 June 1999.

"Making AOL A–O.K." *Business Week*, 11 January 1999.

McHugh, Josh. "Web Warrior." *Forbes*, 11 January 1999.

Mitchell, Russ. "America Online's Here, There, and Everywhere." *U.S. News & World Report*, 5 July 1999.

Nelson, Matthew. "AOL, Sun Team up to Tackle Internet Commerce." *InfoWorld*, 29 March 1999.

Satran, Dick. "RPT–Time–Warner, AOL Deal Leads Shift to Convergence." *Reuters*, 10 January 2000. Available at http://biz.yahoo.com.

Serwer, Andy. "Mother Knows Best: The Word on Dan and Steve Case—from Mom." *Fortune*, 22 November 1999.

"Stephen M. Case." *Business Week*, 27 September 1999.

Swisher, Kara. *AOL.com: How Steve Case Beat Bill Gates, Nailed the Netheads, and Made Millions in the War for the Web*. New York: Times Books, 1999.

Sykes, Rebecca. "AOL Finalizes Acquisition." *InfoWorld*, 22 March 1999.

John T. Chambers

(1949-)
Cisco Systems Inc.

Overview

An impassioned promoter of electronic commerce and all that the Internet has to offer, John T. Chambers heads Cisco Systems Inc., the world's largest manufacturer of data networking equipment. Since taking over as Cisco's chief executive officer in January 1995, Chambers has led the company from annual sales of $1.2 billion to nearly $22.3 billion in fiscal 2001, which ended July 31, 2001. A born salesman, Chambers has helped his company to win control of nearly two–thirds of the international market for the switches and routers that power the Internet and connect networks. He has also positioned the company to compete for a larger share of the telecommunications market with its line of products able to carry data, voice, and video traffic. So effectively has Chambers preached the Net religion that fellow executives in the business have been made to sit up and take notice. Eric E. Schmidt, chief executive of software maker Novell Inc., said of the Cisco CEO: "Chambers has made himself into the No. 1 communicator of the networked vision." Chamber's effectiveness as a salesman for the Internet has not escaped the attention of the nation's top leaders. A few years back, President Bill Clinton and Vice–President Al Gore described the Cisco CEO as "a true leader in this industry, in America's economy, and in the global economy." Clinton and Gore hailed Cisco as "one of the most respected companies, not only in [the networking] field, but in any field."

Personal Life

Chambers was born in Cleveland, Ohio, on August 23, 1949. Shortly after his birth, his family moved to

John Thomas Chambers (left) receiving "Chief Executive of the Year" award from Herbert Kelleher (1999 recipient). (AP/Wide World Photos.)

Charleston, West Virginia, where he grew up. Both his mother and father were physicians. As a boy, he struggled with dyslexia, but his parents hired a private tutor who helped Chambers to overcome this disability. So well did he overcome it, in fact, that he graduated second in his high school class. He attended West Virginia University in Morgantown, where he earned his bachelor's degree in business administration in 1971. He went on to Indiana University in Bloomington for his master's degree in finance and management and later returned to Morgantown to earn a law degree.

Chambers and his wife, Elaine, live in Los Altos Hills, California, not far from the executive suites of

Cisco in nearby San Jose. The couple has two children, a daughter, Lindsay, and a son, John. When not traveling about the country extolling the virtues of the Internet and networking in general, Chambers enjoys fishing and tennis.

Career Details

Chambers began his business career in 1976 at IBM, where he remained for six years before moving on to Wang Laboratories. During his eight–year stay at Wang,

Chambers as vice–president was forced to lay off some 5,000 employees, an experience he found profoundly disturbing. So disturbing, in fact, that he abruptly left Wang, even though he had not yet landed another job. Of the massive layoff at Wang, he later said, "I'll do anything to avoid that again."

In 1991, Chambers joined Cisco as senior vice–president of worldwide operations. The company at that point had annual sales of about $70 million. In the fall of 1994, Cisco's board announced Chambers' appointment as president and chief executive officer, effective in January 1995. By 2001, Cisco had increased its annual revenue to more than $22 billion, a phenomenal increase due in no small part to the leadership of Chambers.

Almost from the start, Chambers began selling the Internet and networking with missionary zeal. In a November 1997 interview with ZD COMDEX, Chambers predicted that "companies that don't adopt networking and the Internet will be left behind, regardless of their size. The productivity gains are too large. Every major aspect of how business will be done will be affected by this new technology." And Cisco has certainly been practicing what Chambers preached. The company transacts more than 80 percent of its business over the Internet. More than that, Chambers has made Cisco a shining example of the productivity gains that can be achieved through use of the Internet, both by speeding up most processes and sharply reducing costs. Every corporate function—including customer support, finance, manufacturing, and human resources—at Cisco is performed through Net systems, winning a reduction of $1.5 billion in costs between 1996 and 1999. Chambers himself is obsessed with customer satisfaction. Every night before he retires, he routinely listens to ten or so voice–mail messages from staffers in the field who have phoned in reports on the status of Cisco's top accounts.

Asked by ZD COMDEX about the challenges likely to face companies seeking to implement a network–centric approach to doing business, Chambers conceded that companies will have to make some significant adjustments. "The first is there are five to maybe ten applications that are the big payback applications. You want to select the right applications at the right time for your industry. . . . The second is to really think about how your network is going to work and what the true cost of the network is. . . . And the third thing is to determine what they are going to do themselves and what they're going to look for their partners to help them do in the implementation of the network."

To speed Cisco's growth and diversify its product base, Chambers has engineered the acquisition of more than 60 companies since becoming the CEO. A key area he has targeted for growth is the telecommunications sector, envisioning a time in the not–too–distant future when "data, voice, and video will be delivered over a single connection in our homes." In Chambers' vision, Cisco's vast data networks could in time become the world's

Chronology:
John T. Chambers

1949: Born.

1971: Graduated with B.A./B.S. in business from West Virginia University.

1974: Graduated with J.D. from West Virginia University.

1976: Began business career at IBM.

1982: Moved to Wang Computers.

1991: Joined Cisco Systems Inc. as SVP, worldwide sales and operations.

1994: Named Cisco's president and CEO.

1995: Assumed position as president and CEO.

1997: Cisco transacted one–third of world's electronic commerce.

2000: Given Internet Industry Leader Award by U.S. Internet Council.

---

leading voice networks. Cisco's maneuvers in the telecommunications arena will not go unchallenged. As the longtime telecommunications leaders become increasingly Internet–savvy, they are moving to head off Cisco's move into the sector. In mid–1998, Nortel bought Bay Networks Inc., a longtime rival of Cisco.

Chambers has traveled the country to promote the new world that has been opened up by the Internet for business and consumers alike. He spends nearly half his time on the road, spreading his message. In his keynote address at ComNet '97 in Washington, D.C., Chambers used several examples to press his case for connecting companies globally and to prove how pervasive both networking and the Internet have become. He pointed out that at a growing number of colleges, the traditional college library has been replaced by the World Wide Web and term papers are submitted via e–mail. He also pointed to the rapidly growing number of company meetings conducted through videoconferencing.

In selling the Internet around the world, Chambers often cites a University of Texas study, commissioned by Cisco, that predicts that by 2010 electronic commerce will account for roughly a quarter of the world's gross national product. Companies that fail to take advantage of the Internet's business potential, he warns, very likely will face irrelevancy.

In August of 2001, Chambers announced major changes in Cisco's organizational structure, changes designed to help the company better serve its customers. At the heart of the changes was a move from Cisco's line of business structure to centralized engineering and marketing organizations. In announcing the restructuring, Chambers said, "Our line of business structure has served us very well in the past, when customer segments and product requirements were very distinct. Today, the differences have blurred between these customer segments, and Cisco is in a unique position to provide the industry's broadest family of products united under a consistent architecture designed to help our customers improve productivity and profitability."

Chambers speaks with a slight southern twang, but nobody is likely to mistake him for a country bumpkin. He was once described as "a West Virginia choirboy who will eat you for lunch." The Cisco CEO expresses unshakable confidence in the future of his company, predicting that "there's no reason Cisco can't be the most successful company in history. Perhaps the highest market cap, but also the most generous with its employees, with payback for its shareholders and also the best giver to the community." One indicator of Cisco's generosity to its employees came when *Forbes* magazine named it the third–best company to work for. ABC News' *20/20* magazine show dubbed Chambers the "best boss in America."

In addition to being a big booster for the Internet, Chambers has been a major cheerleader for the development of San Jose, the California city that serves as Cisco's headquarters. He has proposed massive office complexes on the northern and southern edges of the city, expansions that would allow Cisco to triple its workforce in the San Jose area. Perhaps the biggest project planned by Cisco has been the construction of a $1 billion corporate park in San Jose's Coyote Valley. The complex would house up to 20,000 Cisco employees. Chambers isn't above using strong–arm tactics to get what he wants for Cisco. After he announced his plan for the Coyote Valley office complex in 1999, he made it clear that he could take Cisco's business elsewhere if the necessary approvals weren't handled expediently. "It takes one phone call to North Carolina," he said. "It's a much easier place to do business." Although Chambers' threat ruffled the feathers of some of San Jose's city fathers, "a lot of us were cheering," said San Jose Chamber of Commerce President Steve Tedesco. "Finally somebody could tell the city like it is."

Social and Economic Impact

Chambers has not only guided Cisco to phenomenal success, but he's been a passionate advocate for electronic commerce and the Internet. He's traveled the world to convince government and business leaders how important it is that they embrace the new Net economy. "We're living through the second Industrial Revolution," he tells all who will listen. And for those who may be tempted to ignore his warning and let the Internet bandwagon pass them by, he warns: "You can be Amazoned in a moment."

Chambers has molded Cisco into one of the biggest and most successful companies of all time, while at the same time ensuring that the company's employees look upon their employer as concerned and sensitive about their needs. In this arena, he's been amazingly successful, having won the plaudits of ABC News' *20/20* as "America's best boss" and having Cisco consistently rated among the best places to work in countless surveys. It's not hard to understand when you hear Chambers talk about his personal credo as Cisco's CEO: "Never ask your employees to do something you wouldn't be willing to do yourself."

Chambers hasn't neglected his civic duties either. He has a long and admirable record of philanthropy, ranging from sponsorship of the world's first Internet–based charity concert to forking over $1 million for a San Jose area community center. Among the causes about which Chambers cares the most is education. A couple of years back, he contributed a quarter of a million dollars of his own money to help get a measure making it easier to build and repair schools on the California ballot. An enthusiastic supporter of the Republican Party, he has served as an adviser to President George W. Bush and also co–chaired the Technology Network, which pushes for legislation that will foster the growth of this country's high–tech sector.

Sources of Information

Contact at: Cisco Systems Inc.
    170 W. Tasman Dr., Bldg. 10
    San Jose, CA 95134–1706
    Business Phone: (408) 526–7208
    URL: http://www.cisco.com

Bibliography

"Cisco Sends Mixed Signals." *Communications Today*, 9 August 2001.

"John T. Chambers: Cisco's Live Wire." *Business Week*, 11 January 1999.

Ostrom, Mary Anne. "John Chambers." *Silicon Valley*, 30 July 2000.

Reinhardt, Andy. "John T. Chambers." *Business Week*, 27 September 1999.

Shinal, John. "Networking: Why Cisco's Comeback Plan Is a Long Shot." *Business Week*, 21 May 2001.

Coco Chanel

(1883-1971)
Chanel

Overview

Gabrielle Chanel, known for most of her adult life as "Coco," created a fashion revolution in women's clothing, not once, but twice. In the 1920s, she introduced comfortable, simplistic designs that stood in stark contrast to the popular designs that incorporated numerous frills and ruffles. Again, in the 1950s, she freed women from the trends toward tight–fitting, uncomfortable clothing and returned them to simple elegance and functionality. Chanel was larger than life, a legend before her death and revered after. Over three decades after her death, Chanel remains a highly respected line of clothing and perfumes.

Personal Life

Gabrielle "Coco" Chanel, born on August 19, 1883, in a poorhouse in Saumur, France, was the second of five children born to Albert Chanel and Jeanne Devolle. Her parents did not marry until Chanel was one year old. Her father, a migrant market merchant, moved from town to town peddling his wares, sometimes with and sometimes without his family in tow. In 1894 her mother lost her health after a difficult pregnancy that resulted in the death of the infant. In February 1895, Chanel's mother died. Her father, never known to be dependable, abandoned his five children, never to be seen by them again. Chanel and her two sisters were placed in a boarding school in the town of Moulins run by nuns. Her two brothers were placed with a farm family, as unpaid child laborers.

Many of her memories of her childhood are tainted with feelings of being unloved and unwanted, despite her

Coco Chanel. (Archive Photos, Inc.)

stress. Word circulated of Chanel's adept needlework, and soon she had customers coming directly to her for alterations. She also worked at a tailor shop once a week, where she met several calvarymen who took an interest in the petite, but spunky, Chanel. In their company, Chanel began going to the local cafe, La Rotonde. Amateurs were invited to sing between shows, and Chanel, always known for her boldness, stepped up on stage one night. Chanel's singing voice was marginal, but the support of her escorts encouraged the crowd. According to the tale, Chanel sang of a poor girl who had lost her dog Coco; the crowd began to call back to her "Coco! Coco!" thus bestowing on her the nickname by which she would be known the remainder of her life.

While frequenting La Rotonde, Chanel met Etienne Balsan, a calvaryman from a wealthy French family. When Balsan invited her to visit his racing horse farm in 1903, 20–year–old Chanel accepted and stayed. The young couple enjoyed each other's company, but the relationship was far from perfect. Balsan loved horse racing, women, and parties. Chanel was well aware that men such as the wealthy Balsan did not marry orphaned seamstresses. Nonetheless, during her time with Balsan, she became an expert horsewoman, and was introduced to a social group well beyond her own standing. Through them Chanel first began to draw attention as a fashion designer, primarily at first as a hat designer. When the women appeared at the racetrack with copies of Chanel's hats, the tabloids took note and wrote of the new styles.

As Chanel began making a name for herself within Balsan's social circle, she began to envision herself as a professional milliner with a shop in Paris. Balsan put off her attempts to convince him to finance her idea, but then in 1914 she met the love of her life, Arthur "Boy" Chapel, who found it perfectly fitting that Chanel should want a business of her own. Chapel, an Englishman, and Chanel met during a week–long fox hunt, and when he left to return to England, Chanel caught up to him at the train station, without a bag in hand. Balsan, quite in concert with his nature, decided to live and let live, even allowing Chanel to set up her millinery shop in his Paris apartment. With Chapel's financial help, Chanel opened a new shop at 21 Rue Cambon. Her new simple and comfortable designs became popular, and success soon followed; she soon added clothing to her selection of hats. People were as fascinated by Chanel as they were by her designs, often coming into her shop just to see what she looked like. As she grew in fame, her illegitimate birth and lower class origins gradually disappeared, and Chanel became a full, if unique, member of Parisian society.

Chapel, who never gave up his playboy ways despite his sincere affection for Chanel, eventually married the daughter of a lord. However, he soon renewed his relationship with Chanel, finding he missed her greatly. When he died in an automobile accident in 1919, Chanel was crushed. According to biographer Axel Madsen, Chanel later said, "We were made for each other. That

elaborate and baseless stories of her father's eventual return to reunite the family. In reality, during the six years of her residence there, she slept in the unheated dormitory and sat at the table with the other destitute children who had no family to pay the tuition. She would never accept or admit the extent of the poverty of her youth. Even as an adult, Chanel consistently refused to admit her humble beginnings and talked instead of being raised by her aunts. But always her tales were obscure or contradictory, and the scenario or characters often changed as the moment suited her.

When Chanel was old enough to leave, the nuns found her a job at a local boutique, the House of Grampayre, where she worked as a shop assistant and seam-

he was there and that he loved me, and that he knew I loved him was all that mattered."

Although Chanel had numerous and often well–publicized relationships after Chapel's death, including the Duke of Westminster and a Nazi officer, she never married or had children. She retained her residence and boutique at 21 Rue Cambon the remainder of her life, although she always slept across the street at the Ritz Hotel. She died at the Ritz on January 10, 1971; she was 87 years old.

Career Details

Chanel opened her first business, a millinery, in 1909 with the assistance of Balsan and Chapel. In 1915 Chapel helped Chanel open additional shops in the coastal resort towns of Deauville and Biarritz. It was while spending a leisurely summer with Chapel in Deauville in 1913 that Chanel first invented her famous sportswear design. According to Madsen, "In 1913, knits were considered unsuitable and too limp and lifeless for anything but underwear, flannel too working class or masculine, to be stylish for women. She made jersey chic with her simple gray and navy dresses that were quite unlike anything women had worn before." According to Chanel's later retelling, she cut the front of an old jersey so she would not have to pull it over her head. She then added a ribbon, a collar, and a knot. When people asked where she got her dress, she volunteered to sell them one. Later she told biographers, "My dear, my fortune is built on that old jersey that I'd put on because it was cold in Deauville."

As she would do throughout her career, Chanel created clothing that was backed on functionality and comfort. Unlike the current styles that emphasized frills and tight–fitting corsets, Chanel's new designs emphasized straight flowing lines with plain colors—usually gray, beige, and navy—that displayed an air of simple elegance. The rich flocked to her designs—Chanel single–handedly created a women's fashion revolution.

When Chapel died in 1919, Chanel was crushed, but she was no longer in need of his financial backing. By that time she had a staff of 300 and was selling her dresses for over 7,000 francs (over $2,000 in current terms) each. The House of Chanel was coming into the height of its success. According to the *Smithsonian*, "Harper's Bazaar ran the first picture ever of her couture, 'Chanel's charming chemise dress.' No collar, no bodice, but a deep V–necked, near–masculine waistcoast, no puffs, no frills, with a large hat with a twist of fur. She was stealing on the early march on the flapper look of the upcoming '20s." During the early 1920s, Chanel also designed costumes for the theatre and ballet.

In 1923 Chanel began selling her trademark perfume, Chanel No. 5. Collaborating with well–known per-

Chronology:
Coco Chanel

1883: Born.

1909: Opened first business, a millinery, in Paris.

1910: Moved business to 21 Rue Cambon, where it remains throughout her life.

1913: Designed first women's sportswear.

1923: Introduced new fragrance, Chanel No. 5.

1925: Introduced what becomes known as the classic Chanel suit.

1926: Created the highly praised and often copied "little black dress."

1939: Closed the House of Chanel.

1954: Staged a successful comeback at the age of seventy.

1971: Died.

fume expert Ernest Beaux, Chanel wanted to create a new scent, void of the flowery, rose–water smells of the popular perfumes of the day. Starting with benzyl acetate, a coal tar derivative that smells like jasmine, Beaux added real jasmine. Of the final seven samples, Chanel chose the fifth, thus the name Chanel No. 5. She also designed the simple square–shaped bottle for her new perfume, a drastic change from the fancy bottles on the market. Chanel wanted to make No. 5, which she referred to as "a woman's scent," the most expensive perfume in the world; it definitely became the most popular. To meet the demand, Chanel entered into an agreement with a perfume company to manufacture the product. Although she made a fortune on the perfume, throughout her lifetime she was convinced that the deal had been heavily weighted in favor of the perfumer and that she had been cheated out of a huge sum of money.

In 1925 Chanel introduced what became known as the classic Chanel suit—a collarless cardigan jacket with tight–fitting sleeves and braid trim, matched with a plain but graceful skirt. The following year she created the "little black dress," which was a revolution in color and style, as black was traditionally associated with funerals. *Vogue* called the dress the "Ford" of eveningwear, based on its functionality and enduring quality. She added to her fashion creations by designing costume jewelry, mixing real and imitation pearls and gems. Her jewelry designs added flair and color to her simplistic clothing designs. Chanel, who could not draw her designs, often created them on live models. Her talents were extensive, and along with her standard suit and little black dress designs, Chanel added glitzy eveningwear and cocktail dresses. She created a new trend in women's fashion when she began attending social functions wearing pants—nearly unheard of until Chanel.

During World War II, Chanel's reputation suffered. In October 1939, just weeks after the war began, Chanel closed the House of Chanel and dismissed all her workers. Despite attempts by her employees and the French government to force her to reopen, Chanel remained closed. To add injury to insult, when Nazi forces overran France, Chanel began a relationship with a young handsome Nazi soldier, Hans Gunther von Dincklage, known as Spatz. With German permission, Chanel continued to live at the Ritz. When France was liberated in 1944, Chanel underwent three hours of interrogation by French authorities about her relationship with Spatz. She was released, but her actions had tarnished her public image. For the next decade, she wandered about, living in a self–imposed exile for a time.

In 1954, at the age of seventy, Chanel staged a comeback and reopened the House of Chanel. Complaining that the new lines of clothing coming out were much too constrictive, Chanel later explained that the problem stemmed from the fact that men had taken over women's fashion design, and men, declared Chanel, did not know how to make clothing for women. She debuted her new line of clothes on February 5, 1954, in Paris. The show was highly publicized and highly anticipated, but the affair received shockingly poor reviews, with the *London Daily Express* running the condemning headline "A Fiasco—Audience Gasped!" The European press roundly criticized Chanel for depending too heavily on her previous fashion designs. However, the response in the United States was different; *Life* magazine ran a four–page spread that praised Chanel's comfortable style. The following month a Chanel navy blue suit appeared on the cover of *French Vogue*. When Chanel had another show in May 1955, this time her designs were met with approval and enthusiasm. Triumphant, Chanel had reclaimed her past fame and legendary status.

Social and Economic Impact

When Chanel died on January 10, 1971, at the Ritz Hotel, she left behind an estate worth over $90 million (in present terms). She had nearly single–handedly transformed women's fashion from the frills and constrictive designs to loose–fitting, easy–wearing clothing that provided both style and functionality. After her death, several assistants assumed command of her business, but the business stagnated during the remainder of the 1970s. During the 1980s Karl Lagerfeld took over the design for Chanel fashions and began to focus on a younger customer base. He has been routinely praised for his ability to retain the quality and style of the original Chanel. The company owns 100 boutiques throughout the world and is one of the most recognized names in fashion and perfume.

Chanel never spoke of feminism, but referred frequently to femininity, and yet she challenged and conquered many social limits in women's fashion. Madsen concluded, "Coco Chanel had influence before she had money. She was the Pied Piper who led women away from complicated, uncomfortable clothes to a simple, uncluttered, and casual look that is still synonymous with her name. . . . From beyond the grave, her name is enough to define a pair of shoes, a hat, a pocketbook, a suit, a perfume. It conveys prestige, quality, taste, and unmistakable style. It is a sign of excellence, of fulfilled sensibilities for women who want to be in fashion without screaming fashion."

Chanel's success was powered by the strength of her personality, her desire for independence, and her need to be different. Her impact can be readily seen in the simple but smart designs that dominate twenty–first–century women's fashions. The irony is, of course, that in her desire to be different, Chanel created a trend that was copied by everyone. She became that which she had first rebelled against. And yet her triumph was that she, a poor orphaned girl, influenced and reigned supreme in the highest social circles.

Sources of Information

Bibliography

"Chanel." *Biography.com*, 2000. Available at http://www.biography.com.

"Chanel." Chanel, Inc. Available at http://www.chanel.com.

"Chez Chanel: Couturiere and Courtesan, Coco Made Her Own Rules as She Freed Women From Old Fussy, Frilly Fashions." *Smithsonian*, July 2001.

"Gabrielle Chanel." *Contemporary Designers*. 3rd ed. New York: St. James Press, 1997.

Madsen, Axel. *Chanel: A Woman of Her Own*. New York: Henry Holt and Company, 1990.

"Time 100: Artist and Entertainers. The Designer: Coco Chanel." *Time.com*, 2001. Available at http://www.time.com.

Linda Chavez–Thompson

Overview

Linda Chavez–Thompson's ascension to the highest ranks of the labor movement forms the kind of narrative that might have been scripted by a Hollywood screenwriter or penned by a socially conscious novelist. The inspiring saga takes a 10–year–old Chavez–Thompson from the cotton fields of Texas to the executive council of the American Federation of Labor and Congress of Industrial Organizations (AFL–CIO). During the process, she became an inspirational role model and an effective organizer. Her success is remarkable not only because she's a woman but because she's a member of a minority.

Her career path included stints as a union secretary and a union local representative. She eventually worked her way up to the highest levels of the American Federation of State, County and Municipal Employees (AFSCME), becoming vice president of that organization in 1988. In her current role with the AFL–CIO, she acts as a bridge between the labor movement and minorities, working to bring together those two traditionally hostile factions.

(1944-)

AFL–CIO

Personal Life

Chavez–Thompson is the widow of Robert Thompson. She lives in Washington, D.C., where she relocated after moving from San Antonio, Texas. She has two children from a previous marriage and two grandchildren.

Before she emerged as the leading woman in the national labor movement, Chavez–Thompson, a second–

Linda Chavez-Thompson. *(Archive Photos Inc.)*

generation American of Mexican descent, toiled as a young girl in menial jobs. She was born in Lubbock, Texas, on August 1, 1944, one of eight children born of sharecropper parents. She is no stranger to hard work. When she was only 10 years old, she started working in the cotton fields along with her family. Toiling beneath the hot Texas summer sun for 10 hours a day, Chavez-Thompson only earned thirty cents an hour. When she reached the ninth grade, she dropped out of school to help her parents, who were enduring a difficult period. She was only 19 years old when she married for the first time.

Chavez-Thompson has held the position of executive vice president of the AFL–CIO since her election on October 25, 1995, which came as a result of an insurgent campaign designed not to subvert the AFL–CIO but to infuse the organization with new blood, energy, and direction. Once elected, Chavez-Thompson proved to be more than a symbolic figure. After two years of effective leadership, she was re-elected on September 30, 1997, this time to a four-year term.

When she was first elected, and in accordance with the AFL–CIO's program to work more closely with other community groups, Chavez-Thompson became active in many national organizations. But she wasn't merely following the directives of the federation; this was part of her own vision as well. In addition to her vice–presidential duties, she has served on numerous boards and committees, including The United Way's Board of Governors and the U.S. State Department Advisory Com-

mittee on Labor Diplomacy. She is a member of the Board of Trustees of the Labor Heritage Foundation, an executive committee member of the Congressional Hispanic Caucus Institute, and a board member of the Institute for Women's Policy Research.

Career Details

Following her first marriage, Chavez-Thompson went to work cleaning houses to help supplement her husband's city–employee wages and support their two–year–old daughter. Not long after, she started her trade union career serving as the union secretary for the Lubbock local of the AFSCME, the same labor union to which her father belonged. She held this position from December 1967 to June 1971. It was during that period that she got an up–close glimpse of the inner dynamics of the labor movement, knowledge that she would build upon as she advanced her career and made the transition from being a local to national figure.

From 1971 to 1973, Chavez-Thompson served as an AFSCME international union representative in San Antonio, Texas, at a starting salary of $1.40 an hour, which was only 15 cents above the minimum wage. The role fell to her because no one else in the union could communicate in Spanish with the predominately Latino membership. The role served as her entrance into the AFL–CIO, as the union was part of that organization. The position also placed her in hostile territory, as the union represented members in seven states (Arizona, Colorado, Nevada, New Mexico, Oklahoma, Texas, and Utah) where general opposition to labor organizing existed.

In 1973, Chavez-Thompson became an assistant business manager for AFSCME Local 2399 and soon graduated to the role of business manager. Eventually, she rose to the position of executive director, a post she held from 1977 through February 1995. Her responsibilities included advancing legislative, political action, and education programs. She also conducted every level of grievance procedures for membership representation. In 1986, the Labor Council for Latin American Advancement, AFL–CIO appointed Chavez-Thompson to be its national vice president, a position she held until 1996.

Continuing her rise in the labor movement, in 1988 Chavez-Thompson was elected AFSCME international vice president. She held the position until 1996. In that role she helped organize efforts in the labor–unfriendly seven–state region. Her tenure was highlighted by several significant accomplishments. In Texas, she organized a drive that brought in 5,000 new members. Also, she helped effect the passage of a collective bargaining law for public employees in New Mexico.

On February 4, 1995, she was elected executive director of Texas Council 42, AFSCME, which is made up of 17 locals with 10,000 members. In that role she focused her efforts on undertaking legislative and education programs that would help members in their fight against downsizing, budget cuts, and companies that contract out to non–union sources. Chavez–Thompson continues serving in that capacity.

In October 1995, Chavez–Thompson was elected executive vice president of the 13.6 million–member AFL–CIO. The push to elect her was part of an effort to improve union's relationship with women and minorities, who make up more than 40 percent of membership. As would be expected, her election didn't come without a struggle. She faced formidable opposition as she campaigned for the office by calling for a reorganization of the federation. However, the federation's president, John Sweeney, wanted to increase the number of council members and he wanted that increase to include a woman. Chavez–Thompson's election was seen as a bold step forward for the AFL–CIO in recognizing the nation's increasingly diverse work force at its highest level. In her capacity as vice president and third ranking leader of the AFL–CIO, she is working to forge closer ties between the union and women and other minorities.

During the Clinton administration, former President Bill Clinton appointed Chavez–Thompson to serve on the President's Initiative on Race and to serve as vice chair of the President's Committee on Employment of People with Disabilities.

Chronology:
Linda Chavez–Thompson

1944: Born.

1967: Began her labor union career as a union secretary for the Lubbock local of the AFSCME.

1971: Became AFSCME international union representative in San Antonio, Texas.

1973: Became business manager for AFSCME Local 2399.

1986: Appointed national vice president of the Labor Council for Latin American Advancement.

1988: Elected AFSCME international vice president.

1995: Moved to Washington, DC.

1995: Elected executive director of Texas Council 42, AFSCME.

1995: Elected executive vice president of the AFL–CIO.

1997: Re–elected executive vice president of the AFL–CIO for a four–year term.

Social and Economic Impact

As a woman and as a member of a minority, Chavez–Thompson worked hard to gain the respect of her colleagues. Still, even as she worked hard to be taken seriously, many chose only to see her as a token figure. Others complained that she lacked the necessary experience to take on the responsibilities and pressures of such a high–ranking office. However, Chavez–Thompson would prove the doubters wrong, as she demonstrated that she was a good leader capable of effecting substantial change. Her efforts garnered her the respect and praise of other leaders within the labor movement, as well as other sectors within society, and she became a role model for both women and minorities, as she supplied those two factions with a stronger voice in the federation.

Still, even though she has worked hard for those two groups, her concerns and efforts cross all sectors. And the admiration directed back at her comes from all factions, not just women and minorities. Arturo Rodriguez, president of the United Farm Workers, has said that Chavez–Thompson is "a master at interweaving the Latino culture with the majority culture."

Following her election, Chavez–Thompson became very active and influential in many areas. She is on

the board of governors of the United Way and is a vice–chairperson of the Democratic National Committee. She is also on the executive committee of the Congressional Hispanic Caucus Institute and on the board of trustees for the Labor Heritage Foundation.

Like those who supported her, she sees her election as a big step forward. However, she realized the hard work had only begun and that much still needed to be done. She saw that there was a need for a "mind change" in the AFL–CIO. She credited the organization with creating the position of executive vice president and working to get her elected to fill that position, but she viewed that as only a beginning. Specific needs and changes she wants to bring about include having unions bring more women and minorities into high–ranking positions. Not only that, unions, she feels, need to hire more women and minorities at all levels. The AFL–CIO, she feels, need to diversify not only in its leadership but in its staffing.

She continues trying to build up the union's general membership, which in recent years has been shrinking. Part of her strategy focused on organizing workers in the service sector and on the community at large, as she would like to see the unions become less isolated from the community.

The goals of the AFL–CIO, as she sees it, are to reinvigorate the U.S. labor movement, which she feels has been on a decline due to the lack of organizing and rank–and–file mobilization. She wants members to regain the respect they once had for their unions, while at the same time becoming actively involved in the union. She wants to diminish the infighting and disloyalty. And she doesn't see these problems being solved overnight. The problems must be solved by a series of moderate changes and not by a drastic change.

She has strived to build AFL–CIO coalitions with neighborhood organizations, community groups, civil rights organizations such as the NAACP, the League of United Latin American Citizens, National Council of La Raza, and with women's rights organizations.

Among her many strengths, Chavez–Thompson has demonstrated the ability to recognize new challenges and problems that arose in the 1990s and remained major issues as the country, and its labor force, headed into the new century. These new challenges included the ubiquitous specter of downsizing, the part–timing of the workforce, and the kind of substandard wages and working conditions that were alarming in a modern context. Chavez–Thompson looked to address problems created by the streamlining of the corporate workplace, including the elimination of health insurance and the loss of pension benefits. Above all, she seeks to see that all workers earn wages that will allow them a decent standard of living and are accorded the treatment and respect that their basic rights entitle them to.

At the beginning of the new millennium, she was looking to achieve the goals by helping to develop new methods of organizing workers in such a way that, in her words, would broaden and strengthen labor's base and through obtaining more political representation for workers.

Sources of Information

Contact at: AFL–CIO
815 16th Street
Washington, DC 20006–4145

Bibliography

Biography of Linda Chavez–Thompson. Democratic National Committee. Washington, D.C., 2001. Available at http://www.democrats.org/news/index.html.

Lord, Mary. "A Sharecropper's Daughter Revives Labor's Grass Roots." *U.S. New and World Reports*, 25 December 1995.

Figueroa, Maria. "An Interview with Linda Chavez–Thompson,"

"Linda Chavez–Thompson, Advisory Board Member." *Welcome to the White House*, Washington, D.C., 2001. Available at http://clinton4.nara.gov/textonly/Initiatives/OneAmerica/BIOLCT.html.

"Linda Chavez–Thompson—The Future of Populist Politics." *Cultures in the 21st Century: Conflicts & Convergences*, Colorado 1999. Available at http://www.coloradocollege.edu/Academics/Anniversary/Participants/Chavez–Thompson.htm.

PeaceNet. Available at http://womenshistory.about.com.

Jim Clark

(1944-)
myCFO, Inc.

Overview

James Clark is one of the most renowned and successful engineers and serial entrepreneurs of the Silicon Valley phenomenon. Clark is credited with co–founding and walking away from a trio of billion dollar companies: Silicon Graphics, Netscape Communications, and now WebMD. Clark is arguably the father of the modern–day Internet. After leaving the first company he created, pioneering the use of 3–D graphics, he and programming whiz Marc Andreessen sparked the Internet revolution with their Netscape Navigator browser. This browser software transformed the Internet from an elite domain of technocrats to a vastly important worldwide mass media. Now Clark's springboarding to services that take advantage of the worldwide web. First, he co–founded WebMD, a high profile web–based service for healthcare management. His latest start–ups include myCFO, Inc., a personal money management service; Shutterfly, an online photography site; and DNA Sciences, which studies genetics.

Personal Life

Clark and his third wife, Nancy, live in Woodside, California, and have two children. He lectures widely on technology and business developments in the computer field at major conferences and universities throughout the world. He received the Research Society of America's Annual Gold Medal in physics in 1970, the Annual Computer Graphics Achievement Award in 1984, and the Arthur Young and Company and *Venture* magazine's Entrepreneur of the Year award in 1988.

Jim Clark. *(AP/Wide World Photos.)*

In the spring of 1996, Clark, who likes to sail and fly planes, began working with veteran yachtsman Paul Cayard to create a state–of–the–art racing yacht to win back the America's Cup for the United States at the turn of the century. The vessel, dubbed the *Hyperion*, is one of the largest sailboats in the world and is completely computerized with 25 Silicon Graphics workstations. It was during the building of *Hyperion* that Clark became enchanted by a Lunstroo Schooner and decided that his next yacht would have to be a modern classic. Clark then commissioned Athena, also from the Royal Huisman Shipyard, at 292 feet, and the massive vessel is scheduled for completion in 2004.

A native of Texas, Clark showed little academic promise as a child. He grew up in a single–parent home with few financial resources. He was a self–described hoodlum and was eventually expelled from school. When he joined the navy, Clark again found himself at odds with authority: he marked every question "yes" on a multiple–choice exam, since each one seemed at least partly correct. The navy accused him of trying to fool the computer that graded the tests. Clark had never heard of a computer before.

During Clark's naval stint, his intellectual talents began to emerge. Though he lacked academic training, he scored highest on a math exam and was assigned to teach algebra. Clark later went on to earn a bachelor of science degree in physics in 1970 and a master of science degree in physics in 1971 from Louisiana State University in New Orleans. As a graduate student, he was awarded the Research Society of America's 1971 Annual Gold Medal. In 1974, he completed a Ph.D. in computer science at the University of Utah. His doctoral thesis, the first implementation of what is today known as "virtual reality," focused on building special purpose hardware for graphics applications. In 1995, Clark received an honorary doctorate of science degree from the University of Utah.

From 1974 to 1978, Clark was an assistant professor at the University of California at Santa Cruz, and in 1979 he became associate professor at Stanford University. Even in the academic world, though, Clark's independent thinking sometimes got him into trouble. After he was fired from one teaching job for insubordination, his second wife filed for divorce.

Career Details

At Stanford, Clark and six graduate students worked at the Palo Alto Research Center on ways to enliven computer images with 3–dimensional graphics. They developed a microchip that Clark called the Geometry Engine. When no existing computer companies were interested in this new technology, Clark and his students, using venture capital, started their own computer workstation company, Silicon Graphics, Inc. (SGI) in Mountain View, California. The company's graphical systems appealed first to architects and engineers for use in designing buildings, cars, and rocket engines but soon became essential to filmmakers and animators. Silicon Graphics computers were used, for example, to create the dinosaurs in *Jurassic Park* and the special effects in countless other films. The workstations also were used by defense and aerospace contractors to train jet pilots and tank personnel.

Silicon Graphics thrived and moved into chip development for video game and interactive television markets, but Clark was frustrated in his attempts to accelerate the company's plans to make low–cost, high–volume hardware to connect with the burgeoning information highway. In a highly controversial move, Clark replaced his entire management team in 1984. SGI's profits continued to grow, from $5 million in 1984 to approximately $550 million in 1991. In March 1994, ready to move on, Clark resigned as chairman of the company.

For several months following his resignation from SGI, Clark contemplated investing in a number of business ventures. As he studied the computer technology field, he became fascinated with the Internet. He was especially intrigued with NCSA Mosaic, an exceptionally popular World Wide Web browser software prototype that had been developed by a team of student and staff computer programmers at the University of Illinois and distributed free on the Internet.

In a now legendary e–mail message, Clark, 50, contacted Marc Andreessen, Mosaic's 23–year–old creator, and asked if he would be interested in forming a company to create a commercially viable improved version of the Mosaic browser. In April 1994, Clark invested about $3 million in the new firm, which began life with three employees and offices in Mountain View. The new company originally was called Mosaic Communications Corporation but, after the University of Illinois contested the use of the name, the fledgling firm was renamed Netscape Communications.

By December 1994, Netscape had released its revolutionary browser, Netscape Navigator. Almost immediately, the new browser became the industry standard. Within only one or two months, Netscape claimed 70 percent of the browser market. It offered users speed, sophisticated graphics, and a special encryption code that secured their credit card transactions on the Internet. At first, the new browser faced virtually no competition; within a brief period, however, Microsoft rushed to jump on the Internet bandwagon and soon released its own browser software.

With Netscape's Navigator freely available to the public via downloading from the Internet, how does the company make a profit? It charges fees to create and maintain web servers for the sophisticated software businesses. The fees range from $1,500 to $50,000 for server versions of Navigator, depending on the complexity of a company's home page and the range of services provided to its customers. For businesses designed to conduct much of their business on the Internet, Netscape provides databases of online customers and the ability to secure credit card transactions. Netscape also offers users the option of purchasing the software and thereby receiving customer service.

Though Clark remained actively involved with Netscape, he picked an executive team to manage the company. James Barksdale, whom Clark recruited from McCaw Cellular, AT & T's wireless services division, became head of the company while Andreesen continued with research and development.

The company continues to race to keep ahead of industry giant Microsoft, which introduced its own browser, Internet Explorer, in 1995. Explorer also can be freely downloaded and comes bundled with the Microsoft

Chronology:
Jim Clark

1944: Born.

1974: Completed Ph.D. in computer science at the University of Utah.

1981: Founded Silicon Graphics, Inc. (SGI).

1994: Resigned from SGI and formed Netscape Communications Corporation.

1995: Netscape stock jumped from $28 to more than $74 a share in one day.

1995: Developed Netscape Navigator, an Internet browser program.

1995: Stepped down as chief executive of Netscape but remained chairperson of the board.

1996: Founded Healtheon Corporation, an Internet–based health care service.

1998: Healtheon acquired ActaMed, an electronic databank, and Metis, a developer of online healthcare information services.

1999: Netscape acquired by America Online; announced merger of Healtheon and WebMD; negotiated successful I.P.O. for Healtheon.

1999: Authored *Netscape Time: The Making of the Billion–Dollar Start–up That Changed the World.*

Windows operating system. Netscape remains at the head of the pack, however, and solidified its lead when it became a subsidiary of America Online (AOL) in 1999. Netscape was the first browser to introduce Java, the programming language that animates web sites. It has also expanded its product line to include software that runs inside internal corporate networks.

Clark himself told the story of Netscape's birth and growth in his 1999 book, *Netscape Time: The Making of the Billion–Dollar Start–up That Changed the World.* Critics enjoyed the book's sharp writing and its insights into the machinations of the corporate world.

In June 1996, Clark launched another successful company—Healtheon Corporation, which offers information services online to help medical insurance companies and employers better manage their paperwork.

Healtheon reported $13.4 million in sales for 1997, a 21.6 percent growth from the previous year. In 1998, Healtheon acquired ActaMed and Metis, both Internet–based, health–related companies, and the following year the company announced plans to merge with WebMD, an online provider of medical information, in a deal reported to be worth more than $3.5 billion. By 1999, when Healtheon went public, the company was worth almost $100 million. Clark abruptly left WebMD in 2000.

Clark was key in the development of a new breed of serial entrepreneurs. Starting up companies, taking them public, and then leaving them, once considered a sign of failure, is now part of a booming trend in Silicon Valley. His newest project, announced in 1999, is my-CFO.com, a web site that will provide online financial services to its members. Clark expects myCFO.com to streamline tax preparation, pay bills, and provide quick financial updates. The service is available to individuals with assets of $100 million or more.

Social and Economic Impact

When Netscape made an initial public stock offering of 3.5 million shares on August 9, 1995, an unprecedented stock frenzy ensued. Investors bought the stock in record numbers. Opening at $28 a share, the stock closed at $74, making Netscape's market value $2.3 billion in just one day. By 1999, Clark's personal fortune was worth about $3 billion. That year, he donated $150 million to Stanford University—the biggest single gift in the university's history—for the creation of a biomedical engineering and science center. The Clark Center will occupy 225,000 square feet and will be located across the street from the William Gates Computer Science Building.

Leaving SGI was a risky move for Clark, who left behind 40,000 shares of stock. Speaking to *Industry Week*, Clark recalled, "It seemed a little crazy. No one thought you could build a business around the Internet, but my instincts were if there were 25 million people using it, there was a business to be built." Giving away the software to Netscape Navigator also proved to be a revolutionary idea. "People knew then that I was certifiably nuts—starting this company, hiring a bunch of students, and now giving the software away," Clark said.

By following his instincts, Clark built companies that generated huge profits and transformed business and technology. Silicon Graphics changed the way visual information could be communicated, paving the way for 3–D images and movie special effects. Netscape Navigator was instrumental in making the Internet user–friendly and helped to create the first online generation. Online functions that have become a part of daily life owe much to the pioneering talent of Jim Clark.

Sources of Information

Contact at: myCFO, Inc.
2025 Garcia Ave.
Mountain View, CA 94043
Business Phone: (650)210–5000
URL: http://www.mycfo.com

Bibliography

Clark, Jim. *Netscape Time: The Making of the Billion–Dollar Start–Up That Changed the World*. New York: St. Martin's Press, 1999.

CNET News.com. 30 October 2000.

Current Biography. New York: H. W. Wilson, 1997.

Business 2.0, December 2000. Available from http://www.business2.com.

Holson, Laura M. "Healtheon Is Expected to Join Forces with Internet Provider." *New York Times*, 15 May 1999.

"James H. Clark." *BusinessWeek Online*, 27 September 1999.

"Jim Clark." *Jones International*, 1999. Available at http://www.digitalcentury.com.

"Know Thyself." *The Economist*, 30 October 1999.

Lewis, Michael. *The New New Thing: A Silicon Valley Story*. New York: W. W. Norton & Company, 1999.

"myCFO, Inc." *Hoover's* , November 2001. Available at http://www.hoovers.com.

"The Seer of Silicon Valley Strikes Again." *U.S. News & World Report*, 25 October 1999.

Sherrid, Pamela. "Jim Clark's Hat Trick." *U.S. News & World Report*, 5 October 1998.

"Silicon Valley's Serial Entrepreneurs." *Fortune*, February 2000.

"Richest 100." *Forbes*, September 1997.

Bennett R. Cohen

(1951-)
Ben & Jerry's Homemade, Inc.

Overview

Bennett R. Cohen's name makes up one–half of what may be the world's most beloved ice cream brand, Ben & Jerry's. From its inception in 1978, this business visionary has guided the company from an amateur operation in a renovated gas station to a multi–million dollar world brand that was purchased in 2000 for a staggering $326 million by Unilever conglomerate. But Cohen never really had a taste for the usual corporate ethics. His real interests are improving social causes through responsible business practices. Since the buyout, Cohen continues practicing what he preaches, taking on such business issues as eliminating sweatshop industries, and establishing a fund to purchase companies in low–income communities with the goal of raising wages and benefits.

Personal Life

Cohen is on the boards of several organizations and is an active founding member of Businesses for Social Responsibility. He's a regular on the speaker circuit for colleges, universities, businesses, and non–profit organizations. Over the years, Ben & Jerry's has been nationally recognized for their superpremium products as well as their contributions to the community. In 1984, Ben & Jerry's was named "National Ice Cream Retailer of the Year" by National Ice Cream Retailers Association and *Dairy Record Magazine*. Ben and Jerry are placed on the 1987 *Esquire* Register, the magazine's "annual honor roll of men and women whose accomplishments, values and dreams reflect America at its best." In 1988 the pair

Ben Cohen (right) and Jerry Greenfield, co-founders of Ben and Jerry's Homemade, Inc., eating ice cream. (AP/Wide World Photos.)

scooped up two more prestigious accolades. The first was The Corporate Giving Award from the Council on Economic Priorities. The award soiree was held in New York City, with Joanne Woodward as the host. The second was at the best–known address in the United States at a White House Rose Garden ceremony where the pair was honored as U.S. Small Business Persons of the Year by President Reagan. Then the pair moved on the halls of higher learning, accepting Columbia University's Lawrence A. Wien Prize for corporate social responsibility.

Cohen, divorced, with one son, was born in the New York City borough of Brooklyn in 1951. He met Ben & Jerry cofounder Jerry Greenfield in gym class in a public school in Merrick, Long Island. Both were admitted outcasts and bonded over their shortcomings in the athletic department. Cohen graduated from Calhoun High in Merrick in the late 1960s and enrolled in Colgate University but left school his sophomore year. He studied pottery instead and other crafts at Skidmore College and later at an institution called University Without Walls.

"From the time I was in my teens until I turned 30, I talked to my father about things I planned on doing. He talked me out of them," Cohen told Marian Christy of the *Boston Globe*. As a result, Cohen never really decided upon a career goal and instead took jobs that were interesting learning experiences. "I learned that there are two kinds of bosses, good and bad, and that I worked harder for the boss who trusted me," he told Christy. He had numerous, and varied, jobs on his resume: in high school he had driven an ice cream truck, and during his young adult years he worked in a bakery, drove a taxi, guarded a racetrack, flipped burgers at McDonalds, and was even a staff member in the emergency room of Bellevue Hospital in New York City.

Cohen's casual attitude, artistic abilities, and sense of duty eventually led him into a steady job as a crafts teacher at a camp near Saratoga Springs, New York. He had lost touch with his old friend Jerry Greenfield, who had earned a degree from Oberlin College but then met with rejection when he applied to medical school. The pair rekindled their friendship when Greenfield was working in a New York City research laboratory, and they decided to open a business together. Cohen had some experience making ice cream at the camp with his students, and he and Greenfield decided that this was a product that almost everybody liked and that did not require expensive equipment to produce.

Career Details

Cohen and Greenfield combined their $8,000 in savings, borrowed another $4,000, took a Penn State University's correspondence course in ice–cream–making, and began looking for a location. They liked the college town of Burlington, Vermont, and it lacked an ice cream parlor. With these two requirements, they leased an old gas station there and opened Ben & Jerry's Scoop Shop in May of 1978. They vowed that if their business went under, they would simply become cross–country truck drivers. From the start, Cohen staffed the counter and took care of the financial side, while Greenfield made the ice cream. They both loved to create new flavors, however. As a kid, Cohen used to mix cookies and candy into his ice cream, and from its earliest days in business Ben & Jerry's gained a cult following for their delicious and bizarre concoctions.

Their store was extremely popular in Burlington, but Cohen and his partner were admittedly incompetent when it came to finances. After many late nights poring over accounts and receipts, they hired a Burlington bar owner, Fred Chico Lager, to help out. Lager helped the company expand into ice cream packing operations, and Cohen began delivering the pints to local stores in his Volkswagen station wagon. They opened more stores in New England and eventually went national with their product and their franchise in the 1980s. Greenfield dropped out of the business for a time when his wife went to college, and by 1985 Cohen was experiencing his first taste of corporate burnout. He tried to sell Ben & Jerry's Homemade, but had a change of heart when Greenfield returned to share the burden.

Chronology:
Bennett R. Cohen

1951: Born.

1963: Met Jerry Greenfield in gym class.

1978: Opened Ben & Jerry's Scoop Shop in Vermont.

1981: Opened first franchise.

1985: Established Ben & Jerry's Foundation.

1987: Published *Ben & Jerry's Homemade Ice Cream and Dessert Book.*

1992: Opened first store in Russia.

1995: Retired from CEO position.

1998: Declined offer buyout with Greenfield.

2000: Sold Ben & Jerry's to Unilever.

It was at this point that Cohen and Greenfield decided to make the business work according to their principles, instead of altering their values to suit the profit–driven nature of business. It was a radical idea. When they purchased nuts for their ice creams from South America or blueberries from Maine, they looked to trade directly with the indigenous peoples in the area who often harvested such crops, instead of buying from a corporation in the middle who pocketed most of the profit. In 1992 they launched a Partnershop with a Harlem shelter for homeless men; the store was staffed by residents and its earnings went back into the shelter. In 1999 the newest Partnershop premiered in Chicago. Lawson House is a YMCA that provides low–cost housing and job training assistance for the homeless.

Cohen has taken the occasional sabbatical. He returned the first time and began the 1 Percent for Peace campaign in the 1980s, which urged the U.S. federal government to redirect 1 percent of its budget to positive–minded projects. After another year off in 1993, he announced his plans to look into beginning a graduate business school based on the Ben & Jerry's ethos.

Cohen resigned as CEO in June of 1994, but he remains board chair and still invents new flavors for the famed roster, which includes such experiments as Holy Cannoli! and Smores. Standards in their funky flavors remain Wavy Gravy, Chocolate Chip Cookie Dough, Cherry Garcia, and New York Super Fudge Chunk. When he stepped down, the company announced a campaign to replace him that they named "Yo! I Want to be CEO!" Participants were invited to submit in an essay of 100 words or less why they would be the ideal ice cream company executive.

Eventually, Ben & Jerry's expanded to include frozen yogurt, sorbet and low–fat ice cream for their calorie conscious customers. They regularly add more flavors and limited–edition "Special Batches" during the year. To celebrate their twenty–first anniversary in 1999, they had a record–setting Free Cone Day. Over half a million free ice creams were dispensed across America in 2000 Ben & Jerry's Scoop shops as the ultimate customer gratuity. More importantly, the company also developed an environmentally friendly brown paper pint carton, after determining that the paper bleaching process is a leading national contributor of toxic water pollution.

Cohen devotes a great deal of his time to Businesses for Social Responsibility. He is a founding member of this organization, whose aim is to challenge the way companies do business and to show how profits and ethics are not mutually exclusive areas. Cohen wrote more extensively on this topic in the 1997 book, *Ben & Jerry's Double Dip.* A major ice cream purveyor, Dreyers Grand, offered Cohen and Greenfield a large sum of money to sell Ben & Jerry's in early 1998, but the pair declined. In April 2000, pressured by shareholders, Cohen and Greenfield agreed to sell their beloved brand name to Unilever, a British–Dutch Corporation. After the buyout, the pair retain employee status and sit on a separate Ben & Jerry's board.

Social and Economic Impact

In 1981, *Time* magazine began a cover story on ice cream with an opening sentence stating that Ben & Jerry's was the "best—in the world." Since then, its cult following has expanded to include not just East Coast cognoscenti but residents of Israel and the Netherlands; its pints can be purchased in hundreds of thousands of American supermarkets and convenience stores. But its founders have become role models for entrepreneurs interested in enriching their communities through capitalist ventures.

Cohen and Greenfield call their strategy values–led capitalism. Since the mid–1980s, the Ben & Jerry's Foundation has received 7.5 percent of the ice cream company's pre–tax profits; a nine–member advisory board of employees choose projects and charities that will receive the profits.

They have also publicized concerns about Bovine Growth Hormone (BGH), used in the milk industry, and for many years purchased from a Vermont dairy that did not use the chemical.

Ben & Jerry's employees may indeed be the happiest workers in the state of Vermont. (The company's headquarters have remained in Burlington.) It is consistently cited as one of the best companies in America for which to work offering workers high wages, generous benefits, and three pints of ice cream to take home for every full workday. Though the ice cream business has witnessed ups and downs in the 1990s, the company has found community service projects for the workers and kept them on the payroll.

After the sale of Ben & Jerry's to Unilever, Cohen continues on his path of social activism through capitalism strategy. In September 2001, the business whiz invested in a garment manufacturer, aiming to raise the profile and standards of an industry marred by outright violations and injustices. In August 2001, Cohen established the Barred Rock Fund, a philanthropic venture focused on buying companies in low–income areas, concentrating on improving conditions. The Fund's first acquisition was Sun & Earth, a Philadelphia manufacturer of cleaning products, partnered with a local non–profit. Sun & Earth employees perks included a 23 percent pay raise and obtaining health insurance.

Sources of Information

Contact at: Ben & Jerry's Homemade, Inc.
    30 Community Dr.
    South Burlington, VT 05403–6828
    Business Phone: (802)651–9600
    URL: http://www.benjerry.com

Bibliography

"Ben & Jerry," 14 July 1998. Available at http://www.benjerry.com

<"Ben & Jerry's Co–Founder Establishes Venture Philanthropy Fund." *Philanthropy News Digest,* 7 August 2001.

"Ben & Jerry's Co–Founder Invests in "Sweat–Free Garments." *SRInews.com,* 10 September 2001.

"Ben & Jerry's Company Overview." *The Motley Fool.com,* 7 October 2001.

Christy, Marian. "Ben & Jerry: Here's the Scoop." *Boston Globe,* 26 June 1991.

Gershon, George. "The Art of Taking Time Off." *Inc,* February 1993.

"Takeover for Ben & Jerry's?" *The Associated Press,* 2 December 1999.

William Colgate

(1783-1857)
Colgate–Palmolive Company

Overview

William Colgate, founder of what is now the Colgate–Palmolive Company, revolutionized the American household products industry by discovering new methods for making and selling soap. Colgate–Palmolive Company is a household name and the leading seller of toothpaste in the country. The company also makes personal care products, including shampoo, soap, deodorants, household cleaning products, bleach, and liquid surface cleaners and boasts brands such as dishwashing soap Palmolive and Ajax cleaner, which are brand leaders. Colgate also incorporates a premium pet food division, Hill, which produces the leading Science Diet brand. The company posted $9.3 billion in sales in 2000 and employed more than 38,000 employees.

Personal Life

Colgate was born January 25, 1783, in Hollingsbourne parish, Kent, England, to Robert Colgate, a gentleman farmer, and Sarah Bowles. The family immigrated to the United States in 1795. Colgate married Mary Gilbert in 1811, and the couple had sons Samuel, Robert, and James Boorman. Colgate was a devout Baptist from 1808 on and donated a tenth of his earnings to support missionary work and education. He donated generously to such organizations as the Hamilton Literary and Theological Seminary in Hamilton, New York, which, by 1846, owed half its property to donations by Colgate and his company. The seminary had since become Madison University and was renamed Colgate University in his honor in 1890. Colgate helped organize the American

Chronology:
William Colgate

1783: Born.

1795: Came to the U.S.

1806: Founded William Colgate & Company.

1811: Married wife Mary Gilbert.

1817: Became New York's leading soapmaker.

1817: First Colgate ad appeared in a New York newspaper.

1838: Renamed business Colgate & Company.

1845: Constructed largest soap–boiling pan in existence.

1847: Moved operations to a plant in New Jersey.

1857: Died.

Bible Society in 1816 with the aim of providing Bibles for every household in America. He also assisted in founding the American Baptist Home Mission Society in 1832, to spread the Gospel throughout North America; the American and Foreign Bible Society, serving as the organization's treasurer for thirteen years; and the American Bible Union in 1850, which offered its Revised Version of the Bible that emphasized Baptist beliefs. Colgate died in New York City, New York, in 1857. He withdrew from the Baptist church in 1838 and aided in the organization of a society which built the Tabernacle.

At the age of twelve, Colgate's family immigrated to the United States in order for his father, who spoke out against King George III in support of the French Revolution, to avoid charges of treason. They settled in an estate in Hartford County, Maryland, near Baltimore. They lost the house two years later after a discovery that they did not have clear title to the estate. The family then moved to Randolph County, West Virginia, where his father worked at farming and coal mining. His prospects dim, Robert Colgate moved the family back to Baltimore where he and William partnered with soap and candle maker Robert Mather. William was sparsely educated in England as well as in America and became a tallow chandler at age fifteen, which involved making candles using animal fat, in 1798. The Colgates' partnership with Mather did not last long and ended two years later but steered young William into what would become a very successful career.

After the break–up with Mather, the Colgate family moved again, to Ossining, New York, but William stayed behind in Baltimore, opening his own soap and candle shop. At that time in America, most people made their own soap by boiling a mixture of ash and tallow or fat. The soap was crude and harsh on the skin. Unlike in France and England, commercially–made soap in America at that time was little better, as the scientific process of converting a fat to soap through alkali was little known. Colgate realized there was a need for inexpensive, quality soap that could be mass produced. In 1803, Colgate closed the doors on his business and headed to New York where he joined John Slidell & company, a soap and candle manufacturer. Colgate, who began as a candle maker with the company, worked his way up to business manager.

Career Details

Colgate left Slidell in 1806 to found his own business, William Colgate & Company, on Dutch Street in New York City. To help with costs, Colgate was a one–person act in the business, doing all the manufacturing, buying, selling, delivering, and accounting. He began by selling mainly laundry soap but then began making hand soaps as well. He promoted sales by offering free delivery of his lime and tallow soap mixtures to local housewives. He sold an interest in the company to Francis Smith, who became his partner, in 1807. The 1807 and 1809 passage of the Embargo and Non–Intercourse Acts, respectively, aided the fledgling company by barring most competing European imports from vying with their soap market. From the profits of his growing business, Colgate bought a farm in Delaware County, New York. By 1812 he had amassed $5,000 and considered himself wealthy.

Soap itself was not new but had been produced by people since biblical times, and tallow soap had been made since around the eighth century. Soapmaking, however, even in Colgate's time was hard work. Water had to be boiled in large kettles, and the mixture had to be stirred by hand. Large chunks of soap were produced by this method, which then had to be cut with a knife into smaller pieces. The soaps of the time were harsh and often had a pungent odor. Colgate found a way to produce a better grade of soap, however, through saponification, which allowed the production of a variety of soaps and glycerin from combining tallow and oils.

Over the next four years Colgate's company was steadily producing better quality soap that was affordable, and by 1817, he had grown to become the leading soapmaker in New York as well as a viable competitor abroad. His first advertisement ran that year in a New York newspaper offering "Soap, Mould & Dipt Candles." In 1820 he began manufacturing starch with his brother–in–law John Gilbert. For a time, he had the one of the country's largest starch factories before he later abandoned starch making altogether. Colgate then hit on a way to broaden his market and improve sales: scented soaps. The scented products Colgate formulated caught on and prompted the 1845 creation of what was dubbed "Colgate's Folly," a 43,000–pound capacity soap–boiling pan which several guessed to be the largest of its kind. Critics thought the construction of the pan would sink the company, but by 1847 Colgate was expanding his business even further by moving his company to a bigger, better–equipped plant in Jersey City, New Jersey, and formulating a line of premium hand soaps in 1850. His son Samuel also joined the company, which was renamed Colgate & Co. He remained a vital part of his company until 1856 and died in New York City on March 25, 1857.

Colgate, who has been described as an exceptionally good–natured, generous, and honest man, enjoyed a prosperous business during his entire career with Colgate & Co., which continued even after his death as the business continued to be successfully guided by his sons. Six years after Colgate's death, the company began manufacturing Cashmere Bouquet, the first milled perfume toilet soap to be registered as a trademark. In 1873 the company produced its first toothpaste, which was sold in jars. They revolutionized the product in 1896, when they introduced toothpaste packaged in a collapsible tube, much like modern toothpaste.

Colgate rival B. J. Johnson Soap Company, founded in 1864 and located in Milwaukee, Wisconsin, was about to become part of Colgate's destiny. In 1898 the company debuted Palmolive soap, a product that was selling so well, that B. J. Johnson decided to rename the company the Palmolive Company in 1916. The company merged with Palmolive–Peet Company in 1928 to become Colgate–Palmolive Company, which it remains to this day.

By its 100th anniversary, Colgate & Co. offered more than 3,000 different soaps, dental care products, 625 varieties of perfumes, and related products. In 1906 the company launched a plant expansion at its Jersey City site, and a new eight–story factory was opened on the site. A few years later, in 1910, the entire Colgate operation moved from the original site on Dutch and John streets into Jersey City. The first renowned Colgate clock was installed in 1908 on the roof of one of Colgate's factories in Jersey City. It was 37 feet in diameter and spanned an area of 1,104 square feet. The original Colgate clock, which became a landmark on the New Jersey Waterfront, was moved in 1924 to a new Colgate factory in Jeffersonville, Indiana, and replaced with another, larger clock. The new octagon shaped clock measured 1,963.5 square feet with a 25–foot– 10–inch–long minute hand and a 20–foot–long hour hand. The timepiece is still one of the largest single–faced clocks in the world.

All three of Colgate's sons followed their father's path of success, albeit in different areas. His son Samuel continued running the family business and vastly expanded it during his period of leadership. His son Robert went on to head the Atlantic White Lead Works in Brooklyn, New York, and his son James Boorman founded the banking firm of J. B. Colgate & Co. on Wall Street in New York City.

Social and Economic Impact

Colgate vastly improved soap and the soapmaking process in his day, bringing better quality, affordable soaps to the American market at a price anyone could afford. The saponification process he utilized helped revolutionize the industry in the United States, which grew and thrived as his company was doing the same. He introduced "fancy"soaps, perfumed soaps and toiletries to the market. With an incredible business acumen, he was continuously prosperous throughout his entire career in soapmaking, even through the War of 1812. Through his company, Colgate & Company, he helped create what is today a billion dollar industry which includes detergents, soaps, cleansers, and personal cleaning products like toothpaste. The foundations he laid down for Colgate–Palmolive were key in building the nearly 200–year–old company into a $9 billion dollar industry leader with products and brands known worldwide.

Colgate was not only a renowned entrepreneur but was also a notable philanthropist and one of the most prominent members of the Baptist church for many years. His sizable donations to the Hamilton Literary and Theological Seminary gave the organization more than half its property by 1846 when it had become Madison University. To honor those contributions, the university was renamed Colgate University in 1890. He also donated a tenth of his earnings to various charitable organizations and helped found such religious organizations as the American Bible Union and the American and Foreign Bible Society.

Sources of Information

Bibliography

American Business Leaders From Colonial Times to the Present. ABC–CLIO, 1999.

American National Biography. Vol. 5., Oxford University Press, 1999.

Colgate–Palmolive Company. Available at http://www.colgate.com.

"Colgate–Palmolive Company." *Hoover's*, 2001. Available at http://www.hoovers.com.

"Colgate–Palmolive: Tour—When It Happened" *Colgate–Palmolive Company*, 2001. Available at http://www.colgate.com.

"History." *Colgate–Palmolive Company*, November 2001. Available at http://www.colgate.com.

The National Cyclopedia of American Biography. Vol. 8., James T. White & Company, 1906.

Who Was Who in America. Vol. 1., Marquis Who's Who.

Charles C. Conaway

(1960-)
Kmart Corporation

Charles C. Conaway had been chairman and chief executive officer of the discount department store chain Kmart Corporation since May 2000. A few days before Kmart filed for bankruptcy on January 22, 2002, James Adamson assumed the position of chairman. Dubbed by Kmart insiders as "the Kmart Tornado," Conaway heads the second largest retailer in the United States behind Wal–Mart. It operates 2,171 stores across the United States and more than one hundred 24–hour retail centers that also offer groceries, dubbed Super Kmarts, which Conaway helped establish. According to *The Financial Times*, "Mr. Conaway said Kmart would seek to close stores, cut jobs and consolidate offices." He has also made it a priority to enhance Kmart's brand position. Other plans scheduled for Conaway's five–year contract term included development of the online retail site BlueLight.com, investing in point–of–purchase technology, and revamping the distribution and inventory control systems. Conaway came to the Troy, Michigan–based retailer after a long and successful career at CVS Corporation, which culminated in his appointment to president and chief operating officer of the drug retailer.

Personal Life

Conaway is married to wife Lisa and has two daughters, ages 10 and 12. He enjoys golf and basketball. An avid bow–hunter. the sport has taken him big–game hunting in places such as South Africa. He has served on the board of directors of Linens'n Things, Streamline.com, and Health Connections.

Charles Conaway (left) and Brent Willis reintroducing Kmarts stores "Blue Light Special."
(AP/Wide World Photos/Richard Drew.)

Conaway was born in 1960 in Lapeer, Michigan. Still far from his corporate future, Conaway was raised on a farm in eastern Michigan and leaned how to sail in his youth at nearby Lake St. Clair. After his success, Conaway returned in May 2001 to give a commencement address at St. Clair County Community College, where he encouraged students to ignore the limits other people may set on them. The *Times Herald* reported he told the 564 new graduates, "In spite of what I've accomplished, I still have people challenging my abilities as they attempt to limit my expectations of what I can achieve at Kmart. I must admit I'm getting used to this. In fact (the comments) make me feel right at home . . . I have every intention of leading this company through a historic renaissance and proving my doubters wrong again." He received a Bachelor of Science degree in accounting from Michigan State University in 1982 and earned an master's degree in business administration from the University of Michigan in 1984.

Career Details

When Conaway was only 29, he co–founded Reliable Drug Stores Inc., in Indianapolis, Indiana, in 1989.

He also served as the company's executive vice president and chief operating officer. The company eventually became a $400 million chain. In 1992 he left Reliable to work at CVS Corp., where he was brought on board as senior vice president of pharmacy. After success in that position, Conaway was promoted in 1995 to executive vice president and chief financial officer of the drug retailer and concurrently served as executive vice president and chief financial officer of CVS parent company, Melville Corporation. At Melville, he had a major hand in restructuring the company from a diversified specialty retailer into the country's largest drug chain.

Conaway's coup, however, came when he was given the job of integrating CVS's operation after it bought out Revco DS Inc. in 1997 and Arbor Drugs Inc. in 1998. It was then that he learned the value of accountability and performance measurement that he would later bring to Kmart. After the successful integration which nearly tripled the company's sales and store count within a year, he was rewarded with a promotion to president and chief operating officer of CVS in 1999. As president and chief operating officer for the drug store chain headquartered in Woonsocket, Rhode Island, Conaway headed up the company's merchandising, marketing, and Internet presence and had responsibility for the operations of each of the company's 4,100 stores. Under his leadership, CVS expanded its distribution network, added retail outlets, and developed an Internet presence. The company, which is the second largest drug chain in the country, grew to an $18 billion dollar enterprise under Conaway.

Meanwhile, discount retailer Kmart, which struggled throughout the 1990s after a disastrous move into specialty retail stores, was looking for a replacement for seasoned retailer Floyd Hall, after the company nearly failed in 1995. Hall saved the company from near–bankruptcy with a financial restructuring and introduction of the Big K format that featured food items in the stores. He also brought the popular Martha Stewart Everyday, Sesame Street, and Route 66 brands to the company. Widely credited with turning the company around, Hall left abruptly after five years as its chairman and CEO. While Hall turned the flagging retail giant toward profitability during his five–year tenure, a retail analyst at PaineWebber Group was quoted by the Associated Press as noting that "there is still farther to go." Kmart then began an executive search for a new boss. Although Conaway was on the short list, some on the Kmart board of directors were concerned that the young executive wasn't experienced enough to run the retail giant. Conaway, who had solely been a drug trade executive, also had no previous apparel experience. After meeting with Conaway, however, and seeing his energy and enthusiasm, the board's worries faded. After the announcement of Conaway's appointment in May 2000, investors nudged Kmart stock up 16 percent.

Once installed as Kmart's new chief, the Michigan native began a two–year plan to surpass Wal–Mart and make Kmart the number one retailer. Described as a

Chronology:
Charles C. Conaway

1960: Born.

1982: Received a B.S. in accounting from Michigan State University.

1984: Earned an MBA from the University of Michigan.

1989: Co–founded Reliable Drug Stores.

1992: Joined CVS Corp. as senior vice president of pharmacy.

1995: Promoted to executive vice president and chief financial officer of CVS and its parent company, Melville Corporation.

1998: Successfully integrated Revco and Arbor Drugs acquisitions into CVS.

1999: Became president and chief operating officer of CVS.

2000: Became chairman and CEO of Kmart Corporation.

2001: Reinstated company's Blue Light Special.

2002: James Adamson named chairman of Kmart, but Conaway remained CEO.

2002: Kmart Corporation declared bankruptcy.

no–nonsense businessman who gets the job done, he recalled in *Business Week* his first day on the job and ensuing plans: "When I arrived the first day at Kmart, I arrived with a 30–, 60–, and 90–day plan in detail. Obviously, those plans continue to be changed and altered. The important thing is, I want to communicate how we're running this business. We're running it with an incredible sense of urgency in 30–day increments. I think it forces discipline, accountability and the right tone that we need from a management team and a cultural standpoint for the amount of activity we have to get done." He continues to strive to rectify the company's 2001 net loss of $244 million and measly 3.1 percent sales growth. The three strategies he implemented, according to the company's Web site, are achieving "World Class Execution," maximizing "Sales and Marketing Opportunities," and becoming a "Customer–Centric Culture."

As of April 2001, Conaway had identified and implemented almost 100 restructuring initiatives, meticulously tracking progress of each quarterly. That same month, Conaway also re–instated the company's famous Blue Light Special amid a $25 million advertising campaign. Beginning in the 1960s, the Blue Light Special, a flashing blue police light, was set up to attract shoppers' attentions to unadvertised specials but discontinued in 1991. The new Blue Light Special will be offered every hour on the hour for 25 minutes on popular products at greatly discounted prices. The "Blue Light Always" policy touted in the company's ads offers items like shampoo and groceries, discounted up to 5 percent all the time, to further cut into Wal–Mart's market. The company's BlueLight.com Internet site has already caught on with consumers.

Kmart's customers currently visit the store nine times a year on average. Conaway hopes the Blue Light initiative and Web site will increase current customers' visits to 11, the number of visits Target and Wal–Mart customers currently average. Conaway told *The Associated Press*, "This is no silver bullet. But this will help differentiate us, and drive traffic." Brent Willis, chief marketing officer at Kmart, says if Kmart can merely increase visits from their best customers from 3.2 per month to 4, that alone would increase sales by $2.8 billion. In September 2001, Conaway targeted more than 1,000 of its discount stores for reformatting into supercenters. The strategy will bring the focus to its consumables and commodities categories, which need to be replenished frequently. And with customer frequency the goal, Conaway told *DSN Retailing Today*, the company needs to "turbo–charge food."

Conaway's other strategies for gaining customers include revamping Kmart stores, closing unprofitable stores, increasing customer service through employee incentives, and heavily stocking the stores' more popular items. In order to keep shelves stocked, the company has spent $2 billion on inventory control technology. To keep track of customer service and other customer responses, Conaway introduced a toll–free number for customers to call and provide information on their shopping experience or to register complaints. To encourage participation in the feedback system, Conaway promoted a $10,000 sweepstakes for one lucky caller. Employee incentives have ranged from offering store stock to receiving quarterly cash bonuses.

Finding the right niche for Kmart may be the biggest challenge of all for Conaway. Wal–Mart, with its super–low prices and Target, with its cheap chic appeal, both have very defined markets. Conaway wants to become the authority for moms with kids who buy both for their children and their homes. To accomplish this, he has leveraged Kmart brands such as Martha Stewart Everyday bed and bath line, which has helped boost sales. In 1999 the Martha Stewart line had $1 billion in sales alone. Kmart also has the Sesame Street line of children's clothing, as well as Jaclyn Smith and Kathy Ireland designer merchandise. Although Conaway's initiatives have raised the company's value among some analysts,

not all have had favorable opinions. Of the company's long–term growth, Linda Kristiansen, an analyst for UBS Warburg noted in *DSN Retailing Today*, "Kmart is changing virtually every aspect of its business model, a high–risk undertaking."

Social and Economic Impact

Often dubbed a whiz–kid throughout his years at CVS, Conaway was named chief of one of the largest retailers in the world, Kmart Corporation, before the age of 40. With no prior apparel experience, Conaway took control of the more than 100–year–old, $37 billion company, which is also one of the nation's largest employers. He has already begun to fix many of the problems of the retail giant, including customer service, supply–chain management, inventory control, and marketing with his keen attention to accountability and performance measurement, learned from his many years at CVS. His return to the Blue Light Special has given the Kmart retail brand character again and a unique promotional edge seeped in company history. Intent on growing the company's supercenters to encourage more frequent traffic through the purchase of groceries and related items, Conaway has named 1,000 stores to be overhauled. Making his mark early on, Conaway brought new, young executives from companies like Coca–Cola and Wal–Mart to help redefine Kmart's strategies and image.

Conaway was no less a defining force at CVS, where he helped build the company into the nation's second largest drug chain after acquiring drug retailers Revco and Arbor Drugs. With his fourteen years at the company, Conaway in his twenties and thirties, rose to its top position after working in merchandising, store operations, and logistics departments.

The bankruptcy of the company has forced some people into seeing Conaway in a slightly different light, however. According to Jennifer Dixon reporting for the *Detroit Free Press*, "Under Conaway, Kmart made a series of mistakes that analysts say ultimately forced the company into bankruptcy. Conaway was spending $2 billion on improvements to the stores and Kmart's inventory and distribution system, while cutting prices and advertising." He faces a great challenge to help Kmart, the largest U.S. retailer ever to declare bankruptcy, recover and work its way through bankruptcy.

Sources of Information

Contact at: Kmart Corporation
    3100 W. Big Beaver Rd.
    Troy, MI 48084
    Business Phone: (248)463–1000
    URL: http://www.bluelight.com

Bibliography

Biography Resource Center Online. Gale Group, 2001.

Chandler, Susan. "Kmart Chief Prioritizes Brand-Building Strategy as means to Survival." *Chicago Tribune*, 24 January 2002.

"Conaway to Wall St : Expect Kmart to Grow." *DSN Retailing Today*, 1 October 2001.

"Conaway Leaves CVS to Take Helm at Kmart." *Chain Drug Review*, 19 June 2000.

"Corporate History." *Kmart Corporation*, November 2001. Available at http://www.kmartcorp.com.

Dixon, Jennifer. " Succeed or fail, Kmart chief exec will get $11.5 million." *Detroit Free Press*, 24 January 2002.

Edgecliffe-Johnson, Andrew. "Bankrupt Kmart Becomes Biggest US Retail Failure." *The Financial Times*, 23 January 2002.

"Is Kmart Stock a Blue Light Special?" *BusinessWeek Online*, 11 April 2001. Available at http://www.businessweek.com.

"It Doesn't Get Any Bigger Than This." *BusinessWeek Online*, 4 September 2000. Available at http://www.businessweek.com.

"Kmart CEO to Address SC4 Graduates." *St. Clair Community College*, 23 March 2001.

"Kmart Chairman & CEO Floyd Hall to Retire Charles C. Conaway Named New Chairman & CEO." *Kmart Corporation*, 31 May 2000.

"Kmart Chief Tells SC4 Grads: Accept No Limits." *The Times Herald*, 2001. Available at http://www.thetimesherald.com.

"Kmart Corporation." *Hoover's*, November 2001. Available at http://www.hoovers.com.

"Kmart Plans Overhaul of its Distribution." *Detroit Free Press*, 7 September 2001.

"Kmart Reshuffles Top Management." *The Detroit News*, 27 July 2000.

"A Kmart Special: Better Service." *Business Week*, 4 September 2000.

"Kmart's Bright Idea." *Business Week*, 9 April 2001.

"Kmart's a Challenge and an Opportunity." *MMR*, 21 August 2000.

"Kmart's Covenant." *Retail Merchandiser*, November 2000.

"Whiz Kid Takes Reins at Kmart." *The Holland Sentinel*, 4 June 2000.

Yue, Lorene. " New Kmart chairman has revived troubled companies before." *Detroit Free Press*, 17 January 2002.

Scott Cook

(1952-)
Intuit, Inc.

Overview

Scott Cook, along with Tom Proulx, founded Intuit Inc., the company best known for the personal finance software Quicken. Intuit was one of the first companies to develop user–friendly programs with manuals written in "plain English," and revolutionized online bill–paying and home banking. Intuit has also developed web sites for various financial services through which individual and business customers can maintain their finances and file taxes.

Personal Life

Cook was born in Glendale, California, in 1952. He obtained his Bachelor of Art's degree in economics and mathematics from the University of Southern California and then received his MBA from Harvard University. He was on the board of directors for Broderbund Software from 1993-1997. He is currently on the board for the Asia Foundation, and the Intuit Scholarship Foundation, as well as the online bookseller Amazon.com, which he joined in 1997, and the online auction site, eBay since June 1998. He is also a member of the Young Presidents Organization, an international association of corporate executives dedicated to promoting education, as well as of the board of visitors of the Harvard Business School foundation. In the fall of 2000, Procter & Gamble appointed Cook to that company's board of directors. Cook is married and has three children. In October 2000, his personal worth was estimated to be $1.2 billion.

Career Details

Cook began his career at Proctor & Gamble, a huge manufacturer of household products, where he worked as a brand manager and in other marketing positions. He then went to Bain & Company, a corporate strategy consulting firm, where he managed consulting assignments in the banking and technology areas. After watching his wife tediously write out bills one day, Cook figured that there must be a way to use technology to streamline the process. With the marketing savvy he had picked up at Proctor & Gamble and his knowledge of banking and technology, he set out to find a solution. Teaming up with Tom Proulx, a computer programming student still in college at Stanford University, he began work on a new software program that would allow users to organize their finances by computer.

Although about 20 different accounting products had already been introduced for home computers, they took longer to use than doing everything by hand, and they were expensive. Moonlighting while still at his consulting job, Cook fine–tuned his idea, getting feedback from potential customers by conducting surveys and initiating product tests. He discovered that customers did want software for organizing their personal finances, but it had to be easy to use.

Cook and Proulx formed the company Intuit, Inc. in 1983, named as a shorthand version of the word "intuitive," which indicated that their products would be just that. Cook was named president, chief executive officer (CEO), and chairman of the board for the new firm. Intuit released the first version of Quicken software in 1984. The program cut in half the time it took the average person to pay bills and balance checkbooks.

Cook strengthened Intuit with his excellent marketing skills. It was one of the first firms to actively seek market input for software. Intuit hired product developers to watch consumers—not product testers—use the products in the "real world" of their own homes (this was called the "follow–me–home" program). The company was also a leader in writing simple–to–read software manuals at a time when technical jargon was rampant.

After launching Quicken, Intuit later offered a similar accounting program for small businesses, called QuickBooks, which it introduced in 1992. Intuit also merged with Chipsoft, maker of TurboTax, in 1993, which allowed users to prepare their own income tax returns on their home computers. Soon, Intuit was the leading manufacturer of personal financial software.

Quicken took a couple of years to fully catch on, but Cook relied on an old technique to sell his new product. Intuit was the first to run television commercials for directly ordering the new product from the company. Cook also placed advertisements in magazines such as *PC Magazine* and *Byte*, raising revenues to $33 million by 1990. With sales soaring, Cook decided that Intuit needed savvy business people to help lead its growth. Instead of recruiting consultants, he sought venture capitalists to in-

Chronology:
Scott Cook

1952: Born.

1983: Cofounded Intuit Inc.

1983: Began serving as Intuit president, chief executive officer, and chairman of the board.

1984: Shipped first release of Quicken software.

1995: Intuit and Microsoft called off expected merger.

1997: Intuit introduced online bazaar of financial services.

1998: Opened Online Financial Exchange.

1998: Became chairman of the Executive Committee of the Board.

2000: Appointed to the board of directors of Proctor & Gamble.

2001: Announced plans to expand Intuit's services to mid–sized businesses.

vest in the firm and join the board. "You get a lot of attention from people when you have a few million bucks of theirs," Cook noted in *Fortune*. Four such venture capitalists then joined Intuit, purchasing 20 percent of the company. In 1994, Cook stepped down as president and CEO of Intuit but remained chairman of the board.

By 1995, Intuit and software giant Microsoft were flirting with a merger. Quicken held 70 percent of the personal financial software market in mid–1995, whereas Microsoft Money, the number two package, had only 22 percent. Cook's vision was to expand into electronic banking, allowing customers to access their accounts 24 hours a day. However, he found out that banks were interested in teaming with Intuit with or without Microsoft, and then the antitrust division of the Justice Department blocked the merger, which would have led to a potentially lengthy trial. Microsoft bowed out and paid Intuit $46.3 million to end the deal.

Intuit had been offering Quicken users the option of paying bills electronically since 1990, after forging a deal with CheckFree, but fewer than 10 percent of the customers used the service. In 1994 the company purchased National Payment Clearinghouse (renamed Intuit Services Corporation) as part of its plan to spearhead its own electronic banking service and later teamed with various institutions to let consumers do their banking online. As of

Scott Cook. (Ketchum, Inc.)

July 1995, 17 banks in addition to Smith–Barney and American Express had joined Intuit's program to offer on-line banking to Quicken users, allowing people to pay their bills online without writing checks, to transfer money, and to keep track of balances. BankNow was a joint venture with the online service provider America Online (AOL).

Though Intuit's online banking operation failed and was sold to CheckFree in September of 1996, Cook continued to pioneer home banking with the introduction in 1998 of Open Financial Exchange (OFX), a computer language that became the technical standard in online banking. Microsoft and CheckFree became partners in the venture, which connects home financial software users with their bank computer systems, allowing them to pay bills and make investments. In 1997, Cook also made plans to branch out from software to institute an online variety of financial services on the web. "Just like booksellers and CD stores, Intuit would get a cut of every product sold through its site," explained Kourosh Karimkhany of *Reuters Business Report*. "But Intuit's line of work would be much more lucrative: the commission on a $500,000 life insurance policy is much bigger than the cut on a $10 paperback." Cook told Karimkhany, "We believe there's a huge business opportunity in providing the marketplace where buyers can meet sellers of financial services."

Intuit continued to expand its business with its purchase of 19 percent of the search engine Excite and its establishment of a financial news site, CNNfn, within the CNN web site. In August of 1998, Cook stepped down from his duties as chairman of the board to become chairman of the Executive Committee.

With Cook as chairman of the Executive Committee, William D. Campbell was promoted from CEO to chairman of the board, and William C. Harris was promoted from executive vice president to CEO. Cook continued to remain active in the firm on a full–time basis and, together with Harris and Campbell, began to develop and execute an Internet strategy that would transform Intuit from a packaged software firm into a company that offered Web–based financial services and information.

In 1998, Intuit introduced quicken.com, a web site that offered a range of consumer and business services. By the end of 1999, quicken.com allowed users to view and pay certain bills, look at investment portfolios from TD Waterhouse Group Inc., and see their Discover Card transactions. A five–year agreement with America Online gave AOL subscribers the opportunity to receive and pay their bills from one location. Intuit also developed Web TurboTax, an Internet–based version of Intuit's tax preparation software that let taxpayers prepare and file all federal and state income tax returns over the Internet. Other related sites, developed with different partners, offered quotes on mortgages, life insurance, and auto insurance, referring users to a variety of insurance providers. However, not all Cook's ideas have been completely successful: Quicken Insurance, a venture into Internet–based insurance, was a wash and was sold off to InsWeb in November 2000. In late 1999, Intuit purchased mortgage lender Rock Financial Corp. for $370 million. The acquisition enabled Intuit to actually provide loans and mortgages instead of simply referring customers to other lenders.

With its QuickBooks software dominating the small business market, Intuit began developing Web interactive services for small business owners. QuickBooks 2000 included software that enabled small businesses to build their own web site to give customers and suppliers easy access to company information as well as to manage company finances through the Internet. The company also set up a small business portal on the Web. In 2001, Cook announced that Intuit would soon be offering new services tailored to mid–size businesses.

Wall Street took note of Intuit's Internet strategy, boosting its stock price more than 80 percent in 1999. Intuit's leaders realized that the Web would impact Intuit's business model, and they took steps to make the company a leader in developing Web–based services.

Harris stepped down as Intuit's CEO in September 1999, with chairman Campbell taking on the role of CEO as well. Cook continued to serve as chairman of the Executive Committee.

By 2001, Quicken accounted for less than 15 percent of Intuit's revenue, and Cook was increasingly focused on Web–based financial services. According to Cook, "the great thing about the Internet is it allows your vision to grow." Recognizing that the largest revenue sources lie in small–business services, Intuit has sought to automate critical systems like payroll, buying, selling, and managing information and customers on the Web. For example, QuickBooks 2001's electronic invoicing feature was designed to allow users to pay invoices instantly when they arrive by email. Cook was already envisioning a time in the near future when it would be possible to pay invoices seamlessly from a bank account. And in an interview published in early 2001, Cook noted: "Ultimately, you'll be able to put your finances on autopilot."

Social and Economic Impact

In 1983 approximately 100,000 people used the personal computer to track their finances; less than 20 years later, Intuit is providing its services to almost 25 million customers. The company employs nearly 6,000 people in 13 states and four countries.

Intuit's introduction of Quicken, TurboTax, Quick-Books, and other software revolutionized the way people manage their personal finances. These products have helped millions of users streamline their home and office bookkeeping and made it much easier for people to do their own taxes. Its OFX program may revolutionize the way banking services are conducted in the future. After all, it took 15 years for consumers to get comfortable with automatic tellers machines.

With Intuit's entry into online financial services, the company's goal is to be a "middleman" offering a broad array of product choices. Quicken.com will enable consumers to apply for loans and mortgages and get quotes on health insurance, life insurance, auto insurance, and home insurance online, making it possible to shop around for these services at all hours. Previously, calls and visits to sales offices had to be done during office hours—precisely when most people were on the job themselves. By opening up this area of commerce to online shoppers, Intuit has become a major player in a new era of convenience and flexibility.

Sources of Information

Contact at: Intuit, Inc.
2535 Garcia Ave.
Mountain View, CA 94043
Business Phone: (650) 994–6000
URL: http://www.intuit.com

Bibliography

Claburn, Thomas. "Cooking the QuickBooks—Intuit's Scott Cook sells simplicity." *Ziff Davis Smart Business for the New Economy*, 1 April 2001.

Clark, Drew. "New Intuit CEO Planning to Befriend Banks." *American Banker*, 15 October 1998.

"Code Warriors." *Forbes*, 9 October 2000.

Coursey, David. "Small Biz—How Intuit Plans to Become Your Next Best Friend." Available at http://www.zdnet.com.

Davis, Jen. "Banking on the Future." *The Industry Standard*, February 2001.

Dreyfuss, Joel. "The New Small–Business Portals." *Fortune*, 8 November 1999.

Gillmor, Dan. "Dan Gillmor Column." *Knight–Ridder/Tribune Business News*, 16 July 1999.

Graham, Jed. "Intuit Aiming For 10–Minute Tax Return." *Investor's Business Daily*, 8 February 2001.

Habal, Hala. "Intuit in $370M Deal for Rock Financial," *American Banker*, 8 October 1999.

"Heroes: 10 Unsung Champions of E–finance." *Money*, 15 October 2000.

"Intuit Adds Small–Business Web Site Tools to Accounting Software." *Knight–Ridder/Tribune Business News*, 6 January 2000.

"Intuit Announces Two Million Registered QuickBooks Users; Product Line Continues to Maintain Record 80 Percent Market Share." *Business Wire*, 16 June 1998.

Intuit, Inc. "Corporate Background." Mountain View, CA: Intuit, Inc., 1998. Available at http://www.intuit.com.

Intuit, Inc. "Executive Profiles." *Intuit*, Mountain View, CA: Intuit, Inc., 1998. Available at http://www.intuit.com.

"Intuit, Inc." *Hoover's Online*, 2001. Available at http://www.hoovers.com.

Janah, Monua. "Mountain View, Calif.–Based Firm Plans Full–Service Financial Web Site." *Knight–Ridder/Tribune Business News*, 14 November 1999.

Kang, Cecilia. "Intuit, America Online Make Deal for Bill–Payment Services." *Knight–Ridder/Tribune Business News*, 24 November 1999.

Murphy, Kathleen. "He Wants You to Pay Your Bills on the Web." *Internet World*, 15 August 1999.

"Online Quoting is New Rage." *Best's Review—Property–Casualty Insurance Edition*, July 1999.

O'Sullivan, Orla. "New Quickenmortgage Released." *US Banker*, July 1999.

Ozer, Jan. "Mortgage Web Sites." *PC Magazine*, 1 July 1999.

Power, Carol. "More Than 30 Companies Sign with Intuit to Offer Web–Based Version of TurboTax." *American Banker*, 22 January 1999.

Snel, Ross. "CEO Who Led Intuit to Web Eminence to Step Down." *American Banker*, 27 September 1999.

"Surfing Silicon Valley." *CNN Interactive*, 26 February 1998. Available from http://cnn.com.

Weil, Nancy. "Intuit Buys Mortgagor. *Computerworld*, 11 October 1999.

Stephen R. Covey

(1932-)
Franklin Covey

Overview

Stephen Covey is the author of the best–selling *The Seven Habits of Highly Effective People*, which has sold more than 12 million copies since its 1989 publication. The Covey Leadership Center—a spin–off management–training center that focuses on the book's tenets, merged with Franklin Quest in 1997 to form Franklin Covey. With offices in 60 countries and a 2001 market value of $80 million, Franklin Covey has proved that a product that, for the most part, merely refreshes one's own common–sense good management and leadership principles does, nonetheless, have staying power in the industry.

Personal Life

Stephen R. Covey was born to Stephen Glenn and Louise (Richards) Covey in 1932. Raised on an egg farm outside of Salt Lake City, Covey started out being an athlete but suffered through surgical reconstruction of the bones in his thighs as a teenager, causing him to spend three years on crutches with steel pins implanted in his legs. Covey redirected his energies into academics, taking a particular liking to debate, public speaking classes, and also forensics during high school. He was raised in a devout and close Mormon family, and his parents were exceptionally supportive of anything he engaged himself in. Covey once told a *Fortune* magazine interviewer that he did not drink or smoke while growing up, but he recalled keeping a fifth of liquor for friends who were in trouble with their own parents. He set the bottle in full view on the top of his dresser. Neither parent questioned

him about it nor even mentioned it, because they knew he had no intention of drinking it. He found that event particularly symbolic of their "affirmation."

The 5'7" Covey entered the University of Utah at the tender age of 15 and graduated with a degree in business administration at the age of 20, in 1952. However, his own recollection of those years is of playing ping–pong and cramming for exams. He had vaguely assumed that after graduation he would go into the family business, "Covey's Little America," a hotel and truck stop started by his grandfather in the 1880s. His grandfather, a shepherd, nearly froze to death one cold night in Wyoming and vowed to build a place of refuge if he survived. The business turned into a gold mine later when a highway was built through the area.

But Covey and his brother were both drawn to teaching, and the family business was eventually sold to an outsider, Earl Holding (who, anecdotally, became the owner of Sinclair Oil and the Sun Valley Ski Resort as well). Covey went on to England to serve his two–year term as a Mormon missionary, which set the stage for unfolding events that would change the course of his life.

Career Details

Only a few months into his missionary trip, Covey was redirected to Nottingham to train Mormon "branch presidents" of new congregations. He was reduced to a nonplus by the order, but his mission president encouraged him, telling him, "You can do it." He credits that mission president with getting him started in the business of training leaders. The perilous experience became the root of his future belief in the concept that one learns by teaching.

Covey earned his MBA from Harvard in 1957 and then served three years in Ireland as a missionary for his Mormon faith. As his skills in public speaking were married to the subject matter of preparing Mormon leaders, Covey became increasingly drawn to the human side of successful business. When he returned to Salt Lake City with his family, he became an assistant to the president of Brigham Young University in Provo. He continued with the university in a variety of administrative posts and then was named an associate professor in the business department in 1970. The father of nine children, his business leadership principles also carried into the home. (His son, Stephen M. R., would later relate to *Fortune* magazine interviewers in 1994 that he recalled growing up in a family that had its mission statement hanging on the wall. "From my earliest years I remember we would have family councils, where we would discuss our jobs, and responsibilities, and integrity, and courage, and fairness and sportsmanship. I'm sure that many families implicitly do that; this was a more explicit way of doing it.")

Coinciding with his positions at Brigham Young, Covey returned to the classroom himself to complete his

Chronology:
Stephen R. Covey

1932: Born in Salt Lake City.

1952: Earned B.S. degree from University of Utah.

1956: Married Sandra Merrill.

1957: Earned M.B.A. degree from Harvard University.

1970: Became adjunct professor in business department at Brigham Young.

1976: Earned D.R.E. degree from Brigham Young University.

1985: Founded Covey Leadership Center.

1989: Published *The Seven Habits*.

1997: Merged with Franklin Quest to create Franklin Covey.

doctorate degree with a cross discipline in business and education. Importantly, he chose for his doctoral dissertation the subject of the human side of success in America, as evidenced through "success literature" from 1776 forward. In his studies, Covey found that during the nation's first 150 years, most literature dealing with the subject focused on issues of character and character building—the archetype being the autobiography of Ben Franklin. But according to Covey, following World War II, the focus shifted to the cultivation of certain skills and techniques, behaviors, attitudes, and the promotion of a certain public image in order to be "successful" in the world. Covey began to consider ways to convince people to stop focusing on superficial charm and return to character building. At about the same time, he moved from administrative positions to teaching organizational behavior in the business department.

Covey's *Spiritual Roots of Human Relations* and *How to Succeed with People*, published locally in 1970 and 1971 respectively, serve to reflect those early thoughts and considerations on personal success. Covey's Seven Habits program, taught in his organizational behavior classes, began to draw extraordinary numbers of students (600, 800, 1,000). In 1985, to accommodate a larger and broader audience, he quit teaching and founded the Covey Leadership Center in Provo, putting all his personal possessions up as collateral—including his cabin, his home, his trust money, and all his savings. The investment proved sound for Covey and the seven other investors.

The Center became the nucleus from which Covey grew all else. In 1989 Covey published *The Seven Habits of Highly Effective People*, which stayed on the *New York Times* best seller list for nearly five years. Its principles, honed from Covey's hugely successful seminars and speeches, became the seminal source for future books, CD–ROMs, and the Center's newsletter, *Executive Excellence*. Essentially, the seven habits represented more of a "back to basics" paradigm than a novel approach to management and leadership. They are summarized as follows: 1) Be proactive; 2) Begin with an end in mind; 3) Put first things first; 4) Think win/win; 5) Seek first to understand, then to be understood; 6) Synergize; and 7) Sharpen the saw (engage one's talents and capabilities). Said Covey to *Fortune*'s interviewer at the time, "There's nothing new in all this, I just built the bridge between the theory and the practice."

Simple as it seemed, Covey's message rang true, and his "must read" book was translated into 26 languages. It was followed with his publication of *First Things First*, which capitalized on the same principles stated differently. Later, he published the equally popular *Living the Seven Habits: Stories of Courage and Inspiration*. Covey also is the author of *The Divine Center* (1982); (with Truman Madsen) *Marriage and Family* (1983); *Principle–Centered Leadership* (1991); *Daily Reflections for Highly Effective People* (1994); and *Six Transcendent Events: Using the Lord's Model to Solve Life's Problems*.

By 1996 then–63–year–old Covey had been named one of *Time* magazine's 25 most influential Americans. His list of counselees included Newt Gingrich and then–President Bill Clinton. Later, in December 2000, Covey was invited to appear on National Public Radio's *Morning Edition* to offer advice to president–elect George W. Bush. Said Covey, who thought Bush showed good leadership potential, "His ability to listen, to acknowledge and respect differences and diversity was so evident in his governorship. . . ."

Covey's fees for speaking at conferences were upwards of $55,000, and the list of reservations never seemed to end. More than half of all employees of Fortune 500 companies and the U.S. Postal Service had attended his lectures, and entire communities adopted his management ideas (e.g., Columbus, Indiana, with a population of 36,000). Most of the hugely popular management–training seminars were held 20 minutes away from the Leadership Center, at Robert Redford's more scenic Sundance Ski Resort. Companies were sending employees there for week–long visits at $3,900 a head. There were Covey training tapes and CDs, Covey polo shirts, Covey checkbook covers, and long lines of readers waiting for autographed copies of Covey's books. At the time, Ronald Heifetz, director of the Leadership Education Project at Harvard's John F. Kennedy School of Government, remarked to *Time* interviewers that "he is packaging common sense as if it were original and making a fortune doing it." According to that periodical, Covey's

Leadership Center, comprising eight mock–Georgian style buildings in an office park near a main highway, employed 700 persons and had grossed $78 million the previous year.

In 1997 Covey merged with time–planning Franklin Quest to form the Salt Lake City–based Franklin Covey, of which he is co–chairman. By 2001 the new company, with offices in 60 countries, had already generated $500 million on spin–offs from Covey's book, including audio and video tapes, day–planners, software, and six sequels. This was on top of the more than $500 million Covey had raked in for himself from his best–seller. Another book, promising a fresh approach to management in the 21st century, was scheduled for publication in the spring of 2002. According to *Sunday Business* writer Catherine Wheatley, Franklin Covey has advised more than four–fifths of America's Fortune 100 companies and thousands of small businesses. Notwithstanding, Wheatley's November 2001 article indicates that Covey's merger with Franklin Quest was not particularly smooth. The two entities could not agree on "location, location," and both sides complained that the other was withholding client information. The new company had posted losses for 1999 and early 2000. But Covey was positive. "[I]t just takes time to make a blended alternative," he insisted.

In Spring 2001, Covey authored an article for *Management Quarterly* that applied his seven habits to a technological world. He cautioned his readers to remember that "Technology is a good servant and a bad master." In the article, Covey revisited each of his seven famous principles, citing examples of their application to the challenges of modern technology and electronic communications and advising that they are "as true today as they were in 1989."

Time management is nothing new to Covey; an old friend once told *Fortune* magazine interviewers that he recalled stumbling over Covey at a gym many years ago. Covey was lying on the floor with two or three showers running over him, brushing his teeth and shaving at the same time. Covey's role in Franklin Covey appears to synchronize his management and leadership principles with Franklin's time–management programs. Franklin Covey online (http://www.franklincovey.com) features an interactive service to "create your own Personal Mission Statement," where you may fill out the form, build a mission statement, and have it returned to you by mail. The company also offers palm organizers, planning software, and online software training courses. Other Web sites have praised the products as well. The University of Virginia has summarized the famous seven habits on its "Time Management" site (www.cs.virginia.edu.helpnet/Time/time.html). Online training workshops also include sessions on pinpointing goals, project management, and Covey's "Principle–Centered Leadership."

Covey received the Thomas More College Medallion in 1990 for continued service to humanity; Utah

Symphony's Fiftieth Anniversary Award for outstanding national and international contribution (also in 1990), and the 1991 McFeely Award from the International Management Council for significant contributions to management and education. He also is the founder of the Institute for Principle–Centered Leadership and a guest lecturer at the Brookings Institution in Washington, D.C. A devout Mormon, Covey continues to tithe, live in the same house as he did while teaching at Brigham Young, and drive his Jeep Cherokee to and from his engagements.

Social and Economic Impact

As Stuart Crainer stated in a September 2001 issue of *The Times*, "The business self–improvement master of our times is undoubtedly Stephen Covey, a shave–headed Mormon who has created a business empire on the back of his best–seller. *The Seven Habits of Highly Effective People*." There are similarities between the "effectiveness" movement Covey has spawned and competing organizational improvement programs such as "excellence," TQM, and re–engineering—but none has had the staying power or the broad–band appeal that has been identified with Covey. Because he has focused on the human element of good leadership and management, his principles carry over well into one's personal life. This has added not only to the multi–market saturation of his products but also to the enrichment of persons who might not even be employed or in official leadership roles. By capitalizing on admirable human virtues—whether in the conference room or in the kitchen—he has expanded his potential audience to virtually everyone.

Sources of Information

Contact at: Franklin Covey
    3507 North University Ave., Suite 100
    Provo, UT 84604
    URL: http://www.franklincovey.com

Bibliography

Allen, Debra. "Real Time and How to Manage it Better." *Link–Up*, November/December 2001.

Butler, Charles. "What's the Big Deal About Stephen Covey?" *Sales & Marketing Management*, April 1997.

Cooper, Matthew. "The Bill–and–Newt Gurus." *U.S. News & World Report*, 23 January 1995.

Covey, Stephen. "The 7 Habits 11 Years Later: Applying the Habits in a Technological World." *Management Quarterly*, Spring 2001.

Crainer, Stuart. "Don't Mock the Self–improvement Gurus." *The Times*, 20 September 2001.

Edwards, Bob. "Interview: Stephen Covey Offers Some Suggestions to President–elect George W. Bush. . . ." *Morning Edition (NPR)*, 26 December 2000.

Jackson, Bradley. "The Goose that Laid the Golden Egg? A Rhetorical Critique of Stephen Covey and the Effectiveness Movement." *Journal of Management Studies*, 31 May 1999.

Smith, Timothy. "What's So Effective About Stephen Covey?" *Fortune*, 12 December 1994.

"Time's 25 Most Influential Americans." *Time*, 17 June 1996.

Wheatley, Catherine. "Self–Help Business Management Guru Plans to Release New Book." *Sunday Business*, 11 November 2001.

Jenny Craig

(1932-)
Jenny Craig, Inc.

Overview

Jenny Craig is the creator and founder of one of the most successful weight-loss programs ever marketed. Since the 1980s, her Jenny Craig Weight Loss Centres have helped numerous Americans lose unwanted pounds and learn to eat a nutritional diet that can lengthen their life span. In 1999 there were 661 weight-loss centers bearing her name in North America, Australia, and New Zealand.

Personal Life

Craig was born Genevieve Guidroz in the early 1930s and grew up in New Orleans. Her father, James Guidroz, was a boat captain and part-time carpenter, while mother Gertrude grew her own vegetables to help feed a large family of six children, of which Jenny was the youngest. She studied at Southwestern Business School and worked as a dental hygienist for a time, but by her late 30s she was married to a building contractor and was the mother of two young daughters, Michelle and Denise. The second pregnancy was a difficult one, with Craig having to stay in bed and eat every few hours. After the baby was born, she remained 45 pounds overweight. "I used to look in the mirror and cry," she recalled in an interview with *People* magazine in 1990. "I would just cry and say, 'What did you do to yourself?'"

Having come from a family with weight problems, Craig resolved to take action. Her mother passed away at age 49 from a stroke and had eight brothers and sis-

ters who died before age 50—all of them overweight. Wanting to live a long and healthy life with her family, Craig went to work.

To fix her figure, Craig went on a drastic diet and began attending an exercise classes at Silhouette/American Health. Within a few months, she had lost 30 pounds. She then went to work for the health club in New Orleans and was eventually promoted to management. She began to see a need for health and diet education. The basic foundation for her company's beliefs was formed when Craig herself went through the struggle of losing weight. She was quoted in *Women Entrepreneurs Only* stating, "I began to realize that there was nothing out there telling people that they should eat this kind of food as healthy or avoid that kind of food as unhealthy. I was sure there were a lot of people just like me that want someone to tell them what to do. What really started me off in this business was my own research into what kinds of food I should be eating."

Craig met future husband Sid Craig in 1970 when he arrived in the New Orleans area to expand a chain of failing fitness centers he had just bought. His chain, Body Contour, was going to be positioned as a competitor with Jenny Craig's employer. The California entrepreneur had once been a tap–dancing child in the "Our Gang" series in the 1930s and then went to work as an instructor with the Arthur Murray Dance Studios. He eventually owned several Arthur Murray franchises before getting into the exercise business.

Sid Craig and Jenny Bourcq were still married to respective spouses when they met, but during the 1970s both unions ended in divorce. Craig, having just sold a business, had answered an ad in the paper that Sid had placed for employment with Body Contour. Jenny was hired to work in the new fitness center, and soon their working relationship evolved into a romantic one, and they wed in 1979. After founding the successful diet program that bears the "Jenny Craig" name, the partnership grew into a lucrative financial one as well. Into the 1990s, she held the title of president of Jenny Craig, Inc., while Sid Craig was the company's chief executive officer (CEO) and board chair at headquarters in suburban San Diego. They lived in an impressive beachfront home and were collectors of seventeenth– and eighteenth–century European art. In 1999 she was a millionaire, and some of that wealth funded a health clinic in Mexico for the disadvantaged. The Craigs once sponsored Australia's entire Olympic team. Sid and Jenny Craig also donated a large sum to California State University at Fresno, where Sid went to school in the early 1950s, and as a result its business school was named in his honor. In 1999, The Jenny Craig Pavilion was dedicated at the University of San Diego. The Craigs donated nearly half of the funds necessary to erect the new facility.

The Craigs also own a second home in Aspen, a private jet, and several thoroughbred racehorses. For a time, both Craig daughters from her previous marriage were

Chronology:
Jenny Craig

1932: Born.

1970: Joined Sid Craig in fitness–center company.

1982: Sold Body Contour chain, netted $3.5 million.

1983: Launched Jenny Craig Weight Loss Centres in Australia.

1985: Opened first franchises in United States.

1990: Managed 285 outlets bearing her name.

1991: Initial public offering of stock on the New York Stock Exchange.

1993: Federal Trade Commission (FTC) charged company with deceptive advertising practices.

1994: Revenues reached $403 million annually.

1995: Temporarily lost ability to speak due to freak accident.

1997: Called for health–insurance providers to classify weight–loss programs as a valid medical reimbursement.

1997: FTC complaint resolved with consent agreement.

1998: Replaced by Philip Voluck as president and remains Vice Chairman.

1999: Launched e–commerce on web site.

1999: Announced restructuring plan due to declining revenue and a re–emphasis on basic nutrition beliefs.

2001: Released new cookbook *30 Meals in 30 Minutes*.

multi–franchise owners of Jenny Craig Diet Centers. Craig, a proud grandmother, remained vice chair of the board of Jenny Craig in 2001. She still keeps to the low–fat diet, which launched her weight–loss success, and exercises an hour each day. In 1995 Craig, then 62 years old, suffered a freak accident; after dozing off while watching the news one night, she was startled awake by a loud noise on the television. Her head snapped back so violently that she damaged her jaw muscles. The odd mishap resulted in Craig's loss of speech because she could not control her lower jaw. After extensive surgery and ongoing speech therapy, Craig has regained the ability to speak but can no longer act as the company's spokesperson.

Jenny Craig. *(Reuters NewMedia Inc./Corbis.)*

Career Details

When Sid Craig opened the first Body Contour fitness clubs in the New Orleans area in the early 1970s, Jenny Craig went to work for him. She brought her own ideas about nutrition, diet, and physical fitness to the relationship. Those ideas were not yet popular in the American mindset, and the weight loss industry was just beginning to develop. Nevertheless, Body Contour grew into a $35 million–a–year business. The Craigs pressed their partners to look towards these new ideas and wanted to start implementing them into the Body Contour business. The partners, however, did not see a future there.

In 1982 the Craigs broke ties with business partners and sold Body Contour to NutriSystem. A "non–compete" clause prevented either of them from working in the diet or fitness center industry for two years. The clause, however, only applied to the United States, so the Craigs went to Australia to pursue their plans of combining nutrition and fitness education. Despite cultural barriers, the couple opened 12 Jenny Craig Diet Centres in Melbourne, and they soon were operating 50, which were highly successful. Through hard work, confidence, and dedication—all of which Craig learned through her father—Sid and Jenny Craig made the company name synonymous with weight loss.

With over $50 million in gross income, they brought their idea back to American shores in 1985 and opened the first 14 Jenny Craig Weight Loss Centres in the Los Angeles area. Two years later, they had 46 outlets, and by 1990 the company had grown to number 285. Gregory K. Ericksen, author of *Women Entrepreneurs Only* wrote that, "five years after entering the U.S. marketplace, the company became the sixth–fastest growing private firm in the country."

Jenny Craig continued to grow and finally went public, offering shares on the New York Stock Exchange in October of 1991. To do so, a Wall Street investment bank that saw great potential in their concept of managed weight loss raised $100 million on their behalf to launch the shares. With the success of the offering, the Craigs and their children received $108 million; Jenny and Sid Craig still owned about 60 percent of company stock.

By 1992, Jenny Craig, Inc. was a $400 million company; its biggest competitor was NutriSystem. Weight Watchers and the Diet Center were also top rivals. There were 621 Jenny Craig outlets in 1993, and that year the company posted $467 million in sales. It was perhaps the height of the company's success, and thousands of overweight Americans were attracted to the 16–week program, which offered nutritional counseling and pre–packaged foods called "Jenny's Cuisine" at an extra cost for both. The frozen foods, which provided ready–made meals to clients at a cost of around $70 a week, accounted for about 90 percent of company sales; individual counseling sessions cost about $7 each. The average member spent about four months in the program.

Yet problems arose along with the growth of Jenny Craig, Inc. In 1992 there were allegations and a court case from shareholders of the company's stock who claimed the rapid expansion in the early part of the decade was done to camouflage financial woes. "The suit claims that at the time of its October 1991 public offering, the company knew the market for diet clinics had become saturated but went ahead with expansion plans to boost revenue and create the illusion that Jenny Craig was a prosperous company," explained Denise Gellene in the *Los Angeles Times*. The profit the Craigs earned when the stock went public may have caused some of this dissatisfaction.

In 1993 the Jenny Craig Weight Loss Centres dropped the initial membership fee from as high as $185 for some plans to just $49 in a bid to attract new clients. It was estimated that the diet market in the United States hovered around 50 million at that time, or just under a fifth of the total population. A few franchisers were unhappy with the new lure and claimed that, in some cases, new clients could not afford the pre–packaged foods essential to successful weight loss in the Jenny Craig program. The Craigs bought out many of the franchises that were unprofitable, including some owned by Craig's daughters and their husbands. The fiscal year 1993 saw further problems with the company's finances: the stock had been trading at $34 a share in 1992 but had dropped to $15 a year later. In response, the Craigs restructured the company and brought in experienced executives hired away from other companies, none of whom remained on board for long.

By 1994 the company had posted heavy losses, and many centers had closed altogether. Dieting, as Leslie Vreeland wrote in a 1995 *Working Woman* article, had become "uncool" and cited trends such as a greater selection of low–fat foods on supermarket shelves and the avowal of television personality Oprah Winfrey never to "diet" again after losing a great deal of weight on a liquid diet and then gaining it back within two years. Vreeland also noted the success of anti–diet guru/infomercial host Susan Powter with her "Stop the Insanity" program. Furthermore, the reputations of programs such as Jenny Craig suffered a blow when a popular consumer magazine asked 19,000 people to rate their membership in and weight–loss success at such centers, and a large percentage of them reported dissatisfaction.

According to one observer, the typical experience for a woman who walks into a Jenny Craig Weight Loss Centre is to be immediately asked about her health and how much weight she wants to lose. If she agrees to sign up for the weight loss program, she will leave the center with instructions to consume a 1200–calorie–per–day diet consisting of single–serving meals sold exclusively by the company. This approach to weight loss is based strictly on portion control and calorie restriction. Nutritionist Mark Kantor, Ph.D., of the University of Maryland, explains why it works: "When you eat prepackaged food, you're going on a kind of 'no–thinking diet' in which you simply eat what you're given. You can't help but lose weight."

Jenny Craig, Inc. made headlines of a different kind in 1995 when a group of men who became known as the "Boston Eight" brought a gender discrimination suit against the company. The male employees of a Massachusetts Jenny Craig Centre filed suit in Massachusetts Superior Court for what they felt were condoned workplace practices that denigrated them because of their gender. In what came to be called a "reverse sexual harassment," the men claimed, among other complaints, that they were requested to shovel snow and were not invited for off–premise socializing with their mostly female co–workers.

Despite these setbacks, the company continued to forge ahead in the weight loss industry. In 1997 it introduced its "ABC Program." The program was designed to be an easy, user–friendly plan that made counting calories and fat grams obsolete by placing food into A, B, and C groupings. Jenny Craig believed that healthy eating habits should be easy to maintain and with obesity on the rise, this ease remained a focus of the company. According to government statistics posted on the company's web site, over 100 million people were overweight—54 percent of the adult population in the United States in 1998. Although the company posted continued losses in September 1999, it looked to increased Internet presence and restructuring to get back on track.

In late 1999, in a move intended to improve sales, Jenny Craig entered a 20–year licensing arrangement with Balance Bar to market a line of diet bars under the Jenny Craig name. The joint venture marked the first time the Jenny Craig brand was accessible to consumers outside Jenny Craig centers. And at the end of 2000, Jenny Craig was poised to launch a major effort to differentiate itself based on a more "personalized version of its one–to–one consulting method."

In early 2001, the company announced substantial losses for the last six months of the previous year. According to Craig, the number of new customer enrollments had fallen from that of the previous year "due in part to increased competition and new market entries as well as an unusually high level of competitive advertising." At the end of 2000, the company operated approximately 660 company–owned and franchised centers in the United States, Australia, New Zealand, Canada, and Puerto Rico.

By March 2001, Jenny Craig, Inc. had significantly stepped up its marketing activities. The company's Web presence included a commerce–enabled Web site, online events, and marketing strategies such as search engine positioning and email outreach. In August 2001 the company launched the sale of a new Jenny Craig cookbook, *30 Meals in 30 Minutes*, aimed at the nutritional needs of busy people with demanding schedules.

Social and Economic Impact

Jenny Craig Weight Loss Centres achieved phenomenal success in the 1990s with its diet program that gave clients counseling as well as an easy–to–use meal plan that saved time in meal preparation. In that decade, it was estimated that about 8 million Americans were joining programs such as Jenny Craig and spending about $1.7 billion a year. After Weight Watchers, Jenny Craig became one of the most recognized brand names of the bunch. Like Weight Watchers, the company spent a great deal of its budget on advertising and often enlisted celebrities as spokespeople. Entertainment personalities such as Susan Ruttan (once a regular on *L.A. Law*), Dick

Van Patten, and Cindy Williams, star of the 1970s sitcom *Laverne & Shirley*, have been affiliated with Jenny Craig ad campaigns.

In late 1999, Jenny Craig launched a controversial new advertising campaign featuring Monica Lewinsky, the former White House intern. Stock price jumped 32 percent upon the announcement. But after only five weeks, Lewinsky was gone from the weight loss program's advertising. According to Jenny Craig's VP of Marketing, the company had decided by late 2000 to no longer use celebrities like Monica Lewinsky in its advertising campaigns, "because consumers can identify more with an everyday person than with a celebrity."

One reason for the name–brand identity that Jenny Craig Weight Loss Centres have achieved may be due to the fact that both Craig and the program she designed stress that overweight people need to learn not how to follow a diet but rather how to eat properly for life. Dieting, Craig has emphasized, should not be an occasional drastic measure. Nutritionists agree, but problems arose with some of the company's claims and practices. In late 1993, the Federal Trade Commission cited Jenny Craig, Inc. and four other diet programs for false advertising. Investigators asserted the programs made misleading claims about their effectiveness and the percentage of clients who were able to maintain their weight loss once they had left the program. In the spring of 1997, the company agreed to abide by guidelines that required them to offer proof that their customers were able to lose their desired number of pounds in a certain amount of time, and that those pounds remained off over a specific period of time without rejoining the program at an additional cost.

Federal agencies, however, were not without their own internal missteps. In 1996 the Food and Drug Administration (FDA) allowed dexfenfluramine and fenfluramine (known by the brand name "Redux" and "fen–phen"), the first new prescription drugs for weight loss since the early 1970s, onto the market. Initially, sign–ups and sales at diet programs such as Jenny Craig plummeted, but like some of its competitors, the Centres hired part–time doctors to prescribe the drugs. The drugs were withdrawn from the market in 1997, however, when a Mayo Clinic study linked one of them to heart disease. Concerned about the drug's side effects already and sensitive to critics that charged the company with becoming a "pill mill," Jenny Craig Weight Loss Centres had already ceased the use of the drugs two weeks before the announcement.

Returning once more to their credo, Jenny Craig, Inc. called for a new strategy to help overweight Americans: in response to the controversy, it urged managed healthcare organizations to adopt new rules that would reimburse members for joining weight–loss and weight–management programs such as Jenny Craig. Such health–insurance providers had reimbursed patients for the prescription diet pills before their side effects came

to light. This call for a more health–focused approach to weight management fit in with a new strategy by Jenny Craig, Inc. to position itself as a wellness plan.

The Federal Trade Commission's (FTC) Partnership for Health Weight Management was launched in February 1999. Jenny Craig began her participation in the partnership that was created to develop industry wide standards for advertising and promoting weight loss in the United States. This move cemented the company's goal of being seen as a responsible, consumer–oriented firm.

In early 2000, the company remained focused on educating the public on good health and eating habits. Its redesigned web site allowed for consumers to become acquainted with the company's policies, products, and beliefs. Jenny Craig also introduced a new line of dietary supplements called Advanced Nutrients backed by Dr. Art Ulene, released fitness video cassettes, and produced its first television show, *Jenny's Fit in 15*, that ran on The Health Network in July 1999. According to Craig, "Our goal is to stem the tide of obesity by using a warm, personalized and one–on–one approach to help our clients make positive lifestyle changes. By teaching them how to create a healthy relationship with food, increase their daily activity levels, and maintain a balanced outlook, we give them the tools they need to successfully manage their weight."

In 2001, Craig's company struggled to show a profit, and revenues had dropped for the previous four years. In May 2001, *USA Today* reported that talk was brewing that Craig might sell her company, and in August 2001 the New York Stock Exchange suspended trading shares of Jenny Craig, Inc. Despite the difficult times, not all news was bad: for the fiscal year ending June 30, 2001, Jenny Craig, Inc. posted an operating loss of only $2.7 million on revenues of $238.6 million, compared to a loss of $12.9 million on $291 million the previous fiscal year. Although the year–end total was a loss, the company reported a profit of $4.1 million for the last quarter of the fiscal year.

Sources of Information

Contact at: Jenny Craig, Inc.
 11355 Torrey Pines Rd.
 La Jolla, CA 92037
 Business Phone: (858) 812–7000
 URL: http://www.jennycraig.com

Bibliography
"Ad Follies," *Advertising Age*, 18 December 2000.

Ericksen, Gregory K. *Women Entrepreneurs Only: 12 Women Entrepreneurs Tell the Stories of Their Success*. New York: John Wiley & Sons, 1999.

Farrell, Greg. "Jenny Craig Hires Monica Lewinsky Former White House Intern." *USA Today*, 29 December 1999.

Good, Brian. "What You Can Learn from Jenny Craig." *Men's Health*, January 200_.

Graney, Ed. "USD's New Arena Dedicated; 5,100 Jenny Craig Pavilion to Open in Fall of 2000." *The San Diego Union–Tribune*, 6 May 1999.

Ingersoll, Bruce. "Jenny Craig Settles FTC Charges That Ads Made Deceptive Claims." *Wall Street Journal*, 30 May 1997.

"Jenny Craig Assumes Proud Role on FTC Task Force." *Secure.* Available at http://www.secure.jennycraig.com

"Jenny Craig Diet Centers Stop Using Fenndash & Phen," *CNN.* 11 July 1997.

"Jenny Craig Fortifies Expansion with Balance Bar Debut," *Brandweek*, 8 November 1999.

"Jenny Craig, Inc." *Hoover's Online.* Available at http://www.hoovers.com.

"Jenny Craig Redefines 'Fast Food' With Newest Collection of Recipes Designed for Busy People." *The Financial Times*, 14 August 2001. Available at http://www.ft.com.

"Jenny Craig Reports First Quarter Loss." *Secure.* Available at http://www.secure.jennycraig.com.

"Jenny Craig Reports Fourth Quarter Results." *PR Newswire*, 19 September 2001.

Krantz, Matt. "Jenny Craig to Put Weight–Loss Company Up For Sale." *USA Today,* 14 May 2001.

Rodrigues, Tanya. "Local Firm Jenny Craig Steps Into Online Promotions." *San Diego Business Journal*, 26 March 2001.

Rose, Craig D. "Jenny Craig Expands Focus, Sell Dietary Supplements." *The San Diego Union–Tribune*, 25 March 1999.

"San Diego's Highest Paid Executives." *SDDT.* Available at http://www.sddt.com.

"Strategic Notes." *Health Care Strategic Management*, March 2001.

Thompson, Stephanie. "Two ad pitches for weight loss gain more heft; Weight Watchers and Jenny Craig stress personalized diet programs." *Advertising Age*, 4 December 2000.

Kenneth T. Derr

(1936-)
Chevron Corporation

Overview

Kenneth T. Derr holds the distinction of being the youngest man ever named CEO of Chevron, a position he assumed in January 1989. The position represented a culmination for Derr, who had spent his entire career with the organization. During his 40 years with Chevron, he served for 11 years as chairman of the board and chief executive officer. He is credited with successfully restructuring the company toward a strong investor focus, increasing employee involvement, and facilitating more efficient operations. He also steered Chevron through its transition to an international corporation.

Personal Life

Kenneth T. Derr was born in Wilkes–Barre, Pennsylvania, in 1936. He graduated from Cornell University with degrees in mechanical engineering (BME in 1959) and business administration (MBA in 1960). Following graduation, he joined Chevron and then assumed a series of positions of increasing responsibility.

Derr is a former chairman of the American Petroleum Institute, a trustee emeritus of Cornell University and a member of the Business Council and the Council on Foreign Relations. His community projects included helping to save San Francisco's cable cars and assisting inner–city residents establish a minority–owned Chevron service station.

Aside from his executive responsibilities at Chevron, he has also been a director of AT&T Corp., Citicorp, and Potlatch Corporation. His other memberships include the

San Francisco Golf Club, Orinda Country Club, and the Pacific Union Club. He married Donna Mettler on September 12, 1959, and they have three children.

Career Details

Derr joined Chevron Corporation (formerly Standard Oil Company of California) in San Francisco in 1960. He was elected vice president in 1972 and president in 1979. In 1981, he was elected to be a director of the corporation.

In 1984, Derr headed the company's program to implement the merger of Chevron and Gulf Oil Corporation. During this period, he was noted for providing what was then considered to be an innovative approach, as he utilized the efforts of multiple teams that included hundreds of the company's employees. *The Wall Street Journal* described his approach as a "textbook example of the integration of operations." The following year, he was elected vice chairman of the corporation. Finally, he became chairman of the board and chief executive officer on January 1, 1989.

When Derr took over as CEO in 1989, he placed a sign on his desk that said "Better than the Best." It reflected Derr's goal to make Chevron the most profitable major oil company in the United States in the following five years. He would face some challenges in meeting that goal. By the time he assumed the position, the company had become the oil industry's highest cost producer because of its acquisition of Gulf Oil, as well as steeply falling energy prices and substantial overhead.

In 1990 Chevron was selling approximately $32 billion worth of oil, but the company was also buying twice as many barrels as it was producing, making it the biggest U.S. importer of oil. The spike in oil prices resulting from the unstable situation in the Middle East—which would culminate in the Gulf War in 1991—increased the need for action. Derr decided on a strategy of growth to attain increased profitability. He also worked to make Chevron a global corporation, which would relieve the company of the stringent domestic environmental restrictions that limit productivity. To bring this about, he sold nearly two–thirds of the company's oil and gas properties throughout the United States. These were small wells that generated only 10 percent of production. Also, he nearly doubled spending on overseas exploration. Derr cut the company's work force by 20,000 employees (from 75,000 to 55,000). His plan also included selling $5 billion in non–strategic assets and upgrading the refineries.

Another situation he faced soon after he became CEO was a possible takeover engineered by Pennzoil. Derr frequently took Pennzoil to court in an effort to avert the takeover. Still, Chevron managed to post the best earnings growth in the industry in the first half of 1991. Optimistic, Derr expected to see a decade of stable oil

Chronology:
Kenneth T. Derr

1939: Born.

1960: Graduated from Cornell University with two degrees.

1960: Began 40–year career with Chevron.

1972: Elected vice president of Chevron.

1979: Elected president of Chevron.

1984: Helped implement merger of Chevron and Gulf Oil.

1985: Elected vice chairman of Chevron.

1989: Named chairman and CEO of Chevron.

1999: Retired from Chevron.

2000: Received API Gold Medal for Distinguished Achievement.

prices at the time of a world oil glut. However, the Middle East situation became particularly troublesome. Only 21 months into Derr's tenure as CEO, Iraq president Saddam Hussein entered Kuwait and an oil embargo went into effect.

Derr realized he would have to take some steps to keep moving in the direction he had charted. Right after Hussein's army entered Kuwait, Derr committed an extra $100 million to Chevron's U.S. budget to maximize oil production. Derr's plan was to have Chevron drill approximately 130 more oil wells in existing fields to produce 40,000 additional barrels of crude oil per day. He also tried to set up a joint venture with the Soviet Union to develop the Tengiz field in the northeast Caspian Sea, which would produce high–sulfur crude. The result was worth any risks involved, the company believed.

Chevron did not want to involve other oil companies as partners in the Tengiz venture, as it needed as much crude as the field could yield. It was certainly a risky move financially: Chevron's initial investment was estimated at hundreds of millions of dollars, and the cost was expected to reach more than $1 billion over the following decade. What made it even riskier was the fact that Tengiz would not generate any immediate high financial returns. But Chevron was looking well beyond the 10–year mark. It envisioned the field yielding the world's cheapest oil over its 50 years of projected life. For the immediate future, Chevron was looking to get

Kenneth T. Derr. *(AP/Wide World Photos.)*

25,000 barrels a day in the first year and up to 100,000 within five years.

At the same time, Chevron was involved in offshore drilling with its Port Arguello field, off of the Santa Barbara coast in California. It was the largest domestic discovery in recent years, and it was estimated that it could produce 75,000 to 100,000 barrels a day within a year. Chevron has already written off $445 million in expenses on the field. But after the field was drilled and ready, Chevron was forced to wait for tanker permits from the California Coastal Commission, a situation that resulted from the infamous Exxon Valdez spill. Originally, Chevron did have the permits, but they were rescinded after the spill.

The challenges didn't stop Derr. By 1993, Chevron had posted revenues of $37.1 billion, making it the world's fifth largest oil company. By 1995, foreign revenues accounted for $10.2 billion, or 28 percent of total sales (up from 18 percent of sales in 1989). Return on shareholders' equity was 18.9 percent in the mid–1990s.

In 1996, Derr said his top priority was to outperform Chevron's top competitors: Amoco, Exxon, Arco, Mobil, and Texaco. He also wanted to provide the best stockholder return. To do this he had to find efficient and cost–effective ways to operate. This included reducing per–barrel costs to $6.26. To achieve his goals, Derr set some specific strategies in place. By implementing these plans, Derr essentially reengineered how the company operated. The first strategy involved building a commit-

ted team, as Derr felt that employee commitment was crucial to putting his company in front of the competition. As part of the strategy, Derr sought to establish communication and mutual trust among employees and management, as well as shared objectives, open feedback, and a focus on areas needing improvement.

As his second strategy, Derr sought to continue exploration and production growth internationally, including in Angola, Nigeria, Zaire, Australia, and the North Sea. He also wanted to boost Chevron production in Minas Field in Indonesia to more than 208,000 barrels per day. Chevron would also increase production in the Tengiz Field, which became a joint venture of Chevron and the Republic of Kazakhstan. As part of that particular enterprise, Derr wanted to establish a new export system that would help increase production to 700,000 barrels per day. He also wanted the company to gain a stronger position in the Middle East. By that time, Chevron was providing assistance to Burgan Field in Kuwait, the second largest oil field in the world.

The focus of the third strategy was on generating $1 billion in cash annually from U.S. exploration and production operations. To do this, Derr would cut costs wherever possible and focus on the company's 400 fields in California, Texas, the Rocky Mountains, and the Gulf of Mexico.

The fourth strategy involved having Chevron achieve the top financial performance in U.S. refining and marketing. This involved preventing costly incidents at facilities and continuing to focus on productivity gains and continued cost reductions. In implementing this strategy, Chevron invested in nearly $1 billion in new facilities in Richmond and El Segundo, California, to improve efficiencies and make formulated fuels that improve air quality.

The fifth strategy involved reducing costs across all activities. This included reducing the cost of goods and services by working efficiently with fewer suppliers. Derr's sixth strategy was to keep Chevron's environmental record high by performing self–audits that would ensure compliance with Environmental Protection Agency (EPA) guidelines. By doing this, Derr could help his company avoid costly and unnecessary fines. Chevron was also spending at least $1.5 billion on global environmental protection measures.

Although lauded for his managerial innovations and his effectiveness as corporate leader, Derr often found himself at the receiving end of criticism from various quarters, essentially taking the brunt for the oil industry at large. In 1996, when giving a lecture, Derr felt compelled to answer some of the criticism. Public resentment toward oil companies and CEOs had recently increased. This was during a period when the trend of corporate downsizing and restructuring had become firmly entrenched, and the public felt that CEOs were cutting jobs while accepting large salary increases. During his lecture, Derr told the audience that such restructuring was "necessary to allow American companies to fully become global competitors."

In 1999, before he retired, Derr found himself on the receiving end of pies thrown by members of the Ecotopia Cell of the Biotic Baking Brigade (BBB). The act, which took place outside of the Galileo Academy of Science and Technology where Derr was giving a speech, was a symbolic gesture to protest Chevron's policies. The BBB felt that the company engaged in destruction of indigenous cultures and ecosystems, did not address the issue of global warming, committed labor violations, and was one of the worst polluters in California. The last criticism had some merit. In a study done by the EPA around that time, Chevron's Richmond, California, plant was designated as the nation's biggest toxic waste producer, releasing about a million pounds of toxins into the air.

Derr retired from Chevron in 1999. The following year, he received the American Petroleum Institute's (API) highest award, the Gold Medal for Distinguished Achievement. He was cited for his "extraordinary service to the oil and natural gas industry, as well as to his community and the nation." Derr, the API said, brought "change and innovation to every aspect of his work." Derr had been a member of the API board of directors and played a large role in shaping institute policies, positions, and programs by serving on the senior–level management and executive committees, as well as the committees on public policy and program and budget. Following his retirement from Chevron, he became an honorary member of the institute's board.

Social and Economic Impact

During his tenure as CEO of Chevron, Derr provided the company with innovative, effective leadership that produced quantifiable results. Under his direction, Chevron's market capitalization quadrupled. He also profoundly reengineered Chevron's corporate culture by decentralizing management and increasing employee work force and by diversifying the work force.

Derr also took some risks while at the helm, and they paid off. He developed the partnership in the Tengiz field, and he enabled Chevron to re–enter Bahrain, Kuwait, Saudi Arabia, and Venezuela. He also moved the company into new areas including Argentina, Azerbaijan, China, and Thailand. As an advocate of Africa–America trade, he made Chevron a prominent business partner in Africa. Derr also promoted free–market economics.

Despite criticism aimed at his record, Derr was a strong supporter of public health and education and human rights. During the first Bush administration, he was a member of the Commission on Environmental Quality. During the Clinton administration, he was a member of the Council on Sustainable Development.

Sources of Information

Contact at: Chevron Corporation
  575 Market St.
  San Francisco, CA 94105
  Business Phone: (415)894–7700
  URL: http://www.chevron.com

Bibliography

BBB Press Release. "Chevron CEO Creamed by Pies." *Activism News Bulletin*, 11 March 1999.

Community News. "Ken Derr Receives API Medal for Distinguished Service." *Chevron*, 13 November 2000. Available at http://www.chevron.com/community/whats_new_stories/derr_api_award.shtml.

Darryl Geddes. "Chevron CEO Defends Image of Corporations." *Cornell Chronicle*, 25 April 1996. Available at http://www.news.cornell.edu/Chronicle/96/4.25.96/chevron.html.

Linsenmeyer, Adrienne. "Chevron's Oil Crisis." *Financial World*, 30 October 1990.

Sparks, Debra, and Brooke H. Grabarek. "1994 CEO of the year silver award winners." *Financial World*, 29 March 1994.

Ani DiFranco

(1970-)
Righteous Babes Records

Overview

Ani DiFranco does things her way. To her credit, she has emerged as one of the more influential and inspirational punk/cult music heroines since the 1990s. Impressively, she achieved this without compromising her music to "buy into" Corporate rock, or perhaps more correctly put, without having Corporate rock buy her out. Staunchly independent and uncompromising, Grammy–nominated DiFranco has refused offers from other record companies to take over her music, she releases her records through her own independent label. And through her own independent way, DiFranco has transitioned herself from an underground solo artist to a prolific singer, songwriter, producer, and record company founder. She is the creator of Righteous Babe Records, which, by 2000, had sold more than 1 million copies of her recordings. In 2001, her new release, "Revelling/Reckoning," sold 37,000 copies in a single debut week. Starting with a grass–roots following, Righteous Babes Records finds itself in the position of having to reject or accept the work of other singers who clamor for release through its private label.

DiFranco's acoustic performances are perhaps best described as part pit–party, part hoedown, and part folk–hootenanny, punctuated with stage dives, broken guitar strings, and lyrics that cover controversial issues. DiFranco alternates between a smoldering warmth and an angry explosion of sound, and defies categorization by blending the forthrightness and anger of punk rock with the simplicity, beauty, and poetry of folk music. She uses press–on nails reinforced with electrical tape when performing to bang–strum on her acoustic guitar, and often offers only drummer Andy Stochansky as musical

back up. DiFranco's fans reflect her widespread appeal. They are as diverse and hard to peg as her style, ranging from teenage to middle–aged, and from fans of alternative rock to folk music to punk rock.

Personal Life

Born September 23, 1970, in Buffalo, New York, DiFranco is the daughter of Dante (a research engineer) and Elizabeth (an architect) DiFranco. She began playing music at age nine when her parents bought her a Beatles songbook and an acoustic guitar. Within a few years she was singing "Yesterday" at local coffeehouses with the guidance of a local folk singer/guitar teacher. *Rolling Stone's* Evelyn McDonnell commented in her article, "She met a man named Mike, a 30–year–old 'degenerate folk–singer barfly' at a guitar store in Buffalo, NY. They began playing together and hanging out with other singer/songwriters, who would come up from New York to play." DiFranco's parents were absorbed in their own marital problems at the time, and DiFranco told McDonnell that they "were just happy from the beginning that I was self–sufficient. For me, it was the ideal childhood: complete emancipation."

Befriended by other "artsy" types, including Suzanne Vega and Michelle Shocked, DiFranco gave up music temporarily to study ballet, but that was short–lived. In high school, at the age of fifteen, the independent and spirited DiFranco found an apartment of her own in Buffalo and started writing her own songs to pursue her already mushrooming career. At the age of nineteen, she moved to New York City and began touring the country in a Volkswagen Beetle, performing at college campuses, coffeehouses, bars, and music festivals. She explained to *Guitar Player's* James Rotondi that her percussive acoustic technique "evolved out of twelve years of playing in bars, where people are there to pick up somebody and drink themselves into a stupor, not to listen to the chick in the corner with the acoustic."

Career Details

DiFranco began to develop an impressive following of loyal fans and supporters. Besieged by requests for tapes of her performances, she recorded a demo cassette and pressed 500 copies of it for distribution at future shows. The demo recording, an acoustic collection of personal essays about failed relationships and gender inequities, sold out quickly. In 1990, at the age of 20 and on borrowed money, DiFranco founded Righteous Babe Records. Started as a dining room table operation, the label was intended to fight back against the corporate policies of recording companies interested in her work. As DiFranco told *Billboard's* Jill Pesselnick, "When I was

Chronology:
Ani DiFranco

1970: Born in Buffalo, New York.

1979: Began playing guitar in coffeehouses at age nine.

1985: Moved out on her own and sang in Buffalo coffeehouses and pubs.

1989: Relocated to New York.

1990: Formed Righteous Babe Records.

1995: Released "Not a Pretty Girl," considered her breakthrough album.

1996: Righteous Babe began releasing the works of other artists.

1998: Married her sound engineer, Andrew Gilchrest.

2000: Nominated for Grammy Award.

a teenager playing around Buffalo, already there were guys who would take me out to lunch and say they could make me a 'star.' There were record deal murmurings in the air. It was only after enough lunches with these guys that I really felt an instinctual aversion to marrying myself to business people." She decided she would not contribute to the perpetuation of that system, and buy into "that whole dynamic of commercial, homogenized art," as she stated in a *Canadian Press* article.

DiFranco, a truly independent independent, wanted to record her particular brand of folk/rock whenever and however she wanted, without worry of contractual obligations, censorship, or other modification of her work to properly market it. The reality, as DiFranco continued in *Billboard,* was that, "In the beginning, there was no company—it was my little joke with myself; it became a reality over the course of the next 10 years." She went on, "There's a lot of mistakes I've made along the way and things I would do differently now, but life is about learning."

What those mistakes could be remains a mystery, because, for all intents and purposes, Righteous Babe has slowly but very steadily grown over the years. Early on, DiFranco kept her label floating by recording only one album per year for the first few years, and then followed up with constant touring and grass–roots marketing of each album. The approach worked well, as word–of–mouth advertising spread her name across the country.

Ani DiFranco. *(The Press Network/Albert Sanchez.)*

By the mid–1990s, Righteous Babe had its own office and had expanded its staff to include president Scot Fisher and a sales and marketing team. In 2001, the company had 15 employees, plus a 12–member road crew. Company headquarters was housed in the historic Sidway Building on the corner of Main and Goodell Streets in downtown Buffalo, a location deliberately chosen to express DiFranco's commitment to her hometown.

Described in *MSN Music* as "a folkie in punk's clothing," DiFranco toured the country alone, sporting not only her particular brand of music, but also a shaved head, tattoos, and body piercings. DiFranco created her audience through a gradual build–up of fans over the years. As she commented in *Rolling Stone,* "that's the nature of a career that's built on toting your butt around the country and playing music for people as opposed to commercial air play or national TV exposure." Political and moral themes, often personal in nature, dominated DiFranco's repertoire. One example is "The Million You Never Made" on the album, *Not A Pretty Girl,* in which DiFranco sang, "If you don't live what you sing about, your mirror is going to find out." By including controversial issues in her music, DiFranco hoped to diffuse them, discuss them, and deepen understanding of each topic's nuances.

With a broad emotional palette at her disposal, DiFranco's vocal range fluctuated between gritty and airy. Rolling Stone's Fred Goodman described her as "A wonder to behold: a spiky–haired volcano . . . [whose] songs, though mostly about independence and romance

. . . often take unexpected, jarring turns—as when she recites a poem with disturbing images or controversial overtones." DiFranco told *Out* magazine's Ray Rogers, "I just sing my goofy songs about my goofy little life," underscoring the fact that she was her own person, without regard for those who might take offense at her uncensored output.

DiFranco's most ardent fans were a possessive group. While performing at a concert in New York City in 1996, MTV News cameras filmed the show while DiFranco's fans shouted, "MTV sucks!" at the camera people. DiFranco toned down the angry outbursts with humor, telling the audience that the camera people were from Mutual of Omaha, there to capture her in her natural environment. As DiFranco's popularity grew, she was faced with difficult decisions and growing pains. She was caught between fans who wanted her to remain accessible, and her untapped fans, reached only through more exposure. DiFranco stated in *Rolling Stone,*, "I believe in . . . not just making revolutionary music but making it in a way that challenges the system. . . . The possibility of emancipation and control and independence is so much greater now." Always a favorite on college campuses, DiFranco's music had moved into homes and businesses as well.

In 1996, Righteous Babe began releasing work from other artists. Its first project was a collaboration with DiFranco and folk singer–storyteller Utah Philips. It also put out albums from Brazilian singer–guitarist Arto Lindsay, singer–bassist SaraLee, and poet Sekou Sundiata. While none of the non–DiFranco releases ever sold more than a few thousand copies, the company had always emphasized music before business and product over profit. As DiFranco stated to *Billboard* interviewers, "I guess if there is anything a little inspirational in my story, it is in showing that there are truly viable alternatives to playing the industry game. And that you can make a living at this. I hope I also show that the indie route doesn't have to be a constricting or limiting way of doing things—if you have patience, and if you can come to terms with your life, and if you love your job, and if you are willing to spend 10 years doing what a record company could do in six months." The only constant for her company was not to compromise to fit some slot, be it radio or retail. To that end, in more recent years, Righteous Babe has added Drums & Tuba, an avante–garde improvisational jazz trio, to its roster. Righteous Babe sells its releases through alternative outlets and independent record stores, including Golden Rod Music, Horizon, Zango, and Lady Slipper.

DiFranco has remained true to her original beliefs about artistic independence. "I just don't think that you can say something meaningful within the corporate music structure," she was quoted in a 2000 issue of *Billboard.* "And I know that I don't want to be a part of that structure. I don't want to support it, and I want to do everything I can to actively challenge it on a daily basis." She went on to say that what it would take to move the pendulum out of the commercialism and business priority sphere is moving into independent spheres, as she has, and "realizing that those kind of dehumanizing corporate forces are not fulfilling to us as artists or to the public as fans."

In 2001, Righteous Babe launched its Web site, righteousbabe.com, and started a foray into book publishing, but the label remained true to its artistic objectives. DiFranco was the winner of *Yahoo! Internet Life*'s 2001 Online Music Awards for her "Ani DiFranco at the House of Blues" (hob.com). She still devoted three weeks out of every month to touring, splitting each week between Buffalo, New York, where the label is based, and New York City, where she lives. In addition to "Revelling/Reckoning," DiFranco's other releases include "Ani DiFranco" (1990); "Not So Soft" (1991); "Imperfectly" (1992); "Out of Range" (1994); "Not a Pretty Girl" (1995); "Little Plastic Castle" (1998); and "Swing Set" (2000). DiFranco is quoted in the *Canadian Press* as saying that her heart still lies in performing live. "I've built my life around live performances," she said. "It's an end in itself."

In 1998, DiFranco married Andrew Gilchrest, her sound engineer. She changed her signature hair style from shaved–cropped to dreadlocks, and visibly beamed to interviewers while talking about her husband. But by 2001, that relationship appeared rocky, and the tone of her music appeared more somber, more vulnerable than usual, separated by mood and content into a two–disc release, "Revelling/Reckoning." As Terri Sutton once said about DiFranco in a *Village Voice* article, "DiFranco is still squeezing all her selves into a product."

But that product has continued to be pulled off from retail shelves at an increasing pace, to a wider audience with not–so–much–in–your–face views.

Social and Economic Impact

Like reality TV, reality music has gained a hold on a substantial cross section of the American public. At one time, in–your–face music held an audience limited almost exclusively to the younger set. But Ani DiFranco has been able to negotiate age and gender bridges with her coffeehouse folksy, bluesy style—though with a small following. Moreover, by maintaining her own label, she has been able to bring her honest voice and frank lyrics to the forefront of pop music without commercializing the sound, as did, for example, Eminem. Not to say that her music is any less in–your–face with its lyrics, or would not make jaded audiences wince now and then; it's just that it is simply and purely done *her* way, for the benefit of whoever wishes to listen.

Sources of Information

Contact at: Righteous Babes Records
     PO Box 95, Endicott Sta.
     Buffalo, NY 14205

Bibliography

"Best." *Yahoo! Internet Life,* October 2001.

Gallo, Phil. "DiFranco Bow is Righteous." *Daily Variety,* 20 April 2001.

Gillen, Marilyn A. "Ani DiFranco: Envisioning a Future That Makes Artistic Integrity a Top Priority..." 1 August 2000.

Fuentez, Tania. "Ani DiFranco Focuses Inward on Latest CD, Reflecting Love, Life, Marriage."*Canadian Press,* 2 July 2001.

Linstedt, Sharon. "Development Company Plans Major Rehab of Buffalo, N.Y., Building."*The Buffalo News,* 21 June 2001.

McDonnell, Evelyn. "Ani DiFranco Reflects on her 'Next Bold Move'."*The Miami Herald,* 10 October 2001.

"MSN Music—Ani DiFranco." October 2001. Available at http://music.windowsmedia.msn.com.

Pesselnick, Jill.. "DiFranco's Righteous Babe Grows Up with Ambitious Expansion, Double–CD."*Billboard,* 24 March 2001.

Sutton, Terri. "Girl Uninterrupted." *Village Voice,* 3 October 1995.

Barry Charles Diller

(1942-)
USA Networks Inc.

Overview

Barry Diller is the quintessential risk–taker who sees (and seizes) opportunities before his rivals do, and creates media empires in an already competitive market. The American public may best recognize him for his role in creating the nation's fourth network known as Fox Television (the Fox Broadcasting Company) alongside the powerhouses of ABC, NBC, and CBS. Fox changed television viewing forever with the debut of spike–haired cartoon character Bart Simpson, as well as the then–controversial sitcom, *Married With Children*, and the very successful *Cheers*. He is also credited with playing a role in the creation of made–for–TV movies, "movie of the week" specials, and TV miniseries. But those things are passé for Diller, who bought USA Networks in 1998, a conglomerate which owns the Home Shopping Network and Ticketmaster Online. Diller's long–term goal is to create a true convergence network: combining the Internet with telephone and television—a concept that has been around since the early 1980s but one that has never enjoyed a stronghold in the media world.

Personal Life

Diller was born in San Francisco to Michael and Reva (Addison) Diller in 1942. His father, who ran a real estate company, moved the family to Beverly Hills when Barry was still a boy. He grew up with Danny Thomas and Doris Day, among others, as neighbors.

In 1961, at the age of nineteen, Diller dropped out of college at the University of California, Los Angeles (UCLA) after only four months, and took a job in the

Barry Diller. *(Reuters NewMedia Inc./Corbis/Remy Steinegger.)*

mailroom at the William Morris Agency. After completing a training program, he became a full talent scout for the Agency in 1964. This turned out to be his yellow brick road into Hollywood. According to *Newsmakers 1991,* because of a business strategy "defined by the characteristics of risk–taking, creative decision–making, and tight control over financial strategies, Barry Diller has risen to become one of the most powerful studio managers in Hollywood. Couple that with his personality traits of bluntness, cunning, and intimidation, and you have the essence of Diller." Little has changed from that description in the ten years since, excepting Diller's exodus from Hollywood to New York.

In 2001, the 59–year–old Diller was riding high on a wave of network successes, and always looking to make a new deal. He continues to share his time between a sprawling five–acre Spanish–style estate in Coldwater Canyon, a beach house in Malibu, and a suite in Manhattan's Waldorf Towers. He loves to hike, bike, and play poker—in a long standing game that includes Steve Martin, Johnny Carson. Carl Reiner, Neil Simon, and producer Dan Melnick. He takes annual bicycle trips with Disney CEO Michael Eisner. He plays hard, drives fast, and skis even faster. His long–time friend, Jack Nicholson, told an interviewer for *Los Angeles Magazine* that Diller was "as good as it gets..." Previously a confirmed bachelor, Diller finally married in February 2001 to fashion designer Diane Von Furstenberg in a five-minute ceremony at New York's City Hall. They had been romantically linked for the previous 26 years.

Notwithstanding an aggressive style and personality, Diller typically does not seek the limelight and has refused many groups' requests to honor him with special awards. However, he and former Universal chairman Sidney Sheinberg created the nonprofit group, Hollywood Supports, in 1991, to fight HIV discrimination and homophobia in the entertainment industry and to secure domestic–partner benefits for more than 90 percent of the industry's gay employees. Diller serves on the board of directors for Ticketmaster, Seagram Co. Ltd., the New York Public Library, the Museum of Television and Radio, and the Washington Post. He is a board member for the School of Cinema–Television at the University of Southern California and the Executive Board for the Medical Sciences at UCLA, both the New York University's Board of Trustees and the Tisch School of the Arts Dean's Council, and a member of the Advisory Board for the Center for Health Communications at Harvard University's School of Public Health.

Career Details

Shortly after becoming a talent agent for William Morris in his early twenties, Diller joined ABC in 1966, serving as assistant to the vice president of programming. Two years later, he became executive assistant to the vice president of programming and directing of feature films. Diller was named vice president of feature films and pro-

Chronology:
Barry Charles Diller

1942: Born in San Francisco.

1961: Dropped out of UCLA after four months to become mail clerk at the William Morris Agency.

1966: Joined ABC as assistant to the vice president of programming.

1969: Promoted to vice president of feature films and program development for the East Coast.

1973: Named vice president, prime time television, at ABC Entertainment.

1974: Named chairman and CEO of Paramount Pictures.

1983: Served as president of Gulf and Western Entertainment and Communications.

1984: Named chairman and CEO of Twentieth Century Fox Film Corporation.

1995: Became chairman of Home Shopping Network and CEO of Silver King Communications.

1998: Named chairman and CEO of USA Networks Inc.

---

gram development for the East Coast in 1969. From 1971 to 1973, he served as vice president of feature films and Circle Entertainment, during which time he was responsible for selecting, producing, and scheduling the *Tuesday Movie of the Week*, *Wednesday Movie of the Week*, and Circle Film original features for airing on ABC, as well as acquisition and scheduling of theatrical features for airing on the *ABC Sunday Night Movie* and the *ABC Monday Night Movie*. In 1973, Diller was named vice president of Prime Time Television at ABC Entertainment.

Diller was named chairman and chief executive officer of Paramount Pictures in 1974, serving as chairman for ten years. He next served as president of Gulf and Western Entertainment and Communications Group from 1983 to 1984. In 1984, Diller joined with Rupert Murdoch to develop Fox into the fourth TV network, when the industry said there was only room for the Big Three. Diller served as chairman and CEO of Twentieth Century Fox Film Corporation and TCF Holdings from 1984 to 1985, and chairman and CEO of Fox Inc. from 1985 to 1992.

Diller stunned Hollywood in 1992 when he unexpectedly resigned as chairman of Fox, walking away with an estimated $140 million. He had decided that if he did not make the big leap then, he may never do it. He gave himself one year to travel around the country looking for opportunities. After six months, von Furstenberg took him with her to witness TV shopping on the Pennsylvania–based home–shopping network known as QVC. He was immediately hooked after watching her sell $1.2 million worth of merchandise in less than two hours. Laying down $25 million, Diller took over as CEO of QVC Network Inc.—a position he held until 1994. Using QVC as leverage, Diller next attempted to take over control of Paramount Communications in 1993, but Viacom trumped QVC's bid and Diller moved on. He again lost a bid for CBS, which Westinghouse took over in 1994. Undaunted, Diller sold his stake in QVC for another $100 million, then turned around and seized control of QVC's Saint Petersburg, Florida rival, the Home Shopping Network (HSN). He also seized Silver King Communications—a group of 12 UHF stations, and the flailing Savoy Pictures Entertainment, which had stakes in several more stations.

Buoyed by his new acquisitions, Diller, through HSN, began Internet investing with Ticketmaster and CitySearch, a network of city–based informational Web sites, as well as an Internet shopping site called First Auction. Diller served as CEO of QVC Network Inc. from 1992 to 1994, chairman and CEO of Silver King Communications Inc. from 1995 to 1998, and chairman of the Home Shopping Network from 1995 to 1998. At that time, a new promise appeared on the horizon.

Back in 1995, Seagram's Bronfman had purchased Universal Studios from Matsushita. Two years later, just prior to committing Universal to buy out Viacom's 50 percent share of USA Network, Bronfman invited Diller to dinner and proposed a deal. The complicated details involved Diller's agreement to have HSN buy Universal's cable networks (which included both USA and its sister Sci–Fi Channel) and the TV production arm for $4.1 billion in cash and stock. While Universal would retain a 45 percent stake in the new company—to be called USA Networks Inc., Diller would run it as CEO and chairman of the board. Essentially, the deal gave Diller a large chunk of Universal to merge with his existing local channels. This would allow him to create a cable–broadcast hybrid of local broadcast television stations and Universal's national broadcast television production facilities, along with the Home Shopping Network. Diller's vision was to build a national television network of locally made programming from grassroots neighborhoods on up. His concept included the construction of 13 production facilities in different cities over the ensuing three years (the first opened in Miami). So great was the excitement over Diller's new vision that USA Network Inc.'s share price more than doubled within the year.

Despite the subsequent failure of a proposed deal to merge with Internet portal Lycos (by purchasing 61.5

percent of Lycos stock) to use it as an Internet outlet for HSN and Ticketmaster direct marketing , and an August 2001 reassignment by cable powerhouse AOL Time Warner from Channel 23 to Channel 40 on several systems, USA Network Inc. has done very well. For the first half of 2001, the company reported near 20 percent increase in revenues, to $2.7 billion, and a 13 percent increase in operating income, to $157.4 million. USA shares were up 30 percent.

Moreover, since 1999, Diller has struck more than 30 separate deals to purchase Internet sites, call centers, and warehouses—all intended to create the backbone for the media world of his vision, one which is driven by the interactive sale of goods and services. Diller neared the end of 2001 with a debt–free balance sheet and $2 billion in cash, making no secret that he was searching for his next major media property purchase.

Social and Economic Impact

Barry Diller is not the most powerful or the wealthiest person in the American media business, but he has enjoyed the distinction of having been the most watched. He changed network television forever when he played a major role in forcing the Big Three networks (ABC, CBS, NBC) to move over and make room for a fourth. Additionally, the new network's programming, albeit controversial and on–the–edge by some standards (e.g., the *Jerry Springer Show*), offered a refreshing viewing alternative to the non–cable network audience.

But it is Diller's plan for the future that holds the most interest. Although he is neither the creator nor the prophet of the concept of convergence in the media (television, telephone, and computer), he and his company may be the ones most watched for the concept's ultimate success. To understand the concept at work, one only need look to Diller's July 2001 deal with the Professional Golf Association as a convergence showcase. In the deal, USA Network will broadcast the early rounds of many PGA events through 2007. USA's Ticketmaster will sell the tickets to the events, and USA's e–commerce group will operate PGA.com, which will sell everything from golf shirts to sporting equipment, housed at (and delivered from) the Home Shopping Network warehouses. Already in 2001, USA networks units were running online

commerce sites for the National Football League, the National Basketball Association, and Sportsline.

If Diller is correct, persons may eventually need to venture out of their cocoons only rarely for shopping or entertainment purposes. In July 2001, USA Network purchased Microsoft's online travel site, Expedia Inc.—making Diller the Internet's largest travel agent. With Expedia, Diller hopes to create what may be the media world's first fully functioning convergence entity. His soon–to–debut USA Travel cable channel, his Hotel Reservations Network Inc. Internet site, and his newly acquired Expedia should bring USA Network up to third place (behind Amazon and Priceline) in e–commerce business. If one tosses in a traveler's interest in attending events while traveling, Ticketmaster will handle the transaction online, and if one is looking for a travel partner, he or she can visit USA's dating service, match.com. The impressive array of transaction assets that Diller and USA Networks Inc. have assembled may serve to set Diller up as the revenue role model in the convergence market, with no known competition close behind.

Sources of Information

Contact at: USA Networks Inc.
　152 W. 52nd St.
　New York, NY 10019
　Business Phone: (212) 314–7300
　URL: http://www.usanetwork.com

Bibliography

"Barry Diller." 24 November 2001. Available at http://www.usanetworks.com/people/diller.html.

"Barry Diller leaves home: could a new network built on local programming threaten Hollywood's hold on the television industry?" *The Economist*, 2 May 1998.

Glasner, Joanna. "Meet Barry Diller, Net Mogul." 9 February 1999. Available at http://www.wired.com/news/business.

Kilday, Gregg. "Mr. USA." *Los Angeles Magazine*, March 1998.

"Monitor." *Entertainment Weekly*, 16 February 2001.

"Resume: Barry Diller." 10 September 2001. Available at http://www.businessweek.com/magazine.

"The New Barry Diller." 10 September 2001. Available at http://www.businessweek.com/magazine.

Donna Dubinsky

(1956-)
Handspring, Inc.

Overview

Donna Dubinsky is co–founder and chief executive officer of Handspring, which develops and markets one of the hottest computer innovations, the hand–held computer.

Personal Life

Dubinksy, 46, was born in Benton Harbor, Michigan. Her father was a scrap–metal broker, and her mother was a homemaker who enjoyed playing bridge. Dubinsky attended Yale University, graduating with a bachelor of arts in history. During her years at Yale, her entrepreneurial spirit came to light. Dubinsky and her roommate created a typing service that specialized in overnight turnarounds. The pair quickly realized that they had the power to charge significantly more for their specialized service. Upon receiving her degree, Dubinsky took a job with Philadelphia National Bank as an entry–level financial analyst, balancing spreadsheets by hand. However, before long she had been promoted to commercial lending officer, the youngest in the history of the bank. Dubinsky resigned her position after two years to pursue an MBA at Harvard.

While at Harvard, Dubinsky realized that she wanted to be involved in the creation of a product, rather than the service businesses that most of her classmates were attracted to. She told *Electronic Business*, "I had no interest in service businesses. I longed to create a product, something I could touch and say, 'I helped make this.'" Her dream came into focus in 1981 when she attended a

demonstration of VisiCalc, the first software for spreadsheet applications, developed on an Apple II PC. Seeing her future, Dubinsky completed her MBA and set about getting a job with Apple Computers.

Dubinsky is married to husband Len Shustek; they have one daughter. Dubinsky's success has made her worth approximately $1 billion. Her constant attention to her goal of achieving success has dominated her life and her time. She told *InformationWeek.com*, "I don't even know how to turn on the TV. I've never seen [*Who Wants to Be a] Millionaire*. I never watched *Survivor*. I never even saw *Jerry Seinfeld*."

Career Details

Dubinsky was successful in securing a job at Apple, and for the remainder of the decade she worked within the distribution, logistics, and operations divisions of the company. In 1990 she moved to Santa Clara, California, to take on an assignment as sales and marketing manager at Claris Corp., Apple's application software division. Longing for more independence from the parent company, Dubinsky spent a year pushing Apple to spin off Claris, making it a stand–alone company. When Apple decided against Dubinsky's proposal, she quit to follow her dream of spending a year in Paris. During 1991 Dubinsky lived in France, studied the language and painting, and taught. Finding that her enthusiasm for painting was much greater than her actual ability, she returned to California in 1992.

Upon her return, Dubinsky met Jeff Hawkins, who showed her a hand–held electronic organizer he had developed. In the early 1990s, the Internet was beginning to take off. New innovations in computer and software technology were at the beginning of massive expansion, and Dubinsky was sold on the idea that the hand–held computer was the future of the computer industry. The two decided to go into business together—Hawkins would provide the innovative technology and Dubinsky would create the company to market the product. In 1992 Palm, Inc. was established, with Dubinsky as chief executive officer and Hawkins as chairman.

Over the next three years, Dubinsky struggled to raise money to fund their venture and bring Hawkins' PalmPilot to market. Because of ongoing financial restraints, in 1995 Dubinsky and Hawkins sold Palm to U.S. Robotics Corp., a modem manufacturer based in Schaumburg, Illinois. In March 1996 the first PalmPilot was introduced to the market, accompanied by rave reviews and tremendous sales. It became the fastest selling computer product in history and sold faster than the color television, the cellular phone, the personal computer, and the video cassette recorder. Despite the success of the hand–held PalmPilot, Dubinsky's relationship with U.S Robotics was difficult. She wanted U.S. Robotics to spin off Palm, because she believed it was good

Chronology:
Donna Dubinsky

1956: Born in Benton Harbor, Michigan.

1990: Moved to Santa Clara, California, as sales and marketing manager at Claris Corp., a division of Apple.

1991: Quit Apple; moved to Paris for a year.

1992: Established Palm, Inc.

1995: Sold Palm to U.S. Robotics Corp.

1998: Quit Palm; founded Handspring.

2000: Handspring went public.

business, and she wanted to reestablish the independence she had lost in the sale of the company. However, U.S. Robotics had a hot product in the PalmPilot and was in no hurry to cut it loose. When U.S. Robotics was acquired by 3Com Corp. of Santa Clara, California, in 1997, Dubinsky had no better luck convincing its management team of the benefits of Palm's independence. Dubinsky's and Hawkins' frustration peaked in 1998, and the two abruptly quit.

The success of the PalmPilot helped Dubinsky realize that, while large corporations are helpful in providing resources for new projects, new and cutting–edge innovations often come from smaller independent companies. In an interview with *Forbes*, Dubinsky commented, "I don't think innovation will come from the big guys. The smart ones are those who recognize it."

Dubinsky and Hawkins moved to Palo Alto, California, and started up a new company called Handspring. "We have no customers, no stakes," she told *Forbes*. "We can break the model of everything we've done in the past if we want to." Armed with $18 million in venture capital and a license to use the Palm operating software, the startup company immediately set to work developing its first product. Called Visor, the new device would compete head–on with the PalmPilot. The Visor was released in September 1999, and sales skyrocketed quickly, earning Handspring a 14 percent share of the hand–held market. In fact, the day that Handspring announced its new product, 3Com floated Palm off as a separate company. The key feature of the Visor is its expansion slot, which can transform the Visor into an MP3 player, a digital camera, or a mobile phone. Dubinsky told *ZDNet News*,

Donna Dubinsky. *(Handspring Incorporated.)*

"After we left Palm, we sat down and asked ourselves, 'What are we gonna do at Handspring that we didn't do well at Palm?' Jeff immediately came up with the idea of hardware expansion. We made a list of all the things we would want a Visor to do, and that's where the ideas for the modules came from."

Handspring went public in June 2000; by that August, its initial share price had nearly doubled, and it continued to eat into Palm's dominant share of the market. In 2000 Handspring increased to nearly 20 percent of the market share, whereas Palm fell from 72 percent in 1999 to 64 percent in 2000. However, just as Handspring was charging into the marketplace, economic recession put the brakes on sales and earnings. In the fiscal year 2001, ending in June 2001, sales totaled $371 million, up an incredible 264 percent from the previous year, but net income was a loss of $126 million.

Despite tough economic conditions, Dubinsky has remained upbeat about Handspring's past and future performance and points to new developments and innovation as the key to Handspring's ongoing success. In October 2001, Handspring introduced the Treo, a family of compact communicators that combine a mobile phone, wireless email, messaging, and Web browsing into a small, lightweight hand–held device. The key to the future of the hand–held industry may be hinged to its ability to attract the corporate and business communities rather than individual consumers. However, businesses are not likely to add new innovations to their communications arsenals until economic conditions improve.

Social and Economic Impact

Dubinsky stands out as not only one of the top executives in the digital and Internet business but as one of the top women executives in business. She has not found that being a woman has been an obstacle in achieving her success, maintaining that in the computer industry, gender is not a deciding factor of whether someone will succeed. She believes that in the field of high technology, a glass ceiling does not exist. Dubinsky explained in an interview with NBC's Tom Brokaw: "We're seeing a lot of small companies with women CEOs today, particularly because of the Internet. where. . . business models are very open and fluid and there's such a cry for talent."

Still, Dubinsky recognizes that there are fewer women than men in the technical fields, as women are more likely to be in non–technical areas such as marketing and finance. Dubinsky supports women in technical areas, noting that the initial exposure often begins in middle school or high school when girls become exposed to science and math. Dubinsky feels this is a critical time to promote an interest in such technical studies to girls, areas of study often considered "uncool" by their peers. She hopes that by working hard, running a successful business with integrity, and gaining respect within her field, she will serve as a role model for young women who may follow in her footsteps. She also feels that the opportunities for women, in particular, are exciting. As she explained to Tom Brokaw, "I believe here if a woman is good and she's willing to work as hard as a man does and has the right training and preparation that she can succeed." And as for living in Silicon Valley, Dubinsky told Amanda Hall of the *Sunday Telegraph*, "It's a vibrant, special place, it really is like being in Italy during the Renaissance."

Sources of Information

Contact at: Handspring, Inc.
189 Bernardo Ave.
Mountain View, CA 94043
Business Phone: (650)230–5000
URL: http://www.handspring.com

Bibliography

Entertainment Weekly, July 1999. Available at http://www.entertainmentweeklyonline.com.

Forbes, July 1999.

"Handspring Beats Loss Estimates." *ZDNet News*, 17 October 2001. Available at http://www.zdnet.com.

"Handspring, Inc." Hoover's Online, 2001. Available at http://www.hoovers.com.

"Handspring, The Company: Executive Team." Handspring, Inc., 2001. Available at http://www.handspring.com.

"Handspring, The Company: Background." Handspring, Inc., 2001. Available at http://www.handspring.com.

"Handspring Unites Phone, Messaging and PDA in New Treo Communicator." Handspring, Inc., 15 October 2001. Available at http://www.handspring.com.

Heavens, Andrew. "Handspring Cuts Sales Forecasts in Half." *Financial Times*, 7 June 2001. Available at http://www.ft.com.

Kador, John. "A Hands–On Business." *Electronic Business*, 1 September 2001.

NBC Nightly News with Tom Brokaw, 24 August 1999. Available at http://www.msnbc.com.

Nelson, Matthew G. "CEO Donna Dubinsky Champions Handspring Development." *InformationWeek*, 1 January 2001. Available at http://www.informationweek.com.

Sunday Telegraph, 13 August 2000.

Weingarten, Mark. "Best of the Best: People of the Year." *ZDNet News*, 2001. Available at http://www.zdnet.com.

Robert A. Eckert

(1955-)
Mattel, Inc.

Overview

Robert Eckert is the chairman and chief executive officer (CEO) of Mattel, Inc., the world's largest and most recognized toy maker. After a disastrous step into educational software in the late 1990s, Eckert was selected as the company's new CEO in 2000 and commissioned with the task of bringing profitability back to Mattel.

Personal Life

Robert A. Eckert grew up in Chicago. He attended the University of Arizona and received his bachelor's degree in business administration in 1976. From there, he returned home to enroll in Northwestern University, completing his MBA in marketing and finance in 1977. Eckert is married with four children. He serves on the advisory board of the J. L. Kellogg Graduate School of Management of Northwestern University and is also a member of the board of visitors at the Anderson School at the University of California, Los Angeles.

Career Details

After completing his graduate studies in 1977, Eckert joined Kraft Foods, headquartered outside Chicago in Northfield, Illinois. Initially he worked in the company's marketing department. In 1987 he was promoted to vice president of strategy and development for Kraft's Grocery Products Division. Two years later, in 1989, he became the company's vice president of marketing for the Refrigerated Foods Division. In 1990 he was appointed as the executive vice president of Kraft Foods and general manager of the Cheese Division. He was also responsible for the company's Oscar Mayer Foods and North American Foodservice Divisions. Eckert displayed his leadership and problem–solving skills in August 1991 when confronted with a difficult and embarrassing flub. Kraft ran a promotion that offered to give away a new van to one lucky winner. However, quite by mistake, some 20,000 grand–prize tickets were printed and distributed. Eckert avoided a potentially serious class–action lawsuit filed by disappointed ticket holders by sending out $10 million in coupons, cash, and prizes.

In October 1997, having served at Kraft for 20 years, Eckert was named the company's president and chief executive officer. Kraft Foods is a large and highly diversified company, boasting the largest sale organization of any U.S. food manufacturer. In 1999 Kraft controlled the production and sale of 27 brand names with high sales and four other brands with sales of over $1 billion. During his three years at the helm of Kraft Foods, Eckert earned high marks for his marketing skills; he successfully invented new appeal for old–time favorites that had begun to slip in sales, including Kraft Dinner and Oscar Meyer products. During his tenure, Kraft also introduced fat–free cold cuts and the immensely popular Lunchables. From 1996 to 1998, newly introduced products alone created more than $1 billion in sales.

Eckert was also known for his tenacity to drive his company forward to bigger, better ways. When asked by *Prepared Foods* in 1999 what it would take for Kraft Foods to become the food industry's undisputed leader, Eckert answered: "We'll know we're there when consumers see us as the company, above all others, that makes food a simpler, more enjoyable part of their lives and helps them connect their families the way they want so much to do. . . when our retail grocery and foodservice customers see us as their indispensable business partner. . . when investors see us as the food company that's best at delivering volume–driven earnings growth . . . and when our employees see us as the employer of choice. In many peoples' eyes, we're already there, but we're not letting up on our drive to be the best."

On May 17, 2000, Mattel, Inc., the world's largest toy maker, announced that Eckert had been selected as the company's new chairman of the board and CEO. Mattel's product lines include Barbie dolls, Fisher–Price toys, Hot Wheels and Matchbox cars, American Girl dolls and books, Harry Potter items, and licensed Disney (including *Dinosaurs* and *102 Dalmations*) and *Sesame Street* products. As the worldwide leader in the design, manufacture, and marketing of toys, Mattel's revenues for 2000 topped $5.5 billion. However, despite its incredible name recognition and impressive revenues, Mattel had been through some difficult periods in the nearly five decades of its existence, and Eckert was entering the company at just such a time.

Chronology:
Robert A. Eckert

1955: Born.

1977: Joined Kraft Foods as a marketing executive.

1987: Promoted to vice president of strategy and development for Kraft's Grocery Products Division.

1989: Became vice president of marketing for the Refrigerated Foods Division.

1990: Appointed executive vice president of Kraft Foods and general manager of the Cheese Division.

1997: Selected as the president and chief executive officer of Kraft Foods.

1998: Mattel stock traded at an all–time high of $46.75 a share.

2000: Became chairman and chief executive officer of Mattel, Inc.; earned $12.5 million in compensation in first seven months on the job.

2001: Announced closure of last U.S.–based Mattel factory.

2001: Mattel posted a profit for first three quarters of 2001.

Mattel was founded by Elliot and Ruth Handler in 1955, and just 11 years later, sales totaled $5 million. Sales climbed steadily each year until 1959 when Mattel introduced the Barbie doll, which sent sales skyrocketing. By 1965 sales totaled more than $100 million. But during the 1970s the company overextended itself in less–than–profitable acquisitions, including Ringling Bros. and Barnum & Bailey Circus, and when the management team was found guilty of doctoring the financial records, the Handlers withdrew their involvement in the company under pressure from the courts and the Securities and Exchange Commission. Although under new leadership and a restructured board of directors the company once again became profitable, the tides turned again in the 1980s, and by 1984 Mattel was on the verge of bankruptcy, having lost substantial ground when the electronic game market dried up. In 1987 Mattel posted a loss of $113 million, and stock prices had fallen from a high of $40 per share in 1982 to $10 per share.

Mattel's fortunes were turned around by promoting John W. Amerman to CEO. Amerman cut costs, reduced

Robert Eckert. (Mattel, Inc.)

spent $3.5 billion to acquire the Learning Co., maker of educational software, but the purchase was ill advised, and Mattel lost $300 million, ultimately posting a loss for four consecutive quarters and recording the first annual loss in a decade. The cost in stock market value was measured at nearly $7 billion due to the drastic decline in stock prices. Under pressure, Barad resigned in February 2000.

When Eckert came on board as chairman and CEO in May, investors expected him to clean up the Learning Co. mess and restore Mattel to its former glory. On the day of Eckert's first shareholders' meeting in June 2000, Mattel stock was trading at $14.69 a share, down from a high of $46.75 reached in March 1998. According to Michael White of the Associated Press, the shareholders were looking for answers. "Eckert was grilled for about an hour [about] what he planned to do to restore the world's largest toy company to profitability." Eckert promised to strengthen core brands, bring in top management talent, and cut costs. Although he agreed with Barad's decision to move into high–tech toys, Eckert believed the Learning Co. was not the correct choice for such an endeavor. According to White's report, Eckert noted, "It was the execution that was flawed. It is clear consumers have become more adept at new technology. We need to capitalize on the opportunities that creates."

After less than a year as CEO, Eckert was earning cautious praise from analysts. In March 2001, Katherine Hobson of *U.S. News & World Report*, wrote, "[A]t Mattel. . . it may be too soon to promise a happy ending, but the new boss is enjoying a strong opening act. . . . [Eckert] is taking a back–to–basics approach to turn the company around: He's getting a handle on out–of–control costs, building business around perennially popular brands like Barbie, and keeping a lookout for that next must–have toy. So far, the reviews are good: in a gloomy market, Mattel stock just hit a 52–week high."

Eckert first addressed the issue of the Learning Co. In the end, Mattel basically dumped the company, getting no cash up front but agreeing to settle for a portion of future profits. Another area on which Eckert focused was increasing sales overseas. Global sales had declined for the three previous years, and Eckert was determined to do a better job moving into the vast untapped market of children outside the United States. According to Eckert, it is a matter of great importance, considering that Mattel's take from global sales makes up 30 percent of its revenue—translating into $1 billion from Western Europe alone. Eckert also devised a restructuring plan that implemented cost–cutting measures, including dissolving some unprofitable licensing agreements. Refocusing on Mattel's main product lines, Eckert pushed popular brands like Barbie, Hot Wheels, and Fisher–Price toys to the top of the priority list. Those three product lines alone produced $4.7 billion in sales in 2000.

Eckert has moved slowly but deliberately to stabilize the company, and he has offered conservative but

corporate staff by 150, and refinanced high–cost debt. He then refocused the company on the old standards, like Barbie and Hot Wheels. He also brokered a deal with Disney to provide toys based on Disney films. In 1991 Mattel estimated that 95 percent of all U.S. girls ages 3 to 11 owned at least one Barbie doll. In 1992 sales of Barbie products alone totaled $1 billion, over half of the company's total sales. Mattel continued to post larger profits and higher sales figures throughout much of the 1990s, and stock prices returned to the $40 range. However, the company stumbled badly after Amerman retired. Replaced as CEO by Jill Barad, known for her skills in marketing Barbie merchandise, the new chief promised more than she could fulfill in regard to earnings. She

positive outlooks to shareholders, preferring to over-achieve rather than overreach. William Nygren, a port-folio manager for a major shareholder, told the *Los Angeles Times*, "One of the best things Eckert has done is to refuse to set unattainable goals. You don't need to re–create this company every couple of years. We love those franchises—Barbie and Hot Wheels—they don't need to be transformed; they need to be nurtured." Eckert is the first to agree that the company's future lies in its past by learning from previous successes and failures. "What we need to do today is outperform the toy industry, not change the company," Eckert told the *Los Angeles Times*. "Every time we try to do something else, we haven't done it well. You know, we owned the circus once; that didn't work for us. We've ventured off into electronic games before. That didn't do well. We owned the software company; that didn't do well. I've got it three times, I've seen it and we're not going to give it a fourth time."

Social and Economic Impact

As part of cost–cutting measures, Mattel announced in April 2001 that it would close its last U.S. manufacturing site in Murray, Kentucky. The plant, which was opened in 1973 by Fisher–Price and was acquired in 1993 when Mattel purchased Fisher–Price, employed 980 workers, who manufactured approximately 10 percent of Mattel's preschool products. The plant and jobs were slated for relocation to Mexico. Like other toy manufacturers, Mattel depends on overseas production. Mattel has 15 factories in other countries, including Mexico, Indonesia, China, Malaysia, and Thailand.

Just a week after the news of the last U.S. Mattel factory relocation outside the country to save money, Mattel released information regarding Eckert's salary. According to the Associated Press, for the first seven months of his employment Eckert was paid more than $12.5 million in salary, bonuses, and stock grants. In addition, the company provided Eckert with a loan of $5.5 million that would be forgiven, along with interest, if Eckert remained with the company through May 18, 2004. The reports of the large amount of pay mixed badly in the media in light of Mattel laying off nearly 1,000 U.S. workers. Eckert benefited from the initial arrangement that provided that the majority of his compensation was tied to stock performance, basically tying Eckert's salary to how well he could turn the company around. As stock prices rose, so did Eckert's annual intake.

Improvement has been slow but steady. For the second quarter of 2001, Mattel reported a loss of $4.9 million. However, over the first two quarters of 2000, the loss of $38.9 million on net sales of $1.59 billion showed a considerable improvement compared to the same time period from the previous year in which the loss totaled

$165 million on net sales of $1.51 billion. By the end of the third quarter of 2001, the news was even better. The company posted a net profit of $199.8 million, compared to a net loss of $336.9 million during the same quarter of the previous year. The total for the first three quarters of 2001 showed a net income of $161 million, compared with a net loss of $502 million during the same period in 2000. On October 18, 2001, stock prices were $18.29 a share—nowhere near the all–time low of under $10, but also not yet close to the all–time high of mid–$40. But investors and analysts continue to remain confident in Eckert's ability to lead the company back to substantial profitability. A sluggish economy may prove his greatest obstacle.

Sources of Information

Contact at: Mattel, Inc.
333 Continental Blvd.
El Segundo, CA 90245–5012
Business Phone: (310)252–2000
URL: http://www.mattel.com

Bibliography

Dwyer, Steve. "No Disputing Kraft's Goal." *Prepared Foods*, May 1999. Available at http://www.preparedfoods.com.

Goldman, Abigail. "Mattel Will Shut Down Last U.S. Manufacturing Site." *Los Angeles Times*, 4 April 2001.

Goldman, Abigail. "Toy Repair Man: Mattel's New Chief, Robert Eckert, is Putting the Firm Back in Working Order by Returning to the Basics." *Los Angeles Times*, 15 April 2001.

Gornstein, Leslie. "Mattel Reports $4.9 Million Q2 Loss." *Associated Press*, 19 July 2001.

Hobson, Katherine. "Meet Corporate Turnaround Barbie." *U.S. News & World Report*, 5 March 2001.

"Mattel Chief Earned More Than $12.5 Million." *Associated Press*, 10 April 2001.

"Mattel, Inc." Hoover's Online, Inc., 2001. Available at http://www.hoovers.com.

Michaels, Adrian. "Mattel Names New Chief." *Financial Times*, 17 May 2000. Available at http://www.ft.com.

Montgomery, Bruce P. "Mattel, Inc." In Laura Whitely ed. *International Dictionary of Company Histories*. Vol. 25. Detroit: St. James Press, 1999.

Pruzan, Jeff. "Kraft's Big Cheese Tapped to Mend Mattel." *Financial Times*, 17 May 2000. Available at http://www.ft.com.

"Rebounding Mattel Inc. Reports Third Quarter Porfit." *Associated Press*, 18 October 2001.

"Robert A. Eckert." Mattel, Inc., 24 January 2002. Available at http://mattel.com/about_us/au_vision.asp#bio.

White, Michael. "New Mattel Boss Confronted by Angry Stockholders." *AP Newswire*.

Michael Eisner

(1942-)
Walt Disney Company

Overview

Entertainment executive Michael Eisner is the chief executive officer (CEO) of the Walt Disney Company. He began as an usher at NBC and eventually rose to such positions as head of prime time programming at ABC and president of Paramount Pictures before assuming control of Disney in 1984. Under his leadership, Disney became an entertainment superpower with record profits. Considered a great judge of talent and a shrewd businessman in a tough industry, Eisner is also known as a devoted family man.

Personal Life

Michael Dammann Eisner was born in Mt. Kisco, New York, the son of a well–to–do lawyer, and was raised in luxurious surroundings in his parents' spacious Park Avenue apartment in New York City. His early life was characterized by strict discipline and etiquette, which included wearing a jacket and tie for family dinners. Although raised in wealth, he learned early to treat money seriously. Eisner's father, Lester, was a Harvard graduate and a lawyer who successfully invested the existing family fortune in New York real estate. Lester Eisner also served as a top housing official in the Eisenhower administration.

Eisner and his sister were taught self–discipline early. Among other lessons, they were required to read each day for two hours for every one hour of television they watched. Eisner enjoyed reading "Hardy Boys" mysteries and the works of Jack London, and his televi-

sion favorites included *Hopalong Cassidy*, *Ozzie and Harriet*, and *Leave It to Beaver*. Entertainment for the Eisners often included Broadway, and Eisner marked every special occasion with a visit to the theater.

Eisner attended Lawrenceville School, an expensive New Jersey boarding school, where he was a good student. He tried sports but was largely unsuccessful. He belonged to the Periwig theatrical club and won a lead role in *The Caine Mutiny* as a senior, but illness forced him to withdraw.

After Lawrenceville School, Eisner enrolled in Denison University, a small liberal arts college in Granville, Ohio. His intention was to prepare for a medical career, but by his junior year, he was back in the theater. Shy and not particularly driven to be an actor, Eisner began writing plays. He is known to have completed two plays, one of which was produced by the school's thespian club. Eisner graduated from Denison in 1964.

Eisner and Jane Breckenridge were married in 1967. They have three sons, Breck, Eric, and Anders. Eisner is a well–known family man and prefers pictures of his family in business publications where others will use political shots with public figures. In the critical days leading to his election as chairman of Walt Disney Productions, he delayed meetings because of commitments to his sons.

Chronology:
Michael Eisner

1942: Born in Mt. Kisco, New York.

1964: Graduated from Denison University.

1966: Hired by Barry Diller at ABC.

1976: Named president of Paramount Pictures.

1984: Became chairman of the Walt Disney Company.

1986: Created international division of Disney.

1996: Disney acquired Capitol Cities/ABC company.

1998: Eisner's autobiography, *Work in Progress*, is published.

1999: Purchased InfoSeek and created Go.com.

2001: Number of Disney Channel subscribers reached 70 million.

Career Details

After college, Eisner made a trip to Paris, thinking he would be a writer. He returned home, however, in less than two weeks. Back in New York, he went to work at NBC where he took a job as a clerk who kept track of the number of times a commercial aired. He also worked weekends at an NBC radio station, giving out traffic reports. Not long afterward, Eisner moved to CBS, where he inserted commercials into their slots for children's programs, the *Ed Sullivan Show* and *Jeopardy*.

Somewhat dissatisfied with his career, Eisner sent out hundreds of resumes, looking for a break in the television business. That break came in 1966 when a young executive named Barry Diller called. Diller was only 24 years old but was already a vice president at ABC. At the time ABC was a small network, only about 10 years old and with only 24 affiliates around the country.

Eisner moved to ABC and worked with Diller on ABC's programming. Together, their innovations included the movie–of–the–week and the miniseries. Eisner genuinely enjoyed even the simple forms of popular programming such as sitcoms and cartoon shows. Thus, when he took over Saturday morning programming in 1969, he did not guess at what would sell, he just looked for what he liked to watch.

Eisner's first push for Saturday morning programming was a cartoon series based on the popular singing group, the Jackson Five. Soon, he added another, featur-

ing the singing Osmond Brothers. Within three years, ABC was the top–rated network on Saturday mornings. Within five years, Eisner was put in charge of ABC's prime time schedule, where he was responsible for such hits as *Happy Days* and *Welcome Back Kotter*. Even though the critics complained, the shows were successful and the ratings improved. Eisner understood that the core elements that worked for Saturday morning programming were universal: the importance of the story line, character development, and conflict.

He also was responsible for some serious work at ABC such as the miniseries *Roots* and *Rich Man/Poor Man*. ABC emerged while Eisner was head of programming at the top–rated network, but Eisner had already left for greener pastures.

In 1976 Eisner joined Paramount Pictures, where Diller was the chairman and Eisner became president. Paramount was not a strong company, which is why the parent, Gulf Western, brought in the two successful ABC executives. Paramount had not had a hit movie for several years and lost money. Within a year, Paramount produced *Saturday Night Fever*, and a string of successful movies were to follow that included *Raiders of the Lost Ark*, *Bad News Bears*, *Grease*, *Heaven Can Wait*, and *Beverly Hills Cop*. Two years after Eisner joined Paramount, the studio led the "big seven" studios with nearly one quarter of national box office proceeds.

For six years, Paramount never fell below second in market share. However, two events in 1984 changed Eis-

Michael Eisner. *(AP/Wide World Photos.)*

ner's career direction in a dramatic way. First, his mentor and supporter at Paramount, Gulf Western's chairman Charlie Bluhdorn, died. Bluhdorn's successor, Martin Davis, did not think as highly of Diller and Eisner. Davis has been quoted as complaining that Eisner was not "serious" enough and was "like a kid." Diller had his problems with Davis, too, and left to become chairman at 20th Century Fox.

The second event of 1984 was the culmination of two decades of problems and drift at Walt Disney Productions. Walt Disney had started the company in the late 1920s and, after a few false starts, had found success with the animated character Mickey Mouse. Together with his brother Roy, Disney had built an entertainment giant. Walt Disney's sudden death in 1966 had deprived the company of not only its chairman but of its heart and soul. Using Walt's creative genius and his brother Roy's business acumen, the company had been successful. Yet, like many family–operated businesses, there had been little effort made to groom executives to succeed the founders.

The aftermath of Disney's death was a slowing of growth and, eventually, stagnation in the Disney empire. Attendance dropped in the company's theme parks, and movie production faltered. Earnings dropped, and constant fighting between the "Walt" and "Roy" factions paralyzed the company. While the conflict was visibly between the two arms of the Disney family, the fight was actually between the creative people (Walt) and the administrators (Roy). This fighting actually paralleled conflicts that had existed between the two brothers for years, only now it threatened to destroy their dream.

Disney of the early 1980s was ripe for corporate raiders and take–overs. In the Wall Street climate of the time, it was not uncommon for companies in Disney's condition to be taken over by speculators who would then break up the company and sell the parts for huge profits. Several such profiteers were buying up Disney stock or making overtures to the company and its major stockholders. Disney insiders, including Roy Disney's son, also named Roy, were intent on saving the company.

A group that became known as the "brain trust" was formed. The members of the trust were Roy Disney, Frank Wells, a consultant to Warner Brothers, and Stanley Gold, a Disney board member who ran Roy's company, Shamrock Holdings. The three set out to find a new manager for the company who would restore it to a position of strength, if not to its past glory. Eisner was a leading candidate from the beginning and was seen as articulate, imaginative, enthusiastic, and with values complementary to the company's family identity. It was thought that Walt Disney himself would have loved him.

A protracted battle ensued and, ultimately, then–current chief executive Ron Miller, who was Walt Disney's son–in–law, was fired. Frank Wells was considered a candidate for the top spot, but he recommended Eisner. Finally, with the intervention of major stockholder Sid Bass, a compromise team of Eisner as chairman and CEO and Wells as president was proposed.

Stanley Gold, who was point man for the "brain trust," pushed this team hard. According to Gold, Eisner's reputation as a creative person and a "big kid" was perfect for the head of Disney. Gold said that the problem with Disney since Walt died was that the place had not been run by "crazies." It "needed to be run by crazies again," and Eisner was the man for the job. With the strong businessman Wells as Eisner's partner, Gold was promoting the same type of team that had built Disney in the first place: Walt (Eisner) as the creative "crazy" that drove the company forward while Roy (Wells) applied the common sense and occasional braking that was necessary to satisfy the bankers and Wall Street. Gold's efforts, with Sid Bass's vocal support, proved to be very successful.

Eisner was appointed chairman and CEO of Walt Disney Productions on September 22, 1984. Wells became president, and the new team was off and running to reestablish the Walt Disney Company as the premier entertainment company in America. New blood was brought into the management team, many from Eisner's old company, Paramount. The Disney film archives were utilized to their fullest capacity, the theme parks were restored to profitability with attendance again rising annually, the animation division of Disney returned to making feature–length films, and the stock value rose dramatically.

Over the first decade of Eisner's term as chairman and CEO, Disney produced a string of movie hits including *Down and Out in Beverly Hills* in 1986, *Who Framed Roger Rabbit* in 1988, *The Little Mermaid* in 1989, and *Beauty and the Beast* in 1991. *Aladdin*, the first animated feature to be nominated for an Academy Award for best picture, was released in 1992. Disney has produced a major animated feature nearly every year and got back into television with the hit show *The Golden Girls* and a revised feature, the *Disney Sunday Movie*.

Eisner spearheaded other ventures including a new amusement park, Euro Disney, which opened outside of Paris, although it has never brought in the expected revenues since its opening day in 1993. Disney also acquired independent film company Miramax to produce more offbeat films, and in 1996 Disney purchased Capital Cities, which owned ABC Television and the cable sports network ESPN. Almost 20 years after heading ABC's prime time programming, Eisner now headed the company that owned the network.

Eisner assumed added responsibilities at Disney in 1994 when Wells died tragically in a helicopter crash. For a time, Eisner replaced him with entertainment executive Michael Ovitz, but Ovitz spent just 16 ill–fated months at the network before leaving; many top Disney executives departed as well. Eisner also fought a rather vicious public battle with Jeffrey Katzenberg, a top Disney executive since the early 1980s. Katzenberg departed to become a founding partner in DreamWorks SKG, a studio and multimedia venture with Steven Spielberg and David Geffen. He later filed a lawsuit against Disney, requesting $580 million in compensation. The figure was based on future earnings promised to him by the late Wells for Disney films and other projects that he had developed; the suit was reportedly settled for $250 million.

Under Eisner's direction, greater emphasis has been placed on the construction and operation of company hotels at the theme parks and a cruise ship line is in operation. Merchandising and licensing agreements also brought in steady revenues, with over 700 Disney retail stores on three continents. Disney now owns a professional hockey team named after a modest Disney movie hit, the *Mighty Ducks*, and it has acquired the Anaheim Angels baseball team.

In 2001, with 15 years as chairman and CEO of Walt Disney behind him, Eisner continued to think of Disney as a small family company—though the term family had more to do with the type of entertainment it produced than with who owned the company. And it was not small. In the five years previous, penetration of The Disney Channel rose from 12 million to 70 million US households.

Nevertheless, in 1999, Disney's unbroken record of double–digit annual growth was interrupted as net income dropped from $1.85 billion a year earlier to $1.3 billion. Disney's internet business had suffered increased losses, the consumer products division was stalled, and the film business was struggling with high costs and a saturated market.

In 2000 it was only the company's theme parks/resorts and media networks that were making money. In response to the bad news, Eisner attempted to improve communications, scheduled regular earnings teleconferences, and gave the press greater access. Still, Disney's net profits for 2000 managed to rise by 30 percent. With a new theme park poised to open in California, another near completion in Tokyo, and projects under way in France and Hong Kong, Eisner felt that predictions of more bad news for the company were overdrawn. But in the spring of 2001, Eisner sent out pink slips to 4,000 of his 120,000 full–time employees in an effort to eliminate between $500 million to $850 million from Disney's annual cost structure by fiscal year 2003.

After the terrorist attacks on the World Trade Center and the Pentagon on September 11, 2001, Eisner's company took a major hit on two fronts. First, ABC's advertising dollars decreased because of the stalled economy and because the network maintained many hours of continuous coverage without running commercials. In an interview with the *Financial Times*, Eisner commented: "You don't have to be a genius to figure out that getting zero is not as good as getting something." However, he did note that in the month after the tragedies, advertising dollars were starting to firm up. Second, after the terrorist attacks, the tourism industry fell over drastically, significantly impacting profits at Disneyland and Disney World. By October 2001, Disney had announced that it would cut the hours of some 7,400 employees. Eisner is working hard to maintain the confidence of big investors; nonetheless, stock prices have fallen since September 11. Eisner must also reevaluate the feasibility of purchasing the Fox Family network, a deal first struck in July 2001, which Eisner has since reconsidered due to the sluggish economy.

Social and Economic Impact

Eisner's style is at once casual and friendly, but he is also hardworking, driven, and tough. His creative talent is unquestioned and has served him well, yet there are many stories around the entertainment industry of shrewd deals he has struck to make a movie and attention to detail in the financial end of the business. Eisner understands the need to let the creative juices flow, but he tempers this with the realization that the business must make a profit. In Hollywood, this has turned out to be a very successful formula, and his successes were detailed in his 1998 autobiography, *Work In Progress*.

Eisner is willing to pay the necessary salaries and fees to make use of top talent in Hollywood. This was a radical departure from the older Disney practice of being quite lean in the compensation department. Eisner understood the need to pay top dollar for the services of the likes of George Lucas, but at the same time he looks for promising newcomers that will become the next wave of creative talent in Hollywood.

The strategy has been to make maximum use of the company's strengths in name recognition, reputation, and assets while diversifying into other aspects of the entertainment industry. The growing number of hotel rooms under the Disney name, the cruise ship line, and the sports franchises are examples of this expansion into related areas upon which the Disney name can be capitalized.

For Disney in the twenty–first century, Eisner predicts great revenue potential in DVD sales—just as the launch of its stable of animated classics on Disney Home Video had coincided with the boom in VCR sales in the 1980s—and was eagerly expanding the company's Internet presence. After the purchase of search engine InfoSeek in the summer of 1999, Disney then merged its Internet holdings, which included ABCNews.com, into Go.com, a "portal" in competition to America Online and the Microsoft Network.

Eisner looked forward to a new era for Disney's Internet presence as more households became wired with high–speed Internet connections. "You must have sports and news and entertainment, or you are going to be a Western Union messenger in a fax world," he told Gunther. Consumers would be able to bring Disney content into their homes directly through the site, making premium cable channels and video rental and retail outlets obsolete. "I believe the entire company's product will mostly be distributed through the Internet," Eisner said in the *Fortune* interview with Gunther. New Disney theme parks in Tokyo and Hong Kong were in the works, and many were surprised by Disney's unusual foray into yet another medium: Broadway. The musical version of the *Lion King* was a surprise hit of the 1999 season.

Sources of Information

Contact at: Walt Disney Company
1500 S. Buena Vista St.
Burbank, CA 91521–0001
Business Phone: (818) 560–1000
URL: http://www.disney.com

Bibliography

Fabrikant, Geraldine. "Top Mouse." *New York Times*, 8 November 1998.

Grimes, Christopher, and Robert Thomson. "Disney's Eisner Sees U.S. Television Ad Recovery." *The Financial Times*, 16 October 2001. Available at http://www.ft.com.

Gunther, Marc. *Fortune*, 6 September 1999.

Harding, James. "Disney to Pay Less for Fox Family." *The Financial Times*, 23 October 2001. Available at http://www.ft.com.

"An Interview with Michael D. Eisner." *American Academy of Achievement*, 17 June 1994. Available at http://www.achievement.org.

La Franco, Robert. "Eisner's Bumpy Ride." *Forbes*, 5 July 1999.

Lockwood, Lisa. "Disney Gets Stake In Us Weekly." *WWD*, 28 February 2001.

Mermigas, Diane, and Michelle Greppi. "Disney to cut staff, costs." *Electronic Media*, 2 April 2001.

"Michael D. Eisner: Biography." *American Academy of Achievement, 1998*. Available at http://www.achievement.org.

"Michael D. Eisner, Entertainment Executive." *American Academy of Achievement, 1998*. Available at http://www.achievement.org.

Orwall, Bruce. "Disney's Eisner Seeks to Revive Magic in His Kingdom—He Aims to Assure Employees, Investors Company Will Weather Tough Conditions." *Wall Street Journal*, 5 October 2001.

Parkes, Christopher, and James Harding. "Eisner's Odyssey." *The Financial Times*, 29 January 2001.

Poole, Oliver. "Disney Parks Suffer as Scared Tourists Stay Away." *The Daily Telegraph*, 26 October 2001.

Rublin, Lauren. "Mouse Momentum." *Barron's*, 15 November 1999.

Schurr, Amanda. "A free man in Paris, and a mighty mouse." *Sarasota Herald Tribune*, 28 April 2000.

Streisand, Betty. "Shareholders Smell a Rat." *U.S. News and World Report*, 3 March 1997.

"Walt Disney Company." *Hoover's Online*. 2001. Available at http://www.hoovers.com.

Wetlaufer, Suzy. "Common Sense and Conflict." *Harvard Business Review*, January/February 2000.

Larry Ellison

(1944-)

Oracle Corporation

Overview

A pioneer in the relational database industry, Larry Ellison and two associates founded Oracle Corporation in 1977. The trio had been inspired by a 1976 white paper released by IBM Research in which the potential of the relational database management system (RDBMS) was assessed. Such database systems store information in related tables, allowing the user to view the same data in many different ways. Ellison, partnered with Bob Miner and Ed Oates, following the example set forth in IBM's research paper, decided to develop a database system that could handle ad hoc queries and launched Oracle as the corporate vehicle for their project. Existing database systems all required specific programming for each individual query. Oracle beat IBM to market with a saleable RDBMS product by the early 1980s. Although the company experienced ups and downs, some related to Oracle's tendency to rush to market with new products before they were exhaustively tested, by 1993 Oracle commanded slightly more than a third of the RDBMS market. Oracle, the second largest independent software company and the leading supplier of information management software in the world, reported worldwide sales of nearly $10.9 billion in fiscal 2001, ending May 31, 2001.

Personal Life

As daring and flamboyant in the workplace as he is away from the executive suite, Larry Ellison has earned a reputation as an enigmatic control freak, a wildly ambitious man who is never so happy as when he's bask-

Larry Ellison, introducing Oracle 9i at the Oracle World Conference. (AP/Wide World

Photos/Paul Skuma.)

ing in the spotlight. With three failed marriages behind him, Ellison has been talking for some time of marriage with Melanie Craft, whom he's dated for several years. The Oracle wizard has two children from previous marriages.

Ellison was born in New York City in 1944 and was adopted shortly after his birth by Chicago accountant Louis Ellison and his wife. Young Ellison was raised amid the tenements of Chicago's South Side by his adoptive parents, both Russian Jewish immigrants. Although he was never a particularly eager student, Ellison did show a remarkable talent for science and mathematics.

In the early 1960s, he attended college at both the University of Chicago and the University of Illinois but moved to California's Silicon Valley before he had accumulated enough credits to graduate.

When not in the relative safety of his executive suite at Oracle, Ellison keeps mighty busy with feats of derring–do that would probably intimidate most other businessmen his age. An avid yachtsmen, he sailed the *Sayonara*, his 80–foot yacht, to victory in the annual Australian race from Sydney to Hobart in 1999. Other sailors in the competition were not so lucky; four lost their lives when some of the competing vessels hit a major swell. Although no one disputes Ellison's courage, as demonstrated in some of his recreational feats away from the job, many have suggested that the Oracle executive takes unnecessary chances with his safety. One such incident came in 1992 in Hawaii when he plunged head–first into an enormous wave, despite the presence of red warning flags up and down the beach. The experience cost Ellison a broken neck, punctured lung, and assorted other injuries. To make matters worse, he took a tumble from a bicycle during his recuperation, fracturing an elbow.

Career Details

After attending college, Ellison took a job in 1967 with Amdahl Corporation in Sunnyvale, California. The company provides integrated computing solutions for information technology users, and in his four years with Amdahl, Ellison worked his way up to system architect before leaving to go to Memorex Products Inc. in 1972.

A white paper released by IBM Research in 1976 served as the inspiration for Ellison's big move the following year. The IBM report explored the potential of the relational database management system (RDBMS), an innovative concept in the mid–1970s. Unlike the traditional database, which requires unique programming to handle each query, the relational database is able to field ad hoc queries. Because the information within the relational database is stored in tables, the data may be viewed in a wide variety of ways. Teaming up with two close associates, Bob Miner and Ed Oates, Ellison in May 1977 founded a small company they dubbed Software Development Laboratories to develop such a database. The company's name was later changed to Relational Technologies and finally to Oracle Corporation. Ellison's initial investment in the venture was $2,000. Within a year of the company's founding, Ellison was named president and chief executive officer.

The decision to develop and market a relational database pitted Oracle and its trio of cofounders in a contest against IBM, a formidable foe to say the least. But it was clearly a case of David defeating Goliath, as tiny Oracle managed to develop a product by the early 1980s, besting giant IBM by about three years. And, even better,

Oracle's database was scalable, making it usable with a wide variety of hardware, and portable, allowing it to be moved between different computer operating systems. The Oracle RDBMS caught on quickly with computer users, including the Central Intelligence Agency, which signed a major contract for Oracle's system.

Ellison in 1987 bought into nCube, a manufacturer of advanced symmetrical multiprocessors (SMP). By the end of the 1980s, Oracle products supported the nCube platform. Only a few years later, nCube had managed to stake a claim to roughly two–thirds of Japan's multi-processor market and was doing land–office business with such notable global corporations as Shell Oil and BMW.

One of the consistent complaints about Oracle in its early years was its tendency to rush to market with products before they had been thoroughly tested. Such a case occurred in 1990 when Oracle 6.0 was released. Customer reports that the product was unstable and flaky soon swamped the company's headquarters, and Oracle's accounts receivable soared to more than $65 million, roughly 48 percent of annual sales. The company went back to the drawing board and emerged with Oracle 7.0, a product that successfully addressed most of the problems users had encountered with Oracle 6.0. This managed to pull Oracle away from the brink and helped to push the company to a 34 percent share of the global RDBMS market, substantially ahead of IBM with 26 percent.

Ellison has often been compared by critics and admirers alike to Bill Gates of Microsoft, particularly for his somewhat eccentric behavior. In a 1995 interview with *PC Week,* he dismissed the suggestion that he was eccentric or "a Bill Gates wannabe." Ellison sometimes refers to his arch–rival as "the PC Pope."

"Eccentric? Me eccentric?" Ellison said. "Silly. Certainly I want Oracle to be the largest software company in the world. If I don't, they should get rid of me. That's my job. It's more fun being first than being second. As far as Microsoft is concerned, Microsoft had the benefit and cooperation with IBM for a decade. We [fought] IBM every step of the way. Let's just see what happens. We're growing 50 percent a year. We're very optimistic about our future."

During the late 1990s, Ellison was particularly outspoken about what he described as the "patently illegal" business practices of Microsoft. During a press conference in mid–1998 at the Harvard Conference on Internet and Society, the Oracle CEO blasted Microsoft's "absolute monopoly."

"Think about it," Ellison told reporters. "If you want to build computers, you've got to ask Bill's permission. If Bill wanted to triple the price on Windows, what would you do? You'd pay; you wouldn't have any choice."

Although Ellison has been an extremely vocal critic of Microsoft's business tactics, he came out strongly against government moves to break up the software gi-

Chronology:
Larry Ellison

1944: Born.

1967: Went to work for Amdahl, advancing to system architect.

1972: Began work for Memorex.

1977: Founded Oracle Corporation with two associates.

1978: Named President and CEO of Oracle.

1987: Purchased interest in nCube, manufacturer of a symmetrical multiprocessor.

1990: Company released Oracle 6.0 software.

1992: Injured seriously in beach accident in Hawaii.

1993: Oracle had won 34 percent of global RDBMS market.

2001: Personal wealth estimated at $26 billion by *Forbes.*

ant, contending that market forces could do the job. During the course of Microsoft's lengthy antitrust trial, Ellison, speaking at the San Francisco Bay Area Council's Outlook Conference in January 1999, predicted that in time the personal computer "would become a peripheral product to the Internet, regardless of the antitrust trial." This, he suggested, would bring a market dominated by open standards, effectively ending Microsoft's monopoly. Although District Court Judge Thomas Penfield Jackson ordered in 2000 that Microsoft be broken up, that order was reversed in June 2001 by the U.S. Appeals Court for the District of Columbia, which ordered a retrial.

While there can be little doubt of Ellison's genius for business, critics continue to take potshots at some of his less brilliant moves over the years. The Oracle CEO has acquired a reputation for promising customers products with features that don't even exist and then demanding that Oracle's development team create such products in record time. He's also come under fire for hiring employees who are less than ideally qualified for the positions they must fill. Inside Oracle, some employees in the sales department express unhappiness at some of Ellison's demands for unrealistic increases in the company's sales.

None of this criticism seems to bother Ellison unduly, not surprising in a man who has managed to build a tiny start–up. Ellison's personal fortunes took a pretty serious hit in the early years of the new millennium, due in large part to a general decline in stock prices and an extremely sharp downturn in the high–tech sector. Although *Forbes* magazine in 2000 ranked Ellison as the nation's second wealthiest American with a net worth of $47 billion, by 2001, he fallen to fourth in the *Forbes* rankings with a net worth estimated at only $26 billion. It's doubtful, however, that Ellison is losing any sleep over this temporary slump in his personal fortune.

In the wake of the September 11, 2001, terrorist attacks on the World Trade Center in New York and the Pentagon outside Washington, D.C., Ellison called on the federal government to create a national identification card system. To sweeten his proposal, Ellison offered to donate the software needed to implement such a program, which would involve the fingerprinting of millions of Americans. Such information would then be digitized and embedded on a magnetic strip of the individual's photo ID card. Airport security officials could then use the information to verify the identity of air travelers.

Social and Economic Impact

Ellison's contribution as a pioneer in the relational database industry has been enormous. Oracle Corporation, the company he founded along with Bob Miner and Ed Oates, is now the second largest independent software company in the world and the world's largest supplier of information management software. In the process of building Oracle into the giant that it is, Ellison himself has become one of the wealthiest men in the world, an incredible feat for a college drop–out raised in the tenements of Chicago's South Side. Despite his foibles and eccentricities, of which there are many, he has proved beyond a shadow of a doubt that he is a brilliant businessman, willing to take big risks in his quest for big gains.

It should hardly be surprising that a man of Ellison's stature—incredibly colorful and larger than life—could be guilty of some incredible excesses. Just such an excess surfaced in mid–2000 when Ellison admitted that he had hired some private investigators to sift through the garbage of groups defending Oracle's arch–rival Microsoft. Ellison hinted that his band of probers had uncovered evidence that Microsoft was covertly financing "front groups" in an attempt to sway public opinion in the software giant's favor. He defended his private investigation as Oracle's "civic duty."

In June of 2001, Ellison announced his intention to establish an institute to study the impact of technology on politics and economics. Among the educational institutions believed to be in the running for the money were Stanford and Harvard.

Sources of Information

Contact at: Oracle Corporation
    500 Oracle Parkway
    Redwood Shores, CA 94065
    Business Phone: (650) 506–7000
    URL: http://www.oracle.com

Bibliography

Dodge, John, and Wendy Pickering. "Q and A with Oracle's Larry Ellison." *PC Week*, 24 July 1995.

Hamm, Steve. "The Outrageous Enigma of Silicon Valley." *Business Week*, 26 November 1997.

Read, Stuart. *The Oracle Edge*. Avon, MA: Adams Media, 1999.

Weil, Nancy. "Ellison Calls Microsoft Business Patterns 'Patently Illegal.'" *PC World*, 29 May 1998.

Wilson, Mike. *The Difference between God and Larry Ellison*. New York: William Morrow & Co., 1998.

Roger Enrico

(1945-)
PepsiCo

Overview

Roger Enrico, chief executive officer (CEO) of PepsiCo Inc., is credited with using brand–building to increase sales for the soft drink company and its affiliates. Enrico ran the company with a flair for the dramatic and a keen knack for image–making and profit building.

Personal Life

Enrico was born in 1945 in Chisolm, Minnesota, where his father was a maintenance foreman at an iron–ore processing plant. When Enrico was in high school, his first job was at a local soft drink bottling plant. At the time, he could never have anticipated how soft drinks would ultimately factor into his future. Enrico was an average student, mostly preoccupied with leaving Minnesota. An offer of a full scholarship to Babson College in Massachusetts gave him the chance he was looking for.

While at college, Enrico ran his fraternity and edited the college yearbook; he graduated in three years. Although he had not given much thought to his future, Enrico realized he enjoyed interacting with people, and working in the area of human resource seemed like a logical career choice. He was hired by General Mills to fill an opening in Minnesota. There, he reunited with his high school sweetheart, Rosemary Margo, whom he later married.

What seemed like a good career match turned out to be otherwise. Enrico was bored by the isolation of the personnel division and considered pursuing an MBA. In-

Roger Enrico (right) with Gordon Radley announcing a marketing deal between Pepsi and Star Wars. (AP/Wide World Photos.)

stead, he attempted to join the navy, but that did not work out either because he failed the navy's test for color-blindness. Not wanting to remain stateside, Enrico volunteered for service in Vietnam in 1967. He was stationed in the northern part of South Vietnam and worked transporting fuel. When he returned from Vietnam, Enrico was hired again by General Mills, this time in their brand management division. Although he loved the work, he felt he was passed over for promotions because of his lack of educational credentials. He began sending his resume to headhunters across the country and was offered a job with the Frito–Lay division of PepsiCo in Dallas. Initially, Enrico was wary about moving to Dallas be-

cause of the lingering memories of the recent assassination of President John F. Kennedy, for whom he had once campaigned. Enrico was able to put that behind him when he recognized that both Dallas and Frito–Lay were on the brink of enormous growth.

Enrico and Rosemary have one son, Aaron. The couple enjoys vacationing on Grand Cayman, and Enrico is an avid scuba diver. The couple also owns a ranch in Montana. While in Turkey in 1990, Enrico suffered a heart attack during a company tour. It was a sobering experience for the executive, prompting him to give up smoking.

Career Details

When he first began to work for PepsiCo, Enrico was an associate brand manager for Frito–Lay's onion–flavored snacks, Funyuns. Enrico enjoyed working at Frito–Lay, and when he was 31, he was offered the job of president of PepsiCo Foods Japan. Japan was known to be a difficult and in many ways bewildering market, but Enrico accepted the challenge, as it would be a valuable learning experience.

Despite Enrico's efforts, the Japanese venture was unsuccessful, but PepsiCo understood the difficulties and challenges of that market and did not hold that experience against Enrico. First, he was reassigned to Brazil and then returned to the company's marketing division in the United States. The company's then–president, John Scully, appreciated Enrico's aggressive marketing views. When Scully left the company to take over Apple Computer, Enrico was appointed to his position. He remained president and CEO of beverages from 1983 to 1986. During that time, he began the Pepsi Challenge, forcing long-time rival Coca–Cola to come up with New Coke. Ultimately, his marketing idea boosted Pepsi sales.

In 1986 Enrico's book, *The Other Guy Blinked: How Pepsi Won the Cola Wars*, was panned by critics who regarded Enrico as nothing more than an ego–driven executive. The experience made him leery of the media, and he now shies away from press interviews. It also created additional tension between the two rival companies.

From 1991 to 1993, Enrico worked as chairman and CEO of Frito–Lay and Pepsi Foods International. There, he encouraged the company to push forward with a line of healthy snacks and slashed domestic operations.

In 1994, Enrico took over the position he would hold until he was appointed to CEO job—corporate vice chairman and CEO of Worldwide restaurants, a weak division in the corporate structure. Enrico began streamlining measures and reducing the number of units. The division had a 19 percent profit increase, with savings from operations estimated at more than $200 million. All of this was spearheaded by Enrico.

Not surprisingly, Enrico's efforts had come under the approving scrutiny from PepsiCo's board of directors over the years, and in 1996 he was tapped to take over as CEO when the company's top boss, Wayne Calloway, was diagnosed with prostate cancer. It took Enrico two weeks to decide whether or not he wanted to accept the position, as he was not sure that he wanted the responsibility that a CEO shoulders. The job, he once said, was nothing he had ever aspired to. Financially, PepsiCo made it worth his while, and he accepted. In 1997 Enrico was given a total compensation package of $2.8 million, which included his $900,000 base salary, plus bonuses.

Not long after taking over, Enrico guided the company through a rather spectacular loss: PepsiCo Interna-

Chronology:
Roger Enrico

1945: Born.

1972: Hired at Frito–Lay.

1991: Appointed chairman and chief executive officer of Frito–Lay and Pepsi Foods.

1994: Named corporate vice chairman and chief of Worldwide Restaurants with PepsiCo.

1996: Appointed CEO at PepsiCo.

1997: Divested PepsiCo of its restaurant holdings.

1998: Acquired Tropicana for $3.3 billion; donated salary to scholarship fund.

2001: Left PepsiCo.

tional's bottler in Venezuela, headed by an old friend of his, decided to switch to Coca–Cola. It was a well–publicized defection, symbolic of the company's continued losses in its overseas operations. Yet Enrico also moved quickly to reorganize management and revamp strategic planning processes inside Pepsi headquarters, forcing its sometimes too–dynamic executives to concentrate less on acquisition and more on performance. "I want to make sure that we walk the talk around here, not just on philosophy, but on implementation," Enrico told *Time* writer Frank Gibney, Jr.

Under Enrico, Pepsi continued to evolve. It spun off its entire bottling operations into an independent company, a move that mirrored the highly successful Coca–Cola strategy. The manufacturing and marketing of carbonated beverages is profitable, but the mixing, bottling, and distribution is far less so. "It's a better mousetrap," admitted Enrico cheerfully in the interview with Gibney about copying Coca–Cola. "And there's no pride in this, so why not do it ourselves?"

In the summer of 1998, PepsiCo announced the largest acquisition in company history and one that would further fuel the rivalry with Coca–Cola: Pepsi acquired juice maker Tropicana. With this $3.3 billion purchase from Seagram Co., Pepsi now entered the "orange juice wars" with Coca–Cola, owner of Minute Maid. "This fits in with what we want to be, a company of big brands staying within the beverage and snack business," the *New York Times* reported Enrico as saying upon announcement of the deal. "This is a company that is in great shape.

It's not broken. I think we can add to it, and it will be additive as we go forward." Just a year later, the move resulted in enviable combined retail sales—$11 billion worth of Pepsi, Tropicana, and Frito–Lay snacks.

The company also launched a new Pepsi ad campaign called Generation Next, and introduced a diet drink, Pepsi One. Just two years after Enrico took over as CEO, the soft–drink maker had regained a bit of precious territory in the cola wars: PepsiCo's 1998 sales climbed nearly 7 percent over the previous year, to $22.3 billion.

In late 2000, PepsiCo announced that Roger Enrico would relinquish his role of CEO before the end of 2001 and that he would retire as chairman before the end of 2002. His designated replacement in both capacities would be Steve Reinemund, then president and chief operating officer of the company. But things went more quickly than planned, and by May 2001 both transitions had been completed.

At the beginning of 2001, Enrico was still contemplating his post–PepsiCo career. "If I planned it now, it wouldn't be much of an adventure," Enrico said, as he prepared to turn over the reins of the company to his successor.

Enrico once noted that upon first being appointed CEO, he hoped that he would have the wisdom not to stay on too long, and the perseverance to stay long enough to achieve his goals, which chiefly included restructuring the company and refocusing its activities on the food and beverage market. And true to form, during his tenure as CEO, PepsiCo's restaurant division and bottling operations were both established as independent public companies.

Key accomplishments during his tenure as CEO included beating out rival Coke in the acquisition of SoBe beverages, Quaker Oats, and Gatorade. In Enrico's final year as CEO of PepsiCo, he oversaw increases in operating profits for Pepsi–Cola of North America and Tropicana, which grew 8 percent and 32 percent, respectively.

Social and Economic Impact

Shortly after Enrico took over the CEO position from his relatively staid predecessor, he went into the ballroom of the Laguna Niguel, California Ritz Carlton escorted by a phalanx of white uniformed Star Wars storm troopers. As trumpets blared, Enrico took the stage and announced a coup: PepsiCo would join with George Lucas to promote the 1997 re–release of the smash science fiction trilogy, *Star Wars*. It was a heady moment for the beverage company accustomed to trailing behind rival Coca–Cola. It was also a moment which embodied Enrico's style and his energy.

In a company that values autonomy, Enrico was well suited for the CEO position. Beginning in 1997, he began divesting PepsiCo of its restaurant interests into an independent company. These included over 28,000 Taco Bell, Kentucky Fried Chicken, and Pizza Hut outlets. By doing this, Enrico created a restaurant operation second only to McDonalds. He also elevated the Frito–Lay division of the company, which Enrico has said is like "the Coke of snack foods without a Pepsi."

In a reflection of his personal values about the importance of education, Enrico announced in early 1998 that he would forego his $900,000 salary to contribute the sum to PepsiCo's employee scholarship fund, which provides educational money for employees earning less than $60,000 a year. As Enrico said in a company–wide memo, he had requested that the board cut his salary to just $1 a year and "consider using the savings to benefit our front–line employees," according to the Associated Press. Front–line employees, in corporate lingo, are those who have a hands–on connection to the product itself—in PepsiCo's case, those who bottle, ship, and distribute the soft drink and its auxiliary products. The board agreed to add $1 million to the scholarship fund. Enrico, who still received a $1.8 million bonus for 1997, planned to make the contribution an ongoing one, as a way "to say thanks to our often unsung heroes."

Sources of Information

Contact at: PepsiCo
   700 Anderson Hill Rd.
   Purchase, NY 10577
   Business Phone: (914) 253–2000
   URL: http://www.pepsico.com

Bibliography

"The Advertising Council Names PepsiCo Chairman and CEO as 48th Public Service Award Honoree." The Advertising Council, 26 March 2001. Available at http://www.adcouncil.org.

"Enrico Steps into Pepsi Spotlight." *Beverage Industry*, April 1996.

Gibney, Frank, Jr. "Pepsi Gets Back in the Game." *Time*, 26 April 1999.

Hays, Constance L. "PepsiCo to Pay $3.3 Billion for Tropicana." *New York Times*, 21 July 1998.

"PepsiCo Details Succession Plan." *MMR*, 16 October 2000.

"PepsiCo's Reinemund is New Chairman, CEO as Transition Speeds Up." *The Wall Street Journal*, 3 May 2001.

"Roger A. Enrico." *Business Week*, 8 January 2001.

Emilio Estefan, Jr.

(1953-)
Crescent Moon Studios

Overview

Known as the "godfather of the Miami sound," five–time Grammy winner and singer–producer Emilio Estefan, Jr., has brought Latin music and musicians into the mainstream of American culture. Due to his signature fusion of Latin music and rhythm along with English lyrics, Estefan is one of the most influential voices in contemporary pop music. Through the doors of his $200 million corporation and state–of–the–art Crescent Moon Studios have passed some top recording stars, including Madonna, Ricky Martin, Jon Secada, Marc Antony, Jennifer Lopez, Shakira, Will Smith, Alejandro Fernandez, and others. Estefan is the creator and organizer of the Miami Sound Machine, which also includes his wife, Gloria Estefan, as lead female singer. Through their own music empire, Estefan Enterprises ("the Motown of Latin Music"), the Estefans have also delved into writing and composing, producing, sound and video production and recording, filming, restaurants, and a magazine.

Personal Life

Estefan's success started when he arrived in Miami, a refugee from Cuba at the age of 14. He left Cuba when he was 13, but spent a year and a half in Spain first. Unable to speak a word of English, Estefan found comfort in music—the universal communicator. His first musical instrument was an accordion, given to him when he was 12. His older brother was an engineer, so young Estefan became the brunt of family jokes as the "black sheep" who was going to be a "musician." He belonged to a band

Emilio Estefan, Jr. being interviewed before the first annual Latin Grammys award show.
(Reuters NewMedia Inc./Corbis.)

in Cuba, and when he moved to Spain and the U.S., began playing in restaurants for tips. This was to pay back the $474 his uncle had lent to him for the accordion.

In Miami, Estefan started work as an office boy for the rum importer Bacardi. In the evenings, he attended night school. He would stop to play music in the restaurant almost everyday, and on weekends would play at parties. Unable to afford music lessons, he taught himself to play "by ear." One of his friends at Bacardi advised him that the company was hosting a party and was looking for a band. The friend suggested that Estefan come, and bring two friends. Estefan did exactly that, appearing with a conga player and a guitarist, and bringing his own accordion. They were a big hit, playing mostly old dance music from Cuba, and several bookings for private parties followed.

In 1975, Estefan formed a group called the Miami Latin Boys. He was the band's drummer, and they played traditional Cuban music with a distinctive contemporary flair. They continued to play mostly at weddings and parties. At one of these parties, he met Gloria Fajardo. She was encouraged onto the stage to sing with the band. Estefan was impressed by her voice, and invited her to perform with the band at future gigs. She joined them in 1976, and the group changed its name to The Miami Sound Machine. By 1978, Gloria had married Estefan, and they embarked on a career that would change the world's perception of Latin music forever.

Estefan, asked in a 1998 interview with *Billboard* magazine what he considered to be his biggest professional accomplishment, cited his connection to his roots and his commitment to maintaining his Latin sound. He has worked hard to have a positive effect on how the world views Latinos. At the same time, he remarked that he was an American, and would never return to Cuba to live, even if the country turned away from communism.

Estefan has taken his success in stride, still maintaining his polite demeanor and patient personality. He is known for his loyalty and hard work, and always answers his own cell phone, the number to which is well known in the business. Considered by his wife Gloria to be a workaholic, Estefan starts every morning with a brisk walk along the ocean shore. He and Gloria live in a Star Island mansion–complex in Southeast Florida that he largely decorated himself. Estefan has also designed many of his wife's costumes and jewelry, and likes to shop for her gowns. They have a successful marriage and family, which are important things to him.

In addition to five Grammy awards and two Latin Grammy awards, Estefan has received numerous other awards and recognitions. Estefan was the first–ever recipient of the LARAS (Latin Academy of Recording Arts & Sciences) Person of the Year award in 2000. Said Mauricio Abaroa, executive vice president of the organization, in the *Miami Herald,* "What Emilio Estefan has done in this country to promote Latin music is without dispute. As a producer, as a composer, as a manager, he is one of the greatest ambassadors we have ever had." Estefan is also a two–time Cabale Ace Award winner. Additionally, for his contribution to contemporary pop music and for bringing multicultural music and musicians into the mainstream, Estefan has received an honorary degree of Doctorate of Music from the University of Miami.

Chronology:
Emilio Estefan, Jr.

1953: Born in La Habana, Cuba.

1967: Immigrated to Miami, Florida.

1975: Formed Miami Latin Boys.

1976: Gloria Fajardo joined band, which was renamed Miami Sound Machine.

1978: Married Gloria.

1980: Quit full time job with Bacardi to concentrate on music.

1985: Miami Sound Machine released hit "Conga."

1989: Formed Crescent Moon Productions.

1990: Opened Crescent Moon Studios in Miami.

2000: Received first annual LARAS Person of the Year award.

Career Details

In the beginning, The Miami Sound Machine continued to play at parties, weddings, and all the local benefits in Miami, with only local success. Their first two albums were not successful and they lost their investment when no one would produce it. Estefan credits Gloria with the insistence that they continued to develop their own sound and not try to imitate others, despite the initially poor response from producers. They later recorded "Dr. Beat," which was likewise rejected by Sony Discos (then CBS Discos) as too esoteric. But Estefan insisted that it be printed on the B–side of another record called "Luchare," Then the group engaged in heavy self–promotion, handing out its record to every disco in Miami. The effort paid off and the record rose to the number one spot. Soon they left for England and Holland to promote their record. They only knew two songs at the time, "Dr. Beat" and "I Need a Man." It was enough to please the crowds, if not the producers.

In 1980, Estefan left his full–time job as Bacardi's Director of Hispanic Marketing in order to develop the band's career. Undaunted by their earlier failures, Estefan eventually decided to perform a song written by the group's new drummer, Enrique (KiKi) Garcia. As it turned out, the song, "Conga," was the big break the group had been waiting for. An instant hit, it soon topped both domestic and international charts.

Over the next several years, the group turned out hit after hit, including "Rhythm is Gonna Get You" and "Anything for You." As Gloria added ballads and new dance routines to the program, she became the star attraction for the band, which again renamed itself "Gloria Estefan and the Miami Sound Machine." In 1989, Gloria sold more than 70 million albums worldwide. Estefan dropped back to songwriting and producing, then formed his own label company, Crescent Moon Productions.

In the beginning, financial constraints forced Estefan to do everything—accounting, photographs, publishing—himself. Later, he farmed out these time–consuming tasks and concentrated on managing Gloria's career and producing music for others. Although mostly associated with masterminding the packaged success of his wife's career, Estefan has been largely responsible for the success of many other big names. Of the five most famous "crossovers" in Latino music (wife Gloria, Jon Secada, Ricky Martin, Jennifer Lopez, and Marc Antony), Estefan's name has been on all of their records.

Up until 1990, Estefan had been managing the Miami Sound Machine out of his mother's garage. In that year, he was finally able to open Crescent Moon Studios, located in the heart of Miami, Florida. It is a multi–room facility equipped for audio recording, mixing, and video post. The studio became a "hang–out" for many area musicians and evolved into one of the area's most technologically advanced recording facilities. Estefan owns two restaurants, Larios On The Beach and Bongos, which have been successful. He has also invested in the Cardozo Hotel, which provided the setting for many portions of the hit movie, *Something About Mary.*

Estefan proclaimed in 1999 that he was ready to blaze down new trails. He had signed a $10 million deal with Universal Television Group to develop Latino sitcoms. He was considering a feature film for Universal TV as well. Once he had helped to build a marketplace open to programs with an international flavor, he wanted to use his background to produce those programs. He planned to use his background in both American and Latino cultures to create shows which would appeal to anyone and everyone.

Social and Economic Impact

The Estefans are recognized philanthropists and work primarily through the Gloria Estefan Foundation to help less fortunate persons. The foundation was particularly involved when the Hurricane Andrew disaster hit the Miami community. In memory and thanks for Gloria's recovery from her spinal cord injury following a tour bus accident, the Estefans actively support the Miami Project to Cure Paralysis at the University of Miami School of Medicine.

If there is one thing Estefan is particularly proud of, it is that, according to him, he has been able to elevate Latino music culture in the eyes of the world. What Emilio Estefan has done for the music world is undisputed. When asked about his unique music sound, Estefan stated in a *Miami Herald* article, "I never considered that I was homogenizing Latin sound. I was creating a new sound that is a mixture of cultures, because I am a mixture of cultures. That's where you make history, when you take chances, when you do something that is not commercial, and make it commercial, like what happened with Conga."

Sources of Information

Contact at: Crescent Moon Studios
    6205 Bird Road
    Miami, FL 33155
    Business Phone: (305) 663–8924
    URL: http://www.crescentmoon.com

Bibliography

"2001 Commencement Honorary Degree Recipient Emilio Estefan, Jr." Available at http://www.miami.edu/commencements/honestefan.html.

"Crescent Moon Studios." Available at http://www.crescentmoon.com/idx.html.

Lannert, John. "Emilio Estefan." *Billboard,* 26 September 1998.

Martin, Lydia. "Latin Grammys." *The Miami Herald,* 10 September 2000.

Radelat, Ana. "Leading the Way."*Hispanic,* November 1999.

David Filo

(1966-)
Yahoo!

Overview

David Filo, the quintessential computer geek, made himself a billionaire six times over when he and fellow graduate student Jerry Yang began fooling around on the Internet to create a Web page database of their favorite sites. Thus was the humble and accidental birth of the global Web directory service known as Yahoo! (which originally stood for Yet Another Hierarchical Officious Oracle). Its two genius creators, who called themselves "Chief Yahoos," became the instant darlings of Wall Street analysts and the media. By 2001, Yahoo was attracting more than 120 million worldwide users per month—making it the Big Kahuna of popular Internet portal sites in terms of traffic and global brand.

Personal Life

Filo was born in Wisconsin in 1966 to Jerry, an architect, and Carol, an accountant, but he was raised in Moss Bluff, Louisiana. Moss Bluff was an "alternative community" in which the Filos lived semi–communally with six other families, sharing gardening duties and a kitchen. Filo attended Tulane University in New Orleans, Louisiana, receiving a bachelor's degree in computer engineering in 1988. He continued his education at Stanford University in Palo Alto, California, where he met Jerry Yang. According to Yang, when interviewed in 1997 by online *Newsmakers*, Filo was his teaching assistant in a computer architecture class, who gave him a failing grade (but Filo does not recall this). The two went together to Kyoto, Japan, in a teaching program through Stanford during the early 1990s, where they became

David Filo (left) and Jerry Yang. (AP Photo/Paul Sakuma.)

friends. Filo shared an office with Yang at Stanford during the 1993–1994 academic year. That office became the breeding ground and first home for Yahoo.

Dubbed the "barefoot millionaire boys" by *Newsmakers* because of their tendency to work barefoot in jeans and T–shirts, the young entrepreneurs ran Yahoo out of their trailer office for a year, until the project began to trump study time for the prospective doctoral candidates. After going public in 1996, they were forced to move to larger quarters to accommodate their 200 employees. With a seven–foot Gumby doll greeting them at the door to their new offices and a foosball table upstairs begging for play, Filo and Yang continued to pad around barefoot and treat their new company as a big, fun, cre-

ative toy. They became Silicon Valley icons for all those with a modem and a dream.

Increasingly, as the company grew by leaps and bounds, Filo and Yang developed separate roles in the venture. While Yang gravitated toward the limelight, Filo—the more quiet and media–shy of the two—retreated to the internal workings of Yahoo. He even changed his official title from Chief Yahoo to Cheap Yahoo, a nickname given him when he became insistent on off–the–shelf, no–frills PCs. Filo admitted to *Newsmakers* interviewers that he had become so involved in the minutia of Yahoo that he no longer had time for the simple pleasures he previously delighted in, including tennis, golf, or skiing. Neither he nor Yang completed their doctorate degrees

Nor has immense wealth changed Filo. On the single day of April 11, 1996—the day Yahoo had its initial public offering (IPO)—Filo and Yang each made $132 million. This was followed with another million, then plural millions, and then billions. Richer than Rockefeller, Filo continued to sleep on a futon in his cubicle at corporate headquarters, amid empty pizza boxes and other indicia of cocoonist life. Both he and Yang still flew coach on airplanes and still parked their own cars. As of 2001, Filo remained a bachelor, married only to his brainchild company. Neither he nor Yang had ever wanted to be president or CEO of Yahoo, and Filo was happy to continue as the behind–the–scenes technology guru at the operational level.

In late 2001, Yahoo stock took a tumble, along with several other high–tech entities, and reduced the net worth of the two founders' shares from an estimated $21.8 billion to $944 million—a 96 percent drop. This plunge equated to combined losses of $995 million per month—an almost unfathomable figure for most Americans. Yet Filo remained loyal to his dream and did not sell a single share.

Career Details

In the early 1990s, the World Wide Web was an anarchic mass of data, uncategorized and only accessible via a lengthy address, or URL (universal resource locator; the line that begins with http://). During the 1993–1994 academic year, Filo and Yang were involved with an ostensibly academic project on the computer–aided design of computer chip circuitry. Their office was in a trailer containing a couple of computers, an array of golf clubs, and a sleeping bag. "I was terribly bored," Filo later related in the *San Jose Metro* online. With their faculty adviser on sabbatical in Italy, the pair began playing around with the World Wide Web, a computer network of sites, or "pages," that could be linked together, or "hyperlinked." They created a system of organizing these addresses by subject matter, and the online catalog eventually evolved into what they named Yahoo. Many of the early Web sites were put there by creative graduate students like Filo and Yang, the latter of whom posted his own "home page" (a main site giving general information about a person or a company) with his picture, some golf scores, his name as it appears in Chinese, and hyperlinks to sumo wrestling sites.

One of the problems with the fast–growing maze of sites on the Web was the lack of organization. Filo and Yang, after becoming frustrated when they could not locate a page they found interesting, simply began collecting these confusing codes for their favorite sites so that they could access them again. Others were doing this as well, with some companies publishing books listing numerous sites and describing the content. The Web, however, was changing and growing too quickly. Books

Chronology:
David Filo

1966: Born in Wisconsin.

1988: Earned bachelor's degree in computer engineering from Tulane University.

1990: Befriended Jerry Yang; both travel to Kyoto, Japan, on teaching assignment.

1994: With Yang, created Web directory and calls it Yahoo!

1995: Accepted $1 million investment capital for start–up costs to incorporate.

1995: Yahoo! began selling advertising space online.

1996: Yahoo! Inc. went public.

1996: Gave up director's title at Yahoo! but remained Cheap Yahoo.

1998: Yahoo! began offering Internet service through MCI.

2001: Lost 96 percent value on Yahoo! stock, but hung on.

could not adequately catalog the universe of information, and often sites would "move" to a different server (main computer) or change names, rendering the books outdated before they rolled off the presses. Filo and Yang came up with the idea to provide a kind of road map for online users. They designed some crude software that organized Web pages into topics that could be used immediately to "link" to those pages. In early 1994, "Jerry's Guide to the World Wide Web" was born, and the name was later revised to "Jerry and David's Guide to the World Wide Web." The two provided the service free to all Stanford users. As their list grew, they began subdividing the topics to provide more structure. Later that summer, the system was dubbed Yahoo!, or Yet Another Hierarchical Officious Oracle.

Although Yahoo! was not the first search engine to exist, its categorization was vanguard, and it was the only one to offer whimsy. David Matsukawa in *Transpacific* explained, "Yahoo! had an attitude. It was start–up culture, not corporate. It talked to the folks making the pages. And it talked to the folks venturing out on the waves for the very first time. It said, 'Hey, the Internet is a fun place.'" They built it, and people came. By November of 1994, 170,000 people a day were using the site. By 1998 Yahoo! was counting about 26 million unique visitors out of a staggering one billion "hits" per month, which averaged out to more than 850,000 a day. America Online (AOL), the giant Internet access service, offered a buy–out, and deals poured in from Microsoft and Prodigy as well. Filo and Yang, working 20 hours a day for the sheer enjoyment of it, turned them all down.

However, Stanford University was irked that Yahoo! was tying up their network with all the traffic. "They told us we were crashing their system and that we'd have to move the thing off campus," Yang stated in the *San Jose Metro*. He and Filo began considering starting up a business from a hobby that was becoming overwhelming. "It was a really gradual thing, but we'd find ourselves spending more and more time on it," explained Yang. "It was getting to be a burden," not to mention, they were not making any money off their labor of love. A friend at Harvard, Tim Brady, devised a business plan for Yahoo! for a class project, which allowed the pair to really visualize the potential. In early 1995, the partners packed up, dropped out, and moved on. They accepted a $1 million investment offer from Mike Mortiz at Sequoia Capital, a fund that had financed other Silicon Valley winners such as Apple and Oracle. Filo and Yang rented an office suite, ordered business cards defining themselves as Chief Yahoos, and hired a staff made up of graduate school friends and interns.

By the summer of 1995, Yahoo! began selling advertising space on their pages. Initially frowned upon as "sell–outs" by Web purists who had worked to ban all commercial activity on the new technology, the practice quickly became accepted. Yahoo! teamed up with Reuters news service, based in London, so that users could access news wire stories online with a click of a button. They also added other user–friendly elements, such as links to weather, stock quotes, phone listings, interactive maps, and loads of other information that Web users now take for granted. Their graphics were bright and slick, and they later hired an expert to assist with logical categorization.

Yahoo! also scored points when it developed a "personalized" page called My Yahoo!, which allowed users to customize the Yahoo! page with all of the links that interested them the most. Early in 1996, they started offering a directory tailored to children ages eight through fourteen called "Yahooligans!" They later added a "get local" option, which included sites containing information specific to certain cities in the United States.

Meanwhile, Filo and Yang remained essentially modest with their success. At the start of their mammoth operation, the two paid themselves around $40,000 a year and lived in modest apartments. Filo was driving a beat–up, junk–filled Datsun to the company's headquarters in Santa Clara where his office resembled a dorm–room nightmare, littered with empty cans, Rollerblades, and assorted CDs. He remained reluctant to be in the spotlight, spending most of his time behind the scenes and often sleeping on a blanket in his office. The two were known to donate money to help disadvantaged people learn about computers.

In January 2000, Yahoo! stock closed at an all–time high of a split–adjusted $237.50. Within days, company executives learned that main competitor America Online Inc. planned to purchase media giant Time Warner Inc.— creating a new media empire that would drastically diminish Yahoo's presence in cyberspace. Internal dissention broke out, most of it over whether Yahoo! should try something similar. At first blush, the best strategy seemed to be the purchase of online auction site eBay. Purists Filo and Yang opposed the deal, as did Yahoo's president, Jeff Mallett. Another deal, this time with OgilvyInteractive, was also declined. But Yahoo began to lose advertising revenues to competitors, and by November 2000 Morgan Stanley had downgraded its stock. The first of several internal Yahoo management shake-downs occurred, which continued well into 2001, with the announcement of a new CEO in April. Meanwhile, eBay was recording a 79 percent increase in revenues, up to $184 million. Had the merger gone through, Yahoo would not have needed to rely on advertising for 90 percent of its revenues.

Still, Yahoo! has remained true to its original mission: to guide users through the Internet. It remains patently user–friendly, refusing to sell its search listings to advertisers and prohibiting pop–up or pop–under ads on its home page that would slow down or disrupt user experience. The company believes this will save it, in the end—an admirable goal in the dog–eat–dog world of cyberspace competition. As *Fortune* magazine explained in its November 2001 issue, while Yahoo may not be considered a growth company, it remains a so–called "richly–valued company."

Social and Economic Impact

Were it not for the creative genius of David Filo and Jerry Yang, many would–be Internet users might have remained missing in action in cyberspace to this very day. Since Filo's original mission was to help other users through the maze of Internet sites, rather than to create a business profit, he and Yang have remained true to their customers and created a portal of informational ease not paralleled in the industry.

Sources of Information

Contact at: Yahoo!
    701 First Avenue
    Sunnyvale, CA 94089
    Business Phone: (408)349–3300
    URL: http://www.yahoo.com

Bibliography

Elgin, Ben, et al. "Inside Yahoo!" *Business Week*, 21 May 2001.

Gunther, Marc. "The Cheering Fades for Yahoo." *Fortune*, 12 November 2001.

"How They Stack Up." *Fortune*, 17 September 2001.

Lenzner, Robert, and Victoria Murphy. "Global Crashing." *Forbes*, 29 October 2001.

Madden, Normandy, and Margaret McKegney. "Out of Yahoo!'s Hot Seat." *Ad Age Global*, March 2001.

Pickering, Carol. "A Tale of Two Startups." *Forbes*, 5 October 1998.

Reeves, Richard, and Joan Caplin. "The New Wealth." *Money*, October 1997.

"Web Masters." *Forbes*, 11 October 1999.

Wylie, Margie. "Barefoot Millionaire Boys." *Newsmakers*, 10 November 1997. Available at http://news.cnet/news.

Carly Fiorina

(1954-)
Hewlett-Packard Co.

Overview

President and CEO of Hewlett–Packard Company since the summer of 1999, Carleton S. Fiorina, better known as "Carly," is the highest–ranking female executive in the United States. HP, the world's second–largest computer company after IBM, stands to grow even larger if the company's proposed acquisition of Compaq Computer—engineered by Fiorina—goes through. Fiorina has shaken up the corporate culture at HP, setting aggressive sales goals and assigning a new priority to rapid technical innovation. To accomplish her goals for HP, she has moved aggressively to streamline the company's structure by consolidating its more than 30 units into four basic groups. Under Fiorina, HP has put a whole new emphasis on services and has discontinued marginal operations. However, the ambitious sales goals set by Fiorina have yet to be reached, casting something of a shadow over prospects for her future at HP.

Personal Life

Fiorina lives in California with her husband, Frank Fiorina, a former AT&T executive whom she married in 1985. Her husband, who served as chief information officer of AT&T's corporate business unit, opted for early retirement in 1998 to let his wife concentrate on her career. Fiorina has two stepdaughters, her husband's children from a previous marriage. In addition to managing the family's home, Frank Fiorina serves as a volunteer fireman. Both Fiorinas enjoy boating in their spare time.

Born Cara Carleton S. Sneed on September 6, 1954, Fiorina is the daughter of Joseph (a federal judge) and the late Madeline (an abstract painter) Sneed. She experienced a fairly nomadic childhood, attending five different high schools, because of her family's frequent moves. Prior to becoming a federal appeals judge in San Francisco, her father taught law and served as a deputy attorney general. Fiorina's mother instilled in her "a great zest for life," Fiorina told the *New York Times*.

There's an interesting story behind Fiorina's unusual first name. Because all of the men named Carleton on her father's side of the family died in the Civil War, the family decided to honor their memory by naming one member of each family unit for the fallen Carletons—Carleton for males or Cara Carleton for females.

After graduating from high school, Fiorina attended Stanford University in Palo Alto, California, where she majored in medieval history and philosophy. Interestingly, Stanford is located in the same California city that serves as corporate headquarters for Hewlett–Packard, the company Fiorina now heads. Planning to follow in her father's footsteps, Fiorina began studying law at the University of California shortly after her 1976 graduation from Stanford. After only one semester, she decided that a career in law was not for her and dropped out of law school. She worked in a variety of jobs, including teaching English in Bologna, Italy, before deciding to head back to school. This time, she decided to focus on a career in business, and in 1980 she earned her M.B.A. from the University of Maryland.

With her M.B.A. in hand, Fiorina landed a job as an account executive with AT&T, working first in Washington, D.C., in the company's long–distance phone service operations. Her responsibilities involved selling the company's long–distance services to government agencies. Impressed by her performance, AT&T executives identified her as a likely candidate for a management position and sent her in 1988 to the Sloan School of the Massachusetts Institute of Technology to earn her master of science degree.

Career Details

It was at the Sloan School that Fiorina first met the head of AT&T's Network Systems Group, an equipment division that many considered stagnant. Sensing an opportunity to demonstrate her sales abilities, Fiorina—against the advice of friends—decided to make the switch from long–distance operations to Network Systems. Almost immediately, she was dispatched to the Far East to put together complicated joint ventures for the division. Although business negotiating in the Far East is almost exclusively an all–male preserve, Fiorina found a way to fit in.

Years later, she told Elise Ackerman of *U.S. News & World Report* of one particular incident in South Ko-

Chronology:
Carly Fiorina

1954: Born.

1976: Graduated with B.A. from Stanford University.

1980: Graduated with M.B.A. from University of Maryland.

1980: Joined AT&T as an account executive.

1985: Married Frank Fiorina.

1988: Graduated with Master of Science degree from MIT's Sloan School.

1998: Named president of Lucent Technologies' global service provider business.

1999: Named president and CEO of Hewlett–Packard.

2000: Named chairman of Hewlett–Packard.

2001: Hewlett–Packard announced plan to buy Compaq Computer Corp.

rea. Foreign businessmen visiting South Korea traditionally are invited to visit a *kisaeng* house, where they are treated to entertainment by the South Korean equivalent of geisha girls. Anxious to avoid offending their female visitor, her hosts escorted Fiorina to one of Seoul's finest *kisaeng* establishments but apologized profusely that there were—regrettably—no *kisaeng* boys. Fiorina assured her nervous hosts that the usual *kisaeng* treatment would be just fine with her. So off they went for an evening of food, drink, and flattery. To accommodate the establishment's unusual female guest, Fiorina said later that the hostess "just changed some of the adjectives."

Well before most American businesses began to fully exploit opportunities outside the country, Fiorina pushed her colleagues at AT&T to adopt a more international perspective on business. Before she reached her 40th birthday, Fiorina had been put in charge of Network Systems's North American sales. Shortly thereafter, AT&T broke itself into three separate companies, one of which was made up of the company's long–distance service operations, Lucent Technologies, and NCR Corporation. The focus at Lucent was on telecommunications and networking equipment, much of which is essential for the operations of the Internet. Network Systems was folded into Lucent. Fiorina was chosen to manage Lucent's $3 billion initial public offering (IPO) of stock, one of the largest and most successful IPOs ever. In 1998

Carly Fiorina. (AP/Wide World Photos/Ben Margot.)

Fiorina was named president of Lucent's Global Service Provider Business. Later that same year, *Fortune* magazine named her the most powerful woman in business.

In late July of 1999, Hewlett–Packard, breaking precedent by looking outside its own ranks to fill the top job, tapped Fiorina as its new chief executive officer. Her predecessor in the job, Lew Platt, had been widely criticized for his lack of strategic vision, a failing that kept HP from reaping the full benefits of the Internet boom. Somewhat belatedly, in the spring of 1999, HP had announced plans for its "E–speak" programming language, akin to html or Java. "E–speak" was positioned as a "universal language of services on the Net," according to Allison Johnson, head of brand strategy and communication for HP. Shortly after Fiorina came on board at HP, she spoke enthusiastically about the outlook for E–services and vowed to accelerate "the speed and pace of the business as well as intensify the competitive will to win."

In a statement released upon her acceptance of the job at HP, Fiorina said, "Leaving Lucent was a very difficult decision, but this is a once–in–a--lifetime opportunity for me. Hewlett–Packard is a company of great accomplishment and even great potential." Despite its potential, it was clear from the start that the transformation of HP from a somewhat stodgy engineering company into a fleet–footed Internet competitor would be a formidable challenge for Fiorina. However, she wasted no time in taking steps to shake things up at HP. Among her first moves was an ultimatum to HP sales staffers: produce or leave. She also helped to negotiate exclusive

purchasing agreements with Ford Motor Co. and Delta Airlines and consolidated the company's many decentralized units. She also made clear to HP employees that it was going to be her way or the highway. "If one–quarter of the people in HP don't want to make the journey or can't take the pace, that's the way it has to be," she told *Worth*.

Fiorina's appointment as CEO at HP was welcomed by feminists as a hopeful sign that Silicon Valley, long a male–dominated corporate society, may be ready for a change. Karen Eriksson, CEO of Women in Technology International, a women's networking association, said of Fiorina's appointment: "It shouldn't be an anomaly. We're seeing the fruition of all the years that women have been in management. Between the number of women–led IPOs, board appointments, and the increase in access to capital for women, this is an indication of things to come. . . . this is just another step ahead."

In a bold move, Fiorina announced in September 2001 plans for HP to buy Compaq Computer in a stock offer initially valued at about $25 billion. (This figure tumbled sharply in the wake of the September 11, 2001, terrorist attacks on the World Trade Center and Pentagon.) Under the terms of the proposed agreement, the combined company would carry the HP name and retain Fiorina as its CEO. Michael D. Capellas, chairman and CEO of Compaq, would become the new company's president. With the addition of Compaq's assets, the combined company would rival IBM in size. The Hewlett family, which owns slightly more than 5 percent of the company's stock, announced in early November that it would vote against the proposed merger on the grounds that Compaq is not the right partner for HP. However, in response to the Hewlett dissent, HP released a statement indicating that company management and the HP board of directors remained firmly committed to the merger plan. Only days later, David W. Packard, son of HP co-founder David Packard, announced that he too would vote against the proposed merger, casting more doubt about Fiorina's ability to push it through.

Social and Economic Impact

Although Fiorina has been unable to achieve all of her goals for Hewlett–Packard, she has managed to jolt the company out of its stagnation, making it once again a real competitor in the race with IBM and Sun Microsystems to capture a bigger share of the market for E–business machines and software. Hope is fading, however, for Fiorina's promise to reinvigorate HP's flagging sales, at least in the short term. In the face of a cut–throat price war in the PC market, HP's hardware sales have slipped, and the company has yet to make any significant inroads into the market for services, one of Fiorina's key goals. Two years after her appointment, Fiorina acknowledged the economic climate was hardly favorable for all that she had hoped to accomplish. "Think of all geographies as weak," she told CNET News. "There are no exceptions. I don't think we can call when a recovery will occur."

For its part, HP's board seemed inclined to give Fiorina more time to accomplish her goals. Board member George Keyworth II explained: "In the early summer of 1999, when we were interviewing Carly, we discussed it would take a minimum of three years to turn things around and there would be lots of ups and downs. We are absolutely behind her and know there will be challenges."

One major disappointment came in November 2000, when a proposed HP acquisition of PricewaterhouseCoopers fell through. HP's plan to acquire the giant consulting business was first announced in September 2001 and touted as a way for the company to move more aggressively into the services market. It was hoped that with PricewaterhouseCoopers folded into the company HP could offer customers everything from e–commerce and Internet systems to software, servers, and services. The board was so encouraged by the proposal that it elected Fiorina to a seat only two weeks after the first announcement of the planned acquisition was made.

Almost a year later, Fiorina announced an even bolder plan—the acquisition of Compaq Computer in a deal that could cost up to $25 billion. Members of both the Hewlett and Packard families announced their intention to vote against the proposed merger, opposition which could snowball and eventually derail Fiorina's master plan and spell her undoing.

Sources of Information

Contact at: Hewlett-Packard Co.
   3000 Hanover St.
   Palo Alto, CA 94304–1185
   Business Phone: (650) 857–1501
   URL: http://www.hp.com

Bibliography

Ackerman, Elise. "Silicon Valley Girl." *U.S. News & World Report*, 2 August 1999.

Argent, Lindsey. "Glass Ceiling Shattered at HP." *Wired News*, 19 July 1999.

McDougal, Chris. "The 50 Best CEOs: Carleton Fiorina." *Worth*.

Meyer, Michael. "In a League of Hew Own." *Newsweek*, 2 August 1999.

Newsmakers 2000. Farmington Hills, MI: Gale Group, 2000.

Swartz, Jon. "Another Thumbs Down for H–P Deal." *USA Today*, 8 November 2001.

William Clay Ford, Jr.

(1957-)

Ford Motor Company

Overview

On October 30, 2001, amid cheers from workers who surged to their feet at the announcement, William Clay "Bill" Ford, Jr. introduced himself as the new chief executive officer (CEO) of the automotive giant, Ford Motor Company. For almost two decades, there was no Ford running the company. After Henry Ford II stepped down as chairman in 1979, only professional managers were allowed into the top position. Finally, in 1998, the company declared that chairman Alex Trotman would step down a year earlier than expected to let Bill Ford, Jr., assume control, with Jacques "Jac" Nasser functioning as president and CEO. Nasser was ousted in 2001, following a 58 percent stock tumble, pricey foreign investments, and lawsuits that ended the nearly century-old relationship between Ford and Firestone Tire Company.

Personal Life

Bill Ford was born in Detroit, Michigan in 1957. He was the only son in a family of four children born to William Clay Ford, Sr. and Martha Park Firestone Ford. His father was the grandson of auto pioneer Henry Ford, and his mother was an heiress to the Firestone tire fortune. While other branches of the Ford clan were marred by unstable family relationships, Ford enjoyed a calm upbringing in a home that was as down-to-earth as possible, given the family's household name and incredible wealth. In fact, Ford was often shuttled to less affluent areas of town to play hockey. He excelled at sports, received good grades, and maintained a relatively normal existence without bodyguards or chauffeurs. Though he

did have a nanny, his mother was around at all times. Later, Ford attended the Hotchkiss School in Lakeville, Connecticut, where he gained a reputation as a fierce soccer competitor. He became an avid football fan, no doubt because his father bought the Detroit Lions in 1964. After high school, Ford attended Princeton University, where he earned a bachelor of arts in political science and wrote his senior thesis on labor relations at Ford. Later, he went back to school to obtain a master of science in management at the Massachusetts Institute of Technology in 1984.

Ford married a fellow Princeton student, Lisa Vanderzee, and they have two daughters and two sons. He says since he was not forced into working in the business, he will let his children make their own choices as well regarding their careers. The family lives in Grosse Pointe Farms, an upscale suburb of Detroit, where Ford can be spotted in–line skating through the quiet streets or getting ready for a fly fishing trip. As a nature lover, he likes camping, hiking, and skiing with his family, and he also enjoys tae kwon do, hockey, tennis, coaching soccer, and collecting Civil War documents. He has pledged that his job will not detract from his personal life and has no plans to cut down his involvement with his children. Ford is also a vegetarian who practices alternative healing methods such as acupuncture and herbal remedies, and he does not often drink alcohol. In addition to everything else, Ford is the chairman of the Henry Ford Museum and Greenfield Village in Dearborn, Michigan, and the vice–chairman and a member of the board of the Detroit Greater Downtown Partnership Inc. Though he seems to have as ideal a life as possible, balancing family, hobbies, a football team, and one of the world's largest corporations, Ford admits there are some drawbacks to carrying around his legendary surname. "Whenever I'm at a party," he told *BusinessWeek,* "people are always telling me either to get a new quarterback or make the Taurus back seat bigger."

In November 2001, the Swedish–American Chamber of Commerce announced that Ford would be awarded the 15th annual prestigious Lucia Award in recognition of his efforts to promote world peace through trade.

Career Details

After college, Ford went to work at the family business, starting as a financial analyst and eventually rotating through eleven jobs in his first ten years with the firm. His father wanted him to have a well–rounded education about the business in case he would someday rise to the top. The senior Ford involved his 25-year-old son in labor negotiations because he felt it was an important element in running the firm. Ford also worked in product planning and advanced vehicle development, helping to launch the first Ford Escort and Mercury Lynx, and also led the marketing efforts for Ford in the New York–New

Chronology:
William Clay Ford, Jr.

1957: Born in Detroit, Michigan.

1979: Received a B.A. degree from Princeton University.

1984: Earned a M.S. degree at Massachusetts Institute of Technology (MIT).

1986: Named director of commercial vehicle marketing, Ford Europe.

1988: Became vice president of Ford Truck Operations.

1990: Promoted to director of Business Strategy, Automotive Operations.

1995: Took over the running of Detroit Lions football team from his father.

1999: Named chairman of Ford Motor Company.

2000: Defended Ford Motor Company as tires, and a century–old partnership with Firestone Tire Company, fell apart.

2001: Added duties of chief executive officer to his responsibilities.

Jersey area. In 1986, he worked with Ford of Europe as director of commercial vehicle marketing. The following year, he ran Ford of Switzerland as managing director, succeeding in breathing life into what was previously a sagging enterprise. He was named vice president of Ford Truck Operations in 1988, and in 1990 he became director of business strategy for automotive operations. He has also served as general manager of the climate control division. In 1988, Ford joined the board of directors and eventually led two essential committees, finance and environment/public policy. By the mid–1990s, his name was being considered to take over for Alex Trotman, who had been with Ford since the mid–1950s and held the chairman and CEO positions since 1993.

Speculation simmered for years that either Ford or his cousin, Edsel Ford II, were in line to become the next leader. However, it came to a full boil in 1996 when major business publications proclaimed that Ford would be the next chairman of the board, even if he would not be in charge of day–to–day operations *per se.*

William Clay Ford, Jr. (center), standing with Alex Trotman and Jac Nasser. (AP/Wide World Photos/Carlos Osorio.)

Though his name was probably one reason that, at age 41, he was promoted to lead the world's second–largest industrial firm, Ford still had to work his way up from the bottom and prove his mettle. "I recognize that there are those who think this job was handed to me," Ford remarked to *BusinessWeek*. "But I was under the microscope every step of the way. I had to have drive and ambition because people were looking for me to fail." Ford's immediate mission, in addition to making sure the company remained economically competitive, was to infuse environmental activism into the number two car corporation. He had made it no secret that he hoped to combine his personal devotion to environ-

mental issues with his new position, thereby producing cleaner, more efficient vehicles.

Ford was also becoming involved with his father's enterprise, the Detroit Lions football team. He served as treasurer from 1980 to 1995, then he became vice chairman and assumed responsibility for most of the operations. At his first NFL owners' meeting, he stood up to the threat of having the Lions' Thanksgiving game taken away and given to a better team (they had not won a championship since 1957). His emotional defense preserved the tradition and laid waste to his prior reputation as being somewhat meek. Furthermore, he took immediate steps to give the team a needed lift. First, he fired head coach Wayne Fontes and hired Bobby Ross, formerly of the San Diego Chargers. He then restructured an outdated ticket policy and stepped up marketing efforts. A new web site and weekly radio and television shows added to the facelift. Most importantly, he lobbied to bring the Detroit Lions back to Detroit. For two decades, the team played at the Silverdome, a sports arena located in suburban Pontiac. Crowds had dwindled throughout the years, and the franchise received one of the worst licensing deals in the league with stadium owners: the Lions obtained no revenue from concessions, suites, or parking. With a receptive mayor, Dennis Archer, in office in Detroit and a new baseball stadium being built for Detroit Tigers' owner Mike Illitch, Ford seized the opportunity to contribute to civic pride and arrange a better deal. Ford negotiated to build a new 70,000–seat domed stadium in downtown Detroit next to the new ballpark, with the Ford family and corporate sponsors contributing about half the building costs and government agencies adding the rest.

Observers wondered if Ford's success with the football team would translate to running a gigantic corporation. When mulling over the possibility that Ford would be taking the reins of the automaker, some commentators predicted that it would be a boon for the company. Though Trotman was a respected leader, some thought Ford would soothe stockholders because he has a highly personal stake in the corporation. Not just a "company man," Ford is a part of the firm's history, as is his cousin, Edsel Ford II, who had maintained even closer ties. Edsel Ford II's father was head of Ford for three decades, and many suspected that he would be the successor once Trotman left. Edsel has had a long career at Ford and sits on the board as president of credit operations. Insiders considered Bill Ford a superior choice, due to his diplomacy and previous involvement with the board.

However, some directors were wary. Ford was still enmeshed in managing the Lions and raising four young children, and it was suggested that he would not have the time needed to devote to the job. Others were concerned that the appointment would further inflate the family's influence to the dismay of the rest of the stockholders. The family, however, had the ultimate say on the decision to elevate Ford to the top role. Even though Henry Ford II had stated firmly, "There are no crown princes in the Ford Motor Co.," according to *Newsweek*, the family controlled 40 percent of the voting stock and held three positions on the board, giving it enough clout to make certain things happen.

In the fall of 1998, Ford Motor Company announced that Bill Ford would become the new chairman, effective January 1, 1999, when Trotman retired a year earlier than expected. Although Ford would have the final word on company decisions, many were pleased that Jacques Nasser, former head of global auto operations, would be taking over the day–to–day management of the corporation as president and CEO. This dual manage-

ment is common in Europe and Asia, but most American firms still rely on one person to hold the titles of chairman and CEO. Ford, however, welcomed the concept, explaining in a press conference, "I will lead the board and Jac will lead the company. This will be a partnership." Nasser was results–oriented, with a history of slashing costs more than $4 billion in 1997 and the first half of 1998. The two had worked together before; Ford worked under Nasser in the 1980s, when he was a financial analyst in charge of Venezuela and Nasser was head of finance for Latin America and Asia.

Ford's main goal as chairman was to maintain the company's solid financial record and continue to cut costs and narrow the gap between it and the number one automaker, General Motors. Ford also needed to remain focused on increasing European sales, its largest market outside of the United States. The Asian–Pacific markets were expected to show strong growth as well, and it was essential that Ford Motor Company be competitive there. Ford's other priorities included his long–standing commitment to environmental issues and the production of a high–selling environmentally–friendly vehicle.

Of course, being responsible for keeping the company in business, Ford also saw economic opportunities in being an Earth–friendly company. He predicted an unprecedented ballooning of consumers seeking environmentally sound products in the twenty–first century, and he said that companies that foresee this shift and address it will prosper, while laggards will fail. But his attention to marketing did not drive his activism. "There's no conflict between doing the right thing and the bottom line," Ford noted in *Automotive News*. "I don't see a conflict between shareholder value, customer value and social value." Ford also stated that his great–grandfather, Henry Ford, had always wanted to benefit the world and not adversely affect it, but that the company had, unfortunately, gradually moved away from that. Ford was not afraid to recognize the company's failures in environmentalism. In May of 2000, Ford made an unprecedented statement at Ford's annual shareholder meeting, admitting to the fact that Ford's sport utility vehicles (SUVs) are environmentally unsound. He went further by saying that the company's SUVs should emit no more pollutants than its cars.

Later that year, Ford had to defend his company in the midst of a massive tire recall. In the summer of 2000, Ford and Bridgestone/Firestone jointly set about to recall 6.5 million tires suspected of contributing to vehicle rollovers. Although Ford initially stated that the other Firestone tires with which its vehicles were equipped were safe, it later announced that it had evidence that there were problems on some of those tire models as well. In 2001, Ford announced that it would spend $3 billion to replace all 13 million Firestone Wilderness AT tires on Ford Explorers, Expedition SUVs, and F–150 and Ranger pickups. Meanwhile, Firestone unilaterally announced that it would no longer sell tires to the automobile manufacturer, thus ending a century–long partnership between the two companies. As the great–grandson of both Henry Ford and Harvey Firestone, founder of Firestone Tire Company, Bill Ford understandably called the decision "a painful one."

Social and Economic Impact

It is unusual to think of an automobile baron as an environmentalist, but Ford is just that. As the proud owner of a Ford Ranger electric truck, he volunteered in Earth Day events and became involved with clean–water projects while a teenager. Later, he began reading about green issues and studied the works of nature authors Edward Abbey and Rachel Carson.

Ford is committed to the idea that a company can make things without damaging people or the planet. To that end, he seeks to build worker–friendly, environmentally responsible factories that produce emissions–free cars. He is determined, for example, to eliminate the carbon–dioxide–producing internal–combustion engine by the time he vacates the chairman's office. In 2001, the company announced that it would join with environmental groups to call for consumer tax credits to help subsidize sales of high–mileage hybrid–fuel vehicles, which remain costly to produce. Ford, mean-

while, will begin selling a hybrid–fuel version of its small SUV, the Escape, in 2003.

Sources of Information

Contact at: Ford Motor Company
One American Rd.
Dearborn, MI 48126–2798
Business Phone: (313) 845–8540
URL: http://www.ford.com

Bibliography
"Ford on Ford. . . ." *PR Newswire,* 3 December 2001.

Kerwin, Kathleen, and Joann Muller. "Bill Takes the Wheel." *Business Week,* 12 November 2001.

"Lions' History." Detroit Lions web site. Available at http://www.detroitlions.com.

Wheat, Alynda. "The Top 10 Business Stories." *Fortune,* 24 December 2001.

"William Clay Ford, Jr." *Newsmakers,* issue 1. Farmington Hills, MI: Gale Group, 1999.

"William Clay Ford, Jr. to Receive Swedish–American Chamber of Commerce's 15th Annual Lucia Award. . . ." *Business Wire,* 19 November 2001.

Bill Gates

(1955-)
Microsoft Corporation

Overview

William Henry Gates III became known as "The King of Software" by designing and developing user–friendly software for the personal computer (PC). His innovations revolutionized the computer industry, enabling people without technological training to use PCs in both the work-place and the home. With his high school friend, Paul Allen, Bill Gates co–founded Microsoft Corporation, which he built into a multi–billion–dollar company.

Personal Life

William Henry Gates III was born October 28, 1955, in Seattle, Washington. His father, William Henry Gates, Jr., is a prominent Seattle attorney, and his mother, the late Mary Maxwell, was a schoolteacher, regent at the University of Washington, and chairperson of United Way International. He married Melinda French Gates, a Microsoft manager, in 1994. Together they have a daughter, Jennifer, born in April of 1996, and a son, Rory John, born in 1999.

In his leisure time, Gates enjoys reading, playing golf, and bridge. He has also written two books: *The Road Ahead*, published in 1995, covered his views on the future of the Internet; *Business & the Speed of Thought*, published in 1999, explored how digital technology can help solve business problems. Gates' competitive drive and fierce desire to win have made him a powerful force in business but have also consumed much of his personal life. In the six years between 1978 and 1984, he took a total of only two weeks vacation.

Bill Gates. (Microsoft Corporation).

Gates developed an early interest in computer science in the seventh grade at Seattle's Lakeside School. There, Gates became acquainted with Paul Allen, a teenager with a similar interest in technology, who would eventually become one of his business partners. Gates entered Harvard University in 1973 to study pre–law. By 1975 Gates had decided to pursue a career in computer software and dropped out of Harvard.

Career Details

Gates' early experiences with computers included debugging (or eliminating errors from) programs for the Computer Center Corporation's PDP–10, helping computerize electric power grids for the Bonneville Power Administration, and—while still in high school—founding with Allen, a firm named Traf–On–Data. Their small company earned them $20,000 in fees for analyzing local traffic patterns.

While working with the Computer Center's PDP–10, Gates was responsible for what was probably the first computer virus, which is a program that copies itself into other programs and ruins data. Discovering that the machine was hooked up to a national network of computers called Cybernet, Gates invaded the network and installed a program on the main computer that sent itself to the rest of the network's computers; Cybernet crashed. When Gates was found out, he was severely reprimanded,

causing him to stay away from computers for his entire junior year at Lakeside.

In January 1975, Allen showed Gates a cover story in the magazine *Popular Mechanics* about a $350 million microcomputer, the Altair, made by a firm Called MITS in New Mexico. When he saw the story, Gates knew he wanted to be in the forefront of computer software design. "What first got me so interested in software development, and eventually led to the founding of Microsoft, was the excitement I felt as a teenager when I realized that computers gave me feedback and information like a puzzle to be studied and solved," said Bill Gates.

Gates and Allen developed a BASIC interpreter for the Altair computer while they were still at Harvard. BASIC is a simple, interactive computer language designed in the 1960s and "interpreter" is a program that executes a source program by reading it one line at a time and performing operations immediately.

When Gates dropped out of Harvard in 1975, he ended his academic life and began his career in earnest as a software designer and entrepreneur. He went on to co–found Microsoft with Allen. The partners wrote programs for the early Apple and Commodore machines and expanded BASIC to run on microcomputers other than the Altair.

Gates' big opportunity arrived in 1980 when IBM approached him to help with their personal computer project, code named Project Chess. Gates created the Microsoft Disk Operating System, or MS–DOS, and its related applications can run on almost any IBM compatible PC. By the early 1990s, Microsoft had sold more than 100 million copies of MS–DOS, making the operating system the all–time leader in software sales.

Marketing savvy played a big part in Microsoft's success. Microsoft tripled its sales in the early 1990s with its successful Windows debut. Microsoft Network (MSN) was launched in 1994, Windows 95 was released in August 1995, and Windows 98 made its debut in June 1998. At first, while Microsoft was enjoying these successes, other companies were making inroads in the development of software for the World Wide Web (WWW). But in the fall of 1995, Gates realized that 20 million people were surfing the net without Microsoft software. An aggressive campaign was launched to raise Microsoft's stake in the Web. Staffing was increased, software was bought, and deals were cut—America Online (AOL) was given an icon in Windows 95 in exchange for using Microsoft's Internet Explorer as its principal Web browser. Windows 97 integrates its Internet Explorer browser and MSN into its Windows operating system, creating an active desktop. In 1998 Microsoft gained a significant hold on Web browsers, the NetAction consumer group reported. It found that four of the largest Internet service providers (ISP) distributed only Microsoft's Explorer.

By 1997 Microsoft recorded a net income of $3.4 billion. This made up 41 percent of the profits of the 10 largest publicly traded software companies. This period saw the roll out of Windows 95 and 98, major updates of the world's preeminent computer operating system, Windows. In the first three days of its release, Windows 98 sold more than 500,000 copies, matching the sales of Windows 95 in its debut.

In 1997 Gates entered the world of computer–driven multimedia when he began promoting CD–ROM technology. Gates envisioned the expansion of his business by combining PCs with the information reservoirs provided by CD–ROM and was soon marketing a number of multimedia products.

In addition, Gates invested $1 billion in the cable company Comcast in 1998 in an effort to persuade the cable industry to assist in developing faster connections using cable modems. That same year, Microsoft formed a group—the Cable Broadband Forum—with Intel, TCI, and Time Warner to promote cable modems. The company also invested $425 million to guarantee itself a 20 percent equity stake in the cable access venture, Road Runner. Gates has also invested in Teledesic, a company that plans to expand global two–way broadband telecommunications services through a system of low–orbit satellites.

Gates' strategy has been to leverage Microsoft's desktop operating system to dominate all software sales, from word processing to spreadsheets. Because most new PCs are equipped with the Windows operating system, Gates can place icons for Microsoft software packages on the desktops when a computer is purchased. Also, Microsoft's large cash reserves give it an advantage over its competitors. Microsoft can enter a new market or introduce a new package without needing to make a profit from the outset.

Microsoft's success, however, has brought scrutiny. In April 1995, when Microsoft attempted to make the biggest acquisition in the history of the software industry by purchasing Intuit, a maker of personal finance software, the antitrust division of the Department of Justice blocked the deal and Microsoft backed off. However, competitors continued to complain that Microsoft uses an existing monopoly to retard the development of new technology. It was the bundling of software, such as Web browsers with Windows 95 and 98, that prompted the Justice Department, along with 18 state attorneys general, to file an antitrust lawsuit against the company in 1998. A U.S. Court of Appeals panel ruled that Microsoft was free to bundle its software, but a subsequent finding of fact by Judge Thomas Penfield Jackson in November 1999 ruled that Microsoft was a monopoly. The ruling opened the possibility of numerous private suits being brought against the company by its competitors.

The Microsoft antitrust case made headlines through much of the last half of the 1990s. The U.S. Court of Appeals for the District of Columbia upheld the lower court's conclusion that Microsoft had violated antitrust laws. But, by a 7–0 vote, the appeals court ruled that a

Chronology:
Bill Gates

1955: Born.

1972: Established Traf–On–Data firm.

1973: Developed BASIC computer program for MITS Altair.

1975: Co–founded Microsoft with Paul Allen.

1984: Sold 2 million copies of MS–DOS.

1987: Unveiled Windows software.

1989: Founded Corbis Corp.

1995: Offered the Windows 95 update.

1995: Published *The Road Ahead*.

1998: Became the world's wealthiest self–made man.

1999: Violated anti–trust regulations.

2000: Stepped down as Microsoft CEO; retained position as creative adviser.

2001: Settled anti–trust dispute.

new judge would have to decide what penalty Microsoft should pay because Judge Jackson, who had spoken to the press regarding the case, had given the appearance of having a personal bias against the company.

The on–going negotiations climaxed in 2001. On November 2, 2001, Microsoft announced that it had struck a deal with the Justice Department. However, nine states refused to acknowledge the deal, which did little to revoke Microsoft's software monopoly and was considered by analysts as a slap on the wrist for Microsoft. California attorney general Bill Lockyer told *Time*, "We want real reform, not a fig leaf." When asked by *Newsweek* whether he admitted legal wrongdoing, Gates responded, "I accept that there have been legitimate concerns in reaching this agreement. We're acknowledging those concerns, we're agreeing to make changes, do things in a different way. A lot of this is very new territory, and yet there were concerns, and so new rules had to be created, and Microsoft has agreed to those rules." In August 2001, Gates reflected on antitrust issues for Microsoft to *U.S. News & World Report*, saying, "Remember when AOL tried to block Windows 95?. . . Would the world have been a better place if AOL had been able to block Windows 95? That's an exercise for the reader. Seriously, the whole PC industry was based on that advance."

Despite the distraction of the antitrust case, Microsoft continued to develop Windows, releasing Windows XP in the fall of 2001. The new version completely does away with the MS–DOS format. Windows CE, Microsoft's operating system for its hand–held computers also began to draw more notice, and Microsoft was able to begin chipping away at the dominant hand–held leaders, Palm and Handspring.

In January 2000, Gates announced his resignation as Microsoft CEO, naming longstanding associate Steven A. Ballmer to succeed him. Gates stated that this change represented his wish to focus his personal energies on new development as "chief software architect" of a new type of system encompassing large networks, PCs, and consumer electronic devices connected to the Internet.

Social and Economic Impact

In addition to sparking the PC revolution, Gates created new paradigms for how new products should be created and sold. Accompanying Gates' competitive drive is a fear of losing. A guiding force in Microsoft's economics is Gates' insistence that rather than incurring debt, Microsoft should have on hand enough cash to operate for a year without any revenues. Business associates have argued the point with him and succeeded to a certain extent in acquiring cash for investment in expansion and development; however, as of January 1997, Microsoft had $8 billion in cash and no long–term debt.

Microsoft employs around 40,000 people in 60 countries. A typical Microsoft employee is very intelligent but may only have little if any experience—much like Gates' own background. Employees are typically expected to put in whatever hours are necessary to solve problems and meet new product deadlines, and they become part of the "Microsoft culture." Yet Gates also invites challenge and confrontation to maintain flexibility, and he rewards employees who offer viable new ideas. As a student of business history, Gates came to believe that it is paramount for corporate executives to be sensitive to change in their industries and that they remain flexible in order to respond to change when necessary and to seize opportunities. In *Hard Drive*, James Wallace and Jim Erickson quoted Gates as saying, "I can do anything if I put my mind to it."

Microsoft's influence has spread to banking, retailing, entertainment, and the news. MSNBC debuted on July 15, 1996. This was a joint venture between Microsoft and General Electric's NBC, which offers a 24–hour cable–TV–news channel with a companion Web site. Gates envisions the merging of content and software and with this move has positioned Microsoft to be at the forefront. Real estate is another area that Gates became involved with in 1998, when Cliveden PLC of Britain, a luxury hotel and leisure club operator, agreed to be purchased by Destination USA, a group of U.S. investors, of which Gates owns 10 percent.

Gates also hopes to make Microsoft the number one software provider to China, the world's largest emerging software market. By training technicians at China's universities and centers, developing Chinese–language Windows operating systems, providing Chinese government ministries with PCs that use Windows and DOS, and by developing with Chinese researchers interactive TV and speech and handwriting recognition programs, Gates is laying the groundwork for enormous Microsoft sales.

Gates' other interests encompass medicine and the arts. In 1989 he started a company called Corbis, which owns the rights to 800,000 digitized images. The images are licensed by newspapers and magazines and published by them either in print or electronic form. He has also invested in Teledisc, which is working on a plan to provide worldwide, two–way broadband telecommunications service. Gates sits on the board of ICOS, a biotechnology company, and has invested in others in this field. He believes that, with the Internet, researchers will be able to communicate faster with each other, thus leading to more cures. Finding the best way to treat or prevent illness is important to Gates. He donated $1.5 million in 1998 to the International Aids Vaccine Scientific Blueprint project in the hope of developing a vaccine for Aids.

By late 1999, Gates' net worth was estimated at about $90 billion, making him by far the wealthiest self–made man in the world. Although his personal wealth had declined to about $59 billion by 2001, he remained the world's richest man. Despite criticism that he has done little with his fortune, Gates and his wife Melinda have endowed more than $24 billion for philanthropic causes. Of this amount, more than $2 billion has gone to global health initiatives, $500 million to improving learning opportunities, $200 million to community projects in the Pacific northwest, and $29 million to special projects and annual giving campaigns. In 1996 he and Ballmer donated $25 million to fund computer science work at Harvard University. In 1999 Gates donated $20 million toward the construction of a new computer science facility at Massachusetts Institute of Technology, to be designed by award–winning architect Frank Gehry. Also in 1999, Gates formed the Gates Millennium Scholars Program, which will provide $1 billion for qualified African–American, Hispanic, Native American, and Asian students to obtain undergraduate and graduate degrees in engineering, math, science, and education. The program plans to pay full educational costs through graduate school for qualified students who maintain a 3.0 cumulative average. African–American and Hispanic leaders have hailed the program as an important step in attracting minority students to these fields. In October 2001, Gates' foundation contributed more than $500 million toward wiring schools and libraries. Gates told the *Economist*, "I used to have the notion that I would wait until my 50s or 60s to put substantial resources into the foundation. . . . Seeing how urgent the needs are changed my time line."

Sources of Information

Contact at: Microsoft Corporation
   1 Microsoft Way
   Redmond, WA 98052
   Business Phone: (425)882–8080
   URL: http://www.microsoft.com

Bibliography

Bray, Hiawatha. "Judge Declares Microsoft a Monopoly; Ruling a Near Total Defeat." *Boston Globe*, 6 November 1999.

Brown, Eryn. "Just Another Product Launch." *Fortune*, 12 November 2001.

"The Classroom of the Future." *Newsweek*, 22 October 2001.

Cohen, Adam. "When You Have $24 Million. . . ." *Time*, 5 November 2001.

Corcoran, Elizabeth. "Bill Bites Back." *Forbes*, 12 November 2001.

Corcoran, Elizabeth. "No Regrets." *Forbes*, 26 November 2001.

"The Engineer of a Computer's Soul: Gates Talks." *U.S. News & World Report*, 20 August 2001.

"Gates and the States: Nine Attorneys General Settle with the Software Giant. Nine Soldier On. Has Microsoft Already Won?" *Time*, 19 November 2001.

Kerber, Ross. "Gates Donates $20M to MIT Computer Lab." *Boston Globe*, 14 April 1999.

Markoff, John, and Steve Lohr. "Microsoft Names a New Chief Executive." *New York Times*, 14 January 2000.

"Microsoft Stays Whole." *Maclean's*, 17 September 2001.

Rivera, Elaine. "Bill Gives Big: Mr. Microsoft Will Send 2,000 Minority Students to College." *Time*, 27 September 1999.

"Saint Bill." *The Economist*, 16 June 2001.

"An Unsettling Settlement: Microsoft." *The Economist*, 10 November 2001.

"We'll Move On." *Newsweek*, 12 November 2001.

"William H. Gates." Microsoft Corporation, 2001. Available at http://www.microsoft.com/billgates/bio.asp.

Alan Gerry

(1928-)
Granite Associates LP

Overview

A high school dropout, Alan Gerry transformed a tiny TV repair shop in New York's Catskills region into one of the nation's largest cable television systems. A pioneer in cable television, Gerry started small, providing reliable television reception to 300 subscribers in his hometown of Liberty, New York. Borrowing heavily but wisely, he built his cable system into the eighth largest in the United States. In 1996 he sold it to media giant Time Warner for $2.7 billion. But Gerry was far from through. Two years later, as chairman and chief executive officer of Granite Foundation LP, a venture capital firm he founded, Gerry purchased 2,000 acres of woods and pastureland in his native Sullivan County. It was not just any woods and pastureland, however, but the Bethel, New York, farm of the late Max Yasgur, home to the original Woodstock concert in 1969. Gerry announced plans to turn the near–sacred Woodstock site into a music–themed tourist attraction. Gerry, who has never strayed far from his roots in Sullivan County, made clear that his motives for the purchase had more to do with stimulating economic growth in the moribund Catskills region than any great love of rock music.

Personal Life

One of America's 250 richest people, Alan Gerry lives today with his wife, Sandra, in Sullivan County, New York, not far from the place of his birth. The couple has three children, daughters Robyn and Annelise, both of whom are married and live nearby, and son Adam, a recent graduate of Syracuse University's College of Law. The Gerrys have a second home in Naples, Florida, but spend most of their time in Sullivan County, not far from the Ferndale headquarters of Granite Associates LP, a venture capital firm founded by Gerry after his $2.7 billion sale of Cablevision Industries to Time Warner. It was Granite Associates that purchased the rural site of the original 1969 Woodstock concert for development into a theme park.

Son of a Sullivan County frozen food distributor, Gerry was born in 1928 in Ferndale, New York. During the hard years of the Great Depression, Gerry's father struggled to keep food on the table. Although Gerry and his family lived briefly in New York City's borough of Bronx during World War II, he spent most of his life in and around Liberty, New York, the heart of Sullivan County in the Catskills region. A few months shy of getting his high school diploma in 1946, Gerry dropped out to join the marines. He was not running away from an education but pursuing a specific program of study offered by the U.S. Marines and scheduled to be phased out. That program trained Gerry to service the electrical systems of aircraft. In 1949 he left the military and enrolled in a three–year television repair training course at New York City's Dellahany University. In his spare time, he began repairing TV sets, a business he later undertook on a full-time basis.

Chronology:
Alan Gerry

1928: Born.

1946: Dropped out of high school to join the U.S. Marine Corps.

1951: Opened TV repair shop in Liberty, NY.

1956: Expanded into cable television.

1978: Negotiates $5.2 million loan from John Hancock Insurance to expand cable system.

1989: Converts Los Angeles area cable system to fiber optic.

1995: Received cable–Warner for $2.7 billion in stock.

1997: Purchased 2,000 acres near Bethel, NY, site of original Woodstock concert.

1998: Staged weekend concert at Woodstock site.

Career Details

In 1951, Gerry opened a two–man TV sales, repair, and installation shop in a converted grain elevator in Liberty. One of the common complaints he heard from his customers was the difficulty that most of them encountered in getting decent TV reception in the mountainous resort region more than 100 miles from Manhattan. To supplement his regular business, Gerry began creating tiny neighborhood cable systems, linking 10 to 15 homes to a nearby master antenna mounted on the highest point in the neighborhood. The neighborhood cable systems were not terribly sophisticated, but they worked. In 1955, Gerry met with some representatives of Jerrold Electronics, one of the pioneer manufacturers of equipment for community antenna television systems. He learned that there was technology and equipment available to create large–scale cable systems that could deliver clear TV signals to hundreds of customers.

As a first step, Gerry appealed to Liberty's town fathers for permission to run 15 miles of cable throughout the town so that he could link together all the neighborhood clusters of customers he'd been serving. He then won local approval to erect a massive master antenna atop Liberty's Ravonnah Hill. When everything was finally in place in 1956, Gerry's first city–wide cable service began operations, providing his 300 initial subscribers with crystal clear reception of five TV channels. Pleased with the results in Liberty, Gerry began to ag-

gressively expand to other communities in Sullivan County, obtained franchises in neighboring counties, and paid roughly $300 a subscriber to buy up existing small–scale cable systems in the region.

Convinced that his fledgling business—now dubbed Cablevision Industries—would fly much sooner if he alone were mapping its future, Gerry got a loan so he could buy out his partners in the cable operation. One of his stockholders, he later recalled, was the company accountant, "and he used to declare a dividend every 90 days—so there was no money to run the company." By the early 1970s, Gerry had expanded his cable system into nearby Pennsylvania and was making inroads into Massachusetts, but it was a painstaking process. John Rigas, chairman and CEO of Adelphia Communications, recently recalled the many obstacles faced by cable operators during that period. "To survive in those early years, you had to go to council after council—almost hat in hand—to get a franchise renewed or ask for a quarter increase." Rigas hailed Gerry for his contribution to the industry as a whole, saying: "Alan Gerry's tenacity and his strong commitment to properly serving his customers carried him through some difficult years, helped bring the industry to a higher level, and made him the giant he became."

It was Gerry's practice to finance his regional expansions with loans from banks in the region into which

Alan Gerry. (Granite Associates, L.P.)

he was expanding. Getting to know the local bankers up-front often paid off down the line when he needed community support for his plans or additional funding. As his financing needs became more extensive, he was forced to go to nationwide lenders. In the late 1970s, he negotiated a $5.2 million loan from John Hancock Insurance. When Cablevision passed the 100,000–subscriber mark, it went to the junk bond market for additional financing. Of Gerry's day–to–day involvement in the business, industry colleague Bill Bresnan, president of Bresnan Communications, said: "Alan Gerry really lived his company. He didn't sit in an ivory tower but visited his systems and went into those communities and met the mayors, city councils, and local newspapers. He rolled up his sleeves and got involved. So he got a real appreciation for the business and the people in it—the kind of understanding that you can't get in a distant office."

Gerry also helped to pioneer some of the technology that has allowed the cable industry to grow more rapidly. In the early 1980s, Cablevision installed the first high–powered microwave delivery system, using it to link together the company's cable systems in the Catskills region's Orange, Sullivan, and Ulster counties. Gerry used the microwave technology to link together 17 franchises his company had won in Massachusetts, and similar systems were constructed in the Middle Atlantic States and Florida. Speaking about the company's growth in this period, Gerry said: "For three or four years during the high–growth mid–1980s, we were the nation's

fastest growing cable system, percentage-wise." Cablevision was also one of the first cable systems to use fiber optic cable. In the late 1980s, the company purchased a cable system in the San Fernando Valley outside Los Angeles from a Canadian operator. To try to restore subscribers' faith in the system's reliability, Cablevision in 1989 converted the system to fiber optic, paving the way for many other cable operators across the country to follow.

In 1995, Gerry received the National Cable & Telecommunications Association's (NCTA) coveted Vanguard Award in recognition of his leadership in the cable industry. Each year, NCTA awards two of the Vanguard Awards for Leadership; one called the Larry Boggs Award is awarded to the man the association deems most worthy for his leadership role and the other called the Idell Kaitz Award is given to a leading woman in the industry.

Because Gerry had never taken a major equity partner nor offered Cablevision stock to the public, he owned more than 95 percent of the company himself when Time Warner began showing interest an interest in acquiring it in the mid–1990s. Over the previous four decades, Gerry had transformed the little TV sales and repair shop in a converted grain elevator into the eighth largest cable operator in the nation. The deal finally struck for Time Warner's acquisition of Cablevision brought Gerry approximately $2.7 billion in Time Warner stock. Cablevision, at the time of the acquisition, had 2,500 employees and approximately 1.3 million subscribers in 18 states.

On the far side of 65 after the sale of Cablevision to Time Warner, Gerry might reasonably have been expected to take the billions he'd made in the deal and retire to a sunnier clime to enjoy life away from the frontlines of the business world. But Gerry is not your average guy. Anxious to help others get a leg up in the field that had been so good to him, he founded Granite Associates LP, a venture capital firm that seeks to finance promising entrepreneurs in the technology field. He headquartered the new company, which he serves as chairman and CEO, in Ferndale, New York, the place of his birth, just a few miles down the road from Liberty, scene of his first business triumph.

Social and Economic Impact

As a pioneer in cable television, Alan Gerry helped to shape the industry as it matured into the vast business enterprise it is today. Although he dropped out of high school before getting his diploma, Gerry puts a high value on education and doesn't recommend his course of action to young people looking to make their personal fortunes in the high–tech field that was so good to him. Timing had a great deal to do with his success in the cable industry. By getting on board while the business was still in its infancy, he was able to parlay his modest investments into billions over four decades. A strong supporter of higher education, Gerry still recognizes that an occasional flash of inspiration or creativity can sometimes overshadow the value of a college diploma on your wall. "When you have a brilliant idea, nobody is going to ask your diploma," he once told *Forbes*. "You don't need a four–year college degree if you have burning ambition or a great plan."

Gerry's importance in the development of the cable industry is indisputable, but the folks in Sullivan County, New York, value him for the loyalty he's shown to the place of his birth. In the heart of the Catskills region, once a lively summer and winter playground for people from nearby New York City, Sullivan County and some of its neighboring counties have seen their fortunes reversed in recent years. Many of the big hotels and resorts on the Borscht Belt have been shuttered for a decade or more, including the famed Grossinger's in Liberty. The regional economy has been on the skids since the tourism business began its decline. But Gerry came up with a novel plan to draw more outsiders into the Catskills, especially into Sullivan County. In 1997, he bought up more than 1,000 acres of the Bethel, New York, site of the 1969 Woodstock rock festival, and announced a plan to transform the property into a theme park. Not because he's an unrepentant fan of rock and roll but because he thinks such a development could go a long way toward reviving the economy of the region where he has spent

almost all of his life. It remains to be seen whether Gerry's plan will ever be realized, but it's clear to county development officials that he's doing what he can to help revive the region. And with a record like his, who's going to be against him?

Sources of Information

Contact at: Granite Associates LP
225 Sullivan Ave.
Ferndale, NY 12734–4313
Business Phone: (845) 295–2410

Bibliography
"Alan Gerry, Chairman and CEO, Granite Associates LP," National Cable Television Center and Museum. Available at http://www.cablecenter.org/Main/Museum/Hall_of_Fame. (26 November 2001).

Berger, Joseph. "Theme Park on Woodstock Is Envisioned." *New York Times*, 24 April 1997.

Bianco, Anthony. "Alan Gerry's Woodstock Notion." *Business Week*, 22 March 1999.

The Complete Marquis Who's Who. New Providence, NJ: Marquis Who's Who, 2001.

"Some Billionaires Choose School of Hard Knocks." *Forbes*, 29 June 2000.

Charles M. Geschke

(1939-)
Adobe Systems, Inc.

Overview

Dr. Charles M. Geschke co–founded Adobe Systems, Inc. in 1982 with John Warnock. He served as co–chairman of the board and president of the company until 2000, when he retired as president. He retains his position as co–chair. Geschke and Warnock created a billion–dollar software business based on a handful of highly innovative and successful products, including Adobe Acrobat, PhotoShop, and PageMaker.

Personal Life

The son of a photo engraver, Chuck Geschke grew up in Cleveland, Ohio, was educated in Catholic schools as a child, and spent three and a half years at a Jesuit seminary studying to become a priest. Ultimately deciding to forego the priesthood, he enrolled in Xavier University where he received a bachelor's degree in classics and a master's degree in mathematics. He earned a Ph.D. in computer science from Carnegie Mellon University. Geschke has received honors for his achievements from numerous organizations, including the Association for Computing Machinery, Carnegie Mellon University, the National Computer Graphics Association, and the Rochester Institute of Technology. He is a member of the National Academy of Engineering and the Government–University Industry Research Roundtable of the National Academy of Sciences. He is also a member of the Board of Governors for the San Francisco Symphony. Geschke serves on the computer advisory boards of Carnegie Mellon University and Princeton University and is a member of the Board of Trustees for the Uni-

versity of San Francisco. In 1996 he joined the Board of Directors of Rambus, Inc., which produces high–speed memory interface technology. He is also a member of the Board of Directors of PointCast, Inc.

Geschke married his wife, Nan, in 1964, and the couple, who have three children, lives in Los Altos, California, where they have resided since 1972. In May 1992, Geschke was kidnapped at gunpoint from the parking lot of Adobe's corporate headquarters, blindfolded, and taken to a house in Hollister, California. Five days later, the Federal Bureau of Investigations found Geschke unharmed; the kidnappers, who had requested a ransom, were arrested, tried, and convicted.

Career Details

Geschke began his career as a scientist and researcher in the Computer Sciences Laboratory of Xerox's Palo Alto Research Center. In 1980 he helped establish and became manager of Xerox's Imaging Sciences Laboratory at the same location. His duties centered on overseeing and conducting research activities in the areas of computer science, graphics, image processing, and optics. In 1982 he and John Warnock, who conducted interactive graphics research for Xerox, became frustrated by the difficulty of moving their innovations and research beyond the laboratory and into production. The two decided to venture out on their own; they quit Xerox and created a new company, Adobe Systems, Inc., named after a creek that runs past their homes in Los Altos, California.

Success did not take long. The first product marketed by Adobe Systems was PostScript, a revolutionary, complex computer language that sent information to the printer or other output device regarding the appearance of the electronic document. With PostScript capabilities, highly detailed, professional documents could be easily created using a personal computer and a laser printer. High–quality graphics could be intermixed with formatted text on a single page—an exceptional benefit to such businesses as advertising agencies. Essentially, PostScript introduced the age of desktop publishing.

By 1984, just two years after forming their company, Geschke and Warnock reported Adobe revenues of $1.7 million. The following year they garnered the attention of Apple Computer, Inc., which purchased a 19 percent stake in Adobe and began packaging PostScript with its LaserWriter printer, helping Apple's MacIntosh storm the market as the leading computer for graphic design. In 1986 Adobe partnered with Texas Instruments, Inc., to incorporate PostScript applications into two of its laser printers, which were the first to offer PostScript capabilities to IBM–compatible personal computers.

As a result of the quick success, Adobe expanded rapidly; staff numbers doubled from 27 to 54 between

Chronology:
Charles M. Geschke

1939: Born.

1972: Hired by Xerox Palo Alto Research Center.

1980: Became manager of Xerox's Imaging Sciences Laboratory.

1982: Quit Xerox to co–found Adobe Systems, Inc. with John Warnock; became co–chairman and president.

1983: Introduced Adobe PostScript.

1986: Adobe went public, completing an initial stock offering.

1987: Introduced Adobe Illustrator and Adobe Type Library.

1992: Kidnapped and held for ransom for five days.

1993: Introduced Adobe Acrobat.

1994: Acquired Aldus, owner of PhotoShop and PageMaker.

1999: Introduced GoLive to compete with Quark Xpress.

2000: Retired as president; retained co–chairmanship.

2001: Revenues for fiscal year exceeded $1.2 billion.

1984 and 1985 (and would swell to 3,000 by 2001). By the end of 1986, PostScript had become an invaluable tool for simplifying desktop publishing and reducing costs from the traditional methods of typesetting. Not only did advertising agencies flock to PostScript, but also businesses, corporations, and even the federal government began creating in–house materials that would have been previously farmed out at an increased cost to a printing service.

After the initial introduction of PostScript technology, there was a mad rush to develop complementary applications and uses. Within the first few years, over 15,000 applications were developed. Adobe provided the additional innovation of "Type I fonts" that further increased the range of PostScript uses: Type I could supply fonts in digital form at any resolution. This led to the creation of some 15,000 typefaces. PostScript was also further developed so that it could be used with mainframes, making it accessible to multi–computer networks. Independent software developers used PostScript

Charles M. Geschke. (AP Photo/Richard Drew.)

to create programs that expanded and simplified a wide variety of graphic design applications for all hardware designs and operating systems.

For the first five years, Geschke and Warnock focused on selling their product to original equipment manufacturers (OEMs), a strategy that proved very successful. With its one blockbuster program, Adobe posted a profit of $3.6 million on $16 million in sales in 1986. The same year, Geschke and Warnock took their company public and began selling stock. Despite its rapid success, Adobe was heavily dependent on Apple for its profits. In 1986, dealings with Apple accounted for 80 percent of Adobe's business. Although Geschke and Warnock began selling their product to IBM, the bulk of their business lay with Apple. Retail sales accounted for

a small portion of Adobe's income. However, in 1987, Adobe moved into the retail market with the introduction of Adobe Illustrator, a program able to produce high–quality line drawings. Illustrator was a big hit with graphic designers and technical illustrators.

With one success followed by another, Geschke and Warnock hit the nail on the head again when they introduced the Adobe Type Library, a collection of typefaces developed specifically for electronic application. Initially, the Type Library offered 300 unique typefaces, making it the largest collection available; the 2001 version of the Type Library (renamed as Font Folio) provided 2,750 font choices. In 1989 Adobe also made available Type Manager, a free program that simplified font management and allowed fonts to be resized easily. Having established Adobe as the leading provider of cutting–edge graphics technology, Geschke and Warnock made yet another important advancement when Adobe developed Display PostScript, which provided onscreen confirmation of page layout and design. Basically, what was seen on the screen would come out exactly that way when printed. Display PostScript also allowed users to manipulate and alter graphics.

By the end of the decade, after just eight years in existence, Geschke and Warnock had developed Adobe into big business. In 1989 the company posted a net income of $33.7 million on sales of $121 million. In 1990 revenues reached over $168 million with a net income of $40 million. The following year saw yet another large jump in revenues, up 36 percent to almost $330 million and net income rising to $51.6 million. The co–founders had wisely expanded their interests and clientele. Though Apple remained its largest customer, Apple–generated revenues were down to 33 percent of Adobe's total income. Over 25 PostScript printers were on the market, and 20 computer companies had entered into licensing agreements with Adobe. Geschke and Warnock had also gone international, licensing PostScript to Canon, Inc., of Japan. To protect their interests and new technological innovations, Adobe also made advancements in the legal issues involved in computer development by being the first business to file for a copyright license of a typeface. And, although they distributed licenses for the use of PostScript, Geschke and Warnock wisely maintained exclusive control over Acrobat Reader, the software that interprets the electronic codes.

In the early 1990s, Geschke and Warnock led their company into new areas, including advancements in the optical character recognition, referred to as OCR, which allowed scanned text to be read by a computer, enabling it to be edited. Adobe also entered the multimedia market for the first time by introducing Premiere 3.0, a program that provided desktop video editing and special effects capabilities.

In 1993 Geschke and Warnock took another giant step forward in technology with the Adobe Acrobat software, revolutionizing the future of electronic distribution.

The problem with sending documents electronically was the likely incompatibility of the sending and receiving computers. Although the previously developed computer language ASCII (American Standard Code for Information Interexchange) provided a format for sending and receiving text, all formatting, font styles, designs, color, and graphic components were dumped from the transmission. Adobe Acrobat provided a platform by which those elements could be retained, independent of computer hardware and operating systems. With Acrobat such graphic–rich documents as spreadsheets, reports, brochures, newsletters, and reports could be relayed electronically with all graphics, graphs, charts, pictures, and the like intact. The receiver did not need to have the originating software (e.g., Microsoft Word or Corel Draw); all that was necessary was that both the sending and receiving computers have Acrobat installed. Although the received document could not be edited, it easily could be navigated, printed, and stored.

Between 1992 and 1996, Adobe made 10 acquisitions. Of primary importance was the August 1994 merger with Aldus, a software development company with two headlining programs: PageMaker and Photo-Shop. PageMaker is one of the two dominating desktop publishing packages, along with its main competitor Quark Xpress, and PhotoShop provides extensive image capturing and manipulation capabilities for photo designs. By 1996 PostScript, PageMaker, and PhotoShop were each producing revenues of over $100 million. The three products provided a quality combination, allowing Adobe to expand its offerings to a wide range of needs and interests. And, as the predominance of computer–based communication increased by leaps and bounds, Adobe went along for the ride. When asked in 1995 by *InformationWeek* about any fear that Adobe was too heavily weighted toward the print industry, Geschke replied, "The move from paper–based to electronic documents doesn't worry us. People still want authoring tools." During the last half of the 1990s and moving into the next century, Geschke strongly advocated for his company's continued expansion both in size and scope. The major new focus was toward applications involving the Internet and World Wide Web. Web publishing tools were either added or incorporated into already existing desktop publishing software.

So far Geschke has helped keep Adobe a step ahead of its competition, but in March 2000 he retired from his position as the company's president. In December 2000 Warnock stepped down as chief executive officer, and in May 2001 he also retired from the position of the chief technical officer. Both Geschke and Warnock remain as co–chairs of the Board of Directors. Analysts reserved final judgment on the impact the change in leadership will have on the company. Despite slowed growth in 2001 due to the sluggish economy, confidence remains high that Adobe has the products and the management to withstand a recessive economy.

Social and Economic Impact

Upon the release of Adobe Acrobat, Geschke told *Industry Week*, "We do not expect that paper will vanish. We understand the love affair that humans have with the written word—and the traditional means by which it is delivered. Instead, we believe that print and its electronic counterpart will evolve together so that they will ultimately coexist in forms that are best suited to a particular communication purpose." Geschke, the management expert, paired with Warnock, the technical expert, has gone a long way to merging the printed and electronic word. With close to 3,000 employees and annual revenues topping $1.2 billion, Adobe has grown to become the second largest personal computer software company in the United States. The Adobe motto is "Publish anything, anywhere, on any device." To that end, Adobe's next innovative idea is being tagged "Network Publishing," a phrase that invokes images of cross–applications that move information from a computer to a hand–held to a cell phone to the Web and back again—regardless of platform or device.

By the end of 2001, Adobe was offering close to fifty products covering six major categories: publishing (print and Web–based), digital video, digital imaging, collections, technologies, and Acrobat–based applications called "ePaper" products. Revenues for fiscal year 2001 topped $1.2 billion. The genius of Adobe's leadership team can be witnessed in the combination of successfully numerous long–standing products combined with a continued presence on the cutting edge of technology. PhotoShop, in its sixth version, and Illustrator, in its tenth, are joined by newer programs such as Go-Live, Adobe's Web–authoring program, and InDesign, a professional layout and design application.

According to Geschke, the success of Adobe is based on the people–friendly environment he and Warnock established at the beginning and have deliberately worked to maintain. *Industry Week* noted that Geschke "comes across as a friendly father figure who's most interested in the welfare of his 'family' of [nearly 3,000] employees." Geschke told the publication, "Every capital asset we have at Adobe gets into an automobile and drives home at night. Without them, there is nothing of substance in this company. It is the creativity of individuals—not machines—that determines the success of this company."

Sources of Information

Contact at: Adobe Systems, Inc.
　　1585 Charleston Rd.
　　PO Box 7900
　　Mountain View, CA 94039–7900
　　Business Phone: (415)961–3769
　　URL: http://www.adobe.com

Bibliography

"Adobe, Quark Duke It Out in Boston." *American Printer*, April 1999.

"Adobe Systems, Inc." Hoover's Online, Inc., 2001. Available at http://www.hoovers.com.

"Adobe's Warnock Retires." *American Printer*, May 2001.

Brandt, John, Jr. "Big Ideas, Big Payoffs." *Industry Week*, 5 February 1996.

Chappell Belden, Anne. "A Dramatic Kidnapping Revisited." *Los Altos Town Crier*, 15 October 1997.

"Charles Geschke." Adobe Systems, Inc., 2001. Available at http://www.adobe.com.

Dvorak, John C. "The Future of Adobe." *PC Magazine*, 23 February 1999.

Grant, Alex. "Adobe Caution." *Printing World*, 26 March 2001.

James, Marinell. "Adobe Systems Incorporated." In Paula Kepos, ed. *International Directory of Company Histories*. Vol. 10. New York: St. James Press, 1995.

Leibs, Scott. "Top 50 Software Vendors—Adobe: What We Worry?" *Information Week*, 22 May 1995.

"Rambus Names Adobe Co–Founder/President to Board of Directors; Dr. Charles Geschke Brings 25 Years of Technology Management Expertise." *Business Wire*, 1 April 1996.

Teresko, John. "Can an Acrobat Tame the Paper Tiger?" *Industry Week*, 4 October 1993.

Verespe, Michael. "Empire Without Emperors." *Industry Week*, 5 February 1996.

Ellen Gordon

Overview

After working her way up the corporate ladder to president of the company, Ellen Rubin Gordon used modern business strategies to keep Tootsie Roll Industries, Inc. at the top of the international lollipop business, while still maintaining the feel of a "mom and pop" operation.

Personal Life

Gordon was born Ellen Rubin, the daughter of William B. and Cele H. Rubin in New York. She attended Vassar College from 1948 to 1950. While at Vassar, she met and married Melvin J. Gordon, 11 years her senior, who would later become CEO of Tootsie Roll. The two were married on June 25, 1950, and had four daughters—Virginia, Karen, Wendy, and Lisa.

After her marriage, Ellen Gordon eventually returned to college. She attended Wellesley and ultimately received her B.A in 1965 from Brandeis University. In 1968 Gordon did graduate work at the Graduate School of Arts and Science at Harvard University, which was the same year she started to work at Tootsie Roll.

Gordon has served as president and board of director member of the Committee of 200 and as vice–president and board member of the National Confectioners Association. She has served as director and president of HDI Investment Corporation. She has also sat on the Harvard University Board of Overseers Visiting Committee for the university's medical and dental schools. She has received a number of honors for her contributions and her work, including the Dean's Award from

(1932-)
Tootsie Roll Industries

Ellen Gordon with some Tootsie Roll products. *(AP/Wide World Photos/Beth A. Keiser.)*

the National Candy Wholesalers Association in 1978 and the Kettle Award from the candy industry in 1985.

When the Gordons are not in Chicago, the headquarters of Tootsie Roll Industries, they reside in Center Harbor, New Hampshire. The Gordons eventually hope to turn the business over to their four daughters and to the company's senior managers.

Career Details

Ellen Gordon's involvement with Tootsie Roll began in 1922, a decade before her birth, when the company went

public and Gordon's mother, a schoolteacher, bought some shares of the company stock; she also encouraged all of her relatives to do the same. Gradually accumulating stock, by the 1930s she had a controlling interest in the company because of her stock holdings. Eventually, Melvin and Ellen inherited the business. Melvin joined the board in 1952, and in 1968 Ellen Gordon went to work for the candy company, starting in the areas of pension planning and product development. Two years later, she had moved into the position of corporate secretary. From there, her rise in the company was steady: vice–president of product development in 1974; senior vice–president in 1976, and president and chief operating officer (COO) in 1978, a position she continues to maintain.

By all accounts, Tootsie Roll is a sweet place to work—literally. Employees are encouraged to sample as many of the confections as they would like during the business day, and Gordon is known as a boss who takes a personal interest in her staff and employees. She greets everyone in the company by name.

Tootsie Roll was started in 1896 by an Austrian immigrant, Leo Hirshfield, who brought his secret candy recipe to the United States and began selling his hand–rolled chocolates for a penny a piece in a small store in New York. Hirshfield named his chocolate candies after his daughter, nicknamed Tootsie, who was five years old at the time.

By the early 1900s the candy was manufactured at a small candy factory. Its name was changed to Sweets Co. of America in 1917, and at that time, the company began to advertise its confection nationally. The company was registered on the New York Stock Exchange by 1922. The Tootsie Pop—a hard lollipop with a chewy Tootsie Roll center—was invented in 1931, and within seven years, the company had moved its operation to Hoboken, New Jersey, and began assembly–line mass production of the candy.

As demand for the candy increased, the company opened a West Coast division, in Los Angeles, in 1949. It wasn't until 1966 that the company changed its name to Tootsie Roll Industries, Inc. At that time, the corporate headquarters were moved to Chicago, and a manufacturing plant was opened there, too.

When Gordon was named company president and COO in 1978, she was only the second female president of a company listed on the New York Stock Exchange. She would often get letters, she once said, addressed to Mr. Ellen Gordon or with the greeting, "Dear Mr. Gordon." In 1993, Gordon proved her executive mettle when she won her company $1.4 million in state and local tax exemptions and other incentives, in exchange for keeping the business in Chicago.

Although Tootsie Roll was worth an estimated $245 million at the time, Gordon managed to obtain a lucrative incentive and benefits package for her more than 800 employees, capitalizing on the fact that the city had suffered a major economic blow the previous year. That move had cost the Windy City 2,000 jobs, and officials were willing to negotiate with Gordon to avoid losing another substantial segment of the workforce.

As part of the settlement, Gordon asked for a $1.4 million exemption in both city and state taxes over a 15–year period. In addition, she sought a low–interest loan so the company could buy its manufacturing plant, $200,000 in job training funds, and tax breaks on machinery and processing equipment. In addition to staying in Chicago, Gordon agreed to add an additional 200 workers to the company payrolls and begin a loan program for workers who wanted to buy houses. The negotiations between Chicago and the candy company were said to have been peaceful; to keep the deal sweet, Gor-

Chronology:
Ellen Gordon

1932: Born.

1965: Earned B.A. from Brandeis University.

1968: Attended Harvard University.

1968: Began working at Tootsie Roll Industries.

1970: Promoted to corporate secretary at Tootsie Roll.

1974: Chosen as vice–president, product development at Tootsie Roll.

1976: Named senior vice–president.

1978: Named Tootsie Roll President and CEO.

1993: Bought Warner–Lambert Co.

1996: Celebrated Tootsie Roll Industry's 100th birthday.

2000: Acquired O'TEC Industries and Andes Candies.

2001: Produced 49 million tootsie rolls and 16 million lollipops daily.

---

don reportedly kept chocolates on the table throughout the transaction.

By 1995 company sales topped $300 million—making Tootsie Roll the largest lollipop producer in the world. Since then, sales have continued to rise, to meet the demands of a sweet–toothed public as well as international sales. Net sales jumped from $264.4 million in the third quarter of 1996 to $289.1 million for that same period in 1997. Also in 1997, stocks rose almost 70 percent, and the company had a net profit margin higher than Wrigley's or Hershey's Foods. Revenues for 1999 topped $396 million. In 2001 the company was producing 49 million Tootsie Rolls and 16 million lollipops daily.

Tootsie Roll candies are now sold in Canada and exported to more than 30 other countries, including an office in Hong Kong. In addition to operations in Tennessee, New York, and Massachusetts, the company has a manufacturing plant in Mexico, which produces the confection for the Mexican market.

In 1996 Tootsie Roll celebrated its 100th birthday with a gala celebration at the corporate headquarters that included a huge party and a tour of the manufacturing plant for employees and their families. The mayor of

Chicago declared it "Tootsie Roll Day" in the city, and the story of the company was broadcast, via satellite, to many national television stations.

Social and Economic Impact

There are, in all likelihood, several keys to Gordon's success with Tootsie Roll. For one thing, she has never tampered with the candy's original recipe. Tootsie Roll is a quintessential American product, with virtually universal recognition and a rich history. The candy, for instance, was a staple for troops in World War I. Legendary crooner Frank Sinatra always insisted that there be Tootsie Rolls in his hotel room when he traveled. Sammy Davis, Jr. would pass the candies out to his audience when he sang, "The Candy Man," and Jacqueline Kennedy Onassis reputedly kept a bowl of Tootsie Rolls in her office for guests.

Gordon has paid attention to her product's value and has priced traditional Tootsie Rolls in a variety of prices, ranging from a penny, just as it was when Hirshfield sold it a century ago, to 50–cent varieties. The product is sold both in individual pieces and in bags.

However, Gordon has not relied solely on Tootsie Rolls for the company's success. In fact, since the 1970s, she has acquired multiple other promising candy makers. These have included the 1972 acquisition of Mason Division of Candy Corporation of America, which makes Mason Dots and Crow brands. In 1985, Tootsie Roll bought Cellas' Confection, which makes chocolate–covered cherries. It was the 1988 purchase of Charms Co., a lollipop maker, and the combination of Charms and Tootsie Pops that turned the company into the largest manufacturer of lollipops in the world.

In 1993 Tootsie Roll branched out into a somewhat different arena when it bought the chocolate and caramel brands of Warner–Lambert Co., which included Junior Mints, Sugar Daddy, Sugar Babies, and Charleston Chews. In 2000 Tootsie Roll acquired two more candy companies: O'TEC Industries and Andes Candies. After the O'TEC acquisition, Tootsie Roll began to manufacture Fluffy Stuff Cotton Candy. The Andes acquisition added Crème de Menthe Thins, Cherry Jubilee Thins, Toffee Crunch Thins, and Mint Patties to the Tootsie Roll family. So far, the company has concentrated on other candy companies, choosing not to venture into other products. That is due, in part, to Tootsie Roll's success, but also, Gordon once admitted, to what she calls "the magic of candy. It always brings smiles when we tell people what we do."

In the end, it is still the Tootsie Rolls and the Tootsie Pops that lead the company sales, even after 100 years. As Gordon said in a 1996 interview with *Food Processing*, "the chocolaty chews and the hard candy have remained favorites."

As company president, Gordon has been quick to spot trends, pitching the low–fat content of her products to an increasingly calorie–conscious consumer. She was the first in the confection industry to pick up on what would become a huge marketing trend. In addition, Gordon has never been shy about developing new products. She introduced Caramel Apple Pops in 1996—a mix of sour apple hard candy and milk caramel in a flat pop. This has become very successful, as has the company's redesigned Sugar Blow Pop. In mid–2001 Tootsie Roll had plans to introduce Hot Chocolate Pops, chocolate–flavored hard candy lollipops dipped in marshmallow caramel, later that year. Tootsie Roll was the first to use raspberries, previously popular in drinks, in candies. Its Blue Razzberry Tootsie Pop was voted product of the year in the candy industry. In their other lines, Gordon also proved innovative, introducing a tropical mix in its Mason Dots, which include Jungle Punch, Citrus Safari, Wild Peach Berry, Ape Grape, and Orang–aga–tangy.

In an interview with *Candy Industry* in 2000, Gordon explained her company's commitment to trying new things. "We do see ourselves as innovators. Innovation is coming up with a new way of doing things—be it in technology, ingredients, or marketing. We are developing new ways of doing things all the time," she said. Gordon's innovative ways seem to be paying off; in the fiscal year 2000, her company posted a net profit in excess of $75 million, a 6 percent increase from the previous year, on sales of $427 million. The Gordons own 70 percent of the company's stock, valued at $970 million, and the two earn combined annual salaries nearing $4 million.

While Tootsie Rolls still come in their traditional wrapper, Gordon has changed a decades–old ad of an owl and a turtle to animated, high–tech creatures asking the traditional question: "How many licks does it take to get to the center of a Tootsie Roll Pop?" This is meant to appeal to a younger, more technologically savvy audience. Gordon's management style has been cited by industry watchers as very successful. For one thing, she and her husband emphasize cross–training employees, so workers have a broader understanding of the business and a sense of what goes on in all the other departments. The two attempt to discourage office politics and encourage teamwork, always rewarding creativity. The company maintains a workforce of almost 2,000 employees.

Tootsie Rolls have become a part of American life in much the same way as other household brands. While it can be difficult to sort out fact from myth, it may be that fancy is part of the product appeal. In her *Food Processing* interview, Gordon told this anecdote: "There's one story about a man who went into a convenience store and held up the cashier. Along with the money, he took a bag of Tootsie Rolls. He left the store and began eating them, dropping the wrappers one by one. The police were able to follow the wrappers and caught up with him."

Sources of Information

Contact at: Tootsie Roll Industries
    7401 S. Cicero Ave.
    Chicago, IL 60629
    Business Phone: (773) 838–3400
    URL: http://www.tootsie–roll.com

Bibliography

Amire, Roula. "Innovation and Quality Keep Tootsie Roll On Top." *Candy Industry*, August 2000.

"Bigger Breaks for Small Business." *Working Woman*, November 1993.

Celebrity Register. Detroit: Gale Research, 1990.

Miller, Dan. "The Rich List." *Chicago Sun Times*. Available at http://www. suntimes.com/richlist/index.html.

"On a Roll: Candymakers Ellen and Melvin Gordon, Tootsie Roll's Leaders Keep Brand On Track in Its 100th Year." *Food Processing*, December 1996.

Strahler, Steven R. "Tootsie Roll Industries Inc." *Crain's Chicago Business*. 7 June 2000.

"Tootsie Roll Company." *Hoover's Online*, 2001. Available at http://www.hoovers.com.

"Tootsie Roll Company History: 1896–2000." Tootsie Roll Industries. Available at http://www.tootsie-roll.com/history.html.

Who's Who of American Women. New Providence, NJ: Marquis Who's Who, 1996.

Berry Gordy, Jr.

(1929-)
Motown Records

Overview

Berry Gordy, Jr. founded Motown, the fledgling record company of 1959 that grew into the most successful African–American enterprise in the United States and was responsible for a new sound that transformed popular music.

Personal Life

Berry Gordy Jr., was born on November 28, 1929, and reared in Detroit. He was not the first businessman in the family; both parents were self–employed, his father as a plastering contractor, his mother as an insurance agent. Gordy dropped out of Northeastern High School in his junior year to pursue a career as a featherweight boxer. Between 1948 and 1951, he fought 15 Golden Gloves matches, 12 of which he won, but his fighting career was clipped short when he was drafted to serve in the Korean War.

Berry Gordy married Thelma Coleman in 1953. They had two sons, Berry IV and Terry, and one daughter, Hazel, who married Jermaine Jackson in 1973. Gordy's second marriage was to Raynoma Liles in 1959; they had one son, Kerry. Gordy also had a son with Margaret Norton in 1964 whom they named Kennedy, after John F. Kennedy. He later changed his name to Rockwell and recorded for Motown in 1984. Gordy lives in the Los Angeles area on a Bel Air estate. He highly values his privacy and rarely deals with the press.

Throughout his career Gordy has received numerous awards, including Business Achievement Award

from the Interracial Council for Business Opportunity (1967), the Martin Luther King, Jr. Leadership Award (1969), an award for Outstanding Contribution to the Music Industry at the Second Annual American Music Awards (1975), the Whitney Young Jr. Award from the Los Angeles Urban League, the Black Achievement Award from the Brotherhood Crusade (1988), the National Academy of Recording Arts and Sciences Award (1991), the Trustee Award (1991), Black Radio Exchange Lifetime Achievement Award (1995), the Star on Hollywood Walk of Fame award for Excellence in Music (1996), and the American Legend Award (1998). He was inducted into the Rock and Roll Hall of Fame in 1990 and into the Association for Independent Music Hall of Fame in 2001.

Career Details

Upon his discharge from the army in 1953, Berry Gordy returned to Detroit and used his service pay to open the Three–D Record Mart. His love for the jazz of Stan Kenton, Charlie Parker, and Thelonius Monk influenced his inventory more than his customers' requests for "things like Fats Domino," and his business soon failed.

Gordy worked for his father for a short period and then as a chrome trimmer on the assembly line at the Ford Motor Company. The monotony was formidable, and Gordy's way of overcoming it was to write songs in his head, some of which were recorded by local singers. Decca Records bought several of his compositions, including "Reet Petite" and "Lonely Teardrops" (both recorded by Jackie Wilson), and when Gordy compared his royalty checks to what Decca made from the modest hits, he realized that writing the hits wasn't enough; he needed to own them.

At the suggestion of a friend, teenage singer William "Smokey" Robinson, Gordy borrowed $700 from his father and formed his own company to manufacture and market records. Motown Records was headquartered in a row house on Detroit's West Grand Boulevard, where Gordy slept on the second floor and made records on the first. In time, the company expanded, with nine buildings on the same street housing its branches: Jobete, music publishers; Hitsville USA, a recording studio; musical accompanists; International Talent Management Inc; the Motown Artist's Development Department (the embodiment of Gordy's personal interest in his performers, where they were taught to eat, dress, and act like polished professionals); and the Motown Record Corporation, an umbrella for several labels of Motown, including Gordy, Tamla, VIP, and Soul (the last being reserved for the hit song–writing machine of Brian Holland, Lamont Dozier, and Eddie Holland).

In 1960 Motown released "Shop Around," written by Smokey Robinson and performed by him and the Miracles. The song sold more than a million copies, and with

Berry Gordy Jr. (Archive Photos Inc.)

that gold record, Berry Gordy's company launched the most successful and influential era in the history of popular music.

The Motown Sound was a musical genre that combined classic African–American gospel singing with the new rock–and–roll sound that was being shaped by Elvis Presley and the Beatles. In a sense, this reflected the old "R & B" (for rhythm and blues), but it defined a new generation.

Motown produced over 110 number one hit songs and countless top–ten records, including "Please Mr. Postman," "Reach Out, I'll Be There," "My Girl," "Stop! In the Name of Love," "For Once in My Life," "How Sweet It Is To Be Loved by You," "Heard It Through the Grapevine," "My Guy," "Dancing in the Streets," "Your Precious Love," "Where Did Our Love Go," "Baby Love," "I Hear a Symphony," "I Want You Back," and "I'll Be There." Equally impressive is a list of artists that Gordy brought into the spotlight: Diana Ross and the Supremes, the Jackson Five, Stevie Wonder, Smokey Robinson and the Miracles, the Four Tops, the Temptations, Gladys Knight and the Pips, Tammi Terrell and Marvin Gaye, the Marvelettes, Mary Wells, and Martha Reeves and the Vandellas.

By the mid 1970s, some of the Motown artists had begun to resist Gordy's tight control. Defectors began to break up Gordy's "family" of stars. The first to leave was Gladys Knight and the Pips, and in 1975 the Jackson Five announced that they would be moving to Epic Records when their Motown contract expired.

Chronology:
Berry Gordy, Jr.

1929: Born.

1948: Became featherweight boxer.

1953: Opened short–lived Three–D Record Mart.

1959: Founded Motown Records.

1960: Released Smokey Robinson's smash hit "Shop Around."

1972: Released first movie production, *Lady Sings the Blue*.

1975: Announced much publicized contract with Stevie Wonder for $13 million over seven years.

1981: Superstar Diana Ross announced her defection from Motown to RCA Records.

1988: Sold Motown to RCA for $61 million; retained control of music publishing segment, Jobete Music,

1990: Inducted into the Rock and Rock Hall of Fame.

1994: Released autobiography, *To Be Loved*.

1997: Sold half his interest in Jobete Music to EMI.

2000: Established the Gwendolyn B. Gordy Fund to assist former Motown artists in need of financial assistance.

Although Gordy kept Stevie Wonder at Motown by promising him $13 million over seven years in the famous "Wonderdeal" of 1975, Gordy's public statements usually expressed disappointment that his superstars came to value money over loyalty. This sentiment was heard often from Gordy when, in 1981, Diana Ross announced her move to RCA Records.

Ross' move was particularly surprising and bitter for Gordy in view of the fact that in 1972 he moved his headquarters to Los Angeles to begin a career in film, not only for himself but so he could turn Diana Ross into a movie star. His first production was the 1972 Paramount release *Lady Sings the Blues*, the story of Billie Holiday starring Ross. The picture was nominated for five Academy Awards and grossed more than $8.5 million. In 1975 Gordy directed Ross in *Mahogany*, the story of a African–American fashion model's rise to fame. Although the film did well at the box office, it was not nearly the critical success of *Lady*.

Other Gordy films were *The Bingo Long Traveling All Stars and Motor Kings* (1976), *Almost Summer* (1978), *The Wiz* (1978), starring Michael Jackson and Diana Ross, and *The Last Dragon* (1985).

In June 1988, Gordy sold his company to MCA, Inc. He retained control of Jobete, the music publishing operation and Motown's film division but sold the record label to the entertainment conglomerate for $61 million. He told the newspaper *Daily Variety* that he wanted to "ensure the perpetuation of Motown and its heritage." Although Gordy was less successful in attracting stellar talent in the 1990s, he did score well with a few acts, including Johnny Gill, Boyz II Men, and Queen Latifah. In 1997 Gordy sold half of his interest in Jobete music publishing to EMI.

Social and Economic Impact

Esther Edwards, Berry Gordy's sister, was also interested in preserving Motown's heritage. The brick house at 2648 West Grand Boulevard, once modestly and unknowingly named "Hitsville USA," is now the site of the Motown Museum, thanks to the pack–rat tendency of Edwards. She saved hundreds of boxes of memorabilia, including original music scores, posters, and photographs, and until 1988 most of the mementos were stuck to the walls with thumbtacks. In an effort to have the collection professionally preserved, Michael Jackson, whose ties to Berry were still strong in 1990, donated the proceeds of the Detroit stop of his "Bad" tour—$125,000—to the Motown Museum.

Gordy's autobiography, *To Be Loved: The Music, the Magic, the Memories of Motown*, was published by Warner in 1994. In the *New York Times Book Review*, Milo Miles called Gordy "an African American cultural hero of historic stature." This is partly because Gordy almost single–handedly moved so–called "race music" (the term widely used at the time for recorded music sung by black artists), or "rhythm and blues," into the mainstream of American popular music. Gordy's influence boosted the careers of African–American artists, making them superstars and profoundly shaping musical tastes across racial lines. So important was his contribution to American popular culture that *Entertainment Weekly* pronounced the founding of Motown Records to be the number seventh greatest moment in the history of rock music.

The popularity of the "Motown sound" forced the music industry to stop publishing separate charts for rhythm and blues music and to incorporate all best–selling songs into one list. "Motown was the first bridge between white and black music," noted Smokey Robinson in *Entertainment Weekly* in 1999. "It was one of the great barrier breakers. . . . Berry told us we were going to make music for everybody. I hear it on the radio now, almost as much as I did then—and it still holds up."

In 2000 Gordy established the Gwendolyn B. Gordy Fund to assist former Motown artists, musicians and writers from the 1960s and 1970s who are in need of financial assistance. Gordy donated $750,000 to the charity, which he named in memory of his deceased sister, Gwendolyn. Along with numerous books on the history of Motown, both Berry's second wife and his father have written accounts of their lives with Berry, titled *Berry, Me, and Motown* (1990) and *Movin' Up: Pop Gordy Tells His Story* (1979), respectively.

Sources of Information

Contact at: Motown Records
    6255 Sunset Blvd.
    Hollywood, CA 90028
    Business Phone: (213) 856–3507

Bibliography

Bessman, Jim. "Gordy Sets Up Fund." *Billboard*, 16 September 2000.

Davis, Sharon. *Motown: The History*, 1988.

"The '50s: The 100 Greatest Moments in Rock Music." *Entertainment Weekly*, 28 May 1999.

George, Nelson. *Where Did Our Love Go? The Rise and Fall of the Motown Sound*, 1985.

"Indie Awards—2001 Hall of Fame." AFIM, 13 September 2001. Available at http://www.afim.org/indies.

Miles, Milo. *New York Times Book Review*, 27 November 1994.

Newsweek, 23 May 1983.

Taraborrelli, J. Randy. *Motown: Hot Wax, City Cool, and Solid Gold*, 1986.

Waller, Don. *The Motown Story*, 1985.

Katharine Graham

(1917-2001)
The Washington Post Company

Overview

Katharine Meyer Graham is world renowned for her leadership, particularly during her 10–year reign as publisher of the internationally acclaimed *Washington Post*. During that time, Graham won a United States Supreme Court decision to publish excerpts from the United States government's classified Pentagon study, known as "The Pentagon Papers." She also supported investigative reporting of Watergate, resulting in the resignation of then U.S. President Richard Nixon. "Kay was an extraordinary person," said former *CBS News* Anchor Walter Cronkite to CNN. "As a bereaved widow, she surprised everyone with her strength to take over the *Washington Post* to make it one of the world's great newspapers. She is greatly admired, of course, everywhere in the very competitive world of politics and publishing."

Personal Life

Katharine Meyer was born on June 16, 1917, into a prominent New York City multi–millionaire family of Jewish and German decent. Her father, Eugene Meyer, was a banker who purchased the newspaper *Washington Post* as a hobby and built up a lucrative publishing empire. Her mother, Agnes (Ernst) Meyer, was an author and philanthropist. Katharine's education included the elite Madeira School in Greenway, Virginia, where she pursued her growing interest in journalism by working on the school paper. Her higher education included a year at Vassar College. But she became critical of what she felt was Vassar's conservative climate and transferred to the University of Chicago, considered radical in the

Katharine Graham. (AP/Wide World Photos.)

1930s. During summer vacations, Katharine worked at the *Post*, but after she received her Bachelor of Arts degree in history, she moved to California and worked as a waterfront reporter for the *San Francisco News*. She covered a strike on the waterfront, which would later serve as a valuable learning experience. A year later, Katharine followed through on her father's suggestion to return to Washington, where she became part of the editorial staff on the *Washington Post*. Earning $25 a week, she handled the "Letters to the Editor" department and also wrote some 100 editorials.

In 1939 Katharine met the love of her life, Philip Graham. Philip, two years Katharine's junior, was not a stranger to poverty. His family had struggled until they achieved a more prosperous lifestyle. His father, Ernest Graham, became a successful dairy farmer, later winning a seat in the Florida state senate. His mother, Florence, was a former schoolteacher who instilled in Philip a life-long love of learning. Bright, eager, and with an unaffected, easy–going manner, Philip did extremely well at the University of Florida and went on to Harvard Law School. He later became a law clerk to Supreme Court justice Stanley Reed and then to Felix Frankfurter. Katharine met him at a party where the aggressive and funny Philip immediately got the attention of the more subdued Katharine. According to the *Dictionary of Literary Biography*, Philip told her, "He was going to marry her, and did not want her father's money." Instead, they would ". . . move to Florida. He would go into politics

and they would be so poor she would have only two dresses." The couple was married on June 5, 1940.

Katharine was unprepared for the traditional role of wife. Because of her wealthy upbringing, she had never learned to cook, but she persevered, determined to be a model wife. She willingly deferred to her husband while he encouraged her to retain her job. At the same time, Katharine's father, Eugene, encouraged Philip to consider taking over the *Washington Post*. But when World War II broke out, Philip enlisted. Although Philip's dream was to have a career in politics, he agreed to his father–in–law's offer before he went overseas. Meanwhile, Katharine's father continually ignored his own daughter's interest in the paper. After distinguishing himself in the U.S. army, where he was awarded the legion of merit for decoding Japanese military strategy and identifying bombing sites in the Philippines, Philip returned as a major. Subsequently, he became publisher of the *Washington Post*, and he and Katharine were given 5000 shares of voting stock by her father, assuring the newspaper would remain in the family. Philip received the majority of the stock, while Katharine received the lesser share. Together the couple had four children, and Katharine settled into the role of wife and mother.

Philip had many opportunities to capitalize on his leadership skills and enhance his reputation as a dynamic publisher. He confronted McCarthyism, the unwarranted anti–communism campaign that ultimately persecuted innocent people, with a scathing editorial that likened Sen-

Chronology:
Katharine Graham

1917: Born.

1963: Became president of Washington Post Company.

1969: Became publisher of the *Washington Post*.

1972: Supported Woodward and Bernstein reporting Watergate.

1973: Became CEO of The Washington Post Company.

1973: *Washington Post* wins Pulitzer Prize for public service in uncovering the Watergate conspiracy.

1979: Became chairman of Washington Post Company; ceased to be publisher of *Washington Post*; became first woman publisher elected president of American Newspaper Publishers' Association.

1989: *Fortune* magazine named the Post Company one of 20 most profitable corporations.

1993: Retired as chairman of Washington Post Company.

1998: Won Pulitzer Prize for best–selling autobiography *Personal History*.

2001: Died.

---

ator Joseph McCarthy to a Salem witch hunter. This set the paper's more liberal tone and associated the paper with the Democratic Party. At the same time, Philip aggressively expanded the publishing company over the years, acquiring *Newsweek,* the *News Service,* and several broadcast stations.

Despite his successes, however, Philip became increasingly ill with manic depression, a psychiatric disease little understood in that era. Over the next five years, he engaged in promiscuous behavior, verbal attacks against his wife, outrageous actions, and suicidal thoughts. Although the family provided Philip with the best care then available, he succumbed to depression and shot himself on August 3, 1963. His death left his widow with the doubly formidable task of raising four children and taking care of her family business.

Career Details

After her husband's death, Katharine Graham became president of the publishing business, focusing special attention on the *Washington Post.* One of her most significant changes at the paper was to appoint the innovative Benjamin C. Bradlee as editor. With Bradlee at the helm, the paper attracted fresh new reporting talent. This affected news coverage and gained the *Washington Post* worldwide attention. The paper's reputation was further enhanced when, in 1971, Graham defied a restraining order and pursued publication of the famous "Pentagon Papers," revealing U.S. government involvement in the Vietnam War. Graham fought government efforts to censor the material, which led to a U.S. Supreme Court decision upholding the right for the *Washington Post* to publish the story.

Another opportunity to report controversy came with the 1972 investigation of a burglary at the Democratic National Committee headquarters in Washington's Watergate complex. Courageous *Washington Post* reporters Bob Woodward and Carl Bernstein uncovered the story. After the investigative reporting revealed illegal governmental involvement, a national scandal erupted, and President Richard Nixon was forced to resign to avoid impeachment proceedings. In 1973 the *Post* received a Pulitzer Prize for public service.

Graham's leadership at the *Washington Post* helped to enhance the paper's reputation and boost circulation. When she decided in 1971 to change the privately owned publishing company to a public corporation, her efforts to attract investors succeeded and stock value soared.

Graham made the news again in 1975 when she was faced with a 139–day pressmen strike that disabled presses. Determined to keep the press running, she hired non–union pressmen—a controversial move characteristic of Graham's decisive management style. *Editor & Publisher* reported Graham's remarks on this topic to members of the Southern Newspaper Publishers Association in 1997: "We were not out to bust unions . . . [but] we had to make the fateful decision to replace the union and make sure it was legal. And it was very traumatic . . . It was a really awful thing to have 200 families out of jobs. And we offered them to come back if they would resign from the union, and only 20 did . . . ."

In 1979 Graham turned the title of publisher over to her son, Donald, but remained an enthusiastic advisor and consultant on all aspects of the corporation. She continued as chairwoman of the *Washington Post* until 1993, and even after retirement she remained active as a speaker. At 81 years of age, she authored a best selling and Pulitzer Prize–winning autobiography titled *Personal History*.

Graham passed away on the July 18, 2001, while hospitalized for head injuries sustained from falling on a walk in Sun Valley, Idaho. She was in Idaho for a business conference, still very active and involved at age 84.

Washington Post concluded of her, "Katharine Graham's life ended the way she said she wanted it to: 'The only thing I think any of us want,' she once said, 'is to last as long as we're any good. And then not.'"

Thousands gathered for Graham's funeral. The mourners ran the gamut from the halls of power to friends and fans alike. Such notable statesman and dignitaries included former president Clinton, former secretary of state Henry Kissinger, former secretary of defense Robert Mc-Namara, and President Bush remembered Graham as "the beloved first lady of Washington journalism."

Social and Economic Impact

Katharine Meyer Graham transcended the initial disrespect of her male peers in publishing to become one of the most powerful women in America. Emphasizing freedom of the press, she strengthened the role of newspapers in exposing government actions. Her insistence in publishing the Pentagon Papers and the Watergate story made her a force to be reckoned with in journalism. Graham also exercised effective leadership, developing a reputation as a woman "who mastered the intricacies of profit margins [and] strategic planning," according to the *Dictionary of Literary Biography*. Graham built the Washington Post Company into a thriving media company and secured the *Washington Post*'s reputation as one of the country's leading newspapers.

After breaking the 1975 strike, the *Washington Post* promoted the hiring of minorities and women, and Graham welcomed the newly diverse workforce. She stated at a Women in Communications luncheon in 1984 that she recognized that for women to get ahead in business their close relationships sometimes suffered, adding, "But men in power have always been willing to pay this price." Despite such hard–headed words, Graham remains known as an editor who maintained excellence by supporting her reporters and encouraging those who worked for her.

Sources of Information

Bibliography

"An American Original." *Washington Post*, 30 July 2001.

Childs, Kelvin. "Kay Graham's Side of the Story." *Editor & Publisher*, 15 November 1997.

Epstein, Joseph. "The Colonel and the Lady." *Commentary*, August 1997.

Green, Michelle. "Katharine Graham: A Publishing Power Broker Writes a Very Personal History." *Washington Post*, 24 February 1997.

"Katharine Graham 1917–2001." *The Washington Post Online*, 2001. Available at http://www.washpostco.com.

"Katharine Graham Dies at 84." *Washington Post*, 20 July 2001. Available at http://www.washingtonpost.com.

"Katharine Graham of Washington Post Dies at 84." *The New York Times on the Web*, 20 July 2001. Available at http://www.nytimes.com.

"Legendary Washington Post Chief Kay Graham Dies." 18 July 2001. Available at http://www.cnn.com.

"Media's Katharine Graham, 1917–2001." *People.com*, 20 July 2001. Available at http://people.aol.com.

Nelton, Sharon. *People.com*, 20 July 2001. Available at http://people.aol.com.

"100 Women of the Millennium," *Women.com*, 20 July 2001. Available from http://www.women.com.

Overholser, Geneva. "Katharine Graham." *Women.com*, 20 July 2001. Available from http://www.women.com.

Platt, Adam. "Special Kay." *Harpers Bazaar*, February 1997.

"Remembering Katharine Graham." *The Washington Post Writers Group*, 2001. Available at http://www.washpostco.com.

"A Tribute to Katharine Graham." *BusinessWeek.com*, 20 July 2001. Available at http://www.businessweek.com.

The Washington Post Company. Available at http://www.washpostco.com

"The Washington Post Company." *BusinessWeek.com*, 20 July 2001. Available at http://www.businessweek.com.

"The Washington Post Company." *Hoovers Online,* November 2001. Available at http://www.hoovers.com.

Maurice Greenberg

(1925-)
American International Group (AIG)

Overview

Considered by some to be the most powerful single personality in the insurance business, billionaire Maurice "Hank" Greenberg heads the American International Group (AIG), a multinational giant and the largest underwriter of commercial and industrial insurance in the United States. Having served as the company's CEO for more than thirty years and its chairman for more than ten, Greenberg has been dubbed a legend. Greenberg took the company public during his first year as CEO. Greenberg is widely and enthusiastically admired in the financial world for his management abilities and long–term consistency in keeping AIG an outstanding performer in the industry.

Personal Life

Greenberg was born to Jacob Greenberg and Ada Rheingold in 1925. Although born in New York City, according to *Forbes*, Greenberg was a "farm boy." He is professionally trained in law, having completed a pre–law program from the University of Miami in 1948 and earning a Bachelor of Laws (LL.B.) degree from New York Law School in 1950. His prospective career in law was interrupted by service in the U.S. Army during World War II in the 1940s, and the Korean Conflict in the early 1950s. While serving in the military, Greenberg attained the rank of captain and received the Bronze Star (awarded for heroism or meritorious achievement in ground combat). Upon return to civilian life, he was admitted to the New York Bar Association in 1953. He did not practice law, but instead went into the insurance business.

Eli Broad and Maurice Greenberg (right) shaking hands. (AP/Wide World Photos.)

Greenberg has spent his entire professional career, spanning 50–some years, between two insurance companies—more than 40 of them with AIG. His leadership style (demanding the best) and personal drive has taken him to the top in the insurance industry, and near the top in personal wealth. (*Forbes* magazine rated his personal worth in 2001 at $3.9 billion, and listed him as No. 16 in its overall list of 800 Best Paid CEOs 2001.)

Greenberg is considered an aggressive, demanding, and driven leader who has remained spry and athletic despite his advancing years (upper 70s). He is a fast and skilled downhill skier and tennis player, and works out most mornings. Greenberg is married to wife Corinne Phyllis Zuckerman and has four children. He had built AIG up with the intention of keeping it a "family" concern, but second son Evan, who had been with AIG for 25 years and had been named as intended successor, abruptly resigned while serving as president in 2000. No reason was given for his departure, but he spoke highly of his father and there was no reason to believe a family feud had been the cause for his departure. Another (and the eldest) son, Jeffrey, also served as a senior executive of the company until 1995, when he too left the company only to resurface as head of the risk–capital operation at Marsh & McLennan, the nation's largest insurance broker (which does a great deal of business with AIG).

Greenberg is chairman of the U.S.–China Business Council, the U.S.–ASEAN Council on Business and Technology, The Starr Foundation, and he is the founding chairman of the U.S.–Philippine Business Commit-

tee. He is a member of The Business Roundtable, the White House Economic Roundtable, and the President's Advisory Committee for Trade Policy and Negotiations. He serves as vice chairman of the council on Foreign Relations the Center for Strategic and International Studies. Additionally, he is trustee of The Asia Society and chairman emeritus and member of the Board of Governors of The Society of The New York Hospital, and he is dedicated to several other charitable and civic organizations. Greenberg heads the Starr Foundation (named after company founder), and oversees the disbursement of major financial support to a number of academic, medical, cultural, and public policy institutions. He was honored as the 1998 Insurance Leader of the Year by the New York College of Insurance. He holds six honorary degrees, including from the New England School of Law, Bryant and Middlebury Colleges, and Brown and Pace Universities.

Career Details

Foregoing a career in law, Greenberg began his career in insurance at the Continental Casualty Company in 1952. In 1960, he joined AIG, a company originally founded in Shanghai in 1919 by American entrepreneur Cornelius Van Der Starr (Starr). Under the original name of American Asiatic Underwriters (AAU), then 27–year–old Starr initially represented American insur-

Chronology:
Maurice Greenberg

1925: Born.

1950: Received LL.B degree from New York Law School.

1952: Joined Continental Casualty Insurance Company.

1953: Admitted to the New York Bar.

1960: Joined AIG.

1962: Named president of AIG's subsidiary, American Home Assurance.

1967: Named president and CEO of AIG.

1969: AIG went public.

1989: Named Chairman of AIG.

ance companies offering fire and marine coverages. The money–starved Californian continued to run the company for the next 49 years, until his death.

Two years after joining AIG, in 1962, Greenberg was named president of the company's main subsidiary, American Home Assurance Company. He served in that capacity for five years. In late 1967, the American International Group Inc. was formed to hold the shares of the domestic companies. Shortly thereafter, company founder and CEO Starr decided to groom Greenberg to take over the company. At that time, AIG was a private company with revenues of approximately $300 million. When Starr died a few months later, Greenberg was named the new president and CEO, and within another year, the company went public.

One of Greenberg's most notable contributions to the insurance industry was his encouragement of the risk management movement in the 1960s. At a time when other insurers and brokers were attempting to deter policyholders from keeping large retentions, for fear of losing premium income, Greenberg took the opposite view and encouraged the trend. According to Richard E. Stewart, chairman of Stewart Economics in Chapel Hill, North Carolina, Greenberg "realized that keeping predictable levels of risk was an economically sensible thing to do." Stewart was a principal on the selection committee for the College of Insurance in New York, which named Greenberg the 1998 Insurance Leader of the Year.

That philosophy helped Greenberg pull the company through the latter 1970s and early 1980s, when the property/casualty industry was experiencing rough times. AIG continued to focus on underwriting policies and underwriting results rather than on market share. As a result, in more than 30 years as leader of the company, AIG's stock earnings per share dropped in only one year (1984)—an incredible record of success.

Greenberg is also known for his accomplishments in global expansion of the company. AIG gained a head start in the international arena by having been first established in Shanghai. It was evicted by World War II, then re–entered the area, but was again evicted from the country by Communists. In 1992, after many years of heavy lobbying by Greenberg, AIG again gained access to two Chinese cities, Shanghai and Guangzhou (near Hong Kong). The Asian market represented an untapped market for life insurance products.

Domestically, Greenberg helped create a niche market in the P&C field by specializing in environmental risks and kidnap–and–ransom policies. in addition to supplying the insurance needs of U.S –based multinational corporations. In the late 1990s, AIG began pushing hard into the auto–insurance arena; several years earlier, Greenberg had tried to buy GEICO, but negotiations fell through. Notwithstanding, by 1999, AIG was reporting more than $70 million profits for its auto insurance operations.

It is Greenberg who is credited with building the most powerful insurance company in America over a period of three decades. Greenberg had always been interested in growth and acquisition, but early on, Greenberg began to stimulate internal growth rather than issue new stock. What distinguished AIG from others in the insurance industry was its strong owner management. Nearly 30 percent of AIG's stock is controlled by management, and some of the control is exercised through private companies whose character is only vaguely referenced in proxy statements. A company known as Starr International Co. (SICO) owns 16 percent of AIG, but is an offshore company incorporated in Panama. About 300 top executives at AIG have restricted stock in Starr International but can exercise their stock options only upon reaching the age of 65. Starr International is not to be confused with the C.V. Starr & Company, which is a private holding company that owns about 2.4 percent of AIG, and in which 40 of AIG's top executives own private stock. Of more interest to analysts is that the Starr Company generates policies and premiums for AIG, and gets paid more than $30 million a year for it. Greenberg has a 25 percent interest in Starr, an undisclosed stake in SICO (but estimated to be worth many millions of dollars), and more than 16 million shares of AIG stock. His 2001 net worth was nearly $4 billion.

But AIG has diverse interests outside of the insurance industry as well, which causes both consternation and curiosity from outsiders. AIG was (and is) in the "multiline" business, that is, selling both property and casualty insurance (P&C) as well as life insurance. AIG owns a private golf course, "Morefar," north of New York City, and it also owns Mt. Mansfield Corporation, the proprietor of Stowe, a ski resort in Vermont. Greenberg had foreseen a softening in the P&C business and had jumped the gun to search for auxiliary sources of profits. These have included a commodity and currency trading company and the International Lease Finance Corporation (ILFC), which has $14 billion in airplanes leased out to carriers throughout the world. AIG has also started a credit–card operation in the Philippines. Notwithstanding these diverse interests, AIG reported that 80 percent of its 2000 earnings remained insurance. In 2001, the company operated in 140 countries, with a very large market in Asia.

Greenberg has been called tough, demanding, impatient, focused, tireless, and tenacious, but can be charming as well. His style of management includes a strong penchant for centralization, and he has made his mark as an executive who leads by example and hard–work and usually gets the best performances from his workers. Internal auditing of the staff is routinely conducted by 100 people at AIG. The results (of any misdoings by employees) are directly reported to Greenberg, in writing, as well as some other top–executives who are expected to know the results almost immediately after receiving the reports. It is said that Greenberg spends about 50 hours every fall in budget meetings comprised of at least 25 different operating units. Each unit has its own book containing a business plan, and Greenberg is known to read every one of them and be loaded with questions for the meeting.

Greenberg is the only CEO that AIG has had since it went public in 1969. The company continued to report stable and impressive earnings, reporting 2000 profits of $5.6 billion. As of 2001, the company offered financial services, asset management including aircraft leasing, financial products, trading and market making, consumer finance, real estate investment management, and retirement savings products. Greenberg has told analysts that he would like to expand the retail mutual fund business. He has always made use of AIG stock to make deals and acquisitions, most recently paying $23 billion for American General Finance Corporation (the second largest writer of life insurance policies in the U.S.) in 2001; $1.2 billion for boutique insurer HSB Group in 2000; and $18 billion for asset manager SunAmerica in 1999.

Social and Economic Impact

For shareholders, AIG has been a dream stock for decades. Since 1989, the company boosted earnings per share an average of 15.5 percent per year. During the 1990s, stock prices zoomed nearly 30 percent a year, making it a favorite for investors seeking consistent performance. According to a statement made in the October 2001 issue of *Money* magazine by James Ellman, manager of Merrill Lynch Global Financial Services, "By the end of this decade, we'll have 10 major global financial supermarkets, and AIG will be one of them." Under Hank Greenberg's leadership, AIG has become one of the most profitable and premier commercial insurance providers in the United States.

Sources of Information

Contact at: American International Group (AIG)
    70 Pine Street
    New York, NY 10270
    Business Phone: (212)770–7000
    URL: http://www.aig.com.

Bibliography

"AIG: Aggressive. Inscrutable. Greenberg." *Fortune*, 27 April 1997.

Bowers, Barbara. "Building a Global Platform." *Best's Review/Life–Health Insurance Edition*, August 1998.

"Forbes 800 Best Paid CEOs 2001." *Forbes*, Annual 2001.

Gibbs, Lisa. "Is All Well at AIG?" *Money*, October 2001.

Kafka, Peter, et al. "Billionaires." *Forbes*, Annual 2001.

Souter, Gavin. "Greenberg's Leadership Draws High Praise." *Business Insurance*, 05 October 1998.

Treaster, Joseph. "Dynastic Jitters as Greenberg Successor Bids Farewell." *New York Times*, 22 September 2000.

Robert Greenberg

(1940-)
Skechers Shoes

Overview

The "trendy" know to be seen in Skechers shoes; L.A. Gear is passé. What the trendy do not always know is that Robert Greenberg is the founder of both. The creative, mercurial entrepreneur, who likes to refer to himself as "Captain Marvel," is busy building his second blockbuster company within two decades, both of them dealing with the nation's hottest name in footwear. The company's 2001 revenues were flirting with $1 billion— a 42–percent increase from 2000, and Greenberg hopes to double that by 2005.

Personal Life

Greenberg was described in a 2001 *Forbes* article as "a gregarious, diminutive man with a deep California tan, a thick Beantown accent and an overdeveloped sense of showmanship." All five of his sons work in the business, and his second eldest, Michael, has been groomed to take over. Greenberg still owned 44 percent of the company stock in 2001; Michael had a 5 percent interest.

Greenberg was born into a tough, hard–working Boston family in 1940. As a boy (and the only son), he worked in his father's fresh produce stand. To toughen him up, his father insisted that young Greenberg not wear gloves at work in winter. When he graduated from high school, Greenberg opted for a softer career: hair styling school.

Skechers shoes on display at the Super Show in Atlanta Georgia. (AP/Wide World Photos.)

Career Details

In 1962, young hair stylist Greenberg opened his first beauty salon, called Talk of the Town, in Brookline, Massachusetts. Within a few years, he started selling hair wigs in his salon. Surprised that he could sell $50 wigs for $300, he was struck with the idea of wholesaling and opened his second business, wholesaler Wig Bazaar in 1965. Three years later, Greenberg sold Wig Bazaar and opened up a shop called Wigs 'n Things. Now he was on a roll. When he discovered that $3 women's bangs hairpieces could double as toupees, according to the *Forbes* article, he ran ads for $59.95 toupees in the National Enquirer and began a mail–order business.

Greenberg sold Talk of the Town in 1969, and within 12 months had bought The Europa Group, which became a holding company for his other businesses. In 1971 he bought a publicly traded company called Medata Computer Systems and renamed it Europa Hair. Two years later, he was importing antique clocks from South Korea, buying them for $16 each and selling them for $129. He was hooked.

In 1974, Greenberg sold Europa Hair and started buying men's jeans. He sold them to department stores under the brand name Wild Oats. His next big venture was Removatron, a company that sold electronic tweezers as hair removal devices. He moved to the West Coast in 1978, and within 12 months, had opened up Roller Skates of America, a roller skate sales and rental shop in Los Angeles. He attributes this with leading him into the shoe business.

Always trying to stay one step ahead with a gimmick or "in" item, Greenberg paid $10,000 for a license to sell shoelaces printed with the image of "E.T." in 1982, and grossed $3 million. With some of the earnings, he opened up a trendy women's apparel shop in Los Angeles in 1983 and started importing simple canvas sneakers for his shop. When Reebok cashed in on the aerobics and fitness craze of the early 1980s with its simple black and white sneaker, Greenberg copied the style but attached the name "L.A. Gear" to it. To compete with the big boys, Greenberg relied on his personality and stunts to grab attention. He showed up at a footwear trade show in a 1956 Thunderbird convertible covered with different colored versions of his "L.A. Gear" shoe. When sales took off, he closed the apparel shop to concentrate on shoes full time.

In 1990, L.A. Gear's sales topped $800 million, making it the third largest sneaker vendor behind Nike and Reebok.

Parallel with this development, Greenberg was trying to close the gap that separated him from industry leaders, and he started a habit that became a signature trait. He began to hang around at trade shows, lurking in rivals' booths and studying competitors' shoes. He listened to the sales talk used by competitors, then would try to produce and sell his own version of what he saw. Snooping into competitors' marketplaces became so important

Chronology:

Robert Greenberg

1940: Born in Massachusetts.

1962: Opened Talk of the Town hair salon in Brookline, MA.

1965: Started Wig Bazaar.

1970: Bought Europa Group.

1971: Bought Medata Computer Systems, renames it Europa Hair.

1979: Started L.A. Roller Skates of America.

1983: Started L.A. Gear.

1990: Sales peak at $820 million; L.A. Gear named third largest in industry.

1992: Ousted from L.A. Gear.

1992: Started Skechers with son, Michael.

1999: Skechers went public.

---

to him that he avoided having his picture taken for years, and actually sued an in–flight magazine when it published a picture of him, according to *Forbes.*

Trying to stay in front of the avalanche of sales he inspired, Greenberg made the fatal mistake akin to so many other success stories: market over–saturation. He struck licensing deals for watches, T–shirts, jeans, and other paraphernalia brandishing the L.A. Gear logo. Soon, his goods started piling up in discount stores and warehouses. Retailers with backlogs of merchandise started canceling orders. Desperate to bolster sales, Greenberg signed a $4.5–million promotional deal with Michael Jackson, but that failed miserably.

Moreover, when Greenberg tried to push into men's performance shoes, one of his brand shoes fell apart on the court during a televised college basketball game. L.A. Gear's stock came apart like Greenberg's shoes, dropping to $10 a share (one–fifth of its value the previous year). Worse yet, a 1990 shareholders' lawsuit was settled for $54 million, and L.A. Gear began to default on its business loans. In 1992, Greenberg sold a 34–percent controlling stake in L.A. Gear for $100 million to Trefoil Capital Investors. Four months later, they pushed him out, although he left with $55 million.

Meanwhile, his son Michael, a shoe salesman who was national sales manager for L.A. Gear, telephoned

him to say that he also had been terminated from the company his father started. Soon, the two had decided on the next business: they would form a distributorship for Doc Martens shoes. Starting with $13 million in capital, they sold $40 million in Doc Martens the first year. However, by 1993, relations with the company that owned the Doc Martens trademark soured, and they lost the distributorship.

Greenberg's earlier "copycat" skills that he had honed while building L.A. Gear resurfaced. He started importing Doc Martens look–alikes from an Asian company. The Greenbergs named their lower–priced shoes "Skechers." Although the owner of the Doc Marten trademark later sued Greenberg, the suit was settled with no monetary payment. In 1996, the company introduced a women's sneaker under the Skechers name and sales hit $115 million. One year later, sales had grown to $185 million.

When sales reached $370 million two years later, company executives tried to persuade Greenberg to go public, to raise money to pay off $67 million in debt. Still shaken by the L.A. Gear fallout, Greenberg refused, but after months of prodding, relented. In 1999, Skechers USA, Inc. went public, selling 7 million shares at $11. Wall Street responded slowly, also remembering the L.A. Gear "Titanic." But within a year things heated up, and the company had opened more than 50 of its own retail stores in top locations such as New York's Times Square, Boston's Newbury Street, and London's SoHo district. It also marketed its shoes to 3,500 general retailers in another 25,000 stores.

In 2001, 10 percent of Skechers' revenue was from overseas sales in 35 locations. They opened stores in London, Paris, and Oberhausen, Germany. and hoped to pull in 25 percent revenue from overseas markets by 2004. Skechers had tremendous growth potential in foreign sales, enhanced by its trendy advertisements. Teen idol Britney Spears endorses Energy shoes in overseas advertisements. But the company is careful not to use Britney in U.S. ads—fearful of narrowing its consumer field to teen girls. In November 2001, Skechers announced it had signed a worldwide endorsement deal with L.A. Laker basketball player Rick Fox.

Successful marketing has kept Greenberg in the black. The company builds its image as a lifestyle brand, and spends about one–tenth of its revenues on advertising. Unlike some rivals, Skechers advertises on television, and Greenberg still pulls off memorable stunts at trade shows, such as using "lasers, dancers, and a 30–foot transparent wall displaying tens of thousands of shoes." "It takes flamboyance to build a brand name," he told a *Forbes* interviewer in 2001.

On its Internet Web page, Skechers describes itself as a marketer of "lifestyle footwear for men, women and children," offering "categorical diversity" in boots, shoes, sneakers, and sandals. It is traded on the New York Stock Exchange under the ticker symbol SKX.

Social and Economic Impact

For business students, the lesson taught by Robert Greenberg and his successful marketing career is to aim for being the first to market a new product, or at least as near to first as possible. While Greenberg's success with Skechers relies on a "copycat" mentality, he often "approximates" his look–alike products from overseas markets so that he can be the first in the United States with the "new look." For example, when Greenberg and his chief designer discovered bowling–style shoes made by an on–the–edge Spanish company, they quickly came up with a Skechers version. By the time Kenneth Cole and Prada debuted similar shoes for $100, Skechers had already been selling its $55 version.

Greenberg has offered the public a fresh, trendy way to wear affordable versions of the latest fashions, readily available in area stores. According to an August 2001 *Forbes* review, people just couldn't "get enough of these shoes." The company's advertisements feature young, good looking, trendy groups, wearing Skechers, sitting around talking, and looking, well, rather trendy. But buyers should remember, Skechers are not touted as performance–wear. For example, the company's "Energy" jogger is more for wearing at parties and being noticed than for jogging. The Energy sneaker comes in more than 100 styles and colors, including laceless pull–ons, sling–backs, and roller skate versions. Skechers keeps its prices down by using less expensive leather and other materials. What this means is that the consumer should be a trend–setting spectator at a basketball game, not one of the players, especially if the game is televised.

Sources of Information

Contact at: Skechers Shoes
   228 Manhattan Beach Blvd.
   Manhattan Beach, CA 90266
   Business Phone: (800) 746–3411
   URL: http://www.skechers.com.

Bibliography

"Corporate Profile." Available at http://www.corporate–ir.net/ireye/ir_site.zhtml.

Rotenier, Nancy; and John R. Hayes."Fancy Footwork." *Forbes,* 27 September 1993.

"Skechers USA Footwear Launches New E–Commerce Store..." *Business Newswire,* 26 November 2001.

"Skechers USA Inks Worldwide Endorsement Deal With L.A. Laker Rick Fox" *Business Newswire,* 27 November 2001.

Walker, Elaine. "Manhattan Beach, Calif.–Based Footwear Maker Skechers Outruns Rest of Industry." *The Miami Herald,*19 August 2001.

Wells, Melanie. "Sole Survivors." *Forbes,* 6 August 2001.

Alan Greenspan

(1926-)
Federal Reserve Board

Alan Greenspan is the chairman of the Federal Reserve Board, a position he has held since 1987. In his fourth term, his appointment will expire in 2004. Greenspan is widely known for his intellectual abilities, his introspective and aloof personality, and his ability to finesse the national economy with a light touch.

Personal Life

Alan Greenspan was born on March 6, 1926, in New York City to Herbert and Rose (Goldsmith) Greenspan. His parents divorced when he was five years old, and Greenspan and his mother moved in with his maternal grandparents. The four shared a cramped one–bedroom apartment. Greenspan attended public schools, where he was a good, although not exceptional, student. During his school days, Greenspan developed a reputation for his aloofness and introspective personality—characteristics for which he would be well known throughout his adult life. He developed a keen interest in music, studying the clarinet and saxophone. Greenspan graduated from George Washington High School in 1943.

With dreams of becoming a professional musician, Greenspan enrolled in the prestigious Julliard School of Music as a clarinet major. However, he dropped out in less than a year to join Henry Jerome, who had offered Greenspan $62 a week to play in his swing band. In January 1944, Greenspan began touring the eastern United States. Although a very good amateur musician, Greenspan, by his own definition,

was an average professional. Several months before the band dissolved in 1945, he quit, having decided to pursue a new career.

After giving up on the idea of making a career in music, Greenspan decided to investigate his other serious interest—economics. To that end, he enrolled in New York University, from which he graduated with a B.S. in economics in 1948, with highest honors. He went on to pursue his graduate studies at Columbia University, where he came under the influence of well–known economist Arthur Burns, who would later serve as the chairman of the Federal Reserve Board (also known as "the Fed") from 1970 to 1978. Greenspan completed his master's degree in 1950, but dropped out of the Ph.D. program before finishing due to a lack of funds. In 1977 New York University awarded Greenspan a Ph.D. based on his contribution to economics.

During the 1950s, Greenspan encountered Ayn Rand, a Russian–born philosopher and author of the best–selling novel *The Fountainhead*. For the next 15 years, Greenspan socialized and philosophized within the inner circle of Rand and her followers, called objectivists. Rand preached in the defense of capitalism and free market economy. Later, Greenspan would say that one of the most important things he learned from Rand was that not only did the capitalist system work as an economic model in terms of efficiency and practicality, it was also moral.

In 1952 Greenspan went on a blind date with Joan Mitchell. Ten months later the couple married. However, before their first anniversary, the two decided to split and have the marriage annulled. After the annulment Greenspan and Mitchell remained good friends. On April 6, 1997, Greenspan married NBC news correspondent Andrea Mitchell, after a twelve–year courtship. The two have no children.

Career Details

After dropping out of graduate school, Greenspan began working for the National Industrial Conference Board, later known simply as the Conference Board, a nonprofit organization that studies business practices. Greenspan focused his work on researching issues that affect heavy industry. In 1954, twenty–seven–year–old Greenspan partnered with sixty–five–year–old William Townsend to create the economic consulting firm, Townsend–Greenspan & Company. Townsend, who had been in the business since 1929, needed a new partner, and Greenspan was anxiously awaiting a chance to step out on his own. The new team shared a small office on Wall Street, and Greenspan quickly began being noticed as a man who had an incredible affinity to numbers, data, and statistics. By the late 1950s, Townsend–Greenspan was a well–established name with industrialists, and the company carried some impressive clients on their books, including U.S. Steel, Owens Corning, and Aluminum

Chronology:
Alan Greenspan

1926: Born.

1954: Became a partner in Townsend–Greenspan, an economic consulting firm.

1968: Joined Richard Nixon's presidential campaign as a policy adviser.

1974: Appointed by Nixon as chair of the Council of Economic Advisers.

1975: Appeared on the cover of *Newsweek*.

1981: Appointed by Ronald Reagan as the chair of National Commission on Social Security Reform.

1987: Appointed by Reagan as the chair of the Federal Reserve Board; closed Townsend–Greenspan.

2000: Nomination approved to a fourth term as chair of the Federal Reserve Board, ending 2004.

Company of America (Alcoa). When Townsend died of a heart attack in 1958, Greenspan brought in Kathryn Eickhoff as a new partner.

By the late 1960s Greenspan was a millionaire and living in an apartment at the United Nations Plaza, sharing an address with Johnny Carson and Walter Cronkite. Despite the show of obvious financial success, few if any of Greenspan's friends predicted his coming near–celebrity status as he stepped into the world of politics. Justin Martin noted in his biography, *Greenspan: The Man Behind the Money*, "The general impression among people who knew Greenspan in those days was that he wasn't exactly marked for greatness. . . . He was a success, no question. But no one expected him to rise to dizzying heights. People generally found him modest, reliable, gracious, erudite, and more than a tad introspective. None of these traits seemed to lend themselves to setting the world on fire. His old friends were destined to watch his career unfold. . . in stunned amazement."

Greenspan's first encounter with organized politics came in 1968 when a friend introduced him to Richard Nixon, who invited Greenspan to join his presidential campaign as a domestic policy adviser, a part–time volunteer position. Although Greenspan declined Nixon's offer to join him on staff in Washington after winning the election, Greenspan remained attached to politics by being appointed to numerous commissions, including

Alan Greenspan. (*Associated Press/AP.*)

the Task Force on Economic Growth, the Commission on Financial Structure and Regulation, and the Commission for an All–Volunteer Armed Forces. The latter, referred to as the Gates Commission, ultimately recommended an end to the military draft. Through the early 1970s Greenspan split his time between Washington and New York where he continued to run Townsend–Greenspan.

In 1974 Greenspan was offered a job as the chair of the Council of Economic Advisers (CEA) by the Nixon administration. After steadfastly refusing the position, Greenspan finally was convinced. He turned his firm over to his employees, moved to Washington, and traded his $300,000 salary for the $42,000 the CEA paid. By the time Greenspan's nomination had been confirmed, Nixon had resigned amidst the Watergate scandal, and the economy was in a tailspin of inflation. While chairing a series of meetings on how the economy was affecting a variety of social concerns, Greenspan made his biggest public blunder. When accused by a participant that Ford's policies favored the rich, Greenspan, trying to explain that economy affects everyone, responded, "If you really wanted to examine who percentage–wise is hurt the most in their incomes, it is the Wall Street brokers. I mean, their incomes have gone down the most." Unfortunately, Greenspan's natural propensity to state the numbers was a public relations disaster. He later amended his statement in a joint session of Congress, saying, "Obviously the poor are suffering more."

Greenspan's involvement in bringing the economy back in line, and his strong influence on President Ford, brought him a certain measure of fame in the mid–1970s. In 1975 he appeared on the cover of *Newsweek*. He drew further media attention when he began accompanying Barbara Walters to social events. However, Greenspan receded from the public light after Ford lost the 1976 presidential election to Jimmy Carter. He stepped down from the chair of the CEA and returned to New York and his consulting firm.

When Ronald Reagan made his successful bid for the presidency in 1980, Greenspan reentered politics as an economic adviser to the campaign. He continued to advise Reagan following the election, and in 1981, when social security funding became a divisive topic, Reagan called on Greenspan to chair the newly formed National Commission on Social Security Reform, later known as the Greenspan Commission. Reagan had chosen Greenspan because he was widely regarded for his economic abilities, his ability to be bipartisan, and his skill at remaining calm under intense pressure. When the commission's work was finished, resulting in a social security reform bill passed into law in 1983, Greenspan was once again out of the Washington limelight. But that would all change in 1987.

On June 2, 1987, Reagan announced that he was nominating Greenspan as the next chairman of the Fed. The stock market reacted first; it dropped twenty points, but rebounded quickly, reflecting a general comfort felt by brokers with Reagan's selection. However, international markets reacted more severely; one of the main contentions against Greenspan's nomination was his lack of experience in global economics. Even during his nomination hearings, Greenspan was perfecting his ability to speak without saying too much—a necessary trait when, as Fed chairman, a simple change in his mood, voice, or outlook could cause a major reaction by the economy. For example, according to Martin, when asked a question on antitrust, he responded, "I am, as you point out, philosophically opposed to the Sherman Act. I have been and continue to be. But I understand it, and I understand the legal criteria which are involved in applying it and, hopefully, I am able to separate my own personal views from what is legally required." To which the questioner responded, "That is both very discomforting and very comforting, if you know what I mean."

On July 31, 1987, Greenspan closed the firm Townsend–Greenspan. Days later the Senate approved his nomination by a vote of 91 to 2, and on August 11, he was sworn in as the thirteenth chairman of the Federal Reserve. Greenspan continued to serve as chair of the Fed through Reagan's presidency. He was reappointed to a second four–year term by President George Bush in 1991. Four years later, Bill Clinton awarded him a third term as chair, despite their different party affiliations, and in 2000 Clinton reappointed him to a fourth term, which ends on June 20, 2004.

Social and Economic Impact

The Fed serves as the nation's central bank. Its job is to monitor the growth of the economy and take measures to keep it from growing too fast, which leads to inflation, or from growing too slowly, which leads to recession. The Fed has controls how much money is in circulation, regulates how much money banks must have on hand, and sets the interest rate on money it loans to banks. For example, if the Fed increases the interest rate it charges banks, banks, in turn, increase the interest rates they charge consumers. As a result, fewer people borrow money, less money is spent, and the economy slows. On the other hand, if the Fed decreases interest rates, banks follow, and borrowing becomes more attractive to consumers, thus fueling the economy.

Just two months after his appointment, the bottom fell out of the stock market, and Greenspan had a full–scale economic crisis on his hands. On October 19, 1987, which became known as Black Monday, the Dow Jones industrial average (an index of 30 major stock prices) dropped a record 508 points, sending the economy into a tailspin. Greenspan moved quickly to avoid the Fed's mistakes made during the 1929 crash that led to the Great Depression. Although billions of dollars had been lost in the stock market, the greater issue was the panicky reaction of the largest economy, namely the banks. Greenspan flooded the market with money and pressured banks to continue to make loans despite the uncertain times. His quick and decisive actions were credited with a relatively speedy recovery of the economy.

Although not all his decisions have been popular or, in hindsight, correct, Greenspan has garnered the trust and admiration of the nation. As Bob Woodward wrote in *Maestro: Greenspan's Fed and the American Boom*, "Although his words are almost unbearably opaque, he appears to be doing something very rare—telling the truth. The very act of thinking, the strain in his wrinkled forehead, can be seen in the video footage of him before a microphone. At times it seems painful. But the public has rewarded his caution, reflection, and results with their confidence. That he is the unelected steward of the economy is simply accepted." ABC.com's *Newsmakers* quotes former Representative Frank Ikard of Texas referring to Greenspan: "He is the kind of person who knows how many thousands of flat–headed bots were used in a Chevrolet and what it would do to the national economy if you took out three of them." When his renomination was announced in 1996, *Fortune* commissioned a poll that showed a 96 percent approval rating among the nations top 1,000 executives.

Throughout his career as Fed chair, Greenspan has been a staunch opponent of inflation. He is prone to make small changes rather than dramatic moves, and he is cautious in making statements both of optimism and pessimism regarding the future of the economy. He has seen the U.S. economy through both difficult and prosperous times. However, his lasting legend may be how well he is able to control the recessive economy of the last three years of his term. In 2001, he lowered the interest rate no less than nine times, bringing it to its lowest point since 1960. On October 22, 2001, *Newsweek* ran an article titled "Can Alan Save the Day Again? Probably Not," suggesting that the public and Wall Street both have overestimated Greenspan's power to control the economy. The article's author, Robert Samuelson, noted, "The point is that even zero interest rates can't reinvigorate the economy if other conditions are sufficiently unhealthy."

The significant slowdown in the American economy during 2001 caused some loss of admiration for Greenspan, whom some blame for not lowering interest rates soon enough or fast enough to jump–start the economy. After the terrorist attacks on the World Trade Center and the Pentagon on September 11, 2001, consumer confidence plunged further, and an estimated $1 trillion of wealth was destroyed by the collapse of the stock market in the wake of the attacks. If Greenspan succeeds in averting an all–out recession, he will most definitely find a permanent place among the nation's heroes. As Rob Norton of *Fortune* wrote in 1996, "He will be remembered not only as the best Fed chairman ever but perhaps as the preeminent central banker of the age."

Sources of Information

Contact at: Federal Reserve Board
20th and C Streets, NW
Washington, DC 20551
Business Phone: (202)452–3215
URL: http://www.federalreserve.gov

Bibliography

"Alan Greenspan: Chairman of the Federal Reserve Board." *ABC Newsmakers*, 1997. Available at http://www.abc.com.

Beckner, Steven K. *Back From the Brink: The Greenspan Years.* New York: John Wiley & Sons, 1996.

"Federal Reserve System." The Federal Reserve System, 2001. Available at http://www.federalreserve.gov.

Fox, Justin. "Did He Blow It? We've Long Cursed Deities for our Suffering—Alan Greenspan is No Exception." *Fortune*, 2 April 2001.

Martin, Justin. *Greenspan: The Man Behind the Money.* Cambridge, MA: Perseus Publishing, 2000.

Miller, Rich, and Laura Cohn. "Even 'Free Money' May Not Do the Trick." *Business Week*, 8 October 2001.

Norton, Rob. "In Greenspan We Trust." *Fortune*, 18 March 1996.

Samuelson, Robert J. "Can Alan Save the Day Again? Probably Not." *Newsweek*, 22 October 2001.

Woodward, Bob. *Maestro: Greenspan's Fed and the American Boom.* New York: Simon & Schuster, 2000.

Ellen M. Hancock

(1943-)
Exodus Communications

Overview

Ellen Hancock was the CEO of Exodus Communications, a Web–hosting service, from March 1998 to September 2001. During that time, the company grew tremendously, stock prices soared, and Hancock was on top of the world. Then the bottom fell out of the technology industry, which sent Exodus on an unstoppable downward spiral, ending in bankruptcy and restructuring.

Personal Life

Ellen Marie Hancock, the oldest of four siblings, was born on April 15, 1943, in the Bronx, New York, to Peter and Helen Mooney. Her mother, an Irish immigrant, cared for the children at home, and her father, an Irish American, worked at Audio Productions, a New York advertising agency. Starting out as an errand boy, Hancock's father eventually rose through the ranks to become the company's president. Hancock, a straight–A student, attended an all–girl Catholic school and, for a time, considered becoming a nun. However, strongly influenced by her father, she was drawn to the business world at an early age. She told Ben Elgin of *Business Week* of the evenings when her father would invite his business friends to dinner: "I couldn't cook, but I was just fascinated with the conversation and the range of topics. I remember saying, 'I want to be like this when I grow up.'"

With a strong affinity to logic and math, Hancock enrolled in the College of New Rochelle and earned a

Bachelor of Science degree in mathematics in 1965. The following year she completed her master's degree in mathematics at Fordham University. On September 17, 1971, she married W. Jason Hancock, a fellow employee at IBM. The couple's primary home is in Ridgefield, Connecticut. Hancock is widely known for her love of motorcycles. In the 1970s she owned two small Hondas, but after taking a spill on a back road in Connecticut in the early 1990s that resulted in scrapes and cuts, she decided her motorcycle driving days were done. Letting her husband do all the driving now, she's content to be a passenger.

Career Details

Just one month after graduating from Fordham in 1966, Hancock accepted a position as a junior programmer at IBM, the start of a 29–year–long stint with the company. During the nearly three decades that Hancock spent at IBM, she held a number of increasingly important positions, and by 1995 she was senior vice president and group executive for networking hardware, networking software, and software solutions departments, with 15,000 employees under her charge. She was the first woman ever to achieve the level of senior vice president at IBM. However, her career with IBM came to a bitter end in 1995. Hoping to be named IBM's new CEO, she was passed over when the company brought in Louis V. Gerstner Jr. to fill the position. According to reports, a personality conflict developed between Hancock and Gerstner. Hancock, known for her outspokenness, did not wish to stay with the company in the lesser role, so for the first time since she was a graduate student, at the age of 52, Hancock went looking for a job.

After the stability of her long–term position at IBM, the decade following her departure was filled with numerous notable successes and an equal number of significant disappointments. After leaving IBM, Hancock signed on with National Semiconductor Corporation, a manufacturer of computer chips, as the chief operating officer, where she was responsible for technology and product development. However, two years later, history repeated itself and Hancock was passed up for the vacated CEO office, and she once again went looking for another position. She found it at Apple Computer as the chief technical officer. Her main responsibility was to find or develop an advanced operating system for the Mac computer. But she became unpopular among the staff when she required that they work on developing a new system in–house at the same time that she was working to acquire one from an outside source. The result was that this job, like the one before, proved temporary; when Steve Jobs, the founder of Apple Computers, returned in 1997 as the company's CEO, he cleaned house, and Hancock was out the door once again—with no kind words from Jobs who did not think highly of her abilities.

Ellen M. Hancock. (AP/Wide World Photos.)

During the winter of 1997, Hancock did some soul searching, wondering how, in just three years' time, her professional life had become so fragmented. Her luck changed quickly, however, when Dan Lynch, a longtime friend, introduced her to the board of directors of Exodus Communications, of which he was a member. The company was looking for a new CEO to develop its small Web–hosting operations. On March 10, 1998, five months after being fired by Jobs, Hancock became the president of Exodus. Six months later, on September 9, 1998, K. B. Chandrasekhar, who co–founded Exodus Communications in 1994, announced that Hancock had been promoted to CEO, saying, according to an Exodus press release, "We have tremendous opportunities before us and Ellen has proven that she has the ability to take this company to the next level. Her expertise and leadership have helped us achieve aggressive company milestones and we're confident in her ability to grow our U.S. customer base and expand our business internationally."

Hancock came on board with Exodus during a period of incredible growth. The company basically rented data–center space to companies who conducted business on the Internet. Companies installed and operated their own systems in an Exodus data center, with Exodus providing the space, power, and network broadwidth. In 1998 the demand for data center space was far greater than the supply, and, as a result, Exodus was growing by leaps and bounds. Just nine days after moving into the corner office, Hancock guided the company through its initial public offering (IPO), and in 1998 its revenues

Chronology:
Ellen M. Hancock

1943: Born.

1966: Earned master's degree in mathematics; joined IBM as junior programmer.

1995: Left IBM; joined National Semiconductor as chief operating officer.

1997: Left National Semiconductor; joined Apple Computer.

1998: Became chief executive officer of Exodus Communications; revenues grew over 300 percent.

1999: Exodus stocks traded as high as $70 a share.

2000: Forty–six data centers either open or were under construction.

2000: Acquired rival GlobalCenter for $6.5 million, making Exodus the largest Web–hosting service.

2001: Dot–com businesses failed in large numbers, Hancock resigned, and Exodus filed for bankruptcy; stock prices fell as low as 17 cents a share.

---

grew 308 percent to $215 million. At the end of 2000, revenues totaled $818 million.

At the beginning of 1999, Exodus maintained eight data centers; by the end of 2000, the company had a total of forty–six, either open or under construction. "We're going into the European market. We're going into the Asian market," Hancock told *Computer Reseller News*. "The next two years, we will remain focused on building centers. There is still demand for data center space." Not only were the number of sites increasing but also their size: the first Exodus data center was 14,000 square feet, and by 2000 some new sites were as large as 300,000 square feet. Essentially, Exodus was profiting from the explosion of dot–com companies that flooded the Web in the mid– to late 1990s, and, as Exodus continued to grow at an exceptional rate, Hancock received high praise for her leadership of the company. Harry Blount, an analyst at Donaldson, Lufkin & Jenrette told *Computer Reseller News*, "[Hancock] sees two to three steps ahead, yet she's surrounded with a strong operations team to drive day–to–day operations. They've blown away every comparable company. . . . [She's] done an exceptional job."

By October 1999, just 18 months after completing the IPO, Exodus stock was trading at $70 a share, up more than 1,000 percent from its initial price, bringing its market to $5.6 billion—more than six times its one–year revenues. On September 28, 2000, Exodus entered into an agreement to purchase rival company GlobalCenter for $6.5 billion, making Exodus the largest Internet host with over 5,000 customers, including such well–known names as BestBuy.com, CBS SportsLine, Compaq Computer, eBay, General Electric, Google, Handspring, L'Oreal, MSNBC.com, Microsoft, Merrill Lynch, OfficeMax, Reebok, Starbucks, Sun Microsystems, USAToday.com, and Yahoo!

Despite the incredible growth, Hancock knew she had her work cut out for her. Because of the cost of the massive expansion of data centers, increased revenues did not translate into a bottom line profit. Although revenues increased over 300 percent in 1998, losses grew to 41 percent. Hancock hoped to position the company so that it would start seeing a profit by the first quarter of 2001, with analysts expecting profitability to be reached by 2002. Ultimately both predictions proved much too rosy an outlook. As early as 1999, some analysts were more correctly predicting big troubles ahead for the company.

Social and Economic Impact

When the company was formed in 1994, there was almost no demand for its services; however, as demand mushroomed, so did competitors. In 1999 Cheryl Strauss Einhorn of *Barron's* recognized that increased competition could prove to be a problem for Exodus in the future. Along with Intel, Strauss Einhorn noted, "[C]ompetitors include big, well–known names like AT & T, MCI WorldCom, and GTE. . . . These firms all have greater name recognition, larger customer bases and greater financial, technological and marketing resources than does Exodus. More importantly, they can bundle their Web products with other services, making it more difficult for Exodus to compete." In November 2000, *Business Week*'s Ben Elgin wrote, "Renting data–center real estate has worked fine for Exodus. . . . But, over time, such services are expected to be readily available, and pricing is expected to plummet. To avoid that fate, Exodus is expanding the scope of its services to match a new breed of Internet outsources. These so–called managed service providers offer soup–to–nuts services covering all of a customer's Internet needs, including tending the servers and software for Web sites and e–commerce application."

Even though Hancock was fully aware of the need for Exodus to find new strategic ideas for the future, neither she nor the analysts anticipated the sudden and dramatic downturn in fortunes for Internet–related businesses. As fast as dot–coms entered the market, they were failing just as quickly. The impact on Exodus was immediate and costly. One week after announcing layoffs of 3,000 employees, on August 1, 2001, Exodus stock prices fell to just $1.18, down from a high of almost $90 a share in the spring of 2000. Despite tough times, Hancock continued to talk positively, telling *Business Week Online*'s Olga Kharif on August 3, 2001, "We believe we have not just a viable business, but a great business." In an interview the day before with Corey Grice of *CNET News.com*, she said, "We have sufficient cash and we can stand alone for a long, long time."

Despite her encouraging words, Exodus was taking a beating, and Hancock along with it. In the second quarter of 2001, the company posted a loss of $583 million, a loss ten times greater than the same period of the previous year, even though gross revenues had doubled. As strongly as she was praised prior to the downturn, afterward Hancock found an equal amount of criticism. Mark Veverka of *Barron's* wrote, "What is a tad surprising, if not entirely disappointing, is that among the throngs of disenchanted stockholders running scared from the company's shares has been Exodus chief executive, Ellen Hancock. . . . [She] deep–sixed a large chunk of her holdings just weeks before the rest of us would learn that the company's second quarter [of 2001] was a shipwreck."

In May 2001, the company's chief financial officer, chief operating officer, and chief marketing officer all tendered their resignation. In mid–August, three members of the board resigned. And, on September 4, 2001, chairman of the board L. William Krause announced that Hancock was resigning as CEO. In a press release, Krause said, "We agreed with Ellen that it's time to transition the leadership of the company as it maneuvers through challenging times." The day the news was released, Exodus stock prices fell to a record low of 67 cents. Reacting to the news, Joel Yaffe, a senior industry analyst at Giga Information Group, told *Network World*, "This is a move to appease investors and signal that change is afoot. What it doesn't do is fix the situation. As much as Ellen got a lot of credit for things that weren't beneath her direct control when things were going well, she's now taking a lot of the blame for things that also aren't within her control."

As analysts expected, three weeks after Hancock's departure, on September 27, 2001, Exodus announced that it was filing for bankruptcy. On the morning of the announcement, Exodus shares were down to 17 cents. The company hopes to turn itself around through restructuring its financial debt of over $3 billion and re-bound from bankruptcy to once again operate as a viable business. Not only Exodus suffered impressive losses; rivals Digex, AboveNet, and Intel Online all felt a substantial negative impact.

Hancock's future plans are uncertain. Nonetheless, throughout her career she has made a significant impact as a successful businesswoman in the world of high tech traditionally dominated by men. "I have a lot of respect for Ellen," Ruann F. Ernst, CEO of Digital Island, Inc., told *Business Week*. "She has made it easier for the rest of us."

Sources of Information

Contact at: Exodus Communications
     2831 Mission College Blvd.
     Santa Clara, CA 95054–1838
     Business Phone: (408)346–2200
     URL: http://www.exodus.com

Bibliography

Campbell, Scott. "Ellen Hancock: The Hostess." *Computer Reseller News*, 13 November 2000.

Einhorn, Cheryl Strauss. "Parting the Waters." *Barron's*, 11 October 1999.

Elgin, Ben. "Making Her Own Luck." *Business Week*, 20 November 2000.

"Exodus Communications Promotes Ellen Hancock to CEO." Exodus Communications, Inc., 9 September 1998. Available at http://www.exodus.com.

Grice, Corey. "CEO Hancock Out at Exodus." *CNET News.com*, 4 September 2001. Available at http://www.cnet.com.

Grice, Corey. "In the Eye of the Storm." *CNET News.com*, 2 August 2001. Available at http://cnet.com.

Hagendorf, Jennifer. "CRN Interview: Ellen Hancock." *CRN*, 3 September 2001.

Mears, Jennifer. "Hancock, Exodus Part Ways." *Network World*, 10 September 2001.

Veverka, Mark. "Plugged In: Sharholders are Exiting Exodus, Including CEO Hancock." *Barron's*, 9 July 2001.

"We May Have Hit the Bottom." *Business Week Online*, 3 August 2001. Available at http://www.businessweek.com.

Who's Who of American Women: 2000–2001. Providence, NJ: Marquis Who's Who, 2000.

William R. Hewlett

(1913-2001)
Hewlett–Packard Company

Overview

In 1938, William Hewlett and his college friend David Packard invested $538 dollars to build their company's first "plant" in a garage in Palo Alto, California, starting what was to become the multi–billion dollar Hewlett–Packard Company, a leading manufacturer of information systems and products used in medical, scientific, educational, business, and engineering applications. In 2001 Hewlett–Packard was the nation's 13th largest business, with 88,000 employees in more than 120 countries and annual sales nearing $50 billion. Both Hewlett and Packard were instrumental in creating what later became known as California's "Silicon Valley," dubbed as such because of the rapid growth in that geographic area of companies manufacturing silicon–coated microchips and other electronic components. Moreover, the company's management style (having pioneered decentralized corporate culture) has been widely imitated over the decades and has left its imprint on organizational structure and control far beyond the particular industry.

Personal Life

Born in Ann Arbor, Michigan, to Albion and Louise Redington Hewlett on May 20, 1913, Hewlett's father was then teaching medicine at the University of Michigan. In 1916 he moved the family to California, where he had accepted a position at Stanford University Medical School. Young Hewlett grew up in Palo Alto. When his father died suddenly of a brain tumor in 1926, Hewlett accompanied his mother, grandmother, and sisters to Europe for a year before returning to San Francisco, where

he graduated from Lowell High School. He went on to Stanford University for his undergraduate work, receiving his Bachelor of Arts degree in 1934. He did not think much of his academic talents and even believed he had been accepted at Stanford only because of his father's position. Interestingly, Hewlett's lack of confidence was due in part to his academic mediocrity; he was a slow reader, suffering from undiagnosed dyslexia at a time when the disorder was not widely known or recognized. He compensated by memorizing important facts and figures in an organized, logical way; this ultimately led to his superior skills in math and science. Hewlett's dislike for thick textbooks also contributed to an alternative knack for physically taking things apart to study the composition and function of the individual components. His mother considered it mischief when he frequently disassembled door locks, and during an interview for the *Mercury News* in 1997, he recalled blowing up doorknobs while a student at Stanford. The consummate tinkerer, Hewlett ultimately earned 13 patents over three decades.

It was while a freshman at Stanford that Hewlett began his friendship with David Packard. During their undergraduate days, Hewlett and Packard acquired a mentor, the legendary Stanford professor Frederick Terman, who advised them to gain experience and knowledge before starting their own business, something they had discussed. They both went east after graduation—Packard to work for General Electric and Hewlett to continue his studies at the Massachusetts Institute of Technology. Hewlett received his master's degree in electrical engineering from MIT in 1936. He returned to Stanford where Professor Terman helped him get a contract to construct an electroencephalograph—a device for recording brain waves. When Packard opted to leave General Electric and return to California in 1938, Terman arranged a research fellowship for him at Stanford and encouraged Hewlett and Packard to open their own business in 1939. That year was a milestone for the young Hewlett, during which he also received his engineering degree from Stanford, married Flora Lamson, and first became an official member of his beloved Sierra Club.

While growing up, Hewlett's family frequently vacationed in the Sierra Nevadas, where he eventually met Flora. Young Hewlett developed a lifelong love of the outdoors and became an avid hiker and rock climber. An environmental activist, he later purchased land on the shore of Lake Tahoe in 1971 and then sold it to the U.S. Forest Service to prevent the construction of a proposed massive condominium development. In 1989 he successfully sued the owner of the Squaw Valley ski resort for illegally cutting down 1,800 trees located in a cathedral-like canyon. Hewlett was an amateur botanist, a nature photographer and writer, and an avid fisherman. He and Packard maintained various ranching and cattle-raising operations in both California and Idaho.

Described as a "gentle man" with a good sense of humor, Hewlett was the recipient of several honorary degrees from such renowned institutions as Yale Univer-

Chronology:
William R. Hewlett

1913: Born in Ann Arbor, MI.

1916: Moved to California with his family.

1934: Bachelor of Arts degree from Stanford University.

1936: Master of Science degree in Electrical Engineering from MIT.

1939: Formed Hewlett–Packard Company with friend David Packard.

1947: Hewlett–Packard was incorporated.

1947: Named vice president of Hewlett–Packard.

1957: Elected executive vice president.

1964: Elected president.

1969: Named CEO.

1987: Officially retired, but named director emeritus.

sity, Brown University, University of Notre Dame, Dartmouth College, and the University of California at Berkeley, among others. He was also given an honorary doctor of humane letters from Johns Hopkins University. In 1985 Hewlett received the nation's highest scientific honor, the National Medal of Science, from former President Ronald Reagan. Other awards included the Corporate Leadership Award from MIT in 1970; the Henry Heald Award in 1984; the World Affairs Council Award in 1987; the Degree of Uncommon Man from Stanford in 1987; the National Business Hall of Fame Laureate Award in 1988; the Silicon Valley Engineering Hall of Fame Award in 1991; the National Academy of Engineering's Founders' Award in 1993; and the Eta Kappa Nu Association's Eminent Member Award in 1999.

Hewlett was active in the electronics industry and in the community at large. He served on the board of directors of the Institute of Electrical and Electronic Engineers (IEEE) from 1950 to 1957, and in 1954 he was named president. He was co–founder of the American Electronics Association (formerly the Western Electronic Manufacturers Association), a member of the National Academy of Engineering, and an honorary life member of the Instrument Society of America. Hewlett served as a trustee of Mills College in Oakland, California, from 1958 to 1968, and of Stanford University from 1963 to 1974. He was also an honorary trustee of the California

William Hewlett. *(The Library of Congress.)*

Career Details

Hewlett won the coin toss to see who would get top billing in the new company's name. The Hewlett–Packard Company was formed in 1939. The garage behind Packard's rented house became the first business address, and Mrs. Packard's kitchen oven was where the two men baked their first encapsulated transformers. Their first inventions—including a device for automatically flushing urinals, a shock machine for losing weight, a harmonica tuner, and a foul indicator for bowling alleys—did not do well. They had more success with a resistance capacitance audio oscillator based on a design from Hewlett's graduate school thesis. The device produced variable and stable signals in the low frequency needed for measurements in acoustics, medicine, oil exploration, seismology, oceanography, and many other fields involving low frequencies. A big break came when Walt Disney became interested in using them in the movie industry. Hewlett and Packard sold several oscillators to Disney, who used them in the production of *Fantasia*.

Hewlett and Packard had realized profits of over $1500 dollars in 1939 and built their first building in 1941. During those early years, they swept the floors, kept the books, and took the inventory themselves. From the beginning, they had decided to specialize in electronic measurement and test instruments, and the company did well, with sales of $100,000 by 1941. During World War II, Hewlett was called to serve in the armed forces. He was absent from the company until the end of the war, serving in the Army on the staff of the Chief Signal Officer and then as head of the electronics section of the New Development Division of the War Department's Special Staff. Hewlett was discharged in 1945 and returned home. In 1947, with $1.5 million in sales and 110 employees, the company was incorporated, and Hewlett was made vice president. But the end of the war also meant an end to lucrative defense contracts. A reduction in demand for products caused the company to scale back operations, and a number of employees left, primarily women returning to the home sphere after the war. Distressed by these disruptions, Hewlett and Packard resolved never again to become so dependent upon government contracts. They struggled to develop a wide range of products for a broader market, and by 1959 their product line had grown to 380. Hewlett was made executive vice president of Hewlett–Packard in 1957 and president in 1964.

In accordance with his previously announced plans for management succession, Hewlett resigned as president in 1977 and retired as CEO in 1978. However, Hewlett remained actively involved in the company, serving as chairman of the company's executive committee from 1977 until 1983, then as vice–chair of the board of directors until 1987. Upon his official retirement in 1987, he was named director emeritus. Both he and Packard, nearing their 80s in age, briefly returned to

Academy of Sciences and trustee emeritus of the Carnegie Institution in Washington.

Hewlett's lifelong relationship with Packard, both within the corporate structure as well as on their cattle ranches, invoked widespread inspiration and emanation, and his personal philanthropy and involvement in charitable and other interests created a legacy that continued well beyond his lifetime. At the time of his death at age 87 in 2001, his estimated fortune was approximately $9 billion. Despite his personal wealth, Hewlett remained a publicity–shy, unassuming man, often driving himself to work and sharing lunch in the company cafeteria. Like Packard, he chose to donate most of his fortune to worthy causes. Both men contributed $300 million to their alma mater, Stanford, and another $25 million to set up the Frederick Terman Fellowship to honor their Stanford professor–mentor. Another $70 million endowment went toward the founding of the Public Policy Institute of California, a San Francisco think tank created to research economic, social, and political issues facing the state. In 1966 Hewlett created the William and Flora Hewlett Foundation, which donates approximately $120 million annually to various educational, environmental, and cultural programs. The bulk of Hewlett's estate went to the foundation following his death. He and Flora had five children together. After her death, he remarried in 1978 to Rosemary Bradford, gaining five stepchildren as well. His lifelong partner and friend Packard died in 1996; they remained close and supportive of each other until the end.

the company in 1990 to trim inefficient bureaucracy within its ranks. At that time, company stock had dropped steeply and the organization had become overly centralized. Hewlett and Packard used their influence to reduce the number of committees, which had bloated the company's overhead and weakened the power of individual managers. They also allowed the medical division more freedom in choosing payment policies and gave Lewis Platt, the head of the Computer Systems Group, free rein in building an inexpensive engineering workstation. The project was a great success, and he eventually took over as president and CEO. By 1992 the company again posted a profit while its chief competitors, IBM and DEC, were both in the red.

Social and Economic Impact

Hewlett's personal interest in the miniaturization of electronic mechanisms led to the world's first handheld scientific calculator in 1972, and the company's first consumer product. (It previously had manufactured instruments for primarily academic and professional scientific use only.) The instant success of the pocket–sized calculator made slide rules obsolete for professionals and students alike. Hewlett–Packard went on to produce numerous state–of–the–art cardiac and encephalographic monitors and recorders, scientific measurement and assessment instruments, and information systems, before focusing in the computer and printer industry.

Hewlett–Packard was one of the first companies to make use of semiconductors, and their growth attracted an increasing number of new electronics businesses to Silicon Valley, many of them started by Hewlett's own hand–picked recruits. The company influenced industry in a number of ways, but perhaps most important was the management style fostered by Hewlett and Packard, which encouraged a corporate philosophy committed to people. Hewlett referred to it as "management by walking around." This commitment involved a respect for the individual and expressed itself in management processes that included communications and direct involvement at all levels. Managers made a point of being available to their employees and offering them help as soon as it was needed. Hewlett considered the development of his managers to be his greatest accomplishment at Hewlett–Packard. Messrs. Hewlett and Packard changed the modern workplace and workforce forever by pioneering such employee perquisites as catastrophic health insurance, profit sharing, flextime hours, employee stock ownership, and most of all, the concept of teamwork—from the bottom to the top—in all important company endeavors.

Sources of Information

Bibliography

"Executive Biographies: William R. Hewlett," 23 November 2001. Available at http://www.hp.com/hpinfo/newsroom/hewlett/.

Fuller, Brian, and George Rostky. "William Hewlett, Co–Founder of HP, Dies at 87." *Electronic Engineering Times*, 22 January 2001.

"Hard Drivers." *Forbes*, 11 October 1999.

Hiltzik, Michael A. "High–Tech Pioneer William Hewlett Dies." *Los Angeles Times*, 13 January 2001.

Hewlett-Packard Company. Available at http://www.hp.com.

Seipel, Tracy. "Hewlett Remembered as Generous, Gifted Engineer." *San Jose Mercury News*, 21 January 2001.

Seipel, Tracy, and Therese Poletti. "Electronics Pioneer William Hewlett Dies at 87." *San Jose Mercury News*, 13 January 2001.

Tommy Hilfiger

(1952-)
Tommy Hilfiger Corporation

Overview

Tommy Hilfiger is the man whose name has become synonymous with urban fashion. His fashion label is one of the most recognizable in the world, and he has turned his company into a multi–billion dollar empire that designs and markets clothing, jewelry, and accessories for men, women, and children. Hilfiger's designs—primarily classic styles with a contemporary flair, helped him and his partners build a fashion company rivaling the success of designers Calvin Klein and Ralph Lauren.

Personal Life

Thomas Jacob Hilfiger was born March 24, 1952, into an Irish Catholic family in Elmira, New York, a small town near Cornell University. His father, Richard, was a jeweler, and his mother, Virginia, is a former nurse. When Hilfiger discusses his inspiration for designing such a popular line of clothing, he often mentions his "Leave–it–to–Beaver" upbringing in Elmira. As one of nine children, he grew up in a middle–class five–bedroom home collecting sports equipment, guns, cowboy hats, and wearing Billy–the–Kid brand jeans—all things he views as part of the "American" image. He also recalls how at 16 he loved to wear his service station uniform, which had a large automobile graphic on it. This may have had some impact on his prolific use of large graphics and logos in his designs. Also around age 16, he became interested in clothing, especially the Ivy League look of chinos, madras, and oxfords.

Tommy Hilfiger waving to the crowd after one of his shows. (AP/Wide World Photos.)

Hilfiger started his first clothing business during his senior year in high school, selling bell bottoms and candles in a small shop he opened in Elmira named "The People's Place." The merchandise was bought in New York City, and then brought back to his small town for resale. Tired of this setup, he eventually began designing his own merchandise, and expanded the business to include 10 shops across upstate New York. He found a manufacturer that would make clothing according to his specifications, and began his design career. Unfortunately, his first business venture ended in bankruptcy in 1979, but Hilfiger continued the pursuit of his design career.

By the end of the 1990s, Tommy Hilfiger was a multi–millionaire. The Tommy Hilfiger Corporation posted 2001 sales of $1.88 billion, and had some 4,000 employees. Everyone from teenagers to rock stars to grandmothers could be seen sporting Tommy Hilfiger merchandise. The designer claims he never doubted his eventual success, and was only surprised it took him so long.

Now an established fashion celebrity, Hilfiger has written two books. *All American: A Style Book* was published in 1997. *Rock Style: How Fashion Moves to Music,* which focused on the clothing choices of rock musicians, was published in 1999. The book accompanied a major exhibit of the same name at the Costume Institute of the Metropolitan Museum of Art. Tommy Hilfiger was the major sponsor of the exhibit, which opened

Chronology:
Tommy Hilfiger

1952: Born.

1971: Opened People's Place in Elmira, New York.

1981: Founded 20th Century Survival.

1982: Started to design women's clothing.

1985: Hired by Mohan Murjani to oversee design of Coca–Cola clothing line.

1986: Launched Tommy Hilfiger clothing line, backed by Murjani.

1989: Formed Tommy Hilfiger, Inc. with Silas Chou.

1992: Tommy Hilfiger Corp. is made public.

1997: Opened Tommy Hilfiger store on Rodeo Drive.

1997: Published *All American: A Style Book.*

1999: Named in class–action law suit charging manufacturers of violating workers' rights.

1999: Published *Rock Style: How Fashion Moves to Music.*

1999: Sponsored Metropolitan Museum of Art exhibition of rock music fashion.

---

in New York City in December 1999 and included 100 costumes, accessories, and other items belonging to such stars as Elvis, Madonna, Mick Jagger, Bruce Springsteen, Elton John, Jimi Hendrix, David Byrne, and Sean "Puffy" Combs. "It's so appropriate that at the end of the century we look back at 50 years of outrageousness and excess," the *Daily News Record* reported Hilfiger said about the show.

In addition to his fashion influence, Hilfiger supports several charities, including Race to Erase MS, which focuses on finding a cure for multiple sclerosis; City of Hope, a hospital providing cancer treatment and research; the American Jewish Committee; and the Fresh Air Fund, to which he donated $2.5 million in 1999 to renovate Camp Pioneer in Fishkill, NY. The camp was renamed Camp Tommy during a rededication in 2001. In November 2001, Hilfiger and photographer Anne Menke announced a joint creative limited–edition book featuring photographs of the American flag taken in New York City following the September 2001 terrorist tragedy, with proceeds donated to the Twin Towers Fund.

Hilfiger is married to the former Susan Cirona in 1980, whom he met when she applied for a job at his first store, People's Place. Together they have four children, Abby, Richard, Elizabeth, and Kathleen. Hilfiger resides in a 22–room mansion in Greenwich, Connecticut, and also owns a home on Mustique in the Caribbean's Grenadine Islands.

Career Details

Following the failure of Hilfiger's first business venture, he and his wife moved to New York City to look for design work. By 1985, he was being offered design assistantships for Perry Ellis and Calvin Klein, but declined them both. Eager to start his own label, he needed extensive financial backing, and found it from Mohan Murjani, owner of Gloria Vanderbilt blue jeans and Coca–Cola clothes licenses. Hilfiger and Murjani formed a partnership in which Hilfiger's job was to design men's sportswear similar to Ralph Lauren's, but appeal to a slightly younger clientele and be more modestly priced. As he states in *All American,* "Picturing a more New England, outdoorsy, and classic campus look that I knew would last, I launched Tommy Hilfiger."

When Hilfiger first launched his clothing line, he decided to "self–proclaim" himself a top designer. With the help of a publicity agent, he announced his arrival on the fashion scene in 1985 as one of "the 4 great designers for men," along with Calvin Klein, Perry Ellis, and Ralph Lauren. Critics thought he was incredibly presumptuous and "tasteless." Hilfiger was an unknown who had never attended design school. Analysts were resentful that Hilfiger ads proclaimed Tommy a new star. But Hilfiger continued his aggressive marketing campaigns, commenting in an *Advertising Age* interview "To be successful in this business, you have to be both a designer and a marketer. I am proud to think I have both sides of the brain working at all times."

In 1989, Hilfiger left Murjani International. He began searching for money to expand his own private label. He teamed up with Silas Chou, who had the financial resources to build a company but needed a brand name to sell. The two signed up former Ralph Lauren executives Lawrence Stroll and Joel Horowitz and formed Tommy Hilfiger, Inc. Capitalizing on Polo's success with the "preppy" look, Hilfiger designed men's and boys' sportswear in brighter colors with a more casual, loose fit.

Hilfiger admits it was Silas Chou that pushed the company toward such rapid expansion and success. Tommy Hilfiger, Inc. went public in 1992. In 1995, they licensed Pepe Jeans USA. In late 1997, Tommy Hilfiger opened his first store on Rodeo Drive in Beverly Hills, and a second store in London in early 1998. Soon thereafter, Tommy Hilfiger clothing became available in stores throughout the United States, Canada, Mexico,

Japan, Central and South America, Europe, and the Far East. In November 2001, the company announced the opening of its first specialty store, Soho, in Manhattan, New York —dedicating four stories and 11,000 square feet exclusively to the best of Tommy Hilfiger. Also in 2001, Hilfiger announced that software giant IBM had been chosen to launch Hilfiger's e–business Web sites.

In his book, *All American,* Hilfiger explains his success in foreign markets by saying, "When I started to travel the world, I saw the fruits of American labor everywhere I went, the products and logos that are the trademarks of our industry and our culture. In the most exotic places in the world, you will see people wearing Levi's and drinking Coca–Cola, obsessing over 1950s cars, and sporting cowboy shirts and boots, or wearing the rugged clothes we made for the great outdoors. No matter how different the customs, the world is tuned in to the signature emblems of the American lifestyle."

No longer limited to his men's line, in the mid– to late 1990s Hilfiger began expanding clothing lines to include products for women, children, and teenagers. His company also manufactured its own clothing and was able to keep marketing and distribution costs down. Because of this, Hilfiger was able to offer high quality clothing, comparable to Polo, but at prices more accessible to the American public. He also added a range of accessories, bedding and other home furnishings, cosmetics, and fragrances. Many of these additional product offerings were made possible through licensing agreements. For example, Tommy and Tommy Girl colognes were manufactured by Aramis, to whom he licensed the Tommy Hilfiger name. Hilfiger did not exclude customers seeking more specialized, high–end alternatives. To address that market, Hilfiger designed dressier, more expensive product lines that were marketed through specialty shops.

Hilfiger kept his hand in promoting his designs as well. He hosted fashion shows and autograph sessions, and conducted briefings for sales personnel via satellite. He educated retailers about Hilfiger products and how to display them. Hilfiger also solicited feedback directly from consumers and used that to influence future clothing lines. He was quick to incorporate changes to make his line attractive to teens, African Americans, and Hispanics. Noticing that these young people liked to wear oversized clothes, Hilfiger designed garments in "extra–extra–extra" large sizes. Billed as a "cross–over" artist, Hilfiger's designs were seen on everyone from Bill Clinton to Snoop Doggy Dog to the Spice Girls.

For the 2000 Olympics in Sydney, Australia, Hilfiger was approached by the Olympic Committee to create a new look for athletes at the formal parade ceremonies at all events through the 2004 Summer Games in Athens, Greece. When the Committee rejected his proposed design as too casual, the deal fell through, but not before a multi–million dollar lawsuit was filed by the Committee against Hilfiger in July 2000. Hilfiger's

lawyers defended that a final agreement had never been reached. Meanwhile, U.S. athletes wore Adidas designs for the opening ceremony in Sydney, and were to wear apparel by a different designer for the 2002 winter games in Salt Lake City, Utah.

Social and Economic Impact

Hilfiger has been particularly successful in merging fashion, media, and entertainment. He has sponsored concerts by the Rolling Stones, Jewel, Britney Spears, and Lenny Kravitz, and designed many of the outfits for the Stones' "Bridges to Babylon" tour. In an unusual move, he signed a deal with cable network VH–1 to produce commercials. Hilfiger designs clothes for many top rap artists, including Salt–N–Pepa, Snoop Doggy Dog, and TLC. "We pushed certain buttons within the music world," he said in *Women's Wear Daily.* "Rock and rap stars started wearing my clothes. We dress a lot of athletes and actors. These people send a message of what is hip and what is allowed."

Long before September 2001, Hilfiger believed the nation's colors of red, white, and blue were hip. In early spring of that year, the Hilfiger company conducted a poll on its Website and found that 69 percent of Americans who did not own a flag wished that they did. Hilfiger launched his Stars & Stripes event that offered a top–quality full–sized American flag for $15 with any $50 purchase. The campaign also created a $25,000 opportunity for persons to submit a 20–50 second video that demonstrated what the American flag meant to them; over 700 videos were received, and the winner's was aired on national television in November 2001.

Sources of Information

Contact at: Tommy Hilfiger Corporation
 25 West 39th St.
 New York, NY 10018–3805
 Business Phone: (212) 840–8888
 URL: http://www.tommy.com.

Bibliography
"Designer Tommy Hilfiger and Photographer Anne Menke Join Forces to Publish 'Our New York.'"*PR Newswire,* 04 December 2001.

Doebele, Justin. "A Brand Is Born." *Forbes,* 26 February 1996.

Donnally, Trish. "Hilfiger Rocks." *San Francisco Chronicle,* 21 September 1999.

Donovan, Aaron. "The Fresh Air Fund: Designer's $2.5 Million to Improve Camps." *New York Times,* 27 June 1999.

Goldstein, Lauren. "Tommy Sings America." *Fortune,* 6 September 1999.

Greenhouse, Steven. "Suit Says 18 Companies Conspired to Violate Sweatshop Workers' Civil Rights." *New York Times,* 14 January 1999.

Hethcock, Bill. "USOC Seeks Millions From Tommy Hilfiger." *The Gazette,* 30 September 2001.

Hilfiger, Tommy. *Current Biography Yearbook.* H.W. Wilson Company, 1996.

Hilfiger, Tommy with David A. Keeps. *All American: A Style Book by Tommy Hilfiger.* New York: Universe Publishing, 1997.

Hilfiger, Tommy with Richard Martin, James Henke, and Anthony DeCurtis. *Rock Style: How Fashion Moves to Music.* New York: Universe Publishing, 1999.

"IBM to Provide Technology Behind Tommy Hilfiger e–business Web sites." *M2 Communications,* 11 December 2001.

Knight, Molly and Annmarie Dodd. "Long Live Rock Style: Costume Institute Exhibit to Include 100 of Rock–and–Roll's Greatest Looks." *Daily News Record,* 15 September 1999.

Lockwood, Lisa. "Tommy Hilfiger: Crossing Over; Hilfiger Charts His Course in Women's Wear." *Women's Wear Daily,* 13 September 1999.

Lockwood, Lisa and Anne D'Innocenzio "The Hilfiger Enigma: An Empire in Search of Its Latest Identity." *Women's Wear Daily,* 30 September 1999.

"Tommy Hilfiger Announces Winners of the 'Earn Your Stripes and be a Star' Contest."*PR Newswire,* 14 November 2001.

"Tommy Hilfiger Corporation Capsule." *Hoover's Online.* 2001. Available from http://www.hoovers.com.

Jeffrey R. Immelt

(1956-)
General Electric

Overview

On September 7, 2001, Jeffrey R. Immelt became the chair and chief executive officer of General Electric (GE), following in the footsteps of Jack Welch, who served in the position for the previous 20 years. Welch, so highly admired for his leadership and business skills that he is nearly a legend in his own time, could be a hard act to follow. Immelt is certain that he is up for the challenge.

Personal Life

Immelt was born on February 19, 1956, in Cincinnati, Ohio, where he grew up with his parents, Joseph and Donna Immelt. and his older brother Steve. His father spent 38 years working in GE's Aircraft Engines division, retiring as a mid–level manager; his mother was a school teacher. Showing athletic ability as a youth, Immelt participated in numerous sports and enjoyed an ongoing competition with his brother, who later became an attorney.

Upon graduating from high school, Immelt enrolled in Dartmouth College, where his natural leadership abilities became apparent. During his years at Dartmouth, he played offensive tackle on the college football team, and he was elected president of his fraternity, Phi Delta Alpha. During summer breaks, Immelt worked at a Ford Motor plant in Cincinnati. He graduated from Dartmouth in 1978 with a bachelor of science degree in applied mathematics and worked briefly for Proctor & Gamble in the brand management department before deciding to

Chronology:

Jeffrey R. Immelt

1956: Born.

1982: Hired as an internal marketing consultant at General Electric (GE).

1983: Promoted to district manager of GE Plastics.

1989: Became vice president of consumer services for GE Appliances.

1992: Appointed vice president and general manager of GE Plastics.

1997: Promoted to chief executive officer of GE's Medical Systems division.

2000: Assumed position as GE's chief executive officer.

2001: GE topped *Fortune*'s list of Most Admired Companies for fourth consecutive year.

continue his education. He enrolled in Harvard's graduate school and completed his MBA in 1982.

In 1983, while living in Dallas, Texas, Immelt met Andrea Allen, a GE customer service representative. The two became close, continuing their relationship even after Andrea moved to Chicago. The couple married in 1986, and the following year their daughter, Sarah, was born, since which time Andrea has been a full–time homemaker.

Career Details

Upon his graduation from Harvard, Immelt, like his father before him, became a GE employee. In 1982 26–year–old Immelt was hired as internal marketing consultant at GE's corporate office in Fairfield, Connecticut. The following year he moved to Dallas to become the district sales manager of GE Plastics. In 1989 he left GE Plastics to become the vice president of consumer service of GE Appliances. Three years later he returned to GE Plastics to become the vice president and general manager of the $3 billion division that maintained 5,000 employees. In 1997 he was promoted once again, becoming the CEO of GE's Medical Systems division, located in Waukesha, Wisconsin. Upon his promotion,

GE's Chairman Jack Welch said, "Jeff Immelt is a dynamic, entrepreneurial business leader. We are very excited about the growth prospects for GE Medical Systems, and Jeff is the perfect person to maximize this global opportunity." Immelt maintained this position until being selected as GE's CEO in 2000.

During Immelt's career with GE, prior to being appointed as CEO, he had developed a reputation for excellent leadership and management skills. While at GE Appliances in 1989, he successfully worked through a large recall of refrigerator compressors, delivering motivational speeches to his harried workers on the factory floor in Louisville from atop a forklift. And, true to Welch's prediction, during the time in which Immelt headed GE Medical Systems, sales rose 75 percent and, by many measures, the $7 billion division became the world's most successful imaging company. Immelt discovered that customers wanted more than the line of scanners GE offered, and he set about acquiring 60 smaller companies that offered a broad range of products. Ultrasound, digital x–ray machines, and software all became a part of GE Medical System's product line. The numerous innovations introduced under Immelt include the first digital mammogram system and the LightSpeed CT, a CAT scan machine capable of cutting the diagnosis of trauma patients to just seconds, rather that the minutes required by earlier systems.

As Immelt moved up the corporate ladder, he earned increasing respect and admiration from GE employees and from corporate executives, including Welch. Despite his numerous achievements, Immelt was not always successful in all his endeavors. In 1994 Immelt had difficulties while running half of GE Plastics, missing the division's goals by $50 million due to rising material costs. Immelt recalled the tough period in an interview with *Business Week*: "I didn't move fast enough to get prices up. It was a wacky time with inflation. I knew what I had to do, and I didn't get it done. . . . At the end of the year, we had this management meeting in Boca [Raton]. I'm trying to hide from Jack for three days. He grabs me from behind. He said, 'Jeff, I want you to know, you had one of the worst jobs in the company. I think you are great. I love you. You're going to get this thing right. If you don't, you'e going to have to go.' That was great. . . . The beauty of GE is consequence. . . . Effort is encouraged, but results are what count. He wasn't telling me anything I didn't know." Ultimately, Immelt solved his problems in GE Plastics, later noting that the experience made him a better manager and a more valuable employee because he learned that he could deal successfully with difficult situations.

On November 27, 2000, GE announced that Immelt had been named GE's president and chairman–elect. Not only had Immelt attained the highest rung on the GE corporate ladder, he had been given command of the world's most admired company and was set to replace Welch, one of the world's most admired executives. Welch became chair and CEO of GE in 1981, at the age of 45—

Jeffrey R. Immelt (AP Photo/Marty Lederhandler).

the same age as Immelt when he took over in 2001. Welch made big changes at GE, including selling the housewares business, one of the company's founding divisions, and dramatically altering the GE organizational structure. Firing more than 100,000 employees earned him the nickname Neutron Jack. Building a reputation as one of the best in the business, Welch showed impressive results. During his 20–year tenure, GE's stock rose 3,098 percent, and the company's growth rate averaged 18.9 percent (compared to 896 percent and 12.2 percent industry wide). According to Andy Serwer of *Fortune*, "Welch could be the Michael Jordan of management— the best who's ever played."

In February 2001, *Fortune* announced that GE had topped its Most Admired Companies list for the fourth year in a row: "Tireless innovation. Robust financials. The ability to lure and keep the smartest people. According to more than 4,000 businesspeople *Fortune* surveyed late last year, no company in the nation demonstrates such enviable qualities better than General Electric." At the end of 2000, GE's books showed $130 billion in revenue, earnings of $12.7 billion, and market capitalization close to $350 billion, making it the world's largest company. With 12 different divisions, the company produces a wide array of products, including aircraft engines, locomotive and other transportation equipment, electric distribution, nuclear reactors, plastics, kitchen and laundry appliances, lighting, and medical imaging equipment. GE Capital Services is one of the largest financial services in the United States. The National Broadcasting Network (NBC) is also owned by GE.

The decision to name Immelt the new leader of GE began in 1994 when Welch and the GE board of directors began the formal process of evaluating possible replacements after Welch retired. Each year since 1981, the board would place in an envelope the undisclosed name of the person who would replace Welch in the case of his unexpected death. However, by 1994 they were ready to step up the process. To start, Welch offered 24 possible candidates for his successor. By December 1997, the number was cut to eight, and in June 2000 the final list was cut to three remaining contenders: Immelt; James McNerney, the highly respected head of GE's aircraft engine division; and Robert Nardelli, an executive in GE's electric utilities division. The process was shrouded in secrecy; the candidates were never officially told they were being considered, although most of the company had a fair idea from the rumor mill who was in the running.

Immelt had been hailed as the front runner during most of the process, and although neither Welch nor directors will say exactly why, most analysts believe that one reason was that Immelt was 10 years younger than the other two finalists. He was also the popular choice among GE employees. Finally, on the day before Thanksgiving in 2000, Welch called a teleconference of the directors, and Immelt was officially and unanimously voted in. Determined not to let word leak out to the press or the company until the formal announcement the next Monday, Welch took extraordinary measures. After calling Immelt with the good news on Friday, Immelt and his family flew on a chartered jet (not the GE corporate jet) to meet with Welch in Palm Beach. Afraid to be seen in a restaurant celebrating, on Saturday the two families enjoyed a catered meal, but for added secrecy, it was not provided by the regular GE caterer. On Sunday, Welch boarded his jet and instructed his pilots, who thought they'd be flying to New York, to take him to Cincinnati and then to Albany, where he personally delivered the news to McNerney and Nardelli that they had not been selected. When the official announcement was made on Monday, the news had not been leaked.

Immediately after his selection, Immelt joined the board of GE and the corporate executive office. Initially, Welch was set to retire at the beginning of 2001; however, shortly after the decision was announced, GE began negotiations to acquire Honeywell, a $43 billion deal. As a result, Welch decided to postpone his retirement until January 2002 so that he could oversee the acquisition process. Although Welch was still officially in charge during 2001, he turned over many important responsibilities to Immelt, effectively giving him time to ease into the new role. On July 3, 2001, the European Commission blocked GE from purchasing Honeywell; nine days later, Welch announced that he would move his retirement date up to September 7, 2001. Despite an appeals process, on October 2, 2001, GE officially ended negotiations with Honeywell. Welch and Immelt were duly disappointed; however, some within the company who believed Honeywell was not a wise purchase expressed relief at the dissolution of the deal. On September 7, 2001, Immelt moved into Welch's recently vacated executive office and began his new job as leader of the world's largest company.

Social and Economic Impact

On September 11, just four days after Immelt officially became GE's CEO, terrorists attacked the World Trade Center and the Pentagon. With profits already falling due to a weak economy, the terrorist attacks further rocked the financial profit rates at GE. The New York Stock Exchange closed for the rest of the week; when it reopened, investors began unloading GE stock, causing stock prices to drop more than 20 percent to $30 a share. Despite the uncertainty of the time, GE stock rebounded quickly, coming back up to $35.50 a share by September 25. Nonetheless, GE is not out of the woods, and Immelt readily admits that the path before him may be difficult. Even before September 11, NBC earnings fell 15 percent in the second quarter, compared to the second quarter of 2000. Likewise, GE's lighting and appliance divisions fell off 18 percent and 22 percent, respectively, in the same time period. NBC was subjected to further risk of revenue loss of an estimated $50 million as advertising sales decreased in the slow economy.

GE Aircraft Engines had been a bright spot before September 11, posting an earnings increase of 10 percent in the second quarter of 2000. However, after the terrorist attacks, the airline industry became burdened by a lack of business, causing GE to announce the layoff of some 4,000 employees. The division's losses are expected to total $100 million in 2001 and could rise as high as 200 million in 2002. Also, GE's reinsurance unit, which insured part of the World Trade Center and the hijacked airplanes, posted a $400 million loss. Despite the setbacks, Immelt is holding GE on a steady path. Appliances, Plastics, Medical Systems, and GE Capital continue to post an acceptable profit and are expected to make up for profit loss in the other divisions.

Many analysts are waiting to see if Immelt can live up to his predecessor. So far, he has managed to maintain a good relationship with investors. After 20 years of Welch's robust, no–holds–barred approach, Immelt's quieter demeanor and easy sense of humor will be a change for those inside and outside the company. Immelt told *Business Week*, "My style is that I look at every business from the outside in. My framework is very much the customer and outside market. I'm decisive. I'm accountable. I have good discipline. I believe in people . . . . I love change. I love trying new things. I really bring to the job a complete growth headset. I've had great experiences in technology and globalization, running sales forces and doing acquisitions, and I bring all those things to the job."

Sources of Information

Contact at: General Electric
3135 Easton Turnpike
Fairfield, CT 06431–0001
Business Phone: (203)373–2211
URL: http://www.ge.com

Bibliography

Brady, Diane. "Taking Jeffrey Immelt at His Word." *Business Week*, 26 September 2001.

Brady, Diane. "This is Just About the Best Gig You Can Have." *Business Week*, 5 September 2001.

Cave, Andrew. "Jack Backs His Man as GE Chief Names His Successor." *Daily Telegraph*, 28 November 2000.

Charan, Ram, and Geoffrey Colvin. "Transitions: Making a Clean Handoff." *Fortune*, 17 September 2001.

Colvin, Geoffrey. "Changing of the Guard." *Fortune*, 8 January 2001.

Diba, Ahmad, and Lisa Munoz. "America's Most Admired Companies: How Long Can They Stay?" *Fortune*, 19 February 2001.

Hill, Andrew. "Immelt to Follow Jack Welch as the Head of GE." *Financial Times*, 28 November 2000.

"Jeff Immelt." General Electric Corporation, 2001. Available at http://www.ge.com.

"Jeff Immelt Named President and CEO of GE Medical Systems." *PR Newswire*, 2 January 1997.

"Jeffrey R. Immelt Named President and Chairman–elect of General Electric." *PR Newswire*, 27 November 2000.

Serwer, Andy. "A Rare Skeptic Takes on the Cult of GE." *Fortune*, 19 February 2001.

Useem, Jerry. "Immelt's GE: It's All Yours, Jeff. Now What?" *Fortune*, 17 September 2001.

Betty James
Richard James

(1918-)
(1914-1974)
James Industries

Overview

Richard and Betty James created one of America's most recognizable and enduring toys: the Slinky. More than 250 million Slinkys have been sold, or one for every person in the United States. The Slinky has been sold in all of the continents worldwide, except Antarctica, and the catchy jingle that sold the toy since 1962 is one of the most familiar on television. In addition to its role as a toy, Slinky also has been used for such diverse purposes as therapeutic devices, makeshift antennas, drapery holders, and mail holders. Created by accident when Richard James saw a torsion spring fall on the deck of a ship and fall down some stairs, the Slinky got its moniker when his wife Betty saw the word in the dictionary, which means stealthy, sleek, and sinuous in Swedish. The company they founded, James Industries, developed several other Slinky toys after the original came out, including the Slinky dog, as well as other basic children's toys. After Richard James left in 1960 for Bolivia to join a religious sect/cult, Betty ran James Industries for nearly 40 years as president and CEO, until the company was sold in 1998 to the Michigan–based POOF Products, Inc.

Personal Life

Betty and Richard James were married and had six children. The couple lived in their native Pennsylvania on a 12–acre estate in a suburb of Bryn Mawr until Richard left for Bolivia in February of 1960. In 1974 Betty learned her husband had died there of a heart attack. Betty James retired in 1998 and lives in Hollidaysburg, Pennsylvania.

Betty and Richard James' creation: The Slinky. *(UPI/Corbis-Beitmann.)*

Betty James joined other toy industry greats when she became the 41st inductee in the Toy Industry Hall of Fame on February 10, 2001. The Hall of Fame was established in 1984 to honor individuals who have made outstanding contributions to the toy industry. She has garnered several awards for her business achievements, including the Douglas D. Danforth Award for Quality in Manufacturing from the L.C. Smith College of Engineering and Computer Science in 1995 and the WITTY Award by the Women in Toys organization in 1998. She was inducted into the Blair County Business Hall of Fame for her contribution to the community and named one of Pennsylvania's Best 50 Women in Business in 1996.

Richard James was born in Philadelphia, Pennsylvania, in 1914 and Betty in 1918. Richard graduated from the University of Pennsylvania with a degree in mechanical engineering.

Career Details

While working as a mechanical engineer at a naval shipyard in Philadelphia in 1943, Richard James began work on producing an antivibration device for ship instruments with the goal of developing a spring that would counterbalance the wave motion that rocks a ship. As he observed the torsion spring fall off a table and jiggle as it hit the floor, the idea for the Slinky suddenly sprang to life. Betty recalled in the *Las Vegas Review–Journal*, "He came home and said, 'I think if I got the right prop-

erty of steel and the right tension, I could make it walk.' Over the next two years, Richard experimented with different types of steel wire with the right properties to allow the spring to walk."

Betty was given the task of naming Richard's new invention. Betty told *CNN.com*, "I never named a toy in my life, and some of the things that came to mind were awful. And I said, 'I wonder if I looked in the dictionary,' and I found 'slinky' and that was it." The Swedish word meant stealthy, sleek, and sinuous, which James thought perfectly suited the toy.

In November 1945, the Jameses took their new invention to Gimbel's in Philadelphia where sales were slow at first. In order to generate sales and interest in the toy, the Jameses then returned to the store to demonstrate the toy's stair–walking ability to shoppers. "A Slinky just sitting there isn't very exciting," James recalled in *CNN.com*. "It has to move. If it hadn't been for Gimbel's giving us the end of a counter to demonstrate, I don't know what would have happened." To help sell the toy the day of the demonstration, Betty called a friend and asked if she would go down to Gimbel's and buy one if she supplied her with a dollar, the going price at the time. She reasoned at least one sale would then be made. When Betty and her friend got to the store, they saw the large crowd waving dollar bills, clamoring for the Slinky. The Jameses sold all of the 400 toys that they had in 90 minutes.

The same year they officially introduced the Slinky, in 1945, the couple formed James Spring & Wire

Chronology:

Betty James and Richard James

1914: Richard James born.

1918: Betty James born.

1943: Invented the Slinky.

1945: Founded James Industries.

1960: Betty James becomes CEO; James Industries relocated to Hollidaysburg, Pennsylvania.

1962: Slinky advertising campaign featuring famous jingle launched.

1974: Richard James died.

1998: James Industries sold to POOF Products; Betty James retired.

2000: Slinky inducted into the Toy Industry Hall of Fame.

2001: Betty James inducted into the Toy Industry Hall of Fame.

Company with $500 to mass produce the Slinky. They later founded James Industries to make toys in 1956. Richard James designed and engineered all the equipment used to create the product, which is still made using the original machinery. The first Slinkys were made of an expensive blue–black Swedish steel and sold for one dollar. The company later began using a more silvery–colored steel. The Slinkys were coated and then colored even more silver by the mid–1960s. The Slinky dog was added to the line in 1952 after a suggestion sent to the Jameses by a Mrs. Helen Malsed of Seattle, Washington.

By the late 1950s the Jameses had amassed a small fortune, giving them enough money to purchase their 12–acre suburban estate near Bryn Mawr. Richard, however, became discontent with material success and at some juncture, he became affiliated with an evangelical Christian sect that Betty deemed a cult. He began associating with others in the sect that Betty found dubious, attending revival meetings and making large financial donations to the group. Puzzled and embarrassed, Betty attended one of his revival meetings but failed to convert to his newfound religion. Betty speculated that this sudden change in Richard may have been attributed to the fact that by the mid–1950s, Slinky sales were in a downward spiral and the charismatic Richard, who had grown

used to success, craved more attention. He also felt he needed to confess and atone for his past marital indiscretions that Betty was aware of but tolerated for the sake of their six children.

In February 1960, Richard's involvement in his religious group had grown to the point at which he felt he needed to move to Bolivia to continue their work there. He informed his wife and their two oldest children that they could run the business themselves or sell it as they pleased, but he would no longer be involved in the company. He left in July of that year to perform what Betty considered missionary work, but the exact nature of his mission was unknown. She later learned that at one point he was printing religious pamphlets.

Richard had left the company in a state of near–bankruptcy. He had used considerable company resources to fund his religious activities, and Betty had to contend with millions of dollars of unpaid bills. She kept the company going, however, becoming its CEO, to provide for her large family. She managed to work out a deal with her many creditors, allowing her time to get the company back on track again. Betty periodically received letters from Richard in Bolivia urging her to convert to his religion and join him, at one point even asking that she leave the children to be with him. Betty never replied. She later received the news that he had suffered a fatal heart attack in 1974. After Richard's departure, Betty moved the Slinky plant back to her hometown of Hollidaysburg and began her plan to take the company back to profitability.

One of Betty's most successful initiatives was to launch a highly successful advertising campaign touting the Slinky. The famous Slinky jingle was part of the national campaign that became familiar to the Baby Boom generation: "What walks down stairs, alone or in pairs, And makes a slinkity sound?/A spring, a spring, a marvelous thing, Everyone knows it's Slinky/It's Slinky, it's Slinky, for fun it's a wonderful toy/It's Slinky, it's Slinky, it's fun for a girl and a boy." Betty was also responsible for changing the metal used in the toy at that time. She was also credited with diversifying the Slinky line to include Slinky Jr., Plastic Slinky, Slinky Dog, Slinky Pets, Crazy Eyes (which was a pair of glasses with attached Slinky eyeballs), and Neon Slinky. James claimed the original Slinky was targeted for ages six to 60 but developed a line of brightly colored plastic versions to appeal to younger consumers. There were gold–colored Slinkys, animal and frog Slinkys, and even a Slinky train.

Due to the company's steady success under her reign, Betty regularly received offers from other toymakers to purchase the company she'd built. "Maybe someday I'll take them up on it," James told *Forbes* in 1984. "But it is going to be hard to let go. Slinkys are like my children, and they've been around longer." She did indeed take them up on it in 1998, when she sold the company for a large, undisclosed sum of money to the

Michigan–based POOF Products. POOF assured Mrs. James that they would keep the Slinky plant in Hollidaysburg and its 120 employees. At the time of the sale, the company Betty had headed for nearly four decades had sold nearly 300 million of the springy toys.

of POOF Products, spoke of her legacy to *CNN.com:* "We hold Betty James in the highest esteem. She is to be commended for building a company through very troubled times in the '60s—and in a very male–dominated industry." She "was able to build an American icon."

Social and Economic Impact

The Slinky has become an important part of Americana that is on permanent display in the Smithsonian Institution and was inducted into the Toy Manufacturer's Association's Toy Hall of Fame in 2000. Modestly priced at about two dollars apiece, three to four million of the clever spring toys are sold yearly. Betty reflected on the toy's enduring popularity in *National Engineers Week* saying, "It's the simplicity. There are no batteries, no wind up. And, they are reasonably priced. There's something magic about a Slinky. It sort of comes alive." It has entertained generations of children, and adults have discovered the stress–reducing qualities of the toy for themselves. More than 250 million of the toys have been sold since its inception. More than 3,030,000 miles of wire have been used in the Slinky's production, or enough to circle the Earth 126 times. Available on every continent in the world except Antarctica, the Slinky is recognized by 90 percent of all American households. An original blue–black Slinky sells today for about $100, and the company's 50th anniversary Slinky was also a dark–steel that was packaged in a replica of the original 1945 box.

Slinky has pervaded American culture, appearing in movies such as *Ace Ventura, When Nature Calls, Demolition Man, Other People's Money,* and *Hairspray.* The Slinky dog made a comeback thanks to its appearance in the acclaimed Disney's 1995 blockbuster *Toy Story.* It was also immortalized on a U.S. postage stamp.

Richard James' invention made a difference in the way American's work and play, and his innovation in engineering was celebrated by *National Engineers Week.* The Slinky was thrown into trees to serve as makeshift antennas during the Vietnam War, and NASA even shot the Slinky into space in a space shuttle to test its gravitational properties. Although Richard James invented one of the country's most enduring toys, it was his wife that guided the company through over four decades of prosperity. The year after Slinky was inducted, Betty herself joined the toy in the TMA Toy Hall of Fame during the annual toy fair in New York. The president of TMA, David A. Miller, said after her induction, "It is a tribute to Betty James' leadership, Foresight, and business acumen that 90 percent of U.S. households recognize the Slinky name today...more than 50 years after its introduction. We are proud to honor Betty for her commitment and perseverance, which has allowed children the world over the opportunity to relish the ingenuity and pure fun of a Slinky." Betty was one of the early leaders among women business owners. Ray Dallavecchia Jr., president

Sources of Information

Contact at: James Industries
   45400 Helm St.
   Plymouth, MI 48170–0964
   Business Phone: (734)454–9552
   URL: http://www.poof–toys.com

Bibliography

"Betty James to be Inducted into the Toy Industry Hall of Fame at The First Annual T.O.Y. Awards." *Toy Manufacturer's Association,* 16 November 2000. Available at http://www.toytma.com.

"Betty M. James." *American Toy Institute,* 2001. Available at http://www.toy-tma.com.

"Did the Inventor of the Slinky Join a Cult in Bolivia?" *The Straight Dope,* 6 July 2001. Available at http://www.straightdope.com.

"The Hall of Game." *The Review,* 7 April 2000. Available at http://www.review.udel.edu.

"History." *POOF Products, Inc.,* November 2001. Available at http://www.slinkytoys.com.

"Hot Products with Humble Beginnings." *Ten Online,* 2001. Available at http://www.tenonline.org.

"It Sprang to Mind." *Seattle Post,* 29 January 2001.

"It's Slinky, it's Slinky." *CNN.com,* 11 February 2001. Available at http://www.cnn.com.

"Novel Ideas." *Las Vegas Review–Journal,* 1 March 1998. Available at http://www.lvrj.com.

"Inventors: Slinky." *About.com, Inc,* December 2001. Available at http://inventors.about.com.

"The Slinky FAQ." *The Slinkypedia,* December 2001. Available at http://www.act-one.org.

"Staying Power." *Forbes,* 26 March 1984.

"Zoom Inventors and Inventions." *Enchanted Learning.com,* December 2001. Available at http://www.enchantedlearning.com.

"POOF Products, Inc". *Hoover's,* December 2001. Available at http://www.hoovers.com.

"Slinky—The Spring that Captured the Hearts of Millions." *National Engineers Week,* 17–23 February 2001. Available at http://www.eweek.org.

"Slinky Dog." *Toystory,* December 2001. Available at http://home1.pacific.net.sg/@tldtcchye/slinky.htm.

"Slinky Tidbits." *Phillips Petroleum Company,* December 2001. Available at http://www.teachingtools.com.

"You Shoulda Been There@—Slinky: Zing Went the Spring...." *Discovery Online,* 1997. Available at http://www.discovery.com.

James H. Jannard

(1949-)
Oakley Inc.

Overview

Media–shunning Jim Jannard founded Oakley Inc. in 1975 and created a monopoly in the sunglasses and goggles market that has remained virtually unapproachable by would–be competitors. Celebrities from Michael Jordan to Tom Cruise have sported trendy Oakley sunglasses—often without any endorsement fees being paid—and the company has expanded its product line to include athletic shoes and apparel. More is known about his company than about the reclusive Jannard, who flies a skull–and–crossbones banner above Oakley's headquarters, but one thing is sure: Oakley has made Jannard a billionaire and still counting.

Personal Life

Jannard rarely appears before the media and rarely grants interviews. Much of what is known about him is no more than a collage of informational bits and pieces gathered from various sources over the years. When Oakley first went public in 1995, Jannard refused interviews, and *Forbes* magazine was forced to seek information about him from his ex–wife, Pamela. Although he softened his stance in later years, any granted interviews usually came with strict conditions: no photographs and no printing of any comments made by him that were not in direct response to questions posed.

What is known about him, for starters, is that he was born in Los Angeles in 1949 and grew up in Alhambra. There is a conspicuous gap of information about his childhood and adolescence. According to *Forbes'* 1995 interview with his ex–wife, Pamela, Jannard was a

long–haired freshman at the University of Southern California's School of Pharmacy in the early 1970s, who enjoyed taking his dog with him to classes. Following frequent clashes with his professors over the class attendance of his favorite Irish setter, Jannard left college. Footloose and free, he bought a motorcycle and traveled around the Southwest until he ran out of money a year later and returned to Los Angeles. Jannard traded in his motorcycle for a used Honda and began selling motorcycle parts out of its trunk to Southern California shops that serviced cycles. He also liked to tinker with motorcycles and parts in his garage. In 1975 he designed a rubber grip for off–road motor–cross handlebars and started marketing them, along with his other cycle parts, from his car trunk. He officially formed his company that year and named it "Oakley" after his favorite dog.

In 2001, Jannard still owned 61 percent of Oakley, worth approximately $805 million, and continued serving as its president, chairman, and chief executive officer (CEO). Although he had not taken a salary or bonus from the company for several years, his remuneration in the year the company went public (1995) included a $9.3 million bonus on top of his $380,697 salary.

He runs Oakley's Foothill Ranch headquarters like a college campus; employees move about in shorts or jeans and T–shirts—and so does Jannard. At the company's annual meeting, Jannard showed up wearing a black trench coat, orange Oakley shoes, a beret, and, of course, sunglasses. During one of his rare public appearances outside the company, he gave a store opening speech wearing a gas mask and talking through a megaphone. The May 7, 2001, issue of the *Orange County Business Journal* quoted Jannard as saying that the "Oakley brand stands for mind–blasting creativity and gutsy, even at times deviant, behavior."

The six–foot evasive CEO is considered intense, headstrong, and aggressive but likes to refer to himself as a "mad scientist" or as absent–minded. The atmosphere at company headquarters implies a youthful, laid–back corporate culture, albeit a contrived "cool" image. Jannard once told *Orange County Business Journal* interviewer Melinda Fulmer that Oakley was a "fun, flippin' place to work." The *Journal* has referred to him as "a hippie turned corporate executive," and even the $35 million Foothill Ranch headquarters of Oakley, built in 1997, reflects his nonconforming taste. It is 400,000 square feet of "oversize girders, rivets and valves," according to *Forbes*. "It creates an atmosphere of invention, art and a little bit of mad science," Jannard told the magazine's interviewer. He admitted to being inspired by dark science fiction movies like *Blade Runner* and *Judge Dredd*.

In January 1998, a black and white skull–and–crossbones flag appeared atop Oakley's company fortress on the hill. The company had paid $2000 to obtain county zoning approval for the banner but made no public statement as to its significance. Greg Hardesty of the *Orange*

Chronology:

James H. Jannard

1949: Born in Los Angeles, CA.

1975: Sold motorcycle parts from the trunk of his car.

1975: Oakley formed, named after Jannard's dog.

1980: Oakley first marketed goggles.

1983: Oakley expanded its products to sunglasses, called "Eye Shades."

1995: Oakley went public.

1999: Jannard returned to Oakley as CEO after stock plummeted.

1999: Oakley branched out into watches and wearing apparel.

County Business Journal speculated two likely explanations: one involved a planet Mars line of sunglasses—the magazine advertisements that contained a skull and crossbones on an image of Earth; the other related to an acrimonious relationship with fierce arch–rival Nike, which opened up a subsidiary directly across the street from Oakley. Ongoing litigation between Jannard and former Nike friend, Phil Knight, continued well into 2001, mostly over alleged patent infringements. In any event, the ominous flag was noticed by neighbors, one remarking that it fit the company's "weird image."

But the secretive Jannard could laugh all the way to the bank. *Forbes* magazine rated his 2001 personal fortune at $1.2 billion. His company stock was worth an estimated $805 million in 2001. A cigar aficionado, he is remarried to "Bobbie" and has seven children. He also raises and shows English setter dogs. Little is known about how he spends his money, but he owns a $7 million home on Newport Coast, and in 1997 he paid $22 million for an island off Puget Sound, once known as "Safari Island" for big–game hunters. He has stopped all hunting and has worked to save the rare Ryuku sika deer found on the island. Additionally, Kimberly Brown Seely of *Town and Country* noted in the magazine's July 2001 issue that Jannard may have "quietly bought up" several adjacent multi–million–dollar coastal properties on Crane Island's western shore—part of Washington State's San Juan Islands. Jannard's floatplane, bearing the same skull–and–crossbones flag, has been seen in waters nearby.

Career Details

Jannard does not like to discuss how he built up the Oakley company, preferring instead to discuss his present role in it. But it is known that back in 1979, when he was thirty years old, Jannard designed his first protective eyewear product: high–impact plastic motorcycle goggles that were lighter and more shatter–resistant than their common glass counterparts of that time. Jannard and his salesmen handed out sample goggles at motor–cross competitions and sold them through Oakley's motorcycle parts accounts. The goggles became a hot item, and Jannard advanced to designing hybrid sunglasses–goggles for bicyclists and skiers. In the mid–1980s when champion bicyclist Greg LeMond sported a pair on his way to becoming the first American ever to win the Tour de France, demand for Jannard's new product received a hefty boost. More sunglasses models soon followed, including the trademark Blades model: an interchangeable wraparound lens that slips into a simple carbon–fiber frame.

Coupled with Jannard's unique sunglasses design was his flair for promotion. He and his sales staff had given away many pairs to top athletes during the late 1980s and early 1990s. At a golf tournament, a pair was given to a young golfer/basketball player named Michael Jordan. He has been wearing them ever since, and he now sits on Oakley's board. Jannard's personal friend, tennis's top–ranked Andre Agassi, promotes Oakley sunglasses at no charge. When Nike's Phil Knight was still on friendly terms with Jannard, he was rarely photographed without his Oakleys. Baseball hero Cal Ripken Jr. became another "free" promoter merely by being seen wearing Oakleys. At the 1996 Olympic Games in Atlanta, Oakley placed its sunglasses on 350 competing athletes from around the world—more than half of them unpaid—although Oakley offered cash bonuses if they won events wearing Oakley shades. But Oakley's most high–profile and prolific endorser has been bad boy Dennis Rodman, who originally received neither compensation nor stock for wearing Oakley shades in most of his photo opportunities, from network television to MTV to the cover of *Business Journal*.

At the time of going public in 1995, Oakley had 320 patents issued or pending worldwide, plus 249 registered trademarks. Its sunglasses were selling from $40 to $225 per pair, and availability was limited to specialty shops and sporting goods stores (about 9,500 nationally at the time). Jannard's company posted sales of $124 million for the preceding year (1994) with a net income of $27 million.

Concurrent with the smart marketing and rapid growth, Oakley Inc. developed a reputation as an aggressive litigator, even using it as a marketing tool. In 1995 Oakley's chief financial officer (CFO) told a *Forbes* interviewer, "One of the benefits of being as aggressive as we are is that it deters people from getting into our turf. We work very hard to bust a few chops, make a few examples of people. It makes it easier [for competitors] to copy somebody besides Oakley." Most of the suits involved alleged patent violations.

But Oakley itself soon became the defendant in a series of lawsuits. The company's initial public offering (IPO) in 1995 brought in $69 million for the company and $139 million for Jannard. A few days later, Jannard sold $29 million of his stock, and a few months later (in early 1996) he cashed in on another $214 million of his shares. Stocks plummeted. Thereafter, three shareholders filed a class–action suit alleging that Jannard and his CEO Mike Parnell artificially inflated Oakley's stock price from $17 a share to more than $27 and pocketed more than $200 million through insider trading. In 2000, Oakley agreed to a $17.5 million settlement that would resolve the flurry of shareholder suits filed in 1997, alleging that Jannard and other top executives made material misstatements and omissions about Oakley products and retail distribution practices to induce investment. Notwithstanding the settlement, Oakley denied any wrongdoing.

In 2001 Jannard remained embroiled in federal litigation with Nike that had begun in 1998 when Oakley filed a patent infringement lawsuit against Nike over sunglasses technology. Just before the start of the scheduled February 2001 trial, Nike admitted that it violated the patents but countered by attempting to have Oakley's patents invalidated. The battle had taken its toll on both sides. Jannard initially tried to get even by starting his own line of athletic footwear shortly after he filed suit against Nike. He boldly proclaimed that he would manufacture the shoes in the U.S.—a blatant attempt to cash in on Nike's politically incorrect overseas manufacturing. But by late 1999, Oakley stock had tumbled to $5.50 a share, mostly from its failed footwear, and Jannard started manufacturing them in Asia. He also took over as CEO and bought back 1.2 million shares of company stock. One year later, in 2000, earnings had soared back up to $49 million on a 36 percent sales increase of $350 million. Actor Tom Cruise had sported Oakley's shades in the year's hit movie, *Mission: Impossible 2*, and Oakley glasses had also shown up in the movie *X–men*. In 2001 Oakley lost its largest customer, Sunglass Hut, to competitor Luxottica Group, the maker of Ray–Ban sunglasses. Jannard began signing deals with Champs Sports, Finish Line, and Foot Locker retailers to offset the loss.

Social and Economic Impact

Prior to Jim Jannard, sunglasses were essentially a safety item—and not always so safe at that. Most had glass lenses and often were ill fit for the purpose intended. Jannard's innovative products helped revolutionize the market by customizing the design to fit the intended use, be it motorcycling at high speeds, facing sun glare in downhill skiing, or holding up in changing weather during bicycle marathons. Moreover, Jannard had taken something practical and functional and turned it into an art form, a fashion statement referred to as "eye shades." Instead of spending the least amount of money possible on a pair of functional sunglasses that would reasonably match the contour of one's nose, people were now shelling out unthinkable amounts of money just to be able to look as "cool" as Jordan or Agassi or Rodman. Jannard had cleverly cashed in on one of the greatest consumer trends of the time: an out–of–shape general public trying to look athletic. The limited availability of his sunglasses and goggles and their trendy prices only added to the appeal. And in the end, everyone benefited: the consumer and end–user, the investor, and, ultimately, the man who made it all happen: Jim Jannard.

Sources of Information

Contact at: Oakley Inc.
    One Icon
    Foothill Ranch, CA 92610
    Business Phone: (949)951–0991
    URL: http://www.oakley.com

Bibliography

Berry, Kate. "Oakley Frofit Falls 17 Percent as Orders Plummet." *The Orange County Register*, 18 October 2001.

Earnest, Leslie. "O.C. Business Plus." *Los Angeles Times*, 16 August 2000.

Fulmer, Melinda. "Taking the Shades off Oakley." *Orange County Business Journal*, 2 September 1996.

Hardesty, Greg. "Sunglasses Maker Oakley Hoists New Skull–and–Crossbones Banner." *The Orange County Register*, 11 February 1998.

"Industry." *Orange County Business Journal*, 7 May 2001.

"Jim Jannard." *Orange County Business Journal*, 31 May 1999.

Kafka, Peter, et al. "Manufacturing." *Forbes Annual 2001*.

"Night Falling on Knight." *Forbes*, 19 February 2001.

Pappas, Ben. "Cathedrals to Sunglasses and Other Fantasies of the Very Rich." *Forbes*, 13 October 1997.

Schaben, Susan. "A New Focus." *Orange County Business Journal*, 16 June 2000.

Schaben, Susan. "Oakley, Pacific Sunwear Executive Pay Detailed." *Orange County Business Journal*, 7 May 2001.

Schaben, Susan. "Oakley: What a Difference a Year Makes." *Orange County Business Journal*, 1 January 2001.

Seely, Kimberly Brown. "America's Emerald Isles." *Town and Country*, July 2001.

"Who's Hiding Behind Those Shades?" *Forbes*, 23 October 1995.

Steve Jobs

(1955-)
Apple Computer; Pixar

Overview

Maverick computer innovator Steven Jobs, along with his friend and partner, Steve Wozniak, is considered to be the one of the central figures in the development of the personal computer. Jobs and Wozniak formed the Apple Computer Company in the late 1970s, pioneering the design and development of desktop computers for the general public. The creation of the Macintosh computer in the mid–1980s ushered in a new era of tremendously widespread user–friendly machines. After being ousted from Apple, Jobs went on to form the NeXT Computer Company. He also bought Pixar Animation Studios, where *Toy Story*, the first wholly computer generated and animated film, was created. In the late 1990s, Jobs returned to Apple and oversaw its regeneration with the iMac products.

Personal Life

Jobs was born in 1955 and was placed for adoption by his unwed parents shortly after his birth. Paul and Clara Jobs of Mountain View, California, became his adoptive parents. The elder Jobs was a machinist who worked on lasers, and his wife was an accountant.

Jobs and his parents moved to Los Altos, California, before he entered high school. A statement the pre-teen Jobs made to his parents allegedly precipitated the move: He said that he wouldn't return to school in Mountain View, so his parents decided to move. While a high school student, Jobs showed a special interest in technology. He once went so far as to contact William Hewlett, the president of Hewlett Packard, for some parts

he needed for an electronics project. Jobs not only obtained the parts, he was also offered a summer job at Hewlett Packard.

Jobs graduated from high school in 1972 and attended Reed College in Portland, Oregon, for just one semester before dropping out. In 1974, he went to work for Atari Incorporated as a video game designer. After saving some money from his stint at Atari, Jobs was able to embark on a spiritual sojourn to the Indian subcontinent during the summer of 1974. While in India, Jobs sought to immerse himself in the Eastern way of life. A bout with dysentery in the autumn of 1974 cut his trip short, and Jobs moved back to California and into a commune.

When he was 23 years old, Jobs had a relationship that resulted in the birth of his daughter, Lisa. He reportedly dated folk singer Joan Baez for a time during his twenties. Jobs met Laurene Powell while on a lecture trip to Stanford University; the two married in 1991. Along with daughter Lisa, Jobs and his wife have three children; they live in Palo Alto, California.

By 1975 Jobs started to get involved with the Homebrew Computer Club, which was headed by Steve Wozniak, an acquaintance of his from Hewlett Packard. Wozniak was starting to develop what would become the prototype for the Apple Computer series. Jobs persuaded him to market his designs and prototypes, and the two of them began, in earnest, to develop what would ultimately become the first Apple Computer.

Steve Jobs. *(Archive Photos, Inc.)*

Career Details

Jobs and Wozniak worked on the Apple I in Jobs' parents' garage, and by 1976 they offered models for sale. The most innovative feature of the $700 machine was its single board read–only memory (ROM), which instructed the computer to load and read other programs from outside sources.

The development and sale of the Apple II, which retained the unique features of its predecessor in an updated format, began in 1977. Jobs then got in touch with Mike Makkula, the former marketing manager at Intel, and brought him to Apple as the chairman. Jobs began to encourage independent programmers to create software for the Apple II, and soon over 16,000 programs were available, ranging from business management tools to video games.

First–year sales for Apple were almost $3 million. Impressive as that was, it paled in comparison to the figures reached by the beginning of the 1980s. By 1980, sales had ballooned to $200 million, and the phenomenal success of Apple helped to usher in the revolutionary personal computer era.

Throughout the 1980s, Apple was forced to continually update its systems to stay ahead of the competition. Jobs and Apple faltered a bit with the release of the Ap-

ple III in 1980. The model was riddled with technical and marketing problems and, as a result, sold poorly. However, sales picked up after the bugs were fixed. Nonetheless, the executive organization was restructured; Makkula became president, and Jobs became chairman. Apple went public in 1980, and the company's market value rose to $1.2 billion.

In 1983 Jobs pitched a model he named "Lisa" as the computer for business people who had limited computer expertise. Lisa did not sell well due to its high price and the increased competition from IBM who, by 1983, had gained half of Apple's market share. In the same year, Jobs lured PepsiCo president John Sculley to Apple as the new president and CEO.

In 1984 Apple released the Macintosh computer. Envisioned as the computer that would revitalize not only Apple but the computer industry as well, the Macintosh floundered at first. The initial downfall of the Macintosh in business circles was its lack of a letter–quality printer and a hard drive. The less–than–stellar sales of the Macintosh were instrumental in bringing about Jobs' forced resignation from Apple in 1985. Essentially, Jobs lost a boardroom powerstruggle with Sculley and resigned with $150 million in severance.

Jobs, who still remained chairman of the Apple board of directors, then formed the NeXT Computer Company. The NeXT computer, introduced in 1988, boasted a number of innovations, including extremely quick processing speeds, a superb graphics and sound

Chronology:

Steve Jobs

1955: Born.

1975: Joined Homebrew Computer Club.

1976: Formed Apple Computer Company with Steve Wozniak.

1977: Unveiled Apple II computer.

1984: Introduced Macintosh computer.

1985: Resigned from Apple.

1985: Formed NeXT Computer Company.

1986: Bought Pixar Animation Studios.

1995: Pixar released the animated feature, *Toy Story*.

1996: Rejoined Apple as consultant to CEO.

1997: Named Apple interim CEO.

1998: Launched iMac computer.

1999: iMac sales reached 1 million; introduced iBook portable computer.

2000: Became permanent CEO of Apple Computer Company.

2001: Introduced the iPod, a 1000–song MP3 player; Pixar released *Monsters, Inc.* with Walt Disney Studios.

system, and an optical disk drive. Despite all of these innovations, however, sales of the NeXT computer fell flat due to its steep price, black and white screen, and inability to network. Not to be deterred, Jobs pressed on with NeXT, changing the focus from hardware to software. NeXT eventually gained some prestige by helping to facilitate the establishment of the World Wide Web in the 1990s.

In 1986, Jobs acquired Pixar Animation Studios for $10 million from filmmaker George Lucas. Jobs poured large amounts of his own money into Pixar to develop and establish it as a premiere movie studio. His $50 million investment in Pixar paid off when the first wholly computer–animated film *Toy Story*, released by Walt Disney Pictures, was a certified smash hit when it opened in 1995. By 2000 *Toy Story* had become the second highest domestic grossing animated feature in history. *A Bug's Life*, released in 1998 and using even more sophisticated technology, was the highest grossing animated film of the year. Likewise, the sequel, *Toy Story 2*, which won a Golden Globe award for Best Picture, Musical, or Comedy, was the highest grossing animated film of 1999. The three films combined grossed $1.2 billion worldwide. By 1999 Jobs' 73 percent share of Pixar was worth $1.1 billion.

Hoping to concentrate more fully on developing Pixar, Jobs decided to sell NeXT; Apple bought the company in 1996 for $400 million. At the time, Apple was in need of an updated operating system, and NeXT had one to offer. NeXT had also developed an association with Internet users that Apple desired as well. Apple, which by then had lost about a third of its market share and was struggling to keep afloat, also acquired Jobs as a non–salaried, part–time consultant to Apple's CEO Gilbert Amelio.

The renewed relationship shifted into high gear in 1997 when Jobs agreed to take over as interim CEO of the troubled company after the board of directors ousted Amelio. Jobs implemented the eighth version of the Macintosh operating system, developed a dialogue with Microsoft, and eliminated Apple's clone licensing program. Jobs' leadership proved successful. In less than two years, he had pared Apple's confusing product line down to four basic models and introduced the innovative iMac. With its translucent case, bright color choices, and affordable price tag—just $1,199—the iMac was an astounding success. Launched in 1998, the iMac sold more than 1 million units in its first year and helped boost Apple's market share to about 6 percent. Following on the iMac's success, Jobs introduced the portable version, known as the iBook, in 1999. That year, the combined value of Apple and Pixar reached $6.3 billion.

Following Jobs' success with the iMac, and G3 and G4 PowerMacs, which addressed the needs of the publishing and multimedia markets long dominated by the Macintosh, Jobs brought out a moviemaking application, iMovie, that allowed non–experts to make their own home videos. Next came iTunes, which allowed novices to burn their own CDs. The latest offering is an application that allows users to make their own DVD discs at home. In January 2000, Jobs announced that he was taking over as the company's permanent CEO.

Jobs also remained the chairman and CEO of Pixar, which struck a deal in 1997 with Walt Disney Pictures to co–produce five animated films, sharing all associated costs and profits. *Monsters, Inc.*, the first film under the new deal, was released November 2, 2001. The second film, *Finding Nemo*, is scheduled for release in 2003.

Social and Economic Impact

Jobs was one of the most important figures in the development of the personal computer industry. The Apples and Macs produced by his company were user–friendly, enabling a whole generation of office workers and home users to become comfortable with computer use. Jobs was also instrumental in engineering the joint agreement between Apple and its great rival Microsoft. Both companies agreed to cooperate on selected marketing and technological issues of mutual interest, which helped to simplify choices for consumers.

Jobs' understanding of consumer preferences has been a big part of his success. By pitching his products to young, savvy audiences, he helped dispel the stereotype that computer users were socially inept "nerds." Jobs insisted on being directly involved, for instance, in Apple's "Think Different" advertising campaign, which focused on such cultural icons as Bob Dylan, John Lennon, and Ghandi. And with his introduction of the immensely popular iMac, Jobs proved that consumers would respond to innovative design. "For most consumers," he said in a June 1999 *Advertising Age* article, "color is much more important than the megahertz, gigabytes and other gibberish associated with buying a typical PC."

This focus has served Jobs well in renewing creative energies and profitability at Apple. His leadership was "a superb example of what can happen when a CEO has a simple, focused vision and gets the whole company to focus on and implement that vision," commented marketing executive Allen Olivo in a June 1999 *Advertising Age* article. "He got everyone on the same page, at the same time and for the same goal." As Jobs himself put it in an interview in *Fortune*, "if [great artists like Bob Dylan and Picasso] keep on risking failure, they're still artists. . . . This Apple thing is that way for me. . . . If I try my best and fail, well, I tried my best."

As the PC market slowed down and many of his competitors were already lamenting the death of the PC, Job remained optimistic about its future—despite the fact that Apple's share of the PC market has fallen to 4 percent in the United States and 3 percent worldwide. (In Apple's defense, Jobs points out that no one holds more than 16 percent of the market.) In 2001 he prophesied about the coming age of the digital lifestyle, in which the computer would serve as the hub of a vast array of home appliances. "The personal computer has the power and the memory to do the things that all the devices we are beginning to use will not be able to do. The software will be the glue holding it all together," Jobs told Garry Barker of *The Age*.

Numerous factors are working against Jobs' pleasant predictions. First, Jobs' pet project, the G4 Cube, a more expensive Mac version just one–fourth the size of a regular PC, was a retail flop. Jobs was convinced that the $3,000 model would sell at a rate of at least 200,000 per quarter. In reality, the G4 Cube sold only 100,000 during the first quarter on the market; in the next two quarters, sales dwindled to only 29,000 and 12,000. In July 2001, Apple announced that it would scrap the model and rely on sales the more popular, less expensive regular desktop G4. The significant slowdown of the economy in 2001 also took its toll on Apple's profit. In the third quarter of 2001, Apple posted a 70 percent decline. Nonetheless, cash reserves, just $280 million in 1997, have grown to $4.1 billion under Jobs' leadership. And Jobs isn't resting on his laurels; in October 2001, Apple introduced the iPod, a pocket–sized 5–gigabyte MP3 player able to store 1000 songs and is equipped with an industry–leading 10–hour battery. Charles Haddad of *BusinessWeek Online* predicted, "this new handheld digital–music player will stand tall. Very tall. It's going to do for MP3 music what the original Palm Pilot did for handheld computing in the late '90s—that is, ignite demand like a match to dry twigs."

In Silicon Valley, Jobs remains widely admired, if not universally loved. He is lauded not only for his own ability but also for recognizing and hiring top quality personnel. He has a well–deserved reputation as one of the most demanding and intimidating bosses in the United States, if not the world. Stories still circulate about Apple employees being afraid to ride the elevator with their irascible boss lest they find themselves without a job when they reach their floor.

Sources of Information

Contact at: Apple Computer
1 Infinite Loop
Cupertino, CA 95014
Business Phone: (408)996–1010
URL: http://www.apple.com

Bibliography

"Apple Moves to Scrap Power Mac G4 Cube After Weak Demand." *Wall Street Journal*, 5 July 2001.

"Apple Names Steve Jobs as Interim Chief Executive." *InfoWorld*, 22 September 1997.

"Apple's One–Dollar–a–Year Man." *Fortune*, 24 January 2000.

Barker, Garry. "High Priest of the PC." *The Age*, 4 April 2001. Available at http://www.theage.fairfax.com.au/.

"A Boss's Life." *Business Week*, 11 January 1999.

"Can Steve Jobs Keep His Mojo Working?" *Business Week*, 2 August 1999.

"Creating Jobs." *New York Times Magazine*, 12 January 1997.

Elmer–DeWitt, Philip. "Steve Jobs: Apple's Anti–Gates." *Time*, 7 December 1998.

Haddad, Charles. "For Apple, Sweet Music From iPod." *BusinessWeek Online*, 31 October 2001. Available at http://www.businessweek.com.

Hyatt, Joshua. "Starting Apple Computer Made Steve Jobs Famous. But How Did It Make Him a Legend?" *Inc.*, 18 May 1999.

Johnson, Bradley. "IMAC: Steve Jobs." *Advertising Age*, 28 June 1999.

Legomsky, Joanne. "Investing: Will Pixar Be the Hero of Hollywood Animation?" *New York Times*, 6 June 1999.

Markoff, John. "Jobs Drops 'Interim' From Title at Apple." *New York Times*, 6 January 2000.

"Picking Up the Pieces of a Shattered Dream." *Computer Weekly*, 18 February 1998.

"Pixar: Overview." Pixar Animation Studios. Available at http://www.pixar.com.

"Steven P. Jobs." *PC Magazine*, 16 December 1997.

Schlender, Steve. "Steve Jobs: The Graying Prince of a Shrinking Kingdom." *Fortune*, 14 May 2001.

Schlender, Steve. "The Three Faces of Steve." *Fortune*, 9 November 1998.

"The Sweetest Apples in Ages." *Business Week*, 7 June 1999.

Tam, Pui–Wing. "Apple Unveils Upgrades Despite Tough Market." *Wall Street Journal*, 19 July 2001.

Voight, Tobi, and Joan Elkin. "Steve Jobs: Return of the King." *Brandweek*, 12 October 1998.

"Well, Steve, What'll It Be?" *Business Week*, 30 March 1998.

Robert L. Johnson

(1946-)

Black Entertainment Television

Overview

Robert L. Johnson established the first and only firm that provides basic cable television programming by and about blacks. The founder, chairman, and chief executive officer of Black Entertainment Television, he took BET to the stock market in 1991, making it the first black owned firm to join the New York Stock Exchange. The BET Network created a new genre in television, with 24–hour programming targeted to African–American consumers that reach 90 percent of all black households with cable and air in 65 million homes in the country. Johnson is also the founder, chairman, and CEO of BET Holdings II, Inc., now a division of Viacom, and the first African–American owned and operated media and entertainment company created specifically for African–American interests. BET is made up of Black Entertainment Television; BET On Jazz: The Jazz Channel, the only 24–hour jazz programming service; BET Books, publisher of African–American themed romance novels under the name Arabesque Books; BET International, reaching 3 million subscribers in 66 countries worldwide; and BET Pictures, producer of documentaries and television movies that air on BET networks. BET also owns a large stake in BET.com, the online African–American themed Internet site, and an interest in two XM Satellite Radio channels that play Urban Adult Contemporary and Jazz formats.

Personal Life

Described as intensely ambitious and foresighted, Johnson has also been characterized as gregarious, easy-

Robert L. Johnson. *(AP/Wide World Photos.)*

going, graceful, personal, bright, and articulate. He wears a thick gold bracelet and custom shirts and usually works 15 hours a day during his six–day work week. On January 19, 1969, Johnson married Sheila Crump Johnson, now the BET's executive vice president for corporate affairs, with whom he has a daughter, Paige, and a son, Brett. Johnson and his family live in Washington, D.C., and on the family's 163–acre farm in Virginia.

In addition to his business ventures, Johnson also founded the Metropolitan Cable Club in 1981, a forum for the exchange of information in the telecommunications industry, and served as its president and later a member of its board. He currently serves on the boards of US Airways, Hilton Hotels Corp., General Mills, United Negro College Fund, National Cable Television Association (NCTA), and the American Film Institute. He is also a member of the Board of Governors for the Rock and Roll Hall of Fame and the Brookings Institute. He was named by President Bush in 2001 to serve on a 16–member commission to overhaul the Social Security Program. Among his numerous awards are the President's Award from the NCTA (1982); the NAACP's Image Award (1982); the Capitol Press Club's Pioneer Award (1984); the Business of the Year Award from the Washington, D.C., Chamber of Commerce (1985); the Executive Leadership Council Award (1992); the Turner Broadcasting Trumpet Award (1993); *Broadcast & Cable* Magazine's Hall of Fame Award (1997); CTAM's Grand Tam Award; *Cablevision* Magazine's 20/20 Vision Award; National Women's Political Caucus' Good

Guys Award; and a Distinguished Alumni Award from Princeton University.

Robert Louis Johnson was born on April 8, 1946, in Hickory, Mississippi, a rural town 25 miles west of Meridian. The Johnson family moved to the industrial farming town of Freeport, Illinois, where both parents worked in local factories to provide for their large family. Johnson and his siblings were taught to be self–sufficient. As the ninth of ten children, Johnson told Beverly Smith in a 1992 interview on CNN's *Pinnacle* that he had "a lot of brothers and sisters that I could sort of pick on if I had to for whatever information."

Johnson hoped to become a fighter pilot in the U.S. Air Force but could not meet the physical requirements and concentrated instead on his studies and on college. A good student in high school, he graduated with honors in history and entered the University of Illinois on an academic scholarship, graduating in 1968 with a bachelor's degree in history. Although he lacked the usual qualifications, Johnson was considered a worthy enough risk to be admitted to Princeton University's Woodrow Wilson School of Public and International Affairs in 1969. He graduated sixth in his class in 1972 with a master's degree in public administration.

While at Princeton, Johnson established connections that led to a job as press secretary for the Corporation for Public Broadcasting. After joining the U.S. Army Reserve during the Vietnam War, he became public affairs officer at the Corporation for Public Broadcasting. Johnson then worked as director of communications for the Washington Urban League, press aide for the District of Columbia's city councilman Sterling Tucker, and press secretary for Walter Fauntroy, the District's nonvoting delegate to Congress. From 1976 to 1979, Johnson was vice-president of government relations for the National Cable and Television Association (NCTA).

Career Details

While at NCTA, Johnson developed the idea of starting a cable network company to promote black characters, thought, and philosophy primarily for African Americans. According to the A. C. Nielsen ratings, black viewers watched an average of 70 hours of television per week—compared to 48 hours for whites—but in the late 1970s no networks carried programming specifically for blacks, nor were blacks shown in powerful, dominant roles. He persuaded his NCTA supervisor to promise him a $15,000 consulting contract, which he used to secure a matching loan from the National Bank of Washington. He then borrowed $320,000 from John C. Malone, head of Denver-based Tele–Communications Inc. (TCI), one of the nation's largest builders of cable systems. Malone and TCI also paid him $180,000 for a 20 percent share in the new network.

On January 25, 1980, Black Entertainment Television, which Johnson created from the basement of his home, made its debut on cable with *A Visit to the Chief's Son,* a two–hour movie with an all-black cast that drew an audience of 3.8 million homes in 350 markets. At first, BET kept expenses low by showing low–cost programs that would appeal specifically to blacks, using such black film subjects as *Lady Sings the Blues.* Free music videos from record companies were aired by 1982, and BET soon added black stars, talk shows with black hosts and guests, and black college sports.

BET struggled with several consecutive years of losses. In 1982, Johnson took on a new partner, Taft Broadcasting Company. In 1984 Home Box Office, a cable subsidiary of Time Incorporated (now Time Warner), invested in BET because of its 24–hour telecasting and 7.6 million subscribers. In spite of phenomenal growth, by 1989 BET was still the smallest and least carried of all cable networks. The company also faced legal setbacks from competitors. Johnson began another cable venture in 1984, District Cablevision Incorporated, intended to wire homes and serve the District of Columbia. TCI owned 75 percent of the new company, however, and competitors filed suit to prevent a monopoly, causing more financial pressure. By 1986, the financial burden was eased, but BET did not pay back its investors until 1989.

Johnson then established BET Holdings II Incorporated, the parent company of BET, and on October 30, 1991, BET became the first black–owned corporation

Chronology:
Robert L. Johnson

1946: Born.

1976: Served as vice president of government relations for the National Cable and Television Association (NCTA).

1980: Johnson's Black Entertainment Television debuted on cable.

1991: BET became the first black–owned corporation listed on the New York Stock Exchange.

1995: Moved company to a new $15 million building in Washington's northern industrial corridor.

1996: BET launched the nation's first black–controlled cable movie premium channel, BET Movies/STARZ!3.

1998: Founded BET Pictures II and BET Arabesque Films.

1998: Took company private at $1.3 billion valuation.

2001: BET acquired by Viacom for $3 billion.

2001: BET.com voted Best African–American Community Site by *Yahoo! Internet Life* magazine.

listed on the New York Stock Exchange. Although by then three other black firms had gone public with their stock, none had remained on the public market or had been listed by the NYSE. According to *Current Biography,* the day BET was listed, investors "bid the price up to more than $23 a share, and BET (which reported $9 million in earnings in 1991) had acquired a market value of $475 million." Then Johnson sold 375,000 of his own shares and, in a single day, earned $6.4 million. His net worth after 11 years of work from the increased value of his controlling interest reached more than $104 million. Although the company lost some ground when investors questioned his subscriber count, BET sold some of its stock, clarified the number of subscribers, and later recovered some of its losses. Commenting on his financial progress, the *Network Journal* for June 30, 1995, quoted Johnson's statement to CNN: "Black people will become powerful in this country when they obtain power through control of economic wealth."

In 1991 BET also acquired controlling interest in *Emerge: Black America's News Magazine,* which is aimed at young adults, and began publishing *YSB (Young Sisters and Brothers)*, which appeals to adolescents. BET also established a radio network in 1994 which provides news and music to urban stations nationwide.

The company took a bold step in 1995 by moving its 350 employees to a new $15 million building in Washington's northern industrial corridor. In April of 1995, Johnson added a 50,000 square–foot film and video production facility, one of the largest of its kind on the east coast. In the *Network Journal* for June 30, 1985, Tony Chapelle cited Johnson's plans to become "the preeminent provider of information entertainment and direct marketing services to the Black community."

By 1995, BET reached 41.3 million households. By 1996 the cable network, still the core of the company's holdings, had a children's literature hour, public affairs show, weekly show for teenagers, town hall meetings, and music videos. BET also owned the Cable Jazz Channel and ventures in Africa and England.

In 1996, BET launched the nation's first black–controlled cable movie premium channel, BET Movies/STARZ!3, which offered a lineup of classics that included *To Sir with Love* as well as the newer *Pulp Fiction* and Spike Lee's *Clockers*. Johnson told the *Los Angeles Sentinel* for October 3, 1996, "What we're doing is something that's unique. We're branding movies that appeal to an audience that has demonstrated a tremendous amount of interest in viewing film entertainment." Encore Media Corporation, a cable and satellite movie provider, is another TCI–controlled company. That venture is intended to develop and exhibit black–oriented feature–length films and expand pay–TV households in urban markets. The company established BET Gospel in December 1998, which features inspirational music and speakers. All told, the company was gaining twice the number of viewers Johnson had estimated, at about four million subscribers a year from 1990–1998.

Expanding his cable empire, Johnson founded BET Pictures II and BET Arabesque Films in 1998 to make and promote films, documentaries, and TV movies, with African–American themes. Building on the brand name outside the world of cable TV, BET Holdings II, Inc. also grew its publishing division with BET Arabesque Books, which is the only publisher of original African–American romance novels written by African–American authors; *BET Weekend*, the third largest black publication in the country with 1.3 million readers; and *Heart & Soul*, a beauty, health and fitness magazine.

BET also made its way to the Internet, establishing BET Interactive, LLC (formerly BET.com) in a joint venture with Liberty Digital, LLC, News Corporation, Inc., USA Networks, Inc., and Microsoft Corporation. The BET.com portal contains news, music, health and career Information, and e–mail and chat services for African Americans. The website was voted Best African–American Community Site in 2001 by *Yahoo! Internet Life* magazine. BET Interactive also owns the 360hiphop.com

hip–hop music and culture website. BET Holdings II, Inc. also branched out into a variety of ventures, including the theme restaurant BET SoundStage Restaurant; BET Sound-Stage Club, an entertainment and dance club and joint venture with Walt Disney World Resort at Downtown Disney Pleasure Island in Orlando; BET On Jazz restaurant that specializes in New World Caribbean Cuisine; and Tres Jazz, a French Caribbean fine dining restaurant in the Park Place Las Vegas Resort and Casino.

After being a public company for seven years, Johnson took it private again, at a $1.3 billion valuation in 1998. On November 3, 2000, media giant Viacom announced that it would acquire BET Holdings II, Inc. for $3 billion, which it completed in January, 2001. Johnson, who netted $1.5 billion in Viacom stock for his 63 percent stake, remains as the chairman and CEO of the new Viacom unit. In a Viacom press release, Johnson stated, "Viacom is the perfect home for BET, a healthy, profitable business and the dominant media brand serving the African–American consumer. Combining the assets of BET with the global resources and brands of Viacom will create a platform that is even stronger and better positioned to deliver the wants and needs of BET's core audience. We will be able to continue to push programming to new heights, expand our distribution globally, and leverage the marketing resources of the best advertising–driven media company in the world."

The Viacom deal made Johnson the first black billionaire, ranking 172nd on The *Forbes* 400 list of wealthiest Americans, and gave him a 1.6 percent stake in Viacom that makes him the company's second–largest individual shareholder, behind only Viacom chairman Sumner Redstone. Johnson has come under some criticism as a "sell–out" in the black community for the Viacom deal, especially after a much–publicized firing of BET talk show host Tavis Smiley. While BET is cherished by many as the only black entertainment channel, others complain of a lack of social consciousness and outdated images. Johnson countered the criticism in *Forbes* saying, "We are the only black network in town, so everybody has poured their burdens and obligations on BET, but we can't solve everybody's desires for BET. We have to be focused on running this as a profit maximization business." He also added, "If people would just judge BET for what it is, instead of what they'd like it to be. But nobody will sing our praises." If praise can be measured in viewers and ratings, though, BET's song is on the lips of many. Since BET was acquired by Viacom in early 2001, it has gained 2.5 million subscribers and boosted ratings 23 percent among 18 to 34–year–old blacks from 2000. BET saw record ratings in June 2001, with an average of nearly 400,000 homes.

Johnson's personal success has also allowed him to purchase seven hotels, through his new company RLJ Development L.L.C., from Hilton for $95 million and he also owns a minority stake in Vanguarde. Johnson had also repurchased several of the restaurants previously owned by BET Holdings II, Inc., that he has since sold.

Most notably, in 2000, Johnson had plans to build his own airline, DC Air, with a $200 million investment and discarded assets of the proposed merger of United Airlines and US Airways until the deal fell through when the merger was rejected by the government. *Forbes* reports as of late 2001, he is planning on purchasing more hotels and even a professional sports franchise.

Social and Economic Impact

Johnson's BET Holdings II, Inc., was named by *Forbes* magazine for two consecutive years as one of the Best Small Companies in America. Since he founded BET in 1980, it has grown into a conglomerate that produces television content, films, magazines, restaurants, and other entertainment ventures, pushing it toward his goal of making it the most–valued consumer brand within the black marketplace. Johnson pioneered his company in many areas, beginning with Black Entertainment Television, the first and only basic cable station providing programming by and about blacks. In a landmark billion dollar deal, Johnson sold the company to media giant Viacom, giving him another distinctive first—the country's first black billionaire.

BET also spawned a whole new generation of black executives, producers, and broadcast talent. Curtis Gadson, BET's head of entertainment programming, recalled in *Forbes*, "When I first walked into BET I saw a sea of black people doing the same jobs that I had always seen only whites doing elsewhere. I was almost in tears. The playing field was all of a sudden equal." *Forbes* reports that today, 96 percent of BET's 290 employees are black.

In 1996, Johnson pledged $100,000 to Howard University to help support the School of Communication, and the school responded at its 25th anniversary gala by awarding Johnson the Messenger Award for Excellence in Communications. Jannette Dates, the school's interim dean, praised Johnson for his success and his support of the school. Quoted in the *Washington Informer* for November 6, 1996, Dates summed up Johnson's success: "[H]e showed America that an African American from a not very privileged background can, with the strength of his intelligence and hard work, take a small beginning and become a tremendous success. He has also succeeded in communicating an array of new images of African Americans that are different from those that were portrayed over the years past."

Sources of Information

Contact at: Black Entertainment Television
1900 W Place, NE
Washington, DC 20018
Business Phone: (202) 608–2000
URL: http://www.bet.com

Bibliography

"About Us." *BET.com*, 2001. Available from http://www.bet.com.

"BET CEO Robert Johnson Creates company for Ownership, Operation of Washington, Las Vegas Restaurants." *PR Newswire*, 13 April 2001.

"BET Interactive, LLC." *Hoover's*, 2001. Available from http://www.hoovers.com.

"BET's Robert L. Johnson Slated to Become Owner of New Airline." *Jet*, 12 June 2000.

"The Cable Capitalist." *Forbes*, 8 October 2001.

Notable Black American Men. Gale Research, 1998.

"Oprah Who?" *Forbes*, 27 November 2000.

"Painted Black—Robert Johnson, W.'s Favorite Race Baiter." *The New Republic*, 27 August 2001.

"Robert L. Johnson, Founder." *BET.com*, 2001. Available at http://www.bet.com.

"Suite Success." *Black Enterprise*, April 2001.

"Stories of Entrepreneurs." *National Commission on Entrepreneurship*, 2001. Available from http://www.ncoe.org.

"Taking BET Back From the Street." *Fortune*, 9 November 1998.

"Tavis Smiley's Dismissal By BET Outrages Blacks Across the Nation." *Jet*, 16 April 2001.

"Three Blacks on Bush Panel To Overhaul Social Security Programs." *Jet*, 21 May 2001.

"Viacom Completes Acquisition of BET." *Viacom Inc.*, 23 January 2001. Available at http://www.viacom.com.

"Viacom to Acquire BET Holdings." *Viacom Inc.*, 3 November 2000. Available at http://www.viacom.com.

Samuel Curtis Johnson

(1928-)
S.C. Johnson & Son, Inc.

Overview

Current patriarch of the business founded by his great–grandfather and namesake in 1836, Samuel Curtis Johnson molded S.C. Johnson & Son Inc. into one of the world's largest producers of chemical consumer products. The company, with annual sales of $4.5 billion, is the largest privately owned company in Wisconsin and one of the largest family–owned businesses in America. In 1966, when Johnson became its president, S.C. Johnson's annual sales totaled just over $170 million. The fourth–generation Johnson to head the company, Sam Johnson retired as chairman in 1999, but before leaving his post, he split the company into three units of varying size, giving three of his four children each a unit to operate. Johnson was instrumental in broadening the company's product base significantly during the 1950s and 1960s, overseeing the addition of such well–known brand names as Raid insecticide, Glade air freshener, and Off! insect repellent to the company's core line of wax products. Johnson's accomplishments are all the more remarkable because he triumphed over alcoholism while still at the helm of the family business, a struggle he dealt with frankly in an hour–long film released to the public in 2001.

Personal Life

Sam Johnson, now retired from the day–to–day leadership of the S.C. Johnson international business combine, keeps busy in his hometown of Racine, Wisconsin, where he lives with wife Imogene. Three of the couple's four children remain actively involved in the family business. Curt Johnson, the eldest child, heads S.C. Johnson Commercial Markets Inc., while his brother, Herbert Fisk Johnson, serves as chairman of S.C. Johnson & Son. Johnson Outdoors Inc., a manufacturer of recreational products, is headed by Helen Johnson–Leipold. Winifred Johnson Marquart, the couple's fourth child, is married and lives in Virginia with her husband and four children. Although she has done some consulting work for the family business from time to time, she is not actively involved in the day–to–day management of the company.

Son of Herbert Fisk Johnson and Gertrude (Brauner) Johnson, Samuel Curtis Johnson was born in Racine, Wisconsin, on March 2, 1928. His father was the chairman of S.C. Johnson and Son Inc., and young Sam enjoyed a childhood of privilege. From his early teens onward, he lived at Wingspread, the Racine family home designed by Frank Lloyd Wright in 1941. Two years earlier, the family business had hired Wright to design its Administration Center in Racine, a structure noted for its vast open interior spaces and heralded in the press as a "center of creativity." In 1950 the company's Research Tower, also designed by Wright, opened. Both the Administration Center and Research Tower were placed on the National Register of Historic Places in 1976.

When Johnson was only three years old, his father divorced his mother. The elder Johnson later told his son that his mother's drinking problem had been the main reason for the breakup of their marriage. Young Johnson resolved then and there that he would never be like his mother in this respect. As a boy, Johnson longed for more time with his father, a longing he described in the autobiographical film entitled *Carnauba: A Son's Memoir*, released in 2001. "For a long time I couldn't admit that my father wasn't around enough when I needed him. I guess my biggest doubt about my father was, Does he love me as much as the company?"

The family business was launched in 1886 when Johnson's great–grandfather, also named Samuel Curtis Johnson, bought the parquet flooring business of Racine Hardware Company. In response to demands from its flooring customers, the company brought out Johnson's Prepared Wax two years later. Before long the company's wax business had completely overshadowed its trade in flooring, and for the next several decades, the heart of the family business was its line of wax products. Johnson's father in 1935 made a landmark trip into the jungles of Brazil in search of a stand of carnauba palms that could provide a steady supply of carnauba wax, the hardest variety of wax available, for the company's wax product line. He eventually located a large stand of the carnauba palms near Fortaleza and established a plantation there to supply his company's needs. Years later, Sam Johnson came across a journal his father had kept during the trip to Brazil. It was inscribed, "To Sammy, I hope you make this trip someday."

After graduating from high school, Johnson attended Cornell University in Ithaca, New York, graduating in

Chronology:
Samuel Curtis Johnson

1928: Born.

1950: Graduated from Cornell University with B.A. degree.

1952: Graduated from Harvard University with MBA degree.

1954: Married former Imogene Powers and joined S.C. Johnson & Son Inc.

1956: Oversaw launch of Raid insecticide.

1966: Named president of Johnson Wax.

1967: Named chairman of S.C. Johnson & Son Inc.

1993: Sought treatment for alcoholism at Mayo Clinic.

2000: Retired from S.C. Johnson & Son Inc.

2001: Premiered film entitled *Carnauba: A Son's Memoir.*

1950 with a bachelor's degree in economics. Two years later he received his master's degree in business administration from Harvard University. After his graduation from Harvard, Johnson returned to Racine to join the family business. On May 8, 1954 he married the former Imogene Powers.

Career Details

Johnson joined S.C. Johnson and Son as head of product development, and it was not long before he began developing products that would significantly broaden the company's product line. In a 2001 interview with the *New York Times*, Johnson told about his father's insistence that any new product bearing the family name had to represent a noticeable improvement over similar products already on the market. He recalled emerging from a company lab in the early 1950s with an idea for a new insecticide product. His father asked him to explain how it was different and better than other insecticides already available to the public. Johnson was forced to admit to his father that his proposed new insecticide was really not all that different from those already on the market, after which his father told him to go back and try again. Some time later, when he came back from the lab, it was with the formulation for Raid House and Garden Bug Killer, a water–based insecticide that could safely be used on plants. It soon became one of the company's best–selling products.

Johnson's success with Raid was soon followed by a number of other new products, including Glade air freshener; Pledge furniture polish; Edge, a gel–based shaving cream; and Off! insect repellent. Johnson's diversification of the company's product line was clearly one of his most valuable contributions to the business. He later confided to a reporter that family tradition dictated that each Johnson generation was expected to make a major contribution to the company's fortunes. "My grandfather set the tone in the 1920s, and my father came with international growth and technology. Each generation brings something different."

Early on, Johnson had witnessed the damage that could be done by failure to plan ahead for transition within the company. His grandfather, Herbert Fisk Johnson Sr., had died suddenly in 1928, leaving no will or plan for the transfer of control of the family empire. What followed threatened to rip the family and the company apart. Herbert Fisk Johnson Jr., Sam Johnson's father, fought with his sister for nearly a decade to decide who would control the company. Eventually, a 60–40 split between brother and sister gave H. F. Johnson Jr. control. Sam Johnson vowed that he would do whatever it took to avoid such a rift within the family and company in the future.

In 1965 Johnson's father suffered a stroke, and the following year young Johnson took over as president. In 1967 he was given the added responsibility of chairman. Continuing along the path he had blazed when he first joined the company, Johnson moved aggressively to diversify the company. In the early 1970s he acquired manufacturers of outdoor recreational equipment to form the company's recreational products division. This was later spun off as Johnson Outdoors Inc., the company now headed by Johnson's daughter, Helen Johnson–Leipold. He also founded the Johnson Bank, one of Wisconsin's largest banks. The bank eventually spawned Johnson International, an 850–employee financial services company that Johnson continues to oversee. Of his large–scale expansion efforts in the 1970s, Johnson recently confided that most of this diversification was motivated by uncertainty about the company's core product line. "I thought the wax company might get smothered by Procter & Gamble," he told the *New York Times*. "I also thought these companies might make a good farm team for the children."

Like his mother before him, Johnson developed a serious drinking problem, but he refused to face it for a long time. Three times his family confronted him on the issue, urging him to seek professional help. The first two confrontations did little more than anger him. He said later he was convinced he didn't need help. During the family's third confrontation with Johnson over his drinking problem, "they said, 'honest to God, Dad, you've got to get this fixed,'" Johnson told the *Milwaukee Journal Sentinel*. "I was struggling with that. I was chairman of the Mayo Clinic." Johnson admitted that like a lot of alcoholics who had not had a "moment of truth," such as a drunk driving arrest or a drinking–related mishap, he was reluctant to admit to himself that there was any problem at all. Finally, however, he agreed to seek treatment at Mayo Clinic in 1993. Although his recovery has gone smoothly since his stay at Mayo Clinic, Johnson is a strong believer in the importance of continuing support for recovering alcoholics. To help others get the help that had put him on the path to recovery, he established All Saints Healthcare Center for Addiction Recovery in Racine.

For most recovering alcoholics, the twelfth and final step on the road to recovery is helping others. For Johnson, his twelfth step was the Racine addiction recovery center and the making of *Carnauba: A Son's Memoir*, the film in which he speaks candidly about his alcoholism and his difficult relationship with his father. Another important way station in his recovery was his retracing of his father's 1935 trip to Brazil in 1998. It was a family voyage of discovery. The Johnsons flew to Brazil in a replica of the S–38 Sikorsky amphibian aircraft flown by his father. His father's wish, unknown to him until years after the original journey, was at last fulfilled.

Social and Economic Impact

Sam Johnson's contribution to the family business goes far beyond his sound stewardship over more than three decades at the company's helm. As the company's president and chairman, he oversaw a sharp expansion in company revenue from about $170 million annually in 1966 to a total of more than $6 billion a year for all the Johnson family companies.

Even more important, his careful planning ensures that the company will remain under the control of the Johnson family, headed now by fifth–generation Johnsons. In advance of his retirement in 1999, Johnson laid out a plan to break the company into three separate units, each of which would be given to one of Johnson's three interested children to run.

Johnson has also been instrumental in seeing that another long–time family tradition has been upheld. The Johnson reputation for benevolence and generosity to employees and the communities in which it operates has been enhanced under Sam Johnson's direction. Long before such donations were fashionable, the company gave 5 percent of its pre–tax profits to charities, a practice it continues. In 1917 the company launched a profit–sharing plan that gives its employees 25 percent of the company's earnings. In the decade from 1990 to 2000, the company contributed more than $120 million and countless volunteer hours to charitable programs. The company has also been a pioneer in efforts to sustain and protect the environment, setting specific goals to reduce pollution and waste in its products and processes.

Sources of Information

Contact at: S.C. Johnson & Son, Inc.
    1525 Howe St.
    Racine, WI 53403–5011
    Business Phone: (800) 494–4855
    URL: http://www.scjohnson.com

Bibliography

Barboza, David. "At Johnson Wax, a Family Passes On Its Heirloom; Father Divides a Business to Keep the Children United." *New York Times*, 22 August 1999.

Barboza, David. "SC Johnson Promotes Corporate Family Values." *New York Times*, 13 November 2001.

Hajewski, Doris. "Johnson's Mistakes a Lesson for All." *Milwaukee Journal Sentinel*, 26 August 2001.

Johnson, Samuel Curtis. *The Essence of a Family Enterprise: Doing Business the Johnson Way*. Indianapolis: Curtis Publishing, 1988.

"Our Family Story: Samuel C. Johnson." SC Johnson, 11 November 2001. Available at http://www.scjohnson.com/family/fam_our_sam.asp.

Michael Jordan

(1963-)

Overview

Twice retired and three–times returned to the world of the National Basketball Association (NBA), Michael Jordan is one of the greatest basketball players of all time, as well as part–owner and the President of Basketball Operations for the Washington Wizards. His status as a basketball legend is equaled only by his global celebrity status. He has won an NCAA basketball championship, two Olympic gold medals, and six NBA championship titles. Jordan is considered the person who has almost single–handedly altered professional sports in the late twentieth century. "What was once a clubby parochial business with relatively narrow appeal is today a thriving, global, high–tech industry that attracts fans of all ages, ethnic groups, and cultures," reports *Fortune* magazine. "Stadiums are multimedia marketing platforms. Games are valuable programming, fought over by broadcasters around the world as networks and cable channels proliferate. And Jordan is at the center of it all." Desire, drive, and determination has made Michael Jordan one of the most successful, most popular, and wealthiest celebrities of his generation. And he just keeps bouncing back for more. . .

Personal Life

Jordan was born on February 17, 1963, in Brooklyn, New York, and was raised in Wilmington. North Carolina. Growing up, he excelled at sports. Jordan has many fond memories of youth baseball, especially when he hit the game–winning home run in a Babe Ruth tournament. Reportedly, Jordan's father, James, always dreamed that his son would become a professional baseball player.

In what has become a classic contemporary sports legend, Jordan was cut from the varsity basketball team during his sophomore year in high school. Jordan himself cites that incident as one of the most important in his life. Not making the team encouraged Jordan to work for his goals. He made the team his junior and senior years, and after high school accepted a scholarship to the University of North Carolina.

After playing for three seasons at North Carolina, Jordan made himself available for the NBA draft in 1984. The Chicago Bulls chose him as their number one draft pick that year—third overall. The young draft pick turned out to be a good choice for the Bulls. Jordan was named the NBA's Rookie of the Year in 1985, averaging 28.2 points per game for the 1984–1985 season. His abilities in basketball were further proven the next season. After sitting out 64 games with a broken foot, Jordan returned to score a playoff–record 63 points in his first game back.

In 1989 Jordan married Juanita Vanoy, and they have three children: Jeffrey Michael, Marcus James, and Jasmine Mickael. Jordan's family, particularly his father, have always played an important part in his personal and professional life. In July of 1993 his father was murdered in North Carolina—less than two months after the Bulls won their third straight NBA championship. Three months later, Jordan announced his retirement from the NBA, citing the desire to spend more time with his family and friends and the desire for some sort of life outside of the spotlight.

Although always in the public spotlight for his professional talents, some aspects of Jordan's private life were initially kept from the public. In 1988 he had a son with Juanita Vanoy, but he did not marry her until the boy was almost a year old. It was also rumored that Jordan was a heavy gambler. And for years he endured criticism about his endorsement deal with athletic–gear maker Nike because of allegations of its mistreatment of employees, especially women and children, in its Asian plants. Nevertheless Jordan is an idolized figure and has been a role model for more than one generation.

Winning awards and honors such as MVP of the All–Star Game, numerous slam–dunk contests, and being named league MVP was only the beginning for Jordan in 1988. During that year the player who was originally viewed merely as an offensive weapon ended up being named Defensive Player of the Year as well as the MVP of the league. That season he was the first player to ever lead the league in both scoring and steals. Through 1998, Jordan was named to the All–NBA first team 10 times, and named to the All–NBA Defensive First Team eight times. In 1999, following his second retirement, Jordan was named Athlete of the Century by ESPN, trumping the long–time held previous status of baseball's Babe Ruth.

Personally, Jordan earned more money from endorsements than he did from playing basketball. Companies like Nike, Wilson, Gatorade, Coke, McDonald's,

Michael Jordan. (Reuters/Corbis-Bettmann)

Hanes, and General Mills all wanted him to be associated with their products. Between *Air Jordans* and other shoes and apparel, it is estimated that Jordan products have brought in $2.6 billion for Nike. Michael Jordan's endorsement of Hanes underwear was expected to exceed $10 million annually. A cologne from Bijan as well as a popular Chicago eatery have also carried his name. It has been estimated that such endorsements net Jordan another $42 million annually.

Michael Jordan's money is also put to humanitarian uses. He personally established several charities, including the Jordan Institute for Families and Night Ministry. After his father was murdered, Jordan and the Chicago Bulls established the James Jordan Boys and Girls Club and Family Life Center, which aids Chicago–area youth. The Michael Jordan Flight School was established to serve as a summer basketball camp for boys and girls between the ages of eight and 18. When Jordan returned to play in 2001, he donated his initial $1 million salary to relief funds for victims of the September 2001 terrorist attacks.

Career Details

Like most professionals in the NBA, Michael Jordan prepared himself for his career by playing college basketball. In his first season at North Carolina he became only the second Tarheel player to start every game

Chronology:

Michael Jordan

1963: Born.

1983: Named All–American first team while playing for the University of North Carolina.

1984: Picked third overall in the NBA draft as the Chicago Bull's No. 1 draft pick and led the U.S. Olympic Team to gold medal.

1985: Named NBA Rookie of the Year, averaging 28.2 points per game.

1986: Returned from an injury to score an NBA playoff–record 63 points in a single playoff game.

1987: Won first of seven straight NBA scoring titles.

1991: Led the Chicago Bulls to the first of six NBA Championship Titles.

1993: Retired from the NBA to pursue career in professional baseball.

1995: Returned to NBA.

1998: Led Bulls to sixth league championship in eight years.

1999: Announced retirement from NBA.

2000: Became part–owner and president of basketball operations for the Washington Wizards.

2001: Returned from second retirement to play for the Wizards.

---

as a freshman and was named the Atlantic Coast Conference (ACC) Rookie of the Year in 1982. Jordan led the ACC in scoring during his sophomore and junior years, and was also named the College Player of the Year by *Sporting News* after both seasons. Although he had three outstanding college seasons, the success Jordan was to have in the NBA was not entirely apparent, for he was only the third player chosen in the 1984 draft, trailing Hakeem Olajuwon and Sam Bowie.

Jordan, however, experienced immediate success in the NBA. He was named to the All–Star Team in his first season and also became Rookie of the Year. A broken foot, the only serious injury of his career, sidelined Jordan during most of his second season. He returned in time for the playoffs, and set a NBA playoff scoring record with 63 points in his second playoff game. He av-

eraged 37.1 points per game during his third season, winning the first of seven consecutive scoring titles. Jordan's run was only interrupted by his first retirement in 1993.

In 1989 Jordan led the Bulls to the conference finals. Although it would be two more seasons before the Bulls would win the championship, the team had arrived. The Bulls won the NBA championship three successive years, from 1991 to 1993, defeating the Los Angeles Lakers, the Portland Trailblazers, and the Phoenix Suns. Jordan was voted MVP of the finals all three times.

After winning the 1992 finals, Jordan led a group of NBA players who played for the U.S. Olympic basketball team. This team—which paired Jordan with other superstars like Magic Johnson, Larry Bird, Patrick Ewing, David Robinson, and Karl Malone—became known as the "Dream Team." The team easily won the gold medal, winning by an average margin of victory of 43.7 points.

One month after watching his son lead Chicago to its third straight NBA title in 1993, James Jordan, Michael's father, was murdered. Stating that he had nothing left to accomplish, Jordan announced his retirement from the NBA in October of 1993. He left the sport as the all–time leading scorer in the history of the Chicago Bulls.

The next year he moved onto a different playing field, joining the Chicago White Sox minor league baseball team. He spent 17 months in the minors, with the media again scrutinizing his every move. All in all, his career as a baseball player was short–lived and unspectacular, but it did provide a much–needed respite from basketball as well as an opportunity for Jordan to regain his passion for the game. His return to the NBA was chronicled in two bestsellers: Bob Greene's *Rebound: The Odyssey of Michael Jordan*, and Sam Smith's *Second Coming: The Strange Odyssey of Michael Jordan: from Courtside to Home Plate and Back Again*.

When Jordan first returned to the Bulls in the 1994–1995 season, both he and his team played inconsistently at first. The Bulls reached the playoffs and advanced to the conference semi–finals to face the new talk of the league, Shaquille O'Neal, star of the Orlando Magic. Jordan prevented the Bulls from winning the first game by making two errors in the final 18 seconds. At this point the great Michael Jordan was viewed as only human. The Orlando Magic defeated the Bulls four games to two.

The 1995–1996 season was built on the type of playing on which records are made: the Bulls finished the regular season 71–10, an NBA record, and Jordan earned an eighth scoring title. The Bulls won their fourth NBA title that season, defeating the Seattle Supersonics. The following season Jordan led the Bulls to another title, this time defeating the Utah Jazz. In the 1997–1998 season, it looked like the Bulls might not even make the finals, for Indiana pushed the Bulls to seven games in the Eastern Conference Finals. But Jordan and the Bulls endured and met the Jazz again, emerging as six–time league champions.

During a contentious lockout that blemished the 1998–1999—the first–ever work stoppage in the 52–year history of the NBA—Jordan found himself increasingly at odds with Bulls management. In January of 1999, he again announced his retirement from the game, this time assuring fans that he meant it. He left the league as one of its three all–time scorers, with 29,277 points to his name. "Mentally, I'm exhausted," Jordan said at a press conference announcing the departure, according to a *New York Times* report by Mike Wise. "Right now, I just don't have the mental challenges that I've had in the past to proceed as a basketball player. This is perfect time for me to walk away from the game. And I'm at peace with that." Even President Bill Clinton commented publicly on Jordan's decision to leave the game.

But he had not planned to leave it entirely: a year later, Jordan became part owner and president of operations for the Washington Wizards, one of the NBA's more underachieving franchises. Formerly known as the Washington Bullets, they were last in their division at the time of the announcement, with a record of 12–28, and had only one championship title (dating back to 1978) to their name. The move was immediately heralded as the best thing that could ever happen to such a team, and it was welcomed with tremendous fanfare in the city. Jordan declared his intention to practice with the team, which boasted some young players of great promise, and it was rumored that both this unusual plan as well as the mere presence of Jordan in the front offices might attract some stellar free agents to the Wizards' roster.

For the 2000–2001 season, Jordan was seen several times practicing hard with his team. By 2001, rumors began to surface that he might again return to the court. In June 2001, as president of the Wizards, Jordan made history by selecting the first ever high school player (Kwame Brown) with the top pick in the NBA draft. Within ninety days, it was official: Jordan was returning from his second retirement to play for the Wizards. Much press coverage and speculation surrounded his return, but by December 2001, he had led the team to a 10–12 season record. Considering that the ten–year cumulative record of the team was 344–648, 2001 represented substantial progress.

see the potential in producing movies centered around the sport.

Michael Jordan's success initially meant more money for the Chicago Bulls, who began selling out their games at home and on the road. Yet during the first years of his career he was under a long–term contract that did not net him anywhere near as much income as other stars of the game. Finally Jordan received the contract he deserved, a one–year, $30–million agreement for the 1997–1998 season; it was the highest single–season contract in the history of professional sports. Though that figure may seem high, the Bulls' five (and that year, six) league championships forever banished the city's bruised civic pride at its poorly performing teams: Chicago's Bears football franchise last won a Superbowl in 1985, Blackhawks hockey players hadn't skated to a Stanley Cup victory since 1961, and the last time one of its two baseball teams had won a pennant race, America was fighting in World War I.

Jordan's success not only meant more money for the Bulls, it meant more money for the NBA, especially in marketing Jordan's jersey, with his old number 23 and the new number 45 after he returned from baseball. Jordan reportedly did more for the financial success of the NBA than Larry Bird and Magic Johnson did in the late 1970s. Industry analysts theorize that Jordan's presence alone in the game was responsible for around $500 million in additional revenues for the NBA.

Jordan has been referred to as "Jesus in Nikes." Marketing surveys show that he possesses one of the most recognizable faces on the planet, known even by children living in some of the most impoverished rural corners of the planet. At Chicago's United Center, home to the Bulls, visitors sometimes kneel at a statue of Jordan that graces the entrance. He has been the subject of not only sports biographies, but of serious tomes that examine his impact on professional sports. Among these are *Michael Jordan and the World He Made*, by David Halberstam, and *Michael Jordan and the New Global Capitalism* by Walter LaFeber. "To [some], Jordan personified not only the imaginative, individual skills that Americans dream of displaying in a society that adores graceful and successful individualism," wrote LaFeber, "but the all–out competitive spirit and discipline that Americans like to think drove their nation to the peak of world power."

Social and Economic Impact

When Jordan was drafted by the Chicago Bulls, they were a lackluster team, seldom drawing more than 6,000 fans to a home game. Jordan quickly turned that around. His style of play, incredible leaping ability, and his hang time thrilled fans in basketball arenas across the country. Both he and the hugely popular "Air Jordan" sneakers from Nike have ushered in a new era of popularity for the once–moribund pastime; even Hollywood began to

Sources of Information

Bibliography

Clarkston, Michael. "Air Jordan: Older, Wiser but not Grounded Yet." *Toronto Star*, 16 December 2001.

Clines, Francis X. "For the Wizards' Fans, an Ambassador of Hope." *New York Times*, 20 January 2000.

Greene, Bob. *Rebound: The Odyssey of Michael Jordan.* New York: Viking Penguin, 1995.

Holstein, William. "Jordan Hits the Road." *U.S. News & World Report*, 2 February 1998.

LaFeber, Walter. *Michael Jordan and the New Global Capitalism.* New York: W. W. Norton, 1999.

MacMullan, Jackie. "What's to Like, Mike?" *Sports Illustrated*, 24 January 2000.

"Michael Jordan Chronology." *Los Angeles Times*, 26 September 2001.

"Michael Jordan Goes Young as Wizards Pick High–Schooler Kwame Brown." *Canadian Press,*, 27 June 2001.

"Michael Jordan Sues Owners of Popular Chicago Restaurant Named for Him." *Jet*, 15 November 1999.

"Mike's Timely Rebound." *Christian Science Monitor*, 27 September 2001.

Rhoden, William C. "A Very Cold Send–Off for the Hottest Athlete." *New York Times*, 14 January 1999.

Samuels, Allison. "Mike on Mike." *Newsweek,* 22 September 1997.

Andrea Jung

(1958-)
Avon Products

Overview

Andrea Jung is the young, dynamic chairman and CEO of Avon Products, Inc., the world's largest producer of mass–market perfumes, cosmetics, and fashion jewelry. An early achiever, Jung's career was already on the fast track before she ever got to sit in the big chair at Avon. Once planning on a career in law, Jung credits her understanding of psychology and the anatomy of a female shopper's brain as being instrumental in her success at creating markets within markets in this highly competitive industry.

Personal Life

The elder of two children, Jung was born into an ambitious family in Toronto, Canada, in 1958. Her Shanghai–born mother was one of Canada's first female chemical engineers, as well as a concert pianist. Jung's father was a prominent architect who met her mother at Hong Kong's University. When Jung was just two years old, the family moved to Wellesley in Massachusetts after her father accepted a teaching position at the Massachusetts Institute of Technology (MIT). Her brother Mark runs a San Francisco software company.

As an Asian–American child, Jung was enrolled in Mandarin classes at an early age. When she turned five, her mother sat her down at the piano and began teaching her basic chords. By her own admission, she was not born a good student. Jung recalled to a *Fortune* magazine interviewer that when she was in fourth grade, she badly wanted a box of 120 colored pencils. Her parents

Andrea Jung. (AP/Wide World Photos.)

made a deal with her: she could have the pencils only if she earned straight As in school (no A–minuses or B–pluses). She holed herself up in her bedroom, missing birthday parties and tennis games, but by year's end, she presented her parents with a report card of straight As and got her colored pencils. She never forgot that experience and attributes much of her drive and determination to that and similar incidents.

Piano study also played a role in developing her determination. Weekday afternoons were spent practicing and weekend evenings were spent at music recitals. By the time she entered high school, her rigorous extracurricular activities had developed in her a strong work ethic and personal drive. She spoke Mandarin fluently, could engage in conversation in Cantonese, and could communicate in conversational French as well. She became interested in her high school class politics, serving as class secretary and then president of the student body. Upon graduation, she went immediately to Princeton, where she studied English literature and graduated magna cum laude in 1979.

It was her intention to pursue a career in law, but Jung planned to work two years in retail prior to attending law school. At a college career fair, she interviewed with a recruiter from Bloomingdale's and was hired into the management–training program. She had anticipated that the retail experience would help prepare her for the demands of a law career by educating her in real–world, real–people savvy.

Career Details

Using their studies in demographics and psychology, Jung and her team of young merchandisers at Bloomingdale's tried to create associations in the minds of consumers between certain products and basic human drives. For example, certain fabrics could be linked to memories of childhood intimacy or warmth; a certain cut in a dress could stimulate romantic wishes. Combining instinct with good business acumen, creativity with analysis, made the retail career very interesting to her.

Her parents did not share her enthusiasm for the retail field. In truth, they complained bitterly that she had wasted her education and had lowered herself into a working class akin to used car salesmen and street hawkers. "No one in my family had a retail or marketing background," Jung told interviewers for a *Goldsea* online article. "After I started, though, it got into my blood. I knew this was what I wanted."

Jung had a mentor along the way, who had become the company's first female vice president. She was confident, articulate, and aggressive, and Jung saw in her the kind of executive she wanted to be. Jung felt that she had carried over from her childhood some submissive tendencies, and she hoped to learn from this woman the finer points of tactful aggression. Moreover, Jung's mentor showed her that a marketing career held more potential for women than many other careers because only women could grasp the mindset of the female consumers who make most household purchasing decisions.

Jung found this to be true. She also concluded that businessmen had limited insight into women's abilities and often considered them fragile beings with shaky self–images that could easily be shattered with a well–delivered insult or put–down. Jung further found that women did not support other women as much as she thought they should. "Some people just wait for someone to take them under their wing," she told *Goldsea* interviewers. "I've always advised that they shouldn't wait. They should find someone's wings to grab onto."

She followed her own advice, and under mentor Vass' guidance, moved up to merchandising manager and then vice president of intimate apparel in the mid–1980s. When Vass was wooed over to swanky retailer I. Magnin with offers of becoming the first female chief executive officer (CEO) in the department store's history, she asked Jung to go with her. Jung relocated to San Francisco in 1987 to work under Vass.

During her five years at I. Magnin, Jung advanced rapidly to general merchandising manager and then to senior vice president. Neiman Marcus began to notice her and eventually approached her with an offer she could not refuse: executive vice president. It was a bigger company and a bigger job. She moved to Dallas, Texas, in 1991 to begin her new position as the voice of fashion for Neiman Marcus. But Jung's infatuation with the ritzy retailer began to fade when she realized that her products, fashions, and talents were reaching only three per-cent of Americans—those at the top of the income bracket. Jung decided she would rather try her hand in a notably less glamorous but far larger sector of the general population. In May 1993, Jung left Neiman Marcus to consult for Avon Products. Seven months later, in January 1994, she accepted a full–time position there as president of the U.S. marketing group.

Almost immediately she felt more at home. Avon's corporate culture particularly appealed to her. She had noted that women formed one–fourth of the company's board of directors and nearly half of its senior officers. There was no "glass ceiling" to interfere with her upward mobility. The way that companies treated women had always played an important role in her decision–making.

In 1993, the year before Jung came on board, Avon's domestic sales had actually dropped by one percent, although the foreign market (especially in Asia) had increased. Jung's psychology and marketing background had taught her that by the time most American women had reached their mid–30s, they had already picked the cosmetics brands they would remain loyal to. So Jung began to direct her focus on this particular segment of the consumer market to bolster sagging domestic sales. Next, she delighted Avon's long–time customers by expanding the number of products offered. Avon was the first to come out with an alpha hydroxide acid product; virtually all competitors eventually added the skin–rejuvenating agent to their own products. Jung then introduced a line of lingerie and casual wear, which cleverly generated new revenue within the already–established customer base.

Another task was to create a global brand, with attendant name–recognition, in the marketplace. At the time, Avon's company logo, packaging, and advertising varied from country to country. Jung created a new "Let's talk" campaign to phase out the old familiar "Ding–dong, Avon calling" jingle that dated from 1953. She also created a new corporate tag, "The company for women." Finally, Jung redesigned Avon's packaging to create more modern and sophisticated–looking bottles and jars that were more in line with Avon's upscale department store competitor products.

By the time Jung was promoted to second in command at Avon in 1998 (behind new CEO Charles Perrin, an outsider from Duracell International, Inc.), company stocks had climbed 48 percent. However, U.S. sales—representing about 30 percent of Avon's business—still lagged. When Perrin resigned less than six months later, all heads turned to the three highest–ranking females in Avon management. Jung's four years with the company did not look positive to the search committee, compared with over 27 years of experience for each of the other two. Notwithstanding, then–41–year–old Jung made the greatest impression on the search committee.

Four weeks into her new position as CEO in 1999, Jung laid out her plan at an analysts' conference. She

Chronology:
Andrea Jung

1958: Born in Toronto, Canada.

1960: Moved to Massachusetts, USA.

1979: Graduated from Princeton University.

1979: Began retail career at Bloomingdale's.

1987: Followed her mentor to I. Magnin.

1991: Moved to Neiman Marcus in Dallas.

1993: Joined Avon as a consultant.

1997: Promoted to president at Avon.

1999: Became CEO.

wanted a top–to–bottom makeover of Avon's face and image. With plans to launch an entirely new line of businesses, develop blockbuster products, and commence selling Avon in retail stores, she had her work cut out for her. At the same time, she promised to meet company goals of cutting millions in research, development, and manufacturing costs by the end of 2000. Her vision "has a high probability of disappointment," stated a Paine Webber analyst report at the time.

Jung got on the fast track and started setting up very specific goals with her executives. Almost doubling the research and development budget, she gave that department two years to come up with a breakthrough product (three years was standard). She challenged the manufacturing and packaging operations to really consider how they spent their money; they responded with an automation revamping of the department, saving Avon $400 million annually. Another $60 million was cut from operating costs after the number of suppliers was reduced from 300 to 75. Jung also set up a leadership program for recruiting and maintaining the best sales staff. The program offered incentives and a percentage of sales profits for each new recruit that a current representative brought in.

By the end of 2000, Avon had launched its new "Retroactive" anti–aging skin cream that winter, and it was the runaway hit of the season, expected to bring in $100 million in 2001. Previously, Avon had negotiated a special licensing program with Mattel, Inc., and the resulting special edition "Winter Velvet" Barbie doll became the company's biggest–selling non–cosmetic product ever. In the spring, Avon began selling vitamins, yoga mats, and aromatic therapy oils under a line called

"Wellness," which was expected to bring in another $75 million in sales. In August 2001, Jung made good on her promise of retail sales when 75 J.C. Penney stores began selling a new line of makeup and skin cream, anticipated to net $300 million in five years. Jung had gotten what she wanted and made the world notice her in the process. According to *Hoover's* company capsules for investors, Avon's fiscal year 2000 sales were $5.7 billion—up 8 percent from the previous year. Impressively, the company's net income grew 58.2 percent, to $478 million. After September 11, 2001, New York–based Avon's stock fell 10 percent, as U.S. consumers cut back on discretionary spending.

In addition to her key role at Avon, the 5'8" Jung also sits on the Board of Trustees of the Fashion Institute of Technology and the Board of Directors of the American Management Association. She is married and has one daughter. Her husband, Michael Gould, has been chairman of Bloomingdale's since 1991. Jung walks her daughter to the bus stop when possible and then walks to her mid–Manhattan office by 8:00 A.M. She insists on turning the key to her front door no later than 7:30 P.M. every night so that she is able to share dinner with husband and daughter. But piano playing, novel reading, and socializing with friends are pleasures that have been mostly forfeited.

Social and Economic Impact

In her signature black suit and three–strand pearl necklace, the well–heeled Jung is the quintessential female executive—and a deserving role model and mentor to other aspiring women. Against all odds, she has proved what a difference can be made by breathing new life into an old corporate body. Moreover, she has been an outspoken promoter of professional networking among women, and she encourages all women to align themselves with companies that are committed to the advancement of women in the work place. "I think it's critical that you feel you're working for a person who is committed to advancing your career," Jung remarked in *Goldsea's* article. "That's why I've gotten where I am today."

Sources of Information

Contact at: Avon Products
1345 Avenue of the Americas
New York, NY 10105–0196
Business Phone: (212)282–5000
URL: http://www.avon.com

Bibliography

"Avon Products, Inc." Hoover's Online, Inc., 9 December 2001. Available at http://www.hoovers.com/co/capsule.

Brooker, Katrina. "It Took a Lady to Save Avon: Elegant and poised, with a will of iron, Andrea Jung knows how to win." *Fortune*, 15 October 2001.

"Executive Sweet." *Goldsea*. Asian American Supersite, undated. Available at http://goldsea.com/WW/Jungandrea/jungandrea.html.

"Remaking the Avon Lady: Andrea Jung must show U.S. women that her brand hasn't gone out of style." *Money*, 1 February 2000.

Sellers, Patricia. "The 50 Most Powerful Women in American Business." *Fortune*, 12 October 1998.

Herb Kelleher

(1931-)
Southwest Airlines Company

Overview

Herb Kelleher, resorting at times to somewhat unorthodox techniques, has led Southwest Airline Company to nearly three straight decades of profits in a financial climate that has brought many other, larger passenger air carriers to their knees. Capitalizing on its low–cost, no–frills approach to air travel, Southwest has grown from a short–haul carrier serving cities in Texas to a robust multi–regional airline serving about 60 cities in 29 states. Kelleher prides himself on creating a unique corporate culture at Southwest that allows for extensive employee participation in corporate decision–making. One measure of Kelleher's success is the fact that Southwest experienced only one strike in the first 30 years of its existence. In mid–2001, Kelleher stepped down as Southwest's CEO but retained his position as chairman.

Personal Life

Kelleher lives in San Antonio, Texas, with his wife, Joan. The couple, who married on September 9, 1955, have four children, Julie, Michael, Ruth, and David, as well as two grandchildren.

The fourth child of Harry and Ruth Moore Kelleher, he was born in Camden, New Jersey, on March 12, 1931. He grew up in a close family and as a boy worked after school in a Campbell's Soup Company factory, where his father was employed as a general manager. Kelleher's father died when Herb was only 12, and shortly thereafter an older brother was killed in combat in World War II. The loss of father and brother in such quick

Herb Kelleher at Southwest Airlines Chili Cook-off. (*AP/Wide World Photos.*)

succession brought young Kelleher closer to his mother. In an interview with *People*, Kelleher recalled that he and his mother "became very close. We'd sit up until 4:00 A.M. talking about business, politics, everything."

During his high school years in Camden, Kelleher excelled at sports and served as president of the student body. After graduating from high school, he attended Wesleyan University in Middletown, Connecticut, where he majored at first in English literature, planning eventually to get into journalism. He later switched to pre–law, graduating cum laude in 1953. He pursued his law studies at New York University and sampled the high life in New York City's Greenwich Village, where he maintained a small apartment. Of his law school years,

he later told *Fortune* magazine: "I had a little apartment on Washington Square, and you could just open your door and entertaining people would walk in and you'd have an instant party." In 1955 Kelleher married Joan Negley, whom he had met while attending Wesleyan.

After his 1956 graduation from NYU's Law School, Kelleher went to work as a clerk for a New Jersey Supreme Court justice. In 1957 he was admitted to the New Jersey State Bar, and two years later, he left his job as clerk to practice law with the Newark, New Jersey, firm of Lum, Biunno & Tompkins, where he remained for the next two years. Kelleher's wife was originally from Texas, and he found himself increasingly attracted to the Lone Star State when he and his wife visited her parents there. Finally, in 1961, Kelleher pulled up stakes and headed south to Texas, where he joined the San Antonio law firm of Matthews, Nowlin, Macfarlane & Barrett as a partner. Although he was happy to be living in Texas, Kelleher found law practice less fulfilling than he'd hoped. Of his early years in San Antonio, he later told *People*: "Every day I went to work, I felt my shoulders droop a little more."

Career Details

Things began looking up for Kelleher after a client, banker Rollin King, came to him with an idea for launching a short–haul airline, serving cities in Texas and operating out of Love Field in Dallas. King's plan, sketched out on a cocktail napkin as attorney and client threw back a few bourbons, called for establishing frequent, low–cost air service, linking the Texas cities of Dallas, Houston, and San Antonio. King's proposal so excited Kelleher that he scraped together enough of his own money to buy 1.8 percent of the proposed airline and signed on as a legal consultant for the project. In March of 1967, Kelleher incorporated Air Southwest Company, the name that was later changed to Southwest Airlines Company.

As good as the idea sounded to Kelleher, he found that getting the project off the ground was to be a real challenge. Other regional airlines serving cities that Southwest hoped to serve pulled out all the stops in an effort to block the airline's launch. They repeatedly hauled the company into court to argue that the market was already adequately served and could not absorb yet another carrier on these intrastate routes. And the obstacles didn't disappear when Southwest finally did begin flying in 1971, as it faced restrictions that limited how far Southwest's jets could fly.

Interviewed in 1998 by *Your Company*, Kelleher was asked how he had become convinced that a short–haul intrastate airline was a viable proposition. "I admit I was skeptical at first, so I did some research," Kelleher recalled. "I went to California and visited the operations of Pacific Southwest Airlines and Air California. Both were young intrastate carriers. After some due diligence, I concluded that an airline based on their model could be successful in Texas. After all, consumers began flocking to the California intrastate carriers almost immediately, because they loved the convenience of short–haul flights."

In the late 1970s, Southwest's competitors mounted one challenge to the new carrier that ended up backfiring. The Wright Amendment, named after Texas Congressman Jim Wright, blocked airlines flying out of Dallas's Love Field from serving states other than the four that bordered Texas unless they first touched down at an airport within the neighboring states. Far from clipping Southwest's wings, it fit precisely with the company's

Chronology:
Herb Kelleher

1931: Born.

1953: Graduated with B.A. from Wesleyan University.

1955: Married Joan Negley.

1956: Graduated with law degree from New York University.

1966: Joined fledgling Southwest Airlines Co. as a legal consultant.

1971: Southwest Airlines began commercial flights.

1978: Named President of Southwest Airlines.

1979: Congress passed Wright Amendment, intended to clip Southwest's wings.

1982: Named CEO of the year by *Financial World* magazine.

2001: Stepped down as CEO but retained chairmanship.

short–haul strategy, paving the way for decades of robust growth. Starting in 1973, Southwest has posted profits every year, a record envied by the airline's competitors.

As successful as it has been, Kelleher's management style is nothing if not unorthodox. Southwest's long–time chairman and CEO often rode to work on his Harley and once settled a legal suit with an arm–wrestling match. And for special occasions, Kelleher was known to dress up as Elvis Presley or the Easter Bunny, just to keep his employees smiling. And smile they did, as Southwest built for itself a reputation as the nation's most profitable airline, posting 2000 sales of nearly $5.7 billion and a profit of $603 million, up more than 27 percent from the previous year.

Asked by *Your Company* about his personal management policy, Kelleher said, "Being an underdog is a lonely undertaking that takes a lot of sweat equity, but a leader's fighting spirit infects an entire organization and drives everyone to succeed." As to what it takes to be a good leader, Kelleher observed: "You have to be a good follower to begin with, because you have to show that your real focus is on the well–being of your people and the organization as a whole. Above all, employees come first. That means you have to be willing to have your people tell you you're full of crap or your idea stinks and accept that for the betterment of everyone. You also have to have a clear set of values that you implant in the company. It's up to the CEO to set an inspirational example of how workers should behave."

In 2001, 30 years after Southwest first took to the skies, the company announced some major organizational changes. Effective June 19, 2001, Kelleher handed over his responsibilities as CEO to James Parker but retained his position as chairman. Colleen Barret, a long–time member of Southwest's executive management team, took over as president and chief operating officer. Shortly before stepping down as CEO, Kelleher was interviewed by Mark Haines of CNBC's *Squawk Box*. He outlined his hopes for Southwest's long–term future, saying, "With Southwest Airlines' low cost and very strong balance sheet we're going to be able to continue to expand and to do so for years to come." Also interviewed by Haines was Parker, who said, "There is not going to be any change of course or change in direction in Southwest Airlines. Herb, Colleen, and I have worked together for 22 years, and we have a very experienced and mature management team at Southwest that has worked together for a long time, and we have a very common understanding of what the Southwest Airlines business model is."

Asked by *Your Company* which one of his offbeat antics was his personal favorite, Kelleher didn't miss a beat, answering: "A spoof of litigation: The arm–wrestling match I had with Kurt Herwald, the chairman of Stevens Aviation, to decide the rights to an advertising slogan. Stevens, an aviation sales and maintenance company in Greenville, South Carolina, had been using 'Plane Smart' as its slogan at least a year before Southwest unknowingly began running its 'Just Plane Smart' campaign. Rather than pay a team of lawyers, Herwald and I decided to wrestle it out at the Sportatorium in Dallas. It was a hoot. The whole world focused on it. BBC called to interview me in London. I told them I was too busy training. In the end I got trounced."

Social and Economic Impact

In an economic arena that has seen far more failure than success, Herb Kelleher has piloted Southwest Airlines to nearly three straight decades of profitability. This is an achievement of which any corporate executive could be proud, but it is doubly impressive because it was achieved in the volatile airline sector, an area of the economy where profits have been especially scarce.

To accomplish this feat, Kelleher developed a staff totally dedicated to the company's success and took drastic measures to keep costs down. *Fortune* magazine reported: "Kelleher personally approves every expenditure over $1,000—'not because I don't trust our people but because I know that if they know I'm watching, they'll be just that much more careful'—and he constantly monitors the key industry standard, cost per available seat mile, to make sure he stays a penny or two below the pack." Part of the air carrier's success was credited by *Time* magazine to "Southwest's labor–union contracts, which permit an easy, largely voluntary cross–utilization of workers. Thus pilots and flight attendants occasionally help clean up planes, ramp workers sell tickets, and counter agents unload bags. Flight crews are paid by the trip rather than the hour."

Another important element in Kelleher's strategy for success has been turning Southwest's planes around quickly. Schedules often call for a complete turnaround in 15 minutes from the time an incoming plane arrives at an airport gate until it pulls back with a new set of passengers for an outbound flight.

Kelleher's brilliance as a manager has been widely recognized. In 1992 he was named CEO of the Year by *Financial World*, only to receive a similar award two years later from *Fortune* magazine. In 1996 he received the Outstanding Business Leaders Award from Northwood University, and in 1997 University of Michigan's Business School honored him with its Business Leadership Award.

Sources of Information

Contact at: Southwest Airlines Company
   2702 Love Field Dr.
   Dallas, TX 75235
   Business Phone: (214)792–4000
   URL: http://www.iflyswa.com

Bibliography

Brooker, Katrina. "Can Anyone Replace Herb?" *Fortune*, 17 April 2000.

Haines, Mark. "Southwest Airlines, Chairman, CEO, and CEO–Elect." *CNBC Squawk Box*, 8 June 2001.

Huey, John. "Outlaw Flyboy CEOs." *Fortune*, 13 November 2000.

Ioannou, Lori. "The Best of Herb Kelleher." *Your Company*, 1 August 1998.

Newsmakers 1995. Detroit, MI: Gale, 1995.

Jamie Kellner

(1948-)
Turner Broadcasting System, Inc.

Overview

Jamie Kellner, currently chairman and CEO of Turner Broadcasting Systems, Inc., achieved his prestigious status in broadcasting by building networks that appealed to the young—the demographic most dearly desired by advertisers. He launched the Fox Network and steered it into new TV territory, with such popular and youngndash;skewing shows as *The Simpsons*, *In Living Color*, and *Melrose Place*. He then went on to similar success, founding The WB and bringing the successful *Buffy the Vampire Slayer* to throngs of bloodthirsty young viewers. By appealing to teenagers and twenty–somethings, he's defined not only an advertising niche but two separate and successful television networks. His outstanding efforts at both networks caused AOL Time Warner executives to sit up and take notice. He was promoted in March to chairman of Turner Broadcasting System, where he oversees such aging properties as CNN, TNT, and TBS, while keeping his responsibility for The WB.

Personal Life

Kellner is married and has a son. He lives in Atlanta, Georgia. Kellner received the distinguished Humanitarian Award of the National Conference for Community and Justice. He was the first recipient of the Founder's Award of the Broadcast Cable Financial Management Association in 1997 and was named among Electronic Media's list of the Most Powerful People in Television News in 2001.

Jamie Kellner (left) with Susanne Daniels. (AP Photo/E.J. Flynn.)

He was born in 1948 in Brooklyn, New York, and raised on New York's Long Island. He was educated in the East. He began his practical training to become one of the small–screen's big powerhouses in 1969. It was then that he joined the CBS executive training program at age 21. Of his early experiences there, he told AOL Time Warner, "I spent a month at a time in various departments to learn how the company's units operated. I worked in the music department, licensing and merchandising, and in the syndication and cable sales departments, which at the time was called Viacom. After working in these various areas, it was my responsibility to find a mentor that would take me into their department. In my case, that person was Hank Gillespie, a legendary executive in the syndication and cable sales world, who gave me my first big break. I will always be grateful to Hank, with whom I shared a wonderful relationship."

Career Details

After Kellner cut his teeth in the entertainment industry at CBS, he went on to become vice president in charge of first–run programming, development, and sales for Viacom Enterprises, until he left in 1979.

Kellner then worked at Orion Pictures as president of the Orion Entertainment Group, where he served from 1979 to 1985, before his legendary career as a television executive. He was in charge of network programming, home video, pay television, and domestic syndication. Going against the grain, Kellner decided to leave his position at the company for the challenge of starting a whole new television network. He told *Electronic Media* in 2001, "Let me assure you, back about 14 or 15 years ago, when I told my mother I was quitting my job to start the Fox network, she told me there was no way that could ever succeed." There were several critics who offered the same opinion that Fox would never succeed. After his 2001 appointment at Turner, he recalled, "Every time I do anything, people generally say it can't be done."

For eight years, from 1985 to 1993, Kellner was president and chief operating officer of Fox Broadcasting Co., owned by Rupert Murdoch. Kellner launched Fox and steered it into becoming the "fourth" network, introducing shows like, *The Simpsons, Beverly Hills: 90210, Married...With Children, America's Most Wanted,* and *Melrose Place.* He also created Fox Kids Network. Among the team Kellner led, there was Garth Ancier, who would follow him to the WB and Turner. Suffering from burn–out, Kellner, who had achieved what he set out to do with the network, left Fox and took nearly one year off.

Time off soon made Kellner restless, and in June 1993 he partnered with Warner Bros. and the Tribune Company to form The WB Television Network. The network was part of the Time Warner conglomerate. The WB was officially launched on January 11, 1995. At first the young network had trouble finding its niche, but Kellner soon realized the direction in which it needed to go. The WB became unique in that Kellner targeted the programming for a demographic he felt was being ignored by the other major networks at the time: teenagers and young adults. Kellner's goal was to dominate in the 12–34 demographic, especially girls and young women. That resulted in a slew of programming aimed at youths, including *Buffy the Vampire Slayer, Charmed, Felicity,* and *Dawson's Creek.* It also launched a bevy of new young stars, including *Buffy*'s Sarah Michelle Gellar. The network also began working on the family audience, with shows like *Seventh Heaven.* Kellner courted the very young with his creation the Kids' WB!, which provided weekday morning, afternoon, and Saturday morning programming for children and included the popular *Pokemon* series. In 1997 the WB made further headway in its goal of becoming TV's fifth network by managing to acquire five Sinclair Communications Inc. stations from rival United Paramount Network (UPN). Since its launch, the WB also had the distinction of launching eight series into syndication, something no other network was able to accomplish in such a short time frame. After five seasons on the WB, *Buffy,* one of the network's most successful shows, moved to Viacom's UPN in 2001. The network that Kellner built is expected to show a profit in 2002.

At the same time Kellner launched the WB, he also announced plans for his own station group, ACME Com-

Chronology:
Jamie Kellner

1948: Born.

1969: Began broadcasting career at CBS.

1979: Became president of the Orion Entertainment Group.

1985: President and chief operating officer of Fox Broadcasting Co.

1993: Partnered with Warner Bros. and the Tribune Company to form The WB Television Network.

1995: The WB officially launched.

1997: WB acquired five Sinclair Communications Inc. stations from rival United Paramount Network (UPN).

1997: Became CEO and chairman of company he founded, ACME Communications.

1999: ACME went public.

2001: Named chairman and CEO of Turner Broadcasting Systems, Inc.

munications. Kellner has served as the company's CEO and chairman since 1997 and remains in that position today. While simultaneously running the WB, Kellner grew ACME into a 10–station group that went public in 1999. The 10 ACME stations are all WB affiliates. For the past two years, ACME's KPLR–TV affiliate in St. Louis has been the WB's highest–rated. With Lorne Michaels, Kellner also owns the syndication rights to *Saturday Night Live* and has invested in technology companies.

Founded by TV mogul Ted Turner, Turner Broadcasting and its group of basic cable channels was reorganized by parent AOL Time Warner in March 2001, which grouped it with the WB, naming Kellner as the boss of this new division. Kellner will remain very active in the WB, retaining his title of CEO and his 11 percent ownership of the company. Ted Turner became vice chairman of AOL Time Warner after the merger was announced and handed over control to Terence F. McGuirk. McGuirk ran the company for less than a year before being named vice chairman when Kellner's promotion was announced. After McGuirk, Kellner became the only person, outside of Turner himself, to run Turner's group of stations founded over thirty years ago. In his current position at Turner, Kellner is responsible for corporate oversight of the Turner domestic and international entertainment networks, including TBS Superstation, Turner Network Television (TNT), The WB Network, Cartoon Network, Turner Classic Movies, Turner South, Boomerang, TNT Latin America, Cartoon Network Latin America, TCM & Cartoon Network in Europe, TCM & Cartoon Network in Asia Pacific, and Cartoon Network Japan. Kellner also oversees the CNN News Group, which includes CNN Headline News, CNN/U.S., CNNfn, CNN/SI, CNNRadio, CNN Newsource, CNN Airport Network, and CNN.com. Additionally, he is responsible for all news and entertainment advertising and distribution in the United States and abroad, for all corporate administrative functions, Turner Sports, the Atlanta Braves, the Atlanta Hawks, and the Atlanta Thrashers.

AOL Time Warner hopes that by centralizing its TV stations, it can better compete with rival Viacom Inc., who are able to keep a wide variety of viewers tuned in with stations geared to all ages, including Nickelodeon for children, MTV for teens and young adults, and CBS for older viewers. Kellner, who is known for being able to attract the youth audience, was tapped to help integrate the older–skewing Turner networks. He was also hired to bring new cable stations to the division, possibly including a rival for Viacom's MTV. CNN has become an area of concern after the recent emergence of some strong competition. Bringing more viewers to the news leader will be somewhat more of a challenge for Kellner, who lacks a solid news background but who welcomes the challenge. He has already made such controversial moves as hiring former *N.Y.P.D. Blue* actress Andrea Thompson as a *Headline News* anchor. AOL Time Warner's co–chief operating officer said of Kellner, "He has the unique combination of being a programmer and a sales person and a business person all rolled in one."

Social and Economic Impact

Jamie Kellner has changed the face of television with the youth–related shows he ushered in on the two fledgling networks he helped get off the ground. He introduced ground–breaking programs at Fox, including *The Simpsons*, *Married...With Children*, and *In Living Color*. At his stint at the WB, he launched shows such as *Buffy the Vampire Slayer*, *Charmed*, *Dawson's Creek*, and *Felicity*, which have created a new niche of programming and brought new young stars into the public eye. Much has been written and published about the recent youth movement that Hollywood started, and Kellner is certainly one of the men behind it. In the process, Kellner helped build the Fox network into a solid competitor to the Big 3 broadcast networks, an unprecedented broadcasting feat that several thought could not be accomplished. His accomplishments at the WB were equally well respected in the industry and garnered him

a top Hollywood power position at conglomerate AOL Time Warner's Turner Broadcasting.

In his current position at Turner, Kellner wields amazing power as head of such mature and distinguished networks as CNN and the entire group of Turner cable stations. Recently named as one of the most powerful people in television news, he has already taken risks in his quest to integrate the sometimes disparate group of networks, including re–tooling the well–respected CNN News division as well as revamping several of the programming on its other stations. He plans to further grow the company through the introduction of new cable stations. Kellner still heads the WB as well as the broadcasting company he founded, ACME Communications.

Sources of Information

Contact at: Turner Broadcasting System, Inc.
1 CNN Center
100 International Blvd.
Atlanta, GA 30303
Business Phone: (404)827–1700
URL: http://www.turner.com

Bibliography

"Acme Communications, Inc." *Hoover's*, November 2001. Available at http://www.hoovers.com.

"AOL Combines TV Networks Under a Chief." *The New York Times*, 7 March 2001.

The Complete Marquis Who's Who. Marquis Who's Who, 2001.

"Cowabunga! Kellner Gives Fox its Twist." *ADWEEK Eastern Edition*, 22 October 1990.

"Executive Biography: Jamie Kellner." *Turner Broadcasting System, Inc.*, November 2001. Available at http://www.turner.com.

"A Gentler Jamie Kellner?" *Broadcasting & Cable*, 12 March 2001.

"Jamie Jostles in Newsie." *Variety*, 25 June 2001.

"Jamie Kellner." *Electronic Media*, 13 January 1997.

"Jamie Kellner." *Television Digest*, 5 May 1997.

"Kellner Boldly Assumes Hot Seat at Turner." *Electronic Media*, 12 March 2001.

"The Kellner Connection." *Brandweek*, 11 June 2001.

"Kellner's Latest Surprise: The WB Gets New Legs." *Broadcasting & Cable*, 11 August 1997.

"Losing *Buffy* a Winning Move for WB, Kellner." *Electronic Media*, 30 April 2001.

"Making the Peace At Turner and WB." *MEDIAWEEK*, 12 March 2001.

"Showman Speeds the Makeover of Ted Turner's Empire." *The New York Times*, 15 July 2001.

"Talking With...Jamie Kellner." *AOL Time Warner*, 2001. Available at http://www.aoltimewarner.com.

"TBS' Kellner Makes His Presence Known." *Multichannel News*, 11 June 2001.

"The 10 Most Powerful People in TV News." *Electronic Media*, 10 September 2001.

"Turner Broadcasting System, Inc." *Hoover's*, November 2001. Available at http://www.hoovers.com.

"Turner Turnover." *Multichannel News*, 12 March 2001.

"WB Network Chief Takes Over Turner Operation at AOL Time Warner." *The Wall Street Journal*, 7 March 2001.

Calvin Klein

(1942-)
Calvin Klein, Inc.

No single individual has helped American fashion come into its own more than designer Calvin Klein. In the late 1960s, Klein re–invigorated the fashion industry just when it appeared to have been abandoned by a generation of anti–fashion youth. In 1972 Klein began creating his flexible collections of interchangeable separates that were elegant as well as casual. Known as a designer of perfumes, underwear, jeans, and provocative advertisements, Klein has succeeded in reinventing himself and American fashion with each passing year.

Personal Life

Calvin Richard Klein was born in the Bronx, New York, on November 19, 1942. The son of Leo and Flore Klein, Calvin showed an early interest in fashion design. He rejected more traditional boyhood activities and chose to spend his time on sewing and drawing instead. He also spent a great deal of time at Loehmann's, a high–fashion discount store in the Bronx, looking at the Norman Norell samples and other designer garments. Winning a place in both high school and college, Klein attended New York's High School of Art and Design and graduated from the Fashion Institute of Technology in 1962.

Klein has been married twice. From 1964 to 1974, he was married to Jayne Centre, by whom he has a daughter, Marci. In 1996 Klein separated from his second wife, Kelly Rector, whom he had married in 1986.

Career Details

After leaving school in 1962, Klein apprenticed for designer Dan Millstein in New York City's celebrated garment district. In 1968, with backing from his childhood friend Barry Schwartz, Klein founded his own company called Calvin Klein Ltd., which was later changed to Calvin Klein Inc. Focusing at first on outerwear, Klein prospered after receiving a substantial coat order from retailer Bonwit Teller. Within several years, Klein was successful enough to buy out his former mentor, Millstein, and occupy his offices.

In 1972 Klein expanded his offerings to include women's sportswear. Working in a neutral palette that Barbara Lippert of *Adweek* once described as "modern, subdued, [and] monochromatic," he introduced a signature line of separates such as sweaters, skirts, dresses, shirts, and pants that could be intermixed for a complete day and evening wardrobe. "I felt that the American lifestyle had changed," Klein explained. "For the most part, women today spend their time and energy working, in addition to participating in all aspects of home and community. Their lives have changed and there is little time for wardrobe planning." His clothes were perfectly suited for women who wanted the look of an outfit with the versatility of separates.

In the late 1970s, Klein was known as a young, wealthy, handsome, and talented designer who often appeared in his own advertisements. Sales of his blue jeans began to slow down, however, until he unveiled a controversial new advertising campaign. The advertisements, which first ran in 1980, featured teenage model Brooke Shields delivering the tag line, "Nothing comes between me and my Calvins." Though many were offended by Klein's use of an adolescent model in a sexually suggestive advertisement, the campaign was highly effective and sales of Calvin jeans nearly doubled.

With the success of the 1970s, Klein's brand appeal led to a host of licensing agreements for such lines as menswear, accessories, lingerie, hosiery, and eyewear. He subsequently expanded into fragrances, including such scents as Obsession, Eternity, Escape, CK One, and CK Be. Of these, his unisex fragrance CK One has been particularly successful. He was successful in transforming men's underwear into a fashion statement. Using now famous actors Antonio Sabato, Jr. and Mark Wahlberg as models, Calvin Klein underwear, introduced in 1982, became a sign of masculine sexuality. Klein also developed a line of housewares.

In the early 1990s, Calvin Klein sold his company's underwear and jeans divisions to reduce debt. Since that time, the firm has prospered and expanded into global markets. Klein is known for his marketing talents and has hired such famous photographers as Richard Avedon, Diane Arbus, Bruce Weber, and Irving Penn for his photography shoots and television commercials.

Calvin Klein. (Archive Photos, Inc.)

Calvin Klein has enjoyed acclaim throughout his career. As early as 1973, Klein was chosen by 400 fashion reporters as winner of the Coty American Fashion Critics Award. The citation commented on Klein's "innate but nonconformist sense of classic line . . . and his unique understanding of today's blend of casualness, luxury, and moderate price." Klein went on to win two more Coty awards in 1974 and 1975, and on June 25, 1975, he was elected to the American Hall of Fame of Fashion. Professional honors continued in the 1980s when Klein won Council of Fashion Designers of America (CDFA) awards in 1982, 1983, and 1986. In 1994 the CDFA presented Klein with unprecedented dual awards for both men's wear and women's wear. In 1996 he was named one of *Time* magazine's 25 most influential Americans.

Even with numerous awards and enormous commercial success, Klein found himself at the center of controversy again in the mid–1990s. A Klein advertising campaign featuring young, nonprofessional models in intimate poses drew condemnation in 1995. After critics likened these images to child pornography, Klein eventually withdrew the advertisements.

By the end of the 1990s, Klein was at the helm of a thriving global enterprise. His various lines held worldwide appeal, and Klein boutiques provided retail presence in the United States, Europe, the Middle East, and Asia. In 1999 he opened his first freestanding jeans store in Kent, England, and planned additional boutiques in France, Italy, Spain, and Saudi Arabia. By 1999

Chronology:
Calvin Klein

1942: Born.

1962: Graduated from Fashion Institute of Technology.

1968: Established Calvin Klein Ltd.

1972: Introduced sportswear line.

1973: Won first Coty award.

1975: Inducted into the American Hall of Fame of Fashion.

1994: Received dual CFDA awards for women's wear and men's wear.

1996: Named one of *Time* magazine's 25 most influential Americans.

1999: Chosen as one of Fashion Center Business Improvement District's first Fashion Walk of Fame honorees.

2001: Received a lifetime achievement award at the American Fashion Awards.

almost 38 percent of his $5 billion in total annual retail sales came from markets outside the United States—a figure Klein hoped to increase to 45 percent by 2001. As Klein told Lisa Lockwood in *Women's Wear Daily*, "Global expansion is a strategy that will take us beyond 2000 to accomplish what we've set out to do."

In 1999 Klein announced that he and Schwartz, still his business partner, were looking for a buyer for their company—a move that analysts believed was consistent with Klein's wish to further expand his product lines and global markets. Calvin Klein, Inc. is a private company, with sole ownership in the hands of Klein and Schwartz. In 2000 the company had $170 million in sales but pulled in a total of almost $5 billion through licensing agreements between manufacturers of jeans, underwear, and fragrances and its 40 retail stores worldwide.

Social and Economic Impact

Calvin Klein almost single-handedly elevated the status of the United States in the world of fashion de-

sign. He brought simplicity, elegance, and luxury to clothing at a time in the early 1970s when gaudy economy was the trend. He used natural fibers like cotton and wool in place of the popular and less expensive synthetics of the day such as polyester and rayon. Klein also rejected the wild use of color so prevalent at that time; he favored neutral earth tones.

In terms of fashion design, Klein's greatest innovation could be the look referred to as "casual chic." This style relied on the use of separates that could be mixed and matched to create a variety of outfits. Klein gave these casual clothes the same fine attention to detail that had been previously reserved for formal couture. He told Lockwood in *Women's Wear Daily*, "I've always had a clear design philosophy and point of view about being modern, sophisticated, sexy, clean, and minimal. They all apply to my design aesthetic."

Klein has also been an innovator as a marketer of fashion. His costly and controversial advertising campaigns have, throughout his career, thrust the fashion world into popular culture. The resulting publicity has undoubtedly helped Klein expand his empire from clothing to fragrances and housewares. In the process, he has changed the way fashion is marketed industry–wide. In 1994 he told Bridget Foley of *Women's Wear Daily*, "If people set out to be controversial, they'll never make it. But if something is really good, interesting, and thought–provoking, you get into risk–taking and pushing boundaries and questioning values, and it can be, in the end, controversial. We need newness and excitement in fashion. That's what it's about—that's what puts the fun in clothes." He is known to be the designer of choice for such stars as Julia Roberts, Gwyneth Paltrow, Sandra Bullock, and Helen Hunt and has influenced the work of other well–known designers, including most notably Donna Karan and Miuccia Prada.

In addition to his significant influence on fashion and marketing, Klein has supported several philanthropic causes, including the Rape, Abuse, and Incest National Network (RAINN) and various AIDS charities.

Sources of Information

Contact at: Calvin Klein, Inc.
205 W. 39th St.
New York, NY 10018
Business Phone: (212)719–2600

Bibliography

"Calvin Klein: Biography." *AskMen.com*, 2001. Available at http://www.askmen.com.

"Calvin Klein, Inc." *Hoover's Online*, 2001. Available at http://www.hoovers.com.

Edgecliffe–Johnson, Andrew. "Calvin Klein Invites Bids for Company." *Financial Times*, 7 October 1999.

Foley, Bridget. "Back on Top." *Women's Wear Daily*, 4 February 1994.

Friedman, Arthur. "Fashion's Famous: Bill, Ralph, Calvin." *Women's Wear Daily* 28 October 1999.

Ingrassia, Michelle. "Calvin's World." *Newsweek*, 11 September 1995.

Jacobs, Laura. "Pret–a–Poor Taste." *New Republic*, 2 January 1995.

Kaplan, James. "The Triumph of Calvinism." *New York*, 18 September 1995.

Lippert, Barbara. "Calvin Between the Covers." *Adweek*, 9 May 1994.

Lockwood, Lisa. "Calvin's Credo.' *Women's Wear Daily*, 22 July 1997.

Ozzard, Janet. "CK Jeans Rides Again: Global Push Planned to Cap the Comeback," *Women's Wear Daily*, 30 May 1996.

Prud'homme, Alex. "What's It All About, Calvin?" *Time*, 23 September 1991.

Raper, Sarah. "Calvin's Designs on Europe." *Women's Wear Daily*, 22 February 1999.

Timothy Koogle

(1951-)
Yahoo!

Overview

Tim Koogle, vice–chairman and former chief executive officer (CEO) of the Yahoo! Web portal, will be remembered (along with Jeffrey Mallett) as half of the management duo that built the company into one of the mightiest on the Internet. He once told Saul Hansell in the *New York Times,* "I just love speed. And I love well–built, highly engineered machines." Though the former engineer used to build and race cars, most of Koogle's drive was channeled into creating a quick, high–performance Internet search engine. As head of the very popular Yahoo! Internet portal service, Koogle was in charge of one of the rare Web companies that turn a profit, and a handsome one at that. In January 2000, Yahoo!'s stock had peaked at a split–adjusted $237.50. In May 2001, Koogle left the top post but continued to serve as vice–chairman on the company's board of directors. Once listed on *Forbes'* 400 Richest People list, Koogle, who had company stock worth $365 million, was removed from *Forbes'* list in 2001 when his stock plunged.

Personal Life

Koogle was born on July 5, 1951, in Alexandria, Virginia. His father (both parents are now deceased) was a fire fighter and Navy machinist who taught him a strong work ethic early on. "He said nobody owes you anything, so go out and earn what you want," Koogle related to Hansell in the *New York Times.* Starting at the age of seven (with a crew of other seven year olds that he gathered) he earned cash doing gardening and delivering newspapers. His father also taught him to repair engines.

As a 15–year–old teen too young for employment, Koogle obtained a special work permit so that he could fix machines at the local McDonald's and help his father repair cars. He was able to put himself through undergraduate college by doing engine repairs for professors.

In 1973, Koogle graduated at the top of his class from the University of Virginia's School of Engineering and Applied Science with a bachelor's degree in mechanical engineering. He worked his way through school by rebuilding race cars and restoring antique cars, and he also won a full scholarship for graduate studies at Stanford University. There, in 1975, he obtained his master of science and, in 1977, he earned a doctorate degree. In addition to rebuilding engines, as a graduate student Koogle started up his own industrial design business making controllers for electronics manufacturers. He later sold the operation to Motorola. By the time he earned his doctorate, he had saved enough money to buy a house.

Before Koogle's fast–paced career with Yahoo!, he played in various rock bands and continued to have the image of "an aging rock–and–roller," according to the article by Hansell, who described him as sporting "black jeans, a denim shirt and a mane of gray hair." Another reporter, Umberto Tosi of *Forbes,* described him as having a "GQ look, which runs to hand–painted Italian ties or black turtlenecks." Yahoo! marketing head Karen Edwards told Hansell, Koogle "is not one of those ego–CEOs who try to micromanage everything. He is easy to talk to, but it always seems like he's pondering life's true meaning." As a further testament to Koogle's artistic bent, his circle of friends included a group of glass blowers outside of Venice, Italy.

With Yahoo!'s irreverent image and youthful staff (the average age of Yahoo! employees at the company's peak was 29), the graying and somewhat conservative Koogle was decidedly more low–key. He refused to spray paint his hair with the company's yellow and purple logo for a photo shoot, and he never tattooed the Yahoo! logo on his rear end, as had at least one other executive. However, Koogle was known for being willing to take risks, a quality that was essential when he decided to leave his stable job to join the staff of six at the tiny startup in the earlier days of the Web.

Koogle, who is known casually as "T.K.," has an older brother, Grayson, is divorced, and has no children. He owns homes in Saratoga, California, and on Lake Washington in Seattle, near the home of Microsoft founder Bill Gates. In addition to driving fast cars (his Mercedes reportedly could reach 170 miles per hour), in his spare time he enjoys playing guitar and collects vintage auto models such as a 1972 Stratocaster, a Beatles' Rickenbacker, and an acoustic D–41 Martin.

Career Details

In 1983, Koogle went to work for Motorola, an electronics corporation specializing in communications

Timothy Koogle. *(Reuters NewMedia Inc./Corbis.)*

equipment. He worked there for nine years in management in its operations and venture capital groups. During this time he was responsible for deciding whether to sink millions of dollars into business plans, thus learning all about risk–taking. However, Koogle never felt comfortable in his marble–floored office in an imposing tower. "I never could stand it," he commented to Linda Himelstein in *Business Week.* He left in 1992 to take a job as chief engineer at Intermec, a Seattle–based subsidiary of the Raytheon corporation making automated data collection and data communications products such as bar code machines. He was soon promoted to president of the ailing company and, in that post, more than doubled the firm's sales to $370 million. Also during that time he served as vice president of Intermec and Raytheon's parent company, Western Atlas, which boasted annual revenues of $2 billion.

Yahoo! began as a search engine in 1994 when Stanford University engineering students Jerry Yang and David Filo created a guide to assist fellow researchers in retrieving information from the Internet. Initially it was simply a list of their favorite sites, but as it grew they created categories for the listings. They developed software to help them locate and label material in order to categorize it, and the site became a useful database, grouped by umbrella categories such as "Business & Economy," "Education," and "Science," then getting more specific (such as "Astronomy," "Ecology," and "Physics"). Soon it was one of the best–known sites on the Web.

Chronology:

Timothy Koogle

1951: Born in Alexandria, Virginia.

1973: Graduated top of class from University of Virginia School of Engineering.

1975: Earned Master of Science degree in mechanical engineering from Stanford.

1977: Earned doctorate degree from Stanford.

1983: Joined Motorola.

1992: Joined Intermec as chief engineer, later became president.

1995: Recruited to Yahoo! as president and CEO.

1997: Yahoo! posted first profits.

1999: Named chairman of Yahoo!.

2001: Removed as CEO but stayed on as vice–chairman.

In 1995 Yahoo! sent a headhunter to Koogle, and he accepted the offer to become their president and CEO. Though many would balk at leaving an established company to head up a fledgling business in an uncharted field, he was excited. "I like building stuff," he remarked in the *Daily Telegraph.* "This looked great. It was going back full circle to my roots in Silicon Valley and start–ups. It looked like fun; joining something with a clean slate, six people, no business plan, the ability to craft a brand new enterprise in the face of a market which was probably going to be all about a major shift going on in the world." He added, "I have always had a lot higher tolerance for what most people would consider risk." In 1999 he was made chairman of Yahoo!.

Soon after he took over at Yahoo!, Koogle pioneered the idea of making money by signing companies to post banner advertisements directly on the site's pages, instead of charging users, which other sites were doing at the time. As it turned out, his plan became the standard way of business, and the Yahoo! site carried as many as 3,800 such advertising banners at one time. Also, Koogle broadened Yahoo! from being a search site into being a "portal," offering services such as free e–mail accounts, chat rooms, online auctions, and areas focusing on real estate, finance, health, and more. To use many of these services, Web surfers needed to register demographic information with Yahoo!, which the site then provided to businesses.

More notably, Koogle decided that Yahoo! would retain its independence, making it the "Switzerland" of the Web, while other sites teamed up with bigger corporations or signed exclusive agreements with advertisers. For example, the Excite search engine was sold to the At Home Corporation, owned largely by AT & T and cable firms, and competitor Infoseek was acquired by the Walt Disney Company. But these deals caused various problems for the parent companies. And, as Koogle mentioned to Kara Swisher in the *Wall Street Journal,* "When an Internet–based company combines with one that is purely one kind of access or one provider of content, the offering for user is a little bit more narrow. That may be totally viable, but it's not what has made us successful."

Instead, Koogle chose to do the buying, rather than allowing his company to be put on the auction block. Yahoo! purchased Geocities in 1999, a Web service that hosts a vast number of home pages, and then bought broadcast.com, an Internet audio and video service. In addition, Yahoo! teamed with Kmart to provide a free Internet service provider called Bluelight.com. It also began making money by charging retailers a fee for sales generated via its Web site, which allows Yahoo! to collect a commission on sales without the cost of stocking warehouses or paying customer service employees. However, after a deal in early 2000 in which AOL announced plans to purchase Time Warner Inc., many wondered if the iconoclastic portal would be able to keep its pace. Steve Rosenbush wrote in the May 2000 issue of *Business Week,* "The tremendous scope of Time Warner's assets seems likely to widen the gap. Most important right now, Koogle has to catch up in e–commerce."

Thanks to Koogle's leadership, Yahoo! began to turn a profit in September 1997, which was unusual considering the bulk of Internet ventures, including behemoth operations such as Amazon.com, had yet to operate in the black as of mid–2000. Koogle noted in the *New York Times* in 1999, "I still have conversations with people asking, 'Why do you bother with profits?' But I've had enough experience to know at a gut level that if you don't build a company from the start to be profitable, you're never going to be able to get profitable later." The company went public in 1996, earning about 90 percent of its revenue from ad sales at the time of its initial public offering (IPO).

Though other search engines came into existence, Yahoo! continued to grow, adding elements such as free e–mail, chat rooms, news, auctions, and business services. By 1998 they were the most–visited site on the Web, with some 40 million users logging on each month. Their 1999 sales reached $588.6 million, according to *Hoover's Online,* with a net income of $61.1 million. By this time, the firm boasted almost 2,000 employees, a far cry from the handful on board just five years earlier. Though they later lost their lead to American Online

(AOL), in May 2000 they were still the second–most visited Internet site with 48.3 million visitors per month as opposed to AOL's 59.8 million, according to Steve Rosenbush in *Business Week*. But by 2001, Yahoo was attracting more than 120 million worldwide users per month—making it the most popular Internet portal site in terms of traffic and global brand. Koogle once asserted to Andrew Cave in the *Daily Telegraph,* "We are trying to build Yahoo! into the only place anyone would have to go to find or get connected to anything or anybody."

But "Paradise Lost" was on the agenda for the following year. In January 2000, Yahoo! stock closed at an all–time high of a split–adjusted $237.50. Within days, company executives learned that main competitor America Online Inc. planned to purchase media giant Time Warner Inc., creating a new media empire that would drastically diminish Yahoo's presence in cyberspace. Internal dissention broke out, most over whether Yahoo! should try something similar. At first blush, the best strategy seemed to be the purchase of online auction site eBay, a move that Koogle opposed. But Yahoo! began to lose advertising revenues to competitors and, by November 2000, Morgan Stanley had downgraded its stock. Friction developed between Koogle and Yahoo! president Jeffrey Mallett. The first of several internal Yahoo management shakedowns occurred, which continued well into 2001 with the announcement that Koogle would be replaced as CEO. Meanwhile, water under the bridge, eBay was recording a 79 percent increase in revenues, up to $184 million. Had the merger gone through, Yahoo would not have needed to rely on advertising for 90 percent of its revenues.

Social and Economic Impact

Timothy Koogle demonstrated his risk–taking and entrepreneurial skills and his passionate drive for success by taking on a fledgling company and building it into one of the strongest search engines on the Web. Unfortunately, his managerial style and the decline of the Internet "boom" companies caused his departure from Yahoo!. Koogle once told *Christian Science Monitor'*s Shelley David Coolidge, "The No. 1 thing my father taught me was to try to find what I really feel passionate about. If you feel passionate about something you'll probably be good at it, and if you're good at it, the rest will follow." He went on, "Never, ever turn it around . . . ." Koogle lived by his father's advice, and it carried him far. It is most likely good advice for all.

Sources of Information

Bibliography

Coolidge, Shelley David. "Bottoms Up!" *Christian Science Monitor,* 11 May 1998.

"Dropouts." *Forbes,* Annual 2001.

Elgin, Ben, et al. "Inside Yahoo!". *Business Week,* 21 May 2001.

Lau, Debra. "Forbes Faces: Yahoo!'s Timothy Koogle." *Forbes,* 29 January 2001.

Tosi, Umberto. "Yahoo!'s Tim Koogle." *Forbes,* 7 October 1996.

Harry M. Jansen Kraemer, Jr.

(1955-)
Baxter International, Inc.

Overview

Harry Jansen Kraemer is chair and chief executive officer (CEO) of Baxter International, Inc., a $30.8 billion company with some 45,000 employees worldwide. A medical technology company, Baxter provides products and services related to medically critical conditions. During Kraemer's tenure, Baxter's stock prices, earnings, and market value have risen markedly.

Personal Life

Harry M. Jansen Kraemer Jr. was born in 1955. A high achiever in school, he attended Lawrence University in Appleton, Wisconsin. He graduated with highest honors with a bachelor of science degree in mathematics and economics in 1977. Over 20 years later, Lawrence mathematics professor Bruce Pourciau remembered Kraemer as a student, telling *Investor's Business Daily*, "He was a perfect combination of being very smart and very hardworking, combined with having a great personality." After graduating from Lawrence, Kraemer pursued an advanced degree at Northwestern University's J. L. Kellogg Graduate School of Management. Two years later, he earned a master of management degree in finance and accounting. Kraemer is also a certified public accountant.

Active in many roles in business and civic affairs, Kraemer serves on numerous boards of directors, including Comdisco, Inc., Evanston Northwestern Healthcare, and Science Application International Corporation. He also serves on the Dean's Advisory Board of North-

western University's J. L. Kellogg Graduate School of Management and on the Board of Trustees of Lawrence University and Northwestern University. He is a member of the Business Roundtable, the Business Council, the Healthcare Leadership Council, the Chicago Club, and the Commercial Club of Chicago. In 1996 he was presented with the Schaffner Award from Kellogg Graduate School of Management for outstanding leadership and service.

Kraemer lives with his wife, Julie, and their four children in Wilmette, Illinois. Julie was an investment banker until the birth of their fourth child at which time she stepped back to spend more time with her family. Kraemer takes an active role in the lives of his children and prides himself on being a strong family man.

Career Details

Early in his career, Kraemer worked for Northwest Industries in the field of planning and business development. He was also employed as a corporate banker for the Bank of America. In 1982 Kraemer began his career with Baxter International, Inc., a worldwide leader in blood–related critical therapies for life–threatening conditions. Kraemer started out at Baxter as the director of corporate development. Over the next eleven years, he was assigned to an array of positions within the company, holding senior positions both in domestic and international operations. In 1993 he advanced to the position of senior vice president and chief financial officer (CFO). Kraemer's assigned responsibilities included all financial operations, business development, communications, and European operations. Over the course of the next four years, he also became responsible for the Renal, Medication Delivery, and Fenwal divisions, along with operations in Japan. Kraemer enjoyed the four years he served as the company's CFO, telling *CFO.com*, "I loved to dig through the numbers, challenge the assumptions, and play with my calculator."

In 1995 Kraemer was appointed to the Board of Directors, and in April 1997, he was named president of Baxter. The move, widely expected, was welcomed by investors and employees alike. Vernon R. Loucks Jr., chairman and CEO at the time of Kraemer's appointment as president, noted in a company press release, "For over 15 years, Harry has played key roles in furthering Baxter's global leadership in its chosen fields. And, since becoming CFO in 1993, he has spearheaded Baxter's financial strategies and operational discipline, which has resulted in the company's delivering solid returns on a consistent basis." Kenneth Abramowitz, an analyst for Sanford Bernstein, told the *Wall Street Journal* that the company's stock was "very lackluster" prior to Kraemer's appointment as CFO. "Since Harry," Abramowitz commented, "it still hasn't been a stellar performer, but it has been a solid one."

Chronology:
Harry M. Jansen Kraemer, Jr.

1955: Born.

1982: Joined Baxter International, Inc. as director of corporate development.

1993: Appointed senior vice president and chief financial officer.

1996: Presented with the Schaffner Award from Northwestern J. L. Kellogg Graduate School of Management for outstanding leadership and service.

1997: Named as the company's president.

1999: Appointed chief executive officer.

2000: Added the duties of chairman.

2001: Faulty filters manufactured by Baxter and used in dialysis linked to 51 deaths worldwide; Baxter offered production of smallpox vaccine.

Less than two years later, in January 1999, Kraemer was tapped to become the company's CEO, after Loucks announced his retirement from the position. One year later Loucks also retired from his position as chairman, and Kraemer became both CEO and chairman of Baxter. On the occasion of the announcement, in November 1999, of Loucks's pending retirement at the end of that year, Loucks remarked, "Baxter is fortunate to have Harry as its chairman and CEO. He has continually demonstrated leadership and a passion for driving significant value both at Baxter and in the health–care industry. His integrity, intellect and enthusiasm make him the perfect person to lead Baxter. I couldn't leave Baxter, or the board, in better hands."

Kraemer entered the office of CEO and chairman with three specifically stated goals. His first key objective, according to a Baxter press release, was to create an environment "that challenges, motivates and supports Baxter team members worldwide." Second, Kraemer committed himself to maintaining and further developing Baxter's position as the worldwide leader and first choice of people around the world. Finally, Kraemer asserted his desire to continually seek to increase Baxter's profitability. It appears that Kraemer has done a better than adequate job fulfilling his goals.

First, Baxter, considered a member of the "new generation of CEOs," is widely known for its employee–friendly working environment. As a result, in 1999 *Industry Week* named Baxter to its list of the world's 100 Best–Managed Companies because they "invest in their employees, new technologies, the environment, safety, and their local communities." Employee programs include resource and referral services, adoption assistance, back–up child– and elder–care, and alternative work arrangements like working part time, shortened (compressed) work week, flexible office hours, and telecommuting. Kraemer walks the talk, too. He leaves his office regularly by six o'clock in the evening to get home in time to have dinner with his wife and children. "In any company, people are looking for signals," he told *Forbes*. "When they see me leave at a reasonable hour, they know this isn't being done for effect." To ensure company–wide cooperation, Kraemer allows employees to rate their superiors on how well they do in promoting a work/life environment and then ties the responses to managerial raises and promotions.

Second, when it comes to protecting Baxter's favored position as the worldwide leader in the medical technology industry, the deck is stacked in Kraemer's favor. Baxter can be divided into four major businesses—intravenous fluid, renal therapy, blood therapy, and cardiovascular–related products and services—each branch very successful in its own right and together posting combined sales of nearly $7 billion. Baxter has been in the intravenous fluids business for over five decades. As one of the first companies to provide hospitals with sterile intravenous fluids and the associated equipment, Baxter holds the largest worldwide share of the market.

The company has also pioneered the development of renal therapy, primarily kidney dialysis, and is the worldwide leader in this business. Blood therapy entails breaking down blood plasma into separate components useful in a variety of illnesses, and Baxter is the largest fractionator of plasma in the world. Although Baxter does not lead the market in the production of cardiovascular products, such as tissue heart valves, valve repair rings, critical care catheters, and oxygenators, this leg of the business pulls in close to $1 billion in annual sales and was spun off as a separate company, Edwards Life-sciences, in 2000. "Three quarters of our sales come from products that have market leading positions," Kraemer told *The Wall Street Transcript*. "Now, looking at the geographical diversity of the company, more than 50 percent of our sales and almost three quarters of our earnings come from outside the United States. . . . So basically we've got a portfolio of very strong market leading positions, providing therapies for patients suffering from life threatening illnesses."

Finally, Kraemer has managed to keep shareholders happy with consistent earnings. For the fiscal year ending in December 2000, Baxter posted a net income of $740 million on sales of $6.9 billion, representing an increase of over 8 percent from the previous year. Figures for 2001 continued to improve. For the first nine months of 2001, earnings rose by 15 percent to $739 million, compared to $645 million reported for the first three quarters of 2000. According to *Market News Publishing*, on the announcement of third quarter sales and earnings gains, Kraemer noted, "We will continue to build on our strong momentum with continued focus on operational excellence while significantly increasing our sales and earnings growth rates over time. In order to achieve these goals, we will increase our investments in research and development and capital expenditures." In 2001, Baxter was named third among health–care companies on *Fortune*'s list of most–admired companies. Also worth noting, Baxter's market capitalization increased approximately 67 percent in the first two years of Kraemer's tenure as the company's leader.

Social and Economic Impact

Baxter has been providing life–saving technology since 1931. During World War II, the U.S. Armed Forces used Baxter's blood collection devices and solutions for treating injured soldiers. Throughout the years, Baxter made significant advancement in kidney dialysis, was one of the first companies to produce plasma for commercial sale, and was the inventor of the plastic IV bag. Also, in 1962 Baxter delivered the first disposable total–bypass blood–oxygenator, which made open heart surgery possible. In 1991 the company introduced the InterLink IV Access System, the first "needleless" IV system, thus protecting health care workers from needle–stick accidents. In the twenty–first century, Baxter provides a wide array of products and services in areas of critical care, which have been developed through research or obtained by acquiring other companies. Baxter makes the equipment that collects and separates blood and blood components; the company developed plasma protein therapies to treat such conditions as hemophilia, and it operates more than 200 kidney dialysis clinics in twelve countries outside the United States. In all, Baxter's products and services are used by health care professionals to treat critically ill patients in 112 countries.

In 2001 Baxter stepped forward after the September 11 terrorist attacks on the World Trade Center and the Pentagon and the ensuing war in Afghanistan. Having acquired Immuno International AG, an international leader in infectious disease research in 1997, Baxter had the ability to manufacture vaccines and other drugs. In mid–October 2001, Baxter announced that it could produce just about any vaccines required within a six– to nine–month time frame. With the U.S. population in fear of the possibility of biological terrorist attacks, Kraemer declared his company was ready if called upon. In *Reuters Business Report*, Kraemer said, "We have the ability, given the production and the manufacturing we have, to be able to ramp up very quickly the necessary vaccines. So for example, when Secretary Thompson talks about the fact that he may need hundreds of millions of doses of smallpox vaccines, that's something we could ramp up to help with very quickly, and we're prepared to do that."

In the month following Baxter's pledge to help protect the United States against bio–terrorism, tragic news hit: the deaths of 51 people around the world had been linked to the use of a faulty dialysis filter, called a dialyzer, manufactured by Baxter. All victims—23 in Croatia, 15 in Spain, seven in Taiwan, two in Columbia, and two in both Texas and Nebraska—were using dialysis filters. At first Baxter denied any connection to the deaths, but it did shut down a plant in Sweden, suspend the production of the product, and issue a recall on three models of dialyzers; however, in early November, the company confirmed that a chemical solution used to test for leaks in the filters during production was not completely removed and the solution, known as 5070, may have entered the victims' bloodstreams.

In a widely covered story, CNN reported Kraemer's response: "We are greatly saddened by the patient deaths, and I would like to extend my personal sympathies to family members of those patients." By the end of November, Baxter had settled a lawsuit brought by ten families of patients in Spain; Baxter agreed to pay each family $289,000. According to *AP Online*, Kraemer commented on the settlement: "Our goal is to do the right thing. While nothing we do will replace the loss these families have experienced, we understand their need to bring closure to this tragedy. Our hope is that this settlement helps to minimize the distress to the families involved."

Kraemer, known for his sincerity and compassion for others, has done his best to bring his company through the difficult days. Although earnings dropped off after the announcement of Baxter's liability in the deaths, Kraemer believes the company is strong enough to weather the storm and rebound quickly with no long–term negative effects. The key to his business approach? He told *Investor's Business Daily*, "An awful lot of it for me I think comes down to understanding everybody's perspective. . . . Nothing I've done since second–semester calculus is that complicated. Most of what you do in business is common sense. How do you lead? By example, so people know you're not just talking."

Sources of Information

Contact at: Baxter International, Inc.
1 Baxter Pkwy.
Deerfield, IL 60015
Business Phone: (847)948–2000
URL: http://www.baxter.com

Bibliography

Barr, Stephen. "CFOs–Turned–CEOs: The View From the Other Side of the Desk." *CFO.com*, 27 September 2001.

"Baxter CEO Harry Kraemer Elected to Additional Post of Chairman, Vernon Loucks to Retire as Chairman and Director." Baxter International, Inc., 16 November 1999. Available at http://www.baxter.com.

"Baxter Elects Harry M. Jansen Kraemer, Jr. President." Baxter International, Inc., 14 April 1997. Available at http://www.baxter.com.

"Baxter International, Inc." Hoover's Online, Inc., 2001. Available at http://www.hoovers.com.

"Baxter International, Inc. Delivers Strong Third Quarter Performance." *Market News Publishing*, 19 October 2001.

"Baxter Prepared to Boost Vaccines Production." *Reuters Business Report*, 18 October 2001.

"Baxter Settles with Spain Families." *AP Online*, 29 November 2001.

"Baxter's Kraemer Plans to Add Chairmanship to His Posts December 31." *Wall Street Journal*, 17 November 2001.

"Dialysis Filters May Have Played a Role in Deaths." *USA Today*, 5 November 2001. Available at http://www.usatoday.com.

"Dialysis Product May Be Behind Patient Deaths." *CNN.com*, 5 November 2001. Available at http://www.cnn.com.

Edwards, Douglas J. "The Best 100." *Industry Week*, 16 August 1999.

Grover, Mary Beth. "Daddy Stress." *Forbes*, 6 September 1999.

"Harry M. Jansen Kraemer Jr." Baxter International, Inc., 2001. Available at http://www.baxter.com.

"Harry M. Jansen Kraemer Jr." The New York Stock Exchange, 2001. Available at http://www.nyse.com/pdfs/kraemer4.pdf.

Howell, Donna. "CEO Harry Jansen Kraemer Jr. at Baxter International, He Touts Balance of Work and Life." *Investor's Business Daily*, 22 August 2001.

"Medical Device Firm Baxter International's CEO Talks About His Firm's Future." *The Wall Street Transcript*, 24 May 1999. Available at http://www.twst.com.

Sandra L. Kurtzig

(1947-)

ASK Computer Systems, Inc.

Overview

In 1974 Sandra Kurtzig, just 24 years old, took $2,000 from her last paycheck before quitting her job and started a software company, ASK Computer Systems. By 1985, ASK had sales of $450 million, and Kurtzig was being touted as the queen of Silicon Valley.

Personal Life

Sandra L. Kurtzig was born in Chicago, Illinois, in 1947. Her father Barney Brody, the son of Russian immigrants, was raised by his mother after his father abandoned the family when the boy was a young child. Brody dropped out of school during the Great Depression to help his mother pay the bills and later began his own business building houses. Kurtzig's mother, Marian (Boruck) Brody came from a wealthy Chicago family, graduated from the University of Illinois, and worked for a time as a police reporter in Chicago. In the early 1950s, when Kurtzig and her brother Greg were still young, the Brody family moved to Los Angeles, California, where Kurtzig's father built houses that her mother then advertised and sold. As a result, Kurtzig grew up watching both her parents working odd hours, starting from scratch, and setting their own schedules.

Kurtzig attended the University of California at Los Angeles (UCLA) and graduated with a bachelor of science degree in mathematics. She was then accepted into the Stanford Ph.D. program in aeronautical and astronautical engineering, one of just two women in a class of 250. However, after a year, having completed her mas-

ter of science degree, Kurtzig had serious doubts about her future as an engineer. She took a job with IBM in Palo Alto, California, but the job didn't meet her expectations, and she quit after the first day and spent the summer of 1968 touring Europe. Arie Kurtzig, a recent Ph.D. graduate from Stanford, proposed marriage upon her return to the United States. The two were married on December 1, 1968, and moved into a cramped apartment in Short Hills, New Jersey. Three years later, homesick for her home state of California, Kurtzig convinced her husband to move to Mountain View, California. The couple, who have two sons, Andrew and Ken, divorced in 1983. In the divorce settlement, Kurtzig gave her husband an estimated $20 million—one of the largest settlements ever given by a wife to a husband.

Career Details

Kurtzig began her career after her wedding and a short Acapulco honeymoon. Particularly interested in sales, she took a job with a start-up company, Virtual Computing. In the 1970s, most companies could not afford the expense of owning their own computer systems, so they rented time from computer companies, such as Virtual. Kurtzig was hired to sell these so-called time-shares. But her time at Virtual was barely longer than at IBM. When she arrived on the job, she found herself assigned to writing computer programs, not sales. Three months later, the company instituted a nondisclosure and noncompete agreement (forbidding employees from taking another job with a competitor). When Kurtzig refused to sign it, she was promptly fired.

Still wishing to find a job in sales that would make use of her computer and mathematic knowledge, Kurtzig was able to convince General Electric's (GE) Computer Time-Sharing Service to hire her. She was assigned to the Bell Labs account in Murray Hill, New Jersey. Basically, all engineers and researchers were dependent on programmers who were responsible for all data input and output. Although many researchers had computers at their desks, few had knowledge of or access to useable software. Instead, a researcher would submit data to the programmer who would enter it into the computer system. Results could take a day or a week to finally make their way back to the researcher. Working the Bell Lab account, Kurtzig discovered ways to train the engineers to use their own computers and provided them help in finding or creating productive software, by tapping into the mainframe through which they had access to a number of financial and engineering analysis applications. She went on to work with industrial companies, helping them become more efficient and thereby saving money by enabling them to rely more fully on the fast work of computers.

When Kurtzig decided to return to California, she transferred to the GE Time-Sharing Division in Palo

Chronology:
Sandra L. Kurtzig

1947: Born.

1972: Founded ASK Computer Systems.

1979: ASK sales reached $2.8 million.

1981: ASK became a publicly traded company.

1983: ASK sales soared to $39 million.

1985: Retired as chief executive officer; remained chairwoman.

1989: Returned as chief executive officer and chairwoman.

1992: Retired from ASK.

1994: ASK sold to Computer Associates.

1996: Founded eBenefits with son Andy.

Alto. Her life was set on a new course after she made a sales call at Halcyon, a fast-growing company that built telecommunications equipment. What Kurtzig learned was that Halcyon definitely needed computers but that they also needed expanded and specialized software applications that could track the entire operation of the company, including inventory, orders, and materials used in the assembly of each product—software that GE didn't have. When Halcyon CEO Larry Whitaker asked Kurtzig to write the application he needed, despite nervous doubts, she decided to do it. In 1972 she quit her job with GE and set up her new business in the spare bedroom of her apartment using her $300 advance from Halcyon and a $2,000 commission check from GE. She intended for her new venture to be a part-time job while she started a family. It grew into so much more. ASK Computer Systems was founded with its name based on A for Arie, S for Sandra, and K for Kurtzig, appropriately short and close to the beginning of the alphabet for easy marketing.

Kurtzig's assignment from Halcyon took five weeks, and she earned $900. Scouting out more business proved difficult, but after numerous rejections, she landed her second assignment with Suburban Newspapers. She wrote software that would keep track of some 1,200 mostly school-age paper deliverers, keep the subscription list up-to-date, and organize the process of dividing up the papers and routes among the deliverers. With this job, Kurtzig not only wrote the application but also managed all data input and output. In so doing, ASK took a step from being a programming company to becoming a service bureau, which provides services beyond writing applications.

According to Kurtzig, she made two crucial decisions early in the life of her company that helped steer it toward success. First, after her experience with Suburban, she focused on developing a service bureau. In this way, she would get paid a lump sum for writing the program, and then servicing the account would bring in a smaller but steady monthly income. Second, she decided to target manufacturing companies for business. She wrote in her autobiography, *CEO: Building a $400 Million Company From the Ground Up*, "It was becoming increasing clear that as varied as [manufacturers'] products were, their needs were more similar than dissimilar. Perhaps I could use the code I'd written for one manufacturer as a foundation to build upon for another. . . . Focusing on the basics, I could get in, get out, get paid, and not be a slave to a single company."

In 1974 Kurtzig launched her masterpiece application, MANMAN (a play on *man*ufacturing *man*agement). It was one of the first universal language programs written to track inventory. To date, Kurtzig had provided her clients with custom applications. Although one program might be similar to another, the two were not interchangeable. Universal application had been used to some extent, for example, in the financial and engineering applications Kurtzig had sold through GE, but the concept of large–scale universal programs had not yet taken hold. MANMAN provided tools to track inventory, parts needed, ship dates, and so on but was not limited to any specific inventory. It could be used to track electronic parts as easily as it could automobile parts. Essentially, MANMAN would eliminate the seemingly archaic method of tracking inventory on cards, each listing an individual part number. Kurtzig linked with a successful time–share computer company that provided MANMAN to its customers. Before long, Kurtzig had such big name customers as Coca Cola, General Cable, and Borden Chemical.

Before the end of 1974, Kurtzig was being courted by Hewlett Packard, a highly respected computer company that wanted to include MANMAN on its new minicomputers. Being in the right place at the right time, Kurtzig was able to profit from the increasingly important link between computers and software. With two other programmers she had hired to help with her growing business, Kurtzig spent nights at Hewlett Packard offices rewriting the MANMAN program to operate on an HP computer. Kurtzig's deal with HP gave ASK enough financial cushion to take some needed risks to grow over the next five years—some that worked and some that didn't.

Eventually, ASK took off. Between 1979 and 1983, sales soared from $2.8 million to $39 million. In 1981 Kurtzig took her company public, offering stock for sale. By 1983 the stock was trading at $20 a share. Because Kurtzig retained ownership of 28 percent of the 11.6 million ASK shares, she became worth over $65 million. Kurtzig's personal fame also grew. She appeared on the covers of the *Wall Street Journal*, *Forbes*, and *Fortune*. In 1985, *Business Week* named her on its list of the top fifty corporate leaders. By 1985, sales reached $79 million. To highlight the rapid expansion on ASK's value, consider that in 1976, when Kurtzig offered to pay back a $25,000 loan from her father in ASK stock, her father took the cash instead. If he would have taken the stock, that $25,000 would have been worth $12.5 million at the height of ASK's success.

By 1985 Kurtzig was ready for a break from her 20–hour days. She resigned as CEO, but retained her position as chairwoman. She spent the next two years traveling around the world with her two children, taking trips to Africa, China, Japan, and Singapore. She also dabbled in studying French Impressionist painting. In 1986 Kurtzig explained her decision to resign to *Forbes*, "I was in such a hurry I never had time to smell the roses. ASK was wonderful, but I never got wrapped up in the power trip of it all." However, Kurtzig had difficulty watching as her company began to lose value and the board failed to heed her warnings. In 1989 she resigned as chairwoman and abandoned all ties to the company she had created. However, before the end of the year, with stock prices continuing to depreciate, the board asked Kurtzig to return as CEO and chairwoman. Kurtzig couldn't resist the challenge and returned to her troubled company.

Upon her return, Kurtzig cleaned house and restructured the company leadership. She then redirected ASK's energies to new projects, programs, and developments to catch up to the ever–changing and expanding computer software market. By 1992, Kurtzig had proven herself again, leading ASK to sales of $450 million, making it the largest publicly traded company ever founded and run by a woman. Satisfied with her accomplishments and the position of her company, Kurtzig retired a second time in 1992. However, after her second departure, ASK began to struggle again as competition in the market continued to increase. In 1994 Computer Associates International purchased ASK for $13.25 per share, or $310 million.

Kurtzig's most recent endeavor is in a joint project with her son Andy. In 1996 the two formed eBenefits, which offers human resource, payroll, and benefit services to small businesses online. Kurtzig serves as chairwoman, and her son is the CEO and president. Kurtzig's other son, Ken, also works for the company in business development. Talking about creating the company with his mother, Andy Kurtzig told the *San Francisco Chronicle*, "We had a very good working agreement. I did all the work; she did all the agreeing."

Social and Economic Impact

During the prime of ASK's existence, Kurtzig was considered one of the most influential women in the United States. She has been widely heralded for her tremendous success in a world dominated by men. However, Kurtzig is not quick to play the gender card. In her autobiography, Kurtzig noted, "I've always tried to make being a woman a non–issue. I worked hard because I wanted to succeed, not to prove I was better than a man. I never felt I was competing with anyone but myself." Still, Kurtzig laughs when she remembers her early days with ASK; when she told people she was in software, most thought she made women's underwear.

Aside from Kurtzig's personal success that began with $2,000 and became multiple millions, ASK rode one of the first waves into the computer age. At a time when computers were huge and hugely expensive, Kurtzig discovered a need and filled it. As computers became smaller and more affordable, Kurtzig guided her company through changes that kept up with the changing needs of businesses and consumers. Kurtzig was one of the first to develop a software company based on universal usage. She led her self–made company to incredible success, retired, and then returned to reestablish its dominance on the market. ASK's fall from high stock prices may be due to economic conditions, but clearly, the company prospered under the tender care of the one who gave birth to it.

Sources of Information

Bibliography

Beauchamp, Marc. "Report Card." *Forbes*, 30 June 1986.

Bernstein, James. "Computer Associates Adds On." *Newsday*, 20 May 1994.

"The First Lady of Software." *Entrepeneur*, 2001. Available at http://www.entrepeneur.com.

Glater, Jonathan. "ASK's Kurtzig Returning to Retirement." *San Francisco Chronicle*, 18 July 1992.

Kurtzig, Sandra. *CEO: Building a $400 Million Company From the Ground Up."* New York: W. W. Norton & Company, 1991.

Mitchell, James J. "Online Health Services Firm is Family Affair." *San Jose Mercury News*, 27 February 2000.

Pitta, Julie. "Mommy Track, Revised." *Forbes*, 19 March 1990.

Sasseen, Jane. "A Most Successful Part–Time Job." *Forbes*, Fall 1983.

Sinton, Peter. "Lean on Me: Mother–and–Son Team Rely on Each Other in Building eBenefits." *San Francisco Chronicle*, 16 August 2000.

Who's Who in America, 1999. New Providence, NJ: Marquis Who's Who, 1998.

Emeril Lagasse

(1959-)
Chef

America's favorite "Bam!" man, Chef Emeril Lagasse has taken Louisiana–style cuisine and "kicked it up another notch." Chef Emeril commands a $65 million dollar Creole culinary empire that includes six restaurants, two hot cooking shows on cable's Food Network, cooking correspondent for ABC's *Good Morning America*, and cookbook sales that tally in the millions. In fall 2001 this Cajun crossover served up his own, self–titled sitcom on NBC.

Personal Life

In the early 1980s he was divorced from his first wife, Elizabeth, a schoolteacher with whom he had two daughters, Jillian and Jessica. He married fashion designer Tari Hohn in 1989, who helped him in design and development, but they divorced in 1996. In a small private ceremony in New Orleans, on May 13, 2000, Lagasse married Alden Lovelace, a real estate broker. The next day, they celebrated with guests at a *fais–do–do,* a Louisiana–style dance party, held at one of Lagasse's eateries.

The critical raves for Emeril's establishments were immediate and overwhelming. Emeril's Restaurant won a "five bean" rating from critic Gregory Roberts and in 1990 was named "Restaurant of the Year" by John Mariani of *Esquire* magazine. Emeril was dubbed "Best Southeastern Regional Chef" by the James Beard Foundation and also received the prized Ivy Award. His restaurant NOLA has garnered top honors from *Travel*

Emeril Lagasse. (AP Photo/Robert Button.)

& Leisure, Traveler, and *Southern Living* magazines. Zagat also named Emeril's New Orleans Fish House "Best Restaurant in Las Vegas."

Before becoming one of the best–known celebrity chefs, Lagasse was born October 15, 1959, and raised in the small town of Fall River, Massachusetts, where his French–Canadian father, Emeril Jr., worked in a textile mill and his Portuguese mother, Hilda, was a homemaker who loved to cook. The family also included an older sister, Delores, now a computer operator, and younger brother Mark, a sewing machine mechanic. At age seven, after assisting his mother with a pot of vegetable soup, Lagasse realized the joy of cooking. "I was kind of

viewed as a weird kid because I liked food," he told *People Weekly.* Active in sports and music, Lagasse played in a Portuguese band with older musicians. He taught himself to play trombone, trumpet, and flute but especially favored the drums. However, he always gravitated toward cooking and baking.

Lagasse's first job at age ten was washing dishes in a Portuguese bakery. He gradually became skilled at baking breads and cakes, enjoying the fact that customers took pleasure in his products. "I would just see how happy people were when they came into the bakery," he recalled to Molly O'Neill in the *New York Times Magazine.* After graduating from high school, he turned down

Chronology:
Emeril Lagasse

1959: Born.

1978: Graduated Johnson and Wales University with a doctorate degree in culinary arts.

1993: Published first cookbook, *New New Orleans Cooking*.

1994: Began taping *Essence of Emeril*.

1997: Started production on *Emeril Live*.

1998: Made the "Most Intriguing People of the Year" list by *People* magazine.

2000: Publisher Harper Collins announced Chef Emeril's books top the 2 million mark.

2001: Chef Emeril reached the 1000th show milestone for the Food Network.

2001:: NBS premiered Tuesday night sitcom starring Emeril Lagasse.

---

a scholarship to the New England Conservatory of Music to pursue his dream, trading in his drums for pots and pans. He worked his way through the culinary program at Johnson and Wales University, graduating with a doctorate degree in 1978. After learning the classic techniques in the kitchens of Paris and Lyons, France, Lagasse returned to the States, perfecting his craft in restaurants in Boston, New York, and Philadelphia.

Lagasse's expertise caught the eye of Ella Brennan, the noted queen of the New Orleans restaurant scene. Her family owned the landmark restaurant Commander's Palace and was seeking a new chef to replace the legendary Paul Prudomme. In the early 1980s, Brennan became Lagasse's mentor when he was taking the reins as new executive chef at the Washington Avenue eatery. Lagasse was thrilled with the city and its epicurean attitude toward food. There, he learned the secrets of the spicy cuisine and how best to interpret the flavors through his Portuguese background. "After coming to New Orleans," Lagasse remarked to Mary Beth Romig–Price in *New Orleans Magazine*, "I instantly fell in love with this place, the heritage, the culture, the food, and the music. The city resembles my own years growing up in Massachusetts, especially the warmth of the people, and I am very lucky to have enjoyed tremendous acceptance in the community."

Career Details

But times weren't always "happy happy"" for Lagasse. After seven–and–a–half years working with Brennan, Lagasse was critically acclaimed as a leading recipe wrangler, and he decided to set off on his own gastronomic venture. Living in the city's trendy new Warehouse District, he realized the area was dotted with art galleries but only offered one restaurant, and that only open for breakfast and lunch. Seeing the possibility, he obtained an empty space and began drawing evening visitors to the neighborhood. It was an uncertain time for Lagasse. He had established a sedate clientele at Commander's Palace and was moving into unfamiliar territory. No financial institution was willing to take a risk on the budding entrepreneur; however, due to his persistence and self–reliance, one bank finally relented. In a small borrowed office space, the chef–proprietor developed his business concepts. The list included the budgets, the interior design, the kitchen layout, the demographics, and the wine list. In 1990 along with a devoted staff of 34, he opened the doors of what would become his flagship business *Emeril's Restaurant*. By years end, the critics were dazzled and Lagasse was primed for prominence. In 1992 he branched out to another location with NOLA, a hip bistro in the French Quarter. In 1995 he added a third annex with Emeril's Fish House in the majestic MGM Grand Hotel in South Las Vegas, Nevada. Later he opened Delmonico Restaurant and Bar in New Orleans Garden District, Emeril's Restaurant Orlando at Universal Studios City Walk, and lastly Delmonico Steakhouse in the Venetian/Resort/Hotel/Casino.

Lagasse's menus feature "new New Orleans" cuisine, which is based on traditional Cajun and Creole dishes, but with his own twists inspired by Asian, Italian, and regional American cuisines. Some of his concoctions include stir fry of crawfish over fried noodles with sesame and ginger sauce, corn cakes with caviar, smoked duck with wild mushroom gumbo, crawfish–stuffed filet mignon, foie gras bread pudding, and pork chops with tamarind glazed roasted sweet potatoes and green chile mole sauce. Desserts are equally rich, as exemplified by the goat cheese cheesecake with Creole cream cheese coulis. All of the items are made from scratch. He makes his own cheese and ice cream, and he raises hogs so that he can produce farm–fresh andouille sausage, ham, and bacon. Lagasse believes in using only organically grown produce and the finest of all ingredients, keeping a base of ranchers, farmers, and fisherman on hand to supply him with top quality goods. Lagasse commented to Rick Marin in *Newsweek*, "America got so wrapped up in healthy, healthy, healthy, they forgot what eating was like." Although he seems to be the arch enemy of heart–smart promoters, he asserted to Carolyn Walkup in *Nation's Restaurant News*, "Moderation is everything. I take health into consideration in my cooking." Lagasse convinced his parents to move south from Massachusetts to join him in making the business a family operation. His father, nicknamed Mr. John, regularly helps out in all aspects of the day–to–day operations.

Chef Lagasse has emerged as a top national TV chef. In 1993 the cable channel The Food Network tapped the congenial chef to host his own televised cooking show, *Essence of Emeril*. Until then, Lagasse's recipes were a regional treat, accessible only to those who visited him on location. The show propelled the chef into the nation's living rooms and became the highest rated program on the network. Never using a script, the ragin' Cajun bustles around the onstage kitchen with gesticulations and proclamations, slam–dunking ingredients with a "Bam!" or "Hey Now!" and encouraging viewers to "kick it up a notch," which means to be generous when adding spices. He flies to New York to tape the show, where he always invites members of the audience to taste his creations. Each day, Chef Emeril turns up the heat in 50 million homes nationwide. *Essence* received two Emmy nods for 2001 and was voted by *Time* magazine as one of the "Top 10 TV Shows" in 1996. *Live* has won a Cable Ace Award for "Best Informational Series." In 1998 he created his own website, Emerils.com, which gets more than 300,000 hits a month.

Chef Emeril has penned six books including *Emeril's New New Orleans Cooking, Louisiana Real and Rustic, Emeril's Creole Christmas, Emeril's TV Dinners, Every Day's A Party*, and his latest *Primetime Emeril*. He also plans to begin reaching the public at a young age with a children's book, *There's a Chef in My Soup*, reportedly in the works.

In 2001, NBC announced that Lagasse would star in a sitcom loosely based on the chef's real life. The half hour comedy was developed by top TV talent Linda Bloodworth and directed by her husband Harry Tomason (*Designing Women, Evening Shade*). "We have a show featuring great food and the wonderfully charismatic Emeril who is surrounded by self–assured, terminally opinionated women," reported Bloodworth to NBC. "What's not to like?" Lagasse sees the jump to primetime as just another challenge. "It shouldn't be too difficult," he exclaims to NBC. "I play myself—passionate about food, cooking and making it all fun. Life should be fun. This type of show hasn't been done before and I'm excited to see the outcome."

Social and Economic Impact

Chef Lagasse oversees a Southern–style food empire that employs 975 people and has taken his Cajun

creations across the nation. With his everyday approach, he's made haute cuisine feel more homestyle. No longer the domain of snooty gourmets, food programs have been transformed into a world of fast–paced, down–to–earth fun and entertainment. Lagasse has helped, spark new interest in the art of food, adding zip to the usually sedate world of the how–to cooking show. Throughout his career, he's served up his success with a zesty concoction of comedy and cooking.

Sources of Information

Contact at: Emeril Lagasse
    638 Camp St.
    New Orleans, LA 70130
    URL: http://www.emerils.com

Bibliography

"About Emeril." *The Food Network*, 11 July 2000. Available at http://www.emerils.com.

"Chef Emeril Lagasse Biography." *The Food Network*, 3 April 1998. Available at http://www.foodtv.com.

The Cincinnati Post. 23 June 2001.

"Emeril Biography." *NBC*, October 2001. Available at http://www.nbc.com.

"Emeril Lagasse." *January Magazine*, November 2000.

"Emeril Lagasse, NBC Cook UP a Sitcom with Fizzle not Sizzle." *The Detroit News*, 23 July 2001.

"Emeril Lagasse Ready for Role as Sitcom Chef." *New York Daily News*, 27 July 2001.

"Emeril Review." *Variety*, 24 September 2001.

Lagasse, Emeril, Marcelle Bienvenu, and Felicia Willett. *Every Day's A Party*, William Morrow & Company, Inc., 1999.

Nation's Restaurant News, January 1997.

Newsweek, 31 March 1997.

People Weekly, 28 May 2001.

People Weekly, 28 December 1998.

"Recipe for Success." *Entertainment Weekly*, 13 November 1998.

Restaurant Report, 2001.

Charles Lazarus

(1923-)
Toys "R" Us, Inc.

Overview

Charles Lazarus is one of the nation's most enterprising and successful entrepreneurs. A retail and merchandising genius, he had the foresight to see the potential in specializing in toys alone and to invest in a revolutionary computerized inventory system. This system kept the company he built from scratch on top of the most important trends in the toy industry. The company would remain the number one toy retailer for decades. Lazarus's homogenization of the huge warehouse–like stores and unprecedented selection of some 18,000 toys combined with deep discounts from bulk buying took the company from a single toy store begun in his father's basement to an $11 billion business enterprise with more than 1,450 stores worldwide.

Personal Life

Lazarus married wife Joan Regenbogen in 1995. He was widowed from his previous wife of 16 years, Helen Singer–Kaplan, the famous sex therapist who died of cancer in August 1995. A messy legal suit ensued after Kaplan notified Lazarus of her intention to seek a divorce the day before her death in order to trigger a post–nuptial agreement ordering Lazarus to give her a sum of $20 million that she intended to go, after her death, to her children from a previous marriage. Lazarus has two daughters from his first wife, Ruth and Diane. He was inducted into the Toy Industry Hall of Fame in 1990 by the American Toy Institute.

Charles Lazarus was born in 1923 in Washington, D.C. His father sold used bicycles out of the family's

Charles Lazarus. *(Reuters NewMedia Inc./Corbis.)*

house, purchasing broken bikes and repairing them for resale. When young Charles asked his father why they didn't sell new bikes, his father told him something he never forgot—that he couldn't compete with the large chain stores that could sell them for much less. He went on to serve as a cryptographer in World War II, and when he returned from the army in 1948 he considered enrolling in college on the G.I. Bill but felt he was too old at 25. Searching for a career of some kind, Lazarus didn't have to look beyond the very house he was born in and with $5,000 began a business selling baby furniture out of his father's Washington, D.C. bike shop. Other servicemen were returning from the war and starting families, and Lazarus planned to supply the growing de-

mands of these new parents. Customers then started asking for toys for their babies as well, so Lazarus began to stock toys. He called his business Baby Furniture and Toy Supermarket with a backward "R" to give the name a unique quality.

The turning point for the business came when one customer came back to buy another toy after the infant had broken the first one. Lazarus realized that toys were the better business. After all, furniture, lasting many years, was usually a one–time purchase, whereas toys needed to be replaced much more often. He began to sell toys almost exclusively and renamed his store Children's Supermarket, retaining the backward "R."

Chronology:

Charles Lazarus

1923: Born.

1948: Started a baby furniture business in his family's home.

1957: Renamed his new toy business Toys "R" Us.

1966: Sold his four toy stores to Interstate Stores.

1975: Became CEO of Interstate after they file bankruptcy; Toys reached $200 million in sales.

1978: Interstate renamed Toys "R" Us with Lazarus as CEO.

1983: Lazarus opened Kids "R" Us.

1985: Toys "R" Us had $2 billion in sales.

1994: Lazarus retired as CEO and president while remaining chairman.

2001: Toys "R" Us had seven divisions.

Career Details

The 1950s were a good time to be in the toy business. Mr. Potato Head become the first toy advertised nationally on television in 1952, and it sparked a toy selling boom. Lazarus's toy business grew along with it, and he decided the name of his company was too long and the letters, therefore, too small. In 1957 he changed the name to Toys "R" Us, using the backward "R" he had devised. Businesses such as E. J. Korvette that offered deep discounts, now allowed by the fair trade laws abolishment, began emerging. Lazarus decided this was the way to go with his business and, upon opening his second store, employed the self–service discount method. It was a huge success and not long after, he opened the third store and adopted this as the policy for all future stores. To cap off the decade, Barbie emerged in 1959, becoming the best–selling doll ever.

Lazarus had a total of four stores by 1966, with $12 million in sales annually. He then sold the business to Interstate Stores for $7.5 million and a promise of growing the chain, which Lazarus still headed. The sale proved advantageous to the business—over the next eight years, the franchise grew to 47 stores under the name TOYS. However, in 1974 Interstate's poorly managed, premature venture into discount retailing drove them into bankruptcy. In order to save the toy business that accounted for 85 percent of Interstate's sales, Lazarus was named CEO of Interstate in 1975. He began to sell off the company's other assets and expand the toy store business. Three years later, Interstate was turned around and reorganized under the name Toys "R" Us, with Lazarus as its CEO.

In the late 1970s, Toys "R" Us went public. In an unprecedented decade of growth, the company, which had $200 million sales in 1975 grew to $2 billion in annual sales by 1985. Some of the keys to the chain's success may be found in the sheer volume of toys available to shoppers, with about 18,000 items in each of the stores. Since toys are stocked year–round, unlike department stores, they are able to obtain big discounts from suppliers, allowing them to keep prices low. Each of the items is priced up to 50 percent below retail, and the stores rarely offer sales because of this. Another of Lazarus's demands was uniformity: all the stores are virtually identical—large and warehouse–like, near high–traffic shopping centers, with shelves stacked almost to the ceiling with the same toys on the same shelves in each. Another thing keeping prices down was that employees were usually students earning minimum wage, whose main job was stocking shelves, not customer service.

Lazarus also demanded daily sales analyses from each store with a computer system that sent such sales data from the cash register to company headquarters. This computer system was an invaluable aid in purchasing decisions and was the most advanced computer system in retailing. Lazarus didn't always agree with the computer, telling *Forbes* in 1988, "I thought Cabbage Patch Kids dolls were ugly. I don't think my granddaughter would want to hold one," but when the system caught one of the toy industry's hottest trends early, Lazarus had the sense to go with the computer. Lazarus made a policy of rewarding his employees for good performance. In 1978 he revived employee stock options as incentives for good work. They had been around for years but had not been used in some time. The strategy proved to be very successful, with many of the company's managers and executives remaining loyal to the toy giant for their entire business careers.

The high degree of centralization, in which all decisions are made at headquarters, turned into yet another of Lazarus' successful strategies. *Chain Store Age* coined the phrase the "Lazarus Factor" to describe his bright and creative nature combined with his love of the toy business. Toys "R" Us changed the toy business itself, with toymakers redesigning toy packaging based on how it would be shelved at the retailing giant and how it would stack together. By the mid–1980s, nearly 16 percent of all toy sales were made at Toys "R" Us. In 1984 the company also took its first stores into England, the Far East, and Canada. With little competition, the company had been selling children's apparel since the mid–1970s but not seriously until 1981. In 1983, Lazarus opened Kids "R" Us stores, which sold children's clothing and were managed much like Toys "R" Us, with low–priced, high–quality merchandise and a huge selection. The success of that company further boosted Toys "R" Us' stock prices. By 1988, Kids "R" Us had 112 stores and $300 million in annual sales. Later that year, however, Toys ran into some trouble with sales up a mere 5 percent during the vital Christmas season, down from 1987's 12 percent increase in the same period.

In 1990 the company's sales hit $4.8 billion, boosted by the hot new product from Nintendo—Game Boy, a handheld game. In 1994 Lazarus retired as president and CEO. The company's sales began to slump and discount chain competition heated up, with Wal–Mart, Target, and Kmart expanding into Toys' territory, often with lower prices. Lazarus named Michael Goldstein as his successor. Lazarus still serves on the company's board and has a major say in all the company's decisions. Once cornering the toy market, competition continued to keep Toy "R" Us on its toes as eToys opened online. Furthering its growth, the company launched Babies "R" Us in 1996 with 150 stores selling everything from apparel to furniture for new parents. With continuing growth, Toys "R" Us had more than 1400 stores in more than 20 countries by 1998 but was surpassed as the largest toy retailer that year by Wal–Mart. Goldstein stepped down as CEO.

Nakasone was named CEO in 1998 but left after only 18 months as Toysrus.com struggled to deliver. To turn its fortunes around, in 1999 the company took advantage of the new market for educational toys and opened Imaginarium, an educational chain of toy stores, with 200 stores planned and 700 more inside Toys "R" Us by 2002. To improve the website, Toysrus.com teamed up with Amazon.com. John Eyler took the reins in 2000 with plans in place for proprietary toys, better customer service, and revamped, more modern stores, which it touted in the 2001 advertising campaigns. By 2001, Toys "R" Us, the empire Lazarus built, had grown to include a total of seven divisions: Toys "R" Us USA, Toys "R" Us International, Kids "R" Us, Babies "R" Us, Imaginarium, Toysrus.com, and Babiesrus.com. There are a total of 700 stores in the United States and 450 stores in 27 other countries. Kids "R" Us is one of the largest kids clothing chains, with more than 200 stores. Lazarus said to *Forbes* of the unprecedented growth of his company, "The one enormous advantage that we have over other retailers is that we are in a business that we love."

Social and Economic Impact

Charles Lazarus revolutionized the retail world with his one–stop toy shopping concept, combined with deep

discounting that changed the entire toy industry from manufacturing and packaging to retailing. One of the most successful entrepreneurs of his time, Lazarus had the foresight to specialize in toys at a time when no one else did, and with his unique concepts of standardization, giant selection, and self–service atmosphere, he cornered the market on the toy industry for many years. He put in place the most advanced computer system of the time to track sales and pinpoint the ordering process, putting him far ahead of any of his competitors. His shrewd business acumen led to such ground–breaking decisions as selling from large warehouse–like stores, located near shopping malls, but not in them, to reduce overhead and making all company decisions centralized using sales information coming from each of stores, further driving down costs and streamlining ordering.

Toys "R" Us began as a single store but grew to more than 1,450 stores due to Lazarus' fierce drive and love of the business. In its heyday, the company grew 30 percent a year. By the end of the 1980s, the company drove its two biggest competitors into bankruptcy. Of the continuing expansion, first wife, Helen Singer–Kaplan once referred to Lazarus as having an edifice complex. Lazarus confirmed to *Forbes* this was indeed the case: "I like to have an expanding kind of business." He added, "I like opening stores."

Sources of Information

Contact at: Toys "R" Us, Inc.
461 From Rd.
Paramus, NJ 07652
Business Phone: (201)262–7800
URL: http://www.toysrus.com

Bibliography
"52 Years of Toys 'R' Us." *Business Week*, 4 December 2000. Available at http://www.businessweek.com.

"The Growing Gets Tough." *Forbes*, 13 April 1992.

Hamilton, Neil A. *American Business Leaders*. ABC–CLIO, 1999.

Ingham, John N., and Lynne B. Feldman. *Contemporary American Business Leaders*. Greenwood Press, 1990.

"Post–Mortem." *Wall Street Journal*, 20 September 1996.

"R History." *Toys "R" Us*. 2001. Available at http://www.toysrus.com.

"Turmoil in Toyland." *Time*, 19 October 1998. Available at http://www.time.com.

"Will Toys 'B' Great?" *Forbes*, 22 February 1988.

Bernard Marcus

(1929-)

The Home Depot, Inc.

Overview

In a classic all–American rags–to–riches story, billionaire Bernard Marcus ascended from a childhood in the tenements of Newark to the co–founding of the world's largest home improvement retailer, The Home Depot, Inc., making him one of the richest men in America. Equally impressive is the fact that success has not changed the friendly, sincere, and popular "Bernie," who still gives hugs to his achieving employees, and donates the bulk of his money to charity.

Personal Life

Marcus was born in 1929 in Newark, New Jersey, to Russian immigrant parents. After receiving a degree in pharmacy from Rutgers University in 1954, Marcus instead chose a career in the retail field. After being summarily fired, along with another key executive, from Handy Dan Home Improvement Centers for experimenting with wholesale do–it–yourself merchandise, the two men formed The Home Depot. The easy–going Marcus is married with three children. He enjoys golf, swimming, and the Atlanta Hawks professional basketball team. As far as do–it–yourself projects around the house go, Marcus told *Nation's Business* interviewers that he wouldn't do plumbing repairs even if he had the time. He is co–author of the book *Built from Scratch,* which is about founding The Home Depot.

Marcus is the chairman of the Center for Disease Control Foundation and is on the board of directors of many organizations, including the New York Stock Exchange. He is active in several community organizations,

Bernard Marcus (left) and Arthur Blank at the Home Depot annual shareholders meeting.
(AP/Wide World Photos.)

including the Shepherd Spinal Center and the City of Hope cancer research center. Marcus, with his wife, Billi, is the founder of the Marcus Foundation. The Foundation contributes to Jewish causes, medical and health care issues, free enterprise systems, and children's issues. In 2001, the Foundation announced a $4.5-million contribution to establish the Marcus Chair in Vascular Medicine and the Marcus Vascular Research Fund for Emory University's School of Medicine. Marcus also created the Marcus Developmental Resource Center, a support services resource for children with mental impairments; Marcus made a $45-million donation to the Center in 1998. In November 2001, he gave $200 million to build one of the world's largest aquariums in Atlanta, Georgia.

Marcus was named Most Respected CEO in 1990 by *Georgia Trend* magazine. He also has been honored with induction into the Horatio Alger Association of Distinguished Americans, and in 2000, was inducted into the Rutgers University Hall of Distinguished Alumni.

Career Details

Following graduation from college, Marcus began working at Vornado, a drugstore and cosmetics company. The retail experience appealed to him more than the pharmaceutical aspect of his job, and he instead chose to

Chronology:
Bernard Marcus

1929: Born in New Jersey.

1954: Graduated from Rutgers University with a pharmacy major.

1954: Worked for Vornado, a drugstore and cosmetics company, after graduation from college.

1968: Left Vornado for presidency at Odell, Inc.

1970: Joined Daylin, parent company of Handy Dan.

1978: Fired, along with Arthur Blank, from Handy Dan.

1978: Partnered with Blank and Pat Farah to form The Home Depot.

1979: The first The Home Depot store opened in Atlanta.

1981: The Home Depot went public.

1999: Home Depot earned a place on the Dow Jones Industrial Average.

2001: Marcus pledged $200 million to build one of the world's largest aquariums in Atlanta, GA.

---

continue his career in retail. Moving up through the ranks at Vornado, Marcus was vice president when he left the company in 1968. He moved because he was offered the job of president of Odell, Inc., which he accepted. In 1970, Marcus again moved to a position as vice president of a much larger company, Daylin, Inc. Daylin owned a chain of local home improvement stores known as Handy Dan Home Improvement Centers, Inc.. Marcus found his mark.

By 1972, Marcus had moved through the ranks of retailer Handy Dan and struck up camaraderie with the vice president of finance, Arthur Blank. The pair began experimenting in discounted merchandise within the Handy Dan chain. When Marcus moved up to chairman of the company, he and Blank developed a plan to sell discounted goods in a "do–it–yourself" retail store. They began experimenting with the idea, with local success.

Meanwhile, venture capitalist Kenneth Langone had heard from a friend that Marcus found success with his new marketing strategy at Handy Dan. Langone arranged to meet Marcus. He saw a man with an insatiable drive to make things better, even when things were good. As he told *Forbes* magazine interviewers, "He [Marcus] was—and still is—a warrior."

Langone began buying Handy Dan stock and visiting some of the 60 area stores. He noticed that all the employees knew Marcus as "Bernie." Said Langone in the same interview, "When he put his arm around a clerk and said, 'How's your baby?' he really wanted to know how the baby was." So impressed was Langone that he and a group of Invemed clients bought up about 14 percent of Handy Dan shares. Then Langone began to put pressure on Sanford Sigoloff, head of Handy Dan's parent company, Daylin, Inc. At the time, Daylin controlled approximately 84 percent of Handy Dan stock. Notwithstanding, Langone felt that Sigoloff was not giving Marcus the support he needed. So Langone "put Sigoloff on notice that I was going to hold him accountable, as majority stockholder, for my interest." Sigoloff offered to buy Langone's interest out. Langone held out, then sold.

In 1978, with Langone off his back, Sigoloff fired Marcus and Blank. It was the best thing that ever happened to either of them. As Marcus related in *Forbes,* "I remember calling him [Blank] on a Friday night. He said, 'You've just been hit in the [rear end] with a golden horseshoe. Let's go into business for ourselves.'" That is exactly what they did.

Marcus and Blank joined with a third fired executive, Pat Farah, and developed their vision for The Home Depot. Langone provided an initial investment of $100,000 working capital for them. Unable to finance construction of a prototype store, the men bought two defunct Treasure Island Discount stores in Atlanta and set up shop as The Home Depot. They stocked the shelves with 18,000 different items, priced them low, and hired knowledgeable staff.

On the day of their grand opening, June 22, 1979, Marcus and Blank came up with the idea to have their children hand out $1 bills at the store entrance as a thank you gift to shoppers. By evening, the kids were out in the parking lot, trying to find people and offer them $1 to come into the store. The second day was like the first. Marcus, Blank, and Farah met for lunch. As Marcus later recalled in an interview with *Nation's Business,* "We just sat there in stunned silence. We didn't even eat. It looked like curtains for us." Marcus continued, "My wife wouldn't let me shave for days. She didn't want me to have a razor in my hands."

However, a couple days later, according to *Nation's Business,* Marcus became hopeful when a satisfied customer returned with a bag of home–grown okra as her way of saying thank you for the good shopping experience she had at The Home Depot. New Yorker Marcus didn't know what to make of the okra, but the gesture made him believe he was on the right track. Soon, word spread and the customers poured in—so much so that within twelve months, two more stores had opened. The year after that, 1981, The Home Depot went public and issued its first stock.

During the following 10 years, the company exploded with growth, and it had toppled the nation's leading home improvement chain, Lowes, as the country's biggest warehouse home center retailer. Marcus' and Blank's stock was then worth $780 million. By 1987, The Home Depot had 75 stores and had earned $54 million on sales of $1.5 billion. By 1991, the company had 158 stores in 14 states, and more than 30,000 happy stock–holding employees. Eight years later, in 1999, The Home Depot was added to the selective Dow Jones Industrial Average, when such respected firms as Sears, Chevron, and Goodyear were removed.

But co–founders Marcus and Blank never forgot the day they were terminated from Handy Dan. They had been running the most profitable home center store in the country at the time. But then, unexpectedly, one day, they were fired without reason. As Marcus recalled in *Nation's Business,* "what we learned is this: You never turn your back. You always question success. And that experience gave us one of the things that is critical to running the company today: humility."

That humility translated into customer service for the new The Home Depot chain. Marcus and Blank often made time in their busy schedule to wear an orange apron and walk the floor in one of their stores, helping customers just like any other employee. Further, they always were open for suggestions, whether from customers or employees. These early practices have stayed with the company since the beginning. But, as a result of listening to customers, their stores have not remained the same. The stores have nearly doubled in size and carry twice as many items as those first envisioned.

From the beginning, Marcus served as The Home Depot's chief executive officer (CEO), and Blank was its president (the third partner, Farah, has since retired). But they have always treated the company as though it was a large entrepreneurial interest involving *all* their employees. In 1992, when interviewed by *Nation's Business,* Marcus stated, "Among our 30,000 employees, we probably have 10,000 people who are entrepreneurs. And we have an environment that allows the entrepreneur to function. That is very rare for a company our size." He cited an example of an employee who took it upon himself to learn sign language to better assist hearing–impaired or deaf customers. As a result, the number of deaf customers turned into a steady stream, and the employee began teaching sign language to other sales clerks. All employees of the company are graduates of employee training at The Home Depot University.

Since going public, The Home Depot suffered the exposure that often attracts competitor copycats. But Marcus and Blank believed that their successful recipe involved "chemistry," particularly between customers and employees. And there was chemistry between Marcus and Blank as well. Blank is the more detailed and organized of the two; Marcus is the more gregarious, casual one. His formula for success, as he told *Forbes* interviewers, is that "Every customer has to be treated like your mother, your father, your sister or your brother."

Social and Economic Impact

The Home Depot Inc. reported fiscal 2001 revenues of $45.7 billion, with a one–year's sales growth of 19 percent. That year, they employed 227,000. The chain had grown to 1,100 stores in 48 states and Canada, Puerto Rico, Argentina, and Chile. In 2000, the company acquired plumbing distributor Apex Supply, which had operated 21 facilities in South Carolina, Georgia, and Tennessee. The company planned to open 600 stores by early 2002. For six consecutive years, The Home Depot was ranked by *Fortune* magazine as America's Most Admired Specialty Retailer.

Marcus has been praised in many magazines for his social responsibility, citing him as one of the most generous philanthropists in the world. The Home Depot co–founder Arthur Blank spoke of his relationship with Marcus on the occasion of the Rutgers University Distinguished Alumni award in 2000. Said Blank, "For more than 20 years, we have shared a labor of love at The Home Depot, and my admiration for Bernie has grown through the seasons. Bernie carries within him a sincere respect for people of all origins and situations, and his passion for life and compassion for others has inspired thousands, including me. I am proud to call him my partner, my friend, my mentor, my brother."

Sources of Information

Contact at: The Home Depot, Inc.
    2455 Paces Ferry Rd.
    Atlanta, GA 30339–4024
    Business Phone: (770) 433–8211
    URL: http://www.homedepot.com.

Bibliography

Billips, Mike, et al. "100 Most Influential Georgians." *Georgia Trend,* January 2001.

"Billionaires." *Forbes,* 18 October 1993.

Bachman, Justin. "Entrepreneur Gives $200 Million for Aquarium." *Associated Press Online,* 20 November 2001.

Button, Graham. "The Man Who Almost Walked Out on Ross Perot." *Forbes,* 22 November 1993.

"Hall of Distinguished Alumni–2000." February 2000. Available at http://info.rutgers.edu/University/alumni/HDA2/2000/marcus.html.

"Home Depot." Undated. Available at http://www.wetfeet.com/asp/companyprofiles.asp?companypk=1555&pxID=2831.

Kafka, Peter, et al. "Retail." *Forbes Annual 2001.*

"Marcus Foundation Gives $4.5 Million for Vascular Research." Available at http://www.emory.edu/EMORY_REPORT.

Thompson, R. "There's No Place Like Home Depot." *Nation's Business,* February 1992.

James F. McCann

(1951-)
1–800–FLOWERS.com, Inc.

Overview

From one small flower shop, James McCann established an international retailing empire. His familiar face appears in the ads for 1–800–FLOWERS, the telephone retailer that he purchased and transformed into a business with worldwide sales of over $400 million and more than 2,000 employees. McCann's success can be attributed to his insistence on impeccable service, his smart marketing, and a unique management style. One of the pioneers of toll–free telephone number sales, McCann continued exploring new territory by becoming the first seller on America Online and further expanding the company's click–and–order power with its own Web site as a major sales channel of the company's floral products and gifts.

Personal Life

McCann lives on Long Island, New York, with his wife Marylou. They have three children: Erin, Jimmy, and Matthew. His hobbies include golf and jogging, but surprisingly not gardening, and credits his wife as the green thumb in the family. He revealed to *Fast Company* in 1997 that one of his favorite online bookmarks was the Web site for the television show *Seinfeld*, and added, "A *Seinfeld* quiz is one of the final steps in our hiring process." McCann serves on the board of several companies, including PETCO, Inc., Gateway 2000, OfficeMax, Inc., and the National Retail Federation. Active on the speaking circuit, he was named Toastmaster International's Outstanding Business Speaker in 1997. He has gained many other honors over the years, including Merrill Lynch and *Inc.* magazine's Entrepreneur of the Year award, *Chain Store*

Executive magazine's Retailer of the Year award, Direct Marketer of the Year from *Direct Marketing Day New York*, Advocate of the Year award from Ernst & Young and the Long Island Association, and has been named among the Top Business 100 in *Irish America Magazine*. Among his humanitarian efforts, McCann supports programs for the developmentally disabled.

McCann was born July 28, 1951, in Queens, New York. His father was a painting contractor and his mother was a homemaker. He is the oldest of five siblings, several of whom work for 1–800–FLOWERS.com, including youngest brother Christopher G. McCann, who is president and director of the company. Of their work relationship, McCann told *Management Review*, "Because there's 10 years' difference between us, we were never rivals. We've always had a good relationship. We've never had an argument that we'll admit to. We disagree all the time, and I defer to him more often than not because he's one of the most talented operations managers there is." McCann's siblings compare growing up with the clean–cut young entrepreneur to growing up with Alex P. Keaton from the television series *Family Ties*. McCann remembers often getting in trouble as a child for daydreaming, which he credits as part of the reason for his success.

His first job was working for his family's painting business. Stuck with doing many of the dirty and exhausting chores the other men didn't want to do, McCann told *Management Review* that as he walked by a clothing store and saw a man with a shirt and tie on, he remembered thinking, "I want to get a job like that." McCann did achieve his one–time goal of becoming a retail clothing salesman briefly, but had a new goal in mind: becoming a policeman. McCann graduated with a bachelor's degree in psychology from the John Jay College of Criminal Justice of the City University of New York in 1972. Of the working class Queens neighborhood he was raised in, McCann told *Chief Executive* magazine, "Where I grew up, an Irish–American kid became a priest, a cop, a bartender, or a bad guy." McCann's brief stint as a part–time bartender almost qualified him as filling two of those professions before he eventually landed a position as a counselor at the St. John's Home for Boys in Rockaway, New York, earning a mere $18,000 a year. It was at the home—working with "at–risk," underprivileged inner–city youths who were exposed to gangs, drugs, and poverty—that McCann learned the important lessons that shaped his management style. He realized that success in business is dependent on personal relationships with people. He used those lessons successfully when he eventually began his first business.

Career Details

While Jim McCann continued to work at St. John's, the imminent arrival of his own children prompted him

Chronology:
James F. McCann

1951: Born.

1972: Graduated with B.A. from John Jay College.

1976: Bought first flower shop in New York.

1986: Acquired rights to 1–800–FLOWERS number.

1992: Began selling flowers online through Compuserve.

1994: Became first vendor on America Online.

1995: Established 1–800–FLOWERS.com Web site.

1995: Changed company name to 1–800–FLOWERS.com, Inc.

1999: 1–800–FLOWERS.com went public.

to think about starting up his own business on the side for extra income. He chose to go into real estate, buying rental properties and repairing them himself. Although he continued with the venture, the business was not as lucrative as he had hoped, so he decided to look into buying a franchise of some kind. While scouring the classified ads, he found a flower store called Flower World. McCann liked the fact that selling flowers provided a service that made people happy and uplifted, and he knew that people would continue to enjoy receiving flowers long into the future. McCann had unknowingly found his niche.

In order to buy the little flower shop in Manhattan, New York, McCann borrowed $10,000 from his family and friends and approached the limit on all of his credit cards. In 1976, at the age of 25, he had enough money to buy his first flower shop, but little else, at one time being unable to afford even toothpaste. He later told *Success* that the key for entrepreneurs to become successful is to recognize their potential and to live below their means. Not afraid to do either, McCann grew to love the flower business. With hard work and dedication to the business, he began acquiring one store after another until he had a chain called FloraPlenty, which numbered 14 stores by 1986.

In his biography *Stop and Sell the Roses*, McCann recounted the event that changed his life. In 1984 he heard a radio ad for 1–800–FLOWERS and was immediately intrigued by the flower company named after a toll–free telephone number. Soon after, FloraPlenty was busily fulfilling orders from 1–800–FLOWERS, and the chain really began to bloom. During this time, the orders were so large that McCann had to finally leave his job at St. John's and devote himself to his business full–time. In time, though, orders from 1–800–FLOWERS began to taper off. This firm was struggling to stay afloat under losses of millions of dollars. To revive itself, 1–800–FLOWERS offered McCann a management position. Rather than accept their offer, McCann opted instead to buy them out for $2 million. He immediately sold off all the company's assets, leaving him with the rights to the 1–800–FLOWERS telephone number and $6 million in debt. Ironically, he didn't even have phone service for the toll–free business because this service had been cut off.

McCann learned from his successors' failures: the lack of a reliable network of florists and consistent service during periods of heavy orders spelled the loss of business, particularly from returning customers. This knowledge enabled him to base his strategy on repeat business, which costs much less than expensive advertising, promotion, and overhead aimed at attracting new customers. In sum, relationships with customers were the key.

McCann and his brother Chris ran the 1–800–FLOWERS business from the basement of some of his flower shops. About the brothers' expectations for the fledgling business, Chris McCann told *RETAILTECH* in 2000, "We knew our investment in 800–FLOWERS would be our future, so I started learning about e–commerce, computers and applications."

In the mid–1980s, toll–free numbers were not as familiar and accepted as sales outlets as they were in later years. So McCann hired operators who were friendly and efficient as a way of alleviating the anxiety of customers who were troubled by the security issues involved with providing their credit card information in this new way. As people gradually warmed up to the growing trend of buying goods over the telephone, the business steadily began to grow through the early 1990s.

Marketing savvy and McCann's dedication to excellent service explain why the company, once $6 million in debt, became a $75 million–a–year business by 1993. Heavy television marketing of the 1–800–FLOWERS brand name fueled recognition of the company and its expanding services. Commenting on company service and reliability, McCann told *Success*, "To make sure the experience is perfect every time, we work exclusively with about 2,500 hand–picked florists in a network we call BloomNet. We give the top 100 members of BloomNet 120 orders per month, so when we call a flower shop with an order, we're that shop's best customer. We get good service and monitor each order. We're open 24 hours a day, seven days a week. We need people to trust us, so we offer a 100 percent guarantee." The easy refund policy was another of McCann's successful strategies to win repeat customers.

At the same time, McCann was building the tools for great service: the telephone and computer ordering systems. The company kept detailed records of the sales history and performance of shops near each customer, data that was easily accessible to operators when a customer calls to place an order. The company also began its expansion into the concept of selling gifts other than flowers with 800–BASKETS for gift baskets and 800–GROWERS for fruit.

Using the same foresight he had applied to toll–free retailing, McCann ventured into the relatively new arena of Internet sales by entering into an agreement with Compuserve in 1992. Two years later 1–800–FLOWERS became the first vendor on America Online, and online sales climbed. In 1995, with Internet technology growing rapidly, McCann jumped with both feet into cyberspace by launching his company's own Web site and changing the company's name to 1–800–FLOWERS.com. Utilizing the same philosophy that had made his company successful, he focused once again on building customer relations. He stressed that customer email must receive prompt response. He also ensured that the online ordering process was reliable and easy to use. Finally, he wanted the Web site to be entertaining.

On August 3, 1999, 1–800–FLOWERS.com went public with shares offered at $21 each. The price rose slightly to gain $1.25 per share that day, then dropped 13 percent below the offering value for a day–end price of about $18 per share. The rapid decline was attributed by some to bad timing, as many Internet companies saw their stocks tumble during these months. Yet even two years later, 1–800–FLOWERS.com still hadn't recovered. As of October 12, 2001, its stock price was valued at $12 per share.

Stock price doesn't always tell the whole story, though. With its three sales channels—online, telephone, and storefront—1–800–FLOWERS experienced more than 50 percent growth throughout the 1990s. In 2001, with sales of $440 million and more than 2,000 employees, McCann continued to look to future technology for growth and ease of use for customers. In June 2001 he told *RETAILTECH* that the company is now looking toward mobile commerce.

Social and Economic Impact

James McCann is a retailing pioneer, making his company one of the first not only to utilize the toll–free 800 number, but also to take it to a new level by building his entire company and all of its brands around the novel concept. Savvy marketing strategies also contributed to success. One example is long–distance sales and delivery. McCann realized that few people knew whom to call when they needed flowers sent to someone out of town. The national advertising campaign that he launched, with himself as spokesperson, imprinted the

1–800–FLOWERS name and phone number on the public's mind as a source for flower delivery, across town or overseas. By embracing the power of technology, McCann was also one of the first to sell his flowers and gift products online, and the first retailer of any sort on America Online. The other significant area where McCann's influence has been felt in the world of retailing is his unique dedication to customer relationships, learned from his early experiences in social work and transferred to the big business environment. He is dedicated to continually looking for news ways to please customers and encourage them to remain loyal.

Sources of Information

Contact at: 1–800–FLOWERS.com, Inc.
 1600 Stewart Ave.
 Westbury, NY 11590
 Business Phone (516)237–6000
 URL: http://www.1800flowers.com

Bibliography

"Be Perfect or Die! How 800–FLOWERS Thrives on a 3–percent Margin." *Success*, June 1993, 14.

Chadderdon, Lisa. "My Favorite Bookmarks—Jim McCann." *Fast Company*, December 1997. Available at http://pf.fastcompany.com

"Flower Talk: A Talk with Jim McCann." *Management Review*, March 1995, 9.

Goldman, Jane. "War of the Roses." *The Industry Standard*, 9 August 1999.

"Jim McCann." Westbury, NY: 1–800–FLOWERS.com. Inc., 2001. Available at http://www.1800FLOWERS.com.

"Jim McCann CEO, 1–800–FLOWERS.com." *RETAILTECH Online*, 1 June 2001. Available at http://209.11.43.217/retailtech.com.

"Jim McCann: Making 1–800–FLOWERS Flourish." 6 May 1998. Available at http://content.techweb.com.

McCann, Jim, and Peter Kaminsky. *Stop and Sell the Roses: Lessons from Business and Life.* New York: Ballantine, 1998.

Pellet, Jennifer, and George Schira. "This Bud's For You." *Chief Executive (U.S.)* March 1997, 24.

Warshaw, Michael. "Invest in Yourself; Get Professional Help and Diversify Your Fortune, Says the Owner of Industry Giant 1–800–FLOWERS." *Success*, April 1997, 27.

White, Erin. "Growing Pains on the Web: 1–800–FLOWERS.com's IPO Lesson: Coping with Wilt." *Wall Street Journal, Eastern Edition*, 19 August 1999, B1.

Billy Joe McCombs

(1927-)
Clear Channel
Communications, Inc.

Overview

Billionaire Billy "Red" McCombs has often been referred to as a "one–man conglomerate," having acquired an unusual portfolio consisting of, among other things, car dealerships, radio stations, a movie financing company, cattle, oil interests, banking, insurance, and real estate. In the business world, he is primarily known for co–founding Clear Channel Communications, the largest radio station owner in the United States and one of the leading outdoor advertising companies in the world. But his name became known in considerably more households after his July 1998 purchase of the Minnesota Vikings professional football franchise for $206 million. He turned the team around with his winning management style, leading them to remain the National Football Conference's only undefeated team for two years, and propelling them toward their first good chance at playing in the Super Bowl. McCombs was honored as the 2001 Gold Medal Recipient of the National Football Foundation and College Hall of Fame.

Personal Life

Billy Joe "Red" McCombs was born in 1927 in the small western Texas town of Spur, about 75 miles east of Lubbock. His father was an auto mechanic, but the younger McCombs, the eldest of four children, expressed little initial interest in automobiles. Ironically, that market eventually facilitated his entrance to the world of big business, fame, and fortune.

In 1943 Red and his family moved to Corpus Christi, Texas. An entrepreneur at an early age, 10–year–old

Billy Joe "Red" McCombs. (AP Photos/Jim Mone.)

McCombs began selling peanuts, but quickly discovered that he was taking in no more money than he was spending on peanuts. He soon figured out what was necessary to clear a profit, and the lesson learned stayed with him throughout his life. At the age of 17, his love of sports took him on a hitchhiking tour of schools in the old Southwest Conference, searching for a college that would grant him a football scholarship. He started playing ball at Corpus Christi Junior College but later realized his dream of playing true college football by moving on to Southwestern University in Georgetown, Texas, where he played lineman and receiver for the university's team.

McCombs's college career was interrupted by a call to military service, and he spent 1946 and 1947 in the U.S. Army. After completing his military obligations, McCombs enrolled at the University of Texas, attending the business school and law school. Academia was again detoured when a Corpus Christi friend persuaded him to try selling cars. He was immediately successful, and acquired his first dealership at the age of 25. That same year he spent $10,000 to purchase his first professional sports team, a minor league baseball team called the Corpus Christi Clippers. Four years later, in 1957, McCombs became the youngest Edsel automobile dealer in the United States, and his franchise was one of only a few to show a profit from the ill–fated Ford model. After an impressed Ford Motor Company invited him to fly to Los Angeles to teach a sales seminar for California dealers,

Chronology:

Billy Joe McCombs

1927: Born.

1950: Began career at a used car dealership.

1954: Bought his first professional team, the Corpus Christi Clippers.

1960: Made his first million in car sales.

1972: Co–founded Clear Channel Communications.

1973: Purchased the San Antonio Spurs.

1982: Purchased the Denver Nuggets.

1988: Repurchased the San Antonio Spurs.

1998: Purchased the Minnesota Vikings.

McCombs began buying into distressed dealerships and turning them into profitable centers. By 1960 he had made his first million and had begun to diversify into cattle breeding, oil exploration, and real estate. During the next several decades, McCombs ventured into more than 300 business undertakings, including Clear Channel Communications, making him a billionaire along the way. In the 2000 issue of *Forbes*, McCombs was ranked among the top 400 wealthiest people in the nation.

McCombs earned and spent his money wisely, mostly by returning it to the community. In May 2000 Red and his wife Charlene donated $50 million to the University of Texas School of Business, which was re-named the Red McCombs School of Business. Thanks to this endowment, some expect that the school will become one of the top five in the nation. At the May 2000 press conference announcing the gift, an emotional McCombs stated that, aside from his family, anything he had ever been involved with "paled" in comparison to his ability to make the donation. "This is truly the defining moment of my life," he told his audience.

Other charities and interests have included his roles in bringing the World's Fair to San Antonio in 1968; helping to create Sea World of Texas; co–founding the Texas Research Park in San Antonio; contributing to the construction of the Alamodome, the renovation of his-toric buildings, and the building of new roads; and in-creasing the popularity of basketball. In 1997 he and his wife donated the largest gift ever, $3 million, to the University of Texas women's athletics to fund a new soft-ball complex. Southwestern University has also been the recipient of McCombs's gifts, and he is a member of its board of trustees as well. The McCombs Foundation con-tributes up to $8 million annually to more than 400 char-ities, colleges, and universities across the state of Texas. It has also made major donations to special aid programs for elementary and high school students, and a prison halfway house assisting released inmates. Outside of the academic world, McCombs has supported Kosovar refugees by paying for medical teams to travel to the war–torn areas of Albania and Macedonia.

Among his many honors, McCombs is a Distin-guished Alumnus of The University of Texas at Austin, a recipient of the Automotive Hall of Fame's Distin-guished Service Citation and the Colonel W. T. Bon-durant Distinguished Humanitarian Award, and an in-ductee of the Texas Business Hall of Fame. He is a member of the University of Texas's Austin Capital Campaign Executive Council; chairman of the univer-sity's M. D. Anderson Cancer Center Board of Visitors; and a member of both the university's San Antonio Board and the San Antonio Health Science Center Development Board. McCombs is also an alumnus of one of the uni-versity's fraternities, Alpha Tau Omega. Since leaving college he has avidly supported the fraternity's local Austin chapter and currently serves as a member of the chapter's housing corporation.

At six feet three inches tall and 215 pounds, with a thunderous baritone voice and small–town Texas charm, McCombs commands respect and attention with both his appearance and demeanor. According to his wife, he has never accepted mediocrity in anything he has attempted, with the possible exception of fly fishing. After nearly losing his life to hepatitis in 1977, McCombs stopped drinking and shifted focus to improving his health. In later years, he regularly worked out on a treadmill, where, according to him, he did his toughest thinking and deci-sion–making because he hated the treadmill. Notwith-standing, his management style transferred well from running a car dealership to rallying his Vikings through their best back–to–back winning seasons in the fran-chise's 39–year history. The National Football League labeled him as one of the top five most influential own-ers, and he and his entire family, including his three daughters and eight grandchildren, tried to attend every game, even if it involved flying to Minneapolis from their suburban home in San Antonio.

Career Details

Billy Joe McCombs's strong business acumen, cou-pled with honesty, integrity, and salesman–like charm, would likely have ensured success no matter what he had pursued. As it was, he succeeded in more unrelated and diverse concerns than even the most savvy of business-men would have attempted. Starting in 1958 when he and his wife moved to San Antonio, he partnered with Austin

Hemphill in a Ford dealership from which McCombs would build an empire of more than 50 dealerships nationwide, the sixth largest automobile conglomerate in the country.

McComb ventured into broadcasting in 1972, when he and investment banker L. Lowry Mays purchased a San Antonio radio station. The partners' success prompted them to purchase three additional stations the following year, and another soon after that. In 1975 the burgeoning radio ownership company adopted the name Clear Channel Communications. In 1984, with approximately one dozen stations under ownership, the company went public. It ventured into television ownership, acquiring seven stations by 1992. Under the leadership of McCombs and Mays, Clear Channel expanded its portfolio to 175 radio stations and 18 television stations by 1997.

Also in 1997 the company made its foray into outdoor advertising through its first acquisition in that industry. As a direct result of this and several other similar purchases, Clear Channel enjoyed a 93 percent jump in revenue. Continuing its strategy of growth via acquisition, the company became the nation's second–largest radio station owner in 1999 by spending $4 billion for Jacor Communications. The following year it assumed the number–one position by purchasing AMFM Inc. for $23.8 billion.

As of 2001 Clear Channel Communications held stakes in 1,200 stations in the United States and abroad. Its outdoor advertising empire reached 700,000 displays worldwide and investments in companies spanning 43 countries. McCombs remains a director on Clear Channel's board, while Mays guides the company as its chairman and chief executive officer.

McCombs's business interests are not limited to automobiles, broadcasting, and advertising. Expanding into Texas Longhorn cattle, he acquired a 50 percent interest in Brink's Brangus, one of the world's largest and most respected Brangus bull operations. McCombs is the sole owner of McCombs Oil Corp. in Houston, and through McCombs Enterprises is involved in numerous other business interests. His portfolio has included a Colorado ski resort, a stake in San Francisco's Stanford Court Hotel, 44,000 acres of ranchland and a Brangus breeding operation, a Coors beer distributorship, a weekly newspaper, contract drilling and oil exploration companies, a partnership interest in an insurance company, ownership of 114 "Mr. M." food shops, an interest in a Texas savings and loan operation, and an office building in San Antonio. He also financially backed a movie company involved in two Hollywood hits, *Poltergeist* and *The Verdict*.

McCombs's personal and professional interests coincide in professional sports. He was twice the owner of the National Basketball Association's San Antonio Spurs, most recently from 1988 through 1993. Following his second purchase, he orchestrated a team turn–around that doubled per–game attendance and produced two conference championships. He also became majority owner of another professional basketball team, the Denver Nuggets, which he sold for a $16 million profit in 1985. McCombs purchased the National Football League's Minnesota Vikings in 1998 and has been credited with restoring "Purple Pride" to the Minneapolis community. The team finished 15–1 in McCombs's first year as owner and had its highest attendance in team history, averaging over 63,000 fans per game.

Social and Economic Impact

When Red McCombs does something, he does it "Texas style"—big time. His commitment and involvement with each of his investments has made him an admired businessman and leader. From Clear Channel Communications to the Minnesota Vikings, he remains determined until his mission proves successful.

In under three decades, McCombs turned a single radio station into a global broadcasting and advertising empire. Yet Clear Channel Communications is not content to hold the leading positions in these industries. In 2000 the company ventured into entertainment promotion, followed the next year by an announcement of its intention to offer online music subscriptions through its radio stations.

In 1999 the Vikings attracted a record of over 500,000 fans to their games, and the Metrodome has become the NFL's noisiest stadium, with Texas–style bear–hugs and "yee–haws" overtaking the crowds. McCombs's personal touch, respect for, and interest in his team have played significant roles in the Vikings' successes. In part, his purchase of the team trimmed its ownership from ten people to a single owner, allowing for more focused involvement and input. He is credited with teaching fans the importance of expressing their support for the Vikings. McCombs himself has mingled with the fans, attended pre–season games, and sent flowers to the coaches' wives. When wide–out Cris Carter hurt his right ankle, McCombs personally telephoned him at home to see how he was faring. Carter, a 12–year veteran, stated that it was the first time anyone from the "front office" had ever called to see how he was doing.

According to the National Football Foundation, McCombs once figured he spent about 35 percent of his time working on opportunities, about 35 percent on existing operations, and 30 percent on community interests. He summed up his secret of success by stating, "Make decisions, take chances!"

Sources of Information

Contact at: Clear Channel Communications, Inc.
    200 E. Base
    San Antonio, TX 78209

Business Phone: (210)822–2828
URL: http://www.clearchannel.com

Bibliography

"Billy Joe 'Red' McCombs." National Football Federation, November 2001. Available at http://footballfoundation.fansonly.com.

"Billy Joe 'Red' McCombs." University of Texas at Austin Business School. Available at http://www.bus.utexas.edu.

"Clear Channel Communications, Inc." Hoover's Online, Inc., December 2001. Available at http://www.hoovers.com.

Losefsky, Pam. "Red McCombs: The Man, the Money and the Mission." *McCombs School of Business Magazine*, Fall/Winter 2000. Available at http://www.bus.utexas.edu.

"The Purple Tide Has Turned." *Sports Illustrated*, 26 October 1998, 62.

Patrick Joseph McGovern, Jr.

(1937-)

International Data Group

Overview

Patrick J. McGovern Jr. is the founder and chairman of International Data Group (IDG), an information empire that is a leading technology, media, research, and event company worldwide. IDG published the popular *For Dummies* series, the helpful books with bright yellow covers that began with computer topics for the technologically challenged and branched out to include topics from antiquing to dating. Though later sold, the *For Dummies* line helped IDG make its mark in publishing. The company publishes some 300 magazines and newspapers with more than 100 million readers in 85 countries. Its titles include *PC World, Macworld, Computerworld, InfoWorld, Network World*, and *CIO*. In 2001 IDG had over $3 billion in sales and ranked among the top privately held companies in the United States.

Personal Life

Patrick McGovern is married to Lore Harp McGovern, an entrepreneur who co–founded Vector Graphics, one of the earliest personal computer companies, and who is now involved in numerous Silicon Valley start–ups. Described by many as driven, McGovern first saw Ms. Harp on the cover of *Inc.* after she founded Vector, arranged to meet her, and the rest is history. He is divorced from his first wife, Susan Odell, an early *Computerworld* employee.

Affiliated with many organizations, McGovern is a trustee of the Massachusetts Institute of Technology (MIT) and the Whitehead Institute, and has served as

Chronology:

Patrick Joseph McGovern, Jr.

1937: Born.

1959: Graduated from MIT with a degree in biophysics.

1964: Founded International Data Corp.

1967: Began publishing *Computerworld*.

1972: Launched Japanese computer magazine *Shukan Computer*.

1972: Started employee stock plan.

1980: Established the first joint venture between a U.S. company and the People's Republic of China.

2000: Donated $350 million to MIT for the creation of the McGovern Institute for Brain Research.

2001: Sold Hungry Minds, publisher of the *For Dummies* book series.

director of the Information Industry Association, the Magazine Publishers Association, and the American Management Association. Among his numerous awards are the James Smithsonian Bicentennial Medal from the Smithsonian Institute, the Entrepreneur of the Year award from Ernst & Young, Business Publisher of the Year from *The Delaney Report*, Communicator of the Year from the New York Chapter of the Business and Professional Advertisers Association, and the Entrepreneurial Leadership Award from the MIT Enterprise Forum of Cambridge, Inc.

Born in 1937, he was raised in Philadelphia, Pennsylvania. In high school McGovern became so interested in computers that he built one, a device that could beat any human challenger at tic–tac–toe. His invention earned him both a hometown reputation and a scholarship to MIT. His studies there reflected his interest in the brain and its impact on human behavior. He majored in life sciences with a special interest in neurophysiology and the organization and function of the human nervous system. He also took computer science courses to contribute to developing computational models for the function of neural networks. After graduating with a degree in biophysics in 1959, McGovern launched his career in publishing as associate publisher of the country's first computer magazine, *Computers and Automation*.

Career Details

In 1964 Patrick McGovern attended a press conference for RCA Corp., which was launching a new type of random–access memory. He later met with the head of Univac who complained about the lack of good information on the fledgling computer market. These events prompted McGovern to establish a firm that offered an initial research project that other companies could purchase. McGovern recalled in *Forbes*, "That weekend I wrote up a proposal and sent it out to about 20 companies, not really expecting to hear anything else about it. To my amazement, within ten days I had 12 people send a check for $10,000, half–payment in advance. That was the only capital we actually ever put into the company, those initial customer deposits." International Data Corp. (IDC) was thus born that year.

IDC was initially a market research firm, collecting and selling information with the goal of providing the industry with timely and reliable statistics on information technology. It remained a market research organization for its first three years until McGovern noticed a large untapped market for computer periodicals. He wanted to call his first magazine *Computer World News*, a title derived from the existing *Medical World News*. At the last minute, however, he discovered that the name would not fit across the top of the cover. The shorter titled *Computerworld* began publication in 1967.

Five years later McGovern expanded his *Computerworld* concept by launching the magazine *Shukan Computer* in Japan. With a motto of "think globally and act locally," he strove to ensure that the Japanese magazine would not simply be an alternate language copy of its U.S. counterpart. To this aim, he hired a Japanese staff to edit and manage the publication with the goal of satisfying readers through a superior product tailored to the local market.

In 1980 McGovern continued to expand into new markets, establishing the first joint venture between a U.S. company and the People's Republic of China. As IDC grew, it was transformed into the research subsidiary of the newly formed International Data Group (IDG), which in 2001 had more than 20 million publications in China.

The larger–than–life IDG chairman is known for his long–standing commitment to a decentralized management style and a risk–taking mentality. Once, during a business meeting in Anchorage, Alaska, McGovern dressed up as Nanook of the North and rode into the meeting room on a dog sled as a way of encouraging his executives to relax and enjoy their work. According to *The Wall Street Journal*, one employee said of McGovern's cheerleading tactics that "the guy's spirit really is pervasive in this place."

His unwillingness to rule with a heavy hand allows his employees to stretch their capabilities and absorb some of his day–to–day responsibilities, freeing McGovern to steer the company in new directions. "The big advantage of that," he told *Forbes*, "is that you don't have a lot of internal staff meetings and go to a lot of internal political discussions. You can spend all your time going out and visiting customers; they'll tell you what they need."

This decentralized management style was in part responsible for one of the company's most successful ventures. When McGovern's staff presented him with the initial *For Dummies* concept, the *DOS for Dummies* title, he was far from enthusiastic about the idea, but nonetheless trusted the opinion of his editors and approved the project. The book was so successful that the company first began publishing other technology–related titles, then expanded into non–technology subjects like contracts, cats, and house–buying. One title that McGovern himself consulted was *Weddings for Dummies*. "My daughter was married recently," he told *Success*, "and I needed a little refresher." In 2001 the company sold its 75 percent stake in Hungry Minds, formerly IDG Books Worldwide, publisher of the *For Dummies* series.

IDG also has a research arm, and its event activities subsidiary produces more than 168 information technology conferences and events, including the international series of ComNet, Linuxworld Conference & Expo, and Macworld Conference & Expo.

Due to his laid–back management style and the drive to enter new markets, McGovern propelled his company to vast proportions, with a staff of more than 12,000 and a stable of some 300 publications, including *PC World* and *The Industry Standard*. Not content with merely 100 million readers, McGovern told *Success* in 2000 that he hoped to increase that number fivefold by the year 2005. When reminded that this figures amounts to half a billion, he replied, "Yes. But the world has six billion people now, and there is a real need for useful information."

Social and Economic Impact

Armed only with the knowledge that there was a serious need in the marketplace for technology and computer information, Patrick McGovern started a small company with very little money in 1964. This small market research firm grew into the International Data Group, which produces hundreds of computer publications reaching an international market. This business, along with its market research services and trade show production subsidiaries, generate over $3 billion in annual revenue. Not only did he achieve his goal of providing the information technology sector with reliable information, his *For Dummies* series and consumer computer publications also dispelled some of the fears that many people had of the burgeoning personal computer world.

In early 2000 Patrick and Lore McGovern pledged $350 million over the next twenty years to the Massachusetts Institute of Technology (MIT) for the formation of the McGovern Institute for Brain Research. At that time, this donation was the largest gift ever to a university and made the McGoverns among the most generous philanthropists in the country. The couple had decided to donate such a large portion of their fortune to brain research because their interest in brain science led to their belief that neuroscience is on the threshold of making major strides in the area of the relationship between behavior and the human mind. As quoted in *MIT News*, Charles M. Vest, president of MIT, remarked, "Creation of the McGovern Institute for Brain Research will launch one of the most profound and important scientific ventures of the next century and what surely will be a cornerstone of MIT's scientific contributions in the decades ahead."

Part of a new breed of entrepreneurs who profited from the technology boom of the late 1990s, McGovern is committed to donating a major portion of his wealth for the greater benefit of society in general. Long of the mindset that technology has the potential to improve the quality of life worldwide, McGovern has set out to make that theory reality.

Sources of Information

Contact at: International Data Group
1 Exeter Plaza, 15th Fl.
Boston, MA 02116
Business Phone: (617)534–1200
URL: http://www.idg.com

Bibliography

"About IDG." Boston, MA: International Data Group, November 2001. Available at http://idg.com.

Barlow, Saideh. "Who Will Gobble up Hungry Minds?" *Indianapolis Business Journal*, 28 May 2001, 1A.

Carroll, Paul B. "Magazine Magnate." *The Wall Street Journal, Eastern Edition*, 6 April 1987.

Contavespi, Vicki. "Tips from Winners in the Game of Wealth." *Forbes*, 22 October 1990, 32.

Dennis, Kathryn. "Above the Crowd." *MC Technology Marketing Intelligence*, October 1999, 38.

Gallagher, Paul. "On Top of the PC World." *Success*, October 2000, 16.

"The Heroes: A Portfolio." *FSB: Fortune Small Business*, October 2001, 42.

"IDG's Pat McGovern Enjoys a High–Tech Boom in China." *Management Review*, August 1995, 17.

"International Data Group." Hoover's Online, Inc., November 2001. Available at http://www.hoovers.com.

Laberis, Bill. "IT Century MVPs: Five Leaders Who Made a Difference." *Computerworld*, 6 December 1999, 32.

"A New Way of Giving." *Time*, 24 July 2000, 48.

"Patrick J. McGovern, Jr., Lore Harp McGovern Commit $350 Million to MIT to Establish Institute for Brain Research." Cambridge, MA: *MIT News*, 28 February 2000. Available at http://web.mit.edu.

"Speaker: Patrick McGovern." Boston, MA: International Data Corp., November 2001. Available at http://emea.idc.com.

Vincent Kennedy McMahon

(1945-)
World Wrestling Federation Entertainment, Inc.

Overview

Vincent McMahon transformed the World Wrestling Federation (WWF) into an international multi–media and marketing conglomerate. The WWF, in fact, has become virtually synonymous with professional wrestling. His promotion of "sports entertainment" encompasses more than just televised matches and live events. It spawned an entire industry based on magazines, videos, and action figures. The wrestlers themselves, such as Stone Cold Steve Austin and Jesse Ventura, have also transcended the sport and become mainstream entertainers, celebrities, and politicians that are known worldwide. In the process of making professional wrestling one of the most popular forms of entertainment, McMahon has established himself as both a savvy businessman and a colorful character.

Personal Life

Vincent McMahon is married to Linda, who serves as president and CEO of World Wrestling Federation Entertainment. The couple's two children, Stephanie and Shane, both work for the company as well.

McMahon was born August 24, 1945, in Pinehurst, North Carolina. His parents divorced when he was very young and he grew up in a trailer with his mother and a succession of five stepfathers, some abusive. Vince, who suffered from attention deficit disorder and dyslexia, carried his domestic problems into school, where he was expelled for fighting and drinking. Rejecting the notion of state reform school, McMahon opted to enroll in Fishburne Military School in Waynesboro, Virginia, and be-

Vince McMahon (left) and Jerry Mimnaugh holding a San Jose football jersey. (*AP Photos/Paul Sakuma.*)

came the first cadet in the history of the school to be court–martialed.

Vincent was introduced to the world of wrestling when, at the age of 12, he met his birth father, Vincent James McMahon, a well–known promoter. His family's legacy of professional wrestling extended even farther back, as his grandfather Jess was a wrestling and boxing promoter in the early 1900s. Vincent Sr. owned Capital Wrestling, a small wrestling league active in the northeastern United States during the 1940s and 1950s. Capital televised some of its wrestling events, but professional wrestling was not yet considered a mainstream sport. Yet young McMahon was so impressed after this first meeting with his father that he was determined to become a wrestler. His father, however, did not think this career would be a wise choice, and forbade him from ever entering a ring, hoping that after attending college his son would go into another line of work.

McMahon graduated with a bachelor of science degree in business administration from East Carolina State University in 1968. He told *U.S. News & World Report* that the only way he got through college was to take classes in the summer for each of the five years of his enrollment and to persuade professors to raise his grades. "Even today I can't spell," he said. He worked at various jobs, selling adding machines and paper cups, until 1971, when this headstrong man entered the family business after all.

Career Details

In 1971 Vincent McMahon became a television announcer for Capital Wrestling and oversaw the company's operations in Bangor, Maine. His success in Bangor developed into a position in New England, where he led the company to even greater prosperity. Things were going so well that McMahon's father retired and sold the company to his son in 1982. As Capital's new chairman, McMahon quickly began expanding the regional company by acquiring competing wrestling leagues throughout the country and by recruiting the opposition's talent. Until then, all wrestling concerns were territorial and operated only in certain areas of the country. Soon after, McMahon's newly formed national operation took the name World Wrestling Federation under the parent company Titan Sports Inc. McMahon's vision for a nationwide league was thus born.

McMahon began promoting the World Wrestling Federation with his now legendary techniques. He played upon the entertainment side of the sport and developed distinctive personalities for the wrestlers, complete with story lines that enhanced the competition. He was active in getting the matches televised. Showing a keen business sense, he called his new creation "sports entertainment," readily acknowledging that the matches had predetermined winners. That sort of promotion also freed the league from state regulations.

Chronology:

Vincent Kennedy McMahon

1945: Born.

1968: Graduated from East Carolina State University.

1971: Began to work for Capital Wrestling.

1982: Bought Capital Wrestling and formed the World Wrestling Federation.

1987: Staged the record–setting Wrestlemania III.

1999: World Wrestling Federation Entertainment went public.

2000: Formed the XFL football league.

2001: Acquired World Championship Wrestling.

McMahon took the concept to another level in 1984 when he launched the "Rock and Wrestling" concept, using such rock stars as Cyndi Lauper and Aretha Franklin to promote his shows. The concept increased the popularity of wrestling, and by 1985 matches were regularly aired on the major television networks. By 1987 the WWF's live matches routinely sold out large arenas and generated $80 million in ticket sales for the year. Contributing to this sales boom was Wrestlemania III, an event held at the Pontiac Silverdome in Pontiac, Michigan, and featuring the WWF star Hulk Hogan in a match against the famed Andre the Giant. The event broke the world record for indoor–audience attendance and attracted a huge pay–per–view cable television audience as well.

Growing numbers of loyal fans in the United States were attracted to McMahon's brand of sports entertainment, so he began expanding the live shows and broadcasts internationally, venturing into Australia, France, Germany, and India. The charisma and appeal of McMahon's wrestling stars themselves also fueled the popularity of professional wrestling. Hulk Hogan was the first breakout star from the federation during its rise in popularity, and the merchandising of his likeness on products ranged from action figures to lunch boxes. Other WWF celebrities soon followed suit.

McMahon's company faced new challenges in the late 1980s and early 1990s. A string of negative publicity began when a steroid investigation involved Hulk Hogan and other WWF wrestlers. McMahon was charged with conspiring to provide the wrestlers with anabolic steroids from 1985 to 1991. Hogan testified that they were encouraged to use steroids and that he had frequently used them, a fact that he had publicly denied in the past. McMahon, who pleaded innocent, admitted to using steroids before they became illegal in 1988. He was found guilty on one charge of conspiring to defraud the U.S. Food and Drug Administration, but avoided serious punishment when he was found innocent of the rest of the charges.

During WWF's trials and tribulations, Ted Turner decided to form his own wrestling federation, World Championship Wrestling (WCW). The WCW began luring away such WWF talent as Hulk Hogan, and its *Monday Nitro Live* aired opposite WWF's *Monday Night Raw*. Initially, the WCW was declared the victor, capturing the most viewers for the following year and a half. During the rest of the 1990s, however, the WWF revived, winning the majority of ratings and profits, and grossing $84 million compared to the WCW's $50 million in 1995. As of 2001, a lawsuit that McMahon had filed against Turner for theft of ideas was unresolved, but the fierce competition between the two seemed to benefit both leagues, allowing them both to enjoy unprecedented popularity.

Viewership for professional wrestling reached all–time highs in the late 1990s. During this time the persona of the wrestlers altered into something that was more arrogant and anti–establishment. Stone Cold Steve Austin, for example, was modeled after a number of serial killers. McMahon realized a childhood dream and climbed into the ring himself, inventing the character of a business tycoon bent on revenge against any wrestler who crossed him.

The World Wrestling Federation went public in October 1999, raising millions of dollars. As part of the process, Titan Sports became World Wrestling Federation Entertainment, Inc. In 1999 and 2000, such shows as *WWF Smackdown!* and *Raw* were ratings winners on cable television. Female wrestlers like Chyna began to enjoy both recognition and popularity. Other wrestling stars such as The Rock made appearances on television and in movies.

In 2000 McMahon ventured into the arena of professional football, starting a new league, the XFL. As a joint venture with NBC, the much–hyped league adopted the entertaining style of the WWF. The XFL, however, proved a disaster, and folded after only one season. This sent WWF's stock plummeting from a high of $22 in January to $10.95 as of October 2001.

McMahon faced more trouble when a British court ruled that the WWF acronym used on its Web site belonged to the World Wildlife Fund. In 2000 and 2001 McMahon was also involved in a contract dispute with DirecTV, a satellite broadcasting company, for ceasing the broadcast of WWF's pay–per–view events. Undeterred, however, Linda McMahon told *Business Week*, "We're still the strong entertainment brand we've been for 50 years."

These words do not belie the actions of the company, which continued to expand. In 2000 the WWF opened its first store, restaurant, and television studio in New York, and announced plans to unveil a line of cookbooks and children's stories. It launched its own record label, Smackdown! Records, to produce original rock and hip–hop recordings. In 2001 the company acquired both the WCW and Extreme Championship Wrestling, forming the basis for a new franchise called The Alliance. That year plans were unveiled for a live, two–hour magazine–style show called *WWF Excess*. World Wrestling Federation Entertainment's revenues jumped 20 percent to $456 million, and it was ranked third of *Business Week*'s 100 Best Small Companies.

Social and Economic Impact

Vince McMahon took professional wrestling from cult status and elevated it to pure Americana, complete with comic book–esque heroes and villains. Along the way he rode a wave of controversy all the way to the bank. Larger–than–life athletes/entertainers became so popular that they made appearances on television and in arenas, motion pictures, music videos, and toy stores across the nation and around the world. McMahon's unique contribution has been to meld entertainment and sports, creating a mixture that has attracted fans worldwide.

Sources of Information

Contact at: World Wrestling Federation Entertainment, Inc.
1241 E. Main St.
Stamford, CT 06902
Business Phone: (203)352–8600
URL: http://www.wwfecorpbiz.com

Bibliography

Anderson, Steve. "Transcending Wrestling." *Wrestling Digest*, December 2000, 46.

"Fact Sheet." World Wrestling Federation Entertainment, Inc. October 2001. Available at http://www.wwfecorpbiz.com.

"Forbes Faces: Vince McMahon." *Forbes*, 13 February 2001.

"If You Dream It, Then Do It." *Sports Trend*, October 4, 2000.

Rosellini, Lynn. "Lords of the Ring." *U.S. News & World Report*, 17 May 1999, 52.

Thompson, Clifford, ed. "Vince McMahon." *Current Biography Yearbook 1999*. New York: The H.W. Wilson Company, 1999.

"Those Smackdowns Are Taking Their Toll." *Business Week*, 3 September 2001.

Scott McNealy

(1954-)
Sun Microsystems, Inc.

Overview

The story of Scott McNealy and his company Sun Microsystems is a textbook example of Silicon Valley success. McNealy co–founded Sun Microsystems in 1982, and the company became the leading global supplier of network computing systems, generating sales of over $18 billion. Since taking the helm as CEO in 1984, McNealy has spurred the company to even greater expansion and profit. McNealy's mission is to prove the company's slogan: "The network is the computer." Sun Microsystems specializes in network computers (NCs), as opposed to personal computers (PCs), and hopes that its Java software will succeed in breaking up the near–monopoly of Microsoft's Windows operating system.

Personal Life

Scott McNealy and his wife Susan were married in 1994 and gave birth to their son, Maverick, the following year. Characterized as brash, fun–loving, and extremely energetic, McNealy enjoys creating catch phrases to explain his business philosophy ("have lunch or be lunch") and strategies ("the network is the computer"). His motto, "kick butt and have fun," sums up his general approach to work. In fact, humor is an important part of Sun's corporate culture. For example, elaborate April Fool's Day pranks have become a corporate tradition, with company engineers targeting McNealy and other executives.

Scott McNealy was born on November 13, 1954, to Marmalee and Raymond McNealy. He grew up in the

Scott McNealy at the Java Internet Business Expo. (AP/Wide World Photos.)

Detroit suburb of Bloomfield Hills with his two brothers and a sister. His father, who rose to the level of vice chairman of American Motors Corporation, often engaged his teenage son in discussions about business. He even took him golfing with Lee Iacocca, former chairman of Chrysler Corporation, Raymond McNealy's later employer.

Although Scott McNealy has an impressive educational background, he was not a model student. After attending Cranbrook Kingswood, a private preparatory school where he served as captain of the tennis team, he earned a degree in economics from Harvard University in 1976. But his initial applications to the graduate business schools at both Harvard and Stanford universities were met with rejection. Finally, McNealy was admitted to Stanford on his third try. A manufacturing major, he received his master's degree in business administration in 1980.

Career Details

While awaiting acceptance to graduate school, Scott McNealy took a job as foreman and plant scheduler for Rockwell International at a plastics facility that produced truck hoods for the company's automotive operations. Anticipating a labor strike, Rockwell officials ordered its employees to work double shifts in order to maintain pro-

duction. McNealy contracted hepatitis two months into the accelerated schedule and was hospitalized for six weeks. In the meantime, he was admitted to Stanford, prompting him to quit his job in Ohio and head for California.

McNealy's first job after receiving his MBA was at a tank manufacturing facility owned by FMC Corp. of Chicago, Illinois. He resigned from this position 10 months later, however. As he later told a reporter for *Fortune* magazine, "FMC put me on a strategy team, and I wanted to be a plant manager. I wanted to make something."

In 1981 McNealy was hired as the director of manufacturing for Onyx Systems, a minicomputer company based in San Jose, California. Assigned to improve quality control, he achieved this goal by meeting with employees, talking about the difficulties that they faced, and encouraging them to solve problems on their own. Yet he was still not quite satisfied with the way his career was unfolding. Though his passion for manufacturing had not waned, his commitment to the demands of corporate life was not as strong. In fact, as he revealed to *Industry Week*, McNealy dreamed of owning a small machine shop. "If it all worked out," he explained, "I figured my kids would run it someday and I'd get out when I was 45 or 50 years old and play golf."

McNealy's plans underwent a sudden and dramatic change, however, when a former Stanford classmate and

Chronology:
Scott McNealy

1954: Born.

1976: Received degree in economics from Harvard.

1980: Received MBA from Stanford.

1982: Co–founded Sun Microsystems, Inc.

1984: Became president of Sun Microsystems.

1984: Became CEO of Sun Microsystems.

1995: Unveiled Java computer language.

1998: Entered partnership with chipmaker Intel.

1999: Introduced StarOffice software suite.

2001: Launched Jini technology.

---

engineer named Vinod Khosla invited him to become involved in a new computer company that he planned to establish with product designer Andreas V. Bechtolsheim and programmer William N. Joy. Although he knew very little about computers, McNealy accepted his friend's offer and began work as head of manufacturing for the newly–formed company. In the end, the creation of Sun Microsystems, Inc., in 1982 catapulted McNealy to the ranks of an elite group that *Forbes* magazine dubbed "high tech's new royalty."

McNealy proved to be highly skilled at his new job, enabling the company to meet the explosive demand for its products that propelled sales from $9 million in 1983 to $39 million in 1984. Soon McNealy was also running the sales department and actively seeking funds to help the company expand. In 1984 Eastman Kodak Co. agreed to invest $20 million in the company if McNealy were promoted to president. Around the same time, Khosla left Sun and McNealy was named interim president. Within a few months the company's fortunes took off and McNealy, at the age of 30, was named Sun's CEO.

Under McNealy's leadership, Sun made its name by manufacturing computer workstations of the type traditionally favored by sophisticated users like engineers and scientists. When a network links such computers, their resources are multiplied geometrically, making them more powerful than individual personal computers or terminals served by a mainframe computer. McNealy's commitment to network computing paid off during the 1990s, as major business clients turned to the format in

increasing numbers. Among the firms Sun supplied with networks for their internal operations were Federal Express, the Gap, AT & T, Universal Card Services, and Charles Schwab.

Network computing proved to be an important Internet tool as well. In 1996, for example, some 35 percent of World Wide Web servers were Sun computers. These servers, the type of machines on which companies tend to install all of the software that run their business, proved to be more reliable, versatile, and powerful than those driven by software developed by Sun's competitors, chiefly Microsoft Corp.

Sun Microsystems created two other important products that catered to the needs of Internet users and large businesses. The first and most revolutionary one was Java, a universal computer language that enabled all networked computers to communicate with each other and share applications, regardless of which operating systems they were using. Unveiled in 1995, Java created quite a stir in the computer industry as enthusiastic programmers marveled at the notion of writing software that could flow without restriction from machine to machine along a network. Furthermore, Sun engineers demonstrated that Java mini programs, called "applets," could spice up Web pages with the ability to program motion with words and images. Java thus had the potential to generate revenue for Sun in several ways—as a licensed language, as the language used in Sun–authored programs, and as its own operating system.

Sun Microsystems was one of the first computer companies to offer network computers (NCs), disk–less machines made especially for working on the Internet. With an NC, a user's files and applications were stored at a remote location that was accessible via the Internet. A second–generation version of this machine, the Sun Ray 1 enterprise appliance, was launched in late 1996. Called a "thin client" in Silicon Valley parlance, the $800 Sun Ray was both a new era for the network computer and a return to the early age of computers. Before microprocessing chips revolutionized the desktop computer, such units didn't even possess the capability to store major software systems. The thin clients' access to the retrieval capabilities of the Internet, in fact, might someday even render the disk drive obsolete.

Some critics speculated that the Sun Rays were not likely to appeal to the average consumer. McNealy, impervious to such criticism, remained a staunch champion of this and all of his company's product introductions. He theorized that in the end, a bit of negativity only adds to the product's value. "I mean, if everybody thinks breathing is a good idea, how do you differentiate yourself in the market?" he queried in *Maclean's*. "So I want everybody to think it's a dumb idea. I do. There's plenty of time and the customers will decide, not some writer who doesn't know."

McNealy was among those excited about Sun's prospects. Others expressed a hint of caution, noting that even though Bill Gates and Microsoft lagged behind Sun in the world of networked computers, it would be dangerous to downplay the threat that they posed. "We're not going to make any money on Java, but that's all right," McNealy admitted in *OEM Magazine*. "We'll make money selling servers and desktops and network–management software. We just want the world to be free from having to write to Windows." Indeed, Sun's sales rose to over $762 million by the end of 1997.

Over the years McNealy became one of the most vocal critics of Microsoft and its business tactics, fervidly supporting the U.S. Justice Department's anti–trust suit against Bill Gates' company. "If anyone can loosen Microsoft's choke hold on the future of technology, it may well be Scott McNealy," declared *Forbes*. The head of Sun Microsystems served a number of volleys, some through legal channels, in the war against Microsoft. He voiced strong objections to Microsoft's increasing investment in telecommunications and cable companies. Many of these innovative firms, poised to earn daily fortunes with the digital revolution of the twenty–first century, were lucrative clients of Sun's. Their systems typically used Sun servers and the Solaris operating system, developed in partnership with Unix, and stood as the primary competitor to Windows 2000, formerly Windows NT.

Microsoft's purchase of stakes in such telecommunications companies as AT & T raised McNealy's ire. Other telecom giants, including Qwest, Comcast, and Nextel, were also seduced by a Microsoft investment, and some of them switched from Sun's platform to Windows NT. "The way McNealy sees it, this is all a grand strategy to kill his company," explained David Kirkpatrick in *Fortune*.

McNealy's firm was far from distressed, though. Sun's revenues continued to climb throughout 1999, and its stock performance rose likewise, jumping from $30 a share to $120 a share in the span of 12 months. The company forged a partnership with former Microsoft partner Intel to create a new chip, the Merced, for its Solaris system—a working partnership that posed a greater threat to Microsoft. Several e–commerce sites remained loyal to Sun, among them the Internet auction site eBay and bookseller Amazon.com. McNealy and his company also ventured into the software business with the acquisition of a German company and the launch of its StarOffice product. Considered a competitor to the Microsoft "Office" suite of word–processing, spreadsheet, and communications software, Sun offered free downloads of StarOffice over the Internet, and at the end of 1999 some 40,000 people were downloading the software daily.

By September 2000, when the Internet technology market peaked, Sun was valued at $210 billion, roughly 10 times its revenues and 100 times its earnings. Over the preceding 18 months, the company's revenues had climbed 60 percent to $15.7 billion, and profits had increased 150 percent to $1.9 billion. The chief reason for this explosive growth lay in the nearly exclusive use of Sun computers wherever Internet applications ran, whether in e–commerce firms, telecommunications service providers, or traditional companies.

With the rapid collapse of the Internet technology market, in particular the dot–com companies, in the early months of 2001, Sun's fortunes took a dramatic downturn. In the first three months of 2001, revenues had fallen 20 percent from the previous quarter, and profits were down 43 percent from the previous year. In response, the company's stock declined in value by about 70 percent.

Nevertheless, McNealy managed to remain optimistic in the face of the dire news. After all, Sun Microsystems had seen its fortunes rise and fall before, and it had survived through worse. In fiscal years 1989, 1992, and 1993, earnings had also declined significantly. And in 1998, before Internet sales began to take off, the company had posted only a 14 percent gain in revenues. By mid–2001 Sun was still in good shape, as it had not made any layoffs, it had a manageable inventory, and it had already cut its sales, marketing, and overhead expenses by $40 million in the first quarter of the year. At the end of fiscal 2001, Sun's sales made an impressive turnaround, up 16 percent to over $18 billion.

In 2001, after months of anticipation, Sun Microsystems launched its new Jini technology. Using the Java language as its foundation, Jini software sought to make computers and other devices as easy to use as plugging in a telephone. Sun held a press conference to announce that 35 companies, including Sony, Philips Electronics, and Hewlett–Packard, were licensing the technology, but industry insiders cautioned that it was still in its early stages.

Social and Economic Impact

With both its Java software language and the network computer (NC), Scott McNealy made a concerted effort to challenge the near–monopoly of the Windows operating system and its creator, Microsoft. McNealy was determined that his company remain poised as a competitive threat and avoid becoming merely another of Windows' many vendors. Sun's unique Solaris system and Intel partnership gave his company the ammunition necessary to fulfill McNealy's aims. Brent Schlender observed in *Fortune*, "He has forced Microsoft to rethink basic aspects of its business and play a little catch–up." For that alone, McNealy stood out in an industry that had seen its share of big names, including IBM, Apple, and Netscape, that took on Bill Gates and Microsoft and lost. It is a fate that McNealy had no intention of sharing.

After the U.S. Justice Department's announcement of an anti–trust investigation into Microsoft's business practices, Sun's corporate nemesis increasing became a target of the McNealy wit. A regular speaker at industry gatherings, McNealy gained a reputation for a vast roster of jokes that poked fun at Microsoft, Windows, and Gates himself, whom he referred to as "Billy Big Bucks." Interviewed by *Fortune* in 1997 at the height of Sun's Java launch, McNealy kidded the editors about Gates' frequent appearances on the magazine's cover, and asked what he would have to do to make it there himself. The editors responded that he should wear a Superman suit with a "Java" logo on it, to which the self–assured CEO readily agreed. "That cost me about an hour to do the shoot," McNealy told *Maclean's*. "And a little dignity, but that ain't so expensive. We got a wonderful article out of it."

Sources of Information

Contact at: Sun Microsystems, Inc.
901 San Antonio Rd.
Palo Alto, CA 94303
Business Phone: (650)960–1300
URL: http://www.sun.com

Bibliography

"The Adventures of Scott McNealy: Javaman." *Fortune*, 13 October 1997.

Hutheesing, Nikhil. "Suntel Inside." *Forbes*, 14 December 1998.

Kirkpatrick, David. "Scott McNealy's Plan to Punish Bill Gates." *Fortune*, 25 October 1999.

Laver, Ross. "The Mouth That Roared." *Maclean's*, 11 October 1999.

Miller, Michael J. "View From the Top: Interview with Scott McNealy." *PC Magazine*, 4 September 2001.

Nee, Eric. "Life after Dot–Coms." *Fortune*, 28 May 2001.

"Scott McNealy." *Silicon Valley Magazine*, 30 July 2000.

"Scott McNealy." *Time Digital Archive*, 1998.

"Scott McNealy, Chairman and CEO." Palo Alto, CA: Sun Microsystems, Inc., October 2001. Available at http://www.sun.com.

Southwick, Karen. "The War Escalates." *Forbes*, 29 November 1999.

"Sun Microsystems, Inc." Hoover's Online, Inc., November 2001. Available at http://www.hoovers.com.

"Sun Unleashes Jini." Reuters News Service, 2001.

Yang, Dori Jones. "Bill's Pain Is Sun's Big Gain." *U.S. News & World Report*, 6 December 1999.

Gary G. Michael

(1940-)
Albertson's

Overview

Gary Michael was the outgoing CEO and chairman of the board for Albertson's—the second largest grocery chain in the United States, with approximately 2,500 stores nationwide. Albertson's is considered by industry watchers to be one of the most progressive grocery chains in terms of branding its stores nationwide and trying innovative marketing to keep customers satisfied. Upon his retirement in June 2001, Michael left a legacy of innovation and dramatic growth, capped by the massive acquisition of the 780–store American Stores chain in 1999.

Personal Life

Gary G. Michael was born in 1940. He graduated from the University of Idaho in 1962 with a bachelor's degree in business. Upon graduation, he served as a First Lieutenant in the U.S. Army for two years (until 1964). When he returned from the military, Michael began his career as a staff accountant at Ernst & Ernst. Staying there only two years, Michael joined Albertson's as a staff accountant in 1966.

Michael was known for his "Team Albertson's" concept and "Service First" attitude toward customers. His tenure as CEO was characterized by first–hand involvement with store personnel and customers. Even a 1987 battle with cancer could not keep him away. He spent four days each week out in the field, visiting stores, and could recite average weekly sales volume of specific supermarkets. After biting into a $1.99 pizza at one of the stores (that allegedly tasted like cardboard) and an episode of cake frosting that stuck to the roof of his

Chronology:
Gary G. Michael

1940: Born in Laurel, Montana.

1962: Received bachelor's degree from University of Idaho.

1964: Released from military and joins Ernst & Ernst.

1966: Joined Albertson's as staff accountant.

1972: Promoted to vice–president.

1974: Promoted to senior vice–president.

1976: Named executive vice–president.

1984: Named vice–chairman and CFO.

1991: Named CEO and chairman.

2001: Retired.

mouth, Michael began serving store deli foods to Albertson's board members for quality feedback. To monitor consumer trends and opinions, he employed the use of telephone surveys, focus interviews, and one–on–one interviews to assess performance.

In addition to his responsibilities as CEO, Michael also served on the board of directors for the Boise Cascade Corporation and for Questar Inc. Michael became part of the formation of Idaho's Continental Basketball Association (ICBA) in 1996, which brought professional basketball to Idaho with the establishment of the Idaho Stampede team. He is a former chairman of the Federal Reserve Bank of San Francisco and is a member of both the Financial Executive Institute and the Food Marketing Institute. After his announcement of retirement from Albertson's in 2001, he was appointed to serve on the Harrah's Entertainment Inc. Board of Directors. Still yet, in November 2001, Michael was elected to the board of directors for the Clorox Company. It was unknown whether these new responsibilities would help or hurt the 15.6 golf handicap he carried in 1998, according to *Golf Digest*'s "Handicapping America's CEOs."

Career Details

With borrowed money, founder Joe Albertson opened his first grocery store in Boise, Idaho, in 1939.

But it was no ordinary grocery store. From the beginning, Albertson's was penned "Idaho's largest and finest food store" and that first store was 10,000 square feet in size and space, nearly eight times larger than the typical store in 1939. On hand to greet the first customers were nearly 30 employees, "a scratch bakery filling the store with the aroma of fresh baked bread, an ice cream shop offering double–dipped cones called 'Big Joe's,' fresh roasted nuts and popcorn, and an automatic donut machine serving hot pastries," according to the corporate Web site. The intent was to overwhelm customers with a totally new shopping experience. Albertson's was an instant success, reporting a first–year profit of nearly $10,000 on sales of $179,000. In the 1950s, corporate headquarters were established next to the original Boise store and, in 1959, the company went public with its first stock offering to raise capital for operations and to establish a market value for the business.

By the time Michael joined Albertson's in 1966 as a staff accountant, the company was a booming success. In 1963, it had celebrated the opening of its 100th store in Seattle, Washington. The following year, continued the corporate Web site, Albertson's celebrated its silver anniversary by acquiring a 14–store chain of markets in the Los Angeles, California, area. The average size of each store had increased to 20,000 square feet. That growth continued through the end of the 1960s, by which time the company had 200 stores operating in 9 states. At that time, the publicly traded company had sales of $420 million, some 8,500 employees, and 7,200 stockholders. It was the 38th largest merchandising firm in the country.

Michael was promoted to an assistant comptroller position in 1968 and to controller in 1971. He became a company vice–president in 1972. Also during 1972, Albertson's purchased a wholesale company in Boise—a big step toward establishing its own distribution system. The following year, a full–line facility was constructed in Brea, California, followed by a fully integrated 346,000 square foot warehouse in Salt Lake City, Utah, in 1976.

In 1974, Michael was promoted to senior vice–president. There were other major management changes during those years that would greatly impact the future of Albertson's. In 1972, founder Joe Albertson moved from president to chairman and, in 1976, Warren McCain took over as chairman and CEO. Also in 1976, Michael was named executive vice–president of the company, a position he held until 1984.

Michael was named vice–chairman and chief financial officer (CFO) of Albertson's in 1984. He also assumed the title and responsibilities of corporate development officer. As Albertson's continued to develop a name as a highly regarded supermarket chain, Michael also continued to develop a name for himself. Interviewed in 1991 by *Corporate Board* magazine, Michael promoted the advantages of having corporate headquarters for such a large company as Albertson's in such a remote location as Boise, Idaho. He told interviewers, "We like our remoteness. It allows us not to get caught up in nonproductive time where all companies follow each other closely. We're simply not influenced by surrounding companies." Later that year, Michael was named CEO of Albertson's. His total compensation package for the first full year as CEO was $2.44 million, including stock. He had been with the company 25 years at that time.

Within three years of becoming CEO, Michael was named a Bronze Award Winner on *Financial World*'s 1994 CEO of the Year list. Michael had developed a "Service First" slogan and principle that served the company well. He also had implanted a Team Albertson's concept that had enhanced his reputation as a highly efficient leader. Albertson's continued its impressive growth pattern, and in 1997 the company began testing fuel centers at store sites. Its stores continued to meet the shopping needs of customers with a mix of merchandise and services, all contained in a theatrical presentation that would be both entertaining and functional. This approach paralleled the original vision of Joe Albertson in 1939 when he strove to give shoppers a unique experience upon visiting his Boise store.

In August 1998, Michael announced the company's pending $8.3 billion purchase of American Stores Company, which owned and operated stores under the names of Acme, Jewel, and Lucky stores. Although the acquisition/merger was delayed for ten months by federal regulatory complications, it served to displace the Kroger Company as the nation's leading supermarket chain. (The displacement proved to be short–lived; Albertson's was bumped back to second place in 2001.) In any event, the deal was historic for another reason. The original founder of the American Stores Company was Samuel Skaggs. Skaggs was the person who lent Joe Albertson the money to buy his first grocery store. In 1999, sixty years later, Albertson's was buying out the entire 780–store American Stores chain. The combined assets of the two companies gave Albertson's more than 2,470 stores in 37 states. Michael cited increased competitive pressure and cost efficiencies as reasons for the merger. Albertson's also announced its expectation of a one–time, though significant, reduction in profits following the merger. Another aspect of the merger related to retail expertise. Albertson's, under Michael's stewardship, had maintained its reputation for well–managed operation of food stores. American Stores had the most experience in running free–standing drug stores, operating under the Sav–on and Osco names. Although some analysts noted that drug store operation posed a whole different set of shopping patterns and other issues, Michael dismissed such notions, telling *Associated Press* interviewers that drug stores presented an opportunity to gain a significant foothold in the health care market. The merger was also projected to save Albertson's $300 million in overhead reduction, as well as enhanced buying and distribution efficiency.

Under Michael, Albertson's pursued aggressive growth with the development of their prototype store in Florida. It had a unique look that included colorful displays, specialized dairy and pharmacy departments, and large overhead signs.

At the May 1999 shareholders' meeting, Michael announced plans for 750 new combination food/drug stores, 500 stand–alone drugstores, and 600 fuel centers to open over the subsequent 5 years. The estimated cost was projected at $11 billion. Michael also announced plans to remodel another 730 stores.

The plans proved tenuous. Whereas Albertson's basked in an 18 percent annual growth in earnings per share in the early 1990s, the growth slowed to 12 percent by 1994 and continued at that rate or less for the remainder of the decade. After the acquisition/merger with American Stores went on for ten months in 1999, Albertson's was forced to sell off 145 stores. This became the largest grocery divestiture ever required by the Federal Trade Commission. Michael suffered severe stress during this time.

In December 2000, Michael announced that he would retire in June 2001, and he began assisting the company's executive search committee in the assessment process for his replacement. His salary throughout the years had grown, but his total compensation package had reflected only modest increases over the years. Michael's retirement came at a turbulent but hopeful time when Albertson's continued to struggle with the effort to integrate the American Stores chain with its own stores. The massive undertaking was expected to be ongoing for many months to come. In April 2001, Albertson's named Lawrence R. Johnston, a senior executive of General Electric Company, as its new chairman and CEO. Johnston was Albertson's first top executive to be named from outside the company's ranks.

Social and Economic Impact

Michael's ten–year post as CEO of Albertson's was one of innovation and growth. Because of his aggressive stance on expansion, Albertson's was able to acquire the huge American Stores drug store chain, making Albertson's one of the world's largest food and drug retailers.

Sources of Information

Bibliography

"1994 CEO of the Year Bronze Award Winners." *Financial World*, 29 March 1994.

Albertson's. Available at http://www.albertsons.com.

"Albertson's, Our Heritage." Available at http://www.albertsons.12.7.179.54/corporate/oc_heritage.asp.

Barron, Kelly. "Albertson's Gets a Makeover." *Forbes,* 6 September 1999.

Brown, Matthew. "Albertson's Bags American Stores, Moves Up to No. 1." *Boulder News,* 4 August 1998.

"Forbes Super 500 Paychecks." *Forbes,* 14 May 2001.

"Gary Michael, Albertson's Chief, to Retire." *Drug Store News,* 15 January 2001.

"Gary Michael and Jan Hurley Elected to Clorox Board of Directors." *Business Wire,* 28 November 2001.

"Gary Michael Joins Harrah's Entertainment Board of Directors." *Business Wire,* 13 November 2001.

Halkias, Maria. "Albertson's Names GE Executive to Top Post." *The Dallas Morning News,* 24 April 2001.

"Handicapping America's CEOs." *Golf Digest,* June 1998.

Heenan, David A. "The Small Town: Corporate USA's New Frontier." *Corporate Board,* July/August 1991.

Longo, Don. "Looking for a CEO with a Few Basic Instincts." *Discount Store News,* 3 April 1995.

Muret, Don. "Idaho Stampede Banks on Community Suppport." *Amusement Business,* 2 September 1996.

"What 800 Companies Paid Their Bosses." *Forbes,* 25 May 1992.

White–Sax, Barbara J. "Cross–channel Giant, Albertson's, is Big on Beverages." *Beverage Aisle,* 15 February 2001.

Patricia Edenfield Mitchell

(1943-)

Public Broadcasting Service

Overview

Patricia Mitchell became the first female president and chief executive officer of the country's largest and only noncommercial broadcasting service, Public Broadcasting Service (PBS), in March 2000. Mitchell, who had worked for all three of the major commercial television networks, was recruited by the public network to inject it with a fresh perspective. She has been credited with ushering the well–respected broadcaster into a new era, focusing on attracting younger viewers and delivering relevant programming to people of all ages. Famously well–connected, Mitchell opened the door for Hollywood to bring its best, less–commercial work to PBS's table, producing new ideas, energy, and projects to supplement a lineup that featured such timeless classics as *Sesame Street* and *Masterpiece Theater*. By placing the focus on reality shows and U.S. productions over the glut of British fare and period dramas, Mitchell hoped to reinvent the channel for the new millennium.

Personal Life

Patricia Mitchell and husband Jay Addison Mitchell were married August 20, 1964, and divorced in June 1970. The couple has one child, Mark Addison. Mitchell's interests include hiking, biking, riding and reading.

She is active in several nonprofit and community organizations, and serves on the boards of the Women's Leadership Advisory Council of the Kennedy School of Government at Harvard University and Radcliffe

Patricia Mitchell. *(AP/Wide World Photos.)*

College's Schlesinger Library on the History of Women. She is a founding member and president of the environmental organization Global Green USA. She serves as a board trustee of the Sundance Institute, the Atlanta Metro YMCA, the Advisory Board of the University of California Santa Barbara School of Communications, and the High Museum in Atlanta. Mitchell's dedication to her long broadcasting career earned her several awards, including an Emmy Award for Best Host—Daytime in 1971 and another for Best Daytime Program in 1984. She also won several film festival awards for her work between 1989 and 1992.

Patricia Mitchell was born January 20, 1943, in Swainsboro, Georgia, to James Otis and Bernice Tucker Edenfield. She graduated magna cum laude with a bachelor's degree in English from the University of Georgia in 1964, and the following year obtained a master's degree in English from the same university. Mitchell embarked on a teaching career as an English instructor at her alma mater, where she worked for four years. She then held the position of English and drama instructor at Virginia Commonwealth University in 1969 and 1970. Additionally, Mitchell taught a Women in Politics course at Harvard University's Institute of Politics. A change of career followed when she moved to New York to work as a researcher and writer for *Look* magazine in 1970. For the next year, Mitchell was a speech writer for Garth Associates, also in New York.

Career Details

In 1971 Patricia Mitchell began her 30–year television career at Boston's local broadcast station WBZ–TV. She was producer of the show *Impact News Specials*, as well as host, reporter, and news anchor of a women's program. In broadcasting, Mitchell had found her calling. She stayed at the Boston station for six years before relocating to Washington, D.C. in 1977 to serve as host of a two–hour live news and interview show, *Panorama*. The show's first female host, Mitchell won an Emmy Award for her work in this role.

Patricia Mitchell's break into the major networks came in 1979, when the National Broadcasting Corporation (NBC) made her a correspondent and substitute host for Jane Pauley on the *Today Show*. She remained at NBC until 1982, and then moved first to CBS, as arts correspondent for *Sunday Morning*, and then to ABC, as reporter and producer of *Home*. Later, for Group W television, she created several nationally syndicated shows, including *Hour Magazine*, which she also hosted.

Mitchell formed a production company, Pat Mitchell Productions, in 1983. By doing so, she created for herself the freedom and opportunity to develop programming geared toward women. One such show, *Woman to Woman*, was the first all–female talk show. It became syndicated and aired on more than 100 stations, and earned Mitchell an Emmy for Best Daytime Talk program.

With three other partners, Mitchell also founded VU Productions, an independent production company based at Paramount Studios. VU Productions was active in producing a number of specials, documentaries, and reality series for broadcast and cable stations. Its noteworthy shows include *Shattered Lullabies*, which aired on Lifetime Television, and *Women in War: Voices from the Front Lines*, which aired on Arts & Entertainment Television.

In 1992 Mitchell joined TBS Inc., and was named president and executive producer of the CNN Productions and Time, Inc. Television division. She served as executive producer of *CNN Perspectives*, and also orchestrated the development of a number of lauded specials and documentaries for CNN and TBS. Among the 500 hours of programming produced under her leadership are *Cold War*, *Moon Shot*, *Dying to Tell the Story*, *A Century of Women*, *The Coming Plague*, and *National Geographic EXPLORER*. The documentaries produced during Mitchell's tenure won more than a hundred major awards, including 41 Emmys, seven Peabodys, and 35 CableACE awards. Another of Mitchell's major achievements at the company was the development of an international licensing strategy to give the programs worldwide coverage, and she forged relationships with such overseas concerns as the British Broadcasting Corporation (BBC), Canal Plus, Channel Four, and the Japan Broadcasting Corporation (NHK).

In 2000 Mitchell joined the Public Broadcasting Service (PBS) as its president and CEO. The company that

Chronology:
Patricia Edenfield Mitchell

1943: Born.

1964: Graduated magna cum laude with a bachelor's degree in English from the University of Georgia.

1965: Earned a master's degree in English.

1965: Began teaching English at the University of Georgia.

1969: Taught drama and English at Virginia Commonwealth University.

1971: Began working at WBZ–TV, a local Boston broadcast station.

1977: Host of the two–hour news and interview show *Panorama*.

1979: Correspondent and substitute host for Jane Pauley on NBC's *Today Show*.

1983: Formed Pat Mitchell Productions.

1992: Named president and executive producer of CNN Productions and Time, Inc. Television division of TBS, Inc.

2000: Named president and CEO of Public Broadcasting Service (PBS).

---

she stepped into was in dire need of resuscitation. PBS's viewership and membership were both depressed, 347 member stations were struggling under their membership dues, and the network was facing the expensive upgrade from analog to digital transmission. Mitchell realized that the key to increasing revenue was to attract more viewers, thereby multiplying the number of potential contributors.

No easy task at any time, increasing viewership while cable television loomed as an ever–growing competitor was particularly difficult. Apart from the very popular and successful *Antiques Roadshow*, the line–up at PBS hadn't changed in nearly 15 years. Mitchell, however, quickly developed programming concepts to shake the dust off of the classic PBS programming and better equip the station to compete.

To attract teen audiences, Mitchell purchased the edgy and fast–paced *American High*, a former FOX documentary series featuring teenagers coming of age in a Chicago suburb. Another teen show added to the line–up was *Senior Year*, a documentary set in a Los Angeles high school. Jumping on the "reality show" bandwagon that was sweeping other networks, PBS began work on *Public Square*, a two–hour weekly reality show focusing on politics, arts, science, history, and performance. Mitchell had high hopes for the series. "If this is done right, this will be the single biggest initiative that will really break out for public television," she said in *Current* magazine. "It will really make a statement about distinctiveness and differentiation, and our unique way of delivering value."

As well as introducing new fare, Mitchell also examined PBS's classic programming. In a controversial move, she worked to breathe new life into the beloved *Mystery!* show. This series, traditionally featuring imported, British–produced detective dramas, began incorporating U.S. versions in 2002 and will become predominantly U.S.-inspired by 2004. Of her decision, Mitchell said in *U.S. News & World Report*, "We need American drama. We need diversity; we need to take a few risks." Although some viewers were fiercely loyal to PBS's existing programming, others agreed with Mitchell that the glut of British–produced fare was a drawback for the station.

The cornerstone of Mitchell's plan to revamp PBS's prime–time schedule was the show *Life 360*, hosted by *ABC News* correspondent Michel Martin. The show featured a weekly theme that was illustrated through documentary, personal narrative, and musical formats. The series' first episode, entitled *Six Degrees of Separation*, premiered October 5, 2001. *Life 360*'s executive producer Janet Tobias told the *Los Angeles Times*, "By basing the show on themes, I think it's a blend of news, entertainment and great storytelling. I don't think that this exists on television." She added, "It's all part of Pat Mitchell's efforts to revitalize PBS, and I think there is a huge untapped audience on Fridays that we can catch."

Mitchell also intended to adopt a strategy of commercial networks by increasing the number of hours dedicated to PBS programming by its local affiliates, thereby unifying the station and promoting its series on a broader scale. She became active in recruiting shows that were more typical of HBO, ShowTime, and TNT than the traditional PBS. She also planned to develop partnerships with commercial and international broadcasters to produce a wider range of shows.

Despite Mitchell's lofty goals, public television's limited budget kept her realistic. "We can't tell Aaron Sorkin [producer of NBC's acclaimed *West Wing*] 'here's your $35 million to produce your series,' but we're working on strategic partnerships that will make it possible to produce quality shows," she explained in *Variety*. To that end, Mitchell had approached some high–profile Hollywood entertainers about developing projects for PBS.

Though her emphasis was clearly on bringing in fresh, new programming, Mitchell recognized the important assets already in PBS's stable. The network dominated the afternoon timeslots with its acclaimed educational and children's shows, such as *Arthur*, *Dragon Tales*, and *Clifford The Big Red Dog*. Mitchell's motto is, "Let's keep the best and reinvent the rest."

Social and Economic Impact

Bringing new ideas to a 30–year–old institution where tradition is entrenched was no easy task, but one that Patricia Mitchell boldly accepted. This attitude was nothing new for Mitchell, who had forged her place in the male–dominated world of broadcasting by earning respect and popularity in the leading networks and by forming her own production companies. On her path to prominence, Mitchell held positions at all levels, from host and reporter to producer and president at the three major commercial networks and in cable, producing a slew of award–winning programming along the way.

As president and CEO, Mitchell began shaking up the Public Broadcasting Service with bold and controversial moves. With her plans to give an American facelift to such classic British–produced dramas as *Mystery!*, Mitchell hoped to bring quality television back home. She also aimed to attract a new audience with groundbreaking shows like *Life 360*, *American High*, and *Senior Year*, as well as offer loyal viewers a wider variety of programming. Embracing change, along with the ability and dedication to deliver quality programming. were the twin assets of the dynamic Mitchell, dubbed by PBS station relations chief as "Our Lady of Perpetual Motion."

Sources of Information

Contact at: Public Broadcasting Service
1320 Braddock Pl.
Alexandria, VA 22314
Business Phone: (703)739–5000
URL: http://www.pbs.org

Bibliography

Barnhart, Aaron. "The Little Picture: PBS Has Big Prime–Time Plans." *Electronic Media*, 11 June 2001, 9.

Bedford, Karen Everhart. "Mitchell's First PBS Changes Move toward Airtime." *Current*, 12 March 2001. Available at http://www.current.org.

Bernstein, Paula. "Not Your Parents' PBS." *Variety*, 16 April 2001, 13.

"Pat Mitchell." Alexandria, VA: Public Broadcasting Service. March 2000. Available at http://www.pbs.org.

Soichet, Emannuelle. "A New Point of View at PBS." *Los Angeles Times*, 16 September 2001.

Szegedy–Maszak, Marianne. "Hey, Miss Marple, Meet Ms. Mitchell." *U.S. News & World Report*, 7 May 2001, 48.

Who's Who in America. New Providence, NJ: Marquis Who's Who, 2001, 3676.

Dineh Mohajer

(1972-)

Hard Candy Cosmetics

Dineh Mohajer founded Hard Candy Cosmetics, Inc., a line of cosmetics that targets teens and young adults. Starting the business with her sister and her boyfriend after receiving positive comments on a nail polish she had created to match a pair of sandals she wore shopping, Mohajer, just 22 years old at the time, suddenly found herself at the helm of a multi–million dollar business.

Personal Life

Dineh Mohajer (pronounced *mo–HA–zher*) was born on September 2, 1972 and grew up in Bloomfield Hills, Michigan, a wealthy suburb of Detroit. She has one older sister, Pooneh. Her parents, Reza and Shahnaz Mohajer, immigrated to the United States from Iran before Mohajer was born. Her father was a gynecologist specializing in cancer research, and was the first single practitioner in Michigan to offer on–premise outpatient surgical services. Mohajer observed her father's determination and how hard he worked to overcome people's suspicion of a foreigner from the Middle East. He had to convince people that in spite of his heavy accent, he was good at his job. Mohajer's mother worked as the office manager of her husband's practice. She told *Forbes*, "I never allowed my daughters to set up a lemonade stand, and my husband didn't even allow them to babysit. In Iran, where we come from, it is utterly inappropriate for teenage girls to work." But no matter, said Mohajer's mother, Dineh "wasn't into working, she was into spending money."

Chronology:
Dineh Mohajer

1972: Born.

1992: Spent a summer working for clothier Fred Segal.

1995: Started Hard Candy Cosmetics, Inc.

1998: Revenues reached close to $10 million.

1999: Sold Hard Candy to LVMH; retained position of creative director.

Mohajer's parents had high hopes for their daughters. Older sister Pooneh became an entertainment lawyer in California. With the financial ability to offer her excellent educational opportunities, Mohajer's parents enrolled her in an elite private school. Eventually, she transferred to the Interlochen Arts Academy, located in northern Michigan and famous for its fine arts program and its long list of famous alumni including actress Meredith Baxter, musician Peter Yarrow, and *60 Minutes* veteran Mike Wallace.

During her time at Interlochen, Mohajer met boyfriend Benjamin Einstein, who was also a student at the academy. Upon graduation, the two moved to Boston and enrolled in Boston University. Mohajer decided to pursue a career in medicine like her father: she planned on becoming a plastic surgeon, a decision that her father considered a mixed blessing. Although pleased with his daughter's interest in medicine, he did not feel that surgery should be performed for purely cosmetic reasons. Mohajer told *Time,* "My dad does not believe medicine should be used for high–class fashion—it puts patients at risk. But I think it's O.K. to use surgery to feel better about yourself."

After just one year in Boston, Einstein transferred to the University of Southern California and Mohajer followed suit. Lured by the beautiful weather and the beautiful people, Mohajer loved her new environment, which played well with her love of fashion. She enrolled as a pre–med student and Einstein took up his musical studies. Although she enjoyed science, Mohajer was drawn to fashion and even landed a job at the boutique of super–chic Los Angeles clothier Fred Segal during the summer of 1992. She found she had little in common with her pre–med classmates, most of whom she considered

consummate nerds. She told *USA Weekend*, "I'd think, 'Hey, wash your hair! Put on some lipstick!'"

Career Details

Early in the summer of 1995, Mohajer accidentally stumbled into a new career. She had planned to spend her break from school kicking back and taking it easy. "I had decided that summer to blow everything off and do a very unpremed–like thing and just relax before I had to go off to medical school and never have another chance to be a kid," she told *Entrepreneur.* Preparing for a day of shopping at the fashionable boutiques with her sister, Mohajer couldn't find a nail polish that matched her pale blue sandals so she decided to concoct her own. Mixing a bit of blue dye with white polish in her kitchen, she came up with the baby–blue color she wanted, painted it on, and went shopping. Dozens of passersby noticed the unique shade, and many asked where she got it. When the sales staff at Charles David became enthralled with Mohajer's polish because it was a perfect match for the upscale shoe designer's spring line, Mohajer and her sister decided they were onto something. Deciding that they could sell Mohajer's concoctions, the two sisters went to lunch, came up with a product name, developed a plan to pitch their product to local boutiques, and sketched out some basic packaging designs.

Thinking that perhaps she could make a couple hundred dollars, Mohajer returned to her kitchen and created prototypes of four shades: sky (pale blue), sunshine (yellow), mint (green), and violet (lavender). Mohajer and Einstein took the samples to Fred Segal in Santa Monica, but at first the store's owner was not overly excited about Mohajer's offbeat colors. However, a teenager, who had been dining in the adjacent cafe, wandered over to check out the polish and altered the course of Mohajer's future. She re–created the scene for *Entrepreneur.* "We were talking about how much we would sell it to [the owner] for, and how much the store would have to sell it for, and then this girl, who was, like 16 came running over and said, 'Oh my God, I love these! I have to buy these. How much are they?' We didn't know, but a salesgirl immediately said $18 a bottle. The girl's mother's eyeballs practically dropped out of her head, but the daughter was having a fit and the mother bought them.... The owner turned to me and said, "OK, bring me 200 more tomorrow.'" From that moment, Mohajer had no time to pursue her medical studies.

Although Mohajer had an eye for trendy fashions, she had absolutely no business experience. Delighted with the sale, she quickly realized that she had no plan for production, packaging, or distribution. Nonetheless, she was up for the challenge. After stopping off at beauty supply stores to purchase hundreds of bottles of white polish and then to a pigment supplier for dyes, Mohajer and Einstein drove back to Mohajer's apartment and went to work mixing. At break–neck pace, Mohajer managed to deliver the 200 bottles within two days. When the order sold out, the owner called for more; other boutiques, solicited by Einstein, also came on board. Mohajer enlisted the help of her friends to keep up with production orders. Mohajer's apartment became production central, with polish production going on in every room. As orders increased Mohajer continued to add phone lines until she had seven. At one point, Mohajer had a dozen friends producing polish from a two–bedroom guest house located behind Mohajer's apartment.

Business continued to pick up steam, and Mohajer's life was extremely hectic but manageable for a while. Then with a suddenness that astonished almost everyone, the top blew off sales. Orders skyrocketed quickly after such superstars as Alicia Silverston and Drew Barrymore started showing off Hard Candy colors. Hollywood was hooked. Pamela Lee Anderson, Tori Spelling, and Courtney Love all wore Hard Candy polish. Dennis Rodman painted his nails with Mohajer's specialty line of men's polish. By the end of the summer, Hard Candy had garnered national attention from such publications as *Seventeen*, *Vogue*, and *Elle*, and the company was producing 10,000 bottles of polish a month and bringing in gross revenues of $70,000.

Mohajer's sudden success was overwhelming, literally. Orders were coming in faster than could be filled, and Mohajer was spending every waking moment trying to keep up. Although she had an innate sense of fashion, Mohajer's self–admitted major weakness lay in her lack of business knowledge and experience. The company was growing so fast that she had no chance to learn along the way. She soon found herself over her head and sinking fast. Silvia Sansoni noted in *Forbes*, "[Mohajer] had never seen a balance sheet or a financial statement, and she kept no record of inventory, orders, sales, or invoices. Predictably, Mohajer began to lose control of distribution. Hard Candy polish started popping up on the not–too–exclusive shelves of drugstores and tattoo shops.... Making [the polish] was a groovy pastime, but having to deal with the nuts and bolts of running a real company was not for her."

The first person to come to Mohajer's rescue was her mother, who flew out to California to help. Using her experience as an office manager, she was able to organize the business, straighten out the paperwork, and establish an operational system. Pooneh was put in charge of riding herd over the daily operations. Mohajer's parents also put up $50,000 to facilitate the relocation of the company to an actual commercial site in Beverly Hills. Although Mohajer credits her mother with saving her from throwing in the towel, Mohajer slipped further and further into depression and exhaustion, eventually landing in the hospital with what was diagnosed as adrenal exhaustion. Her hospital stay became a turning point; Mohajer decided to seek outside assistance.

Knowing she needed assistance with the business end, Mohajer did not let her ego stand in the way. She

hired William Botts as Hard Candy's chief executive officer. In his early sixties, Botts had been educated as a nuclear engineer. Ending his engineering career in 1978, Botts had started a software company, which he later sold. He then worked with several start–up companies. In the midst of his experiences was assisting in the sale of Creative Nail Design, a maker of artificial nails, to Revlon for $30 million. Once on board, Botts set about quickly to clean house: he employed suppliers to streamline production cost and time, he established a sales force, and he computerized the company's bookkeeping records. While Botts put things in order, Mohajer took the opportunity to step back a bit and relax. However, she soon found herself ready to be back at the helm and released Botts in the spring of 1997. "My goal is to expand into a cutting–edge, full cosmetics company," she told *Time*. "I want to dominate." In the first step toward that reality, Hard Candy developed a line of lipsticks to complement the polish.

By 1999 Hard Candy was being distributed throughout the United States—including to Bloomingdale's, Nordstrom, and Neiman Marcus—and had expanded into Japan and France. The company had 40 employees, and annual revenues topped $10 million. On May 12, 1999 Mohajer announced that she had accepted a buyout offer from Louis Vuitton Moet Hennessy (LVMH). She explained her decision to Donald van de Mark on CNNfn's show "Entrepreneurs Only:" "Basically the business just became too much for me to handle. I mean, I just couldn't attain the potential of the business that I wanted. It just wasn't, it wasn't running the way I wanted it. And I tried for four years. I built up something that was really kind of, like, it created a brand. There was a lot of brand equity. There just was so to speak, the back office was just not up to par." After the sale, both Mohajer and Einstein retained positions within the company as creative directors.

Social and Economic Impact

Mohajer considers herself an accidental entrepreneur. She had no idea that day she mixed up a bottle of baby–blue polish that it would so radically alter her life's path. She was able to create a hip, Generation X trend–setting cosmetic line simply because she herself was a hip Gen-Xer. Mohajer expresses those generational traits in her offbeat colors, packaging, and eye–catching names. Her original four colors—sky, sunshine, lime, and violet—have been followed by such on–the–edge names as Dork, Sissy, Pimp, Pussy Cat, Porno, Trailer Trash, and Jailbait Vagas. The men's polishes bear such names as Super Man, Testosterone, and Dog. Referring to her just–for–fun specialty line for men called Candy Man, she told *PBS*, "[T]his is not about makeup. This is about fashion. It's about fun!" Names are chosen by Mojaher and Einstein, with the help of brainstorming sessions with friends. Mojaher told *Los Angeles Magazine* that she selects names for her products "based on what I interpret as cool or hip right now. It's more kitschy and funky."

Mohajer's success reflects the power of social trends. Her polish wholesales for $9 a bottle, up to three times as much as other polish distributors, and retails for $12 a bottle. Yet Mohajer can sell her product because she has developed an image that comes along with that small bottle with the cheap plastic red heart–shaped rings on the cap. She has encountered criticism for her outlandish names, considered by some to be tacky, if not offensive—especially since her target audience is 12 to 25. Some wonder how responsible it is to sell polish named Pimp and Porno to teenagers. In *Time* Mohajer explained how she responded to such accusations in the past: "I thought, 'O.K. You're taking yourself wa–a–ay too seriously.' Like, pimp is slang for cool. As in 'Oh, my God, that's so pimp!'" And she smirks at the longstanding cosmetics companies trying to keep up with trends, "Their ads are, like, 'We'll tell you what's hip.' I'm, like, 'O.K., Grandma, tell me about it!'"

Sources of Information

Contact at: Hard Candy Cosmetics
    110 N. Doheny Dr.
    Beverly Hills, CA 90211
    Business Phone: (310)275–8099
    URL: http://www.hardcandy.com

Bibliography

"Best Entrepreneurs." *Business Week*, 30 December 1997. Available at http://www.businessweek.com.

"Give Her a Hand: Dineh Mohajer Cashes in with Her Hot and Cool Hard Candy Nail Colors." *People Weekly*, 12 August 1996.

Hornblower, Margot. "A Princess of Polish." *Time*, 9 June 1997.

"LVMH Has Acquired Hard Candy, an American Cosmetics Company Targeting Teenagers." LVMH, Inc., 12 May 1999. Available at http://www.lvmh.com.

Mournian, Thomas. "The Ultimate Polish Joke." *Los Angeles Magazine*, July 1996.

"Name Game." PBS, Inc. News Hour, 2001. Available at http://www.pbs.org/newshour/infocus/fashion/namegame.html.

Sansoni, Silvia. "Fashion Renegade." *Forbes*, 10 March 1997.

Sansoni, Silvia. "Lemonade Stands." *Forbes*, 9 August 1999.

Stodder, Gayle Sato. "Dineh Mohajer and Her Partners Found Unexpected Success Right at Their Polished Fingertips."*Entrepreneur*, February 1997.

van de Mark, Donald. "Entrepreneurs Only." CNNFN, Inc., 1 July 1999.

Who's Who of American Women, 2000–2001. New Providence, NJ: Marquis Who's Who, 2000.

Zaslow, Jeffrey. "Straight Talk." *USA Weekend*, 26–28 June 1998. Available at http://www.usaweekend.com.

Gordon E. Moore

(1929-)
Intel Corporation

Overview

Gordon E. Moore helped to spawn the personal computer revolution and the ensuing rise of Silicon Valley, arguably the global center of high technology, by contributing to the invention of the silicon chip, which runs personal computers (PCs). Moore also co–founded the world's leading chipmaker, Intel Corporation, a multi–billion dollar giant that employed more than 85,000 people and controlled over 80 percent of the PC microprocessor market. His namesake in technological circles is "Moore's Law," which states that the number of transistors fitting on a silicon chip would double every year while becoming cheaper to manufacture, and which became a guiding principle for the industry. Dubbed the "reluctant entrepreneur," Moore, the nation's fifth–wealthiest man, always maintained that his intention was not to build a manufacturing empire, but that "events simply propelled him in that direction."

Personal Life

Gordon Moore lives in Woodside, California, with his wife Betty, whom he married on September 9, 1950. The couple has two sons, Kenneth and Steven. Moore is an avid fisherman, conservationist, and golfer.

Moore serves as director of Varian Associates, Gilead Sciences Inc., and Transamerica Corp. He is a Fellow of the Institute of Electrical and Electronics Engineers (IEEE), a trustee of the California Institute of Technology, and a member of the National Academy of Engineering. In 1990 he received the National Medal of

Gordon E. Moore. (*AP Photo/Ben Margot..*)

Technology from President Bush for the development of "Moore's Law." He also received the Founders Medal from the IEEE in 1997, the Founders Award from the National Academy of Engineering, the Distinguished Citizen Award from the Commonwealth Club, and numerous other awards. He is an active conservationist and is involved in Conservation International. Along with his wife, Moore contributed half of his stake in Intel Corp., valued at the time at approximately $5 billion, to create the Gordon E. and Betty I. Moore Foundation in 2000. This foundation benefits the environment, scientific research, higher education, and the San Francisco Bay Area.

Gordon Moore was born on January 3, 1929, in San Francisco. He was raised in the nearby town of Pescadero, which he described in an interview with Stanford University as a "little farm town kind of community." He moved to Redwood City at the age of 10 when his father, a deputy sheriff, was promoted. During junior high, Moore decided that he wanted to become a chemist. He attended Sequoia High School and spent his first two years of college at San Jose State where he met his wife. Moore then transferred to the University of California at Berkeley, where he received his bachelor's degree in chemistry in 1950. Four years later he received a Ph.D. in chemistry and physics from the California Institute of Technology.

Moore left his native California for a job in Baltimore, Maryland, doing basic research in the Applied Physics Laboratory at Johns Hopkins University. He was unhappy there, however, longing instead to do research that had a practical application. As he stated in an interview conducted in association with the Tech Museum of Innovation, "I guess, by inclination, I was more of an engineer than a scientist in that having some practical outcome from what I did was important. With my chemistry set, I had to get a good explosion at the end or I wasn't happy." He soon headed back to California, and in 1956 took a position as a research chemist with Shockley Semiconductor, whose founder, William Shockley, co-invented the transistor. Moore soon left the company due to differences with Shockley, but it was there that he met Robert Noyce and eight other engineers who would team up to form Fairchild Semiconductor.

Career Details

In 1957 Fairchild Semiconductor was born just south of San Francisco in the up–and–coming area later known as Silicon Valley. The enterprising Robert Noyce took the helm as president while the quiet chemist–turned–engineer Gordon Moore became head of research and development. Fairchild began manufacturing semiconductors just as computer technology was taking off around the world. A market for U.S.–made computer components grew when Russia launched the first space satellite, *Sputnik I*.

Fairchild's first big break was an order of 100 silicon transistors from the computer leader International Business Machines (IBM). The manufacturer's next boost came when Noyce invented the integrated circuit in 1959 just as one was also developed at Texas Instruments. The invention was revolutionary, making it possible for a single silicon chip to hold several electronic components, thereby reducing the number of chips needed and facilitating the design of smaller computers. Six years later Moore developed and published in *Electronics* "Moore's Law," which stated that silicon chips would double in power and complexity every year while decreasing in cost for the next 10 years. At the time the law was simply a rule of thumb, but its truth was proven throughout the industry in the years that followed. Fairchild Semiconductor grew quickly, eventually reaching $150 million in revenues, but as sales tapered off in the mid–1950s, Noyce and Moore found themselves at odds with the rest of the company.

Interference from their financial backer, Fairchild Camera & Instrument, prompted Moore, Noyce, and another employee, Andrew Grove, to leave Fairchild in 1968 when they founded Intel Corporation. The new company was initially a shoestring operation with a one–page business plan and a small warehouse as its headquarters. Noyce again took the leadership reins as Intel's CEO and Moore served as executive vice president. The contrasting personalities of the two entrepreneurs worked to Intel's advantage. Grove recalled of their differing styles in *Computer Reseller News,* "Bob [Noyce] spewed off ideas that Gordon [Moore] outlawed. Bob was more of a risk taker, and Gordon was more conservative."

Intel unveiled its first product, a bipolar memory chip, in 1969. This chip, smaller than a fingertip yet holding 4,000 transistors, became the industry standard for computers. The revolutionary product enabled the company to post a profit in 1971. That same year the entrepreneurs introduced another groundbreaking product, the first microprocessor consisting of a small computer on four chips designed to work in calculators. The invention sent Intel's stock soaring, tripling in value between 1971 and 1973. By 1973 the company's revenues exceeded $66 million; a mere six years later revenues increased nearly ten–fold to $650 million and the company's staff numbered 14,000. In 1975 as Noyce began to give up some of his responsibilities, Moore was named president and CEO.

Moore's leadership abilities were immediately tested when, that same year, Intel introduced a digital wristwatch, the Microma. The product proved a disaster, losing $15 million in the three years that it was on the market. Moore wore the watch from that point on to remind himself of the mistake, dubbing it his "$15 million watch."

Moore became chairman and CEO in 1979, and Andrew Grove was named president. Their struggling com-

Chronology:
Gordon E. Moore

1929: Born.

1950: Graduated with a bachelor's degree in chemistry from the University of California.

1954: Earned a Ph.D. in chemistry and physics from the California Institute of Technology.

1957: Co–founded Fairchild Semiconductors.

1965: Formulated "Moore's Law."

1968: Co–founded Intel Corporation.

1975: Became president and CEO of Intel.

1979: Elected chairman of Intel.

1987: Stepped down as CEO.

1997: Named chairman emeritus of Intel.

2001: Stepped down as chairman emeritus.

pany received a much–needed boost when IBM chose Intel's microprocessor for its early personal computer in 1981. Moore also sold IBM a 12 percent stake in Intel for $250 million. At the time, Intel needed to raise money and Moore was confident that IBM would not hinder the company's progress in any way. The infusion of capital was timely as Japanese chipmakers began appearing as competitors in the U.S. market. Intel's profits fell and it was forced to lay off 2,000 employees in 1986.

Realizing that Intel must streamline its focus, Moore steered the company away from memory chips and toward microprocessors. Soon Intel developed a high–powered microprocessor. Over the decades as these products became more powerful and less expensive, they were used not only in computers, but also in a variety of everyday devices, enabling them to become "smarter" and make human life easier through technology.

Moore remained CEO until 1987, when he named Grove as his successor. Noyce passed away in 1990, leaving Moore and Grove to run the company without their long–time partner. In 1997 as Moore was named chairman emeritus, Intel unveiled the powerful new Pentium II microprocessor. In 2000 the company recorded its 13th consecutive year of growth, as revenues increased by 15 percent to $33.7 billion and employees numbered 86,000. Moore resigned as chairman emeritus in May 2001 when he reached the age limit for board members.

Social and Economic Impact

Gordon Moore had a huge impact on transforming computer technology, bringing his smaller, more powerful chips to smaller, more powerful computers and into the homes of millions. The two legendary technology companies that he helped establish, Fairchild Semiconductors and, more famously, Intel Corporation, spawned a giant industry built around technology in the Silicon Valley, employing millions, and creating a new economy. Moore must be satisfied that his desire to employ his research for "practical applications" was a resounding success. Few would disagree that PCs provide a host of practical applications, allowing for the everyday use of information technology and the rise of the Internet. Moore's Law remains at work, powering computers, the Internet, cell phones, and a host of other products that continue to get better, smaller, and less expensive. The influence of Moore's theory, his companies, and his inventions has interconnected and changed the world.

Sources of Information

Bibliography

Aragon, Lawrence. "Moore Power." *The Business Journal*, January 1998, 14.

Clancy, Healther. "Gordon Moore—The Intelligence of Intel." *Computer Reseller News*, 13 November 2000.

Gillmor, Dan. "Intel Co–founder Reflects on Accomplishments." Knight–Ridder/Tribune News Service, 20 May 2001.

Gordon Moore, "Silicon Genesis: Oral Histories of Semiconductor Industry Pioneers," interview by Rob Walker, Program in History and Philosophy of Science, Stanford University, 3 March 1995.

"Gordon E. Moore." *Scientific American*, September 1997.

"Gordon E. Moore." *Scientific American*, October 1997.

Hamilton, Neil A. *American Business Leaders*. Santa Barbara, CA: ABC–CLIO, 1999, 475.

Intel Corporation. Available at http://www.intel.com.

"The Intel Economy?" *Newsweek International*, 29 January 2001, 22.

"Laying Down the Law." *Technology Review*, May 2001. Available at http://www.techreview.com.

Norr, Henry. "Moore Foundation Will Join Ranks of the Philanthropic Elite." *San Francisco Chronicle*, 22 July 2001, E1.

O'Reilly, Brian. "From Intel to the Amazon: Gordon Moore's Incredible Journey." *Fortune*, 26 April 1999, 166.

Port, Otis. "Farewell, Mr. Moore—and Thanks." *Business Week*, 30 April 2001, 42.

Who's Who in America. New Providence, NJ: Marquis Who's Who, 2001.

Rupert Murdoch

(1931-)
The News Corporation

Overview

Rupert Murdoch has been credited with single-handedly creating the concept of a modern media empire. With his chain of newspapers, a television network, holdings in book and magazine publishing, part-ownership of 20th Century-Fox, and expansion into satellite television services around the world, Murdoch has mastery over an enormous array of information providers. He created The News Corporation from a few small newspapers inherited from his father, and by the late-1990s his 30 percent share of the company was estimated at $3.9 billion, making him one of the world's richest private citizens. Politically conservative, Murdoch has been accused of wielding his power unfairly. He has been compared to the lead character in the 1930s Orson Welles film *Citizen Kane*, which, in turn, was loosely based on the career of William Randolph Hearst, considered by many as the founder of tabloid-style journalism.

Personal Life

Rupert Murdoch was born Keith Rupert Murdoch in 1931 in Melbourne, Australia. He was named for his father, Sir Keith Murdoch, an Australian newspaper magnate who had been a well–known war reporter during World War I. His mother, Elisabeth, was later honored with the title Dame of the British Empire for her welfare activism. Murdoch and his three sisters were raised in a suburb of Melbourne in a prosperous home and also spent time on the family's sheep ranch in the country. When he was 10 years old, Murdoch was enrolled in boarding

Rupert Murdoch. *(AP/Wide World Photos.)*

school, and as a young adult traveled to England to earn his college degree.

At Worcester College of Oxford University, Murdoch studied economics and political science and earned an Masters of Arts in 1953, the year after his father died. He married and had a daughter, Prudence, but by 1967 the marriage was over, and he wed Anna Torv, a Sydney newspaper reporter with whom he would have three children. The couple separated in 1998 and divorced the following year. Murdoch then married Wendi Deng, a former TV executive, in 1999. In May 2001 the two announced that they were expecting their first child.

Two of Murdoch's three adult children work for him; his second son is involved in the record industry. In 1999 Murdoch commented that the arrival of additional children would not change the succession plans for his media empire. He had described his elder son Lachlan "first among equals" among his children.

For recreation, Murdoch swims, plays tennis, and skis, and also travels frequently to keep tabs on his global empire. When not traveling, he lives in New York City and Beverly Hills and is a generous contributor to the Republican Party. Though considered one of the world's wealthiest private citizens, Murdoch shuns a lavish lifestyle in certain respects. He is known to prefer taxicabs to limousines and did not purchase a Gulfstream jet for his private use until the late 1980s. Among his luxuries, however, is a 155–foot yacht, the *Morning Glory*.

Career Details

Murdoch took his first job in journalism while still in England, when he was hired as a reporter for a newspaper in Birmingham. He then spent time at London's famed *Daily Express*, where he served under the tutelage of its equally newsworthy owner, Lord Beaverbrook, a friend of Sir Keith Murdoch. After his father's death, Murdoch inherited his holdings, including the *Adelaide News*. But when he returned to Australia in 1954, he realized that his father's empire was far smaller than the family had realized, and inheritance taxes had taken a large share. Murdoch set out to revive the *Adelaide News* as its owner and publisher, and he implemented circulation-boosting tactics that he had learned at the *Daily Express*. He is credited with bringing London's "Fleet Street" style to Australia and was known in these early days for writing some of the paper's colorful headlines himself.

In 1956 Murdoch purchased an Australian paper in Perth, and four years later he entered Australia's largest market when he acquired two lackluster Sydney papers, the *Daily Mirror* and *Sunday Mirror*. Critics of Murdoch, mostly his more conservative competitors in the field of journalism, expected him to fail. Instead, circulation rose dramatically, due in part to his operation's particularly racy style. He continued to receive criticism, but it became evident that crime and sex stories did indeed sell papers, as did such attention–grabbing headlines as "Queen Eats a Rat." In 1964 Murdoch lured some of the country's top editors and reporters away from competitors' papers to launch *The Australian*, a serious paper with an esteemed reputation.

Murdoch set his sights on England as his next conquest. In 1969, he bought the weekly *News of the World*, the best-selling newspaper in the English language, and later that year he acquired another Fleet Street staple, the *Daily Sun*. Murdoch more than doubled *Sun*'s circulation in the first year by featuring a photograph of a topless woman every day on page three. Such enticing tactics aside, the paper's characteristic melodramatic tone and excerpts from tell-all books made it the best-selling paper in Murdoch's empire. Over the next decade, the politically conservative Murdoch would use his editorial power to make this and his other papers platforms of support for the Tory Party (conservative) politics in England.

Murdoch entered the U.S. market in 1973 with the purchase of the *San Antonio Express* in Texas. The next year he launched the supermarket tabloid *Star* as a competitor for the *National Enquirer*. His most famous acquisition, however, occurred in November 1976, when he bought the *New York Post*, a bastion of liberal politics and the city's oldest newspaper, founded in 1801 by Alexander Hamilton. This purchase rocked the journalism circles.

Murdoch introduced into the *New York Post* many of the same tabloid-esque tactics that had been so successful overseas. Perhaps most famously, the paper once featured the headline "Headless Body in Topless Bar" for a 1983 crime story. Murdoch also wanted to bring his page-three pin-up concept to American readers, but his wife Anna was adamantly against it. She feared that their three children, who were living in New York City by then, would see the paper on their way to school. For a time, Murdoch himself was somewhat of an outcast in New York, and the children were even refused admission to a certain elite private school.

Murdoch's empire gained further notoriety in 1977, when he bought in a somewhat underhanded manner the New York Magazine Corporation, publisher of the *Village Voice* and the well-regarded weekly *New York*, from a onetime friend. A court case ensued, and *New York* magazine writers went on strike to protest the possibility of having Murdoch as their boss; 20 of them later quit when the deal was settled.

By this time, Murdoch's fortune and clout were enough to enable him to become owner of one of Britain's most venerable papers, the *London Times*, along with its weekly edition, the *Sunday Times*. Although Murdoch shifted the paper's focus to a more conservative slant, he allowed editors there to run stories unfavorable to the conservative government of prime minister Margaret Thatcher. On one occasion, the owner of Harrod's department store, Mohamed al Fayed, objected to a story in the *Times* about one of his homes, the former Paris abode of the Duke and Duchess of Windsor. As former editor Andrew Neil recounted in his book about the Murdoch empire, *Full Disclosure*, al Fayed threatened to cancel his advertising with the paper unless a retraction was printed. Instead, Neil rejected all further advertising from Harrod's, the paper's biggest account. Murdoch gave his blessing to the decision, citing his displeasure that al Fayed would assume that he could "be bought for 3 million pounds [Sterling]."

During the 1980s, Murdoch began focusing more energy on electronic media, and in 1983 he invested in the European satellite television market. His primary goal, however, was to launch a fourth network in the United States, and to meet one of the legal requirements to do so, he became a naturalized citizen in 1985. After purchasing a large share of the movie and television behemoth 20th Century-Fox and several local affiliate television stations, Murdoch launched the Fox Network in 1986, the first competitor to the broadcast giants ABC, NBC, and CBS since the 1950s. A decade later, Fox TV was a serious presence in broadcast television, with a string of highly-rated shows that catered to young viewers. A major coup was its successful bid to the broadcast rights for National Football League (NFL) games, including the ratings plum of the Superbowl. Making its mark on the motion picture industry as well, the company's Fox Entertainment branch boasted six of the top 10 grossing films ever made through 1999.

In 1988 Murdoch cut a $3 billion deal with media mogul Walter Annenberg to purchase several publica-

Chronology:
Rupert Murdoch

1931: Born.

1953: Earned degree from Oxford University.

1960: Bought major Australian newspaper.

1969: Became publisher of two major English tabloids.

1974: Purchased *London Times*.

1976: Bought *New York Post*.

1985: Became a naturalized citizen of the U.S.

1986: Launched Fox Television network.

1997: Bought Los Angeles Dodgers baseball team; Fox Entertainment released *Titanic*.

1998: Bought Manchester United, most popular soccer team in Britain.

1999: Announced acquisition of Healtheon/WebMD.

tions, including *TV Guide*, the best-selling magazine in the United States. By this point, The News Corporation had already acquired several other dailies in the nation's major markets, including the *Boston Herald* and *Chicago Sun-Times*. In the late 1980s Murdoch expanded into book publishing by becoming chairman of the Harper-Collins empire. Meanwhile, acquisitions of satellite broadcast services around the globe continued, and a decade later Murdoch added Asia–based Star TV and India's ZeeTV to his holdings. In 1995 he financed the launch of the conservative American magazine *The Weekly Standard*.

Murdoch flexed more media muscle in Europe in the 1990s when he acquired broadcast rights for Champions League soccer games, among the largest sports events on the continent. In 1998 he paid $1 billion for Manchester United, the most popular soccer team in Britain. Fans and former players protested by threatening to withdraw support for the team.

By the end of the 1990s, Murdoch controlled a global empire that sold media content worth more than $12 billion annually. Still, he had missed some big opportunities. Earlier in the 1990s, for example, he decided against investing in America Online. Since then, however, he has concentrated on capturing his share of cyberspace business. In Australia, News Corporation launched online career and auction sites, and in the United Kingdom it established a free Internet service provider, CurrantBun. In 1999 Murdoch paid $1 billion to acquire an American health-oriented website, Healtheon/WebMD. At the same time, the media tycoon divested himself of many of his print publications. When he sold *TV Guide* to Gemstar International Group in 1999, the deal left *The Weekly Standard* as his sole remaining magazine.

Social and Economic Impact

Rubert Murdoch's wealth has enabled him to exert influence in politics around the world. An outspoken libertarian, Murdoch has never been shy about flexing his media muscle to promote his friends and wound his foes. He once commented about a liberal administration in power in Australia, "I elected them. And incidentally I'm not too happy with them. I may remove them."

Over the years, Murdoch has faced much criticism for his competitive business practices and political conservatism and has been accused of "dumbing down" print and broadcast journalism in general. Even so, some competitors have adopted his tabloid style in order to compete with his empire.

America writer Terry Golway described Murdoch as a "media baron who is destined one day to employ a third of the world's journalists, actors, authors, editors, and scriptwriters." Some have asserted that such control in the hands of one private citizen is unfair and in the end stifles the spirit of the printed word.

During the 1980s Murdoch was an enthusiastic supporter of British prime minister Margaret Thatcher and her Tory government. One aspect of Thatcher's regime was to dismantle many of the country's socialist policies—including the weakening of Britain's powerful trade unions. The Murdoch chain became embroiled in a union squabble when a strike from 1986 to 1987 hit the printing presses at the *Times*. A decade later the high-tech printing plant was non-union, saving Murdoch's company huge labor costs.

In 1997, with the scheduled return of the British colony of Hong Kong to the Chinese government, Murdoch—hitherto a staunch anticommunist—faced criticism for giving in to the Communist leaders in Beijing. The British Broadcasting Corporation (BBC) newscasts, which reflected unfavorably on the Chinese government, were taken off Murdoch's Star TV satellite network. The following year, the News Corporation entered a deal with the *People's Daily*, China's national, party-controlled newspaper, to create an information-technology partnership that would include online services. Murdoch defended the deal as a victory for freedom. "Advances in the technology of telecommunications have proved an unambiguous threat to totalitarian regimes everywhere," a BBC report quoted him as saying.

Yet freedom of speech seemed less important to Murdoch when HarperCollins canceled its deal to pub-

lish the memoir of former Hong Kong colonial governor Christopher Patten. Critics charged that Murdoch canceled the book because Patten's accounts of his dealings with Communist leaders over the years were too critical of mainland China. The book was later published by a competitor, and the incident was considered by some to have damaged HarperCollins's credibility in the book publishing world.

In addition to his media holdings, Murdoch has also invested heavily in the sports industry. He triumphed over long-term business rival Ted Turner in 1997 when he purchased the Los Angeles Dodgers professional baseball team. Murdoch has also bought a partial interest in the New York Knicks, the New York Rangers, and Madison Square Garden. In Australia he owns an entire rugby league and in England a professional soccer team. Still energetically pursuing business at the beginning of the twenty-first century, Murdoch is poised to exploit new technologies that will expand his empire ever further.

By the latter part of 2000, there was speculation that Murdoch was hoping to use sports offerings to tempt millions of cable TV viewers to switch to satellite dishes. The News Corporation had its sights on a controlling stake in Hughes Electronics' DirecTV, the largest satellite television provider in the United States. Murdoch had already been successful in similar schemes in parts of Europe, Asia, and Latin America. But the challenge in the United States was slightly different because most customers there were already tied into the cable infrastructure. However, the number of U. S. satellite-equipped homes was expected to increase from 14.5 million in 2001 to 25 million by 2005, and DirecTV already controlled a 66-percent share of the market in 2001.

In 2001 Murdoch suffered a setback when his bid to merge Sky Global, the holding company for his digital business, with Hughes Electronics, parent company of DirecTV, failed. Such a merger would have produced a $70 billion global satellite network that could pose stiff competition to cable TV in the United States.

By 2001 Murdoch's $30 billion media empire circled the globe and included vast sections of U.S. interests, including the Fox Network, 23 TV stations, the cable networks Fox News Channel, Fox Sports Net and FX, the 20th Century Fox film studio, the *New York Post*, and book publisher HarperCollins. If completed, the DirecTV acquisition would make Murdoch the most powerful media mogul in the world.

Sources of Information

Contact at: The News Corporation
1211 Avenue of the Americas, 3rd Fl.
New York, NY 10036
Business Phone: (212)852-7000
URL: http://www.newscorp.com

Bibliography

"BBC News." British Broadcasting Corporation, 1998. Available at http://www.news.bbc.co.uk.

Burt, Tim, and James Harding. "Murdoch Strips Assets Out of Sky Global." *The Financial Times*, 20 June 2001.

Colford, Paul D. *Knight&dashRidder/Tribune Business News*, 22 June 2001.

Crainer, Stuart, and Des Dearlove. *Business the Rupert Murdoch Way: 10 Secrets of the World's Greatest Deal–Maker.* AMACOM, 1999.

"Duopolies are Good." *Worth*, October 2000.

"From Murdoch, a Health Bulletin." *Business Week*, 20 December 1999.

Harding, James, Nikki Tait, and Richard Waters. "Murdoch's Birthday Cake Without Icing." *The Financial Times*, 10 March 2001.

James, Steve. "Murdoch's Dodgers Start Era of Rupert Ball in L.A." *Detroit News*, 8 April 1998.

Kuczynski, Alex. "*TV Guide* Sold for $9.2 Billion in Stock Deal." *New York Times*, 5 October 1999.

Lefton, Terry, and Berhard Warner. "He's Got Global Game." *The Industry Standard*, 19 February 2001.

Lewis, Mark. "Murdoch Needs DirecTV to Realize His Vision." *Forbes*, 17 August 2001.

Lippman, John, and Ken Brown. "After Bid Fails, What's Next for Murdoch?" *The Wall Street Journal*, 30 October 2001, C1.

"Media Magnate Rupert Murdoch to Be Father for Fifth Time." *AsiaPulse News*, 11 May 2001.

Neil, Andrew. *Full Disclosure*.

Roberts, Johnnie L. "The Man Behind Rupert's Roll." *Newsweek*, 12 July 1999.

"Rupert Does the Cyberhustle." *Business Week*, 12 July 1999.

"Rupert Murdoch." *Time Digital Archive*, 2000.

"Rupert Murdoch Picks Sides between Money and Honesty." *Herald*, 3 March 1998.

"Rupert's Misses." *The Economist*, 3 July 1999.

Shawcross, William. "Rupert Murdoch." *Time*, 25 October 1999.

"Still Counting." *The Financial Times*, 9 March 2001.

Jacques Albert Nasser

(1947-)
Ford Motor Company

Overview

Cosmopolitan and personable, former Ford Motor Company president and chief executive officer (CEO) Jacques A. Nasser mapped his road to success in the high octane world of the number two automaker. Nasser developed his career skills as he worked his way back and forth around the world as a top executive for the car manufacturer. During the course of his 33–year career with Ford, the multi–lingual Nasser was stationed in 10 countries across six continents—a truly global career. He earned a reputation as a hard working executive, full of common sense and drive. He is credited with saving the company billions of dollars and with turning around the company's faltering operations in Australia and Europe. His career with Ford ended when a recall and gloomy economic environment clouded the company's current condition and future prospects.

Personal Life

Jacques Nasser makes his home in Bloomfield Hills, Michigan, where he lives with his wife, Jennifer, an Australian–born schoolteacher. The couple have three daughters and a son. Nasser enjoys reading books, biographies in particular, and his musical tastes run to 1960s rock–and–roll. He is a connoisseur of fine cigars and vintage cars. His automobile collection includes two prized Jaguars, an Aston–Martin, and a rare 1966 Mustang convertible fitted with a right–hand steering column, one of only 20 such cars built to this specification.

Nasser was born in 1947 in the town of Amyoun, Lebanon, located north of Beirut. During the Great De-

Jacques Nasser speaking about Ford's future. *(Archive Photos/John C. Hillery.)*

pression and World War II, his parents moved several times to a number of different countries, including the United States, in search of better economic opportunity. Ultimately they returned to Lebanon during the war, but retained their international disposition by speaking French in the home. Thus Nasser adopted French as his mother tongue, with Arabic as a second language.

Post–war economic conditions were no better than earlier in Lebanon, so in 1951, when Nasser was not quite four, the family packed their meager belongings, boarded a Greek ocean liner that was converted to a troop transport, and sailed for four weeks to Melbourne, Australia. There Nasser, his parents, and his infant brother settled into a working class neighborhood, and Nasser grew up playing tennis, squash, football, and cricket. He was an enterprising child who started a number of different businesses while still in his teens, each with his father's hearty encouragement. As time passed, Nasser became dissatisfied with private entrepreneurial pursuits, as they restricted his inner need to be involved in global commerce.

Career Details

In 1968 Jacques Nasser enrolled at the Royal Melbourne Institute of Technology and secured a job in an undergraduate training program with the Ford Motor Company in Australia. He worked as a financial analyst with Ford while pursuing a degree in business, and by

the 1980s he was in charge of Ford's finances in Latin America and Asia Pacific. In 1982 Nasser was stationed in South Africa, and in 1983 he moved to Ford's headquarters in Dearborn, Michigan.

With his international flair and global orientation, Nasser did not stay in Dearborn for long—he was clearly destined to see the rest of the world. In 1985 he saw more than he cared to see, however, when Ford sent him to Buenos Aires, Argentina, as the head of finance and planning. He had barely arrived at the Ford facility when the entire plant came under a month–long siege by a guerilla band that was protesting President Raul Alfonsin's harsh and oppressive policies toward the Argentinean workers. Nasser spent the first month of his assignment in negotiations with the government and the General Confederation of Workers, initially to secure the release of his employees who were held hostage, and ultimately to hammer out a peace agreement between the two factions.

After that first harrowing month, Nasser's Latin American sojourn was more focused and routine. By 1987 he was the head of Autolatina, a Brazilian and Argentinean finance holding company for Ford and Volkswagen. For the duration of the 1980s, Nasser worked for Ford Motor Company Europe, which was suffering under a recession. Nasser implemented drastic economic measures that included a strategy of aggressive job elimination at the European facilities. His personnel cutting tactics earned him the dubious nickname "Jac the Knife."

Chronology:
Jacques Albert Nasser

1947: Born.

1968: Joined Ford Motor as financial analyst.

1982: Stationed in South Africa.

1985: Sent to Buenos Aires as Head of Finance and Planning.

1990: Named president of Ford Australia.

1993: Promoted to Executive VP and Chairman of Ford Europe.

1994: Named Ford Motor Group VP of Product Development.

1996: Became president of Auto Operations.

1999: Named President and CEO of Ford Motor Company.

2001: William Clay Ford, Jr. is announced Nasser's successor as CEO.

Ford Motor Company transferred him back to Australia in 1990 to head Ford Australia, another enterprise in dire financial straits. Nasser, true to his track record, restored that venture to a profit–making status by the time he left Australia in January 1993. From there he headed back to Europe, where downsizing had begun during his absence. In London the situation was grim and universally described as "hemorrhaging." He worked out of Brentwood, England, as the chairman of the board of Ford of Europe for one year, restructuring the European operation for greater efficiency. In all, Nasser traveled to and worked in 10 countries during the course of his career with Ford.

Nasser proved so capable as a leader, that by 1994 Ford promoted him to group vice president for product and development. He orchestrated such cost–cutting innovations as buying out independent dealers and turning their distributorships into superstores. Additionally, he moved the Lincoln–Mercury headquarters from Michigan to Irvine, California, for a breath of "fresh air," as it was a less conservative environment.

As early as 1995 corporate observers speculated that Nasser was in line to become CEO of Ford Motor. Among his qualifications were his impeccable reputation around the world, his affinity for speeding products to market, and his ability to implement effective cost–

cutting measures. In 1996, in the wake of a restructuring at Ford, Nasser assumed a dual responsibility as Chairman of Ford of Europe and Vice President of Operations for Ford Motor Company

By July 1997 Nasser had restored Ford to profitability and sent its stock price soaring. His successful tactics included the permanent halt of production of several rear–wheel drive products over the course of the spring and summer months of 1997 Observers praised Nasser for slashing the company's operating costs by $4.3 billion during 1997 and the first six months of 1998. Key to Nasser's strategy was a program to develop Ford products with consideration for safety and the environment. Nasser's management and problem–solving abilities, combined with his personable yet sophisticated manner, led to his promotion to President and CEO of Ford Motor Company on January 1, 1999. Nasser was the youngest CEO in Ford history not to have descended from the company's founder, Henry Ford.

In an interview given in December 1999, Nasser predicted that the twenty–first century would be an "incredibly fortunate" time for all industries, but especially for the automotive industry. He foresaw vehicle communication systems—navigation systems, security systems, communication systems, e–mail—as strong growth areas for the industry, noting that there was no reason that one's office or home could not be duplicated in a car. Nasser also questioned whether there was any such thing as stability in a world that was changing so quickly. "The only thing that is predictable today is that the world is unpredictable," he opined.

The picture remained bright for Ford Motor and Nasser until August 2000, when the company issued a limited recall of the tires on its Explorer sports utility vehicle. The Firestone tires that came factory–installed on the Explorer had been found to contribute to vehicle roll–overs. By November the tires were linked to 119 deaths and more than 500 road injuries. This statistic not only expanded the recall to 6.5 million tires, it also prompted the U.S. Congress to conduct its own hearings on regulations related to vehicle safety

To Nasser's credit, Ford responded to the crisis by attempting to get the tires off the road as quickly as possible. When Firestone requested at least six weeks to replace the tires, Ford found this length of time unacceptable and turned to Goodyear, Michelin, and Continental to deliver replacements. Meanwhile, Ford closed its Explorer plant at a cost of $500 million in lost production.

The recall, however, precipitated a downward spiral for both Ford and Nasser. Ford was forced to cut its century–old ties to Firestone, and the recall of 20 million tires cost $3 billion. The cost to the company's image was immeasurable. To add to Ford's economic difficulties, a recession contributed to the loss of both market share and profitability. Ford failed to post profits for two straight quarters, and didn't foresee a return to profitability in the immediate future. As a result, Nasser and

Ford Motor parted ways by mutual agreement on October 29, 2001. The following day, the company announced that Henry Ford's 44–year–old great–grandson William Clay Ford, Jr., would succeed Jacques Nasser as CEO.

Social and Economic Impact

When Nasser took its helm in 1999, Ford Motor Company was firing on all cylinders, overflowing with cash and new products, and was hot on the heels of the world's number one automaker, General Motors. Nasser was viewed as the best and brightest executive to occupy the company's famed Glass House since Lee Iacocca. His cost–cutting tactics and effective management style propelled Ford to even greater success, and Nasser was considered a model leader.

However, Nasser fell from grace during the Firestone tire recall on the Ford Explorer. As the head of the automaker, he was held accountable for the company's financial losses and injured reputation. Ford's directors concluded that Nasser could not effectively lead the company out of its problematic condition, and he was replaced in 2001. In his wake, the company's new Chief Operating Officer Nick Scheele initiated a broad restructuring that would cut thousands of jobs and scale back manufacturing operations in an effort to offset the sluggish economy and increased competition.

Sources of Information

Bibliography

"The 50 Best CEOs." *Worth*, 2001.

Brierley, David. "Ford's Man Facing an Uphill Struggle." *The European*, 13 March 1997.

Deb, Sandipan, and Bharat Ahluwalia. "The Future Lies in Personalised Cars." *OutlookIndia.com*. 6 December 1999. Originally posted on http://www.outlook.india.

Ellis, Michael. "Ford CEO Warns of More Cost Cuts to Come." *Forbes*, 19 August 2001.

Ford Motor Company. Available at http://www.ford.com.

"Ford Motor Company." Hoover's Online, Inc., November 2001. Available at http://www.hoovers.com.

"Ford's CEO Expects Restructuring Plan in 60 Days." *Forbes*, 29 August 2001.

"Ford's Nasser Upbeat Despite Firestone Fallout." *Ward's Auto World*, December 2000.

Holstein, William J. "A Driven Man at Ford: Jacques Nasser, Possible Future CEO, Faces Tough Tests." *U.S. News & World Report*, 19 January 1998.

"It's Curtains for 'Jac the Knife.'" *The Wall Street Journal*, 31 October 2001.

"The Prince and the Pauper." *The Economist*, 19 September 1998.

Robinson, Aaron. "New CEO Has an Eye for Talent." *Automotive News*, 14 September 1998.

Robinson, Edward. "The Re–Education of Jacques Nasser." *Business 2.0*, May 2001.

Smith, David C. and Greg Gardner. "Nasser: Savior or Slasher? Why This Man Has Ford on Edge." *Ward's Auto World*, February 1997.

Truby, Mark, and Daniel Howes. "Ford's Board to Grill Nasser." *The Detroit News*, 11 July 2001.

White, Joseph B., and Norihiko Shirouzu. "A Stalled Revolution by Nasser Puts a Ford in the Driver's Seat." *The Wall Street Journal*, 31 October 2001, 1A.

Rosie O'Donnell

(1962-)
The Rosie Show,
Rosie Magazine

Overview

Dubbed "The Queen of Nice" (a term which she staunchly denies), Rosie O'Donnell is the host of a top–rated, syndicated television talk show, *The Rosie O'Donnell Show*, which has a viewing audience of nearly four million and has forever changed the face of daytime television. In April 2001 the outspoken entertainer launched the publication of her own magazine, *Rosie*, and just a few months previous to that, had released her first Christmas album—selling 500,000 copies immediately. She is a movie star, a stand–up comic, a Broadway alumna, an author and publisher, a one–person industry, and one of *Time* magazine's 25 most influential Americans. Increasingly so, she is also a political activist— which has earned her both applause and criticism. Undaunted, she has put her money where her mouth is, speaking out and contributing millions of dollars to causes she believes in and leaving the rest behind.

Personal Life

Born Roseanne O'Donnell on March 21, 1962 in Commack, Long Island, New York, she is the daughter of Edward O'Donnell, Sr. and Roseanne O'Donnell. Her father immigrated to the United States from Belfast, Northern Ireland; he was an electrical engineer who designed spy satellite cameras. Her mother, after whom she was named, encouraged her eldest daughter's penchant for telling jokes and doing imitations. She also introduced young Rosie to Broadway musicals, which she soon embraced with a passion.

O'Donnell's world changed forever on March 17, 1973 when her mother died of pancreatic and liver cancer. She was buried on her daughter's eleventh birthday. O'Donnell's father became emotionally distant from his children after his wife's death, leaving Rosie and her four siblings (two older brothers, Edward, Jr. and Daniel; one younger sister, Maureen; and one younger brother, Timothy) to fend for themselves. O'Donnell's preferred outlet for dealing with her grief was performing. At school, O'Donnell was always a cut–up. Bubbly and popular, she was the prom queen, homecoming queen, and president of her class. She also did some acting as a member of the drama society and played sports, including baseball. When she graduated in 1980, her goal was to become a Broadway actress.

Comedy, however, proved to be O'Donnell's true calling. She made her stand–up debut in 1978 at the age of 16 when, on a dare, she performed on amateur night at a Round Table restaurant in Mineola, Long Island. She was immediately enthralled by the experience and continued to perform while still attending high school. When O'Donnell appeared at Huntington's East Side Comedy Club, which later relocated to Farmingdale, New York, its manager, Richie Minervini, was smitten. He told Nancy Harrison of the *New York Times*, "She came in and went on stage, and I'll tell you what. She had talent right off the bat. She wasn't really funny but she had a charisma. She had a presence. She had a desire."

Today O'Donnell rides the waves of success as if she had always been on top. Her talk show earns her more than $25 million, giving her a second–place ranking (below Oprah; above David Letterman and Jay Leno) in *Forbes*' 2000 listing of the top 100 highest paid celebrities in the talk show business. Her success helped O'Donnell become a household name across the United States. Thereafter she began to use her immense popularity and celebrity status on behalf of many causes, including breast cancer awareness, pro–choice initiatives, AIDS benefits, and homelessness. In 1997 she founded "For All the Kids Foundation" to raise money for children's charities. She also promoted children's literacy through "Rosie's Readers" in 1999—a joint project with eToys. But her vehement anti–gun stance cost her at least one endorsement when she quit as a K–Mart spokesperson during the late 1990s after discovering that the discount chain sold guns.

The latter issue also caused her viewers some heartburn. In one highly reported incident, actor Tom Selleck appeared on her show to plug his new movie. Because he had previously filmed a commercial for the National Rifle Association (NRA), O'Donnell turned the conversation to gun control and directed her anti–NRA opinions toward him—on the air. The *Miami Herald* later quoted Selleck as saying that it was "an act of moral vanity" for O'Donnell to assume that someone who disagreed with her cared any less about the issue of gun control.

Chronology:
Rosie O'Donnell

1962: Born in Commack, NY.

1978: First stand–up comic debut at age 16.

1980: Graduated from high school.

1984: Rosie is "discovered" on television's *Star Search* competition.

1986: Television debut on *Gimme a Break*.

1992: Feature film debut in *A League of Their Own*.

1996: Launched *The Rosie O'Donnell Show*.

1999: Released her first Christmas album.

2001: Launched *Rosie* Magazine.

O'Donnell—unlike her colleagues, also revealed her political affiliation (Democrat, liberal) shortly after her show first aired and since has spent many televised minutes directing peppery put–downs toward Republicans, conservatives, New York's Rudy Giuliani, and anyone else who disagrees with her views. Regarding her activism, O'Donnell told *National Review* interviewers, "I have a responsibility as well as an opportunity to speak to millions of people on a daily basis. It's sad that celebrities' opinions are given so much weight, but they are, in the culture we live in." There are, of course, millions of Americans who would beg to differ, but O'Donnell is not concerned with demands for equal time for opposing views. "I never enter it into the equation," she went on.

Off screen, O'Donnell continues to work for the causes she supports—whether it's sponsoring the Florida gubernatorial candidacy of former Attorney General Janet Reno, serving as emcee for the Million Mom March, or fighting for national health care and national day care for children. She spends her private time between residences in Miami, Florida; Nyack, New York; Manhattan; and (until 2001) a 12–acre Greenwich, Connecticut spread, which she sold for an estimated $8 million.

The recipient of many awards—including four consecutive Emmys for her talk show and several American Comedy Award nominations, O'Donnell's serious side is directed toward child welfare advocacy. As she stated in a June 2000 *National Review* article, "I always knew that if I were in a position to have an effect on society, I would use it to benefit kids." And she has—donating literally millions of dollars to children's charities through

Rosie O'Donnell. *(Archive Photos.)*

a foundation she personally set up. O'Donnell hinted in the November 2000 issue of *Ladies' Home Journal* that she planned to quit her highly profitable *Rosie* show when her contract ran out in 2002 in order to concentrate more on her first love, facilitating the adoption of children. In 1995 O'Donnell, who had never married but very much wanted a family, decided to adopt a child. She now has four. "Being a mother is the most difficult and beautiful experience anyone can have," O'Donnell once remarked to a *People* reporter. "...I have a greater capacity to love and feel life." In 2000 O'Donnell opened the Rosie Adoptions office in New Jersey, and by the end of the year, she claimed responsibility for nearly 40 adoptions, including a son for former *Charlie's Angels* star Kate Jackson. Jackson told a *Time* magazine interviewer, "I call Rosie my son's 'angel mom,' because God used her as the conduit to bring him to me."

Career Details

Following graduation from high school, O'Donnell began touring as a stand–up comedienne. Though she loved being on the road, she also wanted to pursue her education. She spent short periods at Dickinson College and Boston University but by 1981 her college days had come to an end.

In 1984 O'Donnell received a break when she appeared on the television show *Star Search*, which fea-

tured up–and–coming talent. She won five televised competitions and made it to the finalist level before losing to another contestant. But she won about $14,000, which enabled her to move to Los Angeles. O'Donnell then struggled to make it as an actress while continuing to do stand–up comedy.

O'Donnell made her television debut in 1986 when she appeared in the final season of the situation comedy *Gimme a Break* starring Nell Carter and Joey Lawrence. After *a Break* was cancelled in 1987 O'Donnell joined the adult music video channel VH–1 as a "veejay" around 1988. When veejays were phased out a year later she stayed with the network as the host of *VH–1 Stand–Up Spotlight* beginning in 1990. For the next four years, O'Donnell produced the show and helped select the featured comedians. She returned to the television situation comedy format in 1992 as one of the stars of *Stand By Your Man*, a short–run show about two sisters who move in together when their husbands go to prison.

O'Donnell also made her feature film debut in 1992 in *A League of Their Own*. This popular comedy about an all–women's baseball league that was formed during World War II also starred Geena Davis, Tom Hanks, and Madonna. In 1993 she played the confidante of star Meg Ryan's character in *Sleepless in Seattle*. That same year, she also appeared in the buddy comedy *Another Stakeout* with Richard Dreyfuss and Emilio Estevez. O'Donnell's film career really shifted into high gear in 1994. In addition to appearing in a movie version of the classic television series *Car 54, Where Are You?* and in the film *I'll Do Anything*, she took part in a live–action version of the television cartoon *The Flintstones* in the role of Betty Rubble, Wilma Flintstone's best friend. Also in 1994, her lifelong dream came true when she made her Broadway debut as Rizzo in the musical *Grease*.

By 1995 O'Donnell had adopted her first child and decided that as a new mother, she needed a more stable working environment. She returned to television. Later that year she cut a deal for a new syndicated talk/variety show for which she would serve as both host and executive producer. Inspired by the talk shows she used to watch after school as a child such as *The Dinah Shore Show* and *The Mike Douglas Show*, she promised a fresh view and no violence.

Launched in June 1996, *The Rosie O'Donnell Show* was an immediate hit and it went on to change the face of syndicated daytime talk television. Much of its success had to do with O'Donnell herself. Critics and audiences alike found her engagingly ordinary. She freely admitted her love of junk food, displayed an encyclopedic knowledge of television and popular culture, and worshipped celebrities (especially actor Tom Cruise) as any fan would. Writing of her appeal, Betsey Sharkey of *Mediaweek* observed, "O'Donnell's essential charm is her kick–off–your–shoes–and–stay–awhile sensibility. [She] is a master at making everyday life a laughing matter."

O'Donnell also used her success to promote interest in the theater. She often featured performers from Broadway musicals on her show, for example. She hosted the Tony Awards on CBS–TV in 1997 and again in 1998 and gave a tremendous boost to the program's typically anemic ratings. O'Donnell also presided over the Grammy Awards (which honor those in the recording industry) in 1999 and 2000.

Despite her many personal and professional responsibilities, O'Donnell still managed to find a little time to devote to films. In 1998 she played a nun in *Wide Awake*, and in 1999 she provided a voice for the animated feature *Tarzan*. In mid–2001 there were rumors that she was looking into the syndicated version of *Who Wants to Be a Millionaire?* "I don't have any illusions that people aren't going to get sick of me," she told Paula Span of the *Washington Post*. "I know it's going to happen." Until then, she doesn't appear to be losing any sleep over it.

Social and Economic Impact

For many, Rosie O'Donnell introduced a refreshing change to daytime television—avoiding sex, violence, backstabbing, and condescension. Although she since has promoted her own political, opinionated, and often esoteric agenda, she has remained "the girl next door," whom many viewers can identify with even if they do not share her opinions. The approachable, loveable persona she has developed keeps her in demand, in the spotlight, and of-

ten in hot water. But for those whose causes find kinship in O'Donnell's own agenda, they could not have a better, more loyal, or generous friend.

Sources of Information

Contact at: The Rosie Show, *Rosie* Magazine
   30 Rockefeller Plaza, Suite 800E.
   New York, NY 10112–0002
   URL: http://rosieo.warnerbros.com/pages/rosieo/home.jsp

Bibliography

"AP Top News at 10 p.m. EDT." *Associated Press Online*, 19 May 2000.

Ault, Susanne. "Rosie's lifeline?" *Broadcasting & Cable*, 4 June 2001.

Johnson, Tricia. "Gimme Shelter." *Entertainment Weekly*, 17 August 2001.

"Not–so–Rosie Times for Women's Mags." *U.S. News & World Report*, 18 June 2001.

"People in the News." *The Miami Herald*, 20 May 1999.

"Rosie O'Donnell, Political Activist—A celebrity and her platform." *National Review*, 10 June 2000.

"Talking Heads." *Forbes*, 20 March 2000.

Tyrangiel, Josh. "People: Father Flanagan Meets Mia Farrow." *Time*, 16 October 2000.

Pierre M. Omidyar

(1967-)
eBay Inc.

Pierre Omidyar (pronounced oh–MID–ee–ar) created eBay Inc., the world's first and largest person–to–person online auction website, in 1995 as a way for his girlfriend Pamela to connect with fellow Pez candy dispenser collectors and traders. The company, which boasted the largest number of traders online and was the web's most popular shopping site, made Omidyar a billionaire in the process. eBay evolved from a black–and–white Internet start–up to a community of individuals and businesses forming the largest online marketplace in the world.

Personal Life

Pierre Omidyar married Pamela in a private ceremony at the Bellagio Hotel in Las Vegas in February 1999. He presented his new bride with an extremely rare Pez bride and groom set that he found on eBay, which was his favorite purchase from the auction site he founded. The couple lives in Las Vegas, Nevada. Omidyar enjoys racquetball, backgammon, and reading, and was awarded the Ernst & Young's Entrepreneur of the Year award in 1999.

Pierre and Pamela established The Omidyar Foundation, designed for a new style of philanthropy dubbed venture philanthropy. The foundation benefited a small number of causes that followed solid business plans and met certain criteria, including earning enough to sustain the nonprofit side of their work. The couple planned to eventually donate most of their $3.75 billion fortune to the foundation.

Omidyar was born June 21, 1967 in Paris, France. His parents were Iranian nationals who moved to Paris

Pierre M. Omidyar with Meg Whitman. *(AP/Wide World Photos.)*

to attend school in their teens. When Pierre was six, the family moved from France to Maryland when his father began a residency there at John University Medical Center. Omidyar, who had become a naturalized American citizen, discovered his passion for technology at an early age, sneaking out of gym class in high school to play on a computer. At age 14, the school library hired him, paying him $6 an hour to write a program to print catalogue cards. "I was the typical nerd or geek," Omidyar told *Time.* "I forget which one is the good one now."

In 1988 he received his bachelor's degree in computer science from Tufts University in Medford Massachusetts, where he met his wife. After graduating he landed a position as a software developer at Claris, a subsidiary of Apple Computer Inc., where he wrote the Mac-Draw application. His next move was to become an engineer for General Magic, Inc., an innovative Silicon Valley maker of interactive, online software.

Omidyar tasted entrepreneurial success in 1991 when he and three friends founded Ink Development Corp. Later renamed eShop Inc., the company was one of the early pioneers of online shopping. In 1996 the partners sold the venture to Microsoft Corp.

Career Details

During a casual dinner conversation with his girlfriend Pamela, Omidyar learned that she was having trouble finding and trading with other Pez collectors, and thought it would be a great idea to be able to do that online. Omidyar realized that collectors needed a central location to get together to trade and chat about their hobbies. He was still a General Magic employee when he launched Auction Web, an online person–to–person trading website, on Labor Day 1995. Omidyar later renamed the site eBay, short for "electronic Bay" in honor of his San Francisco Bay area home. The basic, black–and–white website was free to use. Omidyar, who viewed the early venture as simply a hobby, didn't even draw a salary at the time. Publicized largely through word of mouth, the business quickly caught on and in 1996 his Internet service provider, Best Internet, informed him that he needed to upgrade his $30–a–month system due to heavy traffic. Omidyar quit his day job that year to devote himself to eBay's burgeoning business full–time.

The site was easy to use: sellers and buyers came together to trade a wide variety of items from antiques to collectibles. Omidyar settled on the auction format as a way of creating an efficient market. He told *Visions,* "A great example was a man that was selling a daguerreotype [a photograph made by an early type of process] he had in his possession; I think he was asking about $450 for it. He wasn't aware of the true market value. The thing ended up selling for $9,000. If he had just offered it for sale at $500, he would have sold it at that price. The auction really created an official market for him in this case."

The auction process was fairly simple. After registering, sellers placed an item up for auction for a specific

Chronology:

Pierre M. Omidyar

1967: Born.

1988: Graduated from with a bachelor's degree in computer science.

1991: Founded Ink Development, later sold to Microsoft.

1995: Founded Auction Web, later renamed eBay.

1996: The company incorporated as eBay Inc.

1997: Three million items sold on eBay.

1998: eBay went public.

1998: Meg Whitman named president and CEO of eBay.

2001: eBay had 34 million registered users and 8,000 merchandise categories.

---

length of time, from three to 14 days. They could also set a minimum bid, or reserve price. Interested buyers confidentially input the maximum amount that they were willing to pay for the item. eBay automatically bid on their behalf, as well as that of competing buyers, until their maximum was reached. If a bidder was outbid and the auction's time had not lapsed, eBay allowed them to enter a new, higher maximum offer. At the conclusion of a successful transaction, the seller and buyer were given each other's e–mail addresses to arrange for payment and shipping of the item. Afterward, both buyer and seller were invited to provide feedback on the other. Omidyar implemented this feedback system as a way to build trust among participants and to weed out any dishonest or unreliable users.

In time, eBay's users suggested charging small fees for placing an item for sale to keep people from posting items with little value. Omidyar concurred and in February 1996 eBay began charging sellers a placement fee, starting at 25 cents, as well as a percentage of the item's closing price. The fee system also served to make the company profitable.

eBay was incorporated in May 1996. At the time its staff consisted of only Omidyar and Chris Agarpao, a part–time employee. Later that year Omidyar, who was still running the business out of his home, recruited Jeff Skoll to serve as vice president of strategic planning and analysis. It was Skoll who formulated the company's first business plan. Omidyar, meanwhile, focused on educating himself about the evolution of the website he created—who was buying what and what people wanted.

In 1996 the company moved its operations to Skoll's home and then to a temporary office in Sunnyvale before settling in San Jose, California. One year later, the volume of e–mail that the three employees were getting became unmanageable, so Omidyar hired approximately one dozen customer support personnel. In mid–1997 eBay held nearly 800,000 auctions a day. By late 1997 more than 3 million items had been sold, valuing $94 million, and generating $5.7 million in revenue for eBay.

Skoll and Omidyar realized that the company needed more direction than they could provide so they turned to the venture capital firm Benchmark Capital. After receiving a $5 million investment from Benchmark, they immediately began searching for a CEO that could provide eBay the leadership that it required. They set their sights on Meg Whitman, general manager of the pre–school division at Hasbro Inc. Whitman was skeptical about leaving the toy giant to join the small upstart, but after meeting with Omidyar and realizing eBay's potential, she accepted the position in 1998.

eBay went public in September 1998 with an initial offering price of $18 per share that climbed to $47.38 by the end of the first day of trading. With all its success, though, eBay was not without its problems. The ever–expanding list of registered users and items for auction left eBay scrambling to update its technology and outages were frequent. Omidyar handed the company's day–to–day responsibilities to Whitman in order to pursue outside interests, particularly philanthropy.

eBay constantly endeavored to improve its site. Its roster of merchandise categories and sub–categories expanded frequently. For example, the addition of eBay Motors, an automobile category, was a major success for the company. It added new features, like the popular "Buy it Now" option that enabled bidders to buy an item for a set price without waiting for the auction to end. It also added chat rooms and bulletin boards to help users connect with each other and talk about their hobbies, interests, or what they were looking to buy next. The company also expanded into new ventures, acquiring the auction house Butterfields and launching a fixed–price shopping site called Half.com.

According to Media Metrix's September 2000 results, people spent more time on eBay than on any other website. In 2001 eBay boasted more than 8,000 categories of items with 34 million registered users. It also had country–specific sites in Austria, Australia, Canada, France, Germany, Ireland, Italy, Japan, Korea, New Zealand, Switzerland, and the United Kingdom.

Ironically, Omidyar was originally drawn to the Internet for its anti–establishment values and noncommercialism. He was opposed to the idea of becoming yet another corporation pushing products that people didn't necessarily need. "I really wanted to give the individual the power to be a producer as well," he told *Time*. Omidyar also spoke to *Time* about the morals he learned growing up. "My mother always taught me to treat other people the way I want to be treated and to have respect for other people. Those are just good basic values to have in a crowded world." Omidyar incorporated these values into the company he founded, since the eBay experience is wholly dependent on how the users interact with each other. His motto: "Empowering people and helping them be the best they can be."

Social and Economic Impact

What began as a hobby for Pierre Omidyar, who was looking for an interesting way to please his girlfriend and to dabble in cyberspace, spawned one of the Internet's most successful companies, surviving in an environment where many failed in the dot–com downturn. eBay was the first person–to–person trading site and enabled millions of users to create a unique marketplace for themselves. The website evolved with the various needs of its community, adding more categories as new interests emerged and old ones became crowded, and empowering people in the process. The most popular shopping site on the web, eBay's growth prospects remained strong. *Business 2.0* quoted the soft–spoken, modest Omidyar as he addressed a group of Pez collectors: "What eBay is today is what you've built. What eBay will be tomorrow is what you'll create."

Sources of Information

Contact at: eBay Inc.
 2145 Hamilton Ave.
 San Jose, CA 95125
 Business Phone: (408)588–7400
 URL: http://www.ebay.com

Bibliography

Cohen, Adam. "Coffee with Pierre." *Time*, 27 December 1999.

Cohen, Adam. "Creating a Web Community Made Him Singularly Rich." *Time*, 27 December 1999, 78.

Hardy, Quentin. "The Radical Philanthropist." *Forbes*, 1 May 2000.

Kavanaugh–Brown, Justine. "Going Once...Going Twice..." *Visions*, February 1999. Available at http://www.govtech.net/magazine/visions.

Moran, Susan. "The Candyman." *Business 2.0*, June 1999.

"Pierre Omidyar." *1st Person*, Available at http://www.tbwt.com.

Swisher, Kara. "EBay Founder is Bidding on a Sense of Community." *The Wall Street Journal*, 29 October 2001.

Paul Orfalea

(1947-)
Kinko's, Inc.

In 1970 Paul Orfalea opened his first copy center in a small store near the campus of the University of California at Santa Barbara and put his nickname on the door: Kinko's. Over the past 30 years one store has grown to over 1,000, and Orfalea has gone from being a near dropout due to his severe dyslexia to a highly successful, if somewhat eccentric, businessman. Kinko's stores function as temporary, high–tech offices for the creative, the self–employed, and small businesses—offering a wide range of copying services, high quality laser printing, and document management. Kinko's also rents computer time and offers e–mail, faxing, teleconferencing, and other services.

Personal Life

Paul Orfalea (pronounced Or–fa–la) was born in 1948 to Lebanese parents who owned and operated a factory in the garment district of Los Angeles. Orfalea's childhood experience was plagued by his inability to learn to read. As a second–grade student in a Catholic school classroom, Orfalea could not recite the alphabet. "We were supposed to learn to read prayers and match letter blocks to the letters in the prayers," Orfalea told author Jill Lauren (*20 True Stories About People with LD*). "By April or May I still don't know the alphabet and couldn't read. I memorized the prayers so the nun thought I was reading. Finally she figured out that I didn't even know my alphabet, and I can remember her expression of total shock that I had gotten all the way through the second grade without her knowing this."

Orfalea's parents paid his brother and sister $50 to teach their brother the alphabet but the project failed and so did Orfalea. He flunked second grade; when he repeated the grade the following year he still was not able to master the alphabet or learn to read.

After that experience Orfalea's mother began a mission to discover the source of her son's learning disability. She took Orfalea to numerous clinics and colleges for testing. The resulting diagnoses were varied. For two years Orfalea worked with an eye doctor who, believing Orfalea's problem stemmed from bad eye muscles, coached Orfalea through eye exercises. A speech teacher suggested that Orfalea had a lazy tongue. He spent his vacations in summer school. During the school year he found himself assigned to a variety of special groups and spent the third grade in the class reserved for mentally handicapped students. According to Orfalea, in the third grade, the only word he could identify was *the*. He would follow group reading sessions by making the jumps on the page from one *the* to the next.

Finally Orfalea's mother found a highly respected remedial reading teacher who was the first to understand and diagnose Orfalea's dyslexia. "Back then," Orfalea told *Wired.com*, "they didn't even have a word for 'dyslexia.'" Despite finding the correct source of Orfalea's difficulties, his school performance did not improve. In constant trouble for his rebellious attitude and poor performance, Orfalea was expelled from a succession of high schools and failed the ninth grade. He did, however, begin to adjust to his situation. "By the time I was 15 or 16," he told Lauren, "I could get by in a class with reading. But I could never spell. I was a woodshop major in high school, and my typical report card was two *C*'s, three *D*'s, and an *F*. I just got used to it." Still, he has painful memories. For example, according to *People Weekly*, Orfalea recalled a school administrator telling his mother, "Maybe he could enroll in a good trade school and learn to lay carpet." After quitting his after–school job at his father's factory because someone had commented on his inability to read, Orfalea began earning money by painting addresses on curbs.

Orfalae eventually made it through high school with a low–D average, graduating eighth from the bottom in his class of 1,500 "To be honest," Orfalea confided to Lauren, "I don't even know how seven people got below me." Fearing that he was unemployable and might end up drafted into the Vietnam conflict, Orfalea enrolled in a junior college. The following year, thanks to his parents' financial ability to pay the tuition, he became a student at the University of Southern California. He majored in finance but never took his studies very seriously as his dyslexia kept him from ever completely mastering the written word. According to *Forbes*, Orfalea reminisced about his first college philosophy class: "I said, 'God, I don't understand any of that.' I put my pen down and said, 'I'm never going to make it in this world'." Not all his experiences were bad. A professor of an investment strategies course, once he learned of Orfalea's learning

Paul Orfalea. (AP/Wide World Photos.)

disability and stopped taking note of Orfalea's continuous spelling errors, realized that the content of Orfalea's paper was close to brilliant. It was a shining moment in a lackluster academic performance that consisted primarily of taking classes from professors known to be easy graders.

While he attended college Orfalea made extra money by operating a roadside vegetable stand near his parents' home. Even though Orfalea continued to perform poorly in school, he had a natural interest in business and was infatuated with current affairs, often discussing events with his parents. He learned about business from Donald Gogel, a stockbroker and friend of the family. Occasionally, Orfalea would skip school and

Chronology:
Paul Orfalea

1948: Born.

1970: Opened first Kinko's.

1972: Opened second Kinko's.

1979: Kinko's branches totaled 80, covering 28 states.

1989: At the end of the year, 420 branches existed.

1994: Teleconferencing capabilities added to 150 branches.

1995: Kinkonet is launched, providing electronic document transfer.

1996: Kinko's was featured by Jay Leno.

1997: Kinko's was featured on David Letterman; sold 30 percent interest in the company to an investment firm.

2000: Stepped down as chair, took on title of chairperson emeritus; kinkos.com is launched.

2001: More than 1,100 Kinko's branches, located in nine countries, were in operation.

California's Marshall School of Business. In 2001 Orfalea committed $8.5 million over the next 10 years to the child development program at the City Community College of San Francisco (CCSF). According to a CCSF press release, Orfalea, who is dedicated to improving the nation's childcare services, noted, "Our passion is to support the best in child development centers and early childhood education in California. We want to help City College become a model for child care in America."

Career Details

In the late 1960s, Orfalea moved to Santa Barbara and commuted back to Los Angeles until he eventually completed his degree in 1971. Although he paid little attention to his college classes, he did find the inspiration for his future business: a copy machine in the university library. "I saw it and I thought, 'This is a cool machine'," Orfalea told *Forbes*. "I had taken a marketing course and studied product life cycles, and I just thought, 'This thing here is going to go for a long time.'" In 1970 with a loan of $5,000 from the Isla Vista branch of the Bank of America near the campus of the University of California Santa Barbara campus (recently rebuilt after being burned down by protesters in the 1960s), Orfalea leased a one hundred–square–foot garage at the back of a taco stand located on the main road through campus. According to "Our Humble Beginning" found at the Kinko's Web site (http://www.kinkos.com), Orfalea cut a hole in the wall connecting to the taco stand so he could order lunch without leaving his shop. He decided to name his business Kinko's, using his nickname given him because of his curly red hair.

Orfalea leased a Xerox 2400 photocopier, an AB Dick 360 printing press, and a film–processing machine, not sure which machine would attract the most people. Years later Orfalea told *Fortune*, "Back then I didn't know if the business would become a photo store, a stationery store, or a copy center." It was soon clear that the copy machine was hands–down the most popular machine. To make Kinko's even more attractive to students, Orfalea charged 4 cents per copy, undercutting the university library, which charged 10 cents a page. Before long the place was so busy that on some days Orfalea had to wheel the copy machine out onto the sidewalk to make room for all the customers. He also stocked a supply of pens, highlighters, and notebooks that he displayed on the sidewalk so students on their way to classes would stop to make purchases.

Orfalea developed his business and management philosophy, consistent throughout his career, very early in the life of his company. Because he couldn't read well, from the start Orfalea acknowledged that both business documents and the machines themselves could be better run by other people. He knew that he would have to rely on others to help his business succeed: delegation would

show up at Gogel's office where Gogel would tutor the youth on various aspects of business, stocks, and investing. Well before Orfalea graduated from college with a *C* average, he had decided that he would go into business for himself. Because he figured no one would hire him, Orfalea figured he'd have to be his own boss. He was also heavily influenced by his parents who were self–employed, as were many of their family friends. He attributes much of his success in life to his parents, who were always supportive and never demeaning. As *People Weekly* noted: "What saved a curly–haired boy nicknamed Kinko from despair was his own cockiness and a mother and father who refused to accept his teachers' insistence that their son was as dumb as a stone." "Without my parents," Orfalea said, "I'd be a skid row bum right now." Referring to the amount of money spent on tutors throughout Orfalea's school days, his parents joke that they've spent $50 for every word their son has ever read.

Orfalea is married to wife Natalie; the couple have two children. In an effort to assist other young people interested in business, Orfalea has endowed the Kinko's Chair in Entrepreneurship at the University of Southern

be a requirement. According to Rhonda Abrams, author of *Wear Clean Underwear: Business Wisdom from Mom*, Orfalea referred to his dyslexia as an advantage rather than a disadvantage. "Do you think I've got the motto 'I can do it better than you can'?" asked Orfalea. "No, my motto is, 'Anybody else can do it better...'. It's other people's precious hands that build my business.... Because of my advantage in life, where I couldn't read and had no mechanical ability, I always defined my job in the business as one where things had to run beautifully without me."

Staffing his small shop with his hippie friends who agreed to work for a cut of the take rather than a salary, Orfalea spent his days making copies and his nights hawking pens and notebooks through the girls' dormitory. "I had nothing else to do," he told *Wired.com*, "and I wanted to meet girls anyway." As Kinko's popularity and business grew, Orfalea commissioned his partners to expand into new territories. Dennis Itule, Orfalea's cousin, established a Kinko's in Van Nuys, California. His friends followed suit, and new Kinko's locations began to spring up in college towns around the nation.

In 1975 there were 24 Kinko's storefronts; by 1979 that number had grown to 80, covering 28 states. A decade later, 420 stores were in operation, and at the end of 2000 Kinko's had grown into an international chain totaling more than 1,100 stores covering North America, Asia, Australia, and Europe. Orfalea, twice a flunky, was running a $1 billion–a–year business and had a net worth of a quarter of a billion dollars. Thirty years after opening the first store, Kinko's was making 16 billion copies annually.

Until 1997 all Kinko's stores were privately owned by individuals or partners. Orfalea only owned one store outright, which served as the parent organization for the entire chain. Rather than selling franchises, Orfalea retained a financial interest in every individual store, which operated as a corporation. By 1997 Kinko's had grown into a 128 corporate relationship, including joint ventures, small companies, and partnerships. To consolidate control and streamline the cumbersome system, Orfalea sold one third of Kinko's to New York investment firm Clayton, Dubillier & Rice for $214 million, who helped reorganize the company under one corporate umbrella, with Orfalea and other owners holding the remaining equity (with Orfalea retaining 34 percent share). Although he has considered taking his company public, it remains a privately held firm. Under the terms of the restructuring a chief executive officer was hired, and Orfalea ceased to take as active a role in daily operations. In 2000 he stepped down as chairman and assumed the role of chairman emeritus, although he prefers the title "chief wanderer," referring to his ongoing visits to Kinko's stores worldwide to keep in touch with his coworkers (never called employees—Orfalea believes it sounds demeaning) and customers.

Social and Economic Impact

With over 24,000 employees throughout nine countries, Orfalea believes strongly that a manager's job is to serve the workers in the field so that they are enabled to serve the customers. For this reason, coworkers can buy stock in the company. Orfalea told *Sales and Marketing Management*, "It's the fundamental right of workers in America to have the ability to own a piece of where they work." Referring to his employee–friendly stance, he continued, "I think it's responsible citizenship; it's just the right way to treat people. You must take care of your precious assets. You take care of them, they'll take care of you." As for other hopeful entrepreneurs, Orfalea's advice is simple: play to your strengths and turn your disadvantages into advantages. As he told *Business Week*, "Keep your nose to the window long enough, and they are going to let you in."

Kinko's has grown into a lot more than a copy center. Kinko's now offers Internet access, computer access, a wide range of specialized copying, collating, and binding services, e–mail access, and laser printing. Kinko's prides itself on staffing its centers with well–trained, skilled workers who can offer top quality customer service. In 1995 Kinkonet was launched as a platform for the electronic transfer of documents. In 1996 video teleconferencing services were added to 150 sites. In 2000 Kinko's added Kinkos.com, which offers services over the Internet. Large or small orders can be placed via the Internet, which are then electronically distributed to appropriate stores and completed in quick fashion. Orfalea's vision formed as he reacted to the needs of his customers; as needs changed, so did Kinko's services. As a result, Kinko's has become something of a national cultural phenomenon. Jay Leno shot a segment, "My Night at the Copy Shop," and David Letterman tapes a show that features his favorite places in New York City, one of which is a Kinko's store. Kinko's has also been spotted in an episode of *Seinfeld*.

Like most highly successful people, Orfalea is bright, creative, and a natural leader; he possesses seemingly endless energy and was in the right place at the right time. When Kinko's first opened, seven million people in the United States worked out of their homes; by 2000 that number had swelled to over 40 million. Although at first Orfalea planted most new stores in college towns and catered to students, as the number of self–employed and small businesses grew, Kinko's began reaching out to a new market. *Fortune*, which named Kinko's to its "100 Best Places to Work" list two consecutive years, noted that Kinko's "has been at the epicenter of the small–business explosion.... Open 24 hours a day, Kinko's has become a clean, well–lighted place where a driven soul can work on a project deep into the night. Millions of small–business owners and fledgling entrepreneurs have made it their second home. Countless business plans have been crafted, revised, debated, and printed on its premises. Kinko's can rightfully claim to be the birthplace of a legion of enterprises." How appropriate, then, is Kinko's long–serving motto: "Your Branch Office That Never Closes."

Sources of Information

Contact at: Kinko's, Inc.
255 W. Stanley Ave.
Ventura, CA 93002–8000
Business Phone: (805)652–4000
URL: http://www.kinkos.com

Bibliography

Abrams, Rhonda. *Wear Clean Underwear: Business Wisdom from Mom.* New York: Dell, 2000. Available at http://www.businessweek.com.

Cheakalos, Christina, Bruce Frankel, William Plummer, and Susan Schindehette. "Heavy Mettle." *People Weekly*, 30 October 2000.

"Heroes of Small Business." *Fortune*, 13 November 2000.

Lauren, Jill. *Succeeding With LD: 20 True Stories About People with LD.* Minneapolis: Free Spirit Publishing, 1997. Available at http://www.ldonline.org/first_person/orfalea.html.

"Man of Few Words." *Sales and Marketing Management*, March 1997.

Marsh, Ann. "Kinko's Grows Up—Almost." *Forbes*, 1 December 1997.

Moore, Pat. "Orfalea Family Foundation Gives $8.5 Million to Child Care Programs at City College." *City Currents*, 30 April–6 May 2001. Available at http://www.ccsf.cc.ca.us.

Moukheiber, Zina. "I'm Just a Peddler." *Forbes*, 17 July 1995.

"Original Copy Cats." *Wired News*, June 1995. Available at http://www.wired.com.

"Our Humble Beginnings." Kinko's, Inc., 2001. Available at http://www.kinkos.com.

"Paul Orfalea to Assume Chairperson Emeritus at Kinko's." Kinkos, Inc., 8 March 2000. Available at http://www.kinkos.com.

Roberts, Paul. "Free Agent, Free Spirit: Why Kinko's Founder Wanders and Wonders." *Fast Company*, December 1997. Available at http://www.fastcompany.com.

Seaburn, Paul. "Paul Orfalea." *Y & E: The Magazine for Teen Entrepreneurs*, 2000. Available at http://ye.entreworld.org.

"Why Paul Orfalea Didn't Franchise Kinko's." *Business Week*, 23 September 1998.

Paloma Picasso

(1949-)
Lopez–Cambil Ltd.

Overview

Paloma Picasso, the daughter of the legendary Spanish painter Pablo Picasso, has achieved her own renown as an internationally famous jewelry designer. She also achieved success on a global scale with a line of cosmetics and a multi–million–dollar accessories company. Befitting the progeny of a famous artist, Picasso possessed abundant visual flair, evident in the design of her jewelry, which is noted for its distinctive shapes and color combinations. Her social skills, artistic talents, and professional savvy helped establish a long–standing professional relationship with Tiffany & Company, which introduced her first exclusive collection of jewelry in 1980. Picasso's success in jewelry design resulted in her expansion into cosmetics, fashion accessories, and china. Her designs have been sold all over the world and include eyewear, cosmetics, and leather goods. Picasso's personal visual stamp can even be found in the packaging and advertising of her products.

Personal Life

Paloma Picasso was born in Paris, France, on April 19, 1949, to Pablo Picasso and Francoise Gilot. Her father was the world famous Spanish painter best known for developing the "cubist" style, and her mother was a French artist and writer. She is represented in many of her father's works, including *Paloma with an Orange*.

Pablo Picasso and Gilot were 61 and 21, respectively, when they first met. The couple lived together for ten years but never married, as Pablo Picasso was pro-

Paloma Picasso. (AP/Wide World Photos.)

hibited by Spanish law from divorcing his first wife. He and Gilot had two children together, Paloma and her older brother Claude. In 1961 Picasso legitimized his children's status by legally giving them his name.

Paloma, the Spanish word for "Dove," grew up in Paris and the south of France among artists and intellectuals. She never received any formal instruction in painting from her artistic parents, but was encouraged by them to draw. Rather than setting out on a career path similar to her parents, she first chose to express her own artistic instincts in the way she presented herself. When she was a teenager, she became known in Paris for the personal look she created by matching flea-market finds with designer clothes items. During this period, she became

friends with influential people like designer Yves St. Laurent and John Loring, of Tiffany & Company.

Still, Paloma put aside any notions of an artistic career, fearful that her efforts would always be measured against the output of her famous father. However, after graduating from the Université de Paris in Nanterre, she became a theatrical costumer and stylist for a Parisian theater production company. Some of her creations, particularly rhinestone jewelry, caught the eye of appreciative critics. Encouraged by the attention, she began formal schooling in jewelry design and fabrication.

In 1969 she presented her first efforts to St. Laurent. Her work so impressed him that he commissioned her to design a collection of jewelry to go with his fashions. When Pablo Picasso died in 1973, Paloma temporarily lost all interest in designing. She put her career on hold to catalogue and authenticate her father's large estate. This proved an especially difficult task, as her father had left no will and lawsuits were filed for shares of the estate, which was valued at $250 million. Paloma's eventual share was estimated to be close to $90 million. At this time, she also helped the French government establish the Musée Picasso in Paris, which opened in 1983.

In the mid-1970s she met Rafael Lopez-Cambil, an Argentine playwright and director whose work she admired. She began to work with him, designing costumes and sets for two of his Parisian stage productions. The relationship went from professional to personal, and the two were married in 1978. Their wedding ceremony was described as an event, as Picasso wore a St. Laurent design that featured her trademark red, white, and black, and the reception was held in a disco. After the marriage, Lopez-Cambil left the theater and became Picasso's business partner.

Two decades later, in 1999, Picasso divorced Lopez-Cambil. At the time, annual sales of their fashion and perfume products were estimated at $825 million. Picasso told *Women's Wear Daily* that she had to turn over a $100 million because she had unwisely attributed much of her company's success to her husband. In May of that year she wed French gynecologist Eric Thevenet. In January 2001 the couple moved to Switzerland, settling in the Lake Geneva region. There she established the Paloma Picasso Foundation to promote the works of her parents, especially her mother's, of whose work very little was known in Europe.

In 1988 Picasso won the MODA Award for design excellence from The Hispanic Designers, Inc. She was also honored that year by The Fashion Group as one of the "Women Who Have Made an Extraordinary Impact on our Industry." Additionally, she was inducted into The Hall of Fame International Best Dressed List. Her works are featured in the permanent collections of two United States museums. The Smithsonian Institution's National Museum of Natural History displays a 396.3-carat kunzite necklace that she created. Adorned with diamond "lightning bolts", her 408.63-carat moonstone bracelet is housed at The Field Museum of Natural History in Chicago.

Career Details

Like many people born to a world–famous parent, Paloma Picasso was always determined to make it on her own. She never wanted to use her father's name or her inheritance to further her career. As a result, she demanded much of herself. Ultimately, she would harness her own natural creativity toward success in a number of diverse professional and artistic activities.

Picasso's talents for jewelry design first became evident when she worked as a stage designer assistant for a Paris theater company. Her skills attracted notice when she was asked to find a necklace for a leading lady. Displaying an artistic resourcefulness, she turned some Folies Bergere rhinestones into a remarkable choker. Soon after, St. Laurent helped her launch her career when he commissioned her to design fashion jewelry for sale in his Rive Gauche boutique. Energized by the opportunity, she developed her skills further and, in 1971, designed gold jewelry for the House of Zolotas. Again, critics were impressed, and her reputation began to grow.

Her career took a brief sidetrack, however, in the early 1970s after her father died. In 1974, during the period when she had temporarily given up on designing, Picasso acted in *Immoral Tales (Contes Immorreaux)*, directed by Walerian Borowczyk. The movie was lauded by critics and won the coveted Prix de l'Age d'Or. Picasso earned praise for her performance as an evil Hungarian countess with unusual desires. But it has been her only foray into the acting profession, even though she said she enjoyed the experience and would like to star in a film about legendary French fashion designer Coco Chanel. After her marriage to Lopez–Cambil, Picasso resumed her designing career in earnest, paving the way for her most significant achievements.

In 1979 she began her long–standing association with Tiffany & Company when the firm's design director, John Loring, invited her to present a table setting for an exhibition. She was excited about the opportunity, as she had always wanted to design for an American store. Her jeweled creation, titled the *End of Summer*, featured a silver ribbon and a mushroom–shaped cake. The setting received good notices, and Tiffany asked Picasso to create jewelry for the company. The next year Tiffany unveiled Picasso's first exclusive collection of jewelry. Her works were applauded for their imagination, innovation, boldness, and use of brilliant color contrasts, and it is generally acknowledged that she redesigned the direction of modern fine jewelry design. Characteristic pieces included chunky necklaces of marble–sized gemstones, sculptured bracelets, and a fan ring that spread over three fingers. She also produced the oft–copied and extremely popular "hugs and kisses" jewelry that fea-

Chronology:
Paloma Picasso

1949: Born.

1969: Designed jewelry for Yves St. Laurent.

1971: Designed jewelry for the House of Zolotas.

1974: Starred in movie *Immoral Tales (Contes Immorreaux)*.

1978: Married Rafael Lopez–Cambil.

1980: Began association with Tiffany and Co.

1984: Enters cosmetics field.

1987: Established Lopez–Cambil Ltd.

1989: Designed china for Villeroy and Boch.

1990: Produced anniversary collection for Tiffany.

tured Xs and Os in gold and silver on pins, bracelets, and necklaces. Picasso's pieces ranged in price from $100 to $500 thousand.

Picasso ventured into the cosmetics field in 1984, when she and Lopez–Cambil produced a fragrance named *Paloma Picasso*. Picasso's decision to produce her own fragrance was somewhat appropriate, as her maternal grandfather, Emile Gilot, was a chemist and perfume manufacturer in Grasse, France. Picasso recalled how, as a child, she was fascinated by her grandfather's workshop as well as the art of perfumery itself. She described the fragrance as a "jewelry for the senses." The fragrance itself was a blend of florals and amber. The success of the perfume, which was produced by L'Oreal and was priced at over $150 an ounce, encouraged Picasso to expand her collection to include lipstick, called Mon Rouge. The cosmetic's distinctive red color became closely associated with Picasso's own visual style, and it came to be called "Paloma red." Picasso even designed the red–and–black packaging for the product.

Further energized by the success of their joint ventures, the husband–and–wife team expanded its efforts into fashion accessories. In 1987 they founded a New York City–based company, Lopez–Cambil Ltd., to produce and distribute imported designer handbags, belts, umbrellas, and small leather goods. The company had offices and a showroom in New York City, and the products were manufactured in Italy. The collection, called Couture accessories, became known for its high quality and artistic design. The pieces were described as simple and understated, with a playful splash of color. The leather handbags were sleek and angular with bracelet–style handles, and they were tastefully studded with gems. In 1990 this venture was followed up by a less expensive line of accessories called *By Paloma Picasso*, which made Picasso's work available to a much larger market.

In 1990, Picasso also introduced an anniversary collection to commemorate ten years of designing jewelry exclusively for Tiffany & Company. The extraordinary collection featured necklaces mounted with some of the world's rarest and most beautiful gemstones and, again, her work was praised for its innovation.

Picasso continued to expand into new collections. In 1989 she branched into the home furnishings market when she designed china for Villeroy & Boch, creating porcelain and ceramic place settings and tiles. Three years later she and Lopez–Cambil entered the world of men's cosmetics with the launch of the successful Minotaure fragrance line. For this product, Picasso put her design talents toward the bottle and packaging, while her husband developed the concept, the name, and mounted the advertising campaign.

Social and Economic Impact

Throughout her life, Paloma Picasso has been a trendsetter in the world of design. The rich variety of Picasso's output is available all over the world. There are Paloma Picasso boutiques in Japan and Hong Kong, and her accessories are available throughout the United States, Europe, and the Far East. In Europe, her creations include cosmetics and fragrances for L'Oreal in France, and sunglasses and optical frames in Germany. She also creates hosiery for Grupo Synkro in Mexico, and bed ensembles, towels, bathrobes, and dressing gowns for KBC in Germany.

Sources of Information

Contact at: Lopez–Cambil Ltd.
37 W. 57th St.
New York, New York 10019

Bibliography

"Celebrities in Switzerland: Paloma Picasso." *Switzerland.isyours.com*, 2000. Available at http://switzerland.isyours.com.

Johnes, Baird. "Celebrity Art." *artnet.com*, 5 May 1999. Available at http://www.artnet.com.

McGee, Kimberley. "Paloma: Picasso's Daughter Uses Jewels As Her Medium." *Las Vegas Sun*, 5 September 2001.

"Paloma Picasso." *Ciao–magazine.com*, 23 August 1999. Available at http://www.ciao–magazine.com.

"Paloma Picasso." *GreatWomen.com* 2001. Available at http://www.bee–trader.com/ipp/women/picasso.html.

Przybys, John. "The 'Other' Picasso: Painter's Daughter Creates Her Own Artistry in Jewelry to be Displayed at Tiffany's." *Las Vegas Review–Journal*, 30 August 2001.

Ronald M. Popeil

(1935-)
Ronco Inventions, LLC

Overview

Infomercial legend Ron Popeil has pervaded pop culture in the more than 35 years that television viewers have watched him hawk products of his own invention. He founded Ronco Inc., an operation run virtually single–handedly by the charismatic Popeil, who invents, markets, and serves as the consummate pitchman for such well–known products as the Veg–O–Matic, the Pocket Fisherman, Mr. Microphone, and the infamous GLH Formula Number 9 Hair System, a "spray–on toupee." Arising from humble beginnings, the entrepreneur has sold more than $1 billion of his gadgets and become a cult icon in the process.

Personal Life

Ronald Popeil lives in Beverly Hills with his fourth wife, Robin, whom he married in 1995, and has four daughters: Kathryn, Shannon, Lauren, and Contessa. He enjoys fishing on his boat, the *Popeil Pocket Fisherman*, and, not surprisingly, spending time cooking. Popeil serves on the board of directors of Mirage Resorts with close friend and inspiration, chairman Steve Wynn.

Born in Chicago in 1935, he was raised by his paternal grandparents after his parents Samuel and Julia divorced when he was four. Ron and his older brother Jerry were sent to a boarding school in upstate New York. In what Popeil described as an unhappy childhood, he recalls seeing his mother only once at the school and never seeing his father until moving to Chicago at age 13. When he was seven years old, his grandparents, Isadore and

Ronald Popeil demonstrating the Chop-O-Matic food processor. *(AP/Wide World Photos.)*

Mary, took the brothers from boarding school and brought them to their home in Florida. "I grew up in my grandmother's kitchen, always watching her cook," Popeil told *People Weekly*. Life at his grandparents was not always happy, however, as his grandfather often doled out harsh and undeserved punishment. Even with a home life that was lacking and the legacy of his father's abandonment, Popeil refused to hold a grudge. Looking back on his own business success, he still credits his father among his two inspirations. "My father was all business," he simply told the *New Yorker*. "I didn't know him personally."

Popeil's knack for invention came from a long line of entrepreneurs and salesmen. His father, Samuel Jacob Popeil, or S.J., as he was called, started out working for his uncle Nathan Morris, a kitchen–gadget entrepreneur who sold Acme Metal products on the New Jersey boardwalk, employing several other family members to do the same. Nathan's company, N.K. Morris, sold such products as the Morris Metric Slicer and the KwiKi–Pi. After his apprenticeship on the Atlantic coast, S.J. started a Chicago–based company, Popeil Brothers, which produced the Dial–O–Matic, Chop–O–Matic, and, in 1960, the slicer/dicer Veg–O–Matic. The Morris–Popeil family were famous in their day for their inventions and marketing savvy, as well as their fierce competition with one another—S.J. sued his uncle in 1958 over the Roto–Chop, which Popeil claimed was very similar to his Chop–O–Matic.

At the age of 13, Ron was sent to work in the Popeil Brothers factory on weekends, when his father wasn't there. When he started selling his father's products at Chicago's Maxwell Street Flea Market, he was struck by revelation. "I saw all these people selling products, pocketing money, making sales, and my mind went racing. I can do what they're doing, I thought. But I can do it better than they can," Popeil wrote in his autobiography, *The Salesman of the Century*.

Popeil was a natural salesman, sometimes earning $500 in a single day, more money than he had ever seen. Ron, in his late teens, began selling at state and county fairs during the mid–1950s. Soon after, he bargained for a demonstration space at the Chicago Woolworth's—the nation's top–grossing branch. With his good looks and polished performance, Popeil's demonstrations of the Dial–O–Matic and Chop–O–Matic brought in big money, and soon he was earning more than the store's manager, making $1,000 a week. Popeil's friend Mel Korey told the *New Yorker*, "He was mesmerizing. There were secretaries who would take their lunch break at Woolworth's to watch him because he was so good–looking. He would go into the turn [the end of the pitch and the start of the solicitation for money], and people would just come running." Popeil soon enjoyed the fruits of his success, sporting a new Rolex watch and dining at Chicago's finest restaurants. In 1955, after attending one year at the University of Illinois, Popeil dropped out to devote himself full–time to his budding sales career.

Career Details

Standing in front of a crowd selling the Veg–O–Matic, Ronald Popeil realized the potential of the simple yet ingenious and effective device. The machine, which went through pounds of produce per minute, needed a much wider audience and different format to fully demonstrate its ability. Intrigued by the rising medium of television, Popeil teamed up with his college buddy Mel Korey to form Ronco in 1964. Their first order of business was to film a $500 commercial for the Veg–O–Matic. The partners bought a several week run for the two–minute ad at a local television station. The gamble paid off, as stores that stocked the Veg–O–Matic were selling out and reordering plenty more. Television and Popeil's products emerged as a perfect match. Soon Ron began selling his products exclusively on television without the use of a script, relying on the skills honed from years of live practice.

Popeil then turned to marketing another product, The Ronco Spray Gun, a nozzle that fit over a garden hose to disseminate fertilizer, insecticide, and the like. As that product began selling well, Ronco generated $200,000 in sales in its first year alone. By 1968, the company had blossomed into a multi–million dollar enterprise, making $8.8 million in revenue from a diverse array of products: Chop–O–Matic, the Smokeless Ashtray, the Pocket Fisherman, Mr. Microphone, Inside the Eggshell Egg Scrambler, Popeil's Pasta & Sausage Maker, GLH Formula Number 9 Hair System, and rhinestone and stud setters for jeans. Ronco Inc. went public the following year.

Popeil became a late–night television regular, pitching Ronco's gadgets throughout the 1970s and early 1980s. His products became familiar symbols of American ingenuity, and his memorable commercials became fair game for mockery among comedians and talk–show hosts. Proof of his status as a pop icon, Popeil himself was spoofed by Dan Aykroyd on *Saturday Night Live*, demonstrating a "Bass–O–Matic" complete with Popelian catch phrases like, "It slices! It dices!" and "But wait! There's more!" This sort of publicity didn't tarnish Popeil's image nor hurt sales; in fact, it only added to his products' popularity. Not all of his products were successful, however. Cellutrol failed to rid the user of cellulite, and the Inside–Outside Window Washer failed to work outside. Yet these were only occasional failures in an overall booming business.

In 1984 Ronco was forced into liquidation when nervous creditors called in the company's notes. Strapped to find a buyer, Popeil himself bought the rights to Ronco's products at auction from the bank for $2 million of his personal fortune. The transaction left him disillusioned about running the company, however, so he passed the daily operation of Ronco to others and retreated to his home laboratory to test new inventions.

Another turning point for Ronco also occurred that year. The Federal Communications Commission softened

Chronology:
Ronald M. Popeil

1935: Born.

1955: Dropped out of college for a full–time sales career.

1960: Ron's father invented The Veg–O–Matic.

1964: Formed Ronco Inc.

1968: Ronco posted $8.8 million in sales.

1969: Ronco went public.

1984: Purchased Ronco after its liquidation.

1990: Began selling products on infomercials.

1995: Published autobiography, *The Salesman of the Century*.

limit lengths on television commercials, giving rise to the half–hour infomercial. With the dawn of the 1990s, Popeil was back on television with his new Ronco Food Dehydrator, which made the country look at beef jerky in a whole new way. The infomercial format was perfect for the pitchman. As in his early days of selling, Popeil had an audience to interact with as well as the opportunity to fully explain and demonstrate each detail of the product, his specialty.

With the rise of the Internet, Popeil continued to inspire and intrigue the public via several websites devoted to him by fans who either idolized or reviled him. One rabid Popeil fan website raves, "The sound of his voice is harmonious. His face is not beautiful in the way the conventional people consider beauty. It is the contorted face of genius. Years of torment at the hands of critics have hardened his features and made him statue–like. He is more than a man, he is part god. Hercules has nothing on him."

In the 1990s Popeil teamed up with the home shopping television network QVC, selling the Ronco Showtime Rotisserie & BBQ and the New and Improved Popeil Automatic Pasta and Sausage Maker, among other products. In 2000 Ronco posted $250 million in sales.

Despite all of his success, Popeil remained driven, and when not selling his products, was hard at work formulating new ones, such as a countertop meat smoker and an automatic bread–and–batter machine in the works in early 2001. Although Ronco had some 200 employees,

Popeil was still very involved in all aspects of his products. He invented, tested, and was responsible for the research and development of all products, as well as overseeing the packaging, manufacturing, sales, and marketing aspects of the business. He conceived of his own commercials and wrote them, in addition to starring in them. "I'm different than most people and most companies in a lot of ways," Popeil said to *Sales & Marketing Management*. "In the development of products, companies throw a lot of ideas up against the wall. That is, they'll work on a hundred different projects and hope one will work. I don't waste my time or money. I work on one project at a time. I have total focus on that one thing— and I come up with winner after winner. Then I take the product from start to finish."

Social and Economic Impact

Part inventor, part television pitchman, Ronald Popeil is an American pop culture icon. With the dozens of everyday gadgets he invented and sold on television, Popeil changed the retail world with the unique way he presented his products and the catchy, omni–present commercials he created. In and of themselves, the products were not particularly socially relevant or life–changing, but as an entire line of products, together with their inventor and chief promoter Popeil, they came to represent good ol' American ingenuity. Demonstrating capitalism at its most basic level, Popeil built his fortune—literally—with his own two hands, a good idea, and a can–do attitude from the beginning and throughout good times and bad. "This is the ultimate late 20th–century guy," remarked Robert Thompson, associate professor of television at Syracuse University, in *NewStandard*. "What Henry Ford was to industrial strength and genius, Ron Popeil is to the next generation of American ingenuity. He's figured out the very complex negotiations that go on between what American culture produces and how we consume it. People 100 years from now are going to be writing dissertations on him."

Sources of Information

Contact at: Ronco Inventions, LLC
21344 Superior St.
Chatsworth, CA 91311
Business Phone: (818)775–4602
URL: http://www.ronco.com

Bibliography

Donoho, Ron. "One–Man Show." *Sales & Marketing Management*, June 2001, 36.

Gladwell, Malcolm. "The Pitchman: Ron Popeil and the Conquest of the American Kitchen." *New Yorker*, 30 October 2000.

Gliatto, Tom. "He Yells! He Sells! Amazing! Pitchman Ron Popeil Strikes Gold with His Spray–On Toupee." *People Weekly*, 3 May 1993, 154.

"Inventor Profile: Ron Popeil." *The Great Idea Finder*. 30 April 2000. Available at http://www.ideafinder.com.

"My Personal Hero: Ron Popeil." October 2001. Available at http://www.worldofchristopher.com.

"Pitcher Perfect: Infomercial King Ron Popeil's Chickens Have Come Home to Roost." *People Weekly*, 23 October 2000, 125.

Popeil, Ron. *The Salesman of the Century.* Delacorte Press, 1995.

"Ronco and Ron Popeil." *Ronco, Inc.*, October 2001. Available at http://shop.ronco.com.

"Ronco Inventions, LLC." *Hoover's Online, Inc.*, October 2001. Available at http://www.hoovers.com.

Miuccia Prada

(1950-)
Prada

Miuccia Prada is the director of design for Fratelli Prada, the Milan, Italy, fashion design empire. She is the youngest granddaughter of Prada founder Mario Prada. She and her husband Patrizio Bertelli took over the family's luxury goods company in 1978 and turned it into a trendy fashion powerhouse which posted revenues of $1.4 billion in 2000.

Personal Life

Born Miuccia Bianchi Prada in a large apartment on Milan's Corso di Porta Romana, Prada is the second of three children. Her father headed a company that made mowers for putting greens, while her mother, Luisa, was the second generation descendant of the Fratelli Prada fortune. Founded by Miuccia's grandfather, Mario Prada, in 1913, Fratelli Prada sold "oggitti di lusso," or "luxury objects" to the very wealthy—the Italian royal family was among its clients. The company competed with the French houses of Hermes and Louis Vuitton. Many of Mario's designs were based on a movement called Stile Liberty, the Italian version of the Arts and Crafts movement. "He was very eccentric," Miuccia Prada told *Financial Times* writer Alice Rawsthorn. "If you look at his work from the 1920s, there are lots of strange images and details. It was very adventurous for the era."

Prada grew up in relative luxury and comfort in Milan, although the Prada firm had fallen on hard times by the end of World War II. Under grandfather Mario's watch, the female Pradas were not allowed to work in

Miuccia Prada. (AP/Wide World Photos/Luca Bruno.)

the shop "My grandfather said women should stay at home," Prada explained to *Forbes* writer Nancy Rotenier; but when Mario died in the late 1950s, his son wanted nothing to do with the company and let his wife assume the helm. Under Luisa's direction, the Prada business was revived and maintained a semblance of success over the next few decades.

Meanwhile, young Prada led the life of the daughter of a wealthy Milan family. She skied in Switzerland, bought her clothes in Paris, and studied political science at the University of Milan, graduating in 1973. There she became active with the Italian Communist party, and often participated in political demonstrations after becoming a card–carrying member. She also studied mime for

a number of years at Milan's Teatro Piccolo, eventually joining the troupe itself. Despite her rather bohemian activities, Prada always felt a pull toward stylish clothes. "I'd always loved fashion," she recalled for Rawsthorn in the *Financial Times*. "Yves Saint Laurent was my favorite. I wore his things all the time in the 1970s—even to political protests. People looked at me strangely when I handed out pamphlets in my expensive clothes."

Always independent–minded in politics and fashion, she was known for mixing flea market finds with high–end designers Chanel and Yves Saint Laurent. "For me, the thing that is most important about fashion is expression," Prada said in an interview for *Vogue*. "Because in your clothing you express not only social things and the aesthetic of your time but also who you are."

In her day–to–day life, Prada's professional achievements are irrevocably intertwined with the personal. She and Bertelli live, with their two young sons, in the same large apartment compound where she was born. Family members are nearby at home and at work—brother Alberto can be found in Prada's financial executive offices, while her sister Marina is in charge of coordinating special events for the growing number of Prada shops. In her spare time, Miuccia collects modern art and glass, and haunts flea markets for more inspiration for her designs. She also appears at fabric stores that are going out of business, buying up their large bolts at a discount. But then Prada is too hesitant to cut them up, instead draping their swaths artfully around her Milan home. Such acquisitions are more important than others: she's driven the same dark blue Fiat for almost two decades.

Career Details

In 1978 Luisa Prada decided to retire, and she cajoled her daughter into taking over for her. At the time, only the original shop in Milan's Galleria Vittorio Emanuele remained of the house of Prada Miuccia's sole experience in the business was a stint managing this store that primarily sold luggage and handbags. Almost instantaneously, the 28–year–old Prada injected a jolt of Eurochic style into the staid company with her first product: a small bag made out of military–tent nylon, "with a glitzy gold strap that made it look like a post–modern parody of the classic Chanel bag," as Rawsthorn described it in the *Financial Times*. Within a few years the $450 bags had become ubiquitous status symbols toted by the stylemakers in Europe and the United States and "put life and prestige back into the business," wrote Sischy in the *New Yorker*. Years later, replicas of the same bag, made from similar industrial strength nylon, could be found in department stores from London to Los Angeles for $10.

Though she saw fashion as "women's work," as she later commented in *Vogue*, Prada found herself designing more and more. Though Prada told the *New Yorker*'s

Sischy that she "wanted to be something more" than a designer, she admitted, "... I am what I am. Not everyone can be Albert Schweitzer or Karl Marx."

The bag attracted more and more customers and the attention of Patrizio Bertelli, a fellow bag maker from Florence whom Prada had met at a trade show. He had started his business at the age of 17 making beaded hippie bags, but the company had grown into a well–regarded manufacturer of leather goods. The Prada company contracted out some of the manufacturing of their own line of bags to Bertelli's well–run factory. Upon meeting, Prada commended him on the workmanship and quality of his company's products, and the professional relationship between the two firms flourished. Gradually, Bertelli became Prada's business mentor of sorts, and the relationship turned more personal. The couple formalized their partnership in a 1987 marriage; by that time Bertelli had brought much of his expertise to the Prada company. One of the first issues on the table was a natural step after the success of the nylon bag: to modernize the company's line, make it more exclusive, and rid the store of anything but Prada products.

Prada debuted with a bohemian schoolgirl theme that would reappear in subsequent collections. Prada told Sischy in the *New Yorker* interview that the uniforms embodied the attitude she always dreamed of having. "I tried to be bad, but I couldn't be as bad as I would have liked—not as bad as the girls I really admired, and not as bad as the ones who are in my dreams."

Bad girls may have been her inspiration, but her designs quickly became known for quietly exuding "timelessness," "confidence," "quality, luxury, and style," according to *Entertainment Weekly*. Prada's fascination with different materials, processes, technologies, and eras influenced her designs. The couture dresses, the progressive sportswear, the one–of–a–kind items—many from the radical clothing–design days of the 1960s and 1970s—were; sitting in her extensive closets inside the family's Milan apartment compound. Prada's mother is also afflicted with the same need to archive, and together their collection of classic clothes served as the inspiration for Prada's first line of ready–to–wear in 1989. According to *Forbes,* the clothes "look like something you owned 20 or even 40 years ago, only updated ..."

"I never actually decided to become a designer," Prada told *New Yorker* magazine. "Eventually, I found that I was one." As a young woman and Communist, Prada thought of fashion as "basically silly," she said. To the daughter of one of Italy's great luxury goods houses, Fratelli Prada, the idea of working in fashion was unthinkable. But, over time, she found herself reconciling her political convictions with her developing fashion design sense and becoming more involved in the fine leather goods business. In the late seventies, Prada took over the company, and introduced her own line of men's and women's clothes that "[at] first glance ... looks plain and undesigned," said writer Ingrid Sischy in the *New Yorker,*

Chronology:
Miuccia Prada

1913: Family business started by grandfather Mario.

1950: Born in Milan, Italy.

1973: University of Milan, Ph.D. in political science.

1978: Took over family business from mother.

1987: Married business partner Patrizio Bertelli.

1995: Added men's clothing to the fashion line.

2001: Announced plans to go public.

but which, according to *Time,* became "the most cherished name in the fashion apparel industry."

By 1995, there were already 47 Prada stores worldwide and dozens more planned, and the name was a staple in the fashion world. But Prada came into full view that year when actress Uma Thurman wore a one–of–a–kind Prada gown to the Academy Awards. The following day, the Prada switchboard was overwhelmed by calls. To accommodate the widespread interest, Prada introduced a line of clothes that cost less than the Prada line—Prada dresses cost $800 to $3,000; suits, from $1,200. Miu Miu, as the collection was called, appealed to a younger, hipper crowd and allowed Prada to play with her bad girl ideal more freely. She also expanded into men's clothes that year.

Under Miuccia Prada's helm, the house of Prada has become one of the most successful European stylemongers of the 1990s, a feat that used her good mind for business and perpetual creative flair. Items bearing Prada's discreet triangular logo are donned by stylish women—and beginning in 1995, stylish men—around the world and praised by celebrities and the movers and shakers of the fashion industry for their unadorned yet timeless style. Clothes and accessories made by the company are the domain of the fashion elite, with hefty price tags but a classic, clean look that lasts from season to season.

Social and Economic Impact

Twice in 2001, Prada postponed plans to go public due to global economic downturn. There were whispers that the company may have lost some of its elitism by expanding to 150 stores, five alone in Manhattan. But in

December 2001, Prada hosted a lavish party to celebrate the opening of its 24,000 square foot Soho store, with guests at the event as diverse as actor Kevin Spacey, New York City mayor Rudy Giuliani, and actress Milla Jovovich. The company's stated goals are to reach $5 billion in sales by 2010, moving up to the ranks of Gucci and LVMH (Moet Hennessey Louis Vuitton).

"With her long brown hair, no–makeup looks and unassuming manner, Miuccia Prada has more the air of a Bohemian art student than the head of one of the fastest–growing names in the business," commented *Footwear News* writer Sara Gay Forden about this successful Italian designer and head of an international fashion label that bears her family name. "Part of her secret is that she really loves fashion." Prada's astonishing success came despite the fact that she never really planned on entering the family's upscale leather–goods manufacturing business. Nevertheless, she is responsible for turning it into one of Europe's most sought after ready–to–wear labels, prized by fashion critics, and comprising a veritable empire of luxury stores located on some of the world's more stylish streets.

For her fall 2001 collection, Prada, "that most restless of designers," as *New York Times* fashion critic Cathy Horyn called her, returned to sixties–era designs. The move sent the fashion world into a "delicious panic," Horyn wrote. "For better or for worse, [New York] has become a city of Simon Says, and Ms. Prada ... is Simon by default."

Sources of Information

Contact at: Prada
   50 W. 57th St., Fl. 12A
   New York, NY 10019

Bibliography

Dolan, Kerry A., et al. "The World's Richest People." *Forbes,* 9 July 2001.

Guyon, Janet. "Prada Steps Out." *Fortune,* 1 October 2001.

Kahn, Jeremy; and Brian O'Keefe. "Best & Worst 2001." *Fortune,* 24 December 2001.

Trebay, Guy; and Ginia Bellafante. "Prada: A Luxury Brand with World–class Anxiety." *Toronto Star,* 26 December 2001.

Charles Revson

(1906-1975)
Revlon, Inc.

Overview

Charles Revson founded Revlon, Inc. in 1932 with $300. Beginning by selling nail polish, he developed it into a complete cosmetics company with sales totaling nearly $1 billion before his death in 1975. Known for his harsh personality, his drive for perfection, and his extravagant lifestyle, Revson became a legend in his own day.

Personal Life

Charles Haskell Revson was born on October 11, 1906 in Somerville, Massachusetts, outside of Boston, to Samuel Morris and Jeanette Weiss Revson. He grew up in Manchester, New Hampshire, with one older brother, Joseph, and one younger brother, Martin. Both of Revson's parents were Jewish emigrants from Russia. His father relocated to the United States in his early twenties to avoid being drafted into the Russian army; his mother had arrived in the country as an infant. Revson's father (whom all three sons referred to as "the Major") was employed as a cigar roller for R. G. Sullivan Company and his mother worked off and on as a saleswoman at a dry goods store. The family lived in a six–unit tenement house and, although money was not plentiful, there was always food on the table.

Revson did well in school and although he participated in a few activities, including the school play, the yearbook, and the debate team, Revson was considered a loner who stuck close to his brother Joseph, who—although older—was in the same class. Revson, nicknamed "Chick" was short, of slight build, and not par-

Charles Revson. *(Geoffrey Clements/Corbis.)*

ticularly athletic although he did play sandlot baseball in the neighborhood. Only after he graduated from Manchester Central High School in 1923 at the age of 16 did he grow several inches, up to five foot eight and about 140 pounds. His formal education ended with his high school diploma.

Revson was married three times. In 1930 he left behind the girl his parents hoped he'd marry to follow Ida Tompkins, a showgirl, to Chicago. The two married in 1930 but the marriage was brief, and the two divorced within a year. On October 26, 1940 he married Johanna Catharina Christina de Knecht, known as Ancky. A beautiful model and daughter of an important Dutch publisher, she was also the former wife of a French count. Revson agreed to the marriage only after de Knecht threatened to abandon the relationship if he didn't. The couple had three children, again at the insistence of de Knect, who gave birth to two boys and adopted a girl. The marriage lasted 20 years before ending in 1960 when de Knecht filed for divorce, having become fed up with Revson, who was possessive and a constant womanizer, employing prostitutes regularly. He married for a third time in February 1964 to Lyn Fisher Sheresky, 26 years younger than the 58–year–old Revson. Sheresky had three children from a previous marriage. Although Revson was more attentive to his third wife, he decided to file for divorce in 1974 just days after their tenth anniversary.

Over the years Revson gave many millions of dollars to charities. He was particularly supportive of Jewish, medical, and educational causes. Upon his death al-

most half his estate of $100 million was used to establish a charitable foundation. Revson Plaza, located along Amsterdam Avenue in New York and running through Columbia University, was the result of his $1 million contribution. The black marble foundation at Lincoln Center, valued at three–quarters of a million dollars, was built with Revson's money. As biographer Andrew Tobias noted, many of Revson's most touching gifts were spontaneous and unpublicized, such as the $1,000 he gave to the Cuban refugee brother of a manicurist at The House of Revlon.

Although Revson could be generous with his money, he also loved to spend it on himself. During his final years, he was going through $5,000 a day on his personal expenses. A constant presence on the New York social scene, Revson also liked to gamble, usually for high stakes, but always limited the amount of time he would spend at a table. His yacht, the Ultima II, which he purchased in 1967 for $3.5 million, is a prime example of Revson's love for luxury. The third largest in the world at the time, it was 257 feet long (comparable to a New York City block), could house 15 guests, and retained a year–round full–time staff of thirty–one; it cost $20,000 to fill its fuel tanks to capacity. In 1967 he also purchased his Park Avenue triplex for $390,000 and then spent another $3 million to refurbish it with a heavy emphasis on gold accents, including gold–plated dinnerware and a gold–plated telephone. He also retained a live–in staff of eight servants.

By all accounts, Revson was a difficult man to work for. He was a demanding perfectionist who had no qualms about being direct, to the point of being rude and even vulgar. Most employees lived in fear of inciting the wrath of their boss. One person whose company was acquired by Revlon told biographer Andrew Tobias, "In negotiations with us he couldn't have been more of a gentleman. As for working for him—I think I'd rather clean streets." As for his acquaintances, some thought of him as a fine, if misunderstood, human being; others loathed him and considered him a vile, mean man. Revson did manage to alienate most of his family before his death. It seemed his sole truly soft spot was his one granddaughter Jill, whom he loved unabashedly until his death.

Revson died from pancreatic cancer on August 24, 1975 with only one nurse in attendance. Nearly 1,000 people attended his funeral on August 26, 1975. As Tobias noted, "Whatever else he was—nasty, crude, lonely, virile, brilliant, inarticulate, insecure, generous, honest, ruthless, complicated—Charles Revson was a man of single–minded persistence and drive, entirely dedicated to his business."

Career Details

After graduating from high school, Revson disappointed his parents, who hoped he would become a lawyer, by moving to New York City to work as a salesman for Pickwick Dress Company, owned by a cousin. He was eventually promoted to a piece–goods buyer, which allowed him to work with materials and colors, something he found he greatly enjoyed. After his career at Pickwick ended in 1930 when he was fired for overstocking a pattern he particularly liked, Revson moved to Chicago and attempted to sell sales–motivation materials, but with the onset of the depression, the work proved unfruitful and Revson returned to New York nine months later. Moving in with his parents who had since moved to Manhattan, he took a job as a nail polish salesman for the Elka Company. His brother Joseph soon joined him at Elka. When Elka refused to allow the brothers to expand their sales territory beyond New York City, they quit to begin their own business.

On March 1, 1932 Charles and Joseph Revson formed Revlon Nail Enamel Corporation in partnership with Charles Lachman, a chemist who had married into the Dresden Chemical Company, a wholesale manufacturer and distributor of nail polish. (The L in Revlon represents Lachman.) The three put up a total of $300 to form the company and began manufacturing nail polish out of a small $25–a–month room on Manhattan's West Side. Lachman was brought in because of his relationship to Dresden and had no active role in the company, although he continued to benefit financially from his one–third ownership of the company throughout his lifetime.

Dr. Taylor Sherwood of Dresden created nail polish to Revson's specifications—creamy, opaque, and non-streaking. Elka manufactured an opaque polish that had caught Revson's eye because most polishes on the market at the time were transparent, colored with dyes, and came only in three shades of red. Because his "creamy enamel" would be made with pigment, it completely covered the fingernail and provided the possibility for expanding into a wide range of shades and colors.

With prototypes in hand and the business sustained on money borrowed from loan sharks at 2 percent interest per month, Revson peddled his goods to beauty salons as he had no money to launch an advertising campaign. Thus Revson was the salesman and Joseph ran the office. Revson was a natural master of marketing. While with Elka he noted which products sold, which colors people preferred, and how well they were satisfied. Once he had his own formula he would demonstrate his products by painting his own nails or applying the polish to a potential customer's fingertips. Revlon received its first substantial order in 1934 when Marshall Field's purchased $400 worth of polish.

From there, the company grew steadily and rapidly—even during the midst of the onset of the depression. By 1937 it was clear that Revlon was a success: In the last four years, sales had increased by 400 percent, and Revson, in his early thirties, was drawing a handsome salary of $16,500 annually. The following year

Chronology:
Charles Revson

1906: Born.

1932: Formed Revlon Nail Polish Corporation with brother Joseph Revson and Charles Lachman.

1934: Received first major order worth $400 from Neiman Marcus.

1939: Introduced line of lipsticks.

1951: Launched Fire and Ice advertising campaign.

1955: Sponsored hit television show *The $64,000 Question*; became a public traded company; Joseph Revson left company.

1958: Sued by younger brother Martin Revson for fraud; settled out of court.

1966: Purchased United States Vitamin and Pharmaceutical Corporation.

1973: Introduced popular perfume, Charlie.

1975: Died.

the company grew by 300 percent in just one year and Revson's take jumped to $39,000. Revlon's next big jump in sales came in 1939 when lipstick was introduced that coordinated with Revlon's nail polish colors. The slogan "matching lips and fingertips" resulted in sales nearly doubling in 1940. Magazines, printed in color for the first time, showed off the trendy coordinating colors. In 1951 Revlon launched its highly successful "Fire and Ice" campaign that featured a beautiful, somewhat seductive, model who asked, "Are you made for Fire and Ice?"

The company experienced another incredible surge in sales in the mid–1950s when Revlon took on the sponsorship of the television show, *The $64,000 Question*. The show, which aired every Tuesday night, became something of a national phenomenon and Revlon benefited greatly from its popularity. Sales increased by 54 percent and earnings rose almost 200 percent. Revlon was not affected by the negative publicity that ensued in 1959 when the show was removed from the air after it was discovered that it had been rigged—despite the later testimony of others who swore Revson himself explicitly demanded the shows' outcomes be fixed. In those four years sales increased 400 percent to $125 million and earnings jumped eightfold to almost $11 million.

Revson took the company public and the initial stock price of $12 a share increased to $30 within three months.

During this time of rapid growth, Revson came into conflict with both his brothers. Joseph did not agree with the decision to take the company public and quit in protest; Revson bought him out for $2.5 million. Revson brought in his younger brother Martin, who quit in 1958 and sued Revson for fraud and misrepresentation; Revson settled with his brother out of court for $300,000.

During the 1960s and 1970s Revlon continued to expand. The company delved into cosmetics, skin–care products, shampoo, hair spray, and perfumes. Revson, always a master of marketing, developed different lines of products, which ranged in price from expensive to inexpensive, to appeal to different markets. Ultima II and Princess Marcella Borghese targeted the upper end of the market and Charlie, an affordable perfume debuted in 1973, targeted a younger audience and became the best–selling fragrance worldwide, due in large part to Revson's brilliant advertising campaigns. Not every one of Revson's endeavors was successful. His attempt to expand into the fashion field, shoe polish, plastic flowers, and electric razors all failed. Revson owned Evan–Picone for five years but sold the company for a loss of $1.75 million in 1966. However, Revson's decision in the same year to purchase the pharmaceutical company United States Vitamin and Pharmaceutical Corporation (USV) proved very profitable. By 1975, 23 percent of sales and 28 percent of profits came from the health care products associated with USV.

Revson remained in complete command of his company until health issues forced him to step down. In 1974 when Revson named Michael G. Bergerac as his successor, annual sales totaled more than $600 million and annual profits were almost $50 million. Revlon's product line included more than 3,500 items, which were sold in 85 countries. In 1977 Revlon sales figures topped $1 billion and by 2000 Revlon products could be purchased in over 175 countries around the world.

Social and Economic Impact

Revson started with $300 and built a cosmetics empire. Along with the economic impact of such a gigantic business, Revson nearly single–handedly created a social revolution in advertising. His first step was to develop catchy names for his polish colors. Previously Revlon nail polish bottles bore plain names such as dark red. Revson created names that sold both polish and image such as Fatal Apple and Kissing Pink. Then during the midst of the conservative 1950s Revson launched advertising campaigns closely associated with seductive sex-

uality. His ads startled most and offended not a few. While competitors pushed the girl–next–door natural look, Revson's ads featured such offbeat, tawdry slogans as "Who knows the *black lace* thoughts you think while shopping in a gingham frock?" As the sexual revolution of the 1960s and 1970s emerged, Revson's campaigns became even more popular.

Revson also broke new ground in other areas. Because of his drive for perfection he introduced quality control and testing long before it became popular. Although Revson entered the international market later than most of his competitors, he caught up and surpassed them quickly. The tradition had been to alter advertising in other countries to match the style and culture of the specific country. Revson did the opposite: He introduced a purely American–style ad campaign, featuring American models, to foreign lands. The approach, later copied by others, was a smashing success. The "Western look" became chic in places like Japan.

In his biography of Revson, Tobias noted: "He changed the appearance of women throughout the world—both in how they looked to others and how they looked to themselves. He injected a little excitement into what Martin Revson, borrowing from Thoreau, liked to call the 'quiet desperation' of the average housewife's daily life. The irony is that he held women in such contempt. And that he himself, the beauty–maker, was so unbeautiful." He sold image, hope, and glamour to millions of women but always retained a strongly pessimistic attitude regarding the value and abilities of those around him. Seemingly, Revson's drive for perfection was both his greatest asset and his worst trait.

Sources of Information

Bibliography

"The American Experience: The Quiz Show Scandal." *PBS, Inc.*, 2001. Available at http://www.pbs.org.

Bowman, John S., ed. *Cambridge Dictionary of American Biography.* Cambridge: Cambridge University Press, 1995.

Crystal, David, ed. *Cambridge Biograhpical Encyclopedia.* 2nd ed. Cambridge: Cambridge University Press, 1998.

Ingham, John N., and Lynne B. Feldman. *Contemporary American Business Leaders: A Biographical Dictionary.* New York: Greenwood Press, 1990.

"Revlon History." Revlon, Inc., 2001. Available at http://www.revlon.com.

Revlon, Inc. Available at http://www.revlon.com.

"Revlon, Inc." *Hoover's Online*, 2001. Available at http://www.hoovers.com.

Leonard S. Riggio

(1941-)
Barnes & Noble, Inc.

Overview

Starting out with a single college bookshop in the mid–1960s, Leonard S. Riggio went on to become the largest bookseller in the United States. In fact, as of 1998 one in eight books sold in the nation was purchased at Riggio's company, Barnes & Noble. As of 2001 Barnes & Noble's revenue surpassed $4.3 billion and profits rolled in from a network of one thousand stores, more than any other book retailer in the United States. Over the previous 30 years Riggio steadily expanded the company into an empire spanning such peripheral operations as a mail–order catalog, book publishing arm, and a video game retail chain. Its website, Barnes & Noble.com, became one of the largest online booksellers second only to Amazon.com.

Personal Life

Leonard Riggio has two daughters from his first marriage and another with his second wife, Louise, whom he married in the early 1980s. They reside in an expansive apartment on Park Avenue in Manhattan, New York and also have an estate in Bridgehampton, New York. The unpretentious Riggio often socializes with blue–collar friends from his youth, preferring their company to that of the rich and famous. Generous with charity, he donated $1 million to his alma mater, Brooklyn Technical High School, in 1998 and over $700,000 to the Children's Defense Fund for the purpose of building a library on the farm of the late Alex Haley, author of *Roots*. Unlike most philanthropists, though, Riggio is quite low–key about his gifts. For example, instead of putting

Leonard Riggio (left), with Edward Kennedy, wearing an honorary cap and gown bestowed by Bentley College. (AP/Wide World Photos.)

his name on the library, he and his wife suggested naming it after poet Langston Hughes. Riggio is an avid art and wine collector and also likes to golf. His favorite work of fiction is *The Metamorphosis* by Franz Kafka.

Riggio was born February 28, 1941 in the Little Italy section of Manhattan. At age four he moved to the Bensonhurst neighborhood of Brooklyn, where his home housed an extended family of aunts, uncles, and grandparents. His mother was a dressmaker and his father, Stephen Riggio, was a prize fighter who beat Rocky Graziano twice in his career. Many times Leonard Riggio was compared to his father because of what critics called a hot temper and antagonistic nature. Resenting

this characterization as a fighter, Riggio rebutted that quick thinking was just as important as the physical aspect of the sport of boxing.

Politically active throughout his life, Riggio set up copy machines in the basement of his first store so that students could publish antiwar materials. In 1993 he served as campaign finance chair for New York City mayor David Dinkins, and donated $138,000 to Dinkins and New York governor Mario Cuomo in 1993 and 1994.

Throughout his rise to become one of the nation's leading business executives, Riggio stayed close to his roots. His youngest brother, Steve, is a vice–chair of

Barnes & Noble and runs the online sector, and middle brother Jimi is part–owner of a shipping company that handles Barnes & Noble products. "My nationality is New York City," Riggio proclaimed in *Business Week*. "I don't mean I'm a New Yorker like the *New York Times* is a New Yorker. I mean it in the Horatio Alger sense."

A gifted child, Riggio skipped two grades and at age 12, entered Brooklyn Technical High School. Small in stature—he grew to only five feet, seven inches—he played the class clown to make friends, and also excelled in sports, earning a spot on the basketball team despite his height. After high school Riggio enrolled at New York University and studied metallurgical engineering at night but found his day job at the college bookstore to be more intriguing. He eventually switched to the business school but ended up devoting all of his energy to bookselling. He began as a store clerk in 1958 at $1.10 an hour, and by 1965 was an assistant manager earning $140 a week. Like many other employees in various establishments around the country, Riggio held the impression that he could manage the store better than his boss, but unlike most, he actually set out to do something about it.

Chronology:
Leonard S. Riggio

1941: Born.

1965: Opened Student Book Exchange book store.

1971: Bought Barnes & Noble book store.

1986: Bought B. Dalton chain.

1989: Acquired Scriber's chain.

1990: Bought Bookstop superstores.

1997: Established Barnes & Noble.com online bookseller.

1998: Barnes & Noble became the number one bookseller in the country.

2001: Barnes & Noble.com was the second–largest online bookseller.

Career Details

In 1965, with $5,000 in start–up funds from savings and loans, Leonard Riggio opened a competing book shop, the Student Book Exchange, or SBX for short, around the corner from his former employer. By the time he was 30, Riggio had amassed a small chain of campus bookstores on the East Coast but still aspired to do more. In 1971 he made a bid for the failing Barnes & Noble bookstore on Fifth Avenue and 18th Street. Riggio offered $750,000 for this last remaining store of the chain begun in 1873 by Charles Montgomery Barnes and G. Clifford Noble. The offer was eagerly accepted and Riggio immediately overhauled the musty old shop, initiating, among other innovations, a humorous advertising campaign to attract shoppers. He also continued his reputation, started at his college shops, of delivering on every book request imaginable. "We created a crescendo of demand for titles no one else was carrying," he recalled in *Publishers Weekly*. "We included publications from the Government Printing Office, journal reprints. We carried books no matter what the profit margin."

In the mid–1970s one of the company's landmark moves was to open a Sale Annex, featuring tables of books discounted to one dollar as well as selected bestsellers at a discount rate, a concept that revolutionized the business of bookselling. The store eventually sold thousands of titles at big discounts and encompassed 40,000 square feet, a previously unheard of amount of space for a book retailer. Riggio also added restrooms, park benches, and even supermarket carts and grocery store–style checkout lanes. As he explained in a *Forbes* article in 1976, "There are 30,000 mini–delicatessens in American bookselling, and we are the only supermarket." Applying aggressive marketing—a foreign tactic in the polite book industry—the store's slogan was, "If you paid full price, you didn't get it at Barnes & Noble," Riggio told *Publishers Weekly*.

Into the latter part of the 1970s Riggio continued to establish new shops modeled after the Sale Annex, only smaller, ranging from 2,500 to 3,000 square feet. These stores carried a selection of discounted bestsellers and a good deal of remainders. About the same time Barnes & Noble began acquiring several smaller booksellers including Bookmasters, Marboro books, and some college stores. Riggio's company had thus expanded to 37 retail shops and 142 college stores as well as a mail–order business. He really made waves in the industry however, when in November 1986 he purchased the B. Dalton chain of 796 stores from its parent firm, Dayton Hudson.

Riggio began attracting criticism for contributing to the growing trend of the corporatization of bookstores. Some complained that the days of personalized service from well–read clerks were ending and others predicted that smaller and more scholarly works would become obsolete. Some small publishers later pointed out that the larger stores were able to stock a better variety of titles, thereby helping to keep their products viable. Nevertheless, Barnes & Noble epitomized faceless corporate America to many. To make matters worse Riggio continued buying out one small chain after another, including Scribner's in 1989 and Doubleday stores in 1990, then began to shut them down when retailing saw a decrease in mall traffic.

About this same time Riggio took note of the "superstore" concept that was growing in retail, whereby chains like Toys 'R' Us and Circuit City were establishing huge warehouse–style stores that offered a wide selection of goods at low prices. Borders Books, sold to K–mart in 1992, was the first bookseller to try this concept, constructing stores that offered more than 100,000 titles. Recognizing that this was the future, Riggio quickly followed suit. In September 1989 he nabbed Bookstop, a Texas–based chain of 24 superstores. By 1991 he began fervent construction of freestanding buildings reaching 20,000 square feet. Riggio added Starbucks coffee bars, easy chairs, and even cooking demonstrations in order to make his bookstores a social event, something to do as an alternative to a movie or other destination. It was not long before his bookstores began hosting singles' nights, creating a touch of a nightclub atmosphere.

By 1993 Barnes & Noble had grown to become the country's second–largest book chain, next to K–mart's Waldenbooks/Borders. It was clearly leading the pack in superstores, though, with 168 such outlets as opposed to Borders' 35 superstores. That year Barnes & Noble went public. It subsequently suffered under low profit margins and unstable earnings, but by 1998 its fortunes had rebounded. Stock had risen from $13.50 per share in late 1996 to $35 by mid–1998. At the same time, with 483 Barnes & Noble superstores and 528 mall–based B. Daltons, the company boasted annual sales of $2.8 billion, surpassing Borders.

Competitors, particularly independent booksellers, were dismayed at Riggio's enormous success. And they did more than grumble. In April 1999 the American Booksellers Association, a coalition of 4,047 bookstores, filed a federal lawsuit against Barnes & Noble claiming that the chain coerced publishers into giving it price breaks that made it impossible for the small shops to compete. On a cultural level, critics contended that Barnes & Noble was having a negative impact on the industry. They claimed that the chain did not lend itself to individual recommendations from one reader to another as customers often receive at the smaller shops, thereby putting a damper on the kind of word–of–mouth publicity that can make a lesser–known book into a sleeper hit. Other critics charged that Barnes & Noble was "dumbing down" the business of books by offering mainly bestsellers and fad items. However, according to *Business Week*, bestsellers accounted for only three percent of sales at Barnes & Noble in 1997, about the same percentage as at any other bookseller. In addition, many publishers were delighted that Barnes & Noble, thanks to its generous shelf space, could stock an even greater selection, enabling more obscure publications to share the floor.

Riggio, however, had something bigger to contend with by the mid–1990s—the dawning of online book sales, particularly the Internet upstart Amazon.com. Founded by Jeff Bezos in 1994 as a "virtual" bookstore, this website was able to offer a wider selection, sometimes at discounts of up to 30 percent, than any physical store because it was not limited by shelf space. Not to be outdone, Riggio began an online venture, Barnes & Noble.com, in March 1997. Initially, the online venture had its share of snags and was slow to attract large numbers of customers, prompting some to predict that it would fail. But by 2001 Barnes & Noble.com, averaging 5.3 million unique visitors a month, had become the second–largest online book distributor behind Amazon.com, as well as the fourth–largest e–commerce retailer. The website, one of the largest in the world, offered books, music, software, magazines, prints, posters, and other products.

As Barnes & Noble's biggest shareholder, Riggio controls 22 percent of the company and two percent of Barnes & Noble.com. He also owns 80 percent of Barnes & Noble College Bookstores and all of Babbage's Etc., which operates Babbage's and Software Etc. software retailers. Seeking new growth in mid–1999, Riggio announced plans to acquire Ingram Book Group, the nation's largest book wholesaler, for $600 million. This purchase would give Barnes & Noble an edge in distribution and faster delivery, key elements in finding success in the online world. The deal fell through though, when the Federal Trade Commission ruled that it would violate antitrust law. Riggio then focused on different ideas for building distribution networks. Since Barnes & Noble already operated a wholesale facility in New Jersey that accounted for 60 percent of its distribution, Riggio believed that he could increase this warehouse space to surpass Ingram's network.

Social and Economic Impact

Leonard Riggio's passion for bookselling revolutionized the industry. His concept of the superstore, combined with his ideas for making the bookstore a more fun and entertaining place to spend time, set a trend among others. His vision led him to expand Barnes & Noble, acquiring bookstore after bookstore and making his company the nation's leading bookseller. Not content to rest on his laurels, Riggio stepped up to take on the e–commerce giant Amazon.com with his online venture Barnes & Noble.com, which grabbed a large percentage of Amazon's market share and grew to become the second–biggest online bookseller. The GameStop division, which encompasses Babbage's Etc., FuncoLand, and GameStop, has become the leading video game retailer in the country.

With this success, however, has come a backlash from critics who have derided the corporate nature of the book industry and the demise of small, independent shops. Riggio countered with the argument that he has democratized book shops, transforming them from the musty, mysterious institutions of yore into cheery, accessible places where crowds congregate over cups of cappuccino. Such criticism has not deterred Riggio who is always seeking to expand his empire even farther.

Sources of Information

Contact at: Barnes & Noble, Inc.
   122 Fifth Ave.
   New York, NY 10011
   Business Phone (212)633–3300
   URL: http://www.barnesandnobleinc.com

Bibliography

"About Barnes & Noble.com." New York: Barnes & Noble, November 2001. Available at http://www.barnesandnoble.com.

"Barnes & Noble, Inc." Hoover's Online, Inc., November 2001. Available at http://www.hoovers.com.

Dugan, I. Jeanne. "The Baron of Books." *Business Week*, 29 June 1998.

Kemp, Ted. "Barnes & Noble Builds Dual Web Platforms." *InternetWeek*, 31 August 2001.

"Leonard S. Riggio." *Newsmakers 1999*, Issue 4. Farmington Hills, MI: Gale Group, 1999.

Munk, Nina. "Title Fight." *Fortune*, 21 June 1999, 84.

Patton, Susannah. "Barnesandnoble.com Fights Back." *CIO Magazine*, 15 September 2001.

Richard Edwin Rivera

(1947-)
Red Lobster Restaurants

Overview

Richard Edwin Rivera, a tall and striking man known for his affable disposition, is president of the Red Lobster restaurant chain. As one of the highest–ranking minorities in the restaurant industry, he is viewed by many as a role model. His career has been characterized by achievement as well as a demonstrated concern for people, especially women and minorities. He has been honored for his efforts in encouraging women and minorities to develop in their job roles and to advance within an organization and in the industry.

Personal Life

Richard Rivera was born January 6, 1947. He earned his Bachelor of Arts degree from Washington & Lee University in Lexington, Virginia in 1968. Rivera married Leslie Suzanne Pliner on November 18, 1984.

In 1997 Rivera, who held various leadership positions in the restaurant industry for 25 years, took control of the Red Lobster chain, which is owned by Darden Restaurants. When he assumed this position he was determined to turn the moribund chain around by changing the restaurant image and expanding the demographics of its clientele. Rivera's alterations at Red Lobster amounted to a complete overhaul. He moved the once–hidden bar area to a prominent spot in the front of the restaurants, spiced up the food menu, changed such visual elements as the smallwares and employee uniforms, and implemented employee training programs that emphasized customer satisfaction. His efforts not only revitalized the chain but also improved the fortunes of its parent Darden

Restaurants, owner of 1,173 full–service restaurants that included the Red Lobster, Olive Garden, Bahama Breeze, and Smokey Bones BBQ Sports Bar chains.

Career Details

Richard Rivera began his career in the industry working for the Steak and Ale Restaurants of America chain. He was employed by the Dallas–headquartered company from 1971 to 1980, starting as a management trainee and rising to the positions of executive vice president and director. From 1980 to 1982 he was president of the restaurant division for the El Chico Corp. For the next five years he served as chief operating officer for T.J. Applebee's and Taco Villa Mexican Restaurant. In 1987 Rivera joined TGI Friday's Inc., serving as executive vice president of operations until 1988 and as president and chief executive officer until 1994. From 1994 to 1997 he was president and chief executive officer of RARE Hospitality International, Inc. and the owner of Long Horn Steakhouse restaurants. He served as president and chief executive officer of Chart House Restaurants, Inc. from July until December 1997. Since 1997 he has been president of Red Lobster Restaurants, as well as director and executive vice president of Darden Restaurants. During his career he has also served as a Director of the National Restaurant Association. Before he entered the restaurant industry he worked as a credit analyst for National Bank Commerce in Dallas, Texas.

When Rivera joined Red Lobster, he regarded his mission as revitalizing the chain founded in 1968 in Lakeland, Florida. This included changing almost every element of the business involving customer contact, ranging from the bar to tableware and even to television advertising. His focus was nothing less than an entire facelift for the chain's well–established image. His redesign included a shift to highlight the bar, an area typically receiving as much attention, if not more, in other casual–dining restaurants. This change in particular represented a significant break from both tradition and the direction of the former owner, food giant General Mills, which seemingly hid the bar areas in order to de–emphasize beverage sales.

To achieve his aims Rivera engaged the services of industrial psychologist Tom DeCotiis, with whom Rivera had previously worked at TGI Friday's and Chart House Restaurants. Rivera had ambitious plans for Red Lobster and he believed that DeCotiis would be a good resource in helping him revitalize the stagnating chain. Utilizing his "visioneering" process, DeCotiis held extensive interviews with management and store–level employees, ultimately producing a document called *The Compass*, which detailed ways to improve the chain.

As a result, in 2000 Red Lobster remodeled 85 stores at a cost of $250,000 each. The impact of this effort was almost immediate as beverage sales and income in-

Richard Rivera. (Red Lobster Restaurants.)

creased. By the end of that year fiscal revenue for the "New Red" had increased to $2.08 billion.

In its earlier days Red Lobster had once enjoyed a reputation as a leading seafood restaurant. That image had diminished by the late 1990s however, as the chain was hurt by competition from other casual dining restaurants, some of which didn't even specialize in seafood. In response Red Lobster took to offering discounts, and became better known for its price–focused promotions than its menu. The chain's primary aim was to seat and serve as many people as possible. As a result of this approach the menu suffered, as preparation lacked imagination and all items began tasting the same. These were desperate, yet ineffective, measures meant to stem the tide of falling revenue.

When Rivera came on board he recognized the need to improve the hospitality element of the chain, which he felt was sadly lacking. Realizing that something would have to be done about the menu, he directed his chefs to spice up the food with stronger flavors and to make the entrée dishes more interesting. Specific changes included reducing the number of deep–fried items, adding more seafood pastas, and offering more fresh fish dishes. Part of the restaurant overhaul included the installation of a lobster tank as well as the inclusion of the giant lobster tail on the menu, which proved to be a popular item despite its price.

Rivera also wanted to change the "look" of the restaurant and this included alterations in table settings

Chronology:

Richard Edwin Rivera

1947: Born.

1968: Graduated from Washington & Lee University.

1971: Entered the restaurant business.

1980: Became president of restaurant division for the El Chico Corp.

1982: Named COO for T.J. Applebee's and Taco Villa Mexican Restaurant.

1987: Joined TGI Fridays, Inc.

1994: Named President and CEO of RARE Hospitality International, Inc.

1997: Became executive vice president of Darden Restaurants, Inc.

1997: Took over Red Lobster Restaurants chain.

2000: Received Trailblazer award from the Women's Foodservice Forum.

---

as well as the appearance of the staff. He replaced the plain white plates with colorful china. Employees were given a new dress code: out were the black–and–white uniforms and in were colorful print shirts, striped polo shirts, and khakis. "Before, everything was utilitarian," Rivera told *Chain Leader*. "Now, it's mostly about personality, though we still have a lot of work to do."

The employees themselves were retrained in a program that emphasized product knowledge and hospitality. As part of the training program employees were encouraged to take the initiative in creating "personality," providing energy and fun, and demonstrating a more thoughtful attitude toward the diner. Bartenders were taught how to perform tricks for the benefit of the bar customers and they were encouraged to push the appetizers. Rivera also created an employee–satisfaction survey, called "Crews Views" that was released every year. To explain the survey Rivera made videos in English and in Spanish. The bilingual approach was beneficial as Red Lobster recruited many of its summer interns from Puerto Rico and many employees in the Florida restaurants were Hispanic.

Rivera was experienced and savvy enough to realize that change wouldn't come easy. Such drastic measures put both himself and the entire restaurant chain at risk, since the faltering chain would have to go through a critical period before an upturn, if any, could be realized. Rivera knew that success could be achieved only by maintaining a fine balance. On the one hand, revitalization involved an influx of new customers, and a new clientele needed to be established and strengthened. At the same time he attempted not to alienate its established client–base, which might not be comfortable with the changes. The aim was to capitalize on the loyalty of the current customer base as well as the widespread recognition of the Red Lobster brand name, while not jeopardizing either with an overload of drastic changes implemented too quickly. Change could positively impact current customers. "But you need a keen understanding of how far they will let you go," explained marketing expert Karen Brennan in *Chain Leader*.

To walk the median, Rivera felt that he needed to emphasize the benefits of the casual dining experience. He wanted people to recognize that Red Lobster was more than just a seafood restaurant. Rather, it strove to be a place where anyone could come in and enjoy the camaraderie and social experience that the best casual bars provided. Still, Rivera needed for people to know that seafood would always be the predominate element.

Rivera didn't completely do away with the food price promotions but he reduced their number. In 1997 there were nine of these "price point" promotions; in 2000 there were only three. The menu was also improved and expanded. Its changes included the March–April "Lobster Fest" promotion that included such items as Tropical Lobster Chowder. The size of lobster tails offered were larger, as the standard one–and–a–quarter pound tail was supplanted by two– and three–pound lobsters on display in lobster tanks. Some restaurants included more non–batter–fried items, and others offered more fresh fish. Also, the menu expanded its selection of unique non–seafood items, such as a grilled chicken laced with chipotle–flavored barbecue sauce.

Social and Economic Impact

Richard Rivera's overhaul of Red Lobster had a significant and almost immediate impact. Among its 668 units, Red Lobster's average restaurant sales rose from $2.7 million in 1997 to $3.2 million in 2000. Same–store sales and customer volume boasted positive growth for 11 consecutive quarters. Rivera's efforts not only benefited Red Lobster but also Darden Restaurants. Representing 58 percent of its parent company's total units, the seafood chain propelled Darden's stock price to $26 per share, a 45 percent increase, by December 2000. Darden, like Red Lobster, experienced an upturn in its profitability after Rivera's improvements, posting 14 consecutive quarters of positive earnings. "I'm impressed with the turnaround at Red Lobster," said Mark Kalinowski, of Salomon Smith Barney, in *Chain Leader*. "The 'New Red' makeovers seem to have boosted sales."

Rivera's achievements in the industry have been noted as well as honored. He is known for actively recruiting and encouraging women and minorities. In 2000 the Women's Foodservice Forum (WFF) named Rivera as one of its recipients of the 2000 Trailblazer Award, which recognizes individuals with a record of achievement in propelling organizations forward and making a difference in the industry as a whole. Further, Rivera was singled out for demonstrating innovative approaches to business with diversity programs and for making a lasting contribution to furthering opportunities for women and minorities. Specifically the WFF cited Rivera for contributing to and promoting Darden Restaurants' diversity initiatives, such as the Minority Supplier Development Program. The organization also recognized him as being instrumental in repositioning Red Lobster's culture diversity, with respect and fairness as cornerstones. The WFF also pointed out that three of the six people on his executive team were women. Rivera, the WFF stated, embodied the Trailblazer spirit with his equitable approach to individuals without regard to their gender or race.

Sources of Information

Contact at: Red Lobster Restaurants
8815 Southern Breeze Dr.
Orlando, FL 32859–3330
URL: http://www.redlobster.com/

Bibliography

"Darden Restaurants, Inc." Hoover's Online, Inc., November 2001. Available at http://www.hoovers.com.

Farkas, David. "Lounge Act." *Chain Leader*, January 2001.

"The NRAEF Welcomes Eight New Members to Board of Trustees." National Restaurant Association Educational Foundation, 26 October 2000. Available at http://www.edfound.org.

"Richard Edwin Rivera." *Biography Resource Center*. Farmington Hills, MI: The Gale Group, January 2001.

"Women's Foodservice Forum Announces Emerging Leader and Trailblazer Award Recipients." Rich's—In the News, 9 March 2000. Available at http://www.richs.com.

Anthony J. Robbins

(1960-)
Robbins Research Institute, Inc.

Overview

Anthony J. Robbins is a self–help author and speaker who has authored five books. His seminars and instructional audiotapes generate more than $50 million a year in revenues.

Personal Life

Anthony J. Robbins was born on February 29, 1960 in California to Jim and Niki (Shows) Robbins. He attended the University of California in Los Angeles in 1974 but did not stay to graduate. In 1985 he married Rebecca Biggerstaff, an executive, and they have four children: Tyler Jenkins, Jollie Jenkins, Joshua Jenkins, and Jairek. He and his wife later divorced, and Robbins married Sage in late 2001 in the Fiji Islands. He resides in a 10,000–square–foot oceanside mansion in Del Mar, California.

Robbins, whose motto in life is "To live and give passionately" has become known as one of the most popular self–help gurus in the United States. In addition to being the author of five books he has conducted live seminars throughout the world, produced four infomercials, and sold millions of instructional audiotapes and CDs. He is also an entrepreneur and a member of the Young Entrepreneurs Association; he has founded nine companies and owns the luxury Namale Fiji Island Resort. His humanitarian efforts include the Anthony Robbins Foundation and his consulting clients have included President Bill Clinton and several prominent athletes and companies. In recognition of his achievements, Robbins was selected as the 1994 Outstanding Humanitarian and re-

Anthony Robbins. (Hulton/Archive.)

ceived the Justice Brian White Award from the Touch-down Club of Washington, D.C., and was named one of the "Ten Outstanding Young Americans" by the U.S. Junior Chamber of Commerce. In addition, Toastmasters International recognized him as one of the world's top five speakers in 1993 and later he received their most prestigious award, the Golden Gavel Award.

Career Details

Robbins first gained popularity in the 1980s as a motivational speaker who taught people how to walk across hot coals. He wrote two books, *Unlimited Power: Strategies for Personal Excellence* (Premier Publishing, 1984) and *Unlimited Power: The Way to Peak Personal Achievement* (Simon & Schuster, 1986), both of which became bestsellers. During the 1980s he served as president of Achievement Enterprises in Los Angeles (1979–1981) and then as president of Diamond Method (1981–1983). In 1984 he founded the Robbins Research Institute, Inc., in La Jolla, California, for which he continues to serve as president.

In the early 1990s Robbins' fame grew considerably with the advent of his series of four television infomercials, begun in April 1989, on how to improve almost every aspect of one's life: physical health, emotional

Chronology:
Anthony J. Robbins

1960: Born.

1984: Published *Unlimited Power: Strategies for Personal Excellence*.

1986: Published *Unlimited Power: The Way to Peak Personal Achievement*.

1989: First infomercial aired.

1991: Published *Awaken the Giant Within: How to Take Immediate Control of Your Mental, Emotional, Physical, and Financial Destiny*.

1994: Published *Giant Steps: Small Changes to Make a Big Difference: Daily Lesson in Self–Mastery*; became personal advisor to President Clinton.

1995: Published *Notes From a Friend: A Quick and Simple Guide to Taking Charge of Your Life*.

1997: Published *Ebony Power Thoughts: Inspirational Thoughts from Outstanding African Americans* and *Unlimited Power: The Black Choice*, both titles co–authored by Joseph McClendon III.

2000: Launched Website Dreamlife.com; purchased Discovery Toys.

---

well–being, relationships, finances, and professional growth. Referring to other products sold in infomercials, Robbins told *Newsweek*, "With infomercials, you're in the midst of spray–on hair and kitchen mops"; but he decided "the benefits outweighed the downsides." The strategy, used for selling his motivational tapes, paid off: More than a decade later the infomercials continuously aired on average every 30 minutes, 24 hours a day somewhere in North America and had generated sales of over 25 million copies of Robbins' self–help audiocassettes. The infomercials are considered a mainstay of late–night television. Robbins' infomercials have featured such celebrities as former professional football player Fran Tarkenton and actor Martin Sheen.

From there, Robbins began to gain some prestigious clients as a "peak performance consultant." In 1997 Robbins boasted in one of his infomercials that he counseled professional tennis player Andre Agassi; as a result, Agassi moved up from being ranked thirtieth in the world to first in just six months. Other top clients include the entire professional basketball teams of the Los Angeles

Kings and the San Antonio Spurs, basketball coach Pat Riley, and baseball's Tommy Lasorda He also advised members of the British royal family including Princess Diana, and employees of large organizations such as Hallmark, Southwestern Bell, and the U.S. Army. For his high–profile clients, which included President Clinton in 1994, Robbins provides his "cognitive evaluation system." Clients fill out a detailed questionnaire documenting daily events such as diet and mental and emotional well–being. Daily updates are faxed to Robbins who then evaluates the points at which the customers are functioning best. He then assists them in re–engineering their lives to maintain peak performance. For such elaborate services the wealthy pay $1 million or more. Robbins did, however, offer his services to President Clinton in 1994 free of charge.

By the mid–1990s Robbins had written three more books: *Awaken the Giant Within: How to Take Immediate Control of Your Mental, Emotional, Physical and Financial Destiny* (Summit, 1991), *Giant Steps: Small Changes to Make a Big Difference: Daily Lessons in Self–Mastery* (Fireside, 1994), and *Notes From a Friend: A Quick and Simple Guide to Taking Charge of Your Life* (Fireside, 1995). His first three books have been translated into 14 languages around the world.

Despite Robbins' success with late–night television and publishing, his real calling was public speaking. Robbins conducts more than eighty seminars a year in eight nations. He offers a variety of programs from a one–day sales seminar to a nine–day intensive "Life Mastery" program. In seminars that draw thousands of people at a time—many of them salespeople—Robbins espouses his message of "Constant and Never–Ending Improvement" (CANI!). With his 6–foot, 7–inch frame and seemingly endless bounds of energy, Robbins whips participants into a frenzy of hope and inspiration about what they can do and be. Shari Caudron of *Workforce* described a Robbins seminar: "To get an idea of what it's like to attend one of these screaming hug–fests, picture yourself standing on the game floor of a sports arena surrounded by 15,000 other secret achievers, all of whom are wearing some version of khaki pants and polo shirts. Now, picture your hands and 30,000 others balled into fists, punching the air above your heads. You're yelling—hollering, 'Yes! Yes! Yes!' The concrete floor vibrates as you and your new best friends stomp your feet in a fury of motivational passion." Although the participants in his seminars have been compared to fans at a last–minute–win Super Bowl game with the same mania of glee and excitement, the message remains simple as Robbins acknowledged when he told *Forbes*, "I try to keep my ideas simple enough so that they are actionable."

In 1997 Robbins came out with another book, co-authored with Joseph McClendon III, lead trainer of the Robbins Research Institute, titled *Ebony Power Thoughts: Inspirational Thoughts from Outstanding African–Americans* (Fireside). Hoping to reach an audience that had largely ignored his work, Robbins addressed the black community once again with his fifth book, also with McClendon, *Unlimited Power: A Black Choice* (Simon & Schuster), which encourages blacks to overcome social roadblocks and work toward their dreams. Although Robbins, who is white, appears as co–author on the book, the message is dominated by McClendon, who is black. According to *Publisher's Weekly*, "In a relentlessly positive and encouraging tone, [McClendon] uses his own personal experiences and many examples of famous African Americans to explain Robbins' theories." The authors use neurolinguistic programming, which is basically changing how one thinks about things, as the basis for this book; this is the same philosophy that Robbins began with in the 1980s and continues to promote today. As *U.S. News & World Report* noted, according to Robbins, "If you believe you can or if you believe you can't, you're right."

In addition to his best–selling books, Robbins has been extremely successful with his audiotape series "Personal Power," which has sold more than 30 million copies worldwide. Referring to an audio series titled "Powertalk," *Publisher's Weekly* commented, "Robbins' motor–mouth style has particular appeal, and his slightly gravelly voice comes across as direct and engaging, matching the identity projected by his big–toothed smile in the author photo." His next media endeavor, a compact disk set, was titled *Personal Power II: The Driving Force!* and also sold well.

Social and Economic Impact

Robbins has made various societal contributions, including serving as a spokesperson for the Missing Children's Foundation and sponsoring a college education fund in Houston, Texas. In addition, the Anthony Robbins Foundation supplies Thanksgiving dinners for 125,000 people in 65 cities in the United States and Canada. Robbins has also served on the board of directors for Ted Danson's American Oceans Campaign and supplies books and tapes to social organizations such as schools, prisons, and homeless shelters. Robbins' Mastery University, for which he serves as dean, provides a year–long educational experience and utilizes such instructors as General Norman Schwarzkopf on leadership, Dr. Deepak Chopra on psychoneuroimmunology, and Sir John Templeton on finance. More than 10,000 people from 42 nations have attended the university.

Robbins is part of the $7–billion–a–year self–help industry. *Business Week* reported that Robbins' portion of that, from his books, tapes, and seminars, is $80 million a year. He has founded nine companies, including Fortune Practice Management, a practice management company for dentists and other health care professionals; the Namale Fiji Island Resort, a luxury resort in the Fiji Islands; a network marketing business in Asia for nutritional products; and a television production company.

In 2000 Robbins took control of a publicly controlled shell company whose stocks were at only a few cents per share; after announcing his plans to build a self–improvement Website, called Dreamlife.com, the shares rose to $16 a piece. Robbins' portion of that was $300 million. Started as a personal and professional development Website focused on consumers, Dreamlife.com took a different turn in 2001, focusing more on the sales forces of direct–selling organizations. It also began to acquire companies with the purchase of Discovery Toys, a maker of educational products. According to *Business Week*, Dreamlife.com's worth stands at $480 million.

Robbins is not without his critics. In 1995 he settled the last of five lawsuits brought against him by disgruntled distributors of his video seminars who accused Robbins of failing to honor exclusive marketing rights. Without admitting wrongdoing, Robbins forked over $221,000 to close the suits. Others denounce his blatant materialism (on one of his CDs, he tells audiences, "You deserve to have an abundance of money") and the gist of his message of wealth and success. According to *Newsweek*, "Robbins' conspicuous consumption—he presides over an Oceanside mansion in Del Mar, helicopters to his Palm Springs home and dresses in dazzling suits—has also drawn fire." Dr. Douglas LaBier, director of the Center for Adult Development in Washington, D.C., told *Newsweek*, "Robbins' vision of success—money, pools and the like—is outmoded and dangerous."

Professional analysts are particularly critical of Robbins' message that preaches "feel–good–now" only provide a quick fix. For example, Robbins has advised audiences that depression can be overcome by simply staring at the ceiling and smiling. Psychologist Robert Rosen explained to *Sales and Marketing Management*, "One of the dangers of self–help gurus is that their personal experience isn't consistent with the experience of large numbers of people. It may be easy for Tony Robbins to look up at a ceiling, smile, and get over feeling sad, but when a clinically depressed person realizes that that solution doesn't work, he or she may end up feeling worse."

Others are more skeptical than critical of Robbins and the entire self–help industry. "At the very, very worst, these people are charming mountebanks, completely harmless," Nicholas Lemann, author of book on the history of self–help in the United States, told *U.S. News & World Report*, "At their best, they can help a little." Critics aside, millions swear Robbins' techniques and message of self–help enable them to lift themselves up. Judging from his popularity, it seems more people love him than hate him and as a result, Robbins has created a multi–million–dollar business of convincing people that "Reality is the reality you create."

Sources of Information

Contact at: Robbins Research Institute, Inc.
    3366 North Torrey Pines Ct., Ste. 100
    La Jolla, CA 92037
    URL: www.anthonyrobbins.com

Bibliography

"Anthony Robbins." Robbins Research Institute, Inc., 2001. Available at http://www.anthonyrobbins.com/bio2.html.

Berenson, Alex. "Anthony Robbins Makes an Internet Play." *New York Times*, 8 January 2000.

Brewer, Geoffrey. "Is This Guy for Real?" *Sales and Marketing Management*, November 1993.

Caudron, Shari. "Meditations on Motivation." *Workforce*, June 2000.

Cooper, Matthew. "The Bill–and–Newt Gurus." *U.S. News & World Report*, 23 January 1995.

"Dreamlife, Inc." *Hoover's Online*, 2001. Available at http://www.hoovers.com.

Gubernick, Lisa. "The Nemesis Factor." *Forbes*, 9 October 1995.

Kaufman–Rosen, Leslie. "Getting in Touch with Your Inner President." *Newsweek*, 16 January 1995.

Levine, Art. "Peak Performance is Tiring." *U.S. News & World Report*, 24 February 1997.

McGinn, Daniel. "Self–Help U.S.A." *Newsweek*, 10 January 2000.

Morris, Kathleen. "$276 Million: Now That's Motivation." *Business Week*, 13 September 1999.

Nelson, Corinne. "*Unlimited Power: The Black Choice*." *Library Journal*, 1 May 1997.

"One Man's Ted Sorenson is Another's Marieanne Williamson." *Time*, 23 January 1995.

"*Unlimited Power: A Black Choice*." *Publisher's Weekly*, 30 December 1996.

Zinsser, John. "'Powertalk': The Power to Create, the Power to Destroy." *Publisher's Weekly*, 3 August 1992.

Ralph Joel Roberts

Overview

Ralph J. Roberts is the founder and chairman of Comcast Corporation, which he built from a single cable television system into one of the leading communications companies in the world. Comcast Cable is the third–largest cable services provider in the United States. Comcast Corporation develops, manages, and operates a number of broadband services including digital cable and high–speed cable modem Internet access. The company also provides original programming content through its ownership of The Golf Channel, Comcast SportsNet, Comcast–Spectacor, and the home–shopping network QVC, provider of television and Internet shopping in the United States, United Kingdom, and Germany. Comcast also holds a controlling interest in E! Entertainment Television.

(1920-)

Comcast Corporation

Personal Life

Ralph and Suzanne Roberts were married in 1942. They have five children: Catherine, Lisa, Ralph Jr., Brian, and Douglas. The family lives in Fallowfield, Pennsylvania. Roberts enjoys horseback riding on his horse farm in Chester County and fox hunting (of the variety where the fox is merely chased into a burrow, not killed).

A charter member of the World Business Council, Roberts has served on the boards of Philadelphia Electric Co. and CoreStates Financial Corp. and was trustee of the Albert Einstein Medical Center. Active in civic affairs, he holds a seat on the board of the Greater Philadel-

Ralph Joel Roberts (right), Brian Roberts (center), and Charles Lillis at a Comcast/MediaOne Group Inc. news conference. (AP Photo/Mitch Jacobson.)

phia Chamber of Commerce, the Council of Emeritus Directors of the Philadelphia Orchestra, the Brandywine Museum and Conservancy, and serves on the advisory board of the Greater Philadelphia Urban Affairs Coalition. Among the honors bestowed on him during his career are the Distinguished Vanguard Award for Leadership from the National Cable Television Association, and Temple University's Acres of Diamonds Entrepreneurial Excellence Award. He also received the Americanism Award of the Anti–Defamation League of B'nai Brith, and the Brotherhood Award of the National Conference of Christians and Jews.

Roberts was born on March 13, 1920 in New York City to Robert and Sara Wahl Roberts. He grew up in New Rochelle, a picturesque New York suburb. When Roberts was 12 years old, his father died suddenly of a heart attack and consequently, the family moved to a working–class neighborhood of Germantown, Philadelphia. This move to less–desirable circumstances affected young Ralph, who would strive to obtain financial security for his own children later in life. He graduated with a degree in economics from the Wharton School of Business at the University of Pennsylvania in 1941 and served for four years as a lieutenant in the United States Navy during World War II.

Returning from military service, Ralph Roberts got his first entrepreneurial start by joining with an engineer to form a small business. Later, he got a job as an ac-

count executive at Philadelphia–based Aitken Kynett Advertising. One of the agency's clients was Muzak, the company that introduced background music to America in the 1920s. In 1948 Roberts became a vice president for Aitken Kynett and was responsible for advertising, marketing, public relations, and sales promotion. He left the company two years later.

In 1950 Roberts dove into a completely different line of work by joining the Pioneer Suspender Co., the second–largest manufacturer and distributor of men's accessories. Six years later Roberts bought the company, which by then had grown to become Pioneer Industries. Later convinced that beltless men's pants would be the way of the future, he sold the company to Hickok Manufacturing in 1961. Roberts then established the venture capital firm International Equity Corp. (IEC), which dealt primarily in the men's toiletries and cosmetics industry. Through IEC, Roberts helped launch six new businesses over the next three years.

Career Details

In 1963 Daniel Aaron, a business broker, approached Roberts with a 1,900–subscriber cable system that was for sale. At the time, cable was not the sophisticated network of hundreds of stations and alternative programming that it would become, but was merely a means of obtaining clear television reception. Still, its outlook appeared promising to Roberts, so he bought the Mississippi–based system. Although cable was far from Roberts' area of expertise, his economic background prompted him to make the purchase. "I was never, never nervous about buying a cable system," he told *USA Today* in 2001. "You have recurring billing, reasonable rate increases, you keep your costs down and it's like chicken in a grocery store. It's very nice."

Daniel Aaron was recruited to assist in the operation of the business, called American Cable Systems, and later went on to become Comcast's vice chairman. To complete his new team, Roberts also hired Julian Brodsky, who had been employed by an accounting firm that had worked with Pioneer Industries. Brodsky later became Comcast's senior vice president and chief financial officer.

Roberts expanded the company slowly at first, carefully building the franchise over the next ten years. In 1969 the name American Cable Systems was changed to Comcast, a combination of "communications" and "broadcast." The company went public in 1972. Comcast was running smoothly thanks to the management team of Roberts, Aaron, and Brodsky who had built an excellent reputation in the industry for their corporate compatibility. In 1975 the cable industry underwent a significant change when Home Box Office (HBO) began operation, offering subscribers something brand new. The network's launch piqued Roberts' interest in cable television as he had considered cable "dull as dishwater" until that point.

Roberts expanded Comcast via acquisitions throughout the 1980s. His financing and operation of these newly purchased systems was innovative, with each system individually financed and responsible for itself, thereby insulating Comcast from the failure of any of its units. This business practice, among other savvy strategies, drew attention from Wall Street analysts and Comcast began earning a favorable reputation. In 1984 Roberts orchestrated a landmark deal, partnering with Time Inc. and Tele–Communications Inc. (TCI) to acquire the cable operator Group W. This was a major coup for Comcast, which at the time was only the 16th–largest cable company in the nation.

Cable was allowed further expansion during the 1980s when the federal government loosened restrictions on the new industry. Since Roberts had foreseen this change, Comcast was fully prepared to move forward in its new environment. The company made its initial investment in the home–shopping cable network QVC in 1986. Two years later Comcast bought half of Storer Communications thereby increasing its subscription base to more than 3 million and making it the fifth–largest cable operator in the nation. Also in 1988 Comcast entered into the cellular telecommunications industry when it acquired American Cellular Network (AMCELL), which

Chronology:
Ralph Joel Roberts

1920: Born.

1963: Bought American Cable Systems.

1969: Renamed company Comcast.

1972: Comcast went public.

1984: Partnered with TCI and Time to purchase Group W.

1986: Made initial investment in QVC.

1988: Became fifth–largest cable operator.

1989: Stepped down as president.

1996: Formed Comcast–Spectacor.

1997: Received $1 billion from Microsoft to launch networks.

1998: Acquired Jones Intercable.

2001: Bid on AT & T Broadband.

had a base of 2 million customers. In a few years, when the tide reversed and cable regulations, including a maximum on rates, were gradually reintroduced, Roberts had again prepared for the change and had placed Comcast in a position to deal with the new restrictions. Some industry experts have credited his foresight in these and other matters as one of Roberts' greatest assets.

In 1981 his son Brian joined the management team of Comcast, the only one of Roberts' children to follow him into the family business. In 1989 Ralph Roberts stepped down as company president yet retained his position as chairman, and Brian assumed the presidency the following year.

The father and son team continued the company's expansion throughout the 1990s. In 1992 Comcast combined its AMCELL properties with Metrophone, widening the service area to 7 million customers. The next year the company backed an unsuccessful bid by QVC to acquire Paramount Communications, but lost to Viacom. Comcast became the third–leading cable operator when it acquired Maclean Hunter, adding 550,000 subscribers. In 1995 it bought a 57–percent controlling interest in QVC, which would later account for nearly half of Comcast's billions of dollars in sales. That same year it acquired the cable systems of E.W. Scripps, adding 800,000 subscribers and bringing Comcast's total to 4.3 million.

In 1996 Comcast formed Comcast–Spectacor, a sports venture and owner of the Philadelphia 76ers professional basketball team, the Philadelphia Flyers hockey team, the First Union Spectrum, and the First Union Center. Comcast SportsNet, a regional sports channel, was established soon after that. Partnering with the Walt Disney Co., the company bought E! Entertainment Networks in 1997. Comcast was also an early entrant into cable modems and digital television and in 1997 it landed a $1 billion investment from Microsoft Corp. to launch its networks. In 1998 Comcast increased the number of its subscribers by 1.1 million with the acquisition of Jones Intercable.

Never complacent, the company continued to deal, strengthening its central operations while eliminating peripheral businesses. In 1999 its wireless division was sold to SBC Communications for $1.7 billion. Comcast lost to AT & T Corp. in the bidding for MediaOne, but received $1.5 billion and two million AT & T subscribers as part of the termination agreement. Undeterred, Comcast continued its expansion, gaining 1.3 million cable subscribers by acquiring Lenfest Communication in 2000. The following year it acquired Home Team Sports, the Golf Channel, and Outdoor Life Network.

In July 2001 AT & T Broadband, the leading cable operator in North America, was put up for sale. Comcast eagerly put in its bid, as did AOL Time Warner, the Walt Disney Co., Cox Communications, and Microsoft Corp. If Comcast's bid succeeds, its subscription base of 22 million would make it the largest cable operator in the United States.

Social and Economic Impact

Ralph Roberts transformed a single local cable network into one the leading communications and media companies in the nation, operating in the arenas of cable service, broadband Internet access, and television programming. Roberts' bottom–line attitude and solid understanding of business kept the company on sure footing as it steadily grew into the conglomerate that it was in the early twenty–first century. Of the company's confidence in cable as the way of the future, Roberts' son Brian, Comcast president and director, told *USA Today*, "If the most exciting thing happening in the world is the Internet, we're your best connection. If television is the device people use the most every day, we're your connection to television. If it's telephony, we can be in that business, too."

Ralph Roberts told *USA Today* that he has never sold a franchise, and that he still owns the Mississippi operation that started in all in 1963. Thanks to his foresight, keen eye for acquisitions, and willingness to explore new territories, Comcast had 8.4 million subscribers and revenues in excess of $8.2 billion in 2000, and enjoyed its status as the third–largest cable operator in the United States.

Sources of Information

Contact at: Comcast Corporation
    1500 Market St.
    Philadelphia, PA 19102–2148
    Business Phone: (215)665–1700
    URL: http://www.comcast.com

Bibliography

"About Us." Philadelphia: Comcast Corporation. November 2001. Available at http://www.comcast.com.

"Comcast Corporation." Hoover's Online, Inc., November 2001. Available at http://www.hoovers.com.

Eiley, Brahm. "Cable Battles Shaping Up with AT & T's Future in Question." *Financial Post*, 8 November 2001, 15.

Lieberman, David. "Father–Son Odd Couple Make Bid to Rule Cable: One's Calm, One's Wary, Together They're Comcast." *USA Today*, 23 July 2001, B1.

McGraw, Dan. "No Ordinary Cable Guys: Ralph and Brian Roberts, a Father–and–Son Team, Have Wired Comcast for the Future." *U.S. News & World Report*, 8 July 1996, 44.

"Muzak History." Fort Mill, SC: Muzak LLC. November 2001. Available at http://www.muzak.com.

"Ralph J. Roberts." *The Cable Center*, 2001. Available at http://www.cablecenter.org.

"Ralph Joel Roberts." *Biography Resource Center*. Farmington Hills, MI: The Gale Group, 2001.

"SBC Communications Acquires Comcast Cellular." *San Antonio Business Journal*, 20 January 1999.

Stern, Christopher. "A Philadelphia Story: Comcast's Roberts Family Built a Business Poised to Become a Media Colossus." *The Washington Post*, 10 July 2001, E1.

Benjamin Maurice Rosen

Overview

A dynamic genius, venture capitalist, and "angel investor," Benjamin M. Rosen settled into the life of a high–tech mogul after years of unfulfilling work in a variety of well–paid professions—first as an electrical engineer, followed by consultant, analyst, and publisher. He first achieved fame while working as an analyst with Morgan Stanley, where his electronics newsletter became the industry bible. He then invested in two fledgling concerns in fairly rapid succession, and made a fortune in both: Lotus software development and Compaq computers. But dearest to his financial heart was his own private venture, shared with his brother, to develop an automobile motor that would replace the industry's standard turbine engine. The Rosen Motor, based on flywheel technology, came very close to doing just that.

Personal Life

Benjamin Maurice Rosen was born in New Orleans on March 11, 1933, the youngest of three siblings. His father, Isidore J. Rosen, was a dentist and his mother, Anna Vera (Leibof) Rosen, worked as a secretary. Benjamin's parents divorced when he was seven years old. Rosen later attended the Isidore Newman School, one of the finest in New Orleans. By all accounts he was a quiet teenager, a loner of sorts. In addition to playing the trombone in the school band, he began his first business, a mail–order photo–finishing service, at the age of 13.

In 1954 he graduated from the California Institute of Technology with a bachelor's degree in electrical en-

(1933-)
Rosen Motors

Benjamin Rosen. (*AP Photo/Jim Sulley.*)

gineering (B.S.E.E.) He continued is academic pursuits at Stanford University and received a master's degree in 1955. After college, Rosen joined his elder brother Harold in Oxnard, California as an engineer at Raytheon Corporation from 1955 to 1956, and then at Sperry Corporation in Great Neck, New York from 1957 to 1959. Rosen, despite his higher education, felt unfulfilled as an engineer. So in 1959 he uprooted himself, traveled to Europe, purchased a small motor scooter, joined the denizens of the French Riviera, and taught the French to play Frisbee until he ran out of money. When he returned, he went back to school, got his MBA, and embarked on a journey of top–level jobs over the next several decades that would earn him great respect, recognition, and wealth.

Rosen married Alexandra Ebere on September 29, 1967. The couple and their two sons, Jeffrey Mark and Eric Andrew, live in Westchester County, New York. An avid golfer—notwithstanding hip replacement surgery in 2000, he belonged to five golf clubs—Rosen's eclectic New York office for Rosen Motors contained a life–size statue of himself playing golf, donated by a friend. The office also housed an old Wurlitzer jukebox loaded with Ella Fitzgerald, Frank Sinatra, and Stephen Sondheim recordings. In 2001 he continued to sit on the board of overseers of Columbia University Graduate School of Business and serve as a trustee of the California Institute of Technology. He also is on the board of Memorial Sloan–Kettering Cancer Center in New York.

Career Details

Upon his return to the United States from France, Benjamin Rosen enrolled at Columbia University in New York City, where he secured a master's degree in business administration in 1961. For the next four years he served as a vice president at Quantum Science Corporation, specializing in mutual funds associated with the technology industry. In 1965 he joined Coleman & Company as a partner. There, his extensive background as an electrical engineer earned him a vice presidency, as well as a "guru's" reputation in matters of the semiconductor industry.

Despite his career shift, Rosen experienced renewed ambivalence, discontent, and diminished career expectations. In 1975 he joined Morgan Stanley as a vice president and organized a technology newsletter to dispense business news about high–tech industries. His quick wit appealed to a wide audience but he abandoned the lucrative position due to conflict of interest—he wanted to invest in high–tech industries himself. In 1980 he branched out on his own under the auspices of Rosen Research Inc. He wrote a newsletter and hosted forums focused on the personal computer (PC) industry, which was a fledgling startup at that time.

In 1981 Rosen entered into a partnership with L. J. Sevin, a fellow electrical engineer, to form a venture capital fund with $25 million in seed money, of which they personally invested $200,000 of their own capital. Rosen, as chairman of Sevin Rosen Management Company, brought his particular expertise and understanding of marketing and public relations to the firm. By 1983 Rosen had relinquished control of his newsletter and forum businesses, again due to a conflict of interest, and turned his attention to building technology enterprises.

In 1982 Sevin and Rosen funded PC manufacturer Compaq Computer Corporation. Compaq generated revenues of $111 million in the first year and by 1995 it was the world's largest manufacturer of PCs. Also in 1982 Rosen furnished the capital for a fledgling software company called Lotus Development Corporation, the manufacturer of *1–2–3* spreadsheet software. Lotus achieved $53 million in sales that year, overshadowing original projections by a factor of 17. By 1983 Rosen was both chairman of Compaq and a member of Lotus' board of directors, and the perennial conflict of interest issue dictated that Rosen resign from the board of Lotus. In 1983 Sevin Rosen invested $60 million into a second fund, while media observers marveled that venture capital constituted a fifth career for Rosen, after engineer, consultant, analyst, and newsletter publisher. Between 1983 and 1988 Rosen's firm nurtured 10 companies to their initial public stock offerings (IPOs), and by the end of 1989 those combined company values totaled $6.7 billion. Sevin Rosen undertook an average of five ventures per year and accumulated a success record of 35 out of 45 ventures undertaken. Rosen personally sat on the board of five of the ventures.

But the overachieving Rosen and his rocket–scientist brother Harold had yet another venture in mind, this one aimed at the realization of a more personal dream. In 1993 the two brothers formed a partnership to develop a turbine–flywheel automobile. Rosen served as both chairman and deep pocket of the new company, called Rosen Motors, while Harold took the reins of president and CEO of the Woodland Hills, California, enterprise. Harold, a Ph.D. from Cal Tech, was an overachiever in his own right, having developed the technology for stationary satellites while leading the engineering staff at the Hughes Aircraft Space and Communications Group. For four years the brothers canalized their energies and their dreams toward developing a hybrid electric power train driven by two generators, one powered by turbine and the other by a mechanical flywheel. The flywheel turbine they eventually developed was made by another company the Rosens helped found, Capstone Turbine. All that they needed was to find an automobile maker that could house the engine in one of its car models.

Flywheels are battery–like additions to combustion engines that generate power and continue to propel vehicles forward once the regular engines started them moving. Proponents of the technology claim that flywheels can double fuel efficiency and slash emissions. Several automakers had looked seriously into the technology in the early 1990s, including Ford Motor Company and BMW. Chrysler unveiled its prototype flywheel–powered race car, the *Patriot*, in 1994 but never followed through with it because of expense and concern about flywheels breaking loose.

The Rosen brothers were eventually able to pair up with Saturn Corporation for a test prototype model using their engine. The turbine ran on regular unleaded gasoline from a standard size gas tank. When the engine was running, it could spin at 96,000 rpms on ultra–low–friction air bearings and the energy could be stored by the flywheel power train system. The Rosen model used a lightweight fiber composite that allowed spinning at very high speeds. The plan was to produce a system that could reach the energy equivalent of 200 horsepower (hp).

By late 1996 Rosen Motors had attracted more than 60 brainy employees, a remarkable team of engineers, scientists, and technicians, but still no government grants. The Rosen brothers had financed the entire venture, spending approximately $24 million between them and refusing investor inquiries until they could secure interest from a major automaker. In January 1997 they demonstrated their prototype *SC2* Saturn in the Mojave Desert, running it on the test track for a solid two hours at approximately 40 mph. The ultimate plan was to induce a major automobile manufacturer to build a fleet of approximately 25 cars with flywheel turbines by 1998. Eventually, Rosen intended to manufacture the power trains through his company and sell them to the carmakers.

Chronology:
Benjamin Maurice Rosen

1933: Born.

1954: Received bachelor's degree from California Institute of Technology.

1955: Received master's degree from Stanford University.

1975: Became vice president for Morgan Stanley.

1981: Formed first venture capital partnership, Sevin Rosen Management Co.

1982: Funded both Compaq Computer Corp. and Lotus Development Corp.

1982: Became chairman of Compaq.

1993: Formed Rosen Motors with brother.

1997: Rosen Motors ceased operations.

2000: Retired from Compaq.

Despite the successful road test demonstrating the commercial viability of the technology, no carmaker emerged with a firm offer. Major auto manufacturers had their own agendas for alternate energy, several of them leaning toward fuel–cell technology with hybrid gas–electric engines. Although the Rosens had been negotiating with two carmakers to shoulder some of the development costs and help move the technology into a reality, they were unable to secure any real commitments other than research funding. Ben Rosen had made a commitment to himself that he would drop the project if his personal and financial investment did not pay off by the end of 1997. "We needed an automaker to participate at this point, and it became clear to us that they are not interested," Rosen told *Automotive News* reporter Lindsay Chappell. By the end of November 1997, the offices of Rosen Motors were empty and the 70 employees were laid off.

In October 2000 Rosen retired as chairman of Compaq, a position he had held since 1982. His cash remuneration from Compaq for the previous year was in excess of $163 million. Former co–workers remember Rosen for his intelligence and sense of humor. One employee recalls how, once, when a young Compaq exceeded its sales quota, Rosen marched into a sales conference wearing a drum major's uniform and leading a 100–piece marching band.

But retirement has not slowed Rosen down. For private companies in need of startup cash, Rosen, along with other "angel investors," is available to consider investing. He belongs to a group known as the "Band of Angels Fund," comprised of 150 high–net–worth founders or former executive officers of high–tech companies who are available to finance startups. The Silicon Valley–based group backed approximately 20 startups in 2000.

Social and Economic Impact

Rosen helped to transform venture capitalism from a game of chance into the fine–tuned engine that drives much of the high–tech industry. Instead of simply doling out money and then hoping for the best, he eliminated much of the guesswork in his investments by becoming thoroughly familiar with the technologies he was investing in, resulting in both personal wealth and success for the companies. Despite the failure of his own company, Rosen Motors, to secure commercial contracts with major automotive manufacturers, Rosen's efforts helped narrow the gap between available technology and

marketable products. He was ready for the automotive world, it just wasn't ready for him.

Sources of Information

Bibliography

Chappell, Lindsay. "Rosen's Flywheel Grinds to a Halt." *Automotive News*, 24 November 1997.

Fox, Loren. "Heaven Can't Wait." *Business 2.0*, 20 March 2001, 123.

McNatt, Robert, and Steve Hamm. "A Giant at Compaq Goes Softly." *Business Week*, 16 October 2000, 12.

"Now I Think I'll Reinvent the Wheel." *Economist*, 14 September 1996, 70.

"Rosen Motors Folds." *Ward's Auto World*, December 1997, 10.

Taylor, Alex, III, and Edward A. Robinson. "Gentlemen, Start Your Engine." *Fortune*, 30 September 1996, 156.

"Top 200 Salaries & Compensations." *Computer Reseller News*, 22 May 2000, 72.

Vaughn, Mark. "Reinventing the Wheel." *AutoWeek*, 3 March 1997, 16.

Howard Schultz

(1953-)
Starbucks Corporation

Overview

Expressions like "streetwise" and "blue collar" are frequently used when describing the background of Starbucks Corporation chairman Howard Schultz. Raised in the projects in Brooklyn, New York, Schultz was the first in his family to graduate from college. Afterward, he purchased the Starbucks Coffee Company, which he used as a springboard to nationwide success. Within a few years, Starbucks became the first publicly held specialty coffee company and, according to *Advertising Age*, "the darling of Wall Street." The money raised in stock offerings enabled Starbucks to continue its expansion, opening hundreds of new stores and multiplying sales at a fantastic rate—revenue reached $2.3 billion in 2000. Schultz relied on his undergraduate business degree, personal experience, and insight to direct the meteoric rise of the coffee business that he detailed in his 1997 book, *Pour Your Heart Into It: How Starbucks Built a Company One Cup at a Time*.

Personal Life

Howard Schultz lives with his wife Sheri and their two children, Jordan and Addison, in a lakefront home in Seattle's upscale Madison Park district. Yet his upbringing took place along the Atlantic, not the Pacific, coast. Schultz is a native New Yorker, born into the blue–collar projects of Brooklyn in 1953. His father was a cab driver and factory worker, and his mother was a receptionist. Schultz began his college career with a football scholarship to Northern Michigan University and was the first in his family to earn a college degree.

Howard Schultz opening the first Starbucks store outside North America. *(AP/Wide World Photos.)*

In December 1994 Schultz received the Business Enterprise Trust Award for his integrity and philanthropy. Two years later he garnered the International Humanitarian Award for developing an alliance between Starbucks and CARE in support of people in coffee–producing countries. In August 1998 Schultz was honored by the Jerusalem Fund of Aish Ha Torah for his humanitarian achievements worldwide.

Career Details

The inspiration for his phenomenal coffee business was a 1983 visit to Milan, Italy. Schultz perceived a new American way of life in the city's 1,700 coffee bars, and he sought to recreate such forums for people to start their day or visit with friends. Schultz later described the coffee bar as "an extension of people's front porch" in the *New York Times*.

In 1987, at the age of 34, Howard Schultz organized a group of investors and purchased his former employer, Starbucks Coffee Company. The small Seattle–based coffee roaster took its name from the coffee–loving first mate in Herman Melville's novel *Moby Dick*. Schultz renamed his company the Starbucks Corporation.

Schultz's coffee bars were an instant success, fueling rapid growth and expansion, not only for Starbucks but also for the coffee industry as a whole. This new coffee culture supported a proliferation of stores and other sales avenues for Starbucks' beans. The company owns all of its stores, despite the constant stream of franchise inquiries, and has been steadily opening shops throughout the country. In 1992 Starbucks became the first specialty coffee company to go public, a testament to its size and prospects.

Starbucks' first major venture outside of the northwestern part of the nation was Chicago, where mail–order sales were strong. The company's specialty sales division developed new business through Nordstrom's department stores and established Starbucks coffee bars within Barnes and Noble bookstores. Starbucks also formed a partnership with PepsiCo Inc. to create and distribute a new ready–to–drink coffee–based beverage, Frappuccino, as well as entered into a licensing agreement with Kraft Foods. The company even developed a relationship with Capitol Records, releasing *Blue Note Blend* coffee and an accompanying jazz compilation on compact disc.

When Starbucks opened its first stores in New York City, it was a homecoming for Schultz, but he did not act like the conquering hero. The *New York Times* commented, "The soft–spoken Mr. Schultz has barely a trace of a New York accent and a timid, almost apologetic manner. When he comes to visit the 54th Street store his entrance is ultra low–key."

Part of Schultz's success as an entrepreneur is his willingness to nurture his employees. He credits a generous benefits package, offered even to part–time employees, as the key to growth, as it rewards Starbucks with a dedicated workforce and an extremely high level of customer service. It also contributes to a dramatically lower turnover rate—half the rate of the average fast–food business. This creates a financial payoff for the company, since each new employee costs $3,000 in recruiting, training, and productivity losses—the equivalent of two years of premium payment.

Advertisers marveled at Schultz's tactics, including his investments in such "internal marketing" rather than a large external advertising budget. In March 1994 *Advertising Age* noted that Schultz "turned a small chain into a national brand while spending a relatively small amount on advertising." The magazine quoted investor Matthew Patsky as saying, "They don't market . . . they've established a major presence all through word–of–mouth."

In 2000 Starbucks earned $151 million on sales of $2.3 billion. Schultz predicted that the number of Starbucks stores would triple in both the United States and overseas by the year 2005 and that sales and earnings would increase by 25 percent a year. However, Stephane Fitch, writing in *Forbes* in March 2001, questioned whether the company's growth record was sustainable. Some analysts, he noted, argued that Starbucks' profitability reflected growth in the number of stores rather than the popularity of its products. If so, Fitch argued, Starbucks would be waking up to the smell of coffee as soon as the prime locations for new stores were gone.

Chronology:
Howard Schultz

1953: Born.

1975: Received a bachelor's degree from Northern Michigan University.

1982: Hired to head Starbucks' operations and marketing.

1987: Purchased original Starbucks franchise; formed Starbucks Corp.

1992: Starbucks became first specialty coffee company to go public.

1994: Joined with PepsiCo Inc. to produce Frappuccino.

1998: Entered licensing agreement with Kraft Foods.

2000: Formed alliance with resource e–tailer Kozmo.com.

2000: Stepped down as CEO.

On June 1, 2000, Howard Schultz, the visionary behind Starbucks Coffee, stepped down as CEO to assume the post of chief global strategist. Having conquered the domestic markets, Schultz was shifting his gaze toward global expansion. "Five years ago our strategic intent was to build the leading brand of specialty coffee in North America," he told *Nation's Restaurant News*. "Five years later we have fulfilled that promise. And our strategic objectives are now much different, and that is to maintain our leadership position in North America but to build an enduring global brand around the world."

In 2001 Starbucks operated 4,000 establishments worldwide and served 10 million customers weekly. In addition to its coffee houses, Starbucks is available in department stores, grocery chains, airlines, hotels, and bookstores. In the e–commerce arena, the company marketed its name brand coffee through Starbucks.com, as well as through partnerships with the e–tailers Oxygen Media, Talk City, and Kozmo.com.

Social and Economic Impact

With his coffee bars, Howard Schultz stirred up new interest in the coffee culture to the point where it created a vocabulary of its own. Starbucks' employees who make coffee are known as "baristas," and terms like "latte" (half coffee, half hot milk) and "doppio macchiato" (a double shot of espresso topped with milk foam) became part of everyday language by the late twentieth century in the United States.

In 1990 *Forbes* described Starbucks as "bucking an anti–coffee tide." At that time, coffee consumption in the United States was on the decline, but Schultz soon persuaded the public to become coffee connoisseurs. He presented espresso drinks as an affordable luxury, not a beverage reserved for the elite and cosmopolitan. Schultz has also taught coffee drinkers to savor a stronger, richer beverage, as Starbucks uses arabica coffee beans rather than the more common robusta bean.

Schultz's corporate philosophy places great emphasis on supporting Starbucks' employees and on a commitment to community and environmental projects. The company is the largest corporate sponsor of CARE, an international aid and relief organization. In 1995 Starbucks pledged $500,000 to CARE with the stipulation that the money go to the countries that supply Starbucks with its coffee.

Schultz has also attracted considerable attention with his unconventional employment policies. He wanted to give Starbucks' employees "both a philosophical and a financial stake" in the business, according to *U.S. News & World Report*. Employees who worked 20 hours a week or more were eligible for medical, dental, and optical coverage as well as for stock options. At a time when other companies were trimming benefits as a cost–cutting measure, Schultz, who grew up in a family without any medical coverage, believed that his approach is critical to building a better workforce. "Service is a lost art in America," he told the *New York Times*. "I think people want to do a good job, but if they are treated poorly they get beaten down . . . It's not viewed as a professional job in America to work behind a counter. We don't believe that. We want to provide our people with dignity and self–esteem, and we can't do that with lip service." Schultz credits the benefits policy as the key to

the company's growth because it gave Starbucks a more dedicated workforce and an extremely high level of customer service. The chain also achieved a dramatically lower turnover rate—half the rate of the average fast food business. This creates a financial payoff for Starbucks, since each new employee costs the company $3,000 in recruiting and training costs and productivity losses—the equivalent of two years of premium payment.

Schultz has remained firmly committed to employee and community enrichment. As part of his ongoing efforts, Starbucks teamed up with baseball star Mark McGwire and Doonesbury creator Garry Trudeau to promote an adult literacy campaign. Starbucks also partnered with another sports star, Earvin "Magic" Johnson, to service inner city neighborhoods.

Sources of Information

Contact at: Starbucks Corporation
 2401 Utah Ave. South
 Seattle, WA 98134
 Business Phone: (206)447–1575
 URL: http://www.starbucks.com

Bibliography

Forbes, 19 March 2001.

"Howard Schultz." *Nation's Restaurant News*, 31 January 2000.

"Howard Schultz" *Newsmakers 1995*, Issue 4. Farmington Hills, Mich.: The Gale Group, 1995.

"Mr. Howard Schultz." *Nikkei Global Management Forum*, 2000.

"Starbucks Corporation." Hoover's Online Inc., November 2001. Available at http://www.hoovers.com.

"Starbucks in New Net Gambit." *CNET News.com*, 23 July 1999. Available at http://www.cnetnews.com.

"Starbucks, Star Bright." *Far Eastern Economic Review*, 18 May 2000.

"News Releases." Seattle, WA: Starbucks Corporation. Available at http://www.starbucks.com.

Muriel Siebert

(1932-)
Muriel Siebert & Company

Overview

Muriel "Mickie" Siebert has been called many things in her time, but "The First Woman of Finance" may be the most appropriate. She was the first woman to own a seat on the New York Stock Exchange and the first to head one of its member firms. Siebert is the founder and president of a national discount brokerage firm, Muriel Siebert & Company, Inc. The New York City–based firm has offices in Florida, New Jersey, Texas, Michigan, Washington, and California. Siebert continues to oversee the firm's day–to–day operations. As someone who always follows her gut instincts, Siebert built up her company by offering discounted services to customers—a controversial move on her part, but it made her a multimillionaire. Between 1977 and 1982 she served as the Superintendent of Banks of New York. Known for her flamboyance and outspoken manner, Siebert stands as a symbol for women who aspire to careers in the financial industry or who would like to run their own business.

Personal Life

Siebert lives in Manhattan, New York with her pet, a long–haired chihuahua named Monster Girl. She never married, as she believed that remaining single would advance her career. She has never regretted the decision.

Muriel Siebert was born in Cleveland, Ohio in 1932 to Irwin J. Siebert, a dentist, and Margaret Eunice (Roseman) Siebert, a homemaker. She attended Western Reserve University (now Case Western Reserve University)

Muriel Siebert. (AP Photo/Louis Lanzano.)

of Art and the New York State Business Council. She is a member of the Board of the National Council of World Affairs Organization–Long Island Chapter and of the Board of Trustees for the Guild Hall Museum, and is a founder and board member of The WISH List (Women in the Senate and House). Other organizations she has been involved with include the Tokyo Advisory Committee of the Sister City Program of New York City, the Alliance of American & Russian Women, New York City's Minority & Women–Owned Business Enterprise Advisory Board, the Board of the National Association of Securities Professionals, and the Board of Overseers of New York University's Business School. Siebert is also a trustee of Manhattan College and a former director of the United Way of NYC.

The list goes on. Her other memberships include the Financial Women's Association, the Women's Economic Round Table Advisory Council, the National Association of Women Business Owners, and the Ms. America Organization Advisory Council. She is a corporate affiliate of the National Association of State Treasurers, a member of the Twentieth Century Fund's Task Force on Market Speculation and Corporate Governance, and a member of the YWCA's Academy of Women Achievers, The Women's Campaign Fund, The Fashion Group International, and The Capitol Hill Club.

from 1949 to 1952 but she did not graduate, dropping out when her father was diagnosed with cancer.

She moved from Ohio to New York City in 1954 to look for a job. Immediately after relocating, Siebert faced obstacles. She applied for a job with the United Nations but was turned down because she could not speak two languages. Then, because she had an interest in business and the stock market she tried to land a position as a security analyst with a brokerage firm, but was turned down because she didn't have a college degree. Determined to become a financial analyst, however, Siebert lied about having a degree during an interview with Bache & Company. The deception worked, and Siebert launched what would become a phenomenal career in the investment industry, eventually becoming the first woman to hold a seat on the New York Stock Exchange.

As indefatigable as she is successful, Siebert has been involved in many activities and organizations outside of her business. From 1981 to 1984 she served on the Advisory Committee of the Financial Accounting Standards Board. While she was Superintendent of Banks she was also a director of the Urban Development Corporation, the New York Job Development Authority, and the State of New York Mortgage Agency.

Siebert is a founding member of the Women's Forum, an organization of 250 pre–eminent women in the New York area. She is also a trustee of the Citizens Budget Committee and Long Island University, and serves on the Business Committee of the Metropolitan Museum

Career Details

Muriel Siebert advanced her career by making decisions that were bold, even risky. Her initial relocation to New York in search of a career was in itself, a daring move. She arrived in 1954 with only $500 to her name. Lacking a college degree, her chances of finding employment seemed, at best, questionable. However, through pluck and determination, Siebert broke into the brokerage world where her intelligence and intuition proved to be her biggest assets. She landed her first job with Bache & Company where she worked from 1954 to 1957 as a security analyst, studying companies that other analysts weren't interested in, including airlines, radio and television stations, and motion picture studios. From there, she assumed a succession of positions with various brokerage firms. In 1958 she moved to Utilities Management Corporation and soon after joined Shields & Company. In 1961 she moved on to Stearns & Company, where she was made a partner. Then, from 1962 to 1965 she worked for Finkle & Company, and then for Brimberg & Company until 1967. Later, she admitted that the reason she job–jumped so frequently was because she inevitably discovered that her male associates were earning more money than she did. She had good reason to chafe at the inequity as she proved herself to be a shrewd selector of stocks.

By 1967, confident in her capabilities, Siebert decided to go into business for herself and formed Muriel

Siebert & Company. That same year, she made a move that set a historic precedent—she became the first woman ever to become a member of the New York Stock Exchange (NYSE). However, despite her successful work history and the substantial amount of money that she made for her various employers, Siebert was generally ridiculed when she tried to break into the NYSE. In fact, she was turned down by nine of the first 10 men she had asked to sponsor her application. Moreover, the Exchange put her in a "Catch–22" situation. Before it would consider her for membership, the Exchange told Siebert that she would have to get a letter from a bank stating that it would lend her $300,000 of the $445,000 price of a seat. But no bank would consider lending her the money until the Exchange would agree to admit her. Undaunted by the dilemma, she persevered. It took her several months, but Siebert was finally elected to membership on December 28, 1967. For 10 years she was the only woman among the 1,366 NYSE members.

In 1975 Siebert made another bold move when strict regulations that governed the financial industry were loosened. Specifically, a federal law abolished fixed commissions for brokers. She reacted to this price deregulation by announcing that her company would become a discount commission house. Response was both immediate and negative. On Wall Street, discounts were acceptable only for corporate customers. As a result, Siebert was dropped by the clearinghouse that cleared her transactions and her company faced expulsion by the Securities Exchange Commission if she could not find another house in 60 days. Resilient as ever, Siebert managed to find another clearing house right before the deadline and she achieved outstanding success as a discount broker.

As her business was reaching new levels of success, Siebert stepped down from the leadership role in her company to become the Superintendent of Banks for New York State in 1977. The position entailed an enormous amount of responsibility as Siebert would oversee more than 500 banking institutions and manage more than $100 billion in statewide trust accounts. To add to the challenge, Siebert came into the position at a time when the industry was undergoing a great deal of turmoil. Interest rates were climbing steeply, thrift institutions were failing, and an influx of foreign banks was crippling a major municipal credit union. Siebert, however, proved to be a creative administrator adept at solving a host of major problems. Her four years in office earned her praise from the banking establishment though her decisions, as always, generated a great deal of controversy. To deal with the failing credit union, for example, she used state funds to take it over and keep it solvent. She also lobbied state legislators on the behalf of banks, staving off a threatened mass relocation to protest New York's tax rates and usury laws. Additionally she forced some banks to merge and persuaded stronger institutions to help weaker ones.

Siebert resigned as Superintendent of Banks in 1982 to run for the United States Senate on the Republican

Chronology:
Muriel Siebert

1932: Born.

1949: Entered Western Reserve University.

1952: Dropped out of Western Reserve.

1954: Moved to New York City.

1961: Became a partner with Stearns & Company.

1967: Became first woman to join the New York Stock Exchange.

1967: Established Muriel Siebert & Company.

1977: Appointed Superintendent of Banks of New York.

1982: Ran for United States Senate.

1990: Established Siebert Entrepreneurial Philanthropic Plan.

1996: Muriel Siebert & Company went public.

ticket. She failed to be elected in her first and only campaign for political office, however, so she returned to Muriel Siebert & Company. During her absence, the firm had fallen into disarray and Siebert essentially had to rebuild it from the ground up. When Siebert had become the Superintendent of Banks, she had placed her company in a blind trust to be run by her employees. She later admitted that this was a bad move. The employees that she had left in charge hadn't been aggressive enough. Other employees resigned, taking customer lists with them. One former employee even left and started a competing discount brokerage firm. By the time Siebert reassumed the helm, she discovered that new companies that were established during her absence were doing much better than hers. During her first year back, she turned down buyout offers as well as a Wall Street job offer that would have netted her a $1 million annual salary because she was more interested in the challenge of turning her business around. With its founder back in control, Muriel Siebert & Company began flourishing again. By 1985 it was pulling in over $3 million per year in net commissions.

Siebert continued to steer her company with business acumen, determination, and foresight. In 1996 Muriel Siebert & Co. went public as a means to raise capital for a shift in strategy to accommodate Internet trading. By 1999 her firm was rated as one of the nation's leading discount brokerages.

Social and Economic Impact

Muriel Siebert has said that she feels that her greatest accomplishment was becoming the first woman member of the New York Stock Exchange. This was a remarkable feat indeed, especially considering the context of the times, yet it shouldn't overshadow her many other accomplishments. She launched a hugely successful business in a traditionally male–dominated sector in one of the most demanding cities in the world. For that she has become a role model for women, young and old. Nor should anyone underestimate her accomplishments as the Superintendents of Banks. She accepted her appointment to that position from then–Governor Hugh Carey knowing full well that steadily rising interest rates were jeopardizing the banks in her charge. Yet during her tenure she managed to prevent any bank failures in New York. She also restored fiscal order to the Municipal Credit Union, which serves New York City employees.

Siebert is also very much a philanthropist. In 1990 she established the Siebert Entrepreneurial Philanthropic Plan (SEPP), through which she donates to charity half of her company's net profits from new securities underwriting. In its first year SEPP donated a total of $310,000. Donations over the years have climbed over the $4 million mark.

With her success came a great many awards and honors. In 1993 Siebert received an award from the State Employees Federated Appeal for being the highest individual contributor through her SEPP program. The SEPP program also garnered her the Financial Women's Association's "Community Service Award" that same year.

Also in 1993 she received the Greater New York Councils Boy Scouts of America's First Annual "Women of Achievement" award, and New York City Mayor David Dinkens presented her with the "Lifetime Achievement Award" to help celebrate Women's History Month.

Other honors include: the NYU's Stern School of Business Stovall Fellow, as the first woman fellow, in 1992; the White House Conference on Small Business Award for Entrepreneurial Excellence, given to her by President Reagan in August 1986; the first national Emily Warren Roebling Award from the National Women's Hall of Fame, in 1984; the Equal Opportunity Award of the NOW Legal Defense and Education Fund, in 1981; the "Outstanding Contributions to Equal Opportunity for Women" Award of the Business Council for the United National Decade for Women, in 1979; and the Women's Equity Action League Achievement Award, in 1978.

Sources of Information

Contact at: Muriel Siebert & Company
435 East 52nd St.
New York, NY 10022–4834

Bibliography

"Muriel Siebert." Ellis Island Medals of Honor." 1996. Available at http://www.neco.org.

"Muriel Siebert." Michigan: Northwood University Distinguished Women's Awards, 1989. Available at http://www.northwood.edu.

"Muriel Siebert." New York: Women's Financial Network at Siebert, 2000. Available at http://www.wfn.com.

"Muriel Siebert." Utah: FS Capital Markets Group, Inc., 2001. Available at http://www.ipo–merge.com.

Schoenberger, Robert. "Finance World Not Just for Men." *The Clarion–Ledger*, 6 September 2001.

Russell Simmons

(1957-)
Rush Communications

Overview

The explosive entry of rap music onto the national music scene in the late 1980s was greatly due to the effort and vision of Def Jam Records founder and media mogul Russell Simmons. Through the rap label Def Jam, Simmons managed and promoted such top–selling rap acts as Run–DMC, Public Enemy, and L. L. Cool J. Sometimes described as the "Berry Gordy of his time," Simmons took hip–hop and rap music from virtual obscurity to one of the most popular and influential forms of music, spawning a billion–dollar industry that reached movies, clothing, concerts, and Internet sites. According to various sources, as of 2001 one in every 10 records sold in the United States was hip–hop, which surpassed country music in 2000 as the third–largest music category. Often deemed by the media as the "impresario" and "godfather" of rap, Simmons began as a fledgling promoter of a new breed of street music and became founder, chairman, president, and CEO of Rush Communications. Bringing hip–hop to Hollywood, Simmons' multimillion–dollar entertainment conglomerate Rush—encompassing the Def Pictures film and television subsidiary, the fashion labels *Phat Farm* and *Baby Phat*, the magazine *Oneworld*, Internet sites, and the advertising agency dRUSH—became one of the largest black–owned media companies in the United States.

Personal Life

Russell Simmons lives in New York and is married to former model Kimora Lee. The couple has a daughter, Ming Lee. Simmons enjoys yoga and is a vegan.

Russell Simmons. *(AP/Wide World Photos.)*

Simmons was born October 4, 1959, in Hollis, New York to parents who were educators and civil right activists. Simmons, with brothers Danny and Joey, grew up in a middle–class neighborhood in the New York City borough of Queens. He attended August Martin High School in Jamaica, Queens, graduating in 1975.

In the mid–1970s, while studying sociology at the Harlem branch of the City College of New York Simmons first became aware of rap music and its appeal to young inner–city blacks. He noticed that rappers converged in parks and on street corners taking turns singing rap songs to gathering crowds. *Manhattan, Inc.'s* Maura Sheehy depicted the exchange between rappers and their audience in those beginning days of rap: "Rappers, called MCs (emcees) then, told stories and boasted—about street life, tenements, violence, and drugs; about their male prowess, their talents; about 'sucker MCs'; and about women. Their raps romanticized the dangerous, exciting characters of the street, sanctified its lessons into wisdom, made poverty and powerlessness into strength by making rappers superhuman, indomitable. The audience followed, finding their power in dancing and dressing styles of the moment; in mimicking the swaggering, tougher–than–leather attitude; and by worshiping their street 'poets'."

Simmons later took time to give back to the community through a number of scholarship funds, the Rush Philanthropic Arts Foundation, a fresh air fund, and a children's hospital in Brooklyn. He has ties to People for the Ethical Treatment of Animals and teamed up with the

Humane Society for a Fur–Free Fur line of his *Baby Phat* women's clothing. Simmons is politically active in various civil rights causes and encourages political activity in youths. He serves on the board of directors of Brilliant Digital Entertainment, Inc. Simmons has won many awards, including the lifetime achievement award from *The Source* in 1999 and the Moet & Chandon Humanitarian Award for his commitment to supporting inner–city youth.

Career Details

In rap music, Russell Simmons perceived a vast audience untapped by the recording industry. He abandoned his college career and began tirelessly promoting local rap artists, producing recordings on shoestring budgets and conducting "rap nights" at dance clubs in Queens and Harlem. In 1984 he joined fellow aspiring rap producer Rick Rubin to form Def Jam Records. The new company made an immediate impression. One year after its formation, Def Jam caught the attention of CBS Records, which signed Def Jam to a $600,000 distribution deal. Within a mere three years, such Def Jam albums as the Beastie Boys' *Licensed to Ill*, L. L. Cool J.'s *Bigger and Deffer*, and Run–DMC's *Raising Hell* dominated the black music charts.

Simmons acted as manager of all Def Jam acts and emphasized the genuineness of each group. "Our artists are people you can relate to," he told Fayette Hickox in *Interview.* "Michael Jackson is great for what he is—but you don't know anybody like that. The closest Run–DMC comes to a costume is a black leather outfit...It's important to look like your audience. If it's real, don't change it." Some critics, however, found this authenticity somewhat disturbing. "It is the look of many rap artists—hard, belligerent, unassimilated, one they share with their core audience—that puts many folks on edge," noted *Essence.* The group Public Enemy, which represented itself with a logo of a black teen in the scope of a police gun, is representative, Simmons said, of how many black teenagers feel—like "targets that are looked down upon." He added, "Rush Management identifies with them. That's why we don't have one group that doesn't look like its audience."

The lyrics and acts of some male rap artists infuriated women's groups, who claimed that the message in some songs and stage acts was the hatred of women. Public officials have even brought charges of lewdness against rappers in concert. Yet Simmons distances himself from censoring the content of his groups' songs, telling *Essence* that "rap is an expression of the attitudes of the performers and their audience." He ultimately upholds rappers as positive role models for many black youths.

Simmons was insistent on presenting rap images that were true to the tough urban streets from which rap arose.

As a result, his groups don such recognizable street garb as black leather clothes, expensive high–top sneakers, and gold chains. He explained his objectives to Stephen Holden in the *New York Times:* "In black America, your neighbor is much more likely to be someone like L. L. Cool J or Oran 'Juice' Jones than Bill Cosby...A lot of the black stars being developed by record companies have images that are so untouchable that kids just don't relate to them. Our acts are people with strong, colorful images that urban kids already know, because they live next door to them."

As an example of the affirmative position rappers can take, Simmons pointed out to Holden that the members of Run–DMC, which include Simmons' younger brother Joseph, "are more than musicians...They're from a particular community, and have succeeded on their own terms without any compromise...If you take a look at the pop cultural landscape or the black political landscape now, there aren't a lot of heroes. If you're a 15–year–old black male in high school and look around, you wonder what you can do with your life. How do you better yourself? Run–DMC has opened up a whole new avenue of ambition. You can grow up to be like Run–DMC. It's possible."

In 1985, the same year as the CBS deal, Simmons produced his first movie, *Krush Groove,* for $3 million. Starring Run–DMC, Rick Rubin, and Blair Underwood, the movie was loosely based on the founding of Def Jam with Rubin basically playing himself and Underwood in the role of Simmons. Despite poor reviews, *Krush Groove,* which also featured and promoted many of Def Jam's rap acts, made $20 million. With it, Simmons got his first taste of success outside of the music business. Soon he was producing other films, including *The Addiction* (1995), *The Funeral* (1996), *Gridlock'd* (1997), and *Def Jam's How to Be a Player* (1997).

In 1993 Polygram bought a 60–percent stake in Def Jam for $33 million. Six years later, wanting to branch out from his musical roots, Simmons sold his remaining 40 percent interest to Universal Music Group for $100 million. Pursuing other media outlets through Rush Communications, Simmons' efforts included co–producing the very successful *Nutty Professor,* starring Eddie Murphy; producing the long–running black comic showcase *Def Comedy Jam* for HBO; and launching 360hip–hop.com, a hip–hop music, news, and lifestyle website that also sells the company's products. Simmons himself has appeared in a number of television movies and films including *Tougher Than Leather, The Show* and *Tupac Shakur: Before I Wake.* Rush Communications partnered with Brilliant Digital Entertainment to form Digital Hip Hop, a digital production company.

The year 2000 was a banner year for Simmons' ventures. His *Phat Farm* line of men's clothing grossed $150 million. A spin off line for women's clothing, *Baby Phat,* was launched with his wife Kimora serving as creative director of the line. Simmons partnered with Donny

Chronology:
Russell Simmons

1957: Born.

1984: Formed Def Jam Records with Rick Rubin.

1985: Def Jam signed a production deal with CBS Records.

1985: Produced the movie *Krush Groove.*

1993: Polygram bought 60 percent of Def Jam Records.

1994: Produced *Def Comedy Jam Primetime* for television.

1996: Co–produced *The Nutty Professor.*

1999: Universal Music Group purchased the remainder of Def Jam Records.

2000: Formed the advertising agency dRUSH.

2001: Released his autobiography, *Life and Def: Sex, Drugs, Money and God.*

2001: Organized Hip–Hop Summit for rap industry insiders.

Deutsch of Deutsch Inc., the largest independent U.S. advertising agency, to form dRUSH, a youth culture advertising and marketing agency. The agency won the high–profile clients Coca–Cola and HBO, among others. "Everything feeds off everything else," he explained to *Ebony* in 2001. "We're coming off our best year ever." Capping off an eventful year, Simmons penned his autobiography in 2001, *Life and Def: Sex, Drugs, Money and God.* His life was also scheduled to be the subject matter of a Fox Television Studios mini–series.

Long averse to the political scene, Simmons became active in that arena in the late 1990s. In June 2001 he held a "hip–hop summit" for industry artists, executives, writers, and politicians to discuss problems in the industry, as well as to attempt to avert a proposed bill to fine record labels and film companies for marketing adult material to children.

Social and Economic Impact

Many breakout rap moguls, including Sean Puffy Combs, have named Russell Simmons as an inspiration.

Combs had this to say about Simmons in *Ebony*: "If it weren't for Russell Simmons, I wouldn't be in the game. He gave the blueprint for hip–hop. For our generation, the baton was taken by Russell Simmons...He knows how to break down color barriers without compromising who he is." Simmons has helped make what began as music geared toward blacks into something purely "American"—several sources report that, in 2001, 80 percent of hip–hop buyers were white. He has also translated hip–hop music into a number of different genres including movies, advertising, clothing, and the Internet through his media empire, Rush Communications. In essence, he has made rap and hip–hop a lifestyle.

In his role as political activist, Simmons organized rappers and encouraged the industry and its fans to be more politically and socially conscious. He lobbied in Washington for the hip–hop industry's First Amendment rights, meeting with such politicians as Attorney General Janet Reno and Senators Hillary Rodham Clinton and Joe Lieberman. He also led a hip–hop summit, bringing the industry together to carve out its future. In his role as a philanthropist, Simmons enriched the community in many ways, from youth programs to animal activism.

Sources of Information

Contact at: Rush Communications
    530 Seventh Ave.
    New York, NY 10018
    Business Phone: (212)840–9399

Bibliography

"Brilliant Names Russell Simmons to Board of Directors." Los Angeles: Brilliant Digital Entertainment, Inc., 20 August 2001. Available at http://www.brilliantdigital.com.

Brown, Eryn. "From Rap to Retail: Wiring the Hip–Hop Nation." *Fortune*, 17 April 2000, 530.

Carroll, Rebecca. "Russell Simmons and Donny Deutsch Launch dRUSH." *Africana.com*, 14 December 1999. Available at http://www.africana.com.

Chappell, Kevin. "The CEO\$ of Hip–Hop and the Billion–Dollar Rap Jackpot." *Ebony*, January 2001, 116.

Contemporary Musicians. Volume 7. Farmington Hills, MI: Gale Research, 1992.

Decurtis, Anthony. "Russell Simmons Speaks Out." *Rolling Stone*, 13 September 2001.

Elzas, Sarah. "Principals for a Day: Opening Eyes, Forging Bonds." *Education Update*, May 2001. Available at http://www.educationupdate.com.

Farley, Christopher John. "The Pop Life: Hip–Hopping to the Church on Time." *Time*, 28 December 1998, 48.

Muhammad, Tariq K. "Hip–Hop Moguls: Beyond the Hype." *Black Enterprise*, December 1999, 78.

Reid, Shaheem. "Russell Simmons Outlines Goals of His Hip–Hop Summit." MTV News Online, 16 May 2001. Available at http://www.mtv.com.

Roberts, Johnnie L. "Mr. Rap Goes to Washington." *Newsweek*, 4 September 2000, 22.

"Rush Communications." Hoover's Online, Inc., November 2001. Available at http://www.hoovers.com.

"Russell Simmons." *The Internet Movie Database*, 2001. Available at http://www.imdb.com.

"Russell Simmons & Kimora Lee." *People Weekly*, 5 July 1999, 105.

"Russell Simmons Teams With the HSUS to Put Compassion into Fashion." The Humane Society of the United States, 16 January 2001. Available at http://www.infurmation.com.

"Russell Simmons' True Hollywood Story." *Rolling Stone*, 2001. Available at http://www.rollingstone.com.

Simmons, Russell, with George Nelson. *Life and Def: Sex, Drugs, Money and God*. Crown, 2001.

Stark, Jeff. "Brilliant Careers: Russell Simmons." *Salon*, 6 July 1999. Available at http://www.salon.com.

"Taking Responsibility: An Interview with Russell Simmons." About.com, 6 June 2001. Available at http://rap.about.com.

"UMG Finally Obtains Def Jam." *Rolling Stone*, 1999.

Pradeep Sindhu

(1953-)
Juniper Networks, Inc.

Overview

Pradeep Sindhu, through the company he founded, Juniper Networks, Inc., helped revolutionize broadband access, speed, and reliability to Internet service providers with the high–speed router hardware that he developed and marketed. In only five years Juniper became a leader in network technology, boasting an impressive 30–percent share of the multi–billion router core market and standing as the only serious competition for networking leader Cisco Systems. Sindhu's simultaneous involvement in the control of his company and the development of the M40 router was a both a business and technological feat. The M160 router, which was the same size but four times as powerful than the prototype M40, was an unprecedented technological achievement that helped Juniper become one of the forerunners in its field.

Personal Life

Pradeep Sindhu is both a husband and a father. He has received a number of awards, including the Technologist of the Year award from *SiliconIndia* in 2000. His company also received numerous awards, including the Data communications Testers Choice Award, the Nikkei Industry Awards for Superiority, and *PC Magazine's* Best Internet Product Award.

Sindhu was born in 1953 in India. In 1974 he graduated with a bachelor's degree in technology from the Indian Institute of Technology in India, and received a master's degree in electrical engineering from the University of Hawaii. In 1983 he earned a Ph.D. in computer

Chronology:

Pradeep Sindhu

1953: Born.

1974: Received bachelor's degree from IIT Kanpur.

1983: Received Ph.D. in computer science from Carnegie Mellon University.

1996: Formed Juniper Networks, Inc.

1999: Juniper went public.

1999: Juniper generated $103 million in revenue.

2000: Revenue jumped 550 percent to $674 million.

2000: Juniper's M160 router was the fastest on the market.

2000: Juniper acquired Micro Magic.

2000: Partnered with Blue Star to distribute routers in India.

science from Carnegie Mellon University's School of Computer Science. Sindhu then took a job as a principal scientist at the Xerox Palo Alto Research Center, where he developed design tools for high–speed interconnects for shared–memory multiprocessors. He later worked at Sun Microsystems and was involved in the design and development of Sun's first high–performance multiprocessor systems family, incorporating the SS1000 and SS2000.

Career Details

In 1995, while was working at the Xerox Palo Alto Research Center (PARC), Pradeep Sindhu formulated the idea to create a new company. He saw a growing need for high–end Internet routers that was not being met by manufacturers. "I felt networking was an area with maximum growth potential," he told *Indiatimes*. "We decided to focus on the Internet router market because the number of Internet users was doubling rapidly and the cost of bandwidth was coming down, but the routers that were existing back then were very limited in their capability."

Sindhu established Juniper Networks in 1996. Operating the firm from his home, he immediately began securing financial support and recruiting experienced

professionals. Renowned venture capitalist Vinod Khosla, former founding CEO of Sun Microsystems, invested $200,000 for the formation of the Silicon Valley–based Juniper. In a shrewd move, Sindhu, being a technology specialist with no business background, soon hired Scott Kriens as the company's president and CEO. He lured the most talented engineers away from his former employers as well as such rivals as Sun Microsystems, Xerox PARC, and Cisco in order to create a workforce capable of providing the speed to market required of the complex, high–tech products. An increase in the number of Internet users resulted in more data traffic over the lines, and Juniper sought to fill the need for faster and more efficient routers. The new routers that Juniper developed were the most powerful on the market, able to transmit high volumes of data for Internet and telecommunications companies.

In 1999 Juniper Networks went public. Its opening price was $34 per share, and by the end of the year it had jumped tenfold to $304 per share, raising $76 billion for the relatively new company.

One of the keys to the company's success was the advanced technology of its products. Unlike its competitors' decade–old recycled technology, JUNOS router software was specifically designed for Internet use. At the heart of each of its M–series router was the Internet Processor II ASIC. Sindhu described its function on Juniper's website: "The Internet Processor II ASIC's ability to process packets intelligently with uncompromising performance is unique to Juniper Networks routers and is the key to enabling smart IP services. Juniper Networks M–series routers, powered by the Internet Processor II ASIC and controlled by JUNOS software, enable a truly integrated multiservice IP network for the first time in the industry."

The fact that the company specialized in one area, Internet routers, and did it better than any other company was another reason that Juniper became a leader in its field. The third key to Juniper's success rested in the speed at which it could develop and deliver technology. Despite its small size, Juniper was able to execute the difficult task involved in new router technology with greater speed and efficiency. The final explanation for Juniper's meteoric rise to success was that it outsourced all of its manufacturing, enabling it to focus 100 percent on development. Sindhu's role as chief technology officer allowed the entrepreneur to focus wholly on plotting the future of technology at the company, as well as participating in actual design and development of products. Proof of that success: in 1999 the company generated $103 million in revenue. One year later this figure jumped more than 550 percent, to $674 million.

In March 2000 after 18 months of development, Juniper's M160 router was unveiled as the fastest on the market. The new product gave Juniper a distinct advantage over its competition. "The significant thing about this development is that this machine is four times more powerful than the M40 and is the same size as the M40," Sindhu told *The Economic Times Online*. "This is the first time in the history of communications or computing that this has been achieved." As companies lined up to order the M160, such rivals as Cisco, Nortel, and Lucent rushed to build a similar router, though none appeared on the market until early 2001, nearly a year later.

Juniper continued to grow and expand, raising $1 billion in early 2001 for acquisitions, research and development, and marketing. It partnered with LM Ericsson to produce mobile Internet devices and joined with Blue Star Limited to distribute routers in India. Juniper acquired Micro Magic, a leading integrated circuit solutions company, in December 2000.

While many technology companies, including Cisco, warned of a slowdown in the industry in 2001, Juniper raised its yearly forecast by 14 percent to $1.6 billion. However, as of November 2001, Juniper's stock was valued at $21.92 per share, down from the previous year's lofty $185.88. Although it appeared that Juniper had joined the other victims of the technology downturn, its possibilities for future growth remained bright. According to leading researchers, the $2 billion market for high–end routers will soar to $12 billion by 2003. Sindhu believes his company will grow along with it.

Sindhu himself expanded into the field of venture capitalism, investing his company's profits into start–ups not unlike Juniper Networks. His native India had emerged as one of the fastest–growing information technology markets, having blossomed from $100 million to nearly $100 billion in 10 years. Sindhu intended to capitalize on India's healthy market, also benefiting from the fact that the venture capital business was still in its infancy there. Vishuni Varshney, chairman of the Indian Venture Capital Association, said that of the $1 billion in venture capital invested in new Indian technology start–ups in 2000, most came from U.S. investors.

Social and Economic Impact

Only five years after its formation, Juniper Networks became a leader in its field, Internet routers. This business accomplishment was remarkable, yet Pradeep Sindhu's scientific contributions have been equally impressive. His own groundbreaking work, along with that of the specialists that he gathered at Juniper, pushed the outer limits of technology and set the bar for others in the industry by designing the fastest, most advanced products in the least amount of time. "By far the biggest unsung hero is Pradeep Sindhu," said venture capitalist Khosla in *Inter@ctive Week*. "He permanently changed the definition of what a router does and how it is built, and got Internet Protocol on a robust footing."

Sindhu steered his upstart Juniper Networks into uncharted territory, vying with industry giant Cisco Systems, which had a near monopoly in the sector. With his vision of producing faster, more powerful routers and delivering them more quickly to the market, Sindhu was able to grab a healthy share of market and change the face of technology in the process. Building on the success of Juniper, Sindhu quickly dove into the profitable world of venture capitalism, funding start–ups like his own in Silicon Valley and worldwide.

Sources of Information

Contact at: Juniper Networks, Inc.
1194 North Mathilda Ave.
Sunnyvale, CA 94089
Business Phone: (408)745–2000
URL: http://www.juniper.net

Bibliography

Dutt, Ela. "Juniper Unveils Router Four Times More Powerful than Predecessor." *The Economic Times Online*, 2 April 2000. Available at http://economictimes.com.

Fusco, Patricia. "New Juniper Networks Processor Takes on DOS Attacks." *InternetNews*, 18 April 2000. Available at http://www.internetnews.com.

Iwata, Edward. "Juniper Attacks Cisco with 'Smart Bomb' Accuracy." *USA Today*, 21 August 2001.

"Juniper Networks Deepens Expertise in IP Infrastructure Technology." Sunnyvale, CA: Micro Magic Inc., 11 December 2000. Available at http://www.micromagic.com.

"Juniper Networks, Inc." Hoover's Online, Inc., November 2001. Available at http://www.hoovers.com.

"Juniper Networks, Inc. and Blue Star Join Hands." Mumbai, India: Blue Star Ltd., 31 October 2000. Available at http://www.bluestarindia.com.

Korzeniowski, Paul. "Jumpin' Juniper." *Business 2.0*, May 2001.

Mackinnon, Ian. "Web Warriors." *Newsweek*, 16 October 2000, 50.

"Pradeep Sindhu: Vice Chairman, Chief Technical Officer, and Founder." Sunnyvale, CA: Juniper Networks, Inc., November 2001. Available at http://www.juniper.net.

"Routing a Neutral Course." *America's Network*, 1 October 2000, 95.

Shinal, John. "Juniper: The Upstart That's Eating Cisco's Lunch." *Business Week*, 11 September 2000. Available at http://www.diehardindian.com.

"Shining Stars." Pittsburgh, PA: Carnegie Mellon University's School of Computer Science, 2000. Available at http://www.cs.cmu.edu.

Sindhu, Pradeep. "How to Build a Better Router." *Telecom Asia*, September 2000, 68.

Sindhu, Pradeep. "Infotech Interview." *Indiatimes*, 2001. Available at http://www.indiatimes.com.

"Top 25 Unsung Heroes of the Net." *Inter@ctive Week*, 6 March 2000, 35.

"Websmart: Pradeep Sindhu." *Business Week*, 14 May 2001, EB52.

"What is Driving the Need for Smart IP Services?" Sunnyvale, CA: Juniper Networks, Inc., 15 May 2001. Available at http://www.juniper.net.

"Who's Who: Pradeep Sindhu." *Siliconindia.com*, November 2001. Available at http://www.siliconindia.com.

Ollen Bruton Smith

(1927-)
Speedway Motorsports, Inc.

Overview

Known simply as Bruton within the world of motor sports, Ollen Bruton Smith was the first to take racing to the New York Stock Exchange when his company, Speedway Motorsports, went public in 1995. Speedway owns and operates six motorsport facilities—the Atlanta Motor Speedway, Bristol Motor Speedway, Lowe's Motor Speedway, Las Vegas Motor Speedway, Sears Point Raceway, and Texas Motor Speedway. It also owns the Internet auction site SoldUSA.com. The company's Finish Line Events subsidiary provides food, beverages, and souvenir merchandising for the events. Its 600 Racing subsidiary makes and distributes 5/8–scale modified racing cars. Smith also owns the second–largest automotive group in the country, Sonic Automotive, with more than 170 car dealerships and 30 repair centers. Speedway Motorsports is the leading marketer and promoter of motorsports entertainment in the United States.

Personal Life

Ollen Bruton Smith is divorced and has four children. He is absolutely immersed in his businesses. "His hobby is business," said Eddie Gossage, head of the Texas Motor Speedway, in the *Fort Worth Star–Telegram*. "I've got to believe his IQ must be in the genius level, because he never forgets anything. He always does what he says he's going to do. If I need a phone number, I don't look it up, I ask him. He memorizes everything. He never has a schedule, but he can tell you where he has to be on the 13th of next month."

Chronology:
Ollen Bruton Smith

1927: Born.

1960: Partnered with Curtis Turner to construct the Charlotte Motor Speedway, then lost ownership.

1975: Regained majority ownership of the Charlotte Motor Speedway.

1990: Acquired Atlanta Motor Speedway.

1992: Hosted industry's first night race on a speedway.

1994: Established Speedway Motorsports, Inc.

1995: Began construction on the Texas Motor Speedway.

1995: Speedway Motorsports went public.

1996: Acquired Bristol Motor Speedway and Sears Point Raceway.

1999: Sold naming rights of the Charlotte Motor Speedway to Lowe's.

In 1984 Smith founded Speedway Children's Charities, a non–profit organization that has a chapter at each of the six Speedway racetracks. The organization has raised more than $5 million. Smith received the NASCAR Award of Excellence in 1997 for his efforts on behalf of Speedway Children's Charities.

Ollen Bruton Smith was born in 1927 in Oakboro, North Carolina. His poor childhood motivated him to become a financial success as an adult. "Growing up on a farm in the rural South during the Great Depression was extremely hard," he recalled in *Sports Illustrated*. "We had plenty of food, a great family, but no money." He continued, "In high school, I remember seeing this guy from a family that had a little money. Every day at school I'd see him with an Eskimo Pie. I loved em. Plenty of chocolate. Just delicious. You could get em for 10 cents. I couldn't afford one. Once in a while I could afford a Popsicle for a nickel. But I kept saying, 'Someday I'm gonna be able to buy an Eskimo Pie.'"

Upon graduation from high school, Smith worked at a hosiery mill in North Carolina. In the early 1950s he took a job as a car salesman while promoting dirt–track races at the Charlotte Fairgrounds on the side. There, he met the late Curtis Turner, a pioneer in the racing field.

The two partnered on the construction of the Charlotte Motor Speedway. The track opened in June 1960 with a 600–mile race for the National Association for Stock Car Auto Racing (NASCAR). Although the speedway attracted large crowds for this and later events, Smith had trouble raising enough money to cover the costs of operating the track and the Charlotte Motor Speedway was put into court receivership that same year.

Smith distanced himself from the racing industry for more than ten years, turning instead to automobile sales. He saved enough money to purchase a car dealership in Rockford, Illinois, and went on to open other dealerships and business interests in Texas. In 1972, however, he observed the heavy promotion that tobacco giant R.J. Reynolds was investing in stock–car racing events, and predicted that the sport's popularity was on the rise. So he made a bid to acquire his former racing venture, the Charlotte Motor Speedway.

Career Details

By 1975 Ollen Bruton Smith had acquired a majority stake in the Charlotte Motor Speedway by buying out hundreds of investors who had purchased its stock from the courts years earlier. Smith then hired long–time collaborator H. A. "Humpy" Wheeler, who later became president and chief operating officer of Speedway Motorsports, Inc. "We'd both gotten our starts operating dirt tracks," Wheeler told *Sports Illustrated*. "We knew we'd done everything possible to run fans off. We dusted em, gave em lousy food. But not only did they keep coming back, they multiplied. We knew if we could ever fix up a track to be as nice as a modern stadium, this sport would be three or four times as big. We didn't know it would be 10 times as big."

In addition to increasing its audience in general, Smith also wanted to attract more women, knowing that this would likely increase his male audience even more. Smith's novel attention to detail—planting grass, flowers, and some 250 trees around the track—set the bar for all other racetracks. He also upgraded the facility to include VIP suites, chic restaurants, enclosed clubhouse seating, and major grandstand additions. Using unique promotional techniques to gain publicity and large audiences, Smith became famous for his pre–race shows, which included everything from a fire–breathing "robosaurus" to Elvis impersonators parachuting from airplanes. He added a lighting system to the Charlotte Motor Speedway in 1992, enabling it to host the first night race on a superspeedway. Some called the track "the Mecca of motorsports facilities."

A risk taker with keen foresight, Smith announced in the early 1980s that he wanted to construct and sell condominiums overlooking the Charlotte Motor Speedway. Skeptics pounced on the notion. Late–night talk show host David Letterman, a NASCAR aficionado, telephoned Smith on–the–air with sarcastic comments. Even Wheeler, Smith's right–hand man, told him that the enterprise would fail. Undeterred, Smith built the condos— and they sold out within one year for about $125,000 each. "Just a giant extension of tailgate parties," he called the condos in *Sports Illustrated*. "Instead of getting to the speedways early, you wake up there. And your friends come."

In 1990 Smith expanded his ownership to a second track, the Atlanta Motor Speedway, and became its president, chief executive officer, and director. In December 1994 he formed Speedway Motorsports, Inc. as the parent company of his two tracks, taking the reins as its chairman and CEO.

The following year Smith poured $250 million into the construction of the luxurious, 200,000–seat Texas Motor Speedway. As of late 1999 the Texas track was the second–largest sports arena in the country. However, Wheeler was apprehensive about the prospects of the giant new speedway because it wasn't the venue for a Winston Cup race. Smith alleviated this concern by purchasing the North Wildesboro Speedway in North Carolina and transferring one of its Winston Cup races to the Texas track.

The Texas Motor Speedway became one of the most publicized speedways in history, regularly making national headlines. Smith came under fire for the extravagance of the track. Some in the industry argued that he sacrificed the quality of the track surface itself in favor of the facility's luxury. Although Smith regarded this attention not as negative but as simple publicity, he rebuilt the track itself in 1998 for $3.5 million.

In January 1996 Smith acquired the Bristol Motor Speedway and immediately doubled its seating to hold 135,000 fans. In November of that year, he purchased the Sears Point Raceway. Smith continued to implement his novel idea to build condos aside his racetracks. Those around the Atlanta and Texas Motor speedways were more elaborate than his earlier residences, selling for $550,000 to $650,000.

In 1999 the Charlotte Motor Speedway adopted the name Lowe's Motor Speedway in the industry's first naming rights deal. Sponsored by Lowe's Home Improvement Warehouse, the long–term licensing agreement first drew criticism, then followers.

Never one to shy away from controversy, Smith again made waves by proposing to split the Winston Cup into two leagues, the American League and the National League, in order to meet the increasing demand for race dates. Some industry critics argued that the idea would trigger a tug–of–war between tracks competing for racing stars to attract the crowds. "We don't know how many Jeff Gordons or Dale Earnhardts or Dale Jarretts there are out there in America," Smith argued in *Sports Illustrated*. "We do know there are more than 1,200 speedways in America, most of them small, running weekly events. That means there are tens of thousands of race

drivers in this country. Young Joe America is out there running two, three events every week at small tracks, and he has tremendous talent. Bifurcate the series, double the opportunities, and it would bring up some great drivers whom you and I don't know today."

By the turn of the century Speedway Motorsports was one of the industry's leading racetrack operators. Races held at its speedways included 17 NASCAR events, three Indy Racing League, three NASCAR Craftsman Truck Series, and four National Hot Rod Association races, as well as numerous short track racing events. The combined seating of all of the speedways was 712,000.

Social and Economic Impact

Throughout his career, Ollen Bruton Smith amassed a portfolio of some of the premier racing facilities in the United States. He became an innovator in the field of motorsports, one of the fastest–growing sports in the nation. He was a pioneer in promoting NASCAR events by offering sizable purses for the winners and providing upgraded facilities and services for the fans. He was the first to build luxury suites and condos around his lucrative tracks. Smith was also the first to take a motorsports company public.

Smith has gained enormous financial rewards due to his efforts in the motorsports industry. In 1996 he made his first appearance on the *Forbes* 400 list; this magazine recorded his personal wealth at $890 million in 2000. Revenue of Speedway Motorsports, Inc. continued to climb, reaching $354.3 million in 2000. As a reminder to Smith of his original motivation for success, Dove Bars are stocked in the freezers of his speedways' suites. "The Dove Bar is what the Eskimo Pie used to be," he told *Sports Illustrated*. "And I have one every damn day."

Sources of Information

Contact at: Speedway Motorsports, Inc.
    5555 Concord Pkwy. South
    Concord, NC 28027–0600
    Business Phone: (704)455–3239
    URL: http://www.gospeedway.com

Bibliography
"Bruton Smith Donates $5M to Local School." *The Business Journal (Charlotte)*, 12 June 2001.

"Forbes 400: Sports Stars." *Forbes*, 9 October 2000, 240.

Gonzalez, Simon. "Bruton Smith Gets His Kicks." *Fort Worth Star–Telegram*, 25 March 1999.

Hinton, Ed. "Big Wheel: By Staying Ahead of the Curve, Bruton Smith Has Made Himself One of the Most Powerful Men in Racing." *Sports Illustrated*, 22 December 1999, 96.

"O. Bruton Smith." Charlotte, NC: Lowe's Motor Speedway, November 2001. Available at http://www.lowesmotorspeedway.com.

"Speedway Motorsports, Inc." Hoover's Online, Inc., November 2001. Available at http://www.hoovers.com.

"Speedway Motorsports, Inc." Concord, NC: Speedway Motorsports, Inc., November 2001. Available at http://www.gospeedway.com.

Spiegel, Peter. "Life in the Fast Lane." *Forbes*, 1 November 1999, 266.

Suzanne Somers

(1946-)

Overview

Suzanne Somers came to fame as the bubbly, ditzy–but–lovable character of Chrissy in the 1970s situation comedy series, "Three's Company." Despite having established herself as an icon of the era, she abruptly left the series following a salary disagreement—causing her displacement from a star on the A–list to a has–been almost overnight. The buoyant Somers moved on, however, and launched a career as a nightclub performer in Las Vegas before landing new opportunities in television. She and her husband also established a successful business promoting a then–unusual exercise item, the ThighMaster, which grew to become one of the biggest fads of the 1990s. Hugely successful at marketing herself, Somers has continued to keep her name out there with a line of jewelry on the Home Shopping Network, a generous publishing contract for her memoirs, and a series of diet and fitness books that has already sold millions of copies.

Personal Life

Somers was born on October 16, 1946, in San Bruno, California, the daughter of Francis ("Frank") and Marion Elizabeth (Turner) Mahoney. One of four children, she was raised in a family that was ostensibly close and prosperous, but suffered from internal disruption due to her father's drinking. Somers attended Mercy High School, where her studies were affected by her father's all night rages. She had trouble doing her homework due to the environment at home and often fell asleep in class. However, she won the lead in the school musical, Gilbert

Suzanne Somers. (Hulton/Archive.)

and Sullivan's *H.M.S. Pinafore*, and later noted in her autobiographical *Keeping Secrets,* "Thank God for music. It was the only thing keeping me in school. I got A's in music." At the age of 14 she was expelled from school for writing sexually suggestive notes to a boy, even though they were all fantasy, and she never sent them. She then transferred to Capuchino High School in San Bruno. There, she continued to act in school plays and graduated in 1964.

While attending Lone Mountain College on a music scholarship, also known as San Francisco College for Women, she became pregnant and married Bruce Somers, her high school sweetheart, on 15 April 1965. Their son, Bruce Jr., was born in November of 1965. Af-

terward, she began classes at a modeling school and found work as a nurse's aide while her husband attended law school. Unsatisfied with her marriage and her life, she divorced and moved into an apartment in Sausalito, raising her son on her own. Forced to support herself with odd jobs, Somers endeavored to get her modeling career off the ground. Memorably, her first assignment was to lie in traction at an American Medical Association convention. Later, she landed some advertising work and began to get noticed in the industry.

After her first few appearances in box–office–hit movies, Somers met Alan Hamel, a former talk show host and manager, who was married when they began seeing each other in 1968. Their relationship endured, and he divorced his wife and married Somers in 1977. Hamel has two children, Stephen and Leslie, from his first marriage. Somers and Hamel reside in Malibu, California, and have one granddaughter. Her fan site on the Web is at http://www.geocities.com/suzannefar/.

Somers has twice won the People's Choice Award for favorite actress in a new series (1977 and 1991) and was named Las Vegas Entertainer of the Year in 1986. In addition to maintaining her various businesses, Somers has founded the Suzanne Somers Institute for the Effects of Addiction on Families. Its goal is to set up outpatient centers in every major city in the United States for treating addicts and family members of addicts. Somers also presented material on the subject to a U.S. Senate committee in 1991.

Career Details

Somers was starting to scrape up more modeling work and had made a few small appearances in television shows and films when she got her first breakthrough role in a tiny part as the beautiful blonde in a convertible in the 1973 George Lucas film, *American Graffiti.* That same year, she appeared in *Magnum Force,* a Clint Eastwood movie. Both were box office hits, and the *American Graffiti* role, despite being small, won her a legion of admirers and a positive reception in Hollywood.

Though Somers also published a book of poetry in 1973, *Touch Me Again,* her acting work received much more attention than her literary talents. She landed a guest appearance on "The Tonight Show" with Johnny Carson after the release of *American Graffiti,* and eventually moved to Los Angeles to concentrate on her career. In April of 1977 she auditioned for the situation comedy "Three's Company," about two women who share an apartment with a male roommate who must pretend that he is homosexual in order for the landlord to consent to the unusual living arrangement. Somers played Chrissy Snow, the stereotypical more–bust–than–brain blonde, and became one of the biggest icons of the 1970s, on par with Farrah Fawcett, star of the series "Charlie's Angels."

"Three's Company" was a smash hit. It costarred Jack Ritter as Jack Tripper and Joyce DeWitt as Janet Wood, the two roommates. The top–rated series was so big, it landed Somers on the cover of 55 magazines in one year; the news magazine show, "60 Minutes," also profiled her. She won a People's Choice Award for favorite actress in a new series and was nominated for a Golden Globe in 1979. She also signed a deal to appear in two feature films, *Yesterday's Hero* in 1979 and *Nothing Personal* with Donald Sutherland in 1980.

In the meantime, Somers had hired Fawcett's publicist, Jay Bernstein, to work his magic on her as well. However, Bernstein had persuaded Fawcett to leave her series for bigger opportunities, and many at the ABC network held a grudge against him for it; Somers' career suffered because of it. In 1980 her husband took over managing her and helped her forge a new image as a nightclub entertainer in Las Vegas. Somers wanted to gear up for a singing career, so Hamel arranged a deal for her to appear at the MGM Grand Hotel eight weeks a year for two years. After working on the set of "Three's Company" each day, she would rehearse her Vegas act until the wee hours of the morning. These were the golden years for Somers, when her bookings thrived, and her name was high on the neon marquees. She toured various clubs across America and also performed for U.S. Navy troops aboard the U.S.S. *Ranger*, along with Gladys Knight and the Pips and Marie Osmond.

As Somers related in her 1998 book, *After the Fall*, back on the set of the TV series, her relationship with her costars, Ritter and DeWitt, began to deteriorate. When her five–year contract was up, Somers tried to negotiate a monetary raise equal to that of the male costar, John Ritter. Instead of a raise, she was written out of the script. The media characterized her as the "greedy" star, and the stigma remained for nearly a decade. However, the ratings for "Three's Company" plunged after her departure, and the series ended in 1984.

Somers tried to land more substantial roles, but found that she had been branded a troublemaker and could not find work. In 1984 she landed a role in the high–profile musical, *The Moulin Rouge,* being produced at the Las Vegas Hilton—and transformed it from a flop to a sell–out success. She was named Las Vegas entertainer of the year in 1986. By 1987 she was asked to star in a new television series, "She's the Sheriff," about a woman who takes over as the town law officer after her husband's death. However, it was canceled after two seasons.

Feeling fatigued from her whirlwind career and having dropped to about 92 pounds in weight, Somers took some time off from acting. She wrote *Keeping Secrets,* an autobiography that dealt explicitly with her father's alcoholism and its effect on her entire family. Published in 1988, it reached number one on the *New York Times* best–seller list. Subsequently she and her family made a heart–wrenching appearance on the "Phil Donahue

Chronology:
Suzanne Somers

1946: Born in San Bruno, CA.

1964: Graduated from high school.

1965: Married Bruce Somers and has son, Bruce, Jr.

1968: Began dating Alan Hamel.

1973: Played first breakthrough role in *American Graffiti.*

1977: Married Alan Hamel.

1977: "Three's Company" debuted and became an instant hit.

1981: Left "Three's Company."

1986: Earned Las Vegas Entertainer of the Year award.

1988: Published best–seller, *Keeping Secrets.*

1997: Published best–seller, *Suzanne Somers' Eat Great, Lose Weight.*

1998: Published *After the Fall.*

Show", and Somers ended up speaking on a bevy of other talk shows as well, including "Sally Jesse Raphael," "Good Morning America," and "The Tonight Show." She also began giving lectures at hospitals, universities, and corporations, speaking of her experiences and of forgiveness. As she later wrote in *After the Fall*, "During these times, I realized the tremendous opportunity I had been given on 'Three's Company.' The pettiness of my departure seemed insignificant compared with the platform I had been given as a result of the exposure and fame I had won during my years on the show. Chrissy had made me lovable and trusted. That is who my audiences thought they would meet. Instead, they met the real me; and to my good fortune, they were not disappointed." Later she published *Wednesday's Children,* a book of interviews with people from abusive families.

Meanwhile, Somers was seeking a way to keep her career going without the strain of making constant appearances. When her husband came in contact with a man trying to market a piece of exercise equipment that had been in existence for 20 years, Somers was doubtful. Notwithstanding, she agreed to meet with the man, who showed her what he called the V–Toner, an exercise device for shaping up the torso, shoulders, and biceps.

Somers asked if it would work on inner thighs, and he said yes. She and her husband renamed it the Thigh-Master and took a partnership interest in the company.

It was a good match for the leggy Somers, and in no time, the ThighMaster went from being an obscure toning device to a piece of popular culture. "Saturday Night Live" and other television shows worked it into their gigs; and it showed up in a number of popular films including *Heat, Forever Young,* and *The Nutty Professor.* Even then–President George Bush made a joke out of it in a speech. Soon, "ThighMaster" had become an entry in the American dictionary and used in a Trivial Pursuit game question. The product was selling in the millions. Eventually, Somers and her husband bought out the other half of the company, now called "Body Solutions." On a roll, Somers next branched out to sell a line of jewelry on the Home Shopping Network, becoming one of the first celebrities to get involved with home shopping enterprises.

In 1991 she began costarring with Patrick Duffy in a new sitcom called "Step by Step," an updated version of "The Brady Bunch." The show ran until 1998, and in 1991 Somers won another People's Choice Award for her role in this series. Also in 1991, Somers served as executive producer and starred in a made–for–television movie based on *Keeping Secrets.* As time went on, she landed roles in a number of television movies and a cameo in the 1994 John Waters feature "Serial Mom." In 1998 Somers co–hosted a new generation of the hit television series, "Candid Camera," along with Peter Funt, son of the program's original founder, Alan Funt. She also starred in a 1998 television movie, *No Laughing Matter,* playing an alcoholic mother and tried her hand at romantic comedy again in the 2001 film, *Say It Isn't So.*

A few years prior, she began making workout videos and added the ButtMaster to her product line, though later she told Joel Stein in *Time* that "the ButtMaster got a raw deal. There were certain religious groups that picketed stores objecting to the name. We had to repackage it as the Lower Body Exerciser." Then in 1997 Somers penned *Suzanne Somers' Eat Great, Lose Weight,* a book that "isn't a diet; it's how to change the way you eat so you can eat what you want and never put on a pound," she told Craig Modderno in *TV Guide.* It included more than

100 of her personal favorite recipes and remained on best–seller lists through 2001.

Somers' recent focus continues to be on health and nutrition books, including *Suzanne Somers' Get Skinny on Fabulous Food,* and *Suzanne Somers' 365 Ways to Change Your Life,* both released in 1999, and *Somersize Desserts,* published in 2001.

Social and Economic Impact

The resilient Suzanne Somers has always touched people with her candor as well as her humor. She has shared with them her dysfunctional childhood, her be-hind–the–scenes acting career, and, more recently, her bout with breast cancer. Her books have remained best–sellers—evincing a palpable form of "thank you" from a loyal public. With some of the profits from royalties, Somers has founded the Suzanne Somers Institute for the Effects of Addiction on Families, giving back to the community that has supported her through thick and thin.

Sources of Information

c/o Chasin Agency
190 N. Canon Dr., Ste. 201
Beverly Hills, CA 90210

Bibliography
Crute, Sheree. "Breast Defense."*Heart & Soul,* August 2001.

"Health Bestsellers." *Los Angeles Times,* 03 September 2001.

Newsmakers 2000, Issue 1. Farmington Hills, Mich.: Gale Group, 2001.

Sutton, Judith. "Somersize Desserts (Book Review)." *Library Journal,* 1 August 2001.

"Suzanne Somers Biography." Available at http://www.geocities.com/suzannefan/bio.htm.

Terry–Azios, Diana A. "Films for the Perfect Date." *Hispanic,* January/February 2001.

"Where Are They Now?" *Biography,* February 2001.

Roy M. Speer

(1932-)
Home Shopping Network
(HSN)

Overview

Billionaire Roy Speer, along with partner Bud Paxton, formed the first–of–its–kind telemarketing Home Shopping Network (HSN) in 1983. A novel marketing entity, it allowed prospective shoppers to view merchandise on their television sets and order by telephone from their homes. Within a few short years, sales had topped $1 billion and HSN was reaching 60 million households. Speer then sold his interest in HSN and went on to start more than 100 other companies.

Personal Life

Born "dirt poor" in 1932, Roy Speer is a lawyer by training who left full–time practice for a more lucrative career in real estate investing and retail marketing. He considered his early poverty to be his biggest blessing because it forced him to roll up his sleeves and carve out his stake. He received his Bachelor of Arts degree from Southern Methodist University in 1956 and then graduated from Stetson University's law school with a J.D. degree in 1959.

Career Details

Speer practiced corporate law until the late 1960s, although his law practice coincided with other business ventures and real estate transactions. He and his wife (he has three children) established a second residence in the Bahamas and ventured into foreign real estate, including

Chronology:

Roy M. Speer

1932: Born.

1956: Graduated from Southern Methodist University.

1959: Graduated from law school at Stetson University.

1978: Acquired first radio station.

1983: Formed Home Shopping Network (HSN) with Bud Paxson.

1986: HSN has its first public offering.

1992: Sold controlling interest in HSN to Liberty Media.

1998: Merged with PrimeQuest to form LifeScience Technologies Ltd. (LST).

2001: Advantage Marketing Systems acquired collective LST entities.

---

a Puerto Rican vegetable farm and an oil company. He eventually worked his way from a small law partnership in Clearwater, Florida, to the Assistant Attorney General's office for the State of Florida.

He then started building a name as a broadcasting executive, buying properties and setting up businesses, including Aloha Utilities in 1966. In 1978 Speer partnered with Lowell "Bud" Paxson to buy a local FM radio station in Clearwater. They began to buy up several other local radio stations in the Tampa/Clearwater area. After an advertiser on one of the radio stations gave Paxson several electric can openers as payment for the airtime advertisement, Paxson came up with the idea to sell the 112 can openers over the air. He sold them all, over the air, for $9.95 each by the next day. Thus, the Suncoast International Bargaineers Club, a radio shopping show, was born. It was so successful that he and Speer began plans to do the same on cable television.

In 1983 Speer and Paxson launched their Home Shopping Network on cable TV, first from a local cable channel in Clearwater. Speer became the chief executive officer (CEO) of the new company and Paxson its president. Three years later, Speer led HSN to its national broadcast TV debut five hours each day via satellite. In 1986 Home Shopping Network went public. Within months, HSN was labeled the fastest growing company in the United States. At his peak with HSN, Speer set a single–day sales record of 250,000 units of merchandise sold. HSN was distributing and marketing products and producing infomercials in 70 countries and had established name recognition rate of better than 94 percent in the United States.

In 1987 the Home Shopping Network filed a $1.5 billion lawsuit against GTE, its telephone company, alleging that technical problems within GTE made the Network lose telephone calls and, therefore, prospective sales. After two years of litigation and trial, a jury in 1989 denied Home Shopping Network's claims. Worse yet, the jury awarded $100 million to GTE in libel damages. The suit was later settled.

In 1991 Paxson retired as president of the Home Shopping Network and sold his interest to Speer. The following December 1992, Speer sold his controlling stake in HSN to TCI's Liberty Media Corporation (LMC) for $160 million in stock (which ultimately became Bell stock after AT&T merged with TCI). Most of his remaining interest was sold in 1993 for another $100 million. Speer also resigned from his position in the fall of 1993 as chairman and CEO of HSN, although he was retained by the company for the next five years as a consultant. His official resignation followed a lawsuit naming Speer and other top executives, which alleged his involvement in "hush money" payments to potential whistleblowers, ties with organized crime, hidden vendor stakes (involving charges that Speer required vendors to give him a stake in their company in return for having their products offered on HSN) and commercial bribery. At that time, there were nine pending lawsuits in Florida in which Speer was named as a defendant.

Some of the other lawsuits were brought by investors and involved what is referred to as "related party transactions" by company executives that may not be in the best interest of shareholders. For example, HSN leased equipment from Speer's family trust. HSN also entered into two agreements with Interphase, Inc. (a company in which Speer was the sole shareholder) for the leasing of certain communication equipment at a monthly rental fee of $40,000. Interphase was also retained by HSN to construct a television studio for $100,000. HSN also borrowed nearly $400,000 from Interphase at 2 percent above prime rate. HSN leased real property owned by the Speer family for use as the company's accounting and data processing center. While these facts did not constitute illegal activity per se, they reflected poorly on the integrity of the management at HSN and damaged investment interest. In 1994 Speer was issued a court order to pay his former company (HSN) $2 million to fulfill the terms of one (the "7547 Corp.") lawsuit.

During those years, HSN was also being investigated by the Securities and Exchange Commission (SEC) for allegations of improper transactions with related parties, as well as by the Internal Revenue Service. The only well–publicized outcome of those investigations occurred in 1996. The U. S. Tax Court had ruled that Speer and his wife Lynnda did not use a computer software company, Pioneer Data Processing Inc. (owned by Speer's son Richard) to hide income. Pioneer had developed software for HSN from 1986 to 1992 and was paid $14 million for it. The IRS had charged that the money paid to Pioneer as royalties actually constituted HSN profits that were going untaxed and, further, should have been considered gifts to Richard. However, the tax court ruled that the payments to Richard's company were "fair and reasonable," and the case was dismissed.

Not everything Speer touched turned to gold, however. In 1989, for example, Speer claimed losses of $1.1 million and $78 million respectively for a Florida full–service marina and tugboat/barge service in which he had controlling interests.

At one time it was estimated that Speer had ownership interest in as many as 108 different companies and owned ten cable TV stations with a paying subscription of ten million home viewers. In 1998 Speer bought an 80 percent controlling interest in Precision Systems Inc., a producer of voice recognition systems. Precision Systems was another spin–off company from HSN, having handled its computer systems for callers–in, among other things. In the $106 million deal, several of Speer's Nashville companies (e.g., Speer Communications Inc., which controls a company that sells telecommunications technology) contributed several million dollars in cash along with assets and products involved with digital storage, video production, and telecommunications. In 1999 Speer sold his interest in Precision Systems and Vulcan Ventures, another company in his portfolio (which seeded Precision Systems) to Phil Anshutz for $23 million and $106 million respectively.

Another 1998 venture for Speer was the merger of his Speer Communications in Nashville with Celerity Systems Inc., another Tennessee company. Speer Communications at that time had one of the largest digital video storage vaults in the world and offered digitally equipped video studios and on–location video teams across the country. Celerity, in turn, provided interactive video hardware, along with some software and computer systems. The merger intended to combine their capabilities in the interactive video services industry.

Over the years, Speer created a series of broadcasting ventures that required sophisticated digital network systems. After Speer's computer teams developed expertise in those systems, Speer began to market the expertise to the outside world by starting yet another company—Orlando, Florida–based Advanced Datacom Inc., in 1999. Speer wanted to capitalize on e–commerce through an on–line shopping channel and Web production studio. Speer became chairman and owner of both Advanced Datacom and its relative, Advanced Data Designs Ltd. Advanced Data Designs installed high–speed

computer network cable systems, while Advanced Datacom handled Web–hosting, online marketing, computer security systems, and Internet security for other businesses. Organizationally, both companies were subsidiaries of another very large Speer company known as Life Sciences International Inc., a nutritional and skin–care product company based in Orlando, Florida.

LifeScience Technologies, Ltd., a spin–off, was the surviving company resulting from yet another 1998 Speer merger with the former PrimeQuest International. LifeScience specializes in dietary supplements and natural products. One of its key products is "adaptogens," marketed as "a secret blend of plants that the Russians have had for years. " After PrimeQuest was able to secure exclusive rights to the research on adaptogen plants being conducted by Dr. Israel Breckman in Russia, Speer funded the efforts to bring Dr. Breckman to the United States to market the resulting product. Copious information is available on the Internet about LifeScience products, on various web pages maintained by distributors and marketers. Meanwhile, according to Gerry David, vice president of sales, Speer was building a life extension facility in the Bahamas.

LifeScience Technologies was expected to be Speer's second "billion–dollar baby." Ever the telemarketing wizard, Speer had innovatively come full circle with his companies and put together a package that incorporated much of their expertise. According to Speer himself, in his web site message regarding LifeScience, "I've invested all my years of business experience as an entrepreneur in the development of the product technologies, a merit compensation program, and the bringing together of an experienced management team—everything to put you well on your way to creating a successful business." The network marketing company was set up to market and distribute its products through individually held interests purchased by investor–franchisers. LifeScience Technologies had sales of approximately $7 million in 2000. However, in January 2001, Advantage Marketing Systems, Inc. announced to investors that on January 4, 2001, it had acquired LifeScience Technologies Holdings Limited Partnership, LifeScience Technologies Limited, LifeScience Technologies of Japan, LST Fulfillment Limited Partnership, and LifeScience Technologies of Canada, Inc. for an undisclosed amount. LST was thereafter listed as a division of Advantage Marketing Systems.

In 2000 *Forbes* listed Speer's worth at $1.1 billion. Although officially semi–retired, Speer did not disappear from view. Dividing his time between residences in the Bahamas, Florida, and Nashville, Tennessee, he spends his time fishing and looking for new investments. He continues to oversee his real estate investments in Florida, Las Vegas, and the Caribbean and to invest in new technology companies, but he rarely gets involved in their day–to–day business anymore.

Social and Economic Impact

Together with his partner Bud Paxson, Speer changed shopping forever with the advent of his Home Shopping Network concern. He also changed TV viewing forever, as HSN provided not only entertainment but also electronic interactivity: prospective shoppers viewing a product demonstration on their televisions from the privacy of their homes could pick up their telephones and dial directly to the station. For some, hearing their own real-time voices on television (as they telephoned in to ask questions about the product or place an order) was itself enough of a thrill, but the program was often enhanced with celebrity appearances to endorse products and/or with special sales and deals not available to non-HSN viewers. When the focus of telemarketing shifted to e-commerce, Speer was there and ready to capitalize again, with ownership interest in companies that designed websites, set up computer and communication systems, and set up and trained new entrepreneurs. He has remained one step ahead of the market but has often been mired in controversial deals and arrangements involving multiple companies to a transaction and his financial involvement with each of them.

Sources of Information

Contact at: Home Shopping Network (HSN)
1 HSN Dr.
St. Petersburg, FL 33729
Business Phone: (800)284-3900
URL: http://www.hsn.com

Bibliography

Billac, Pete. "Managing Stress." Undated. Available at http://www-swan-pub.com/stress.htm.

Burnett, Richard. "The Orlando Sentinel, Fla., Technology Column." *The Orlando Sentinel, Fla*, 17 January 1999 and 10 July 2000.

"Celerity, Speer team up for marketing." *Nashville Business Journal*, 2 March 1998.

"CEO is Main Attraction." Undated. Available at http://store.yahoo.com/nbj/ceoismainat.html.

Egan, Mary Ellen, Victoria Murphy, and Nicole Ridgeway. "Content Kings." *Forbes*, 9 October 1999.

E.S. "HSN Settles with Former Chairman. " *Direct Marketing*, April 1994.

Gattuso, Greg. "Speer Calls it Quits." *Direct Marketing*, September 1993.

"Investor Relations." Available at http://www.shareholder.com/ams/news/20010109-45404.cfm.

Lewis, Charles, and Bill Allision. "Tax Tips for Tycoons." From *The Cheating of America*. William Morrow: 2001. Available at http://www.weeklyplanet.com/2001-04-19/news.html.

"LifeScience Technologies." Available at http://www.federal-way.com/diet/press.htm.

Mack, Toni. "The Next Quest." *Forbes*, 26 July 1999.

"Media Moguls." *Forbes*, 11 October 1999.

"NBC Buys 32% of PAX." *The Palm Beach Post*, 17 September 1999.

Newcomb, Peter, and Harold Seneker. "Billionaires." *Forbes*, 16 October 1995.

Schilit, W. Keith. "Initial Public Offerings: Identifying 'Turnons' and 'Turnoffs.'" *Journal of Investing*, Winter 1998.

Speer, Roy. "Roy Speer, Chairman of LifeScience Technologies." Available at http://natural-stress-management.com/RoySpeer.htm.

"The Week in Business." *The Business Journal of Tampa Bay*, 12 August 1996.

Torbeson, Eric. "Home Shopping Network Comes to Rescue of St. Petersburg, Fla., Precision." *St. Petersburg Times*, 27 April 1998.

Steven Spielberg

(1947-)
Amblin Entertainment and
DreamWorks SKG

Overview

Steven Spielberg has turned out some of the most popular, highest–grossing films in movie history. With his movie *Jaws*, he played a large part in ushering in a new era in modern cinema: the big–budget blockbuster. His critics claim his movies often depend too heavily on spectacular special effects. His fans call him the king of good storytelling. Whatever the opinion, no one can deny that Spielberg has impacted moviegoers since the 1970s and in the process has built a movie–making empire of unmatched dimensions.

Personal Life

Spielberg married actress Amy Irving in 1985. They had one son before divorcing in 1989. In 1991 Spielberg married Kate Capshaw, an actress who starred in *Indiana Jones and the Temple of Doom*. Between them they have seven children.

Now known as a family man, Spielberg is often described as a giant kid. He typically dresses in jeans and sweatshirts and wears a baseball cap. He admits to a fondness for bad television movies and a love for video games. In a 1994 *New Yorker* article, Tom Hanks described him fondly, saying, "The thing about Steven is he's still the A.V. guy in junior high school. You know, the guy who brings the movie projectors around and knows how to thread them, and all that kind of stuff."

Steven Spielberg was born on December 18, 1947, in Cincinnati, Ohio. His father, Arnold Spielberg, was an electrical engineer who designed computers for RCA, GE,

Steven Spielberg, accompanied by wife Kate Capshaw, holding his American Film Institute award. (Archive Photos, Inc.)

and IBM, and his mother, Leah Spielberg, was an accomplished pianist. Spielberg was the eldest of four children. Spielberg's father moved the family frequently as he pursued jobs around the country, settling in Phoenix, Arizona, from 1957 to 1964. School proved to be difficult for Spielberg. He had trouble making friends because he moved so often, and at school he was constantly teased because he was often the only Jewish student.

At a very young age, Spielberg decided to make movies. His three sisters were his favorite subjects and appeared in many of his earliest attempts at filmmaking. His mother would help with the special effects. By age

13, Spielberg had already won a contest for his 40–minute war movie *Escape to Nowhere*. In 1964 he turned out *Firefly*, an earth–versus–alien epic nearly two–and–a–half hours in length.

Upon his high school graduation, Spielberg had hoped to attend film school at the University of California at Los Angeles, but his *C* grade average was not good enough to gain admittance to the competitive program. Instead, he attended California State College at Long Beach. College held little interest for Spielberg, though, and he spent most of his time at the movies. In a 1996 *Cosmopolitan* article, Spielberg told of the day that he began sneaking into Universal Studios in 1966. "I went back there every day for three months. I walked past the guard every day, waved at him and he waved back. I always wore a suit and carried a briefcase, and he assumed I was some kid related to some mogul. . . . So every day that summer, I went in my suit and hung out with directors and writers and editors."

Career Details

Though he may dress like an overgrown child, Spielberg has a reputation for being a shrewd businessman. Unable to direct all of the products he was interested in, Spielberg formed his own production company in 1980. The company was called Amblin Entertainment, after one of his first films. Movies that have been released under the Amblin banner include *Gremlins, Back to the Future, Goonies,* and *Men in Black*. Amblin also produced several animated films, including *Who Framed Roger Rabbit, An American Tail,* and *Land Before Time*. Amblin was likewise responsible for such television shows as the hit drama *ER* and the animated series *Tiny Toons Adventures* and *Animaniacs*. Many of his early films were made with his close friend, director George Lucas. In 1994 Spielberg merged his company with a new production company. He formed the company with former Disney president Jeff Katzenberg and billionaire music producer David Geffen. The power trio planned to combine their talents and envisioned the creation of their own multimedia entertainment projects. Criticized for its slow start, the company has been involved in making records, films, animated movies, toys, and video games. Despite the diversity of the company's endeavors, Spielberg concentrates mostly on filmmaking. He continues to focus on what he has always done best, directing movies.

Spielberg began his career in 1969 when Universal Television's Sid Scheinberg saw Spielberg's short film, *Amblin'*. Spielberg left school and signed a seven–year contract with Universal. His first assignment was an episode of a 90–minute pilot for Rod Serling's *Night Gallery* series. He then directed episodes of several other television shows. In 1971 Spielberg directed his first movie. *Duel* cost only $350,000 to make, drew rave reviews, and grossed over $5 million in foreign releases alone.

Spielberg made two more television movies before directing his first theatrical film. The comedy–drama, *The Sugarland Express* was released in 1974. The film received positive reviews, even earning Spielberg a best–screenplay award at the 1974 Cannes Film Festival, but it did not fare extremely well at the box office.

Spielberg's next effort was more successful. Entrusted with the screen adaptation of Peter Benchley's best–selling novel *Jaws*, the director unleashed a sensation; the story of an Atlantic seaside town terrorized by a great white shark seized the public imagination. The 1975 film became the highest–grossing motion picture to date. Its big budget and the incredible special effects used to portray the mechanical shark named Bruce set the stage for a new generation of high–budget, megahit movies. Though not every film was a hit, it was clear from the beginning that Spielberg knew how to win at the box office.

In 1977 Spielberg released his next film project, the science fiction story *Close Encounters of the Third Kind*, another enormous box office hit. Spielberg released *Raiders of the Lost Ark* in 1981. The action drama set in the 1930s, with Harrison Ford starring as archaeologist–adventurer Indiana Jones, was so successful that Spielberg released two sequels, *Indiana Jones and the Temple of Doom*, in 1984, and *Indiana Jones and the Last Crusade*, in 1989.

In 1982 Spielberg made movie history again with the release of *E.T.: The Extra–Terrestrial*. The movie, a story about a boy and his friendship with a loveable alien trying to find his way home, is close to Spielberg's heart. He has drawn comparisons between the emotions that are portrayed in the movie and those that he felt when his parents divorced. Despite its overwhelming popularity with fans and critics alike and its many nominations, *E.T.* received no Academy Awards.

In 1986 he made *The Color Purple*, based on Alice Walker's Pulitzer Prize–winning novel of the same name. While the film received some impressive reviews, Spielberg received criticism for patronizing African Americans and for sentimentalizing rural southern poverty. Nonetheless, the movie did well at the box office and introduced two new stars, Oprah Winfrey and Whoopi Goldberg. The movie received a record–tying 11 Academy Award nominations but failed to win in any category, and Spielberg himself was not even nominated. *Empire of the Sun* was released in 1987. Based on a true story, the movie recounted the adventures of a young British boy in Shangai during World War II. The film earned fair reviews and box office attendance. Also in 1987, Spielberg finally received recognition for his work: the Academy of Motion Pictures bestowed on him one of its highest honors, the Irving J. Thalberg Award. The award recognizes a distinguished body of works.

Taking a break from serious films, which had not fared as well as some of his others, Spielberg's megahit *Jurassic Park* was released in 1993. The subject of one of the most intensive pre–release promotions in film history,

Chronology:
Steven Spielberg

1947: Born.

1975: Directed *Jaws*.

1979: Directed *Raiders of the Lost Ark*.

1981: Directed and coproduced *E.T. The Extra–Terrestrial*.

1984: Directed and coproduced *The Color Purple*.

1985: Directed and coproduced *Empire of the Sun*.

1993: Directed *Jurassic Park* and *Schindler's List*.

1994: Established DreamWorks SKG.

1994: Established the Shoah Foundation.

1997: Directed *Amistad*.

1998: Directed *Saving Private Ryan*.

2001: Produced *Band of Brothers* on HBO with Tom Hanks.

---

the story centered on a present–day theme park that featured genetically engineered dinosaurs as the main attraction. Based on a book by Michael Crichton, the film was such a hit that Spielberg could not resist the temptation to do a sequel and subsequently released *Jurassic Park: The Lost World* in 1997, which grossed $229 million.

In the years 1993–1998, Spielberg finally quieted all the critics who did not believe he could make an "adult" movie. His film *Schindler's List*, a black–and–white movie filmed in Poland, was a lengthy Holocaust drama based on the true story of a German factory owner who saved the lives of thousands of Jews who worked for him. The critically acclaimed film earned seven Academy Awards, including awards for best picture and best director. The film held personal meaning for Spielberg, who had shunned his Jewish heritage as a child because he had been an outcast. He described his Jewish awakening at the birth of his son Max in 1985, when he began thinking about his family and the stories about the Holocaust that had been told to him when he was young. He told *Harper's Bazaar* in 1994, "Not since *E.T.* had I felt such a personal calling, to do something I actually feel part of." Spielberg set up two public foundations with his earnings from the movie for the purposes of studying the Holocaust and keeping alive the memory of the Jews who died in it. One of these foundations, the Shoah

Foundation, was established to preserve the testimonies of holocaust survivors and witnesses, and to date has collected more than 50,000 eyewitness testimonies in 57 countries and 32 languages.

A later Spielberg work, *Saving Private Ryan*, released in the summer of 1998, told the story of eight American soldiers during World War II who go behind enemy lines to retrieve a lost paratrooper after it is discovered that all three of his brothers had been killed during the war. The movie received excellent reviews. Spielberg's realistic portrayal of the D–Day invasion of the beaches of Normandy have led many to call it the greatest war movie of all time.

Spielberg's latest foray into film was a collaboration with the late Stanley Kubrick, entitled *A.I.:Artificial Intelligence*. After Kubrick died, Spielberg developed the screenplay from a detailed story treatment and 1,000 storyboards the legendary director had left behind. The science fiction film, based on the short story *Super–Toys Last All Summer Long*, topped the box office at $29.4 million in its opening weekend July 1, 2001.

Spielberg and Tom Hanks reteamed that year to produce a TV project that would honor the hundreds of thousands of "citizen soldiers" that helped turn the tide in World War II. The result was HBO's $120 million 10–part World War II miniseries, *Band of Brothers*. Debuted on September 9, 2001, the series spotlights the men of Easy Company based on the Stephen E. Ambrose bestseller of the same title. *Band of Brothers* is a brutal front line portrayal of members of the 506th Regiment, 101 Airborne division, among the first American paratroopers trained for the war.

Social and Economic Impact

Spielberg entered filmmaking at a time when big budgets that paid for high–tech special effects and major marketing campaigns were not the standard. With the unprecedented success of *Jaws*, that all changed. In a time when no movie had grossed $100 million in the United States or Canada, *Jaws* grossed almost a half a billion dollars. Ticket sales skyrocketed *Close Encounters of the Third Kind* into the top–ten moneymakers up to that time. *E.T.* not only topped box office sales but also became an overwhelming merchandising and video success. The movie made $700 million, the largest box office take at the time, and earned over $1 billion in merchandising. *Jurassic Park* quickly became the highest–grossing film at its release. Spielberg has made big movies into big business. His estimated gross income for 1997 was $283 million. A *Forbes* correspondent asked the question, "Has Spielberg had his hand in every single blockbuster coming out of Hollywood—or does it just seem that way?"

Spielberg has once been accused of making only kids' movies with plots full of action and special effects but without depth. Yet, his success with *Schindler's List* in 1994 and *Saving Private Ryan* in 1998 have changed his image. These movies brought issues to the forefront that spoke to many people. He presented history in ways that no one had before him. In 1998 *Time* magazine named Spielberg in its list of the 100 most influential people of the 20th century. In *Time*'s tribute to Spielberg, film critic Roger Ebert affirmed Spielberg's place on the list. "In the history of the last third of twentieth century cinema, Spielberg is the most influential figure, for better and worse. In his lesser films he relied too much on shallow stories and special effects for their own sake . . . In his best films he tapped into dreams fashioned by our better natures."

Sources of Information

Contact at: Amblin Entertainment and DreamWorks SKG
100 Universal City Plz.
Universal City, CA 91608
Business Phone: (818)733–7000

Bibliography

"'A.I.' Plugs in at No. 1." *E! Online*, 2 July 2001. Available at http://www.eonline.com.

Appelo, Tim. "First Critic." *Entertainment Weekly*, 17 December 1993.

Brown, Corie, and Richard Turner. "Fishing Buddies: As DreamWorks Finally Releases its First Movie, the Partners Are Still Learning to Work Together." *Newsweek*, 29 September 1997.

"Close Combat: HBO's 'Band of Brothers.'" *American Cinematographer Magazine*, 16 September 2001. Available at http://www.cinematographer.com.

Contemporary Authors. Detroit: Gale Research, 1997.

Corliss, Richard. "Hey, Let's Put on a Show!" *Time*, 27 March 1995.

Corliss, Richard. "Peter Pan Grows Up: But Can He Still Fly?" *Time*, 19 May 1997.

Current Biography Yearbook 1996. New York: H. W. Wilson Co., 1997.

Ebert, Roger. "Time 100: The Most Important People of the 20th Century." *Time*, 29 May 1998.

Encyclopedia of World Biography. Detroit: Gale Research, 1998.

Hallett, Anthony and Diane Hallett. *Encyclopedia of Entrepreneurs*. New York: John Wiley & Sons, 1997.

Maser, Wayne. "The Long Voyage Home." *Harper's Bazaar*, February 1994.

Sanello, Frank. "Spielberg: The Man, the Movies, the Mythology." *Cosmopolitan*, July 1996.

Schiff, Stephen. "Seriously Spielberg." *New Yorker*, 21 March 1998

"Steven Spielberg." *E! Online*, 5 October 2001. Available at http://www.eonline.com.

Survivors of the Shoah Visual History Foundation. Available at http://www.vhf.org.

George Steinbrenner

(1930-)
New York Yankees

Overview

George Steinbrenner, the Cleveland shipbuilding magnate who purchased the New York Yankees in 1973, has been one of professional sports' most controversial and quotable figures. Twice suspended by baseball for legal and ethical violations, Steinbrenner nevertheless earned the respect of his fellow owners for his record of success on the field. The Yankees won multiple championships under Steinbrenner's aggressive style of leadership.

Personal Life

George Steinbrenner was born on July 4, 1930, in Rocky River, Ohio. His father, Henry Steinbrenner, owned a Great Lakes shipping company. His mother, Rita, managed their home in Bay Village, the suburb of Cleveland where Steinbrenner spent his formative years. As a child, Steinbrenner delivered eggs to earn spending money. His father, a former collegiate track and field star, instructed him to work hard and urged him to try competitive athletics.

At age twelve, Steinbrenner took up hurdling. Whenever he finished second in a track meet, his father appeared instantly at his side, demanding to know: "What the hell happened? How'd you let that guy beat you?" These scoldings instilled a perfectionist streak in the young Steinbrenner that he often cited as the key to his later success.

Steinbrenner was educated at the Culver Military Academy in Indiana. He then went on to Williams Col-

George Steinbrenner. *(AP/Wide World Photos.)*

coaching career was to be short–lived. In 1957, at the request of his father, Steinbrenner returned to the shipyard, where he was put to work counting rivets in crawl spaces. He married the former Elizabeth Zweig on May 12, 1956.

Career Details

In 1956 Steinbrenner seemed set to take over his father's business. However, the lure of big–time sports proved too powerful, and Steinbrenner invested a considerable sum of money in his first pro franchise, basketball's Cleveland Pipers. The team failed, and Steinbrenner lost all his savings.

Urged to file for bankruptcy, Steinbrenner instead worked to pay off his debt. When his father retired in 1963, he took control of the family shipping business and helped turn around its sagging fortunes. With the money he made, he formed a partnership with a group of investors and bought into the American Ship Building Company. Elected to the company's presidency in 1967, Steinbrenner fetched his father out of retirement to help him run the operation. American Ship Building flourished under Steinbrenner's leadership and made Steinbrenner a multimillionaire.

In the late 1960s, Steinbrenner began to exert his newfound influence on the national level. He used his political connections to become the chief fundraiser for the Democratic Congressional Campaign Committee, raising nearly $2 million over a two–year period. The election of Republican Richard Nixon to the presidency in 1968 made Steinbrenner fear reprisals against him or his business. To hedge his bets, the shipbuilder contributed to Nixon's 1972 re–election campaign. Unfortunately for Steinbrenner, his donations violated several campaign finance laws. He eventually pleaded guilty to all counts and was fined a $35,000.

These charges came just as Steinbrenner was embarking on a new career as a major league baseball owner. In January 1973, Steinbrenner joined with a group of investors to purchase the New York Yankees for $10 million. Once baseball's hallmark franchise, the Yankees had slipped to second–division status in recent years under the ownership of CBS and a management team headed by Mike Burke. Steinbrenner, who at first announced he would "stick to building ships" and let others run the team, promptly forced Burke out and hired Cleveland Indians' general manager Gabe Paul to supervise the rebuilding process.

In November 1974, baseball commissioner Bowie Kuhn briefly returned Steinbrenner to the shipyards by issuing him a two–year suspension for his campaign finance transgressions. In Steinbrenner's absence, Paul made a series of shrewd trades and personnel decisions that laid the groundwork for the Yankees' return to prominence. By the time Steinbrenner returned from ex-

lege in Massachusetts, where he ran track and edited the sports section of the campus newspaper. In the glee club, he stood directly behind future Broadway legend Stephen Sondheim and—by his own account—outsang him. After earning his bachelor's degree in 1952, Steinbrenner joined the United States Air Force. There he took charge of a succession of successful projects that showed his emerging leadership skills. He established a sports program and set up his own food service business on the base.

After three years in the military, Steinbrenner got a job coaching high school football in Columbus, Ohio. He later moved to the college level, becoming an assistant at Northwestern and then at Purdue, but his Big Ten

ile in 1976, the Yankees had a top–flight club poised to contend for a world title. The team won its division going away that season and then relied on a clutch ninth–inning, game–winning home run by Chris Chambliss to secure the American League pennant in a five–game playoff against the Kansas City Royals. Only a four–game sweep at the hands of the Cincinnati Reds in the World Series dampened the spirit of rejuvenation surrounding the Yankees.

In 1977 Steinbrenner opened his checkbook to bring in free agent slugger Reggie Jackson, the former star of the Oakland Athletics. Jackson added considerable star power and clutch hitting to the team, but he also heightened dissension in the clubhouse. He had a stormy relationship with manager Billy Martin and was considered selfish by his teammates. Nevertheless, the talented, if volatile, teammates survived these distractions to make it to the World Series for a second year in a row. This time they were victorious, ousting the Los Angeles Dodgers in six games. Steinbrenner had fulfilled his promise to bring a championship to New York.

Steinbrenner brought a second world title in 1978, though again at a high cost in terms of hostility. The simmering Martin–Jackson feud bubbled over in mid–season, prompting Steinbrenner to fire his manager. On his way out the door, Martin took a few parting shots at both Jackson and the team's owner. "One's a born liar, the other's convicted," Martin observed—an apparent reference to Steinbrenner's campaign finance activity. Relations between the two men would forever be colored by this incident.

Over the next few years, the Yankees continued to contend for the American League pennant. Steinbrenner's increasingly meddlesome management style was blamed for a lack of stability that doomed the team's best efforts. He hired Billy Martin back as manager in 1979—only to fire him at season's end. It was the first of four instances in which the erratic Martin was invited back to take control of the club, only to be let go with assurances that he would never be hired again. In 1980 the Yankees won 103 games under manager Dick Howser, but Steinbrenner fired him after the team was beaten in the play-offs.

In 1981 the Yankees returned to the World Series. However, after beating the Los Angeles Dodgers in the first two games, the Yankees dropped the next three. Following game five, Steinbrenner called a late–night press conference to hold up a flimsily bandaged hand and announce that he had defended the Yankee honor by beating up two Dodger fans in an elevator. The Yankees failed to take a "get tough" cue from their owner and lost the sixth and deciding game. Before the game was even completed, Steinbrenner ordered the Yankee publicity department to issue an apology to the people of New York City for the club's lackluster performance.

The rest of the 1980s proved to be a bleak period for the Yankees and their fans. Steinbrenner signed many

Chronology:
George Steinbrenner

1930: Born.

1967: Became president of American Ship Building.

1973: Purchased a controlling interest in the New York Yankees.

1974: Given a two–year suspension from baseball for violating campaign finance laws.

1977: Signed Reggie Jackson; Yankees win the World Series championship.

1978: Yankees won second straight World Series.

1982: Hired and fired three different managers.

1990: Suspended from baseball for a second time for acts considered harmful to the sport.

1993: Returned from suspension to control the Yankees once more.

1996: Hired manager Joe Torre.

1998: Yankees won World Series, winning again in 1999 and 2000.

1999: Formed YankeeNets LLC with New York Nets owner Lewis Katz.

2001: Yankees won 38th pennant, a league record, and their fourth consecutive World Series.

high–priced players but with seemingly little regard for their adaptability to the pressures of playing in New York. Managers were put under intense pressure to succeed, subject to dismissal at any time according to the owner's whims. Three men were hired and fired during the 1982 season alone. Steinbrenner engaged in protracted contract squabbles with one star player, Don Mattingly, and publicly belittled another, Dave Winfield, by comparing him unfavorably to the departed Reggie Jackson. By 1990 the Yankees were one of the worst teams in baseball—thanks in large part to the instability wrought on the club by its owner.

By that time, Steinbrenner's relationship with Winfield had deteriorated to the point at which he reportedly hired a known gambler to dig up information that would destroy the slugger's reputation. Acting on evidence of this plot, baseball commissioner Fay Vincent suspended Steinbrenner from baseball on July 30, 1990. Control of the Yankees was handed over to limited partner Robert

Nederlander for an indefinite period. Yankee management used this period of "exile" to rebuild the team's shattered minor league system and make a few judicious trades. When Steinbrenner was allowed to regain control of the team in 1993, it was once again ready to contend for a world championship.

Many observers expected Steinbrenner to return to his imperious ways and jeopardize the club's progress, but banishment seemed to have mellowed Steinbrenner. He changed his management style, showing a renewed willingness to let his "baseball people" run the team. Other than ousting manager Buck Showalter after the 1995 season, he made few personnel changes and largely avoided making the kind of public comments that had generated controversy in the past. Under new manager Joe Torre, the team capped a stellar 1996 season with a come–from–behind upset victory over the Atlanta Braves in the World Series. Two years later, the Yankees posted the best record in American League history, going 114–48. They then completed an impressive playoff run by sweeping the San Diego Padres in four games in the World Series. In 2000 they won another championship by beating the New York Mets in what became known as the "subway series." In 2001 the Yankees nearly staged a dramatic World Series comeback; two games down to the Arizona Diamondbacks, the Yankees pulled out extra–inning wins in games four and five after being behind in the bottom of the ninth inning with two outs. The teams entered the seventh game, tied in the best of seven series. The Diamondbacks won the decisive game in the same dramatic fashion—a comeback win in the ninth inning, robbing the Yanks of yet one more World Championship.

During this period of success, Steinbrenner turned his attention more frequently toward the future of the Yankees. He lobbied city and state officials in New York for the construction of a new stadium or at least the refurbishing of the old one. In 1999 Steinbrenner joined with New York Nets owner Lewis Katz to create YankeeNets, a merger of the New York Yankees and New Jersey Nets. By 2000 YankeeNets was also the holding company for the New Jersey Devils hockey team. (Principal owners George Steinbrenner of the Yankees and Lewis Katz and Ray Chambers of the Nets and Devils retained direct control of their respective teams.) In 2001 the firm was working to launch a regional cable sports network called Yankees Entertainment and Sports.

Social and Economic Impact

Steinbrenner owns a team steeped in history and tradition. Since 1903 the Yankees franchise has won a record 26 World Series championships and 38 American League pennant races. Some of the sport's greatest players have worn Yankee uniforms, including Babe Ruth, Lou Gehrig, Joe DiMaggio, and Mickey Mantle. Steinbrenner, through both his good decisions and blatantly

poor decisions on and off the field, has managed to keep the Yankees in the public eye, and his impact on the game of baseball and the New York Yankees in particular, will long be debated. His blustery personality and poor management of the Yankee minor leagues earned him the title of the Most Hated Man in Baseball during the late 1980s and early 1990s; however, success can soften even the hardest of hearts. Valued at over $750 million, the Yankees are the richest team in baseball and maintain a payroll of $91.5 million, the largest in professional baseball. Steinbrenner, who owns a controlling share (57 percent) of the team, can use that money to draw the best players in the game to his team. He has also learned from his past mistakes and now pays much more attention to his farm league teams, grooming quality players from within the Yankee's organization rather than relying on hiring big names from other teams.

Although still outspoken and sometimes contentious, Steinbrenner, now in his 70s, has refrained from firing his popular manager, Torre, for five seasons—no small feat, considering the Yankees had a string of 18 manager changes in a 15–year period. Like the Yankees themselves, many New Yorkers and others around the country, either love Steinbrenner or despise him. His supporters consider his over quarter of a century as the Yankees' owner as just another chapter in the dramatic—and sometimes soap–opera–ish—history of the Yankees. His detractors, who consider many of his past actions as inexcusable, will celebrate the day when control of the team passes from his hands. Steinbrenner continues to defend his hands–on approach. As a friend of the owner told the *Financial Times*, "His life is the Yankees."

Sources of Information

Contact at: New York Yankees
        Yankee Stadium
        E. 161st St. and River Ave.
        New York, NY 10452
        Business Phone: (718) 293–4300
        URL: http://www.yankees.mlb.com

Bibliography

Frommer, Harvey. *The New York Yankee Encyclopedia*. Macmillan, 1997.

Gallagher, Mark. *The Yankee Encyclopedia*. Sagamore Publishing, 1996.

Knight, Rebecca. "George Steinbrenner Fields Options for Yankees." *Financial Times*, 4 April 2000.

Madden, Bill. *Damned Yankees*. Warner, 1991.

"New York Yankees." *Hoover's Online*. Available at http://www.hoovers.com.

Schapp, Dick. *Steinbrenner!* Putnam, 1982.

"YankeeNets LLC." *Hoover's Online*. Available at http://www.hoovers.com.

Martha Stewart

(1941-)
Martha Stewart Living
Omnimedia

Overview

Described as the guru of good taste in U. S. entertaining and the person who has had the biggest impact on the aesthetics of the U. S. household, Martha Stewart has turned her lifestyle and tastes into a business empire. As a domestic arts expert and lifestyle consultant Martha Stewart has left her stamp on the way U. S. citizens currently view cooking, home decoration, gardening, and entertaining. In the process, Stewart has revolutionized how–to and self–help into a state of mind and a way of life.

Personal Life

Martha Stewart was born on August 3 in 1941, in Jersey City, New Jersey, and grew up in Nutley, New Jersey. She is the daughter of Edward and Martha Kostyra, of Polish–Catholic ancestry. Her father was a pharmaceutical salesman; her mother was a sixth–grade school teacher. She was the second of six children. When Martha was three, the family moved to a three–bedroom frame house in suburban Nutley, New Jersey. She recalled, "We were brought up unpretentiously, but with a lot of spirit and a lot of 'You can do anything you want to do' hammered into our heads." Stewart was a favorite of her father, who taught her about gardening, carpentry, and public speaking. She described herself as a child as "very proper, very busy, very driven." She alone among her siblings had a flair for gardening and did not mind spending hours weeding. She was also fascinated by food and cooking and learned a good deal from her maternal grandmother. While still in grammar school, Stewart or-

Martha Stewart. (AP/Wide World Photos)

ganized birthday parties for neighborhood children for fun and to augment her baby–sitting income.

By high school, her blonde good looks earned her modeling assignments in fashionable stores and on television. A straight A student, Stewart turned down a full scholarship to attend New York University to work her way through Barnard College in New York City. She abandoned early plans to become a chemist and decided to study art, European history, and architecture instead. In 1961, while still in her sophomore year of college, she married law student Andrew Stewart. To support them, Martha Stewart took modeling jobs and appeared in television commercials for Clairol, Lifeboy soap, and Tareyton cigarettes. She graduated from Barnard in 1963 and continued to model until the birth of her daughter, Alexis, in 1965.

Stewart contemplated entering graduate school to study architecture but decided that her father–in–law's profession as a stockbroker interested her more. From 1965 to 1973, she worked at the small brokerage firm, Monness, Williams, and Sidel. She was successful and "liked the sales part of it, the human contact," but the 1973 recession was traumatic. As she explained, "I wanted to sell things that were fun to sell. And stocks weren't anymore." In 1973 the Stewarts moved from their apartment in New York City to a home in Westport, Connecticut, that they began to restore themselves. Once the house was renovated, Stewart began to concentrate on another hobby, gourmet cooking. In 1976 Stewart began a catering business, working out of her

home's basement kitchen, which led to her career as a cookbook author and domestic lifestyle expert.

Stewart sustains her many ventures with seemingly boundless energy. As she admitted to *Cosmopolitan*, "I tend to get over enthusiastic, and often that's translated as workaholism. For example, I'm writing a garden book, so I garden 12 hours a day. If people like to characterize that as workaholism, it's their problem. I work at what I do, but to me it's fun. I have the ideal career, because I'm constantly writing about or photographing things I like. Whatever work is involved is something I really enjoy doing. Actually, I think I'd characterize myself more as an enthusiast than a perfectionist. But as far as being a perfectionist, I'm like that in anything I do." To maintain her frenzied pace, she claims that she only needs to sleep four hours nightly. Most mornings begin at 6:00 A.M. with an hour–and–a–half session with a personal trainer before her work schedule begins. As her friend Mort Zuckerman, chairman of *U.S. News & World Report*, has observed, "Martha is a unique combination of the beauty of the orchid and the efficiency of a computer."

Her marriage to Andrew Stewart, who cofounded the publishing company of Stewart, Tabori, and Chang, ended in divorce in 1989. Stewart spends her time at Turkey Hill Farm, her Westport home, with her collection of seven Himalayans cats and four chow chow dogs. She also has an apartment in New York City, a weekend beach house in East Hampton, New York, a 30–acre property in Fairfield, Connecticut, and a home on the Maine coast.

Career Details

With apparent ease, Stewart transformed her personal love for cooking into a career. While on a modeling assignment in the early 1960s, she visited Europe for the first time and studied the restaurants she visited in Italy, Germany, and France. As a stockbroker, she had sampled haute cuisine on expense account meals with clients. In 1976 she placed an advertisement in a local newspaper offering her services as a caterer. Almost immediately she found herself preparing for a wedding for 300. Over the next 10 years, Martha Stewart, Inc., grew into a $1 million business, serving corporate and celebrity clients drawn to her tasty menus and unique presentations. She and a staff cooked meals for as many as 1,500 people at a time. Herbs and ingredients came from her own gardens. She has also contributed articles to the *New York Times*, worked as a freelance food "stylist" for photographers, and served as the food and entertaining editor and cooking columnist for *House Beautiful*.

Stewart's big break came when a client, impressed with her work, convinced her to let his company publish her first book, *Entertaining*, an oversized, lavishly illustrated book of her hostess ideas, published in 1982. The book's introduction served as a declaration of the Martha Stewart style and method, which called for a "new style of entertaining that is informal, relaxed, and expressive, based not on intimidating prescriptions but on personality and personal effort." The personality that is revealed is Stewart's own: casual elegance, natural materials, and hand–crafted sophistication. The book reached a receptive public, selling more than 625,000 copies and going through some 30 printings. A string of successful sequels followed, such as *Martha Stewart's Quick Cook Menus*, *Martha Stewart's Hors d'Oeuvres*, *Martha Stewart's Weddings*, and *Martha Stewart's Christmas*. Other endeavors have included videotapes, television specials, lectures, and seminars.

Stewart's ideas for enhancing domestic life have tapped into a vast market of fans who appreciate the ingenuity of her suggestions, the authority with which good taste is presented, and the deeper dream of elegance and sophistication that her books, programs, and persona project. As she explained to a *New York* interviewer, her success is due to Americans' "interest in self–improvement . . . I'm just approaching it from an aesthetic point of view, rather than a scientific point of view or psychological." Critics have been quick, though, to charge her with overindulgence in materialism, with raising style to an almost religious devotion, and with offering a standard of domestic achievement well beyond the reach of most of her fans. Stewart has defended her approach, saying, "Having something to dream about is very important to most people."

The fantasy has proven to be a potent one and has allowed Stewart to create a business empire around her tastes and lifestyle. In 1987 Kmart signed Stewart as its lifestyle consultant, and she agreed to promote her own line of bed and bath products through Kmart. Martha Stewart's first line of Martha Stewart Everyday products for Kmart, Everyday Blue and White Label bedding and bath products, was launched in February 1997. In the next four years, Kmart introduced five additional product lines: Martha Stewart Everyday Colors, a paint collection for walls; Baby Baby, an infant bedding and nursery line; Garden, a line of plants, seeds, tools, outdoor furniture, and barbecue grills; Kitchen, a collection of cooking accessories; and Keeping, featuring plastic storage boxes, chrome shelving, cedar hangers, glass food canisters, and wooden clothespins.

Collectively, Stewart's Kmart lines were expected to generate $5 billion in total sales between 1997 and the end of 2001. In mid–2001, Kmart and Stewart launched the sixth line of Martha Stewart Everyday products. Taken together, Stewart's Kmart lines were expected to have sales of $1.6 billion in 2001. As Kmart filed for bankruptcy in 2002, analysts were debating whether Stewart would continue to market her products through the chain. If Stewart decided to contract with a different distributor, Kmart would be seriously hard–hit to make up that much revenue.

Chronology:
Martha Stewart

1941: Born.

1961: Married Andrew Stewart.

1963: Graduated from Barnard College.

1965: Began work for a Wall Street brokerage firm.

1976: Began catering business.

1982: Published first book, *Entertaining*.

1987: Named lifestyle consultant for Kmart Corp.

1989: Divorced Andrew Stewart.

1997: Formed Martha Stewart Living Omnimedia.

1999: Raised $129.6 million in Initial Public Offering.

By the late 1990s, Stewart was able to take tighter control of her increasingly complex business. With profits from her association with Kmart, in 1997 she was able to buy her signature publication, *Martha Stewart Living*, from Time Warner, which had launched the magazine in 1991. By 2001 the magazine had 2.1 million loyal subscribers. Stewart took over as CEO of Martha Stewart Living Enterprises, which in addition to the magazine includes a syndicated television show, a web site, a daily radio show, books written by her and the editors of *Martha Stewart Living*, a syndicated newspaper column ("Ask Martha"), a mail–order catalog company ("Martha by Mail"), and retail products. By 1998 Stewart's company made $24 million on sales of $180 million, and analysts predicted 1999 sales to top $225 million. By 2003, experts predicted, the company would approach the $400 million in sales.

In 1999 Stewart caused a Wall Street sensation when she took her company public. Stock prices doubled within the first day, raising $129.6 million for the company and making Stewart a billionaire on paper. Analysts attributed the IPO's phenomenal success in large part to the fact that Stewart is so widely known.

Social and Economic Impact

Successful in her many roles, Stewart has demonstrated a unique entrepreneurial skill in marketing not so much a product as herself and her sense of taste, turning her own life into a business empire. Like any other good businessperson, Stewart has shown that she understands her audience and has captured their imagination. Stewart summed up her influence on the American public when she said, "My books are 'dream' books to look at, but they're practical. Women can take the recipes, the ideas, and use them every day, because what I'm giving them is not a fantasy but a reality that looks like a fantasy."

Stewart has, in a number of ways, helped to change the ways Americans eat, entertain, and decorate. Joining the concept of self–help with consumption, Stewart has instructed a mass audience in the lessons of good taste and the values that she has cultivated in her own life. Indeed, so closely is Stewart's personality identified with her company that some analysts wonder about its future. "I'm a brand," Stewart has noted, but as her empire has grown and she has aged, the lifestyle queen has had to begin delegating some responsibilities. She no longer reads every word that is printed in *Martha Stewart Living*, for example, and has courted top management for the various segments of her business. She remains confident that the company will endure even after she is no longer intimately involved with it. "I have imbued this company with a tremendous amount of my spirit and my artistic philosophy," she told *Business Week* writer Diane Brady. "So much that emerges here now is a combination of that and other people's creativity."

Stewart has taught an entire generation of American women how to cook, garden, and decorate their homes. Through her daily television program, which is syndicated coast–to–coast; her magazines, which reach ten million readers; her 27 books; her weekly newspaper column, which appears in 233 newspapers; her national radio show; and her website, Stewart has become one of the most influential women in the United States.

A hallmark of Stewart's success is that she sees herself not as a traditional publisher but as a source of information, which can be formatted in many ways—in print, on video, on television, or online—and can also be transformed into retail products, as Stewart has done with her lucrative Kmart lines. But the content she produces, which reaches an audience of more than 88 million a month, always remains sophisticated and tasteful; her magazine, for example, does not run articles on such staple subjects as dieting, hairstyles, or dating.

Stewart has remained vigilant in every aspect of her business. As Brady put it in *Business Week*, "She realized from the start that Martha Stewart could live up to its Omnimedia potential only if it controlled every piece of information passing through its universe." Known as a perfectionist, Stewart oversees everything from the details of a TV set design to long–term corporate vision. Controlling 60 percent of her company's shares, Stewart controls 96 percent of its votes.

Eager to expand her lifestyle empire ever further, Stewart is looking to increased Internet sales and expanded revenues from her Kmart partnership. "Our market," she told *Business Week*, "could be as big as everyone who has a house."

In October 2000, *Vanity Fair* magazine ranked Stewart 42nd in its annual list of the top 50 leaders of the Information Age. In the same month, she was named number 274 on *Forbes* magazine's annual *Forbes*' 400 Richest in America list. She has been named one of the "50 Most Powerful Women" twice by *Fortune Magazine* (October 1998 and October 1999) and has been recognized as one of America's 25 Most Influential People by *Time* magazine (June 1996) and as one of New York's 100 Most Influential Women in Business by Crain's New York Business.

Stewart has been awarded six Daytime Emmy Awards: "Outstanding Directing in a Service Show" for the 1997–98 broadcast season; "Outstanding Service Show Host" in both the 1994–95 and 1996–97 broadcast seasons; and "Outstanding Service Show" in the 1994–95, 1998–99, and 1999–2000 broadcast seasons. In May 1998, *Martha Stewart Living Television* received the 1998 James Beard Foundation Award for the Best National Cooking Segment.

In March 1998, the American Marketing Association presented Stewart with an Edison Achievement Award. That fall, she received the HFN 1998 CEO Summit Award and was inducted into the National Sales & Marketing Hall of Fame. In the fall of 1999, HFN named Stewart the top Lifestyle/Designer for her Everyday products. Adweek singled her out as "Publishing Executive of the Year" in March 1996. Stewart serves on the board of directors of the Magazine Publishers Association (MPA).

Sources of Information

Contact at: Martha Stewart Living Omnimedia
    20 W. 43rd St.
    New York, NY 10036
    Business Phone: (212) 827–8000
    URL: http://www.marthastewart.com

Bibliography
"About Martha," Martha Stewart Omnimedia, 2001. Available at http://www.marthastewart.com.

Brady, Diane. "Inside the Growing Empire of America's Lifestyle Queen." *Business Week*, 17 January 2000

"*Fortune*'s 50 Most Powerful Women." *Fortune*, 25 October 1999.

Hitchens, Christopher. "Martha Inc." *Vanity Fair*, October 1993.

Kasindorf, Jeanie. "Living with Martha." *New York*, 28 January 1991.

"Martha Stewart Living Omnimedia." MarthaStewart.com, 1997. Available at http://www.marthastewart.com.

"Martha Stewart Living Omnimedia, Inc." *Hoover's Online.* Available at http://www.hoovers.com.

"$129 Million in Martha Stewart Stock Sale." *New York Times,* 19 October 1999.

Oppenheimer, Jerry. *Martha Stewart—Just Deserts: The Unauthorized Biography.* New York: William Morrow, 1997.

Stewart, Martha. "The Importance of Being Myself." *Cosmopolitan,* July 1997.

Yue, Lorene. "Martha Stewart's New Kmart Line: Keeping Clutter Out." *Knight–Ridder/Tribune News Service,* 13 June 2001.

Clara Mae Lewis Stover

(1882-1975)
Russell Stover Candies Inc.

Overview

Clara Stover, a farm girl from Iowa, was the founder, vice president, and later president of Russell Stover Candies, the company she and her husband began in the basement of their home. Stover worked to perfect her candy, which she and her husband tirelessly marketed until they had built a million–dollar business that produced millions of pounds of candy and became an American favorite. Nearly eighty years after its beginnings, the company is now the country's largest manufacturer of boxed chocolates, chocolate bars, bagged candy, and S'mores. The company's Whitman's Sampler is a drugstore and grocery store staple and one of the company's biggest moneymakers. The candy maker had sales of $471 million and 5,200 employees in 2001.

Personal Life

Stover was born Clara Mae Lewis on September 25, 1893 in Johnson county, Iowa, to Mary Ann and Lorenzo Evan Lewis, a farmer. She married Russell Stover in 1911 and the couple had a daughter, Gloria Virginia, who married Reginald Ingram–Eiser. Stover was the author of a book about her husband, *The Life of Russell Stover*, published in 1958, and she also composed the songs "My Pretty Little Kitty from Kansas City" and "I'll Never Love Again." Her hobbies included swimming and motoring. Mrs. Stover was a Republican and was affiliated with the Linwood Presbyterian Church in Kansas City. Stover served on the board of the Art Institute, the Heart Association, and the Starlite Theatre Association, all in Kansas City, Missouri. She was a member of the Welsh

Society, the Women's Chamber of Commerce of Kansas City, Sigma Iota, Chi Omega, and the Soroptimist Club. Stover made contributions to Saint Luke's Research Hospital and Baptist Memorial Hospitals, in Kansas City, and the Shawnee Mission Hospital. She was a trustee of Research Hospital in 1956. She donated the Russell Stover Memorial Auditorium to what is now the University of Missouri's Conservatory of Music in 1955. After 1931 the couple lived in Kansas City, Missouri and also had a house in Miami Beach, Florida, where Russell Stover died in 1954. Mrs. Stover died over twenty years later in 1975 at the age of 93.

Stover's grandparents, Evan and Rachel Lewis, emigrated from Wales and moved to Aurora, Illinois, before settling in Oxford, Iowa. Clara describes what it was like growing up on a turn–of–the century farm in her book, *The Life of Russell Stover:* "Social competition among families was something unknown to us. We were as 'well off' as anybody, we thought. If someone sported a buggy with a fringe on top, we certainly did not envy him and therefore felt no inner drive to keep up with the Browns. We felt we were a successful farm family with lots of food and warm clothing." The second oldest, Clara had three sisters, Annbert Maud, Cettie Glee, and Hannah Mabel and one brother, LeRoy Evan. The family lived a spare existence, raising hogs and cattle and buying staples such as groceries and clothing with the sale of the livestock.

Stover was educated in the local schools of rural Johnson County. She was able to borrow $300 from a bachelor neighbor to go to college, a huge sum in those days, which she later paid back with interest. She attended the University of Iowa where she studied speech and, later, music. While at the university, Stover taught school near Homestead, Iowa. She also met her future husband while at college, a chemistry major who attended the university for a year after graduating from Iowa City Academy. The studious Stover was also tall, dark, handsome, and popular with the ladies. After graduation, she taught piano to local children in Oxford, Iowa, and then decided to return to Iowa City for further piano study. There, she met up with Stover again. She recalled the meeting in her book: "And surely destiny was at work—our first real meeting in a sweet shop! It wasn't the least prophetic then. We both joshed each other about our weakness for candy and ice cream, unaware that it was to become an abiding habit all through the years, for no matter where we were, Russell passed an ice cream parlor or candy store with only the greatest difficulty." Clara married Russell Stover on June 17, 1911, in Chicago, Illinois.

For a short time, Russell Stover worked as a salesman for the American Tobacco Company. In 1911 the couple moved to Hume, Canada, in the province of Saskatchewan. Russell Stover ran a 580–acre farm there until 1912. Mr. Stover then got a job as a candy salesman, and they relocated to Winnipeg, Manitoba, Canada. To help with the family's expenses, Mrs. Stover took var-

Chronology:
Clara Mae Lewis Stover

1882: Born.

1911: Married Russell Stover.

1912: Began making candy in her kitchen and selling it in Canada.

1923: Founded Mrs. Stover's Bungalow Candies with her husband.

1925: Opened the company's first factory in Denver.

1931: Moved their headquarters to Kansas City, Missouri.

1943: Company renamed Russell Stover Candies.

1954: Became president of Russell Stover Candies.

1960: Sold company.

1975: Died.

ious odd jobs: selling magazines door to door, working in a drugstore, and operating a sewing machine in a factory. Later in 1912 the candy company that Mr. Stover worked for declined to reimburse the salesman for some inedible candy, so the Stovers decided to make their own candy and learn the business of selling it.

Career Details

The Stovers came up with their own recipes for the candy, which they produced with some used equipment they set up in a little storeroom. They sold the candy locally. It became very popular, and their little business flourished. Due to World War I, however, Canada instated wartime rationing in 1916, which hindered the Stovers' candy business. The couple returned home to Iowa. They eventually moved to Chicago, where Mr. Stover found a position as a salesman for the A.G. Morris for a year. After that, he sold candy for the Bunte Candy Co., where he stayed for three years. Mrs. Stover found work as a salesperson at the department store, Carson Pirie's. In 1919, in the kitchen of their Chicago apartment, Mrs. Stover once again began making the candy she and her husband had developed in Canada. She hired an assistant who dipped the candies. She sold the all–chocolate sweets under the name of Stover's Candy. Mr. Stover used his connections in the industry to sell

Window shoppers at a Russell Stover Candies store. (*Corbis/William A. Bake*)

the candies to sixteen local stores. Her husband then took a job as superintendent of the Irwin Candy Co. in Des Moines, Iowa and when the couple relocated there in 1920, Mrs. Stover left the candy business she had established in Chicago behind.

While at Irwin, Mr. Stover helped bring the company out of bankruptcy, but the business was acquired by the Graham Ice Cream Co. of Omaha, Nebraska in late 1920. Mr. Stover remained in his superintendent position with Graham. In 1921 Mr. Stover perfected and promoted what would become an American icon: a frozen treat that he christened the Eskimo Pie. The new confection sold rapidly throughout the following year but, just as quickly, dried up as interest in the new-fangled dessert suddenly waned. The Stovers took their $25,000 from the Eskimo Pie sales and decided to start their own business. In 1923 the Stovers moved once again, this time to Denver, Colorado, where they began their own company called Mrs. Stover's Bungalow Candies. Mrs. Stover became vice president of the company in 1925, a position that she occupied for eighteen years until 1943.

The couple made the candy and ran the business out of the basement of their Denver home. Mrs. Stover trained the company's first employee in the art of producing their candies. Mr. Stover rented two retail stores to sell their confections. In less than a year, the company grew to five stores in Denver, produced 20,000 pounds of candy and had seven employees. In 1925, the Stovers opened a factory in Denver, where Mrs. Stover managed the female employees. In 1931 the couple moved their burgeoning business to Kansas City, Missouri. Some tough times followed with the depression and a sugar shortage during World War II, but the company managed to survive these hurdles. They were doing well enough to open a second factory in Kansas City, Missouri, and a third in Lincoln, Nebraska, in 1942.

Mrs. Stover traveled all over the country, opening and decorating stores that numbered forty by 1943. The company also had offices in Denver, Kansas City, and Lincoln, along with their factories there. The year 1943 also saw a reorganization of the company, which was renamed Russell Stover Candies. That year, the company allowed thirty-five of its employees with the longest service records to become a part of the business. The company grew from seven employees to 900 by 1954 and increased production to 11 million pounds of candy, which was sold in the company's own 40 stores as well as 2000 other department stores and drugstores throughout the United States. In 2001 the company's website stated, "Mr. and Mrs. Stover established principles that were successful then and are still carefully followed today. The three principles of quality, service and value allow Russell Stover to remain 'Only the Finest.'"

Mrs. Stover took over as the company's president after her husband's death at age sixty-six in 1954. Under Mrs. Stover, the business continued its phenomenal growth and production doubled to 22 million pounds by the time the business was sold in 1960 by Louis Ward. Mrs. Stover still enjoyed making candy throughout her retirement and was active in several civic organizations until her death on January 9, 1975.

Social and Economic Impact

Phil A. Koury said in the introduction of the book, *The Life of Russell Stover*, "Though they moved in corporate pastures, the Russell Stovers were in no wise [sic] corporate people in that slim and detached and specific legal sense of the word. The truth is, they possessed a comfortable and rooted love of what corporations are really made of, namely, humans. It is a good love and has served the Stovers well."

Clara Stover was an innovator in the field of candy making and certainly among the earliest women to serve as vice president and later president of a large, national manufacturer. Not afraid of hard work, Stover took a variety of jobs throughout her life—in her college years and later to help support her husband who was trying to establish himself in the candy business. Once he had established himself, the self-starting Stover began making her own recipes and perfecting them in her own home, and she helped her husband sell and market the finished product. Stover traveled extensively throughout the country once her company had been established, in order to personally oversee and direct the atmosphere and other details at the company's retail stores, which grew to forty in her tenure. While Stover served as the company's president from 1955 until 1960, the company's productivity doubled, cranking out 11 million pounds of candy per year.

Stover founded and helped build a company that has lasted for nearly eighty years as the leader in producing boxed candy. Russell Stover's is now an international company, with sales in Canada and Puerto Rico. The candy Stover began can now be found in more than 40,000 drugstores, gift stores, department stores, and related outlets in all fifty states in the United States. The boxed candy industry that Stover helped build is now a $2 billion dollar market and part of a larger $10 billion market for chocolate. Every time one takes a bite of a Russell Stover–made candy, he or she will be tasting almost exactly what Mrs. Stover created back in her Den-

ver kitchen, as the company maintains that each of her recipes remains basically unchanged.

Sources of Information

Bibliography

"Company History." *Russell Stover Candies Inc.*, 2001. Available at http://www.russellstover.com.

The National Cyclopedia of American Biography. James T. White & Company, 1961.

"Russell Stover Candies Inc." *Hoover's*, 2001. Available at http://www.hoovers.com.

Stover, Clara, and Phil A. Koury. *The Life of Russell Stover: An American Success Story*. Random House, 1958.

"Russell Stover and the Chocolate Wars." *The Business Journal*, 28 March 1997.

Pamela Thomas–Graham

(1963-)
NBC, Inc.

Overview

A graduate of Harvard with three degrees, Pamela Thomas–Graham has often been described as a super–achiever. In July 2001 she was named president and CEO of CNBC, the Internet branch of the financial news channel. She is also executive vice president of NBC. Prior to that she worked for 10 years at McKinsey and Company, a prestigious management consulting firm in New York City. When she was 32–years–old she became the first African–American woman to become a partner in that organization. On top of all of her executive duties Thomas–Graham found the time to become a popular author. Her three mystery novels have been published by Simon and Schuster. In addition, she serves on the board of charities such as the Red Cross and the Metropolitan Opera. When she assumed her position with CNBC, she became the highest–ranking woman executive heading a division at NBC.

Personal Life

Pamela Thomas–Graham was born in 1963 in Detroit, Michigan. Her mother was a social worker from Georgia and her father an engineer from South Carolina. She has one brother.

Thomas–Graham's parents were deeply inspired by the civil rights movement of the 1960s and they in turn influenced Thomas–Graham's own values. While growing up in Detroit in the 1970s, Thomas–Graham looked up to civil rights leaders like Julian Bond and Thurgood Marshall. Her parents were also firm believers in the benefits of a good education. As such, they encouraged their daugh-

Pamela Thomas–Graham (left) standing with Maria Bartiromo at the 2001 Glamour Magazine "Women of the Year" awards. (Hulton/Archive.)

ter to reach as high as she could go and Thomas–Graham did not disappoint. Her peers at Detroit's Lutheran High School West named her as the "smartest" and "most likely to succeed." During high school, Thomas–Graham, who liked to sing and dance, was active in the drama club and school choir. She also became the first graduate of Lutheran High to go to Harvard University.

Thomas–Graham initially went to Harvard to become a lawyer. But when she entered college she became interested in economics and business, which would eventually result in her simultaneously attaining a business degree and law degree. She graduated Phi Beta Kappa

from Harvard–Radcliffe College with a B.A. in 1985. While at Radcliffe she received the Captain Jonathan Fay prize, which is the highest annual honor bestowed by Radcliffe. Thomas–Graham won the award for being the student "showing the greatest promise" in her graduating class. She continued on to earn an MBA from Harvard Business School in 1989 and a law degree from Harvard Law School that same year. During her college years, she interned during summers, working in politics, for a professor, and at Chase Manhattan Bank in New York. While in law school, she was an editor of the *Harvard Law Review*.

Chronology:

Pamela Thomas–Graham

1963: Born.

1985: Graduated Phi Beta Kappa from Harvard–Radcliffe.

1989: Graduated from Harvard Business School and Harvard Law School.

1989: Hired by McKinsey and Company.

1992: Married writer/lawyer Larry Otis Graham.

1995: Became first African–American woman partner at McKinsey and Company.

1998: First novel published by Simon and Schuster.

1999: Named as COO of CNBC.com.

2001: Became president and CEO of the CNBC cable network.

2001: Named vice president of NBC.

Her education, intelligence, and ambition landed her high–ranking positions with McKinsey and Company, a prestigious management consulting company in New York City, and with NBC. In 1998, she began writing mystery novels that have proved popular with the reading public.

Thomas–Graham met her husband, Lawrence Otis Graham, a writer and attorney, in the mid–1980s when they were both attending Harvard. They dated for six years and were married in 1992. Thomas–Graham has also worked as a strategist for her husband's congressional campaign. The couple lives in Chappaqua, New York with their son. They enjoy exercise and weekend tennis.

Thomas–Graham serves on the boards of the New York City Opera, the American Red Cross of Greater New York, the Inner–City Scholarship Fund and the Harvard Alumni Association.

Career Details

Thomas–Graham's professional career began in earnest in 1989 when she started her 10–year stint with McKinsey and Company, who first hired her as an associate. She worked 16–hour days but her efforts paid off.

Over the course of the next several years she worked her way up through the firm and became one of the heads of its media and entertainment practice, advising Fortune 500 companies. She would later say that one of her biggest challenges was convincing herself and others that she could effectively advise a corporate CEO about complex business problems.

In 1995, when she was only 32–years–old, she became the first African–American woman partner in the company. In fact, she was one of only three black partners in a firm of approximately three thousand consultants working in thirty–five countries. Thomas–Graham later related how there were no African–American female role models, so she had to set herself up as her own role model.

Thomas–Graham found consulting work to provide great groundwork in advancing her career. In a piece she wrote for *The Black Collegian Online* titled "Reflections on Success," she said, "Going into consulting can be a great choice for people starting out who aren't exactly sure what they want to do. You're helping people solve business problems, and you are at the same time exposing yourself to all kinds of different possibilities."

In 1999 Thomas–Graham felt she was ready to leave McKinsey and move on to the next challenge, so she sent out feelers. One of her mentors at McKinsey and Company then arranged for her to meet Jack Welch, the chairman of General Electric. At McKinsey, as part of the retail and media practice group, Thomas–Graham helped clients build business on the Internet. Therefore, she seemed appropriately suited for General Electric, which owns NBC and CNBC.com. At the time, the CNBC website was serving strictly as a promotional tool for the CNBC cable channel, and Welch wanted to turn it into a full–service financial site. As it turned out, Welch and Thomas–Graham hit it off when they met and a few months later, Welch was offering her a job. Thomas–Graham immediately accepted. She was excited by the opportunity to become involved in the online industry.

At first, Thomas–Graham was in charge of CNBC's online operations. In February 2001 she became president and COO of CNBC. When she took the position, CNBC had risen to be an international leader in business news and operations. Her job for the cable network, as she saw it, was to set the strategic vision of the site and then to make sure it had the adequate resources to allow it to grow, building the value of the franchise. She oversaw a staff of 150. Her duties included managing all aspects of editorial, production, marketing, communications, and technology. On top of all of that, she still managed the website.

When Thomas–Graham was offered the position, some observers were skeptical about NBC's choice. Thomas–Graham had no previous experience in the broadcast industry. However, NBC was confident in its decision. Bob Wright, president and CEO of NBC, said, "I have chosen Pamela for this new COO role because of her management skills and leadership capability, and I am confident that adding her to our CNBC executive team will help CNBC build on its success in the years ahead."

By this time, Thomas-Graham was also confident in her own abilities. In September 2001 she told *Black Enterprise* that she had made it at McKinsey and knew that she could, and would, make it at NBC. But she understood that it would be a challenge. "I knew I had to prove myself coming in," she said.

In July 2001 she became the president and chief executive officer of the CNBC cable network. She was only 38-years-old, a relatively young age to assume such a position with a major, high profile corporation. At the time CNBC was providing business news programming and financial market coverage to more than 198 million homes worldwide, including more than 82 million in the United States and Canada. As the CEO of CNBC, she reports to the president and chief operating officer of NBC, and she is responsible for all CNBC domestic operations, including programming, advertising sales, and coordinating activities across CNBC's television and Internet platforms.

Soon she acquired another title: executive vice president of NBC. In that position, she participates in weekly meetings that involve the high-level strategic direction for the entire corporation. With the job came executive perks. Each morning, she is driven to work at CNBC.com's headquarters in Fort Lee, New Jersey. She also has an office at Rockefeller Plaza in Manhattan.

As she moves into the future with CNBC, Thomas-Graham develops initiatives that will increase revenue and viewers. Near the end of 2001, plans included new programming like "CNBC World," a digital services that offered investors real-time access to comprehensive financial information on a global scale.

As if Thomas-Graham hasn't achieved enough, she has also carved out for herself a career as a successful mystery writer. Her debut novel, *A Darker Shade of Crimson: An Ivy League Mystery*, was published in 1998 by Simon and Schuster, one of the top book publishing houses in the world. It was part of a planned series and featured a main character named Nikki Chase, a young African-American professor of economics at Harvard. In a review of the book, *Publisher's Weekly* remarked the Thomas-Graham "delivers on the promise of her first story" and "skillfully incorporates attitudes toward race and integration." A writer for *Kirkus Reviews* said the book was "an impressive first outing" and "[v]ivid characters, easy dialogue, and fluidly entertaining narrative mark a robustly talented new recruit to the genre."

Her debut novel was followed by a second in the "Ivy League" series, *Blue Blood*. A third one is not yet published.

It seems remarkable that Thomas-Graham could even find the time to be a novel writer, a profession that requires a great amount of time, dedication, and discipline. After all, she has a high-ranking profession in a demanding industry and she is raising a young son. However, Thomas-Graham revealed that, when she is in the process of producing a novel, she gets up at 4:30 a.m. and sits at her computer for several hours, writing until it is time to see to her family and get ready to go to work.

In addition to her literary and broadcasting pursuits, Thomas-Graham serves on the boards of directors of the New York City Opera, the American Red Cross of Greater New York, and Girls Incorporated. She has been profiled in a number of leading publications, including *Fortune, Jet*, and *Time*.

Social and Economic Impact

Pamela Thomas-Graham's life and career have included a number of distinctions. Besides being named as the first African-American woman partner at McKinsey and Company in 1995, she is also the highest-ranking woman executive running a division at NBC, Inc.

She has received many business awards including the 2001 Matrix award from New York Women in Communications for her contributions in the field of new media and the "Woman of the Year" award from the Financial Women's Association. She has been included in *Crain's New York Business* "Forty Under Forty" list of rising young business leaders. She was also chosen as one of the "Top 20 Women in Finance" by *Global Finance Magazine*, and one of the "Top 10 Consultants in America" by *Consulting Magazine*.

In the late part of the 1990s, after Thomas-Graham came on board, CNBC's revenues and popularity rose considerably. Sales went from $196 million in 1996 to $507 million in 2000. One-year sales went from $380 million in 1999 to $507 million in 2000. A good part of the success has been attributed to Thomas-Graham's lead and direction with CNBC.com. When Thomas-Graham joined CNBC in 1999, CNBC trailed behind competitors like CBSMarketwatch.com and CNNfn.com. However, by 2001 she had turned CNBC.com into an award-winning site with 1.5 million visitors per month.

Sources of Information

Contact at: NBC, Inc.
    30 Rockefeller Plz.
    New York, NY 10112

Bibliography

Clarke, Robyn D. "Excellence by the Graham," *Black Enterprise*, September 2001.

"Pamela Thomas-Graham." *NBC.com Corporate Info*, 2001. Available at http://www.nbc.com/nbc/header/Executive_Bios/thomas-graham_pamela.shtml.

"Pamela Thomas–Graham Named Chief Executive of CNBC." *CNEWS Media News*, 24 July 2001. Available at http://www.canoe.ca/CNEWSMediaNews0107/24_cnbc–ap.html.

Roach, Collen. "Compelling Couple: Pamela Thomas–Graham and Larry Otis Graham." *The Westchester Wag*, June 2000. Available from http://www.westchesterwag.com/pastarticles/grahams.asp.

Thomas–Graham, Pamela. "Reflections on Success." *The Black Collegian Online*, 2001. Available at http://www.blackcollegian.com/issues/30thAnn/reflectpgraham2001–30th.shtml.

Charles Lewis Tiffany

Overview

Charles Lewis Tiffany built his "fancy goods" company into what became the nation's preeminent jeweler for over fifty years and a uniquely American symbol of elegance and style. Tiffany pioneered what would become a classic engagement ring style, the raised solitaire diamond, six–prong "Tiffany Setting." Dubbed by the press in his day as the "King of Diamonds," Tiffany has catered to everyone from the likes of presidents including Abraham Lincoln and John F. Kennedy; European royalty; preeminent American families, including the Vanderbilts and the Astors; and celebrities in droves. Tiffany was honored for his dedication to excellence in his day and his trademarked Tiffany Blue Boxes and shopping bags have become familiar and enduring American icons of wealth and luxury to this day.

Personal Life

Tiffany was born on February 15, 1812 in Killingly, Connecticut, to Comfort Tiffany, a cotton goods manufacturer, and Chloe Draper. He married his partner's sister, Harriet Olivia Young on November 30, 1841 and had six children. Son Louis Comfort Tiffany became world renowned for his Tiffany glass. He died of pneumonia on February 18, 1902, in Yonkers, New York.

Tiffany was a founder of the New York Society of Fine Arts, patron of the Metropolitan Museum of Art, and member of the National Academy of Design. He was made a Chevalier of the Legion of Honor by France in 1878 and was bestowed the medal Praemia Digno by the Czar of Russia.

Tiffany & Co.
(1812-1902)

Charles Lewis Tiffany. (*Reuters NewMedia Inc./Corbis.*)

Educated at a school in nearby Danielsonville, Tiffany later spent two years at the Plainfield Academy in Connecticut. At the age of fifteen, Charles' father, a pioneer in the cotton goods industry, put him to work as a manager of a general store near the family's mill. Intermittently schooled in between work, Tiffany ran the store for ten years. He then joined his father's company, which was then christened, C. Tiffany & Son, after Charles' father bought out his partners.

Career Details

On September 18, 1837, with a thousand dollars borrowed from his father, Tiffany and friend John B. Young opened Tiffany & Young at 259 Broadway in New York City. The store originally sold stationery supplies and fancy goods, including costume jewelry. Business conditions were less than ideal at the time with the Panic of 1837, and some thought the company's uptown location would be bad for patronage. The first three days of sales totaled $4.98, but after that rocky start the business soon took off. Tiffany's store was unique for its time, offering fixed prices on items, thus removing the bartering process. The company also refused to extend credit to customers, which had become a problem for many businesses of the day. By 1839 Tiffany added glassware, cutlery, porcelain, and clocks to the company's line of products.

By the time Tiffany married his wife Harriet in 1841, the company had a new partner, J. L. Ellis and became known as Tiffany, Young & Ellis. With the funds Ellis brought to the firm, the company was able to rent the adjoining room, doubling its floor space. Ellis, who brought strong experience in the European jewelry market, became the company's chief overseas operator after his buying trip to Europe. In 1844 the company was importing quality Italian and English jewelry, adding to its already well–respected reputation. That year the company discontinued its costume jewelry line as demand for the imported gems escalated along with their reputation for offering expensive, quality pieces. The company, which focused very little on gems at the time, published its first catalogue in 1845 that some speculate was the country's first mail–order catalogue.

The company's trademark shade of robin's egg blue was also established during the early years of the company and appeared on all company catalogues, shopping bags, boxes, and promotional materials. Regarding the now familiar Tiffany Blue boxes, the company's web site quoted a 1906 article in the *New York Sun*: "Tiffany has one thing in stock that you cannot buy of him for as much money as you may offer; he will only give it to you. And that is one of his boxes. The rule of the establishment is ironclad, never to allow a box bearing the name of the firm to be taken out of the building except with an article which has been sold by them and for which they are responsible." The tradition has continued to this day, with the Tiffany Blue boxes becoming a symbol of elegance and sophistication.

In 1847 the company also began selling silverware. The following year, the company benefited from revolutionary movements in Europe, enabling Tiffany's to acquire historic European jewels from important aristocrats over the next several decades, including some of crown jewels from the French Empire in 1857, when the press dubbed Tiffany the "King of Diamonds." After the European acquisitions, the company's reputation greatly broadened. In 1850 Tiffany opened another store in Paris and hired John C. Moore, a silversmith, to craft silverware exclusive to Tiffany's and also began manufacturing gold jewelry, aided by the California gold strike in 1850. Tiffany was the first U.S. company to use the 925 parts silver per thousand standard for sterling that later became the United States Sterling Standard. The company underwent another reorganization when Tiffany's partners, Young and Ellis, retired, and in 1853 the company was renamed Charles L. Tiffany & Company. Tiffany had a huge statue of Atlas beneath a clock installed at the company's new headquarters at 550 Broadway. The statue, which moved three more times, may still be seen above the company's Fifth Avenue store entrance.

Tiffany was skilled in promotion and steered the company to further growth throughout the rest of the 1850s. Tiffany was able to generate publicity for his company in association with P. T. Barnum on several occasions. Once he crafted a special jeweled horse and carriage as a wedding gift for the marriage of Barnum's Tom Thumb. The most publicized promotional event occurred in 1858, when Tiffany's sold sections of the first transatlantic cable as souvenirs, which generated so much interest that the police were called to keep frenzied buyers in line. In 1861 Tiffany was hired to design a presentational pitcher for the inauguration of President Abraham Lincoln. President Lincoln later gifted his wife, Mary Todd Lincoln, with a seed–pearl jewelry suite from Tiffany's.

In support of the Union forces during the ensuing Civil War, Tiffany's manufactured patriotic items including flags, medals, surgical implements, and swords, and he allowed his store to serve as a depot for military supplies. Tiffany also designed jewel–encrusted presentation swords for Generals Grant and Sherman. After the war, the company, which was incorporated in 1868, opened a London store that same year. Tiffany, who served as the company's president and treasurer, also found a building for its New York operations on Fifth Avenue after several other sites were tried. In addition to jewelry, the company began producing clocks and watches.

As the company's reputation for quality and excellence grew, Tiffany's attracted more than twenty crowned heads of state among its worldwide range of customers. In 1867 Tiffany's was the first American company to win the gold medal for jewelry and the grand prize for silverware at the Paris Exposition. The company opened a factory in Newark, New Jersey, which produced Tiffany's silverware, stationery, and leather goods. Tiffany–designed copper, silver, and niello pitchers were acquired by the Boston Museum of Fine Arts, the first of many of the company's designs currently in museum collections worldwide. Tiffany continued to enhance his company's reputation by acquiring the 128.54 carat fancy yellow Tiffany Diamond in 1878, one of the largest diamonds of its kind in the world. It was later worn by Audrey Hepburn in publicity photos for the movie classic, *Breakfast at Tiffany's*. The gem can be seen to this day on the first floor of Tiffany's Fifth Avenue store.

Innovative jewelry design became a Tiffany trademark early on. The six–prong diamond solitaire engagement ring was created using the "Tiffany Setting," which raised the stone up from the setting, thus allowing the maximum amount of light to set off the diamond's brilliance. Tiffany's son, Louis Comfort Tiffany, established a special department within the company called Tiffany Art Jewelry in 1902.

Tiffany died of pneumonia on February 18, 1902, in Yonkers, New York. At the time of his death, his personal fortune was valued at $35 million and the company was capitalized at $2.4 million. Son Louis took the position of vice president and artistic director of Tiffany & Co. after his father's death and became an accomplished jeweler in addition to the fame he would later acquire for designing stained glass.

Chronology:
Charles Lewis Tiffany

1812: Born.

1837: Charles Lewis Tiffany and John Young established Tiffany & Young.

1845: Tiffany's published its first catalogue.

1850: Began making silverware exclusive to Tiffany's.

1853: Company renamed Tiffany & Co. after his partners retire.

1867: First American firm to win an award for its silverware at the Paris Exposition.

1878: Purchased the 128.54 carat Tiffany Diamond.

1886: Introduced the "Tiffany Setting."

1887: Acquired some of the French Crown jewels.

1902: Died.

In 1905 the store moved again to a sixteenth–century Venetian–style building on Fifth Avenue at 37th, which became a National Landmark in 1978. In 1940 the company moved its New York headquarters to its own building, designed by Cross & Cross, on Fifth Avenue and 57th Street, where it exists today. The company, which went public on the New York Stock Exchange in 1986, continued after Tiffany's death to set standards in the jewelry industry: In 1926 Tiffany's platinum became the official standard for all platinum in the United States: the company introduced tanzanite, a unique blue gemstone, to the world in 1969; and the company innovated a new engagement ring, the Lucida, with a patented cut in 1999.

Social and Economic Impact

Charles Lewis Tiffany created more than just the most well–known jewelry store in the country; he created an enduring American symbol for luxury and elegance. With his early innovative business practices and dedication to excellence in jewelry and fine silver, Tiffany & Co. was the pre–eminent jeweler in the United States for over fifty years. Winning numerous prizes for his silver and jewels from international exhibitions, Tiffany proved to Europeans and others that his American artisans were among the best in the world. His famous acquisitions of some of the world's most desirable gems, including the Tiffany Yellow Diamond and the French Crown Jewels, built his worldwide reputation and attracted many of the country's most prominent citizens to seek out his treasures. From heads of state, celebrities, and royalty, to everyday people, Tiffany's continues to offer something for everyone.

Over a century and a half after opening his "fancy goods" store in New York, the Tiffany's empire has grown to include 225 stores worldwide, its famous catalog, and a Web site. Tiffany's employed nearly 6,000 people and rang up more than $1.6 billion in sales in 2001, with 78 percent of that figure derived from the sales of its legendary jewelry. His company and work are immortalized in such modern–day works as Truman Capote's 1950 novel, *Breakfast at Tiffany's* and the classic 1961 Audrey Hepburn movie of the same name.

Sources of Information

Bibliography

"About Tiffany." *Tiffany & Co*, 2001. Available at http://www.tiffany.com.

American Business Leaders From Colonial Times to the Present. ABC–CLIO, 1999.

American National Biography. Oxford University Press, 1999.

"Charles Tiffany's 'Fancy Goods' Shop and How it Grew." *Smithsonian*, December 1987.

Dictionary of American Biography. Base Set. American Council of Leaned Societies, 1928–1936.

"Jewelry Made By a Tiffany Who Chose A Life of Art." *New York Times*, 9 August 1998.

The National Cyclopedia of American Biography. Vol. 2. James T. White & Company, 1892.

"Tiffany & Co." *Hoover's*, November 2001. Available at http://www.hoovers.com.

"Tiffany's Sparkles After 150 Years." *Seattle Times*, 18 September 1987.

Linus Torvalds

(1970-)

Transmeta Corporation

Overview

Software engineer Linus Torvalds is the creator of the Linux operating system, a program that by the late 1990s was getting attention as a potential competitor to the powerful Microsoft Windows, which runs about 85 percent of the world's computers. This would be intriguing enough if Torvalds was a software guru out to topple Microsoft as a leader in this market, but astonishingly, after cobbling together the project on his own time for his own use as a computer science student at the University of Helsinki, the Finnish programmer posted the system and all its code (the set of instructions used to create it) on the Internet, free to anyone who wanted it. His motivating factor, then, was not to earn money from a superior product but just simply to build a better quality, more reliable operating system. "People have grown used to thinking of computers as unreliable, and it doesn't have to be that way," Torvalds told Amy Harmon in the *New York Times Magazine*. "I don't mind Microsoft making money. I mind them having a bad operating system." Though he is one of the most popular icons among the computer–savvy, Torvalds has not made a cent from his creation. However, Linux companies did give Torvalds stock options, much of which he sold during the technology boom in the late 1990s–early 2000. His reputation also earned him a job at Transmeta, a secretive start–up firm in Santa Clara in 1997. The company is partially financed by Microsoft cofounder Paul Allen and is reportedly involved in chip design or operating systems.

Linus Torvalds. *(Reuters NewMedia Inc/CORBIS.)*

Personal Life

Torvalds is married to his wife, Tove, who was the reigning karate champion of Finland for six years. They have three daughters and live in a tract house in Santa Clara, California, which is filled with stuffed penguins—the mascot of Linux, because Torvalds finds them friendly and sympathetic. He and his family left Finland so he could accept the six–figure salary in Silicon Valley's Transmeta. Torvalds' hobbies include reading and playing snooker. He was named Person of the Year by *PC Magazine* in 1999.

He was born in about 1970 and named after physicist Linus Pauling as well as the intellectual *Peanuts* comic character. He grew up in Helsinki in a family of journalists but his grandfather, Leo Toerngvist, had the biggest influence on him. He was a mathematician and statistics professor at the University of Helsinki who bought one of the first personal computers in order to use it as a programmable calculator. Enlisting his grandson to help out with the Commodore VIC–20, Toerngvist taught Torvalds the basics of writing programs. Before he had reached his teen years, Torvalds was devoting most of his time to writing code for computer games. "I liked the challenge of making a computer do what you wanted it to," he mentioned to Leslie Helm in the *Los Angeles Times*. He also admitted, "I was a geek." His mother, Mikke, recalled in *SiliconValley.com*, "I suppose I have already answered the question of what Linus was like as a son: easy to raise. As Sara [Linus' sister] and I used to say, just give Linus a spare closet with a good computer in it, feed him some dry pasta, and he will be perfectly happy."

As a computer science student at Finland's University of Helsinki in 1991, 21–year–old Torvalds felt he needed a better operating system to perform his work. Microsoft's MS–DOS was simply not technologically up to snuff, but as a poor undergraduate, Torvalds could not afford to spend the $6,000 to $9,000 for the more advanced Unix system, which runs large mainframes in the corporate and academic arenas. So he figured he would write his own version. As Torvalds put it to Elizabeth Simnacher in the *Dallas Morning News*, "Reliability was an issue, but the systems were very messy. There was essentially no philosophy. They didn't fit my notion of what an operating system should be." He explained further, "When you don't have some kind of a plan, the end result is such that nobody can understand how it works and there aren't any clear rules about how to use it."

Career Details

Torvalds was dedicated to his pursuit. "Forget about dating! Forget about hobbies! Forget about life!" he exclaimed to Janice Maloney in *Time*. "We are talking about a guy who sat, ate, and slept in front of the computer." When he mentioned his project to an Internet discussion group, one person offered him some space on a university computer to post the program. He posted first the raw version with the message: "Are you without a nice program and just dying to cut your teeth on an [operating system] you can try to modify for your own needs? Then this post might be just for you." One of the members dubbed the program "Linux," after its original creator and the program he based it on, Unix. The decision to unleash the Linux program for free over the Internet was astounding enough, but Torvalds went a step further when he also posted the source code so that other programmers could play with the version on their own, making modifications at will. This is what is known in the industry as open source software (OSS), a movement that is gaining steam even in the commercial sector because of the fact that more minds being applied to the product will yield superior programs. Sure enough, a few people soon downloaded and puttered around with the code and e–mailed modifications to Torvalds. "When I released Linux, I thought maybe one other person would be interested in it," Torvalds related to Harmon.

Before long, the handful of Linux enthusiasts grew to somewhere between 100 and 200, and by 1994 Torvalds felt it could be considered a complete operating system. At this point about 100,000 people had downloaded it and were running it on personal computers. To keep it free, Torvalds had used the GNU General Public License, a licensing system developed by Richard Stallman, a pioneer in the free software movement, which required anyone who modified the program to offer their code at no charge to anyone else who wanted it. Stallman dubbed this a "copyleft," instead of a copyright, license, in homage to its liberal philosophy.

By 1998 seven to eight million users were running Linux. A following of a few million converts to this renegade system was still along way from the roughly 250 million using Windows, but Linux won over more than just a loose–knit collection of disgruntled techno–geeks. Linux became the operating system preferred by people running Internet servers, the computers that route traffic on the World Wide Web and provide web sites to users. Smaller servers on local area networks began using it, too, and it started to seep into businesses as computer network administrators got word of it and its reliable nature. Soon some big players had begun installing Linux, helping transform it from an underground, cultish product for the techno–elite to one with a promising future for the masses.

In April of 1998 Linux was installed on 68 personal computers combined together into a "supercomputer" at Los Alamos National Laboratory in order to run a program to simulate atomic shock waves. In addition, Linux was installed on machines at NASA, the United States Postal Service, and in administrative offices for the U.S. Navy and the Boeing Company and is also the operating system that runs computers at Digital Domain, a special effects firm hired for the film *Titanic*. The telecommunications giant Southwestern Bell also installed Linux and found that it helped decrease their costs because of its stability—when a network goes down, productivity is stalled, and thus profits are chipped away. Whereas most Windows NT users find they need to reboot their systems at least weekly or more, Linux users are finding that their computers can run for months without a reboot.

Linux still has a ways to go before it will be competitive with Microsoft or Unix. Some naysayers counter that Linux is difficult to install and use and that the only means of technical support is by time–consuming communications with other users via the Internet. A solution to the support dilemma came along when companies like Red Hat and others offered their own version of Linux and accompanying technical support for $50, thus pro-

Chronology:
Linus Torvalds

1970: Born.

1991: Created the kernel of operating system that would become Linux.

1994: Linux completed as an operating system with some 200 users.

1996: Linux version won award for best desktop computer operating system from *InfoWorld* magazine.

1997: Began working at Transmeta.

1998: Linux is run by seven to eight million users.

1998: Linux installed by NASA, the U.S. Postal Service, the U.S. Navy, and Boeing Company, among others.

1999: Dell computers began selling a line of computers running Linux.

2000: Transmeta announced the creation of a line of super–efficient chips for portable computers and hand–held devices named Crusoe.

2001: Published the autobiography *Just for Fun: The Story of an Accidental Revolutionary.*

viding a more efficient way to obtain answers. This made the system more commercially viable. In 1996 a version of Linux released by Red Hat Software won the award for best desktop computer operating system from *InfoWorld*, a trade magazine. Red Hat also began working on a graphic interface it dubbed GNOME to make it more user–friendly.

The future for Linux seemed sealed when technology behemoths Netscape and Intel each purchased a stake in the tiny, North Carolina–based Red Hat in late 1998. Intel vice president Sean Maloney said at the time, "The investment in Linux is clearly a reflection of (its) growing importance and influence in the business community," according to an article by Karlin Lillington in the *St. Louis Post–Dispatch*. In April of 1999 Dell computers purchased an interest in Red Hat as well, and announced it would start selling a line of computers running Linux. Meanwhile, Microsoft Corporation president Steve Ballmer indicated that his firm considered Linux a threat and hinted that Microsoft may even consider eventually making available some of its code for Windows.

Although Linux was sprung from hacker origins (and it shows in its lack of slick graphic design), its more reliable nature and its growing accessibility are helping it gain a wider range of fans, including many businesses and governmental bodies. Many still think it has a while before it becomes a serious contender, especially since it cannot run many of the more popular desktop software programs yet that will be necessary to make it appealing to home users. However, more and more big–name firms are supporting its growth by offering Linux on systems and investing in companies that are selling their versions of Linux, and Torvalds holds the hope that someday it will be a viable option to Windows. In April 2000, LinuxMall.com hosted an online question and answer session with Torvalds about the future of Linux. Torvalds further expanded on the origins of Linux and its creator in his 2001 autobiography *Just for Fun: The Story of an Accidental Revolutionary*.

As well as rivaling Microsoft, Torvalds' work may pose a challenge to another technological institution: Intel. In 2000, Transmeta, the company Torvalds joined in 1997, came out with a line of super–efficient chips for portable computers and hand–held devices named Crusoe after Robinson Crusoe. The chips run virtually all the same programs as the Intel Pentium III chips but don't need as much power, allowing laptop computer users to run them all day without recharging, instead of only a few hours. The chips, which would set the bar high for Intel if they worked as promised, were due on the market in mid–2000. One reason Torvalds took the job at Transmeta, however, was that it allowed him to continue his ongoing work on Linux.

Social and Economic Impact

With mottos like "Do unto others what you would like others to do unto you. And have fun doing it" and "Greed is never good," Torvalds is a unique personality in the computer world where one of its own, Bill Gates, reigns as the richest entrepreneur in the country. His single–minded devotion and honest attempt at creating a better operating system for the benefit of all prompted his decision to open the source code and let others around the world work on Linux for the benefit of the program itself, not for his own personal gain. Linux has made Torvalds a hero among the technically savvy. In 1998, *Time* noted, "Programmers love Linux (rhymes with cynics) because it is small, fast and free—and because it lets them participate in building a library of underground software. Silicon Valley loves Linux because it offers an alternative to Sun, Apple, and especially, Microsoft; in the past month Intel, Netscape, and some of the Valley's richest venture capitalists have invested in Linux operation. Journalists love Linux—and its Finnish eponym—because his is a story in the classic David and Goliath mold."

Torvalds, however, is quick to point out that he only supplied a "kernel" of the program. By opening the source code, users around the globe continue to work on it on a volunteer basis, fixing any bugs that hamper its performance and making enhancements as they wish, as long as they post their code back to the community of users for perusal. Thus, its users claim, Linux runs faster and is more stable than other operating systems, specifically Microsoft Windows NT for networks (the program is far more popular on computer servers than on individual machines) and boasts a roster of clients, which include Fortune 500 companies and NASA. Despite the fact that the system lacks a user–friendly graphical interface and the code remains free, some companies are finding ways to make a profit off it. Red Hat Software, for example, charges $49 for its version of Linux and offers technical support for users. Those who download Linux on their own, on the other hand, have no central source to contact if they need assistance.

Sources of Information

Contact at: Transmeta Corporation
    3940 Freedom Circle
    Santa Clara, CA 95054
    Business Phone: (408)919–3000
    URL: http://www.transmeta.com

Bibliography

"A Boy and His Computer." *Salon.com*, 24 April 2001. Available at http://www.salon.com.

"Giving It All Away." *Metroactive*, 8 May 1997. Available at http://www.metroactive.com.

"An Interview with Linus Torvalds: Free, as in Beer." *ITworld.com*, 8 February 2001. Available at http://www.itworld.com.

"Just for Fun: The Story of an Accidental Revolutionary (Review)." *Publisher's Weekly*, 23 April 2001.

"Learning to Love Linux." *Europe*, July–August 1999.

"Linus the Liberator." *SiliconValley.com*. Available at http://www.mercurycenter.com/svtech.

"Linus Torvalds." *TIME Digital*. Available at http://www.time.com/time/digital.

"Linus Torvalds Featured on Web–Based Q & A; Linux Operating System Founder To Answer Questions." *PR Newswire*, 4 April 2000.

"The Mighty Finn." *Time*, 26 October 1998

"On Being Linus." *NE Online*, April 2001. Available at http://ne.nikkeibp.co.jp.

Newsmakers 1999. Issue 3. Gale Group, 1999.

"Person of the Year." *PC Magazine*, 15 November 1999. Available at http://www.zdnet.com.

"Taking a Chip Shot." *U.S. News & World Report*, 31 January 2000.

"Transmeta Corporation." *Hoover's*, November 2001. Available at http://www.hoovers.com.

Eiji Toyoda

(1913-)
Toyota Motor Corporation

Overview

Eiji Toyoda, the man in the driver's seat of the Toyota Motor Company for nearly twenty years, is virtually unknown outside of Japan's Toyota City, headquarters of "the company that stopped Detroit," according to the *New York Times*. But like a latter–day Henry Ford, Toyoda has made his mark on the auto industry. He not only presided over revolutionary changes in the way cars are built, but he also saw his family–run business become a powerhouse in the world export market and forged an unlikely alliance with an arch–rival, General Motors Corporation. As chairman of one of the most powerful industrial clans in a nation of 120 million people, Toyoda had an almost Western flair as a go–getter and an empire builder that belied his reputation in Japan as a staunch political and economic conservative. The parallels between the Fords and the Toyodas extended from the assembly line to the board room, from which Toyoda retired in 1994.

Personal Life

Toyoda was born September 12, 1913, in Kinjo, Nishi Kasugai, Aichi, Japan, the son of Heikichi and Nao Toyoda. The family worked in the automatic loom business. Toyoda married Kazuko Takahashi, December 19, 1939, and they have four children: Kanshiro, Tetsuro, Shuhei, Sonoko.

Toyoda's uncle, Sakichi, founded the original family business, Toyoda Automatic Loom Works, in 1926 in Nagoya, about 200 miles west of Tokyo. Sakichi's son, Kiichiro, established Toyota Motor Company in 1937 as

Eiji Toyoda. (AP/Wide World Photos.)

an affiliate of the loom works. The family was so involved in the business that Eiji's father Heikichi (younger brother of Sakichi) even made his home inside the spinning factory. "From childhood, machines and business were always there right in front of me," Eiji Toyoda said in an interview in *The Wheel Extended*, a quarterly review published by his company. "By seeing the two together, I probably developed an understanding of both, from a child's point of view." Toyoda describes himself as a combination engineer–administrator: "I don't really think of myself as an engineer, but rather as a manager. Or maybe a management engineer. Actually, I graduated from engineering school, but more important is the work a person accomplishes in the 10 or 15 years after school."

Career Details

After graduating in 1936 with a mechanical engineering degree from the University of Tokyo—training ground for most of Japan's future top executives—the twenty–three–year–old Toyoda joined the family spinning business as an engineering trainee and transferred a year later to the newly formed Toyota Motor Company. The company was a relative newcomer to the auto business in Japan. The country's first car, a steam–powered vehicle, was produced just after the turn of the century, followed in 1911 by the introduction of the DAT model, forerunner of Datsun/Nissan, Toyota's nearest rival today.

The Toyoda family patriarch, Sakichi, the son of a poor carpenter, had invented the first Japanese–designed power loom in 1897 and perfected an advanced automatic loom in 1926, when he founded Toyoda Automatic Loom Works. He ultimately sold the patents for his design to an English firm for $250,000, at a time when textiles was Japan's top industry, and used the money to bankroll his eldest son Kiichiro's venture into automaking in the early 1930s.

Numerous stories have sprung up over the years concerning why the auto company was named Toyota rather than Toyoda. A *Business Week* article claims the family consulted a numerologist in 1937 before establishing its first auto factory: "Eight was their lucky number, he advised. Accordingly, they modified their company's name to Toyota, which required eight calligraphic strokes instead of ten. Sure enough, what is now Toyota Motor Corp. soon became not only the biggest and most successful of Japan's automakers but also one of the most phenomenally profitable companies in the world." But a *New York Times* story notes the family changed the spelling in the 1930s because "it believed the sound [of the new name] resonated better in Japanese ears."

After Eiji joined the family business in 1936, he worked on the A1 prototype, the forerunner of the company's first production model, a six–cylinder sedan that borrowed heavily from Detroit automotive technology and resembled the radically styled Chrysler Airflow model of that period. During those early years, Toyoda gained lots of hands–on experience. "I tried in the past to see how much I could really tell by touch," he said in *The Wheel Extended*. "It was hard for me to recognize a difference of one hundredth of a millimeter. I must have had a lot of free time. Still, I think it is important to know how much of a difference one can sense." It was a philosophy he shared with his cousin Kiichiro, who often told his employees: "How can you expect to do your job without getting your hands dirty?"

In this spare time, Eiji Toyoda studied rockets and jet engines and, on the advice of his cousin, even researched helicopters. "We gathered materials in an attempt to make a helicopter and made prototype rotary wings," he said in *The Wheel Extended*. "By attaching the wings on one end of a beam, with a car engine on the other, we built a contraption that could float in the air. . . . We weren't doing it just for fun. However, the war intensified, and it became hard to experiment because of a shortage of materials."

The war left Japan's industry in a shambles, and the automaker began rebuilding its production facilities from scratch. Recalled Toyoda: "Everything was completely new to us. Design and production, for example, all had to be started from zero. And the competitive situation allowed for not even a single mistake. We had our backs to the wall, and we knew it."

But while Kiichiro Toyoda was rebuilding the manufacturing operations, Japan's shattered economy left the company with a growing bank of unsold cars. By 1949 the firm was unable to meet its payroll, and employees began a devastating fifteen–month strike—the first and only walkout in the company's history—which pushed Toyota to the brink of bankruptcy. In 1950, the Japanese government ended the labor strife by forcing Toyota to reorganize and split its sales and manufacturing operations into separate companies, each headed by a non–family member. Kiichiro Toyoda and his executive staff resigned en masse; Kiichiro died less than two years later.

Eiji Toyoda meanwhile had been named managing director of the manufacturing arm, Toyota Motor Company. In what some automakers must view as a supreme irony, he was sent to the Unied States in 1950 to study the auto industry and return to Toyota with a report on American manufacturing methods. After touring Ford Motor's U.S. facilies, Toyoda turned to the task of re-designing Toyota's plants to incorporate advanced techniques and machinery.

In 1967 Toyoda was named president of Toyota Motor Company—the first family member to assume that post since Kiichiro resigned in 1950. The family power wasn't consolidated until 1981, when Sadazo Yamamoto was replaced as president of Toyota Motor Sales by Shoichiro Toyoda, son of Kiichiro and nicknamed the "Crown Prince" by the Japanese press. A year later, the two branches of the company were unified in the new Toyota Motor Corporation, wih Eiji Toyoda as chairman and Shoichiro Toyoda as president and chief executive officer. A *Business Week* article at the time quoted a Japanese economist as saying the return of the Toyoda family to power was a "restoration of the bluest of blue blood."

At this stage of the company's history, there may be a strong family presence (after a stretch of non–family leadership for most of the postwar period), but not "con-trol" in the Western sense. The top three family members own just over one percent of Toyota Motor stock, according to Britain's Financial Times. In contrast, the Ford family in the United States controls 40 percent of the voting power in the Ford Motor Company.

The Toyodas led their company to a record year in 1984. Toyota sold an all–time high 1.7 million vehicles in Japan and the same number overseas. Profits peaked at $2.1 billion for the fiscal year ending March 31, 1985. Though that performance would certainly earn Toyota a mention in automotive history books, Eiji Toyoda and his company may be better remembered for a distinctive management style that's been copied by hundreds of Japanese companies and is gaining growing acceptance in the United States The Toyota approach, adopted at its ten Japanese factories and twenty–four plants in seventeen countries, has three main objectives: keeping inventory to an absolute minimum through a system called kanban, or "just in time," insuring that each step of the assembly process is performed correctly the first time

Chronology:
Eiji Toyoda

1913: Born.

1936: Received B.M.E., Universiy of Tokyo.

1933: Toyoda's cousin Kiichiro founded company later known as Toyota Motor Corp.; Toyoda worked in management.

1950: Visited United States to tour Ford Motor Co., Rouge plant.

1957: Premiered first model Crown car in U.S.

1960: Named executive vice president Toyota Motor Corp.

1966: Launched Corolla car in U.S. to huge success.

1967: Promoted to president of Toyota Motor Corp.

1973: Oil crisis boosted sales of fuel–efficient models.

1994: Stepped down from Toyota board of directors.

and cutting the amount of human labor that goes into each car.

Despite the predominance of robots and automation at Toyota, the company firmly believes in the principle of lifetime employment; displaced workers are not laid off but are frequently transferred to other jobs. Toyoda believes the day when robots totally replace humans is a long way off. He told *The Wheel Extended*: "At the cur-rent stage, there is a greater difference between humans and robots than between cars and magic clouds. Robots can't even walk yet. They sit in one place and do exactly as programmed. But that's all. There is no way that ro-bots can replace all the work of humans."

Due in part to that sort of philosophy, it's not sur-prising that company loyalty is so high. Toyota's em-ployees in Japan, for instance, are encouraged to make cost–cutting suggestions, an idea that Eiji Toyoda bor-rowed from Ford after his first visit to the United States. Since the system began in 1951, more than ten million suggestions have flooded the executive offices—nearly 1.7 million in 1983 alone. "The Japanese," asserts Toy-oda, "excel in improving things."

In 1986 Toyoda returned to the United States to take another look at the American automotive industry. Upon his return to Japan, he told his employees that the Toy-ota Motor Corporation would produce superior automo-biles, doing it with creativity, resourcefulness, wisdom, and hard work. Among Toyoda's ambitions was the production of a luxury car to rival Mercedes and BMW. This goal was achieved in 1989 when Toyota introduced the Lexus and immediately stole market share from the established luxury automobiles.

Toyoda's 15 years at the helm of the company required successful steerage through the storms of emission control legislation and export restriction in the United States. Faced with the inevitability of export restraints, Toyoda decided to build cars in the United States, a decision that later proved to be one of his most visionary. By 1999 Toyota had sales quotas of 1.5 million cars a year in North America, with more than 60 percent of them produced locally. The company was also beginning to build plants in Europe.

In 1994 Toyoda resigned from the board of Toyota. That same year, he became the second Japanese person, after Soichiro Honda, to be named to the U.S. Automotive Hall of Fame. His photograph now sits there alongside Henry Ford, Walter Chrysler, and the other giants of the automotive industry. Though retired and revered, Toyoda still reports to work daily to witness even further global expansion of the company.

Toyota Motor Corporation's net income rose 82 percent to $2.4 billion dollars for the half year to September 30, 2001, boosted by favorable currency rate gains, cost cutting and concrete sales. Toyota has raised its global sales forecast to 5.85 million vehicles, which would be an increase of 6 percent over last year's sales, 1.71 million of which is projected for North American sales.

Social and Economic Impact

What Toyoda accomplished for Toyota Motor was dazzling success at a time when Detroit automakers were struggling to stay profitable. Toyota, Japan's number one automaker, spearheaded the tidal wave of small, low–priced cars that swept the United States after successive energy crises in the mid– and late–1970s. Enraged by the invasion of Japanese imports, Toyoda's counterpart at the Ford Motor Company, then–Chairman Henry Ford II, vowed, "We'll push them back to the shores." It never happened. Instead, Ford and his lieu-

tenants turned to Toyota to negotiate a possible cooperative venture in the United States—an unsuccessful effort that preceded GM's historic agreement in 1983 to jointly produce Toyota–designed subcompacts at an idle GM plant in Fremont, California.

In addition to running the largest corporation in Japan—and the world's third largest automaker, behind GM and Ford—Toyoda oversaw the development of a highly efficient system known as lean manufacturing that is being copied worldwide. It "represents a revolutionary change from certain tenets of mass production and assembly–line work originally applied by Henry Ford," wrote *New York Times* Tokyo correspondent Steve Lohr. In short, Toyoda's career could be said to echo the company's U.S. advertising slogan: "Oh, what a feeling!"

Today, Toyota Motor Corp. makes cars in 24 countries and sells $90 billion worth of them in 160 countries. Toyoda's 15 years in the driver's seat of Toyota required successful maneuvering through storms of emission control legislation and export restriction in the United States. Faced with the inevitability of export restraints, Toyoda decided to build cars in the United States, a decision that later proved to be one of his most visionary. Toyoda was engaged in the company's auto manufacturing business since the 1930s and his role in production and managerial decisions turned Toyota into one of the world's top auto companies.

Sources of Information

Contact at: Toyota Motor Corporation
   1, Toyota–cho
   Toyota, Aichi 471–8571, Japan
   Business Phone: 81–565–28–2121
   URL: http://www.global.toyota.com

Bibliography

AsiaWeek.com, 2001. Available at http://asiaweek.com.

Automotive Manufacturing & Production. June 2001.

"Eiji Toyoda." *Encyclopedia of World Biography, 2nd ed.* 17 Vols. Farmington Hills, Mich.: Gale Research, 1998.

Time 100, 23–30 August 1999.

Juan "Terry" Trippe

(1899-1981)

Pan American Airways

Overview

The cofounder of Pan American Airways, Juan "Terry" Trippe, was an aviation pioneer who was instrumental in the overall development of the commercial airline industry. When he was a young man, he recognized the potentials of commercial aviation before anyone else, and he turned his visions into reality. He guided Pan Am from its modest beginnings and turned it into one of the largest corporations in the world. As the leader of Pan Am, he established several significant "firsts." Pan Am was the first airline to fly across the Atlantic and Pacific, the first to order and fly American–made jets, and the first to order the Boeing 747 jumbo jet. By the time Trippe retired, Pan Am was flying to 85 nations in six continents. Above all, he brought the world into the jet age and made it possible for the masses to afford air travel.

Personal Life

Juan Trippe was born in Sea Bright, New Jersey on June 27, 1899, the son of Charles White Trippe, an investment banker, and Lucy Adeline Terry. He graduated from the Hill School in Pottstown, Pennsylvania. When he was growing up, Trippe chose to be called Terry, as if he felt the name sounded more appropriate for someone of his affluent background.

Trippe first became interested in aviation at the age of 10, when his father took him to see an air race involving the Wright Brothers. He entered Yale College in 1917, during World War I, but quit after his first year to join the U.S. Navy. He was commissioned a naval aviation ensign and learned to fly while in Florida. However,

Juan Trippe. (Bettmann/Corbis.)

Trippe never experienced any air combat while overseas. Just as he was about to enter the war, it ended.

When he returned to Yale to complete his education, he started a flying club. He graduated from the school in 1922 with a Ph.D. and worked on Wall Street for two years. But aviation remained his primary passion, and when he learned that the navy was selling surplus planes, he bought seven and started an air charter service at Rockaway Beach, Long Island.

He cofounded Pan American Airways in 1927, and he would serve as the corporation's chairman and chief operating officer for 41 years. As chief operating officer, Trippe developed a global network of 80,000 air miles. He remained in control of Pan Am until he resigned in 1968. He remained honorary chairman and an active member of the board until 1975. He worked a full schedule until 1980, when he suffered a cerebral hemorrhage. He died of complications resulting from the stroke in 1981.

Trippe married Elizabeth Stettinius on June 16, 1928. His wife was the daughter of a J. P. Morgan associate and sister of Edward Stettinius, who would later become secretary of state. They had four children.

Career Details

Trippe first entered the commercial airline business in 1923, when he formed Long Island Airways. He fi-

nanced the business by selling stock to his rich Yale classmates and bought seven navy surplus Aeromarine 49-B float planes for $500 each. With these two–passenger planes, he flew customers to Atlantic City and to Honduras and Canada. As self–appointed president and general manager, Trippe involved himself in every part of running the business, including the bookkeeping, flight scheduling, and even carrying bags for passengers. The company folded in 1924. That same year, he formed Colonial Air Transport.

At this time a significant development occurred that would advance Trippe's career: The Kelly Act, or the Airmail Act, of 1925 helped foster the concept of commercial aviation by providing mail subsidies to private airlines for delivering mail in the United States and overseas. Actually, Trippe had pushed for the concept by convincing Congressman Clyde Kelly, chairman of the House Post Office Committee, of the benefits of having private contractors delivering airmail. When Kelly introduced the bill, it was passed. As a result, Trippe formed Eastern Air Transport (with the help of well–heeled friends Cornelius Vanderbilt Whitney, Percy Rockefeller, and William H. Vanderbilt). Then he merged it with Colonial Air Transport. The new company acquired the first U.S. airmail contract and serviced the New York–to–Boston air route.

At Colonial, Trippe became vice president and operations manager. However, in 1927 he had a falling–out with the Colonial directors, who were uncomfortable with Trippe's unorthodox business approach. When he resigned, he formed the Aviation Corporation of America with Whitney and John Hambleton. By this time, Trippe had secured exclusive landing rights in Cuba with an agreement he made with Cuban president Gerardo Machado. To take advantage of this agreement, Trippe merged the airline with two others and formed Pan American Airways, or Pan Am, as it would come to be called. The company made its first flight to Cuba in October of 1927. Trippe would remain with Pam Am for the rest of his career.

By 1930, Pan Am, under Trippe's guidance, had become the world's largest airline. The company purchased the New York, Rio, and Buenos Aires Line, and now its planes flew 20,000 air miles to 20 Latin American countries that were part of a U.S. Post Office contract route. The next year, Pan Am and Trippe achieved one of several "firsts" by becoming the first U.S. airline to buy seaplanes. These huge planes were able to land in harbors without needing a runway, and this advantage spurred more growth for Pan Am. For passengers' comfort, the planes were redesigned to include sleeper berths, promenade decks, and dining compartments. Accommodations included in–flight service.

In 1934 Trippe startled listeners when he claimed that his company would "conquer the Pacific." At the time, no one believed that was possible. There would be nowhere a plane could stop and refuel. Undaunted,

Trippe went to the postmaster general and boldly proposed that if Pan Am could find a way to cross the Pacific, then the government would guarantee his company all airmail contracts to the Far East. The Roosevelt administration agreed, figuring that Pan Am would open the way for American businesses and military. To achieve his ends, Trippe sailed to Wake Island and built an airport. The enterprise cost millions, but in less than a year, the previously uninhabited island became a thriving seaport. It was a big gamble on Trippe's part, but it paid off. Settlement of the island now allowed Pan Am to cross the Pacific. In 1935 Pan Am launched its first scheduled transpacific service with the inaugural flight of the famous *China Clipper*, a Martin M–130 "flying boat." Flights traveled from San Francisco to the Philippine Islands. In 1939 Pan Am launched the first scheduled transatlantic service on its *Yankee Clipper*, with flights from Port Washington and New York to Lisbon and Marseilles.

During World War II, Pan Am became the contract carrier for the U. S. government, flying more than 90 million miles in 19,000 transoceanic crossings. This resulted in Trippe receiving the Medal of Merit in 1946. President Harry S. Truman cited Trippe's organizing capacity, management skills, and cooperation with representatives of the United States.

After World War II, Trippe introduced low–cost air travel on Pan Am's North Atlantic routes and inaugurated the two–class seating arrangement. At first, other companies in the industry opposed such a move. However, all airlines would eventually adopt the concept. Up to this point, transoceanic flight was a luxury enjoyed by the rich and famous. "Tourist Class" seating allowed such a trip to become a reality for the masses. In 1947 Trippe introduced another first when Pan Am began offering around–the–world flights. The company continued to grow, and in 1949 it became Pan American World Airways when the holding and operating companies merged.

In 1955 Trippe brought in the "jet age" when he ordered the first commercial jet planes, purchasing 45 for $269 million. At the time, airline manufacturers weren't interested in building passenger jets, because they felt jet airliners used too much fuel to be cost effective. Trippe disagreed and convinced Boeing and Douglas to enter the jet–building business. In 1958 Pan Am first operated transatlantic service with the Boeing 707 with a flight from New York to Paris.

For Trippe, the 1930s and 1940s were years of risk–taking, innovation, and growth. The 1950s were a boom time for Pan Am. However, the 1960s started a period of decline for the organization. Enormous expenditures for equipment began taking a toll, and competition from international companies began hurting business. Foreign airlines were, for the most part, government–owned and, therefore, weren't as concerned with profit.

Trippe finally retired from Pan Am on May 7, 1968, after 41 years as chief operating officer. He remained an

Chronology:
Juan "Terry" Trippe

1899: Born.

1922: Graduated from Yale.

1923: Formed his first airline company.

1927: Cofounded Pan American.

1935: Pan Am launched first transpacific flight.

1946: Received Medal of Honor.

1955: Purchased first commercial jet planes.

1968: Resigned from Pan American.

1980: Suffered massive cerebral hemorrhage.

1981: Died.

active board member, however, until 1975. Before retiring completely, Trippe took one last gamble in the early 1970s, this time with the Boeing 747. In another first for the company, Pan Am was the first to order the enormous aircraft, which made its inaugural flight from New York to London in 1970. Trippe felt such a large plane would alleviate air traffic problems at crowded airports. By the 1960s air travel had become so popular that airports were having a hard time handling all of the traffic created by the large number of smaller jet planes. But it proved to be a costly move, and the jumbo jet would play a big part in the company's eventual collapse. Trippe bought too many 747s at a time when the airline industry was reeling from the effects of an Arab oil embargo that increased jet fuel prices. Also, the country was suffering a major recession that hurt the airline industry. Pan Am itself suffered a period of ineffective management.

The 1980s were a particularly hard time for the company. By 1980 Pan Am was forced to start selling its assets. The next year, Trippe passed away. By the end of the decade, Pan Am had lost more than $3 billion dollars. Pan Am finally went out of business on December 4, 1991, a decade after Trippe had passed away.

Social and Economic Impact

Trippe has often been referred to as the father of the modern airline industry. This hardly seems an exaggeration. Indeed, he was the man who made commercial long–distance air travel a reality. In doing so, he impacted not just an industry but the entire world. He was a true pioneer with a bold vision. He realized, at an early age, that travel provided the means to connect nations.

He not only opened up the world by creating new air routes, he revolutionized the concept of commercial aviation. He saw that the future in the industry was in tourist class travel, and he made it possible for everyone, not just the rich, to enjoy airline travel.

He reputedly possessed incredible powers of persuasion, and he used this talent to bring the rest of the airline industry along with him. He also possessed entrepreneurial instincts that allowed him to take full advantage of every opportunity that came his way. Trippe helped launch Pan Am in 1927 and, through a combination of risk–taking and resourcefulness, turned the company into an undisputed industry leader. Before its decline, Pan Am was one of the largest and best–known global corporations. (Its logo was prominently displayed in a major motion picture, *2001: A Space Odyssey*.) The Pan Am building became one of the most famous structures in New York City. During its glory years, Pan Am had more international destinations than any other airline, flying to 113 cities in 81 countries.

Trippe's achievements have been recognized around the world. He was said to have been decorated by more foreign governments than any other U.S. citizen. In his own country, he received many honorary degrees, and he was a member of the boards of Visitors of Harvard Business School and Johns Hopkins University. He was a member of the corporate boards of the Chrysler Corporation and the Metropolitan Life Insurance Company. Air trophies he received included the Robert Collier Trophy (1947), the Harmon Aviation Trophy (1937), and the Frye Airline Performance Trophy (1954).

Sources of Information

Bibliography

Branson, Richard. "Juan Trippe: Pilot of the Jet Age."*Time 100: Builders and Titans.* 1998. Available from http://www.time.com/time/time100/builder/profile/trippe.html

Capsule Biographies. "Juan Trippe,"*Aerofiles.* 2001. Available from http://www.aerofiles.com/bio_t.html.

"Juan Trippe."*Aviation Posters.* 2000. Available from http://www.aviationposters.com/juantrippe.htm.

"Juan Trippe."*PBS—Chasing the Sun,* 2001. Available from http://www.pbs.org/kcet/chasingthesun/innovators/jtrippe.html.

Marcus, J., and G. Voss. "Air Apparent."*Boston Magazine.* 2000. Available from http://www.bostonmagazine.com/highlights/airapparent.shtml.

Ivana Trump

(1949-)
Ivana, Inc.

Overview

Ivana Trump, known commonly as Ivana, made a splash across tabloid headlines in 1977 when she married real estate billionaire Donald Trump, to whom Ivana referred to as "The Donald." The couple stayed in the eye of the media, first for their extravagant lifestyle and then for their messy divorce. After the divorce in 1991, Ivana became an independent businesswoman, worth millions in her own right.

Personal Life

Ivana Trump was born Ivan Zelnicek on February 20, 1949 in Zlin, Czechoslovakia to Milos, an engineer, and Maria (Francova), a telephone operator. She was not a particularly healthy child and spent several months in an incubator as an infant. Her father thought that sports might help improve her health and so as a young child, growing up in Gottwaldov, Czechoslovakia, a mid–sized industrial town south of Prague, Ivana began swimming and skiing. She won her first ski race at the age of six. She was an equally good swimmer, but when time constraints demanded she limit herself to one sport, she chose skiing. Deciding she needed more structure and discipline to develop her athletic talents, her father placed her in a strict Communist–run school for child athletes when she was 12 years old. At the age of 15, Ivana began traveling around Europe competing as a member of the Czechoslovakian junior national team. At the age of 18, she enrolled in Charles University in Prague to study physical education; she went on to earn a master's degree. During her college years in Prague she skied on

Ivana Trump. (AP/Wide World Photos.)

both the university ski team and the national team. While a student, Ivana also began her modeling career. In 1971 she was earning $38 a day for photo shoots, a considerable rate at the time in Prague, and she appeared on the cover of the fashion magazine *Moda*. In 1970 she appeared in her first film, a Czech production, *Pantau*.

Ivana began a relationship with Czech skier Jiri Syrovatka and lived with him for a time. Syrovatka made arrangements for Ivana to marry Alfred Winklmayr, an Austrian skier, so that she could obtain an Austrian passport and leave Communist Czechoslovakia, a common method of emigrating from the country. The two married in 1972 and divorced within the same year. During 1972 Ivana fell in love with Jiri Staidl, a rich playboy in the

center of Prague's social scene. However, her relationship with Staidl ended abruptly when he was killed in an auto accident in October 1973. Years later in the midst of her divorce from Trump, Ivana remembered the tragedy, telling *Ladies' Home Journal*. "Before this, I had one tragedy in my life. I had a boyfriend in Czechoslovakia who died in a car crash. I was in love with him. It was a disaster; that's why I went to Canada. I needed to get away and forget...if you ever forget. It took me about five years to be able to even talk about it."

Staidl's death, along with the fact that she had failed to make the Olympic ski team, prompted Ivana to immigrate to Montreal, Canada where she was reunited with her former boyfriend Syrovatka, who owned a ski boutique and sporting goods store. Although her career as a skier had ended, Ivana maintained a life–long love for the sport and continued to ski recreationally. Skiing had been a big part of her life and she felt it had taught her a good lesson in life. Ivana explained to *People Weekly* what she learned from skiing: "When you are going down the mountain at 80 miles an hour, you cannot count on Mama or Papa. You have to count only on Ivana."

For the next several years Ivana and Syrovatka worked as ski instructors to supplement their incomes. Ivana began earnestly pursuing her career as a model and regularly appeared on the runways throughout Canada for the Andrey Morris Agency. Ivana's life changed forever in 1976 when she met Donald Trump while on a photo shoot in New York City, sent to promote the upcoming Olympics hosted by Montreal. During her stay, Ivana found herself sitting at a trendy restaurant, compliments of Trump, whose real estate empire is valued between $1.7 billion and $4 billion. The two hit it off instantly, and nine months later in 1977 they were married; Dr. Norman Vincent Peale, famous for his message of the power of positive thinking, performed the ceremony.

The following year, Ivana gave birth to the couple's first child, Donald, Jr. By 1982 the Trumps had added two more children to their family, Ivanka and Eric. The marriage gained the ongoing attention of the press because of the Trumps' indulgent lifestyle, highly touted during the 1980s. For example, after Trump built the famed Trump Tower in New York City, the Trump family occupied the top three floors. In 1984 they purchased a Greenwich, Connecticut mansion for $3.7 million. The following year they spent $10 million on the Mar–a–Lago estate in Palm Beach, built by cereal heiress Marjorie Merriweather Post in 1927. The mansion consists of 110 rooms with enough plates to serve thirty people for sixty consecutive dinners without reusing a single dish. Among Trump's other possessions, he owned three Atlantic casinos, the famed New York Plaza Hotel, a $29 million yacht, and a Puma helicopter. Because the couple made regular appearances on the wealthy New York social scene as well as other trendy locations around the world (reached on their private 727 Boeing jet), Ivana and her husband regularly appeared in the social and gossip columns. In 1988 Ivana became a naturalized U.S. citizen.

Given their high profile life, it is not surprising that when the marriage began to falter, the tabloid press was quick to make the most of it. On February 11, 1990 Liz Smith, a gossip columnist for the New York publication *Daily News*, broke the story with a front–page headline "Love on the Rocks." According to *Ladies' Home Journal*, Smith reported that Ivana "was devastated that Donald was betraying her.... Intimates say Ivana had every chance to continue being Mrs. Trump by allowing her husband to live in an open marriage so he could see other women. But the bottom line is she won't give up her self–respect to do it."

Chronology:
Ivana Trump

1949: Born.

1973: Married and divorced Alfred Winklmayr.

1973: Immigrated to Canada.

1977: Married Donald Trump.

1985: Became president of Trump's Castle Hotel and Casino in Atlantic City, New Jersey.

1988: Became president of the Plaza Hotel in New York City; gained U.S. citizenship.

1990: Separated from Trump.

1991: Finalized divorce; established Ivana, Inc.

1992: Wrote novel *For Love Alone*.

1993: Began appearing on Home Shopping Network; established House of Ivana company; published *Free to Love*.

1995: Married Riccardo Mazzucchelli; published *The Best is Yet to Come*.

1997: Divorced from Mazzucchelli.

1999: Debuted magazine *Ivana's Living in Style*.

2000: Created Haute Couture & Company.

Those who had followed the Trump's marriage were less than surprised. Rumors had been spreading for several years, especially regarding Trump's alleged multiple affairs. The situation garnered considerable press coverage in December 1989 when Ivana and Trump's mistress Marla Maples, a 26–year–old model, had a confrontation on the Aspen ski slopes. Maples reportedly demanded to know if Ivana loved Trump, telling Ivana that she was in fact in love with him. The all–too–public episode fueled the flames of the media frenzy and signaled the beginning of the end of the Trumps' marriage. *Maclean's* Tim Powis wrote of the marriage: "It was a spectacle of wretched excess. For New York City's flamboyant tabloid newspapers, it was an occasion for lurid headlines and sharp surges in circulation. The highly publicized separation of [Donald and Ivana Trump] became one of the most closely followed marital disputes in history."

After lengthy legal negotiations to establish the validity of the couple's prenuptial agreement, as well as three postnuptial agreements, the divorce became official in March 1991. According to reports of the settlement, Ivana did not get as much as she wanted but she was hardly left with financial worries. The final settlement awarded Ivana a $10 million certified check, with a guarantee of another $4 million when she vacated the Trump Tower. She was also given the house in Greenwich, with a 1992 market value of $18 million and use of the Mar–a–Lago estate for one month each year. Trump also paid child support of $300,000 a year and alimony of $350,000 per year. Ivana retained custody of the couple's three children.

By the end of 1991, Ivana began dating Riccardo Mazzucchelli, an Italian businessman she met in London. The couple married in 1995, but after just 20 months, the marriage ended in divorce. According to *People Weekly* Ivana said of her third divorce, "I'm very sad, I cry. I love Riccardo. This is a tremendously hard time for me." Despite Ivana's pain, she also noted that she was willing and ready to move on, telling the reporter, "Do you think that I'm going to lie down and die? Not a chance, girl. Am I going to marry? Absolutely! What I really need is a little bit of brain—I really prefer that. He might be fat. He might be old. You know, it's a question of the chemistry and of two people being with each other. I have a million deals here and everywhere. I'm going to be just fine, honey."

Career Details

Soon after her marriage to Trump, Ivana was looking for a challenge to undertake. In 1979 Trump named her vice president in charge of interior design of the Trump Organization. In 1982 she took on the title of senior executive vice president. Part of her responsibility was overseeing the decorating of the Trump Tower. By most accounts, Ivana proved herself a diligent and talented decorator, albeit with a whimsy for the overdone, extravagant look. From 1985 to 1988, Ivana was the president of Trump's Castle Hotel and Casino in Atlantic City, New Jersey. In 1988 Trump put her in charge of the Plaza Hotel, which he had recently acquired. Ivana supervised every detail of the hotel's renovation and redecoration. A New York City landmark, the hotel had fallen into disarray, but Ivana's efforts restored it to its former glory as one of the finest hotels in the city. Trump boasted—much to the dismay of feminist–minded people—that he paid Ivana an annual salary of $1 as president of the Plaza Hotel but promised her all the dresses she wanted. For her part, Ivana honored Trump's stipulation, spending nearly $500 million a year on designer fashions.

Ivana retained her position at the Plaza Hotel through the divorce proceeding, eventually stepping down in 1991. She then hit the lecture circuit, giving speeches on topics such as "Women Who Dare" for a reported $20,000

per presentation. In 1992 she became a novelist, writing *For Love Alone*, a thinly veiled autobiography that recounted the life of a young skier who married a rich American and then suffered through a divorce. The following year she published the sequel, *Free to Love*. Although not lauded as a great writer, Ivana found a niche with women who felt wronged by men and empathized with Ivana. Her first book sold over 250,000 copies. In 1991 Ivana created her own company, Ivana, Inc., to handle her speaking engagements and book sales. Later the company also began managing the business of Ivana's advice columns in the *Globe*, *Star*, *Porthole*, *Divorce Magazine*, *Delo Revije*, and *DivorceMagazine.com*.

In 1992 Ivana became inspired after watching the Home Shopping Network (HSN). Believing she had the ability to be successful, she contacted the network and in April 1993 she began appearing as a celebrity promoter. Not willing to settle for the small commission awarded guest hosts, Ivana created the House of Ivana to market her own line of clothing, jewelry, and perfumes. By 1994, hawking her own line of goods, Ivana was bringing in retail sales on the Home Shopping Network between $3.2 and $4 million a month—half of which the House of Ivana kept. *Forbes* reported, "This is not high–glamour stuff. The women's suits, made mostly in the Far East, sell for $180 to $280. Here's a woman accustomed to going first class selling to women who travel tourist. A contradiction?" Ivana responded: "Absolutely not.... I've been used and abused by world–class designers. 'Here's Ivana, let's give her a big bill!' You can have good–quality clothes without paying so much." In her first weekend on the air, her line of pastel spring suits sold out immediately, bringing in $1.2 million. She soon broke the HSN's record for sales per minute by selling her $280–women's tuxedo at a rate of $74,000 per minute.

Despite criticism for her over–the–top style considered in poor taste by some, Ivana continued to find success. By the second half of the 1990s, House of Ivana's gross earnings were $5 million. In 1995 she landed a deal worth millions to market her perfume line at J.C. Penney Co. Committed to proving herself as a sound businesswoman, Ivana spoke to *Forbes* of her commitment to her business endeavors: "I don't sing, I don't dance. I don't tell jokes well.... I am a businesswoman." In 1997 Ivana left HSN and moved her product line to Value Vision, and in 1999 she debuted her magazine *Ivana's Living in Style*, featuring such articles as "The Joy of Not Cooking," "High Heels: Who Should, Who Shouldn't," and "How to Get Out of a Car Elegantly." Ivana told *People Weekly*, "I'm for the modern woman, the woman who wants to juggle all the pieces of herself."

In 2000 Ivana established a third company, Ivana Haute Couture & Company, which conducts business for her licensing deals, her Internet venture (http://www.ivanatrump.com), and distribution of her products over the Internet. Her future plans include developing an Ivana Catalog and "Ivana Boutiques"—retail stores that would market her fashions, jewelry, scents, and publications. She has also appeared in commercials for Coors Light, Pizza Hut, Kentucky Fried Chicken, Cotton Inc., the Milk Campaign, Comfort Inn, and American Express.

Social and Economic Impact

Some would argue the Ivana has made a career out of being famous and that her fame does not come from any particular talent in any particular field but from simply having spent nearly 13 years as the wife of Donald Trump. In the years immediately following the divorce, it appeared that being "The Donald's" wife may have been her only legacy. Ivana played heavily to the press, parading around the talk show circuit as the wronged woman who had overcome devastating personal hardship. Yet her business acumen and strong personality paid off in her numerous successful independent ventures after her marriage ended. Nonetheless, Ivana has never been the poster child of feminism. In many of her writings and appearances, Ivana seemed to be fiercely proclaiming "I am woman!" Yet at the same time, in her 1995 nonfiction book, *The Best is Yet to Come*, which discusses love, marriage, divorce, and children, she offers her readers a toll free number to call to find the perfect plastic surgeon.

Interestingly, Ivana has succeeded in remaking herself—independent of Trump, yet somehow always closely connected. In the 1980s she was the epitome of the decade of self–indulgence and free–flowing money. She lived her life in high society unabashedly. A lot was good, but more was better. Then after her divorce from Trump, she spent the 1990s marketing herself as the everyday woman, one who struggled to balance career, children, and romance. She found a home in the hearts of middle–class women who saw her as the underdog and who championed her cause. Yet, with three personal trainers, six homes, and a 105–foot yacht, Ivana is far from ordinary. In the winter of 2001, she was spotted on the Aspen slopes in a sable–trimmed ski suit, valued at

$4,500. In the end, her overindulgences are forgiven because more important to many who follow her life and career was her steadfast refusal to accept her husband's infidelity. "A lot of women," she told *People Weekly*, "they know what their husband is doing and they say, 'As long as he doesn't embarrass me...' I could not do that."

Sources of Information

Contact at: Ivana, Inc.
721 5th Ave.
New York, NY 10022
Business Phone: (888)694–8262
URL: http://www.ivanatrump.com

Bibliography

Cojocaru, Steven. "Behind the Seams." *People Weekly*, 15 January 2001.

Cooper, Nancy. "For Richer and Richer." *Ladies' Home Journal*, May 1989.

Gerstenzang, Peter. "Fast Food for Thought." *Entertainment Weekly*, 12 May 1995.

Green, Michelle. "Riccardo, We Hardly Knew Ye." *People Weekly*, 21 July 1997.

"How to Live Like Ivana." *Newsweek*, 16 November 1998.

"Ivana Trump." Ivana Haute Couture & Company, Inc., 2001. Available at http://www.ivanatrump.com.

Machan, Dyan. "Ivana Strikes Back." *Forbes*, 23 October 1995.

Machan, Dyan. "Ivana's Revenge." *Forbes*, 7 November 1994.

Meadows, Bob, Anne–Marie O'Neill, and Liz Corcoran. "Time of Her Life: Fab at 50, Ivana has Trumped The Donald and Made her Own Millions." *People Weekly*, 17 May 1999.

Plaskin, Glenn. "Ivana's Heartache." *Ladies' Home Journal*, May 1990.

Powis, Tim. "Trump Warfare." *Maclean's*, 5 March 1990.

Ted Turner

(1938-)
Turner Broadcasting

Overview

Robert Edward (Ted) Turner III, also known as the "Mouth of the South," has put his money where his mouth is to become a multimedia mogul. From his ownership of two professional sport teams and a love of yachting to his empire of seven cable networks and two movie studios, Ted Turner has become a billionaire three times over. He was also named biggest charitable donor in 1997 by pledging to the United Nations $100 million each year for the next 10 years.

Personal Life

Ted Turner was born in Cincinnati, Ohio, on November 19, 1938. His parents, Ed and Florence Rooney Turner, moved Ted and his younger sister, Mary Jane, to Savannah, Georgia, when Ted was nine. Ted's father was described as an authoritarian who, at times, asserted his power by beating Ted with a wire coat hanger. Ted never felt like he could, or would, live up to his father's high standards.

Ed Turner enrolled his son in the Georgia Military Academy where Ted remained until high school. His father then sent Ted off to McCallie, a Tennessee military preparatory school. In 1955 Ted, representing his high school, won the Tennessee state debate contest, but he was also something of a rebel.

After graduating from high school, Turner wanted to attend the U. S. Naval Academy in Annapolis, Maryland. However, his father put his heavy foot down and told Ted that he would attend Brown University and pur-

sue a business degree. Nonetheless, Ted defied his father's authority when he decided to study humanities and the classics instead of business. This show of independence ignited a battle that became public after Turner published, in Brown's student newspaper, a letter that his father wrote, which completely made fun of him and his decision. However, this did not stop Turner's father. Ed continued wielding his influence until Turner finally broke down and changed his major to economics. Yet, Turner would never earn a degree from Brown. He was kicked out of Brown twice. First, he was suspended because of a rowdy party. Although he was allowed to return six months later, after a tour of duty with the Coast Guard, Turner was expelled a second time because he broke Brown's rule forbidding students from having guests of the opposite sex in their dorm rooms. Turner was not asked back.

Turner married three times—first to Judy Nye, with whom he has two children, Laura Lee and Robert Edward IV; second, in 1964, to Jane Smith, with whom he has three children, Beau, Rhett, and Jennie; and third, in 1991, to Jane Fonda. Turner and Fonda divorced in 2000.

Ted Turner. (*Archive Photo/Malafronte.*)

Career Details

Turner actually began a full–time "career" at just nine years of age when his father had him work summers at his billboard company—Turner Advertising. Turner mowed the lawn around billboards and maintained their poles. He continued working summers at his father's company, although by college he had stopped cutting grass and had started working with customers as an account executive. Yet, Turner was not happy. He had wanted to work at the Norton Yacht Club in Connecticut, a club that would let Turner pursue his love of sailing by giving him the chance to race, but his father said no.

In 1960 Turner became general manager of Turner Advertising Company at its branch office in Macon, Georgia. For the next three years, Turner found that he did not have a strong liking for business. As Turner's success grew, so did his confidence, and in 1963, with this newfound confidence, Turner battled his father once again. In 1962 Ed Turner had overextended his budget by buying into the General Outdoor Advertising Company, and by 1963 Ed felt that he had too many financial obligations. He decided to sell his business. Turner became furious and confronted his father. He had become a successful businessman, just as his father had wanted, and he was not willing to simply give up on the business. But, on March 5, 1963, Ed Turner did give up—he killed himself. Turner stopped the sell–out plans and sold two family plantations to help cover business debts. Over the next seven years, Turner worked hard to get the family business, now his business, back on track.

In 1970 after rebuilding the company—now known as Turner Communication Corporation—into a huge suc-

cess, Turner stepped into the world of television. Television would never be the same again. Merging with Rice Broadcasting, Turner bought Channel 17, an independent Atlanta UHF station. With this station, Turner stomped out the local competition by cornering a 16 percent share of the TV audience. He won this huge audience by broadcasting Atlanta sports teams' games, movie reruns, and sitcoms. Just six months later, Turner further expanded his TV audience when he bought a second independent station, WRET–TV in Charlotte, North Carolina. For the next five years, Turner kept an eye on the progress of cable television, and in 1975 his station—now known as WTBS—became the first wholly cable station to be delivered to TV audiences via satellite. By the end of 1976, Turner's "superstation" was estimated to be worth $40 million dollars.

Turner was not solely focused on his work, however. In 1976 he bought Atlanta's baseball team, the Braves, and Atlanta's basketball team, the Hawks. He bought controlling interest in Atlanta's hockey team, the Flames. Turner was also a sportsman in his own right. In 1977 he captained his yacht the *Courageous* and won the America's Cup. This win granted him the title "Yachtsman of the Year." This award also, according to *Les Brown's Encyclopedia of Television*, "earned him the nickname 'Captain Courageous.'" However, "the [TV] industry and press [named him] 'Captain Outrageous,' for Turner's outspokenness, eccentric behavior, and derring–do in the business world." With this "derring–do," the purchase of three of Atlanta's sports teams, and his growing library of network reruns and movies,

Chronology:

Ted Turner

1938: Born.

1960: Took over family business, Turner Advertising Company.

1970: Purchased first TV station.

1976: Bought the Atlanta Braves and the Atlanta Hawks.

1977: Won America's Cup yacht race.

1980: Formed Cable News Network (CNN).

1982: Launched Headline News.

1986: Established Turner Network Television (TNT).

1986: Purchased MGM/UA's movie studio and film library.

1991: Named *Time*'s Man of the Year.

1991: Married Jane Fonda.

1992: Introduced Airport Channel and Cartoon Network.

1994: Began Turner Movie Classics, his seventh cable network.

1996: Purchased ranch acreage in New Mexico, for purpose of ecotourism and bison grazing.

1997: Pledged $1 billion in donations to United Nations causes.

1999: Sold mineral rights on New Mexico land for royalty, allowing drilling.

2000: Divorced Jane Fonda.

2001: Time Warner merged with America Online to form AOL Time Warner; set up Ted Turner Productions.

Turner's WTBS, in 1979, began broadcasting 24 hours a day.

However, Turner was not happy with just one cable station, albeit a "superstation." In 1980 Turner got what he wanted by creating the first U. S. 24–hour news station—Cable News Network (CNN). The television industry laughed at Turner's creation. Some wondered how Turner could profit with a 24–hour cable news station when broadcast networks like CBS, NBC, and ABC could not profit with their daily half–hour newscasts. He

went on to launch a second news channel, Headline News Network, in 1982. This new network offered continuous half–hour news summaries. Both proved to be huge successes.

Still, Turner faced setbacks during the 1980s. He first made an unsuccessful bid to buy CBS. He then closed a $1.6 billion deal to gain control of the movie studio MGM's film library; this acquisition benefitted Turner, but its terms were less than favorable. To finance this deal, he had to give up some of his power when he was forced to sell off parts of his media empire to cable operators such as Tele–Communications, Inc. (TCI) and Time Warner. By 1986 Turner was once again standing tall when CNN began showing a profit and increasing its audience steadily. Also in 1986, Turner established his fourth cable station—Turner Network Television (TNT)—now known for its programming of WCW wrestling matches, theatrical movie reruns, and original movies.

In 1986 Turner's love of sports yet again pushed him into another new venture. Turner founded, financed, and broadcast the Goodwill Games. Turner wanted these Olympic–like games to foster better relations between Russia and the United States. For the next five years, Turner continued building his empire by purchasing the Hanna–Barbara animation studio and its cartoon library. He continued promoting peace through the second Goodwill Games in 1990, even though this endeavor cost him millions of dollars. During these five years, the popularity of CNN exploded due to its accurate and up–to–the–minute reporting of the Persian Gulf War. Thus, Turner was dubbed by some the "King of Cable," and was named "Man of the Year" in 1991 by *Time* magazine. That year Turner also married Academy Award–winning actress Jane Fonda.

In 1992 Turner established two more cable and satellite channels: the Airport Channel, which offered flight information at U. S. airports, and the Cartoon Network, which was supported by his recently purchased cartoon library. Two years later, Turner established yet another channel when he started broadcasting his MGM film library on Turner Classic Movies (TCM).

In a surprise move in a 1995, Turner accepted a $7.5 billion bid from Time Warner to buy Turner Broadcasting. With this deal, Turner became Time Warner's vice chairman and largest shareholder. The purchase in part helped Turner and Time Warner to fend off an aggressive television market attack by holdings of Rupert Murdoch's News Corporation, owner of the Fox network, among many other media interests.

Turner was seldom hesitant to share the fortune he'd made from his many business ventures. Most dramatically, in 1997 he announced that he would donate $1 billion to the United Nations (UN) through a special foundation he created for the cause. His massive contribution came in the wake of his periodic criticisms of other billionaires for not giving enough back to society. Turner had long been associated with environmental and other charitable causes. In an explanation of his gift to the UN, Turner told Howard Fineman in *Newsweek*, "According to Jesus Christ, money is worthless. It won't buy you anything in heaven, if there is one. It might not even get you in." A Turner Networks employee speculated on additional motives behind Turner's unusual pledge to the UN, calling the pledge part of Turner's "Citizen Kane complex." Turner was apparently fascinated by the story of Citizen Kane, and Turner's son claimed that Turner "thought he was Kane, a guy who has everything and ends up with nothing." Turner's friends also suspected that his philanthropy was in part motivated by the fact that Turner didn't want to die rich and alone.

But Turner angered environmentalists in 1999 when he went against his previously stated intentions and decided to allow oil drilling operations on 578,000 acres of private property in New Mexico. Turner had stated when he bought the land in 1996 that it was to be used only by ecotourists and resident bison. He later sold the mineral rights to the property for a 3 percent royalty, which was expected to total $81 million over a period of 21 years.

By early 1999, Turner's wide array of business ventures included a large market share of the bison market, according to *Insight on the News*. Turner owned 17,000 head of bison on three ranches, was a major supplier of the North American Bison Cooperative, and sold $6 million to the federal government to feed poor Native American families. However, a competitor, the InterTribal Bison Cooperative, accused Turner of selling the best cuts of the meat to exotic restaurants and selling the government the fattiest cuts. Appearing embarrassed, Turner attempted a low profile on the issue by stepping out of the spotlight and merging his operations with an Omaha–based meat supplier.

In January 2000, AOL announced it would acquire Time Warner, Inc., for approximately $165 billion in stock, with the exact value to be determined by the stock prices of both firms. The new company would be called AOL Time Warner, with Steve Case serving as chairman. Time Warner's chairman Gerald Levin was to be the new company's CEO, Turner the vice–chairman. The merger would give AOL access to 20 million homes connected to Time Warner's cable lines and 300,000 cable modems already installed in Time Warner's Road Runner network. AOL would then be positioned to deliver its content through cable as well as telephone lines.

The merger took place in January 2001. That April, Turner criticized his boss Gerald Levin in a *New Yorker* magazine interview, saying, "I think he did a pretty marginal job of running [AOL Time Warner]." Turner's main complaint, however, was his relegation to a marginal role—vice–chairman—in the company. In May, AOL Time Warner announced that it was cutting 500 jobs at Turner Broadcasting System, including 400 at CNN. *Reuters News Service* reported on a *Wall Street Journal*

story in October 2001 stating that Turner would likely not renew his employment contract with AOL Time Warner when it expired at the end of the year. He was expected, however, to maintain his place as a member of the AOL board.

In June, Turner, frustrated by the gradual loss of control over his media empire, announced that he was setting up his own production company to produce feature–length films and documentaries. Although the studio planned to work closely with AOL Time Warner, Inc., it also expected to develop projects on its own in cases in which AOL Time Warner was not interested.

Social and Economic Impact

Ted Turner has made an indelible mark on the world's television markets through his founding of several of the leading networks viewed on cable and satellite television. His revolutionary concepts like CNN's all–news format created wholly new and profitable genres of broadcasting that had not previously existed. He has also been a notable personage in international sporting and social causes through his participation in yachting competitions, his ownership of Atlanta–based professional sports teams, and his philanthropy and social activism.

Turner considered himself an ardent environmentalist, and in the year 1998 he gave funds to environmental organizations that totaled $25 million. The Turner Foundation included the Turner Endangered Species Fund, which focused on saving species such as the desert bighorn sheep and the California condor. Turner's environmental foundation funded 450 environmental advocacy groups in 1999. On ranch land that Turner owned in Montana, he planned to reintroduce wolves and falcons as well as native plant life. In addition, he hoped to demonstrate cultivation methods on the land that were environmentally sound. Turner was also concerned with other social issues such as world overpopulation and the impact of consumption on the earth's resources. In his personal life, Turner sought to decrease his own consumption by driving a mid–sized car, walking when possible, and saving on electricity in his home. Claimed Turner of his approach to life, work, and the causes that he supported, "I didn't set out to make a lot of money. . . . I went after the best ideas that would benefit the most people."

In 2001, after Turner's nine–year marriage to Jane Fonda had dissolved and his boss Gerald Levin had eased him out of his top role at AOL Time Warner, Turner reportedly compared himself to the biblical character Job, who went from great wealth to enduring incredible financial and personal hardships. Characteristically, Turner responded by announcing plans to donate money to the UN, fight for environmental causes, and bankroll hard–hitting documentaries.

In March of 2001, Turner responded to questions by students at his alma mater, the McCallie School. In commenting on his philanthropy, Turner said, "I never set out to become wealthy so I could become philanthropic. I set out to have an interesting life and to do well. But as I did better than well, I started thinking about the possibility of reinvesting my wealth in making a better world." When asked if the motivation for his charitable contributions was for personal glory or the greater good, Turner replied that he didn't know. "It's hard to tell. Who cares, as long as it gets done?" he explained. Former spouse Jane Fonda put a different spin on the picture, however: "For some reason, he has a guilty conscience. He went so much further than his father thought he would. So what's left? To be a good guy."

Sources of Information

Contact at: Turner Broadcasting
   PO Box 105366
   Atlanta, GA 30348
   URL: http://www.turner.com

Bibliography

Bart, Peter. "Ted's trail of tears: after five years of ill–fortune in the film business." *Variety*, 31 August 1998.

Dictionary of Twentieth Century Culture, Vol. 1. Detroit: Gale Research, 1994.

Dworetzky, Tom. "Wildlife Scientists Are Having a Field Day On Ted Turner's Western Ranchlands." *National Wildlife*, October–November 1998.

Fineman, Howard. "Why Ted Gave It Away." *Newsweek*, 29 September 1997.

Galletta, Jan. "Ted Turner Blasts President Bush for Environmental Stance." *Knight–Ridder/Tribune Business News*, March 28, 2001.

Glass, Stephen. "Gift of the Magnate." *New Republic*, 26 January 1998.

The International Who's Who. 60th ed. London: Europa Publications, 1996.

Kempner, Matt. "AOL Time Warner Off To Great Start, Boss Says." *The Atlanta Journal–Constitution*. May 18, 2001.

Levine, Samantha. "A Turner for the Worse." *U.S. News & World Report*, March 19, 2001.

Lucier, James P., and Timothy W. Maier. "Controversy Surrounds Turner's Buffalo Empire." *Insight on the News*, 19 July 1999.

Rembert, Tracey C. "Ted Turner: Billionaire, Media Mogul, and Environmentalist." *E*, January 1999.

"Strange Bedfellows Dept." *Business Week*, 5 July 1999.

Summers, Mary. "Turncoat Ted." *Forbes*, 26 July 1999.

"Ted Rips Levin's Leadership Of AOL TW." *New York Post*, 16 April 2001.

"Ted Turner Starts Production Company." *New York Times*, 16 June 2001.

"Ted Turner: The Inventor of CNN Brought the World Dash, Daring and a Feel for the Big Picture." *People Weekly*, 15 March 1999.

"Turner: Times Have Been Tough." *Dayton Daily News*, 17 April 2001.

"Turner Won't Renew Contract." *Reuters*, 5 October 2001. Available at http://www.reuters.com.

Webster, Donovan. "Welcome to Turner County." *Audubon*, January 1999.

Madame C. J. Walker

Overview

Madame C. J. Walker was a washerwoman who became the first female African–American millionaire by founding and running a cosmetic empire for black women. Walker, through her ingenious products, revolutionized the methods for treating black hair, as well as the way business people marketed their products. Through her hard work and business acumen, this daughter of former slaves owned and ran the largest black–owned company in the United States. The Madame C. J. Walker Manufacturing Company produced and distributed a line of hair and beauty preparations for black women, including conditioners to ease styling, stimulate hair growth, and cure common scalp ailments, as well as an improved metal "hot" comb for straightening curly hair. Her self–made fortune allowed for a lavish personal lifestyle and extensive public philanthropic commitments, particularly to black educational institutions.

(1867-1919)
The Madame C. J. Walker
Manufacturing Company

Personal Life

For her contribution to business, civil rights, and philanthrophy, Walker was inducted into National Women's Hall of Fame, Seneca Falls, New York, in 1993. Walker, who was twice married with one daughter Lelia, was a member of the National Association of Colored Women. She died in 1919 at her home in Irvington–on–Hudson, New York.

Named Sarah Breedlove at birth, Walker was born on December 23, 1867, in Delta, Louisiana. Her parents, Owen and Minerva Breedlove, were former slaves who

Madame C.J. Walker. *(The Granger Collection, New York.)*

had chosen to remain as sharecroppers, living in a dilapidated shack on the Burney family plantation near Delta, Louisiana, on the Mississippi River. As a child and an adult, Walker toiled in the cotton fields with other black laborers. Cotton, still ranked as the main source of income for southern farmers, was produced by hand and mule labor and required a warm to hot climate. Working conditions were unbearable for laborers. Hardened, sharp cotton bolls pricked and cut their fingers as laborers picked cotton in the hot sun. With no child labor laws, Walker, a mere child, worked from sunrise to sunset. The family was poor, and both parents died by the time Sarah was seven. She was taken in by her older sister, Louvenia, who worked as a domestic. A few years later they moved to Vicksburg, Mississippi.

Sarah's education was extremely limited, and she was subjected to the cruelty of Louvenia's husband. To escape the oppressive situation, she married Moses McWilliams when she was 14. In 1885, when Sarah was eighteen, her daughter, Lelia, was born. Two years later, McWilliams was killed, and suddenly Walker was a single parent with a two–year–old child to rear. Vicksburg, Mississippi, was not an ideal place for blacks. Blacks had the best chance for employment and education in urban areas, so Walker moved to St. Louis, Missouri, where she had relatives and found work as a cook and laundress. She also joined St. Paul's African Methodist Episcopal Church. Through her long years of hard work, she managed to see Lelia graduate from the St. Louis public schools and attend Knoxville College, a black private col

lege in Tennessee. Walker, who was barely literate, was especially proud of her daughter's educational accomplishments.

Career Details

Shortly after her arrival in St. Louis, Sarah began losing her hair. Like many black women of her era, she would often divide her hair into sections, tightly wrap string around these sections, and twist them in order to make her hair straighter when it was combed out. Unfortunately, this hair–care ritual created such a strain that it caused many women to lose their hair.

To keep her hair, Sarah tried every product she could find, but none worked. Desperate, she prayed to God to save her hair. "He answered my prayer," she later told a reporter for the *Kansas City Star* in a story recounted in *Ms.* magazine. "One night I had a dream, and in that dream a big black man appeared to me and told me what to mix up for my hair. Some of the remedy was grown in Africa, but I sent for it, mixed it, put it on my scalp, and in a few weeks my hair was coming in faster than it had ever fallen out. I tried it on my friends; it helped them. I made up my mind to begin to sell it."

Walker experimented with patent medicines and hair products already on the market, developing different formulas and products in her wash tubs for testing on herself, her family members, and friends. Realizing the commercial possibilities in the under–served market for black beauty products, she began selling her concoctions door–to–door in the local black community.

After perfecting her "Wonderful Hair Grower" in 1905, she moved to Denver, Colorado, to join her recently widowed sister–in–law and nieces. Other products followed, including "Glossine" hair oil, "Temple Grower," and a "Tetter Salve" for psoriasis of the scalp. These products, used along with her re–designed steel hot comb with teeth spaced far apart for thick hair, allowed black women to straighten, press, and style their hair more easily.

Walker's beauty products complemented her belief that one of the ways black women could gain access to business careers and financial power was by looking more "acceptable" to members of the dominant mainstream white society. Using her preparations would not only help improve personal hygiene for many rural black women but also enhance their personal self–esteem. "I have always held myself out as a hair culturist. I grow hair," she once told a reporter whose story was later quoted in *Ms.* magazine. "I want the great masses of my people to take a greater pride in their appearance and to give their hair proper attention."

Soon she had enough customers to quit working as a laundress and devote all her energy to her growing business. In 1906 she married Charles Joseph Walker, a Den ver newspaperman. His journalistic background proved helpful in implementing advertising and promotional schemes for her products in various black publications, as well as through mail–order procedures. Though the marriage only lasted a few years, it provided a new professional name for herself and her company—the Madame C. J. Walker Manufacturing Company.

Leaving Lelia in charge of her burgeoning mail–order operations in Denver, Walker traveled throughout the South and East, selling her products and teaching her hair–care method. In 1908 she established a branch office and a school called Lelia College in Pittsburgh to train black hair stylists and beauticians in the Walker System of hair care and beauty culture. While Lelia managed the school and office, Walker logged thousands of miles on the road. introducing her preparations to black women everywhere she went.

Stopping in Indianapolis in 1910, she was so impressed by the city's central location and transportation facilities that she decided to make it her headquarters. That year she consolidated her operations by moving the Denver and Pittsburgh offices there and building a new factory to manufacture her hair solutions, facial creams, and related cosmetics. She also established a training center for her sales force, research and production laboratories, and another beauty school to train her "hair culturists."

On one of her many trips, Walker met a train porter, Freeman B. Ransom, who was a Columbia University law student working during his summer vacation. After he graduated, she hired him to run her Indianapolis operations, freeing Lelia to move to New York in 1913 to expand activities on the East Coast and open another Lelia College. Walker herself continued to travel and promote her beauty program.

Walker was fast building an empire in the true tradition of American enterprise—manufacturing the products in her own plant, employing a nationwide sales force to sell them, and owning the beauty shops that used and promoted them. At every town she visited in her indefatigable travels, she made sure to meet the leading black business, religious, and civic leaders, knowing that if these influential citizens began using her products, the rest of the populace would follow suit.

By 1917 the Madame C. J. Walker Manufacturing Company was the largest black–owned business in the country, with annual revenues of approximately $500,000. Much of its success was built around the sales force—thousands of black women known as Walker agents. Dressed in white blouses and long black skirts, they became familiar sights in black communities throughout the United States and the Caribbean. Walking door–to–door to demonstrate and sell Walker products, they easily outpaced their competitors in the new-found black beauty field.

Being a Walker agent or hair culturist was a rare career opportunity for black women in the rigidly segre-

Chronology:
Madame C. J. Walker

1987: Born.

1881: Married Moses McWilliams.

1885: Gave birth to daughter Lelia.

1905: Perfected her hair growth tonic.

1906: Married Charles Joseph Walker.

1906: Began The Madame C. J. Walker Manufacturing Company.

1908: Established first Lelia College to train black hair stylists and beauticians in the Walker System of hair care and beauty culture.

1910: Moved the company's headquarters to Indianapolis, Indiana.

1917: Company became the largest black–owned business in the country.

1919: Died.

gated pre–World War I era. It enabled many to become financially independent, buy their own homes, and support their children's educations. Walker herself considered it one of her greatest accomplishments, telling delegates to the National Negro Business League, as recounted in *American History Illustrated*: "I have made it possible for many colored women to abandon the washtub for a more pleasant and profitable occupation. . . . The girls and women of our race must not be afraid to take hold of business enterprise."

Once her agents were making money, Walker encouraged them to donate to charitable causes in their own communities. She shrewdly organized them into clubs for business, social, and philanthropic purposes, stimulating their activities and fostering prestige by offering cash prizes to the most generous clubs. Delegates from local clubs attended national conventions at regular intervals to learn new techniques and share business experiences.

Walker set a good example to her saleswomen by becoming the leading black philanthropist of her day. She contributed substantial sums to promote black education (particularly for women), encourage black businesses, support homes for the aged, and aid anti–lynching legislation. Some of her favorite causes were the National Association for the Advancement of Colored People

(NAACP), the Colored YMCA of Indianapolis, and the National Conference on Lynching.

Walker befriended many famous black leaders of her era and generously supported their efforts, among them Booker T. Washington's Tuskegee Institute, Mary McLeod Bethune's Daytona Normal and Industrial Institute for Negro Girls, Lucy Laney's Haynes Institute, and Charlotte Hawkins Brown's Palmer Memorial Institute. She also built a school for girls in West Africa and continued providing for it. When the National Association of Colored Women appealed to their membership for donations to pay off the mortgage of the late abolitionist Frederick Douglass' home, Walker made the largest contribution. At the group's 1918 convention, she proudly held the candle that burnt the mortgage papers.

Even with her generosity, Walker was able to lead a lavish lifestyle. Shrewd real estate investments complemented her self–made business fortune. A striking woman nearly six–feet tall, big boned, with brown skin and a broad face, she made heads turn by her presence whenever she entered a room. And her extravagant tastes only enhanced her public image. She dressed in the latest fashions, wore expensive jewelry, rode around in an electric car, was seen in the finer restaurants, owned townhouses in New York and Indianapolis and, befitting the first black female millionaire in the country, built a $250,000, 20–room, elegant Georgian mansion, Villa Lewaro—complete with gold piano and $60,000 pipe organ in Irvington–on–Hudson.

By 1918 Walker's nonstop pace and lifetime of hard work had begun to take its toll. Despite orders from doctors to slow down to ease her high blood pressure, she continued to travel. During a business trip to St. Louis, she collapsed and was transported back to her villa in a private railroad car. She died quietly of kidney failure resulting from hypertension in May of 1919 at the age of 52, leaving behind a prosperous company, extensive property, and a personal fortune in excess of $1 million.

In her will, Walker bequeathed two–thirds of her estate to charitable and educational institutions, many of which she had supported during her lifetime. The remaining third was left to her daughter, now called A'Lelia, who succeeded her as company president. True to her beliefs, a provision in the will directed that the Madame C. J. Walker Manufacturing Company always have a woman president. In 1927 the Walker Building, planned by Madame Walker, was completed in Indianapolis to serve as company headquarters. It was later called The Madame Walker Theatre Center, dedicated to nurturing and celebrating the arts from an African–American perspective for cross–cultural appreciation. The center is a National Historic Landmark.

Walker was celebrated by the United States Postal Service, who issued the Madame C. J. Walker Commemorative stamp in 1998, the 21st in the Black Heritage Series. Walker's great–great granddaugher A'Lelia Perry Bundles, honored her life, first in a young adult biography published in 1991, *Madame C. J. Walker— Entrepreneur*, and later in the 2001 biography, *On Her Own Ground: The Life and Times of Madame C. J. Walker*, the first truly comprehensive biography on Walker, based on nearly thirty years of research. Bundles also owns and maintains The Madame C. J. Walker homepage, http://www.madamcjwalker.com.

Social and Economic Impact

Madame C. J. Walker overcame poverty, abuse, and overwhelming odds to become the pioneer for black hair care and cosmetics through her self–made business. Her accomplishments in business, science, and philanthropy were accepted with pride by black communities across the land and were mind–boggling for the average person. Summing up her life, the author of an editorial in *Crisis* said that Madame Walker "revolutionized the personal habits and appearance of millions of human beings." Walker managed the overwhelming struggles that were involved in the management of a company by a black woman in 1904 to unprecedented success. She attained her strong reputation in American business accomplishments by meeting a need prudently and imaginatively. In spite of her fame, she was down–to–earth and remained mindful of her roots. She knew that she rose from a poor, black heritage, and she would not let herself forget it.

Walker not only made herself a millionaire with her ground–breaking black beauty care business but provided opportunities for the many black women, who served as her sales agents, to become financially independent in the rigidly segregated pre–World War I era. Walker became the leading black philanthropist of her day, contributing a large portion of her fortune for the benefit of encouraging black businesses and black education (particularly for women) and other civil rights causes.

Sources of Information

Bibliography

Bundles, A'Lelia. *On Her Own Ground: The Life and Times of Madam C.J. Walker*. Scriber, 2001.

Contemporary Black Biography. Vol. 7. Gale Research, 1994.

"Facts of Science: African Americans in the Sciences."*Princeton University*, 2001. Available at http://www.princeton.edu.

"From Rags to Riches." *The Library of Congress Information Bulletin*, May 2001. Available at http://www.loc.gov/loc/lcib.

"Madame C. J. Walker." *Smith and Associates*, 2001. Available at http://www.madamcjwalker.com.

"Madame C. J. Walker." *The National Women's Hall of Fame*, 2001. Available at http://www.greatwomen.org.

Notable Black American Women. Book 1. Gale Research, 1992.

Jay Scott Walker

(1955-)
priceline.com Incorporated

Jay S. Walker, founder of priceline.com, gave the public the power to "name their own price" online for the first time on goods and services in four areas: travel, with airline tickets, hotel rooms, and rental cars; personal finance, with home mortgages, refinancing, and home equity loans; automotive, offering new cars; and telecommunications, with a long distance calling service. As long as a customer was flexible and pre–paid, he or she could soon be airborne for far less money than ever before. An Internet commerce pioneer, Walker, who is also founder, chairman, and CEO of Walker Digital Corp., came up with the innovative idea of patenting priceline's method of doing business, along with a slew of other patents granted and pending that could revolutionize industries outside the Internet as well. Walker Digital is the largest intellectual property laboratory dedicated to business methodology.

Personal Life

Walker married Eileen McManus on April 18, 1982. They have two children, Evan and Lindsey, and live in Ridgefield, Connecticut. A licensed pilot, Walker also enjoys reading, book collecting, photography, collecting space memorabilia, and fine wines.

Walker is a member of Sigma Phi, where he served as chairman of the board from 1988 to 1990. He was named Ernst & Young's regional Master Entrepreneur and *The Industry Standard's* Most Influential New Business Strategist, both in 1999.

Jay S. Walker. (Reuters NewMedia Inc./Corbis.)

Walker was born on November 5, 1955, in Queens, New York, to Arthur, a real–estate developer, and Jeanette Walker, who had fled Europe at six to escape Nazi persecution. He cites his mother, a golf and bridge champion, as giving him his competitive drive. Indeed, Walker began his entrepreneurial career at a young age. At nine years old, he created and distributed his own newspaper, and at thirteen, he undercut the price of the canteen and sold candy to kids at summer camp. Walker's mother died when he was eighteen.

While Walker's early business efforts were not promising, as a student attending Cornell University in Ithaca, New York, he routinely played the Parker Brothers game Monopoly and quickly became an expert at the secrets of winning. Although Parker Brothers had threatened him with a suit if he wrote a book about his secrets, Walker and a partner wrote one anyway, entitled, *1000 Ways to Win Monopoly Games*. The company did indeed sue, with legal fees eating up the $50,000 profit Walker made from the book. The suit was later dropped. Undaunted by this early setback, Walker obtained financing and began a weekly newspaper, *Midweek Observer*, in Ithaca, during a leave of absence after his junior year of college. The results were disastrous: Gannett, a leading publisher, ran his paper out of business, leaving Walker in debt to the tune of around $250,000, some sources say. He graduated with a bachelor's degree in industrial relations from Cornell University in 1977. That summer, he attended a course in publishing at New York University, with the idea that never materialized of selling a maga-

zine filled only with coupons. Other early ventures, involving selling catalogs at retail outlets and selling advertising in mail–order catalogs, were similarly unsuccessful.

Career Details

The company Walker began in the catalog venture, Catalog Media Corp., saw its first success in 1985, when he made a deal between hundreds of catalog vendors and Federal Express. The deal was that the catalog merchants would subsidize Fed–Ex overnight delivery of their products to customers, thereby extending the Christmas holiday shopping season for the merchants until the day before December 25th.

Fresh from his first big business achievement, Walker then partnered with Michael Loeb in a company they called NewSub Services, which began operation in 1991. Walker's aim for the company was to offer an indefinite renewal service for magazine subscriptions by charging customer's credit cards automatically each year. A common procedure in other countries, the practice had not yet been introduced in the United States. He came up with a software program, which later received a patent in 1999, that allowed publishers to renew subscriptions automatically to a customer's stored credit card number, with the customer's permission. Loeb, whose father was the financial journalist and editor Marshall Loeb, had connections in the publishing industry, and the company sold half a million subscriptions within one year. By 1998 the company, later renamed Synapse Group Inc., had sold 30 million magazine subscriptions and had sales of nearly $300 million.

Walker was already looking for a new challenge to conquer in the early 1990s and set his eye on Internet as his medium. At first, Walker had the idea of starting an Internet casino. Then he began to wonder if he could simply profit from ownership of the idea of Internet gaming. He followed up with patent lawyers who assured him he could patent his idea. Business, at the time, invented many things, like credit cards and frequent flyer programs, and Walker was amazed to learn no one had ever tried to patent these original ideas. With that in mind, Walker began his next business, Walker Digital Corp., in 1994. Walker hired a group of computer engineers, cryptographers, and other technical personnel to devise new methods of doing business on the Internet and to develop the corresponding technology. Patent lawyers were also retained to secure ownership of any ideas that the research division of the company developed.

On April 6, 1998, Walker started his online business, priceline.com, with $20 million from the sale of a third of his ownership of NewSub and $100 million from outside investors, including Paul Allen, cofounder of Microsoft; George Soros, a financier; Jim Manzi, a computer–software executive; and John C. Malone, a cable television executive. Four months later, Walker was granted a patent for its development of a "buyer–driven" business method and the corresponding software. The method entailed allowing prospective customers of goods and services to send a binding purchase offer to a prospective seller over the Internet. This was the driving force behind priceline.com, which first offered consumers the chance to bid for airline tickets. Users would indicate their travel dates and the price they wanted to pay, enter their credit–card number, and participating airlines would review the bids and decide whether to accept the traveler's offer. If they agreed on the price, the traveler was obligated to purchase the ticket. Prospective travelers stood to gain by receiving discounted tickets while airlines gained by being able to fill any as–yet unsold seats. Priceline sold an estimated 40,000 tickets in the first three months of business. The idea caught on because of the appeal of discounts as well as the humorous ad campaigns that starred ex–*Star Trek* cast member William Shatner. Some early complaints noted that the success rate was only about 10 percent but rose as more airlines gradually participated in the process.

During the technology boom, the company went public, and its March 29, 1999, Wall Street debut was a huge success. The offer price of $16 per share ended the first day of trading at $69, making it one of the most successful initial public offerings ever, giving the company a $9.8 billion market value and making Walker an instant billionaire. The stock reached to more than $82 on the next day. At its all–time high, the company's stock reached $165 a share. Just over a year later, the stock reflected the deflated technology market at nearly $30. Though the company has yet to post a profit, like many other former high–flying technology companies, analysts predict priceline will be in the black by 2001 and, in fact, posted a quarterly profit for the first time in late 2001. Its 2000 sales stood at more than $1.2 billion and its loss narrowed to $315 million.

Priceline soon grew beyond merely airline tickets, with customers able to name their price on home financing, hotel rooms, new cars, rental cars, and telephone long distance. Some argued that the system behind priceline wouldn't work with the new products and services it added, but Walker firmly defended his idea to invent new business methods and patent them. "Amazon.com is a wonderful company, but anybody can sell books on the Internet. Same thing with eBay and auctions. What they will ultimately need are proprietary advantages," he told the *Wall Street Journal*. Walker suffered a set–back when he left the day–to–day operations of priceline to others in November 1999, to launch WebHouse Club. The company was not affiliated with priceline but used Walker's patented technology to allow people to bid on gasoline and groceries. The business shut down in October 2000 because of insufficient operating funds. Walker then stepped down as priceline's vice chairman in late 2000, selling off most of his stake in the company, currently leaving him with about 10 percent ownership. He left

Chronology:
Jay Scott Walker

1955: Born.

1977: Graduated from Cornell University.

1991: Started NewSub Services offering automatically renewable magazine subscriptions.

1994: Founded and chaired Walker Digital Corp.

1998: Founded priceline.com.

1999: Priceline's initial public offering one of the most successful in history.

1999: Launched WebHouse Club.

2000: Stepped down as priceline's vice–chairman.

2000: Became CEO of Walker Digital.

priceline to focus on the company he started that came up with priceline's business model, Walker Digital, where he is now chairman and CEO.

Since Walker's departure in late 2000, priceline has struggled amid the publicity regarding complaints about customer satisfaction and increased competition from other Internet businesses. In September 2000, the Better Business Bureau expelled Walker Digital due to complaints that it didn't adequately explain the restrictions on its discount airline tickets, but the company was reinstated two months later when it changed its disclosure policy. Its stock price stood at about $4 as of late 2001.

Walker Digital owns around 60 patents, which provide methods for generating and executing insurance policies for foreign exchange losses, disbursing prepaid phone time, and issuing postpaid traveler's checks. Some of Walker's more than 400 patents pending would allow people to place fast–food orders via Palm Pilot or other digital device. With the company churning out a patent application every two weeks, Walker has lobbied to streamline and speed up the patent process. Critics argue that patenting business methods may not be the best way to go. When Walker asked former CEO of AMR Corp., parent company of American Airlines, why he had never patented his creation of frequent–flier mileage, he said the idea never occurred to him but added in the *Wall Street Journal*, "It seems to me that if business processes were patentable you would very severely limit competition."

Social and Economic Impact

Internet mogul Jay Walker introduced the nation and the Net to a totally new way of buying. His patented system, which allowed users to name their own price on airline tickets, revolutionized the way people do business on the Internet. With one of the most successful IPOs in history, Walker became an instant billionaire off what may have been his greatest idea—priceline.com—and patenting its underlying business system.

Since Walker hit on the novel idea of patenting business systems, that has become his sole order of business through Walker Digital, a new age "think–tank," which creates and patents new ideas in commerce almost weekly. Given that he has many patents in hand and hundreds of patents pending, one of Walker's ideas might well revolutionize business methods in the future.

Sources of Information

Contact at: priceline.com Incorporated
    800 Connecticut Ave.
    Norwalk, CT 06854–9998
    Business Phone: (203)299–8000
    URL: http://www.priceline.com

Bibliography

"Big Idea Turns Priceline's Founder Into a Billionaire." *Wall Street Journal*, 1 April 1999.

"'Business–Method' Patents, Key to Priceline, Draws Growing Protest." *Wall Street Journal*, 3 October 2000.

"Can Jay Walker Pull A New Rabbit Out of His Hat." *Barron's*, 8 January 2001.

The Complete Marquis Who's Who. Marquis Who's Who, 2001.

Current Biography Yearbook. The H. W. Wilson Company, 2000.

"Discounted Out." *Wall Street Journal*, 16 October 2000.

"The Hype is Big, Really Big, at Priceline." *Fortune*, 6 September 1999.

"Inside Jay Walker's House of Cards." *Fortune*, 13 November 2000.

"It's a Completely New Way of Buying." *Business Week*, 16 September 1999. Available at http://www.businessweek.com.

"Jay S. Walker Steps Down From Priceline.com Board of Directors." *Priceline.com*, 28 December 2000.

"Jay Walker's Patent Mania." *Salon*, 27 August 1999. Available at http://www.salon.com.

"Our Company." *Priceline.com*, 2001 Available at http://www.priceline.com.

"Priceline Fires Chief and Shuffles Officials." *New York Times*, 8 May 2001.

"Priceline Founder Sells Stock at Low Price." *Wall Street Journal*, 22 August 2001.

"Priceline Reports Losses and Slow Sales." *New York Times*, 16 February 2001.

"Priceline.com Founder Jay S. Walker Honored By the Industry Standard And Ernst & Young." *Priceline.com*, 23 June 1999.

"Priceline.com Incorporated." *Hoover's*, November 2001. Available from http://www.hoovers.com.

"Priceline's Jay Walker to Sell Bulk of Shares to Hong Kong Buyers." *Wall Street Journal*, 6 June 2001.

"Walker Digital." *Hoover's*, November 2001. Available at http://www.hoovers.com.

Ty Warner

(1944-)
Ty Inc.

Overview

Ty Warner created a billion dollar industry based on an idea for a $5 pellet–filled toy cat that turned into a line of hundreds of avidly collected and traded Beanie Babies. His company, Ty Inc., became the number one toy maker in 1998 using Warner's unique marketing techniques that kept his company shrouded in mystery and his Beanie Babies in high demand with limited volumes of an ever–changing line–up of cuddly characters. The Beanie frenzy of the late 1990s has created an entire industry around the aftermarket sales of the toys, including trading clubs and auction websites, sometimes fetching $5,000 and more for rare or most–wanted Beanies. Selling toys with names like Legs the frog and Chip the cat has made Warner himself a billionaire, ranked on the *Forbes* 400 list.

Personal Life

Warner has never been married and lives in Oak Brook, Illinois, with his long–time girlfriend Faith McGowan and her daughters Lauren and Jenna. He also owns a Mediterranean–style home near Santa Barbara, California. He is an accomplished classical pianist, taught by his mother, and enjoys tennis, baseball, and Italian cuisine. Warner also collects luxury cars.

H. Ty Warner was born September 3, 1944 in Chicago, Illinois to parents Harold Warner, a toy and jewelry salesman and Georgia, a pianist. Warner claims he was named after baseball great Ty Cobb and president Harry S. Truman. Some say the H. in front of his name stands for his father's name Harold, but Warner

Beanie Baby bears. (AP/Wide World Photos.)

claims it stands for nothing, just like the "S" in Harry S. Truman. He grew up in suburban La Grange, Illinois, with his younger sister Joyce, in a house built by famed architect Frank Lloyd Wright.

He was educated at Cossit School in La Grange until fourteen and then Lyons High School in Chicago. After only a few terms at Lyons, Warner was transferred to St. John's Military Academy, a boarding school in Delafield, Wisconsin. He was a member of an elite academic club, the Star and Circles, and was active in football, basketball, and baseball. Warner attended Kalamazoo College in Michigan for one year, studying drama, before dropping out and moving to Hollywood to give acting a try. To support himself, Warner sold cameras door to door and worked at a gas station. Disenchanted, Warner soon moved back to Chicago just before his parents divorced.

Career Details

He got his start in the toy business, in 1962, working with his father as a salesman at Dakin toy company. His former boss told *People*, "He was probably the best salesman I ever met." At Dakin, Warner learned the *in's* and *out's* of toy business by selling the company's plush animals. Warner began dabbling in unorthodox marketing techniques, arriving at distributors in a white Rolls–Royce convertible he had purchased, dressed in fur coat complete with top hat and cane. He guessed, correctly, that that would intrigue retailers enough to see what he had for sale. After eighteen years at Dakin, Warner was making more than $100,000 at the company, but he left in 1980. Warner told *People* he left to pursue other interests, but his former boss told the magazine he was fired for creating a competing line of toys.

Warner traveled to Sorrento, Italy, where he was inspired by the number of unique stuffed toy cats he had seen there. Upon his return in 1983, his father died of a heart attack and left Warner $50,000. With that money, in addition to his savings from his time at Dakin and a second mortgage on his condo home, Warner began to develop a line of toys. In 1986 he formed Ty Incorporated and, after working out of his home, moved to a small office in Oakbrook, Illinois. He hired two employees and on a trip to Korea, found a production plant to manufacture his stuffed animals. His first toy was a white Himalayan cat named Angel. In the first line, there were ten cats, all with different names like Peaches and Smokey in all different colors. "Kids identify with names. In the beginning, I thought of the cute names. Now I take them into the office and everyone makes suggestions," Warner told *People*. He was able to get buyers through his old Dakin contacts and sold the small, loosely filled pellet animal for $20. They sold well. At the Atlanta Toy Fair, Warner sold 30,000 in one hour.

After his success in Atlanta, Warner moved out of the little Oakbrook office and into a 12,000 square foot warehouse in Lombard, Illinois. He began a new line of toys, the Collectable Bears Series, in 1991. They were limited edition bears, each with a numbered stripe on its right foot. Ty, Inc.'s 1992 catalog featured these bears and the original cats, in addition to a variety of new animals like dogs and monkeys in the $5–$20 range. Warner then decided to put his focus on a toy that children could easily afford and would like to collect. He wanted to create a quality toy line for the retail price of $5, which he felt, to that point, didn't exist.

In 1993 the first Beanie Babies were born: Brownie the bear and Punchers the lobster. After tweaking these early attempts, there were nine Beanie Babies all together in the first line unveiled at the New York Toy Fair. Warner called the flagship Beanies Chocolate the moose, Cubbie the brown bear, Flash the dolphin, Legs the frog, Patti the platypus, Pinchers the lobster, Splash the whale, Spot the dog, and Squealer the pig. By early 1994, the little toys with the characteristic heart–shaped tag were in stores.

Warner's marketing genius was keeping stores from carrying all the different kinds of Beanie babies in the line. That way, people went hunting for them and kept demand high. He shunned all advertising, and the toys weren't carried by toy retail giants like Toys "R" Us or Wal–Mart, yet soon Beanies were flying off the shelves of Hallmark stores and smaller retailers that carried the line. Warner also limited each store to a certain number of Beanies they could order each month. Making supply scarcer, he knew, would increase demand from avid collectors. In 1995 he came up with another scheme—retiring certain styles after a while and putting out new styles to keep interest up. Warner himself designed all the different Beanies, except one, Spook, now called Spooky, that was designed by Jenna, his girlfriend's daughter.

The mystique Warner likes to keep around his products, his company, and himself is well known. He has no signs anywhere surrounding his Illinois headquarters and no listed phone number, sometimes frustrating retailers wishing to reorder. Warner claims the unlisted phone number is simply because they can't keep up with demand. He swears his employees to secrecy regarding the company and himself and has only agreed to a very limited number of interviews with the press. Warner's success has allowed him to show his philanthropic side, though. His specially designed Princess bear raised more than $15 million for the Diana, Princess of Wales Memorial Fund. He donated Beanies to refugee children in Kosovo. He also shared the wealth with his workers. In 1998 Warner handed out bonuses to all 300 Ty employees equal to their annual salaries and often gave out special edition Beanies to them, as well.

In 1998 Ty was named the leading toy maker in the country. That year, Ty Inc. partnered with Cyrk Inc., a corporate promotion company to form the Beanie Baby Official Club. The club kit offered a chance to buy the

Chronology:
Ty Warner

1944: Born.

1962: Began career in toys at Dakin.

1980: Left Dakin after eighteen years.

1986: Formed Ty Incorporated.

1993: First Beanie Babies were created.

1994: Beanie Babies hit the market.

1998: Named number one toy maker.

1999: Buys Four Season Hotel in Manhattan, the city's tallest hotel.

1999: Announced retirement of all Beanie Babies.

1999: Held online vote on whether to discontinue Beanies.

2000: Beanies voted to continue.

exclusive Clubby bear. The next year, the partnership began producing BBOC Trading Cards, which only lasted for four series of the cards, and another kit offering the new Clubby II bear. Cyrk also produced a number of promotional items, including calendars, trading card accessories, and the special club bears. Cyrk was unable to produce the Clubby Beanie Buddies within the time when they were advertised, which is illegal, and was fired by Ty.

In August 1999 Ty Inc. enigmatically announced on its website that they would discontinue making all the 325 different Beanie Babies after December 31 of that year. Collectors, who sometimes pay in the thousands for Beanies in aftermarkets like auction sites eBay and Beanienation.com, went wild. Fans e–mailed frantic messages to the company, and prices bid online for the Beanies rose. Even the company's own employees were baffled. Some speculated that the reason behind the decision was that the secondary market had ebbed recently and the move was an attempt to boost sagging sales. Although Ty does not gain from secondary sales, many retailers purchase the Beanies based on the aftermarket values, which were dropping. Stores began stocking up in droves after the announcement. When December 1999 finally arrived, Ty Inc. decided to let the public vote on whether the company should produce Beanies in 2000. The vote was overwhelmingly pro–Beanie, with 91 percent in favor of continuing Beanie production in the new millennium. Votes cost 50 cents each with Ty donating the proceeds to the Elizabeth Glaser Pediatric AIDS Foundation. Year 2000 sales were up 36 percent at 800 million. In 2001 a special edition America bear appeared with 100 percent of the profit from sales to be donated to the Disaster Relief Fund of the American Red Cross in honor of the victims of the attacks of September 11, 2001.

Warner's personal fortune has allowed him to embark on a second career as a hotelier. He has purchased prestigious real estate, including the Four Seasons hotel in New York City, the city's tallest hotel, the Four Seasons Resort in Monetcito, and the San Ysidro Ranch near Santa Barbara, the honeymoon destination of John F. and Jacqueline Kennedy. He has renovated the New York and Santa Barbara hotels, with plans of expansion at the latter.

Social and Economic Impact

Beginning with a single stuffed toy cat, Warner created a line of 325 unique Beanie Babies that were avidly embraced by toy lovers and collectors worldwide. His company, Ty Inc., that began in his small condo in Illinois, grew into one of the largest toy makers in the country, boasting $800 million in sales in 2000. Warner has shared his wealth, generously rewarding his employees and donating a variety of Beanie Baby proceeds to a number of causes.

Warner also revolutionized marketing with his Beanie sensations. With no advertising or big name retailers, Warner managed to make the roughly four–inch, loosely stuffed Beanies a most–wanted collectible for adults and, at about $5 each, popular among children who liked to trade them with friends. The eccentric Warner, perfecting his unique marketing tactics, kept production of the toys a mystery, rotating the line frequently and limiting supply to create demand. While nothing lasts forever, Warner has managed to keep the Beanie craze going by announcing their demise and suddenly reviving them at the last minute. He has created a multi–billion dollar industry with the toys in sales as well as aftermarket, with trading clubs and websites popping up everywhere.

Sources of Information

Contact at: Ty Inc.
    280 Chestnut Ave.
    Westmont, IL 60559
    Business Phone: (630)920–1515
    URL: http://www.ty.com

Bibliography

"All About...Ty Warner: The Man Behind the Magic." *Beany Babys.com*, 2001. Available at http://www.beanybabys.com.

"Beanie Babies Creator Buys Manhattan's Tallest Hotel." *Wall Street Journal*, 15 March 1999.

"Beanie History." *About Beanies.com*, 2001. Available at http://www.aboutbeanies.com.

"Bean There, Done That." *People Weekly*, 20 September 1999.

"Requiem for Beanie Babies. Or Maybe Not." *New York Times*, 1 September 1999.

"There Goes the Neighborhood." *Forbes*, 1 October 2001.

Ty, Inc, 4 November 2000. Available at http://www.ty.com.

"Ty, Inc." *Hoover's*, 4 November 2001. Available at http://www.hoovers.com.

"Ty Puts Beanie Babies' Fate Into the Hands of Consumers." *New York Times*, 25 December 1999.

"Voters Save Beanie Babies." *ABC News.com*, 3 January 2000. Available at http://www.abcnews.go.com.

John Edward Warnock

(1940-)
Adobe Systems Incorporated

Overview

Hailed as a "modern–day Gutenberg," after the man who invented moveable type, John E. Warnock revolutionized the field of visual communication with renowned graphic and multimedia software packages that sparked a desktop publishing revolution. Warnock founded Adobe Systems Incorporated, which pioneered the software technologies that allowed sharing of electronic documents between computers. Some of Adobe's software packages include Adobe Acrobat, Adobe Photoshop, Adobe Illustrator, Adobe PageMaker, and Adobe Premiere. Warnock helped make the $1.3 billion company a widely copied model of integrity, technical excellence, and corporate responsibility; moreover, it is the second largest PC software company in the United States. Warnock, holder of six patents, is one of the most respected computer software innovators in the world.

Personal Life

Warnock married his wife in 1965, and the couple has three adult children. Warnock enjoys painting and photography, skiing, hiking, non–fiction books, and movies. The software developer and entrepreneur also collects first editions of books about famous innovators, including Galileo, Newton, Darwin, and Copernicus.

Warnock is a distinguished member of the National Academy of Engineering, a member of the Utah Information Technology Association, and a fellow of the Association for Computing Machinery. He is a board member of the Octavo Corporation, Entrepreneurial Board

John Edward Warnock standing in the lobby of Adobe headquarters. (AP Photo/Paul Sakuma.)

Advisory Committee, the American Film Institute, the Folger Shakespeare Museum, and past chairman and current board member of the Tech Museum of Innovation. His long list of awards include the Entrepreneur of the Year award from Merrill Lynch, Ernst & Young and *Inc.* magazine; *PC Magazine*'s Lifetime Achievement Award for Technical Excellence; the Cary Award from the Rochester Institute of Technology; Distinguished Alumnus Award from the University of Utah; the Corporate Outstanding Achievement Award and the Distinguished Service to Art and Design International Award, both from Rhode Island School of Design. He was inducted into the *Computer Reseller News* Hall of Fame as one of the "Ten Revolutionaries of Computing" in 1998.

Warnock was born on October 6, 1940, in Salt Lake City, Utah. In an interview with Jill Wolfson of the *San Jose Mercury News* and high school student Denise Cobb, Warnock described his early scholastic aptitude: "When I was in the 9th grade, I flunked 9th grade algebra. I couldn't cope with 9th grade algebra. And then I remember taking an aptitude test when I was a sophomore in high school, and they said, 'You should probably consider not going to college.' Then they said, 'Well, what would you like to do?' At that time I had no idea what I wanted to do, so I said 'Well, maybe something in engineering.' And the counselor told me, 'Your probability of having any kind of success in any engineering–related activity is probably zero.'" In high school, Warnock got back on track due to a particularly influential teacher named Barton,who made math fun and exciting for his students, almost all of whom went on to get master's degrees and Ph.Ds. "That was the thing that turned my life around," he told Wolfson and Cobb. About his early, misguided counseling, Warnock added, "Students should have a healthy skepticism about what they're told."

Transforming into a straight A student in math and science, Warnock went on to attend the University of Utah, where he received a Bachelor of Science degree in math and philosophy in 1961, a Master's degree in math in 1964, and a Ph.D. in electrical engineering and computer science in 1969. In 1963, just before receiving his Master's degree, Warnock took a job recapping tires at Firestone Rubber. He hated it and quickly applied for a position at IBM the same year. He was trained on punch–card equipment before handling programming. The following year, Warnock took a job teaching math with his alma mater. Warnock decided a teaching salary was not enough to support a new family so, in 1965, after his marriage, he started his career in computers in the University of Utah's Computer Science Department. After completing his Ph.D., Warnock and his family relocated to Vancouver, Canada, when he got a job at Computime Canada Ltd. The small start–up company didn't last long, and Computime folded in 1970, but in *USC Networker,* Warnock called his brief time there a "great experience." From there, Warnock moved to nearby Toronto and took a job with Computer Sciences Corp. until 1971. The family then left for Maryland when Warnock went to work at Goddard Space Flight Center in Washington, D. C., until early 1972. Warnock then took a new job that year, working with supercomputers as head of operating systems development, at Evans & Sutherland Corp. at the Ames Research in California. He later worked on real–time flight simulators with the company. In 1978, after E&S asked him to relocate to Utah, Warnock decided instead to stay in the San Francisco Bay area and took a job at Xerox Palo Alto Research Center where he was principal scientist. At Xerox PARC, Warnock helped develop graphic imaging standards. While at both E&S and Xerox PARC, he developed a language that became the basis for PostScript.

Career Details

Warnock was frustrated by Xerox PARC's reluctance to build and support a printing standard based on the early version of PostScript called JaM. In 1982, with Xerox coworker Dr. Charles Geschke, Warnock founded Adobe Systems Inc. The founders named the company after a creek that ran behind their homes. Warnock's aim for the company, which then had just two employees, Warnock himself and Geschke, was to develop applications for their PostScript page description language. They were able to get $2.1 million in seed money to launch Adobe over two years from the company Hambrecht & Quist. Warnock made a now–famous quote when the company first started that Adobe would never have more than 50 employees. He told *USC Networker,* "Obviously we have never expected the success we have achieved. When you start a company you do all kinds of contingency planning for failure events. You never do much planning for success." The company went public in 1986, trading on the Nasdaq National Market under the symbol ADBE.

Warnock's strategy for Adobe was to focus on producing products with the technology they created. He told *USC Networker,* "People are only given extraordinary rewards when their technology makes it into a product." In 1993 Adobe introduced their Adobe Acrobat. In a news release, Warnock said, "Acrobat will fundamentally change the economics of information by removing the critical barriers that have kept electronic documents from moving between computers. Today's paper–based information is hampered by the physical media. Acrobat technology liberates information and the flow of ideas and allows it to enter the electronic age." Other products sprung from Adobe's creativity was the document–layout product Adobe PageMaker, for creating documents that are heavy on graphics and don't change often, including magazines, newsletters, and school yearbooks. After the company's acquisition of Frame Technology, they also owned FrameMaker, a similar desktop publishing product for creating and maintaining documents that required constant updating, like manuals. Adobe grew its company with other acquisitions, including Aldus Corporation and Ceneca Communications.

Warnock wisely began focusing on the Internet during the mid–1990s. In 1996 Adobe had 2,200 employees worldwide with 2 million registered users for their main applications. Accounting for unregistered users, an estimated 10 million were using the company's Adobe Acrobat alone. Acrobat, which utilizes the portable document format (PDF) that helps businesses convert print document into digital ones, has since became prevalent on the Web. By the late 1990s, Adobe Photoshop was used by 93 percent of Web developers. PageMaker 6 was released. Adobe also launched a Web design software platform, Adobe GoLive. The company's range of products used in Web, print, and video publishing included Photoshop, Adobe Illustrator, Adobe LiveMotion, Adobe

Chronology:
John Edward Warnock

1940: Born.

1969: Received Ph.D. in electrical engineering and computer science.

1978: Began as principal scientists at Xerox PaloAlto Research Center.

1982: Founded Adobe Systems, Inc. with Charles Geschke.

1986: Adobe went public.

1993: Adobe Acrobat was introduced.

1996: Adobe had 2 million registered users.

1999: Introduced InDesign professional publishing platform.

2000: Adobe had sales of more than $1.2 billion and employed 2,900 people.

2001: Stepped down as CEO.

Premiere, Adobe FrameMaker, and Adobe After Effects. The products were designed to be used by a wide variety of customers with a range of skill–levels, from graphic designers to home users.

Adobe was threatened by a hostile takeover by rival Quark in the late 1990s. Although Adobe's revenue at the time, $912 million, dwarfed Quark's $200 million, Adobe was restructuring, and its stock prices had almost dropped in half. The takeover bid failed, but a shaken Adobe vowed to build its strength. In 1999 the company came up with InDesign, a product for the professional publishing arena to compete with Quark's dominance in that area. In the new millennium, the company is focused on the next wave of innovation, Network Publishing. Network Publishing involves making visually complex information available to anyone, anywhere, on any device. In 2000, Adobe had sales of more than $1.2 billion and employed 2,900 people. After founding the company nearly 20 years earlier, Warnock stepped down as CEO in 2001, remaining as cochairman of the board with Geschke. In addition to his technical and business leadership, Warnock has contributed articles to many technical journals and industry magazines and is a frequent speaker on computer and publishing industry issues.

Social and Economic Impact

Warnock's contribution to computer graphics, printing and publishing is legendary in the industry. Designing and marketing the tools for transforming paper documents to electronic and back again spawned the era of desktop publishing just in time for the age of the Internet. Of Adobe's influence, Michael P. McHugh said in *USC Networker,* "One would be hard–pressed to find a magazine, newspaper or even a site on the World Wide Web that has not, in some way, been stamped by Adobe technology." Adobe is indeed prevalent on a majority of web sites that were created or modified using one of Adobe's products like Photoshop, Illustrator, Acrobat, GoLive, FrameMaker, or LiveMotion.

The entrepreneur built Adobe from a two–person venture into the second largest PC software company in the United States with over $1 billion in revenue. Millions of users worldwide turn to Adobe software to create a variety of projects on paper, the Internet, and video. In 2001 the *San Jose Mercury News* gave Warnock and his Adobe cofounder more lofty praise: "In Greek mythology, Prometheus brought fire from the gods and gave it to humankind. When John Warnock and Chuck Geschke founded Adobe they did something similar, bringing the power of publishing to anyone with a computer. Others have described the pair as modern–day Gutenbergs whose entrepreneurship transformed the PC from a calculating machine to an artistic platform."

Sources of Information

Contact at: Adobe Systems Incorporated
    345 Park Ave.
    San Jose, CA 95110–2704
    Business Phone: (408)536–6000
    URL: http://www.adobe.com

Bibliography

"Computer Hall of Fame Inducts John Warnock." *Silicon Valley/San Jose Business Journal,* 20 November 1998. Available at http://sanjose.bcentral.com.

"Computer Industry Icon John Warnock to Retire from Adobe." *Adobe Systems, Inc,* 15 March 2001. Available at http://www.adobe.com.

"Corporate Backgrounder." *Adobe Systems, Inc.,* 2001. Available at http://www.adobe.com.

"Executive Profiles: Dr. John E. Warnock." *Adobe Systems, Inc,* 2001. Available at http://www.adobe.com.

"Innerview: John Warnock." *USC Networker,* March/April 1996.

"John Edward Warnock." *The Complete Marquis Who's Who.* Marquis Who's Who, 2001.

"John Warnock Interview: Adobe's CEO Talks to ZDNet." *ZDNet,* 23 July 1999. Available at http://news.zdnet.co.uk.

"John Warnock's Meteoric Rise." *TechTV,* 10 July 2000. Available at http://www.techtv.com.

"A PDF Day 2001 Salute to John Warnock & Charles Geschke." *Planet PDF,* 12 April 2001. Available at http://www.planepdf.com.

"The Revolutionaries: Turned Around by Brilliant' Teacher." *San Jose Mercury News.* Available at http://www.mercurycenter.com.

Daniel Joseph Weinfurter

Overview

Daniel Joseph Weinfurter is the founder, president and CEO of Parson Group LLC, a corporate staffing and consulting service headquartered in Chicago. The company, which he started in 1995 as Current Assets LLC, was one of the fastest growing private companies in the late 1990s. Parson Group specializes in improving organizational effectiveness in the areas of finance, accounting and business systems. With his company, Weinfurter created a new niche in the staffing services market by catering to clients who had high–level staffing and consulting needs.

Personal Life

Daniel Weinfurter was born April 16, 1957, in Milwaukee, Wisconsin, the son of Joseph Thomas and Betty E. (Stanton) Weinfurter. He graduated with a BS/BA degree from Marquette University, in Milwaukee, in 1979. He earned an MBA degree from Marquette in 1984 and did postgraduate work at George Washington University in Washington, D. C. in 1984 and 1985.

Weinfurter began his professional career in 1979 with General Electric Information Services. For the next 11 years he worked for General Electric and Intelogic Trace, Inc. in sales, marketing, and management positions. He joined Altenative Resources Corporation (ARC) in 1990. When he was working for ARC, he developed the idea for his own company, Current Assets LLC, which he founded in 1995.

A Roman Catholic and Democrat, Weinfurter married Martha Marie Brennan on May 14, 1983. They have

(1957-)

Parson Group LLC

Chronology:

Daniel Joseph Weinfurter

1957: Born.

1979: Graduated from Marquette University with a BS/BA degree.

1979: Hired by General Electric Information Services.

1984: Earned MBA from Marquette University.

1989: Joined Alternative Resources Corporation.

1994: Created business plan for Current Assets LLC.

1995: Established Current Assets LLC.

1996: Opened office in Minneapolis.

1997: Changed company name to Parson Group LLC.

2000: Entered partnership with J.D. Edwards.

---

two daughters, Amy Jordan and Andrea Taylor. Weinfurter's recreational interests include running, racquetball, bicycling, golf, and reading. Weinfurter is an active board member of the Chicagoland Chamber of Commerce and the Boys and Girls Club of Chicago.

Career Details

For Weinfurter the road to Parson Group LLC began at General Electric Information Services, in Milwaukee, where he started his career, as a service account representative, in 1979. From that point on, his career path took an upward trajectory. In 1982, he was promoted to senior account representative at General Electric. Continuing his growth within that organization, he became a project manager in Rockville, Maryland. In 1986, he became the acting regional sales manager for General Electric Corporation in Morristown, New Jersey. That same year, he was promoted to district sales manager in Bensonville, Illinois. In 1987, he left General Electric to join Intelogic Trace, Inc., in Schaumberg, Illinois, where he was a regional sales manager. He became area sales manager for the company in 1989.

Later that year, Weinfurter joined Alternative Resources Corporation (ARC), an information staffing company, in Lincolnshire, Illinois. He was hired as the director of business development. In 1990, he was

promoted to vice president of operations. He became president of Alternative Resources Corporation Ventures in 1993.

A former colleague at Alternative once commented that Weinfurter provided the kind of quiet leadership that fosters trust in coworkers. That quality also inspired productivity. In his five years with the company, Weinfurter supervised the opening of offices in 30 new markets. By 1994, when the company went public, revenues had soared to more than $94 million.

However, in 1994, Weinfurter developed an idea that would soon have him leaving ARC to start his own business. The basis of the idea was a market need that he perceived. At the time, established staffing companies were offering generalized staffing and consulting support, or they offered clerical staffing support for accounting departments. Weinfurter observed that few staffing companies could offer more complex and sophisticated help in areas like budget analysis or systems reconstruction. Neither could they provide a temporary replacement for vacant high-level positions. Weinfurter realized there was a large void in the temporary staffing solution marketplace, and he saw an opportunity to start a company that could provide the services of seasoned professionals who could offer accounting and finance operations support and project management to large companies.

The viability of his idea was underscored for him by problems existing within ARC, where Weinfurter had an up-close glimpse of what can happen when successful corporations find themselves with inadequate personnel resources. ARC was a growing company, but its accounting and financial-reporting system couldn't handle the stringent new reporting requirements that came with success. The staff had difficulty meeting deadlines.

Conditions in the corporate world at large were another motivating factor. The corporate downsizing trend in the 1990s had decimated the staffs in the accounting and finance departments of large companies. The idea of outside help from accountants and other professionals began sounding appealing to high-level executives at these companies. So, the need was growing, and the niche was wide-open and ripe for the taking. Weinfurter knew he had to act quickly on his idea.

First, he sat down and composed what was essentially a one-page outline of a business plan in 1994. The plan attracted the interest of two venture capitalists, Samuel P. Chapman and J. Jeffry Louis, who had started a venture capital company called Parson Capital Corp. They wanted to hear more.

All went well when the three men met. The potential investors liked Weinfurter, respected his success at other companies, and, most important of all, they believed his plan had significant potential. They realized that Weinfurter's plan had indeed recognized a new niche.

The business would be called Current Assets LLC, and Chapman and Louis provided $7.2 million funding during its first two years. (Weinfurter contributed another $800,000 to bring the total to $8 million.) In the meantime, Chapman and Louis tried out Weinfurter's idea on high–level executives in the area, who responded positively. After that, they helped Weinfurter design a detailed business plan.

Louis and Chapman, who had numerous contacts in the business community, then set up a board of directors. According to *Inc.* magazine's article in 2000, the high–profile members included "Jerry Pearlman, the former chairman and CEO of Zenith Electronics Corp.; Donald Perkins, the former chairman of Jewel Cos, Inc., one of Chicago's largest grocery chains; and Sam Chapman's father, Alger Chapman, who was vice–chairman of ABN AMRO," the international banking organization.

In July 1995, Weinfurter officially launched Current Assets LLC to provide interim accounting help in the Chicago area. But by the time he launched his service, Weinfurter saw that other companies were already picking up on the idea. Therefore, he implemented some strategies that would make his company different from the others. Most important, Weinfurter decided that Current Assets would not market its employees to customers as a possible temp–to–perm solutions. After all, as Weinfurter pointed out, why would a professional–services firm want its clients to hire away its best people. Also, Weinfurter did not want his company to conduct audits or prepare tax returns. That would have put his company into competition with top accounting firms, and it would have required costly liability insurance. In keeping the overhead down in this fashion, Current Assets could offer more competitive fees.

With everything set in place, Weinfurter next had to find clients. At first, doing so involved the arduous and sometimes tedious process of making "cold calls" to area Fortune 1,000 companies. The board of directors, with all of their contacts, also pitched in. Plus, Chapman and various employees called upon their own contacts to generate referrals. The combined effort and strategy paid off as, in its first year, Current Assets was servicing some of biggest companies in the Chicago area.

Still, Weinfurter did not allow himself any complacency with this early success. He realized he would have to expand the company quickly. After all, he had a good idea, and it would not be long before even more companies would enter the market. What he wanted to do next was establish a national presence and eventually expand into the top 20 markets in the country. The first expansion site chosen was Minneapolis. Weinfurter picked the city in 1995 because it was a relatively small market that was located close to Chicago. In 1996, they opened an office in Dallas. That same year, Weinfurter opened an office in Boston.

Recruiting became Weinfurter's top priority. He frequently travels to interview the best managerial candidates. Realizing just how important good people are to his kind of business, Weinfurter developed an appealing recruiting pitch. His company, he would tell prospective employees, enables accountants to move higher and much quicker than they would in a traditional corporate culture. Current Assets also offered a full–time salary instead of hourly rates as well as equity in the company.

In 1997, Weinfurter, seeing that the accounting–staffing market had indeed become more crowded, implemented several major changes. First, he shifted the company's focus toward high–level consulting. To go along with that, he changed the name of the company to Parson Group LLC. Another motivating factor was the growing number of headhunting services available on the Internet, which cut into his business. Also, the shift toward consulting just seemed to make more sense to him. Earlier in the year, the company had already tried to attract consulting projects. Then, too, customers had always asked his employees to handle more complicated projects. Parson Group LLC also began looking into more complex areas like mergers and acquisitions, integration, risk management, and enterprise resource planning. The company still maintained its staffing business, but it started calling itself a consulting–services company in its new markets. It turned out to be a good move. It brought in $6 million of funding from the Chicago–based Bank One Equity Capital.

Still, the shift in focus involved new concerns. Overhead increased because Weinfurter had to hire more in–house, full–time employees to build a consulting staff. He also realized that it was a risky move, as it is hard to predict market needs. But a year or two after the change, half of the company's revenues was coming from consulting work. At the time, Weinfurter predicted that by the end of 2001 it would account for about three–quarters of its revenues.

By 2000, Weinfurter had met with investment bankers who were interested in seeing the company go public. At the time, Weinfurter felt Parson Group LLC was not ready yet. It still had some more growing to do. And that is what he expected his company to do. He hopes to see it bring in as much as $500 million by 2004. Weinfurter had good reason to be optimistic. In its five years of existence it showed a growth rate of nearly 28,000 percent.

Weinfurter is also taking his company into online world. In September 2001, Parson Group LLC had entered into a strategic partnership with J.D. Edwards and Company, a leading provider of collaborative solutions for the Internet economy. Their alliance, called an Extended Solution partnership, is aimed at helping clients realize lower total cost of ownership and quicker return–on–investment on enterprise software initiatives. More specifically, the new partners intended to provide specialized industry and technical expertise in financial and professional services, business process engineering, systems optimization, and mergers and acquisitions to J.D. Edwards customers worldwide.

Social and Economic Impact

On the surface, it might seem unlikely that someone like Daniel Weinfurter is the founder of what has been called America's fastest growing private company, particularly one that provides high–level financial advice for big companies. After all, he admits that he is not a very good "numbers cruncher." In fact, he says he even has trouble balancing his own checkbook. But what Weinfurter does possess is the ability the grasp the larger picture. Throughout his career, he has been able to recognize new market niches as well as anticipate trends. His remarkably perceptive powers seem to be largely responsible for his company's tremendous growth. Parson Group LLC boasts more than 800 employees, and, in five years, its sales soared from $200,000 to $56 million. Even at the outset, its services had immediate impact on the operations of over 1,000 companies. This dynamic growth resulted in Parson Group being named the number–one Fastest Growing Private Company by *Inc.* magazine in 2000.

From its inception in Chicago, Parson Group LLC has grown to include offices in Atlanta, Boston, Cleveland, Dallas, Denver, Detroit, Houston, Los Angeles, Minneapolis, New York/Northern New Jersey, Santa Ana (CA), San Francisco, and Stamford. Currently, the company serves also 550 national and international clients.

Sources of Information

Contact at: Parson Group LLC
    333 W. Wacker Dr., Ste. 1620
    Chicago, IL 60606
    URL: http://www.parsongroup.com

Bibliography

Caudron, Sharon. "Permanent Solutions for Temporary Staffing." *Controller Magazine.* November 1997. Available at http://www.businessfinancemag.com.

Hansen, Susan, "Ready, Set, Grow." *Inc.* 15 October 2001. Available at www2.inc.com/incmagazine/20745.html.

"J.D. Edwards and Parson Group Enter into Strategic Partnership," *J.D. Edwards Newsroom.* 11 September 2001. Available at http://www.jdedwards.com/NewsRoom/archive/2001/parsongroup.asp

"Parson Group Company Profile." 2001 Available at http://www.parsongroup.com.

"Profile: Board of Directors." 2001. Available at http://www.parsongroup.com/profile_people_board.html.

Jack Welch

(1935-)
General Electric Company

Overview

Jack Welch may be the most respected manager in the business world. It has been estimated that during his tenure as head of General Electric (GE), Welch added $52 billion in market value to his company and, after a tech slump at Cisco, GE is again the world's largest corporation. That is a remarkable turnaround for a man who, during corporate cutbacks, earned the nickname "Neutron Jack" for eliminating 100,000 jobs at GE and radically reorganizing the blue–chip company. But his keen leadership has earned him admiration among his peers as the man they would most want to work for. He has maintained consistent earnings, solid financial performance, and strong commitment to shareholder value. Welch utilized his talents to take GE to the top and into the twenty–first century.

Personal Life

John Francis Welch, Jr. was born November 19, 1935, in Peabody, Massachusetts. He grew up in the small city of Salem, Massachusetts, in a solidly working class Roman Catholic neighborhood. His father, John Sr., was a conductor for the Boston & Maine Railroad and was away from home a great deal. Welch has credited his mother, Grace, with playing the most important role in his life. As he has said in an interview in *Fortune*, "Don't get me started on my mother; she's my whole game." She cheered her son on in sports and fostered his self–confidence, helping him to overcome a serious stammer that she insisted was not a speech impediment but the result of Welch's hyperactive brain that was working faster than his mouth.

Jack Welch. (General Electric.)

Though Welch was an only child, the Welch extended family was his neighborhood: "Kids that didn't have anything," Welch remembered. "You were lucky if you had food on the table." The center of Welch's youth was a makeshift park created from an excavated gravel pit. In the "pit" Welch played basketball, baseball, and hockey in tough competitions. As Welch recalls, "We were jocks of sorts. I mean, we played ball countless hours, played street hockey all night. That was everything. Sports were everything." It was there that Welch learned how to compete, to hate losing, and to negotiate for playing space among the bigger kids. A friend of Welch's at the time explained that the lessons learned helped ensure later success: "Hey, we can do anything. Nothing can be as tough as going to the Pit." Welch attended Salem High School, excelling at sports. His class voted him the "most talkative and noisiest boy." In his school's literary magazine Welch recorded his "repressed desire: to make a million."

Failing to win a Navy ROTC scholarship, which would have paid for a private college, Welch instead attended the University of Massachusetts. His mother wanted him to become a doctor or a priest. He wanted to be a great hockey player, but he was not fast enough and instead took up engineering because, as he recalls, "we only had one person in our whole family that was at all educated beyond high school. He was called an engineer, and he worked at a power plant. So I went to engineering school." Although he was able to graduate with

honors, Welch remembers his college years as a time more devoted to parties and having a good time than for studying. He went on to get his Ph.D. in chemical engineering at the University of Illinois in 1960. Out of three job offers, Welch chose General Electric's engineered materials plant at Pittsfield, Massachusetts. As Welch remembers, "It was like going home in a way. That may sound ridiculous, but in those days that was kind of important." Welch steadily climbed the GE corporate ladder to become in 1981, at age 46, the youngest chairman and CEO in the company's history.

Welch married Carolyn Osburn in 1959, whom he divorced in 1987. He married Jane Beasley in 1989. He has four children: Katherine, John, Anne, and Mark. An avid sportsman, Welch is a devoted golfer, and the lessons he has learned in sports competition have transferred to his business approach, which thrives on challenges and a commitment "to fight like hell before I lose." A demanding and relentless supervisor, Welch has succeeded in creating an extremely competitive structure at GE in pursuit of what he has described in an interview for *Fortune* as the "boundaryless" workplace in which the traditional lines separating workers and departments are blurred in order to expedite the delivery of services and products. Welch's relentless pace was slowed in 1995 when he was diagnosed with heart disease and underwent successful triple bypass surgery. Yet Welch seems reluctant to step down as head of GE, a position he has held since 1981 and repeatedly states his intentions to remain until the year 2000.

Career Details

When Welch came to work for GE, he was about as far from the center of power in the giant company as he could be. He worked in the chemical development area of the organization, charged with developing new chemical businesses. Welch also contradicted the image of the corporate team player. As one of his colleagues recalled, Welch was "the least typical GE guy. Definitely a maverick in his style." Yet Welch's skills as a scientist were quickly complemented by a business insight that enabled him to understand not just a product's design but the sales techniques and production steps required for a product to find a market niche. The small scale and independence of his early experience with GE suited his style and ability and helped to determine his future idea of the giant GE empire. As he revealed in an *Industry Week* interview, "My only business experience came from being an entrepreneur in a small business outside the mainstream of GE: a family grocery store, if you will—the plastics business. My technician and I were partners [working] on the same thing. We had two people, then four people, then eight people, then 12 people, and now we're a $5 billion business! But it started that way. So that's my vision of how people should communicate. Everyone's involved. Everyone knows. Everyone's got a piece of the action. The organization's flat. All these things are from when I was 26 years old." Within three years of Welch's appointment as general manager of GE's worldwide plastics division in 1968, he had turned the fledgling division into a $400 million–a–year business.

Promotions followed rapidly. He was named vice–president in 1972, and in 1977 he was appointed to head GE's consumers goods and services division. He became a vice–chairman in 1979 and was appointed to replace Reginald Jones as GE's chairman in 1981, becoming the youngest CEO in GE's history. Welch found himself managing, instead of a "family grocery store," an industrial giant of diverse businesses that made everything from light bulbs to nuclear weapons. In the 1970s, GE had led U. S. business in hiring huge staffs of strategic planners and, although GE enjoyed sales of $25 billion and profits, which Welch helped triple in eight years, he feared that the company's size and bureaucracy would cost GE flexibility in the modern marketplace. Welch embarked on a radical restructuring, dividing GE into winning divisions that were number one or two in their markets and losing divisions, mostly the company's older, slower–growing manufacturing concerns, and began to sell them off. Welch closed 73 plants and facilities, sold 232 businesses and product lines, and laid off more than 132,000 workers, more than a quarter of GE's labor force. Although GE pioneered generous severance packages and retraining for laid–off workers, Welch was nicknamed "Neutron Jack," an allusion to the nuclear weapon that killed people rather than buildings. Welch continued to defend the move as essential in establishing GE's productivity and flexibility in the rapidly changing future marketplace. By cutting bureaucratic layers and achieving a flatter organization, Welch showed how even a corporate giant like GE could imitate the aggressive innovation of Welch's early experience of turning the company into what has been labeled in an *Industry Week* article a "$60 billion family grocery business."

To reach that goal, Welch cut the work force and reorganized GE's divisions in such a way that management encouraged rather than inhibited product development. Success took some time. By 1984 sales were still only about $28 billion, and annual growth rate in labor productivity was a meager 1.9 percent. However, by the end of Welch's first decade at the helm, GE recorded sales of $58.4 billion and an annual growth rate of over 8 percent, a third better than inflation. By 1999 sales grew to $100.5 billion. Welch did not just cut GE's assets but bought $25 billion worth of new companies, including RCA, the New York investment bank Kidder Peabody, and Hungary's Tungsram lighting company. The 1986 $6.4 billion acquisition of RCA, which included its National Broadcasting Company (NBC), at that time was considered the largest merger in business history outside of the oil industry. The acquisition also broadened GE's base within the services and technology industries, the two growth areas that Welch anticipated would dominate

Chronology:
Jack Welch

1935: Born.

1960: Began career with General Electric (GE).

1968: Promoted as general manager of GE's worldwide plastics division.

1973: Assigned vice–president and chief executive of GE's components and materials group.

1977: Made senior vice–president, consumer goods and services division.

1979: Promoted to GE vice–chairman and executive officer.

1981: Named GE's youngest chairman and chief executive officer.

1986: GE acquired RCA and the National Broadcasting Company (NBC).

1999: Announced plans to retire in 2000 or 2001.

1999: Launched e–commerce initiative for GE.

2001: Retired as chairman and CEO of General Electric.

the future business landscape. Welch had proven that he could not only trim his company down but boost its sales dramatically as well. To Welch, size was synonymous with "sloth, systems, and smugness rather than speed, simplicity, and self–confidence." He disliked talking about the size of GE, claiming to "hate" what a fat bureaucracy could represent. But Welch also admitted that the key to running a company the size of GE was to leverage it rather than manage it.

Leverage was the key to Welch's eventual globalization of GE. According to a *Fortune* article, Welch successfully leveraged his unique human capital and talented management to become a global corporation. Part of the company's eventual transformation to a global presence began with a corporate change in mindset. Up until the early 1990s, GE had looked at the rest of the world only in terms of an export market, and the company had relatively small holdings in Europe. Management later claimed that GE's initial deals with Europe were "defensive," in part because the company had not yet figured out how to transfer their unique brand of management talent overseas. The initial European investments lost money, and Welch was reluctant in the early 1990s to pursue further European ventures. But a European recession caused prices to drop and GE European revenues increased from $9.1 billion to $14.1 billion from 1994 to 1995. Welch and GE eventually smoothed out their European acquisitions processes, using planned restructuring processes and cohesive sales forces to better facilitate overseas acquisitions. Among some of the techniques that GE applied in such acquisitions was the identification of "blockers" (people who impede progress and who are to be removed) and "high–pots" (people to keep). The head of one GE European holdings claimed that these innovations were not necessarily unique to GE, but the speed with which they were implemented was a GE trademark. Welch also saw the globalization of GE as a willingness to "go where the best brains are," whether that meant "using Russian engineering and Indian software— not to arbitrate labor costs but because these are the best people you can find."

Welch introduced other unique management techniques, which were effective both in GE's global and U.S. companies. One corporate innovation, titled the "Work–Out," required that bosses solve problems on the spot without resorting to haggling, meetings, or further delay. The concept was considered cutting edge, particularly in Europe. Under Welch, GE management also pushed their employees to think beyond a predefined box and forced them to consider broader scenarios, such as greater growth than initially predicted. In 1995 the company also introduced an internal standard called "Six Sigma," meaning that there were to be no more than 3.4 defects per billion. Defects could include anything within the range of manufacturing processes, billing, or loan processing.

In 2001 Welch spearheaded a company initiative to delve into e–commerce possibilities, calling it "the biggest revolution in business in our lifetimes—and I've got all the tools to go after it." Welch claimed that online business would change many things, including relationships with employees, customers, and suppliers. Welch declared the worldwide web would save $10 billion in sales and overhead costs. GE has a $7 billion e–business, which is an increase of $1 billion since 1999; however, critics say it's too early to draw any conclusions regarding the bottom line.

Welch tapped star pupil Jeffrey Immelt to succeed him and stepped down as chairman and CEO of General Electric in April 2001. In September 2001, Welch released his autobiography *Jack, Straight from The Gut*. The book deal garnered a 7.1 million advance, earmarked for charity, and jumped straight to number one on bestseller lists including *The New York Times* and *The Wall Street Journal*. Additionally, Welch relishes the challenges of his new career, consulting to a small group of Fortune 500 business CEOs.

Welch's success routinely allowed him to be listed among America's preeminent business gurus. It has been estimated that, during his tenure as the head of GE, Welch added $52 billion in market value to his company. In the late 1990s, GE was the world's most valuable company in terms of stock market capitalization, and it ranked fifth in the Fortune 500. As a research analyst reported to *Kiplinger's Personal Finance Magazine*, "The companies that have the technological skills and the manufacturing expertise are the ones that are going to come out ahead. That is probably the most impressive area of GE—its ability to constantly drive down the cost structure and improve productivity. And for that, Welch is the key."

Social and Economic Impact

Welch has succeeded in radically transforming GE as a giant and venerable company, founded by Thomas A. Edison, allowing it to continue its technological innovations that have invented and manufactured products that Americans use in almost every aspect of modern life. For example, GE's plastics division manufactures almost all of the plastic in personal computers (PC). Like IBM, GE has been synonymous with affecting the course of modern electrical and electronic innovations. As a self–styled corporate outsider and maverick, Welch has shown how modern business can be re–created in a leaner, more flexible structure to encourage productivity and change. As one of the world's largest corporations, GE plays a major role in the U.S. and world economy. As GE showed through the 1980s, modern corporate retooling can be painful. In GE's case more than 130,000 jobs were cut. But Welch had the courage to go through with painful, short–term cuts for long–term productivity and growth that could add even more jobs and a higher standard of living. The new structure at GE has proven to be a model for all other modern businesses.

As Welch explained in an *Industry Week* interview, "The hero is the one with the ideas. So my job is to find great ideas, exaggerate them, and spread them like hell around the business with the speed of light." Welch has made sure that the heroes with those new ideas, whether for new products or increased productivity, can emerge and that his company can act on their inspiration. Welch has shown how a modern corporate giant like GE can still achieve an informality and a sense that everyone is involved in the common goal, an atmosphere that more and more will be needed as large multinational corporations enter the twenty–first century. As Welch has taught U. S. business, "A successful leader can shock an organization and lead its recovery. An unsuccessful leader will shock an organization and paralyze it. So organizations constantly need to be regenerated. There's a constant flow of ideas, excitement, and energy that has to be put into an organization. And it has to keep getting better. The bar has to keep going up."

Sources of Information

Contact at: General Electric Company
    3135 Easton Tpke.
    Fairfield, CT 06431–0001
    Business Phone: (203)373–2211
    URL: http://www.ge.com

Bibliography

"A Bright Idea for GE." *Business 2.0*, March 2001. Available at http://www.business2.com.

Day, Charles R., and Polly LaBarre. "GE: Just Your Average Everyday $60 Billion Family Grocery Store." *Industry Week*, 2 May 1994.

Dolan, Kerry A. "The Jack Factor." *Forbes*, 27 December 1999.

Financial Executive, May–June 1996.

"General Electric Co–Jeffrey R. Immelt Named President and Chairman–Elect." *Market News Publishing*, 1 May 2001.

"General Electric Company." *Hoover's Online*. Available at http://www.hoovers.com.

Goldsmith, Jill. "GE Chief Welch to Retire in 2001." *Variety*, 8 November 1999.

Fortune.com, 17 September 2001. Available from http://www.fortune.com.

"Jack Welch: One Big Pair of Vacant Shoes." *Business Week*, 15 November 1999.

LaBarre, Polly. "The Light's Still On At This Family Grocer.'" *Industry Week*, 20 November 1995.

Loeb, Marshall. "Jack Welch Lets Fly On Budgets, Bonuses, and Buddy Boards." *Fortune*, 29 May 1995.

McClenahen, John S. "CEO of the Decade." *Industry Week*, 15 November 1999.

Michaels, James W. "Jack The Elephant Tamer." *Forbes*, 10 October 1994.

Morris, Betsy. "The Wealth Builders." *Fortune*, 11 December 1995.

"A New Chapter for Welch." *The Financial Times*, 9 May 2001.

"Person of the Year 2000." *Time.com*, 2000. Available at http://www.time.com.

Sloan, Allen, "Judging GE's Jack Welch." *Newsweek*, 15 November 1999.

Stewart, Thomas A. "See Jack. See Jack Run Europe." *Fortune*, 27 September 1999.

"Welch's March to the South." *Business Week*, 6 December 1999.

Margaret Whitman

(1957-)
eBay Inc.

Overview

In 1997 a renowned corporate scout approached marketing whiz Margaret (Meg) Whitman to work for an unknown "online auction community." Whitman was recruited to eBay after a blue chip background at Hasbro, Disney, and Bain & Co. Whitman herself couldn't believe she'd relocate her family across the country to work for the fledgling, black–and–white auction site with 19 employees, but eventually she realized eBay's real potential. Whitman turned eBay from a relatively successful Internet start–up into one of the only profitable Internet companies. Less than two years after taking on eBay, she became the first female Internet billionaire.

Personal Life

Meg Whitman lives with her husband, Griffith R. Harsh IV, a neurosurgeon at Stanford University. They have two sons, ages 13 and 16, and enjoy fly–fishing in their spare time. The family frequently travels to her husband's family farm in Sweetwater, Tennessee. Whitman, who has traded Beanie Babies and Pokemon cards with her children on eBay, named her Burger King Mr. Potato Head as her most treasured collectible. Whitman was named to the board of directors of Goldman Sachs, a leading global investment banking and securities firm.

Whitman was born in Cold Spring Harbor on the north shore of Long Island, New York, in 1957. She is the youngest child of a businessman and an adventurous homemaker. When she was six, Whitman's mother packed her and her siblings into a camper along with a

family friend with five children of her own and took them on a three–month camping excursion through Canada to Alaska. When the kids got unruly, Whitman's mom made them get out and run ahead of the camper, while she trailed them until they got tired. Occasionally, truckers would ask if anything was wrong. "We finally put a sign on the back of the camper that said, 'We're O.K.,'" Whitman related to Laura M. Holson in the *New York Times*.

In 1977 Whitman graduated from New Jersey's Princeton University with a degree in economics. Originally a pre–med major at Princeton, Whitman told *Fast Company*, "I took calculus, chemistry, and physics my first year. I survived. But I didn't enjoy it. Of course, chemistry, calculus, and physics have nothing to do with being a doctor, but if you're 17 years old, you think, This is what being a doctor is going to be about. After that, I had to find something else to do. I began selling advertising for a magazine that was published by Princeton undergrads. It was more fun than physics."She then obtained a master's degree in business administration from Harvard University in 1979. Out of school, she landed a job as a brand assistant with Proctor & Gamble in Cincinnati, Ohio, and worked her way up to brand manager. In 1981 Whitman moved to San Francisco when her husband, a neurosurgeon, began a residency at the University of California. Whitman then found work as a consultant for Bain & Company, where she stayed for the next eight years.

Career Details

In 1989 Whitman became senior vice president of marketing at the Walt Disney Company, where she helped the firm acquire *Discover* magazine. After her husband took a new position as codirector of the brain tumor program at Massachusetts General Hospital in Boston in 1992, she accepted a job as president of Stride Rite Shoes in Lexington, Massachusetts. This children's shoe manufacturer also produces Sperry topsiders and Keds sneakers. In 1995 she left that post to become CEO of Florists'Transworld Delivery (FTD), an alliance of commercial florists. There, she faced the challenge of transforming it to a privately held company. This met with much resistance from higher–ups, and in addition, the federation was facing new competition from Internet floral delivery services.

In 1997 Whitman changed jobs again to go to Hasbro, Inc., one of the largest toy and game manufacturers in America. She was hired as general manager of the Playskool division, the profitable umbrella under which many of the firm's best–known toys reside, including Mr. Potato Head and the Teletubbies. She would not stay there long, though. In November of 1997, a headhunter told Whitman about a job with an Internet start–up in Silicon Valley. Reluctant to uproot her husband and two sons, she turned down the suggestion. However, after vis-

Margaret Whitman. (Reuters Newsmedia Inc./Corbis/Jeff Christensen.)

iting the offices of online auction site eBay in San Jose, she packed up and headed West in February of 1998. "There's no substitute in the land–based world for eBay," she remarked to Kathleen Melymuka in *Computerworld*. "I just had an overwhelming instinct that this thing was going to be huge."

eBay was launched in September 1995 by Pierre Omidyar, a computer programmer in San Jose, California, as a way for his girlfriend, a Pez candy dispenser collector, to find other collectors to buy and sell to. The eBay premise: For a $3.00 fee to eBay, a seller describes an item and sets a minimum bid; then buyers have opportunities to outbid each other until the auction expires,

Chronology:
Margaret Whitman

1956: Born.

1977: Earned B.A. in economics, Princeton University.

1979: Graduated with M.B.A. from Harvard Business School.

1979: Became brand assistant at Proctor & Gamble.

1981: Made vice president at Bain & Co.

1989: Named vice president of Marketing at Walt Disney Company.

1992: Took position as President of Stride Right.

1995: Became president and CEO of FTD.

1997: Worked as general manager of Preschool Division at Hasbro, Inc.

1998: Named president and CEO of eBay, Inc.

with the item going to the highest bidder. eBay later started taking an average 6 percent commission. Visitors to the site became known as "eBayers," and by 1997 eBayers were spending more time on eBay than the average shopper on any other site. The company became too big to handle, so Omidyar sold part of the company to a capital investment firm, who in turn hired Whitman.

Whitman took charge of eBay and started making changes to the company in the interest of profitability. "EBay comes from the roots of an open, sort of libertarian, point of view," she said in *Fortune*. She almost immediately launched an advertising plan for eBay, which up to then had grown only by word of mouth. She then initiated eBay's purchase of Butterfield & Butterfield, a 134–year–old traditional auction house in San Francisco, to add to eBay's profits. In September 1998 she took eBay "public," selling 6.5 million shares to the public in the stock market, which also increased the company's worth.

When Whitman joined eBay as CEO in 1998, she was given options to buy 14.4 million shares of company stock at pennies per share. She chose to exercise these options exactly one month after joining the company and ended up realizing a paper profit of $42.7 million—the difference between her share option price and the proposed IPO stock price—when she took the company public some six months later. But she made her real money

later when she sold all 1.8 million shares that vested March 1, 1999—600,000 in 1999 and 1.2 million in 2000—at prices of between $55 and $171.

Some investors chose to interpret Whitman's readiness to cash in on her eBay stock options as a demonstration of lack of faith in her company, but others, noting that cash compensations for dotcom CEOs tend to be very meager, argued that a certain amount of cashing out was to be expected. Meanwhile, *Forbes* reported in October 2000 that Whitman's salary had risen by 37 percent in 2000, but that she had suffered a paper loss of $900 million during the dotcom shakeout of the previous year.

Although UCLA (University of California at Los Angeles)sociology professor Peter Kollock told *Fortune* that he considered auction fraud a small problem, the National Consumers League's Internet Fraud Watch rated auction fraud the No. 1 problem on the Web, according to *Fortune*. Whitman even had to pay the difference, when a live charity auction was held on the *Today* show and fraudulent bidders drove the price of a jacket up to $200,000 (the highest legitimate bid was only $11,400). To combat the problem, Whitman initiated a "comprehensive trust and safety program" at eBay. It granted eBayers insurance options and the opportunity to have their identity verified by a credit–rating firm. "We have a real corporate feeling that our users need to be treated with respect...," she told the National Press Club in 1999.

There were also occasions when technical glitches caused eBay to shut down. In August of 2000 eBay had to switch to backup servers after auctions were stopped for 35 minutes. But in 1999 the site was down for 22 hours due to a system crash. Tens of thousands of outraged eBayers flooded the site's support board with messages. Whitman responded by closing the board completely, a decision for which eBay was criticized. "There was a joke going around: 'I guess there are no more problems at eBay,'" Scott Samuel, president of Honesty Communications, which measures traffic on online auctions, told *Fortune*. "These are your customers—you don't do that."

Still, in 2001, when most dotcoms were sitting in the doldrums, eBay was making money hand over fist. The company's profits for 2000 had risen nearly 400 percent, to $48.3 million, while registered users rose 125 percent, to 22.4 million. And although eBay's stock price suffered like every other Net stock in 2000, by early 2001, its shares were up 30 percent, unlike those of Amazon, Yahoo, and AOL.

Social and Economic Impact

Ebay's top auctioneer Meg Whitman is a Silicon Valley superpower, helping build eBay from trading Pez dispensers to a $5 billion dollar behemoth. With 34 million registered users, eBay is the world's largest online marketplace for sales of goods and services by a varied community of businesses and individuals. It handles 79 million transactions per quarter and lists more than 5 million items.

Somehow, eBay managed to escape the dotcom downturn, coming out ahead in its second quarter projections for 2001, and according to Forrester Research, it could become a $52 billion dollar industry by 2002. Meg Whitman, who owns about 4 percent of the company she runs, is a multibillionaire and one of the world's wealthiest women CEOs.

Showing that eBay also has a philanthropic side, eBay began the Auction for America after the terrorist attacks on New York and Washington in September 2001, which allowed sellers to list items free of charge, and upon the sale of an item, 100 percent of its value goes to the September 11th Fund. Ebay's goal is to raise $100 million in 100 days, which, coincidentally, ends on December 25th, 2001. Some of the items auctioned have been donated by such public figures as New York Governor Pataki, who put up a picture of himself and Joe DiMaggio after the Yankees had won the World Series, and Andre Agassi, who has a signed tennis racket. Also up for auction is a U.S. flag that flew at the Capitol, signed by every member of Congress. "So we've got musicians, singers, congressmen, politicians, and then every average American. A mom has started a virtual lemonade stand on Auction for America, auctioning off virtual cups of lemonade, and her daughter's artwork," Whitman added in an interview by *FoxNews.com*.

Sources of Information

Contact at: eBay Inc.
    2145 Hamilton Ave.
    San Jose, CA 95125
    Business Phone: (408)588–7400
    URL: http://www.ebay.com

Bibliography

Business Week, 4 October 1999. Available at http://www.businessweek.com.

CBS MarketWatch, 4 October 1999. Available at http:/ /cbs .marketwatch.com.

"The Charlie Rose Interview: eBay's Meg Whitman." *Cisco Systems*, 2001.

Chief Executive (U.S.), January 2001.

"A Conversation with eBay's Meg Whitman" *Business 2.0*, 3 October 2001. Available at http://www.business2.com.

"Ebay Defies Dot–Com Gravity." *The Industry Standard Magazine*, 19 July 2001.

eBay Inc., 4 October 1999. Available at http://www.ebay.com.

"Ebay, Inc." *Hoover's*, November 2001. Available at http://www.hoovers.com.

"Face Time With Meg Whitman." *Fast Company*, May 2001. Available at http://www.fastcompany.com.

Forbes, 26 July 1999; 9 October 2000.

Fortune, 5 July 1999; 19 March 2001.

"Meg Whitman." *TIME Digital Archive*, 2001.

"Meg Whitman Joins Goldman Sachs' Board of Directors." *The Goldman Sachs Group, Inc.*, 1 October 2001. Available at http://www.gs.com.

"Meg Whitman, President & CEO of eBay." *FoxNew.com*, 28 September 2001. Available at http://www.foxnews.com.

"Meg Whitman Speaks." *The Industry Standard Magazine*, 7 October 2001.

Newsmakers 2000. Issue 3. Gale Group, 2000.

"Q & A with eBay CEO Meg Whitman." *Silicon Valley.com*, 27 May 2001.

"Q & A with Meg Whitman." *Worth Magazine*, May 2001.

Tech Law Journal, 4 October 1999. Available at http://www.techlawjournal.com.

Vanity Fair, October 1999.

Wired, 4 October 1999. Available at http://www.wired.com.

ZDNN Online, 4 October 1999. Available at http://www.zdnet.com/zdnn.

Oprah Winfrey

(1954-)
Harpo, Inc.

Overview

Oprah Winfrey revolutionized the talk show market with her unique and natural style and rose to become the host of the most watched daytime show on television, which boasts 22 million viewers daily (three–fourths of whom are women). She is the first African American to own her own TV studio. The multitalented Winfrey is also a millionaire businesswoman, a talented actress, owner of a movie production company, and committed philanthropist.

Personal Life

Oprah Gail Winfrey was born January 29, 1954, on a farm in Kosciusko, Mississippi. She was supposed to be Orpah, from the Bible, but for some unknown reason, she has been known as Oprah almost from birth. Her unmarried parents, Vernon Winfrey and Vernita Lee, separated soon after she was born, leaving her to be raised by her maternal grandmother. "She certainly wasn't an educated woman, but she taught me the shape of letters, and she taught me my Bible stories," Winfrey recalled in *Life* magazine. By the time she was six, Winfrey had moved to Milwaukee to live with her mother. During this time, she was sexually abused by a teenage cousin and then by other male relatives and friends. "I was, and am, severely damaged by the experience [of abuse]. All the years that I convinced myself I was healed, I wasn't," she told *Redbook*. "I still carried the shame, and I unconsciously blamed myself for those men's acts."

Winfrey had a contentious relationship with her mother, often acting out as a bid to gain attention. Once

she faked a robbery in her house, smashed glasses, feigned amnesia, and stole her mother's purse, all because she wanted newer, more stylish glasses. It seemed Winfrey was heading down a road of destruction until her mother sent her to live with her father in Nashville at age 14. Winfrey said her father saved her life. He was very strict and provided her with guidance, structure, rules, and books. He required his daughter to complete weekly book reports, and she went without dinner until she learned five new vocabulary words each day. She joined her school's drama club and became a prize–winning orator, winning a $1,000 college scholarship after delivering a short speech entitled "The Negro, the Constitution, and the United States" to 10,000 Elks Club members in Philadelphia. She was the first black woman to win Nashville's Miss Fire Prevention title. In 1971 she was named Miss Black Tennessee. In 1976 she graduated with a degree in speech communications and theater from Tennessee State University.

In 1986 Winfrey received a special award from the Chicago Academy for the Arts for unique contributions to the city's artistic community and was named Woman of Achievement by the National Organization of Women. The *Oprah Winfrey Show* won several Emmys for Best Talk Show, and Winfrey was honored as Best Talk Show Host.

In addition to her numerous daytime Emmys, Winfrey has received other awards. In 1993 Winfrey won the Horatio Alger Award "given to those who overcome adversity to become leaders in their fields," according to *Jet* magazine. She was inducted into the Television Hall of Fame in 1994 and received the George Foster Peabody Individual Achievement Award, one of broadcasting's most coveted awards, following the 1995–1996 season. Further, she received the IRTS Gold Medal Award, was named one of America's 25 Most Influential People of 1996 by *Time* magazine, and was included on Marjabelle Young Stewart's 1996 list of most polite celebrities. In 1997 Winfrey received TV Guide's Television Performer of the Year Award and was named favorite Female Television Performer at the 1997 People's Choice Awards. In 1998 *Entertainment Weekly* named Winfrey the most powerful person in show business.

Winfrey has used her popularity and influence to advocate for political causes as well. In 1991 the tragic story of a four–year–old Chicago girl's molestation and murder prompted Winfrey, a former abuse victim, to propose federal child protection legislation designed to keep nationwide records on convicted abusers. She did this with the help of former Illinois governor, James Thompson. In addition, Winfrey pursued a ruling that would guarantee strict sentencing of individuals convicted of child abuse. The result was a bill signed by President Clinton that allows child care providers to check the background of prospective employees.

Winfrey resides with her partner, Stedman Graham, in a condominium on Chicago's Gold Coast. She also

Oprah Winfrey. (Archive Photos, Inc./Victor Malafronte.)

owns a house in Tennessee and a Wisconsin condo. In 2001 she purchased a 42–acre seaside estate on the Santa Barbara coast for $50 million. She volunteers time with a variety of nonprofit organizations, churches, shelters, and youth programs.

Career Details

While in college, Winfrey already knew what she would do—pursue a career in broadcasting. As a freshman in college, she was twice offered a job by the Nashville CBS affiliate. Initially, Winfrey refused both overtures, but on the advice of a speech teacher, who reminded her that job offers from CBS were "the reason people go to college," she decided to give the station a try. She became, at age 19 and still a college sophomore, the coanchor of the evening news. When she left Tennessee State, Winfrey headed to Baltimore to become a reporter and coanchor of ABC affiliate WJZ–TV. The station sent her to New York for a beauty makeover, which Winfrey believes was her assistant news director's attempt to "make her Puerto Rican." She also attributes the makeover to an incident when she was told her "hair's too thick, nose is too wide, and chin's too big."

Nonetheless, Winfrey continued to excel. Around 1977 she became a cohost on the *Baltimore Is Talking* show, which, under her leadership, boasted better ratings than Phil Donahue's talk show. After seven years in Bal-

Chronology:
Oprah Winfrey

1954: Born.

1984: Became anchor of *A.M. Chicago*.

1985: Made acting debut in *The Color Purple*.

1986: Debuted *Oprah Winfrey Show* nationally.

1986: Formed Harpo, Inc. production company.

1988: Took over ownership of her show.

1990: Ranked third on *Forbes* list of richest entertainers.

1992: Named highest paid entertainer in the United States.

1996: Began on–air book club.

1998: Named the most powerful person in show business by *Entertainment Weekly*.

1999: Created 12–part series *Oprah Goes Online*.

2000: Launched a new Hearst publication, *O*, a lifestyle magazine.

---

timore, Winfrey was hired by the general manager of WLS–TV, ABC's Chicago affiliate, after he saw Winfrey in an audition tape sent in by her producer.

Winfrey seemed to have a magic touch that could turn humdrum programs into interesting shows with solid ratings. In January 1984 she became anchor of the ailing *A.M. Chicago*, a morning talk show that consistently placed last in the ratings. Winfrey did a complete overhaul of the show, changing its focus to current and controversial topics. The effect was immediate: one month later the show was ranked even with Donahue's program. Three months later it had inched ahead. In September 1985 it was renamed the *Oprah Winfrey Show* and was expanded to one hour. In a matter of months, Winfrey's show was syndicated to television stations in more than 120 American cities. Subsequently, Donahue moved to New York. Just a year after the show was renamed, it made its national debut, and within five months it was rated the third most popular show in syndication—after the game shows *Wheel of Fortune* and *Jeopardy*. Moreover, it was the number one talk show, reaching upwards of 10 million people daily in 192 cities.

"When I first got the job, I was just happy to be on TV," Winfrey told *Jet* magazine. "But as the years

evolved, I grew and wanted to say something without the show, not just be a television announcer or a television performer, but I wanted to say something meaningful to the American public and culture."

The tremendous popularity of her program soon gave Winfrey these opportunities. When Quincy Jones saw her show in 1985, for example, he immediately thought of casting her in a movie he was coproducing with director Stephen Spielberg. *The Color Purple*, based on Alice Walker's novel and starring Whoopi Goldberg, featured Winfrey as Sofia, a proud, assertive woman. Critics praised her performance, and she was nominated for an Academy Award. Though Winfrey had never had any formal acting lessons and little exposure to the theater, she enjoyed acting and went on to take other significant parts.

This exposure piqued Winfrey's interest in television and cinematic productions, prompting her to form her own production company, Harpo, Inc., in August 1986. Harpo has produced several television programs based on stories written by black authors, including *The Wedding* and *Before Women Had Wings*. Winfrey once told *Ms.* magazine that "I'm starting a minority training program ... specifically to bring more people of color into the film and television industry as producers."

Winfrey has committed to stay with her daytime show—which has outperformed every other syndicated talk show in television history—at least through the 2004 season. In a press release, Winfrey noted, "I am finally at a point in my life where I'm doing the kind of shows I've always wanted to do, helping people see themselves more clearly and to make choices that lead to more fulfilled lives. We're still running on." In 1996 and 1997 she was third on the *Forbes* list of the world's highest–paid entertainers, after grossing a combined total of $201 million, and in 2001 she was listed among the 10 most influential people in publishing. In 2001, with an income of $900 million, she placed 250 on the *Forbes* list of the 400 richest people in America.

Winfrey purchased the movie and television rights to several books, including Toni Morrison's *Paradise*, and has an exclusive agreement to produce feature films for the Walt Disney Motion Pictures Group. The first film under the agreement was the 1998 release of Toni Morrison's best–selling novel *Beloved*. In addition to serving as producer, Winfrey also starred in the film, and its commercial failure wounded Winfrey deeply. "I felt like I was behind a wall," Winfrey told *Newsweek*. "I could hear people laughing, and I could feel that I should be happy, but I wasn't because I was so deeply saddened." The film made $23 million, just half of what it cost to make.

Winfrey worked through her despondence by working harder. In late 1998 Winfrey became involved with the formation of Oxygen Media, which includes a cable television station aimed at women, and debuted in February 2000. In conjunction with Oxygen, Winfrey created a series *Oprah Goes Online*, detailing her adventures with friend Gayle King as they learn how to use the Internet. Since its initial debut, the Oxygen Network has stumbled in the ratings, and Winfrey has become less involved in the project. In addition to her media projects, in 1999 Winfrey joined the faculty of Northwestern University's Kellogg Graduate School of Management to teach the course "Dynamics of Leadership." Winfrey's partner, Stedman Graham, is the coteacher. Needing to lighten her daily schedule, Winfrey stepped down from her teaching position in 2001 but is reworking her curriculum for publication on the Internet.

In April 2000 Winfrey was highly successful in launching a lifestyle magazine for women called *O, The Oprah Winfrey Magazine*, with a subscription base of 2.5 million readers. According to Winfrey's website, http://www.oprah.com, *O* "gives confident, smart women the tools they need to explore and reach for their dreams, to express their individual style, and to make choices that will lead to happier more fulfilled lives."

Social and Economic Impact

Winfrey cultivated a reputation for championing causes in her programs and ventures that other leading media and entertainment companies ignore. She is most interested in productions that no one else will do because the topics are not sensational enough. Jeffrey Jacobs, Winfrey's lawyer, manager, and chief adviser, told *Ms.*: "Because of our economic status, and because of Winfrey's other talents, we're going to bring things to the screen that no one else will be able to do ... She can develop or buy something that no one else will think is commercially viable because she thinks the message is important and people should see it.... If we can make money, great. And if we don't, well, there are other reasons to do projects besides making money."

One of the most influential projects Winfrey has tackled is literacy. The on–air reading club she started in September 1996, "Oprah's Book Club," boosted book sales so dramatically that Winfrey quickly became the most important book marketer in any communications medium. Books featured on her show have often been catapulted to the top of the best–sellers list—all the more significant because her choices are often "literary" novels that would not normally attract a mass audience. "Don't confuse Winfrey with Diet Coke," wrote Martha Bayles in *The New York Times Book Review*. "For all her power, she is not part of some blockbuster machine.... On the contrary, she focuses on a category of books voted least likely to succeed in the marketplace.... [Perhaps Oprah's success shows] the difference between pandering to the lowest common denominator and offering people something uplifting."

"Doing this book club has given me the courage to pursue the things I care about," Winfrey told *Life* mag-

azine. That courage has led to many philanthropic endeavors. She established Oprah's Angel Network in 1997. In its inaugural year, Oprah's Angel Network raised over $3.5 million to fund college scholarships for students with financial needs. Beginning in April 2000, the Angel Network has been handing out "Use Your Life" awards every Monday on Winfrey's television show. The awards of $100,000 each are given to people who use their lives to better the lives of others. Winfrey has also entered a partnership with Habitat for Humanity, which has 10,000 volunteers helping to build houses for impoverished Americans throughout the country. She is helping minority students get a better education through her involvement with A Better Chance, a Boston–based privately funded program that provides bright inner–city youth with the opportunity to attend college preparatory schools. She gives proceeds from her inspirational video "Oprah: Make the Connection" to A Better Chance. In June 2001 Winfrey did a tour of self–help seminars entitled "Live Your Best Life." In September 2001 she cohosted a memorial service held at Yankee Stadium for the victims of the terrorist attacks on the World Trade Center on September 11, 2001.

Winfrey has made generous contributions to charitable organizations and institutions such as Morehouse College, the Harold Washington Library, the United Negro College Fund, and Tennessee State University, and in February of 2000 she was honored by Coretta Scott King at the Salute to Greatness Awards dinner at the King Center in Atlanta, Georgia.

"My prayer to God every morning on my knees is that the power that is in the universe should use my life as a vessel, or a vehicle, for its work," Winfrey told *Redbook*. "I feel positive about the future, but I do believe that we are in a time where there are forces of good and evil in TV making themselves known," she commented in *Good Housekeeping*. "I'm always trying to figure out how to take the power I have and use it." Her 1997 comment to her TV viewers is perhaps the best summary of Winfrey's approach to her work: "The opportunity to have a voice and speak to the world everyday is a gift. And I thank you for allowing me this gift."

Sources of Information

Contact at: Harpo, Inc.
110 N. Carpenter St.
Chicago, IL 60607
Business Phone: (212) 633–1000
URL: http://www.oprahshow.com

Bibliography

Bayles, Martha. "Bookends: Imus, Oprah, and the Literary Elite." *New York Times Book Review*, 29 August 1999.

Dedman, Bill. "Personal Business: Professor Oprah, Preaching What She Practices." *New York Times*, 10 October 1999.

D'Orio, Wayne. "Creating Oprah: The Magazine." *Folio*, 1 September 1999.

"Dumbing Up: How Oprah Has Influenced People to Read More Through Her Television Show." *The Economist*, 17 October 1998.

Farley, Christopher John. "Queen of All Media." *Time*, 5 October 1998.

"Harpo, Inc." *Hoover's Online*, 2001. Available at http://www.hoovers.com.

Johnson, Marilyn, and Dana Fineman. "Oprah Winfrey: A Life in Books." *Life*, September 1997.

"Oprah on Oprah." *Newsweek*, 8 January 2001.

Oprah Winfrey Fact Sheet. Available at http://www.oprah.com.

"Oprah Winfrey Named Most Powerful Person in Entertainment Industry." *Jet*, 9 November 1998.

"Oprah Winfrey Raises More Than $130,000 in a Special Benefit Auction At Amazon.com." *PR Newswire*, 7 October 1999.

"Oprah Winfrey Reveals the Real Reason Why She Stayed on Television." *Jet*, 24 November 1997.

"Robert Johnson and Oprah Winfrey Make Forbes' List of 400 Richest People in America." *Jet*, 22 October 2001.

"She's Gotta Have It: Oprah Winfrey Finds Her California Dream House, a $50 Million Estate with Plenty of Ocean Views." *People Weekly*, 2 July 2001.

Smolowe, Jill. "O On the Go: On the Road with Her Message of Uplift, America's First Lady of Chat Preaches the Gospel According to Oprah." *People Weekly*, 16 July 2001.

Taraborrelli, J. Randy. "How Oprah Does It All." *Redbook*, August 1996.

Taraborrelli, J. Randy. "The Change That Has Made Oprah So Happy." *Redbook*, May 1997.

Martin J. Wygod

(1940-)
WebMD Corporation

Overview

Martin J. "Marty" Wygod, chairman of the board of directors and CEO of the WebMD Corporation, is a financier and pharmaceutical executive who has developed a reputation as an incredibly savvy investor. He has often displayed a knack for anticipating investment fads and for turning huge profits on investments in a relatively short time. Throughout his career, Wygod has demonstrated a particular talent for buying small companies, merging them with other companies to form a new company, and then selling the conglomerate for enormous amounts of money.

Personal Life

Martin J. Wygod was born in New York City in 1940. He graduated from New York University, in New York City, in 1961 with a BS degree in business administration. After graduating, he worked as a stockbroker on Wall Street. Later, he formed his own brokerage company, which he sold for $10 million when he was 29 years old. In the early 1970s, he ran his own merchant bank and he eventually entered the health care field in the 1980s, focusing on cost–containment services. In 1992, the *Business Journal of New Jersey* named Wygod as the most highly paid executive in New Jersey, based on his annual salary of $459,028 plus stock options.

When Wygod was young, he developed a love for horses. As a teenager he walked horses at the racetracks at Belmont and Aqueduct. He is involved in racing, boarding and breeding thoroughbred horses, and is Pres-

Chronology:
Martin J. Wygod

1940: Born.

1961: Graduated from New York University.

1964: Invested in Computer Sciences Corp.

1977: Bought Glasrock Medical Services.

1982: Sold Glasrock for $125–million profit.

1983: Formed Medco Containment Services.

1992: Sold Medco to Merck.

1999: Established CareInsite Incorporated.

2000: Became co–CEO of WebMD.

2001: Named chairman of the board of WebMD.

ident of River Edge Farm, Inc., in Bedminster, New Jersey.

Career Details

For Marty Wygod, it all started with a $20,000 seed fund given to him by his mother. Through subsequent investments and acquisitions, he turned that relatively modest gift into approximately $50 million by the 1980s.

One of his early and profitable investments involved Computer Sciences Corporation. It was 1964 and computer technology was starting to develop and grow. Thus, Wygod believed that investors would soon be clamoring for computer software stocks. With that in mind, he put $75,000 into Computer Sciences. Wygod's instincts proved correct. By 1970, the investment returned a profit of $5 million. Wygod made himself even richer when he invested in the private stock of Computax, another computer company. When the company went public, the stock value increased from $10 to $100.

The mid–1960s were an especially prosperous time for the young financier. When he was 26 years old, he started his own brokerage firm and, three years later, he sold it for $10 million. Even though he could have chosen not to work for the rest of his life, Wygod remained active. In the 1970s, he ran a merchant bank.

It was during that period that he first became interested in health care investments. In 1977, he bought, along with fellow investors Bernie Marden and Albert

Weiss, a controlling interest in Glasrock Medical Services, an Atlanta company that produced medical plastics. Wygod's initial investment of $2 million turned into $125 million when, in 1982, he sold most of his interest in the company, along with interest in another company to a British company. Wygod was only 43 years old, and yet he still entertained no thoughts about early retirement. Instead, he used his profits to start Porex Technologies in January 1983.

By then, Wygod wanted to get into the mail–order prescription drug business. He had heard about National Pharmacies, a small, mail–order drug company that provided funded health benefit plans. National Pharmacies, he learned, had revenues of about $25 million and profits of about $400,000. Wygod also learned that it was part of financier Victor Posner's APL Corp. Wygod paid Posner $30 million in Porex stock and cash for it, and then set out to find business for his new company. He merged Porex with National Pharmacies to form Medco Containment Services Incorporated and, in six months, he had signed up several corporate–funded drug benefit plans, including those offered by Alcoa, General Motors and Georgia–Pacific.

Wygod based Medco in Fair Lawn, New Jersey, setting it up as a pharmacy–benefit management company focused on the sale of prescription medicines. With the help of financiers Michael Milken and Drexel Burnham, Medco's market value shot up to $290 million. (Eventually it would become a $2.6–billion company with a net income of $138 million.)

Wygod became more firmly entrenched in health care after his 1985 acquisition of Paid Prescriptions from Computer Sciences Corporation. The move gave Medco access to a national network of 40,000 drugstores that accepted its health care card.

By 1991, Medco had benefited from the robust growth of funded drug benefit plan coverage in the United States. In 1983, only about 5 percent of the population were covered. By the early 1990s, 40 percent were covered. Medco was mailing maintenance drugs through 900 funded benefit drug plans of corporations, unions, HMOs and state retirement systems. Also, it boasted of its exceptional service and lower prices. According to *Forbes's* Howard Rudnitsky, Medco "specialized in maintenance medication drugs," including prescriptions for "blood pressure, arthritis, diabetes, gastrointestinal problems and other chronic ailments." Rudnitsky added, "Medco claimed it was saving customers 20 percent or more" over retail pharmacy prices. At the time, "independent retail pharmacists and state pharmacy boards lobbied to restrict mail order drug services." However, they were unsuccessful.

To make itself even more attractive to customers, Medco created its Prescribers Choice program, which took its service to a higher level. Beyond the maintenance drugs, Medco, with the addition of the new program, was involved in therapeutic drug categories in which drugs were priced at different levels. This is how the program worked: If a prescription for the more expensive brand of drug in those categories was mailed to Medco, while an equivalent drug could be prescribed at a lower price, then a Medco pharmacist notified the prescribing physician. Obviously, some major pharmaceutical companies were uncomfortable with the program. But others felt is was better than cost–containment programs run by HMOs that offered reimbursement for only one or two drugs prescribed for a condition.

In 1992, Wygod made a deal with Merck and Company, a major pharmaceutical manufacturer, to buy Medco for $6.6 billion. As part of the deal, Wygod became a member of Merck's board of directors, and he continued running Medco. It turned out to be another sweet deal. When Wygod eventually left Merck toward the end of the decade, he took with him more than $250 million in stock and fees from the merger. The profit bought him a 100–acre ranch in Rancho Santa Fe, California.

By 1994, nearly 33 million Americans were covered by Medco–administered drug benefit plans, and Medco had become more than just a mail–order company. The major retail pharmacy chains and most independent pharmacies were accepting Medco's benefit card. The card enabled the user to get his or her prescription filled for little or nothing. Medco reimbursed the retailer and charged the benefit plan at its discount rates.

When Wygod left Merck, he became chairman of Synetic, an online medical company that subsequently merged with Medical Manager Corp. In May 1989, Wygod became chairman of the board of Medical Manager, a position he held until September 2000.

In 1999, Wygod, together with a group of former Medco colleagues, helped establish CareInsite Inc., an Internet–based health care corporation. The aim of the web site was to provide physicians, pharmacists, and payers with an Internet–efficient method of accessing and exchanging medical information, as well as claims processing and information retrieval services. CareInsite automated and put online the rules that govern managed care and dictate treatments and drugs that doctors can provide to their patients. Essentially, it was an online Medco. He served as chairman of the board of CareInsite from 1999 until September 2000.

Wygod scheduled an IPO for June 1999, with the system set to debut in strategic locations including New York City in September. Before that happened, however, Merck went to court in February 1999 to stop the site's implementation. Wygod and his partners, Merck claimed, had signed non–competition agreements with Merck's Medco pharmacy benefit manager. Wygod countered that the agreement expired in May 1999 and filed his own suit in July 1999. It was Wygod's contention that Merck was out to eliminate competition.

Despite Merck's lawsuit and the complexity of Wygod's business model, as well as the deeply troubled health care industry, CareInsite made it to the market. In February 2000, it was acquired by WebMD. As a result of other acquisitions and mergers, WebMD became the largest processor of electronic transactions in the health care industry. It was also the top consumer health care web portal as well as a leading provider of software services to physician offices.

Wygod, who entered WebMD via CareInsite, served as co–chief executive officer of WebMD from September 2000 until October 2000, sharing the CEO reins with Jeffrey Arnold. Wygod became sole chief executive of the Atlanta–based WebMD when Arnold resigned. At the time, WebMD, like many dot.com companies formed in the late 1990s, began experiencing significant financial trouble. In May 1999, its stocks had reached a high of $105 a share. Soon after, though, the value plummeted. Wygod took over at a time when WebMD required massive restructuring because of substantial overlap created when WebMD acquired several companies. Besides CareInsite, these companies included Envoy, Medical Manager, and OnHealth Network. The overhaul resulted in the company laying off more than 1,000 employees and eliminating many of its costly strategic alliances. The company said the restructuring could help it save about $250 million by the fourth quarter of 2001.

The restructuring plan included two phases. The first phase involved WebMD consolidating its offices and data centers, reducing marketing and promotional expenses, and eliminating redundant positions. The second phase involved consolidating sales forces and focusing on customer service, generating revenue, and eliminating non–strategic and non–profitable products and contracts.

In April 2001, Wygod was appointed chairman of the board of WebMD. He remained the company's CEO. He was confident the he and WebMD would finally be able to pull off what others couldn't: a profitable e–health enterprise. Wygod's goals, according to *BusinessWeek Online,* included "constructing tight digital links between insurers, doctors, and patients. Analysts said the measures could possibly save WebMD at least $50 billion in processing and other back–office costs."

One of the ways Wygod and WebMD hoped to get out of the red was to offer a new piece of technology: a hand–held device for doctors. The company would charge between $250 and $400 per month for a service that doctors can use to perform tasks that would include writing prescriptions, conducting lab inquiries, and monitoring billing.

Social and Economic Impact

Whenever anyone goes to the pharmacy to fill a prescription, and they present a card that provides them with a substantial discount, they are benefiting, in part, by

Martin Wygod's involvement in the health care industry and cost–containment practices. Wygod helped revolutionize medical billing when he got into the mail order prescription business in the 1980s. As chairman and CEO of Medco, Wygod turned the company into a major player in the mail–order prescription drug industry.

Besides making a great deal of money with his investment strategies, Wygod, in the process, essentially transformed the drug distribution business when he created Medco Containment Services, which was an intermediary between health plans and pharmacies. Medco administered the health plan's rules for prescribing medication. As a result, it saved the payers' money by monitoring doctor's prescriptions and indicated when less expensive drugs were available and appropriate.

Sources of Information

Contact at: WebMD Corporation
    669 River Dr., Ctr. 2
    Elmwood Park , NJ 07407
    Business Phone: (201) 703–3400
    URL: http://www.webmd.com

Bibliography

Barrett, Amy, "Marty Wygod Stuns Health–Care Industry—Again," *BusinessWeek Online.* 15 February 2000. Available at http://www.businessweek.com/bwdaily.

Burroughs, Don L., "Merck's Medicine Man." *U.S. News and World Report.* 21 February 1994.

Businessweek.com, "Marty Wygod," *Business Week Online.* 14 May 2001. Available at http://www.businessweek.com/magazine/content.

Rudnitsky, Howard, "Drugs by Mail." *Forbes* 15 April 1991.

Rudnitsky, Howard "There's Plenty for Everyone." *Forbes.* 11 February 1985.

Jerry Yang

(1968-)
Yahoo!

Overview

Jerry Yang teamed with fellow Stanford student David Filo to make the emerging World Wide Web a place that could be navigated. What started out as a part–time project mostly for their own benefit turned into Yahoo! Inc., the world's most used search engine for the Web, complete with personalized features for shopping, searching, connecting, and using the Internet.

Personal Life

Yang was born Chih–Yuan Yang in Taiwan in 1968, and was raised by his mother, Lily, an English and drama teacher, after his father died when he was only 2. He immigrated to the United States at age 10 with his mother, grandmother, and younger brother Ken, settling in the Berryessa suburb of San Jose. His mother moved the family in 1978 soon after the United States reestablished diplomatic ties with China so that her sons would not eventually be drafted into the Taiwanese army. Yang spoke Mandarin Chinese and hardly any English, but he honed his skills and became a straight–A student. He attended Piedmont Hills High School, where he was class valedictorian, played on the tennis team, and was elected president of the student body his senior year. He was admitted to Stanford University, where he obtained his bachelor's and master's degrees in electrical engineering in 1990, completing both degrees in just four years. There, he met David Filo, who is two years older than Yang, and the two became close friends. Yang and Filo went to Kyoto, Japan, together in a teaching program through Stanford during the early 1990s. While in Ky-

Jerry Yang (right), shaking hands with Jong-Yong Yun. (Gamma Liaison Network.)

oto, Yang met his future wife, Akiko, a fellow Stanford student of Japanese heritage who had grown up in Costa Rica. After returning to Stanford during the 1993–94 academic year, the two shared the office where they would spawn their creation.

Career Details

Doctoral students Filo and Yang in 1993–94 were involved with a project on the computer–aided design of computer chip circuitry. Their office was in a trailer containing a couple of computers, an array of golf clubs, and a sleeping bag. "I was terribly bored," Filo related in *San Jose Metro Online*. With their faculty adviser on sabbatical in Italy, the pair began fooling around with the World Wide Web, a computer network of sites, or "pages," that can be linked together, or "hyperlinked," featuring text and graphics. The Web can be used for uncountable tasks, from accessing photographs of celebrities to finding out more about a company to consulting academic papers. Early on, though, many of the sites were put there by creative graduate students like Yang. He posted a "home page" (a main site giving general information about a person or a company) with his picture, some golf scores, his name as it appears in Chinese, and hyperlinks to sumo wrestling sites.

One of the problems with this maze of pages on the Web was the lack of organization. Akin to entering a library without the aid of a card catalog or other system to direct patrons to the correct shelf, it was difficult, if not impossible, to locate information on the Web without a URL, or domain name. This is the address that begins with "http://" and usually contains the letters "www." for World Wide Web, followed by a word that somewhat describes the topic of the site, such as a person's or company's name, followed by a three–letter code indicating whether the site is a nonprofit site (.org), a company or personal site (.com), an educational institution (.edu), or a governmental branch (.gov). After becoming frustrated when they could not locate a page they found interesting, Filo and Yang began collecting these confusing codes for their favorite sites so that they could access them again. Others were doing this as well, with some companies publishing books listing numerous sites and describing the content. The Web, however, was changing and growing too quickly. Books could not adequately catalog the universe of information, and often sites would move to a different server (main computer) or change names, rendering the books outdated before they were published.

Filo and Yang came up with the idea of providing a kind of road map for online users. They designed some crude software that organized web pages into topics that could be used immediately to "link" to those pages. In early 1994, "Jerry's Guide to the World Wide Web" was born, and the name was later revised to "Jerry and David's Guide to the World Wide Web." The two provided the service free to all Stanford users. As their list grew, they began subdividing the topics to provide more structure. Later that summer, the system was dubbed Yahoo!, or Yet Another Hierarchical Officious Oracle.

Although Yahoo! wasn't the first search engine to exist, its categorization was vanguard, and it was the only one to offer whimsy. David Matsukawa in *Transpacific* explained, "Yahoo! had an attitude. It was start–up culture, not corporate. It talked to the folks making the pages. And it talked to the folks venturing out on the waves for the very first time. It said, 'Hey, the Internet is a fun place.'" They built it, and people came. By November 1994, 170,000 people a day were using the site. By 1998, Yahoo! was counting about 26 million unique visitors out of a staggering 1 billion "hits" per month, which averages out to more than 850,000 a day. America Online (AOL), the giant Internet access service, offered a buy–out, and deals poured in from Microsoft and Prodigy as well. Filo and Yang, working 20 hours a day for the sheer enjoyment of it, turned them all down.

However, Stanford was upset that Yahoo! was tying up their network with all the traffic. "They told us we were crashing their system and that we'd have to move the thing off campus," Yang stated in *San Jose Metro*. He and Filo began considering starting up a business from this hobby that was becoming overwhelming. "It was a really gradual thing, but we'd find ourselves

Chronology:
Jerry Yang

1968: Born.

1978: Immigrated to the United States.

1994: Established Yahoo! with David Filo.

1995: Dropped out of Stanford Ph.D. program; accepted $1 million in start–up funding from Sequoia Capital; began selling advertising space.

1996: Completed initial public offering of stock.

1998: Joined with MCI to provide Internet service.

1999: Yahoo!'s market value reached $70 billion.

2000: Stock peaked at $237 a share.

2001: Stock fell to $12 a share; market value fell to $5.2 billion.

spending more and more time on it," explained Yang in the *Metro*. "It was getting to be a burden." Not to mention, they weren't making money off their labor of love. A friend at Harvard, Tim Brady, devised a business plan for Yahoo! for a class project, which allowed the pair to really visualize the potential. Around March or April 1995, the partners packed up, dropped out, and moved on. They accepted a $1–million investment offer from Mike Mortiz at Sequoia Capital, a fund that had financed other Silicon Valley winners such as Apple and Oracle. Filo and Yang rented an office suite, ordered business cards defining themselves as Chief Yahoos, and hired a staff made up of graduate school friends and interns.

By the summer of 1995, Yahoo! was rapidly establishing itself in the online world. Netscape Navigator, the software most people were using to run the Web on their computers, added a "Directory" button on their interface that linked users to Yahoo! About that time, in August 1995, Yahoo! began selling advertising space on their pages. Initially frowned upon as "sell–outs" by Web purists who had worked to ban all commercial activity on the new technology, the practice was quickly accepted. Also that month, Yahoo! teamed up with Reuters news service, based in London, so that users could access news wire stories online with a click of a button. Since then, they have added other user–friendly elements, such as links to weather, stock quotes, phone listings, interactive maps, and loads of other information that Web users now take for granted. In addition, their graphics were bright and slick, and they later hired an expert to help with logical categorization.

Despite the ballooning success, Filo and Yang suffered some setbacks. A *San Francisco Chronicle* columnist kept a long–standing pessimistic view of the fledgling operation, even printing a litany of anonymous readers' comments that gushed over the legion of Yahoo! competitors, touting the superiority of the many other services. Then, in late 1995, Netscape ditched its Yahoo! link for that of a competing search engine, for which it was paid handsomely. Pundits predicted the off-beat little company would drown in the sea of other search directories, many of which had corporate backing. Though the Netscape back–out resulted in a temporary drop in the amount of traffic on Yahoo!, the numbers rose again. Yang and Filo also approached Netscape with the idea of offering their users a variety of search engines to choose from when they are surfing, instead of limiting them to only one that is willing to pay lots of money for the spot. Netscape agreed, deciding to charge each company a set amount to be included on its directory list.

Yahoo! also scored points when it developed a "personalized" page called My Yahoo!, which allows users to customize the Yahoo! page with all of the links that interest them the most. A popular culture aficionado, for example, could design a page with links to movie and music data and reviews, celebrity sites, online magazines, and more, whereas a business executive might want to pull up business periodicals and other relevant news sources, stock quotes, and competitors' home pages. Early in 1996, they started offering a directory tailored to children ages 8 through 14 called "Yahooligans!" They later added a "get local" option, which included sites containing information specific to certain cities in the United States.

Although the World Wide Web was booming in the mid–1990s, investors were still trying to figure out how to turn a profit. When Yahoo! first offered its stock publicly on April 12, 1996, the value at the end of the day was $848 million. However, by the end of the year, the stock was down 44 percent. *Fortune* magazine, in December 1996, reported that "Internet advertising doesn't seem to work. The search companies are generating paltry revenues and losing money." By late 1997, however, the outlook had drastically changed for the better. In September another *Fortune* writer remarked that Yahoo!'s "stock price has continued to defy gravity," and a *Computerworld* article two months later noted, "Yahoo is still the only search engine company posting profits several quarters in a row now and its revenue this year has more than doubled compared with last year's." As far along as March 1998, the only other search engine boasting a profit was Lycos.

Yahoo! was making money, not only by charging advertisers for space on its pages, but they were also getting a cut from online sales. For instance, if a customer ordered a volume from Amazon online booksellers, Yahoo! would get a flat fee and a commission from that sale. Because of this new avenue for profits, Yahoo! decided to cancel a pending deal with Visa, which would limit its ability to work with other merchants. Other partnerships have been established, however. In 1998, Yahoo! joined with MCI to become an Internet provider as well as a search provider. The strong brand name was expected to be a boon in wooing users. Also that year, Yahoo! teamed up with *National Geographic Traveler* magazine to offer information about cities of the world and expanded its television listings by partnering with Gist.

In 1999 Yahoo! had a market value of $70 billion, with Yang and Filo's wealth measuring approximately $7.5 billion. Revenues doubled in 1999 to $588.6 million, with a profit of over $61 million. The company has local operations functioning in 15 countries and has five times as many regular users as America Online has subscribers. However, by 2001 the bottom had dropped out of the economy, with Internet–related businesses suffering the quickest and most dramatic drops in value. Yahoo!'s market value dropped to $5.2 billion, and stock prices fell from a peak of $237 a share in January 2000 to $12 a share by November 2001. Marc Gunther of *Fortune*, noted, "A onetime darling of Silicon Valley and Wall Street, Yahoo has been hit by a triple whammy: the collapse of the dot–com bubble, a severely depressed advertising market, and the widespread economic uncertainties brought on by the September 11 terrorist attacks." Critics have also pointed to Yahoo!'s cavalier attitude toward advertisers who once would pay Yahoo!'s price for banner ads. Now Yahoo! must lure back advertisers who have moved on or now balk at high–priced space on the site.

Social and Economic Impact

Meanwhile, Yahoo!'s main men, Yang and Filo, have remained pretty much the same. At the start of their mammoth operation, the two paid themselves around $40,000 a year and lived in modest apartments. Yang continued dressing in preppy chinos and button–down shirts, even to business conferences. Though Yang eventually bought a nice home in Los Altos, California, and a new Isuzu Rodeo, he told *Forbes*, "It's nice to know that your family is provided for, but the money isn't that important." He is still very close with his family, spending every Sunday with his brother and mother at her house for dinner. Throughout the company's rise, Yang functioned as the public relations man, happy to grant interviews and appear on television, whereas Filo was reluctant to be in the spotlight, spending most of his time behind the scenes and often sleeping on a blanket in his office. The two have also been known to donate money to help disadvantaged people learn about computers.

According to Brent Schlender of *Fortune*, "Given Yahoo's huge popularity—100 million people browse its offerings monthly—it's no stretch to say that Jerry and Dave's company, as much as any other, fomented the Internet revolution." Acknowledging it was a phenomenon that started out as a part–time distraction, Yang is hesitant to close the books on the significance of his company. He told *Fortune*, "Maybe in a few years we'll be better at this, but at the moment it's really hard for us to objectively evaluate ourselves. I've been very afraid to have Yahoo placed in a historical context this soon, because I don't think we've done it yet. The Yahoo story is still being written."

As long as people are using the Web, it seems there will be a need for the creative, continuously expanding search service of Yahoo! Although there are other engines, Yahoo! has staked its place, perhaps because of its co–founders' passion for their work, which shows in the product, and also because it is easy for even Web novices to use. Yahoo!, claimed Yang in *San Jose Metro*, "conveys the sense of fun involved in all this, the sense of adventure. That is what really distinguishes our site. It is a place for adventures. A place to discover things."

Sources of Information

Contact at: Yahoo!
    3400 Central Expressway, Ste. 201
    Santa Clara, CA 95051
    URL: http://www.yahoo.com

Bibliography

"A Couple of Yahoos." *San Jose Metro*, 11 April 1996. Available at http://www.metroactive.com.

Colvin, Geoffrey. "Shaking Hands on the Web." *Fortune*, 14 May 2001.

Elgin, Ben. "Inside Yahoo!" *Business Week*, 21 May 2001.

Goodell, Jeff. "Jerry Yang." *Rolling Stone*, 30 March 2000.

Gunther, Marc. "The Cheering Fades for Yahoo." *Fortune*, 12 November 2001.

"Jerry Yang." *Newsmakers 1998*, Issue 3. Farmington Hills, Mich.: Gale Group, 1998.

O'Brien, Jeffrey M. "Behind the Yahoo!" *Brandweek*, 28 June 1999.

Schlender, Brent. "How a Virtuoso Plays the Web." *Fortune*, 6 March 2000.

Carl Yankowski

(1948-)
Palm, Inc.

Overview

Carl Yankowski's career is a litany of company giants: over his thirty–year career, he has worked for such well–known brands as Proctor & Gamble, Memorex, PepsiCo, General Electric, Cadbury Schweppes, Polaroid, and Sony. His last stop was with Palm, Inc., the leader of the handheld computing industry.

Personal Life

Carl J. Yankowski was born in 1948 in Butler, Pennsylvania. On June 11, 1977, he married Patricia Pamela Petraglia. They live in Dover, Massachusetts. Along with electronics and aviation, his hobbies include classic automobiles—she is a member of Porsche of America Club—gardening, antiques, and woodworking. He was educated at the Massachusetts Institute of Technology, receiving a Bachelor of Science degree in electrical engineering and management in 1971.

Career Details

Yankowski began his career in 1971 as a computer analyst for Proctor & Gamble. However, he soon found that he enjoyed selling products and ideas rather than analyzing data. Therefore, in 1973 he transferred to a position as a marketing executive, where he remained for the next three years. Included in his responsibilities were marketing campaigns for Pringle and Duncan Hines cake mixes. In 1976 he was hired by Memorex as a product

manager and was part of the development of the highly successful "Is It Live or Is It Memorex?" campaign. After just a year, he left Memorex in 1977 and joined PepsiCo as a marketing manager. In 1978 he became the director of marketing for PepsiCo, and a year later he was promoted to group director of marketing. While at PepsiCo, Yankowski worked on the three–year marketing ploy The Pepsi Challenge, which resulted in the only time that Pepsi outsold Coca–Cola.

Yankowski left PepsiCo in 1981 to become the general manager of marketing for General Electric, where he remained through 1982. While at General Electric, he helped develop the "Spacemaker" line of products and the "We Bring Good Things to Light" campaign. In 1983 Yankowski changed jobs again, this time to become the president of Sodastream. In 1986 he was named president and CEO of Sodamate. Sodastream and Sodamate are owned by beverage producer Cadbury Schweppes. In 1988 Yankowski became a corporate vice president of Polaroid. During his four years at Polaroid, Yankowski's efforts resulted in substantial increases in profits and revenue in the business imaging market globally. In 1992 he was promoted to chairman of the AsiaPacific division of Polaroid and helped establish Polaroid's AsiaPacific headquarters.

In 1993 Yankowski left Polaroid to become president and chief operating officer of Sony, Inc., a position he retained for the next five years. During his tenure with Sony, Yankowski's strong leadership and marketing skills propelled the company forward. Focusing on the development and marketing of new products, Yankowski increased the company's revenues from $6 billion to more than $10 billion—although not everything Yankowski touched turned to gold. In fact, while at Sony, Yankowski oversaw the development of one of the earliest versions of a handheld computer. The Sony Magic Link was a small lightweight device that ran on a newly developed portable operating system developed by a software startup company. However, the product, with wireless e–mail capabilities, was a flop. Yankowski later expressed his disappointment, telling *eWeek,* "I failed with Magic Link. That was mine. I invested $12 million."

In 1998 Yankowski was named president and CEO of Reebok International Ltd, renamed Reebok Unlimited during his tenure. Although he spent less than two years at Reebok, Yankowski led the company through significant restructuring and global expansion. Yankowski implemented his strongest skills at Reebok—longterm vision and a clear, objective company mission. As Reebok's leader, Yankowski was critical of the manner in which Reebok had followed in the footsteps of Nike, its chief competitor, which resulted in the myriad of very similar products, one indistinguishable from the other. In 1999 Yankowski told *SGB UK*: "There has been a certain sameness in the technology that has existed over the last 20 years, and that is a long time to run down the same street. The market is struggling with a wall of white and it is very difficult for the consumer to figure out the

Carl Yankowski. (AP/Wide World Photos/Richard Drew.)

benefits from many different products. . . .We have chased the competition too much and tried to be a mini–Nike or Adidas, rather than Reebok."

Yankowski spent much of his time at Reebok focusing on global expansion and reorganization. He also pushed the company to develop innovative strategies for the future designs of the products and their marketing. In an effort to make Reebok a global company, Yankowski traveled extensively to Reebok's markets around the world. Over the first nine months of his tenure, he visited about 90 of Reebok's global markets. His experiences included a ride on an elephant and hanging a python around his neck. Because of Nike's dominance

Chronology:

Carl Yankowski

1948: Born.

1971: Hired by Proctor & Gamble as an analyst.

1973: Moved to Proctor & Gamble's marketing department.

1976: Became a production manager for Memorex.

1977: Joined the marketing department of PepsiCo.

1981: Became general manager of marketing for General Electric.

1983: Hired by Cadbury Schweppes to run Sodamate and Sodastream division.

1988: Named corporate vice president of AsiaPacific market of Poloraid.

1993: Hired as president and chief operating officer of Sony.

1998: Named chief executive officer of Reebok International Ltd.

1999: Became chief executive officer of Palm, Inc.

2001: Resigned from Palm, Inc.

in the U.S. markets, Yankowski was looking to take advantage of the global possibilities for his company. Although he continued to pursue Nike as the market leader in the United States, Yankowski saw global expansion as vital to the future of his company. To objectify Reebok's commitment to a market with no boundaries, the company's name was changed to Reebok Unlimited.

One of his first acts as CEO was to restructure the company into six strategic business units: performance footwear, classic footwear, kids footwear, apparel, business development, and retail. Yankowski made his expectations for each division clear: be accountable for the U.S. and global markets and be accountable to customers. He laid out five operating principles to achieve these goals: focus on customers; innovate and be willing to take risks; look to the future, not to the past; always go beyond what the customer expects; and build up a positive corporate environment based on team building. Yankowski also worked hard to get to know his employees and to be sure that the right people were in the right position. As he explained to *Business Week*: "This is why I travel so much to ensure that I personally have

the opportunity to learn more about each country. I try to know and ensure that everybody from the janitor to the board of directors is saying that this is the direction in which Reebok is moving. Then, everyone is proud to move in the same direction. It is as simple as that."

Yankowski also envisioned a new future of the sports shoe industry as technology continued to make advances. "If you think about it," Yankowski told *Business Today*, "in the 1950s, 1960s, and 1970s, the basic shoe was the sneaker. In the 1980s and the 1990s, we discovered segmentation, which meant we had running shoes, walking shoes, tennis shoes, and adventure shoes. And now in 2000 and beyond, we will shift to the era of personalization of products, and focus the benefit of technology on the product." According to Yankowski, the athletic shoe of the future will be custom made to each customer, offering a perfect fit based on electronic measurements of each individuals foot. To usher in this new age of shoes, Yankowski adopted what he termed "humanity positioning" under the catch phrase "Are You Feeling It? " The goal was to redirect consumers' thoughts to the comfort of the shoe and to the love of sports and away from the dominance of athlete hero worship used so extensively in marketing campaigns during the last two decades of the twentieth century.

In the fall of 1999, Yankowski began being courted by the leadership of 3Com, of Santa Clara, California, who wanted Yankowski to head Palm Computing. A world leader in providing computer networking services and equipment around the world, 3Com had inherited Palm when it bought U.S. Robotics in 1997. Palm, the leading manufacturer of handheld computers, was originally created by Donna Dubinsky and Jeff Hawkins who later sold the company to U.S. Robotics and then left to create its main competitor, Handspring. With Palm's products flying off the shelves, garnering some 75 percent of the market share, and 3Com already committed to spinning it off as an independent company, Yankowski could not refuse the challenge: On December 13, 1999, he became the new CEO of Palm.

When Palm was cut loose by 3Com in early March 2000, its initial public offering of stock pushed prices from $38 a share to $95 a share. According to *Money*, that left Yankowski holding more than $1 billion in stock options. Over the first year, the new CEO received high marks from analysts. In November 2000, *VARBusiness* reported, "Yankowski has made remarkable progress by successfully taking Palm public and transforming that 3Com division into an independent company with a $30 billion–plus market cap. He has repositioned the company from a manufacturer of personal digital devices to a supplier of wireless Internet solutions. . . .He's even helped transform Palm from an emerging U.S. operation to a cash–positive world leader." *The Economist* reported, "[Yankowski] is a big, dressed–in–black gadget guy with just the right combination of the consumer–marketing experience and technology savvy to straddle the gap between computing and consumer electronics."

Palm operates under two different umbrellas. First, it makes many models of handheld computers. As the first successful handheld introduced to the market in 1996, Palm almost instantly acquired nearly 90 percent of the market. Over the next several years, competitors ate into that number, but in 2001 Palm still retained a 56 percent market share. Second, Palm owns and licenses the Palm operating system (OS), used by many of its competitors, including Acer, Handspring, IBM, Nokia, Samsung, and Sony. Palm then licenses developers to write software applications that operate on the Palm OS. In 2001 nearly 175,000 developers—up from just 30,000 in 1999—registered with Palm to develop software. By the end of 2001, the work of these independent agents had resulted in more than 12,000 software applications and 100 add–on devices.

The first bad news came in March 2001 when Palm announced that it was being affected by the economic slowdown. Because sales had been so strong the previous year, Palm sped up production but then found itself with too much inventory and not enough buyers. Then in May the company reported a delay in the production of its newest devices, the Palm m500 and m505. Now, not only were the shelves full, but they were full of soon–to–be–outdated models—and with no new models to replace them. In the first five months of 2001, Palms stock price plunged 78 percent.

Some analysts acknowledged that many of the problems that emerged in 2001 were either due to the economy and out of the control of Yankowski or already in place within the company when Yankowski arrived. Nonetheless, the high praises heard in 2000 evaporated and criticism of Yankowski escalated. He was blamed for focusing on the corporate market rather than the consumer market; he was accused of not paying close enough attention to the internal inefficiencies of his management team; and he was criticized for pushing new innovation without a plan for its implementation. As early as June 2001, questions were being raised about Yankowski's future at Palm. Rob Cihra, an analyst at ABN Amro in New York, told the *Wall Street Journal*, "Palm's management is under the gun to prove they should even be at the company. And ultimately, the buck stops with their head guy. Will the same management team be in place in a few months? Maybe, maybe not."

Although Yankowski told the *Wall Street Journal* that he was "up to the challenge," the company's situation failed to improve. In a speech in July 2001, according to *Twice*, Yankowski told his audience, "We realize there are things we could have done better but many of the problems were market–wide." "Of course," he added, "it is certainly fair for us to be scrutinized but we're heading in a good direction. The Palm economy is vibrant and growing—and committed." The same month, Palm split its hardware and software divisions, establishing the Platform Solutions Group, which handles the Palm OS platform, as a wholly owned subsidiary. Despite the brave talk and continued changes, by mid–October 2001, the stock price, which started the year at $28.75 a share, had fallen more than 90 percent to $2.09.

On November 8, 2001, the seemingly inevitable occurred—Yankowski stepped down as Palm's CEO. In a press release picked up by the *PRNewswire*, "Yankowski stated that once the company was divided into two separate entities, he would be left with only half under his control. My role has changed, and it no longer matches my aspirations." He concluded, "It has been an honor to lead Palm." Despite widespread concurrence among analysts that Yankowski was pushed out, he did not leave empty–handed. Although details of his severance package are undisclosed, he was entitled to a lump–sum payment equal to two times his annual salary ($666,667 in fiscal 2001), along with stock options and paid health benefits. Following the November 8 announcement of his resignation, Yankowski did not discuss his future plans.

Social and Economic Impact

Yankowski clearly saw the future of computing in the development of the handheld computer. According to *Twice*, Yankowski told a convention audience in January 2001 that "the future of handheld computing had arrived. Handheld computing has changed the way we work and live," Yankowski declared. "The handheld will do for computing what the Walkman did for music." He went on to say that, although handhelds would probably never completely replace the desktop personal computer, handhelds were making new inroads, while the mainline computer industry had stagnated on creating faster and bigger machines with little regard for the usability of their products. "Computers were never designed with average people in mind," Yankowski told his audience. "Why should a consumer know what a C drive is? The computer is great for spreadsheets and word processing, but you don't have instant access to information you need daily. "

Because the handheld computer allows the user mobility, a major jump in the access to information takes the form of access to the Internet. Yankowski was aware of the importance of Internet capabilities for the handheld industry. In an interview with *Interactive Week*, Yankowski argued that "a tethered PC model has dramatic limitations in terms of the mobile shifts that we're seeing in our culture today. People are on the go and want to access information anytime, anywhere. . . .It's very difficult to get that, even with a larger notebook or a smaller notebook. But you can get that with a very thin client elegantly tied wirelessly to a server or Internet–type structure, and people are gravitating towards this. They are gravitating to e–mail on these devices, Internet access on these devices, [and] personal schedule management."

Yankowski's enthusiasm and far–reaching predictions were not without merit. The industry has pushed technology to the edge and caused an incredible out-pouring of creative and technical energy to make computing an everyday, every minute, everywhere affair. As a result Palm generated more than $2 billion in revenue in 2000. The holiday season of 2000–2001 showed a growth of 165 percent over the same period of the previous year. Yet suddenly and with tremendous force, the bottom dropped out. Now the question remains: can the handheld transform itself into a common personal and professional accessory, such as the cell phone has become? Can Palm create an image and a product that is not seen by the business or consumer markets as a handy yet extravagant expense, making it the first on the list of purchases to be crossed off the list when the economy is slow? Like Yankowski, the future of Palm and the handheld computer industry in general remains in question.

Sources of Information

Bibliography

Baskin, Sarah. "Interview: Palm's Carl Yankowski." *Interactive Week*, 23 February 2001.

"PBS CEO Exchange: Episode 202: Carl Yankowski." *PBS, Inc.*, 2001. Available at http://www.pbs.org/wttw/ceoexchange/episode_202/

"Carl Yankowski—CEO, Palm." *VARBusiness*, 13 November 2000.

"Former Sony Exec to Head Palm." *ZDNet News*, 2 December 1999. Available at http://www.zdnet.com.

Fried, Ian. "Palm Chief Admits Mistakes." *CNET News*, October 2001. Available at http://www.cnet.com.

Hartnell, Neil. "Are You Feeling It?" *SGB UK*, 18 March 1999.

McCormick, Gavin. "Palm CEO: Stay Out of Hardware." *Boston.Internet.com*, 22 February 2001. Available at http://www.boston.internet.com.

"One Palm Flapping." *The Economist*, 2 June 2001.

"Online, Everywhere, All the Time: How It Will Change Our Lives." *Pop!Tech*, 1921 October 2001. Available at http://www.poptech.com.

"Palm CEO Carl Yankowski Resigns." *PRNewswire*, 8 November 2001.

"Palm Chief Executive Quits." *CNET News.com*, 9 November 2001. Available at http://www.cnet.com.

"Palm, Inc." *Palm, Inc.*, 2001. Available at http://www.palm.com.

Rafi, Natasha. "The Ledger." *Money*, 1 May 2000.

Safer, Will. "Yankowski Says Palm Evolving into Personal Network Devices." *Twice*, 9 July 2001.

Scoblete, Greg. "Yankowski Bows Me-Commerce in CES Keynote." *Twice*, 22 January 2001.

Skaria, George. "Never Ask What Is or Was, But Always Ask What Can Be. " *Business Today*, 22 July 1999.

Tam, Pui–Wing. "Carl Yankowski is Under Pressure to Turn the Ailing Palm Around." *Wall Street Journal*, 4 June 2001.

Tam, Pui–Wing. "Palm's CEO Quits Amid Slowing Sales, Mounting Losses." *Wall Street Journal*, 9 November 2001.

Zimmerman, Michael R. "For Palm, What a Difference a Year Makes." *eWeek*, 15 December 2000.

Who's Who in the World, 1991–1992. Wilmette, IL; Marquis Who's Who, 1990.

James M. Zimmerman

Overview

James Zimmerman is the chairman and chief executive officer (CEO) of Federated Department Stores, Inc., an Ohio–based company that owns such well–known upscale department stores as Macy's and Bloomingdale's. Zimmerman, who had been with the company since 1965, took over leadership of the company in May 1997.

Personal Life

James M. Zimmerman was born in 1944. He graduated from Rice University in Houston, Texas, with a Bachelor of Arts degree in liberal arts in 1966.

Zimmerman ranked 143rd on *Forbes'* "800 Best Paid CEOs" for the year of 2001, up from his 197th place rank in 2000. Among the rankings of the retail industry, Zimmerman placed fifteenth in 2000, with a base salary, not including bonuses, of $1.25 million, and he moved up to seventh place within the retail industry in 2001. Zimmerman, who has been a member of the Board of Directors since 1988, serves on the Executive and Finance Committees. He also serves on the Board of Directors for Goodyear Tire & Rubber, Chubb Corporation, Convergys Corporation, and H. J. Heinz Company.

Career Details

Zimmerman began his four–decade–long career with Federated Department Stores when he joined Fed-

(1944-)

Federated Department Stores, Inc.

Chronology:

James M. Zimmerman

1944: Born.

1965: Began career with Federated Department Stores, Inc. at Foley's store in Houston, Texas.

1984: Appointed chairman of Rich's Department Store in Atlanta, Georgia.

1988: Named president and chief operations officer of Federated.

1990: Federated filed for bankruptcy.

1994: Federated acquired Macy's Department Stores.

1997: Appointed chairman and chief executive officer of Federated.

1999: Purchased Fingerhut, the nation's second largest catalog–based retailer.

2001: Ranked 143rd on *Forbes'* list of 800 highest–paid executives.

---

erated–owned Foley's Department store in Houston, Texas, in 1965. Zimmerman rose through the ranks of Federated's management. Eventually, he was appointed president of Rich's Department Store in Atlanta, Georgia, which is also owned by Federated. In 1984 he added the position of chairman to his job title. In 1988 Zimmerman became president and chief operations officer of parent company Federated, which was at the time saddled under a heavy debt load. In 1990 Federated applied for bankruptcy restructuring, and by 1992 the company had reorganized to include under its umbrella 220 department stores in 26 states with annual sales of $7 billion. In December 1994 FDS acquired R. H. Macy & Company, making it the largest department store retail in the United States.

In May 1997 Zimmerman was appointed chairman and chief executive officer, replacing Allen Questrom, who resigned after having served in those positions since 1990; Terry J. Lundgren replaced Zimmerman as president of the company. By the end of 2001, Federated was operating 460 stores in 34 states, along with Guam and Puerto Rico. Federated–owned stores include Bloomingdale's, The Bon Marche, Burdines, Goldsmith's, Lazarus, Macy's, and Rich's. Federated also operates mail–order and electronic businesses for Bloomingdale's By Mail, bloomingdales.com, and macys.com. In 1999

Federated acquired the Fingerhut Companies, Inc., a direct–marketing and electronic commerce business. Federated appears on *Fortune*'s list of the 100 largest corporations in the United States.

Federated came into existence in the early 1990s, when a group of retailers decided to band together under one corporation. Its flagship businesses have long been Bloomingdale's and Macy's, with Macy's celebrating its 75th Macy's Thanksgiving Day Parade in 2001. The corporation hit a major stumbling block in 1988—the same year that Zimmerman arrived at corporate headquarters—when Canadian real estate developer Robert Campeau acquired the company in a leveraged buyout in a poorly executed deal that saddled the company with an incredible debt load equal to 98 percent of its total capital. Two years later, Federated was forced to file for bankruptcy. In 1990 Questrom, previously a Federated executive, was called back to the company to help Zimmerman and chief financial officer Ronald W. Tysoe restructure and reorganize some $8 billion of debt.

Over the next six years, the executive team methodically brought Federated back from the brink. They focused on consolidating divisions, centralizing administrative functions, and greatly increasing the technology necessary to handle the management of the large volume of inventory and distribution. Cost–cutting measures were put in place, and the savings produced were used to renovate stores and lower prices of goods. Then, in 1994, Federated purchased Macy's, a high–end department retailer with 123 stores. Analysts declared the acquisition to be a brilliant move. The purchase positioned Federated as the largest retailer in the United States. Macy's provided a profitable addition to the Federated family, and it appeared Federated was moving in the right direction again.

However, the financial outlook took a significant hit just eight months after the acquisition of Macy's. In a highly criticized move, Questrom organized the purchase of Broadway, an 82–store chain of department stores based in California. With Broadway just days away from filing for bankruptcy, Questrom doled out a whopping $1.6 billion for the chain, which was widely considered to be in run–down shape. The $1.6 billion purchase price reflected a cost of $8 a share, whereas shares were trading at $2 on Wall Street. The purchase also increased the company's long–term debt to $5.5 billion, equal to 60 percent of total capital. Commenting on the Broadway acquisition, Chris Ohlinger, president of Service Industry Research Systems, which studies the retail industry, told *Fortune*, "Either Federated is trying to corner the market on submediocre retailers, or they've adopted the high–risk, Evel Knievel style of retail expansion." Largely due to the close proximity of time between the purchase of Macy's and Broadway, the combined cost of which totaled $5.7 billion, Federated posted a loss of $63 million on sales of $13 billion in the twelve months ending October 31, 1996.

By 1996, 52 of the Broadway stores had been converted to Macy's stores, six became Bloomingdale's stores, and the others were closed or sold. Questrom's far–reaching plans did not mix well with the coming economic recession. The following year, he resigned as CEO and was replaced by Zimmerman, who stepped into a difficult situation. Soon Broadway was not Zimmerman's only concern; in 1998 Federated was forced to pay $10.6 million to settle complaints that it had wrongly collected debts from credit card holders who were bankrupt. His purchase in 1999 of Fingerhut, a direct distributor with catalog and Internet sales, was another challenge to be dealt with. Fingerhut, the second largest catalog retailer behind J. C. Penney, was losing money, and Zimmerman was forced to restructure and downsize operations. Plans were announced in late 2000 that Federated would eliminate approximately 550 employees from Fingerhut's payroll, with expected savings of $40 million annually.

In February 2001 Federated decided to close its 19 New Jersey– and New York–based Stern stores, announcing that most locations would be converted to a Macy's or a Bloomingdale's; five stores would remain closed. Zimmerman has also had to address the problems related to Federated's Web presence. At the end of November 2001, Zimmerman announced that Federated would close its Bloomingdale's e–commerce Web site. The site was instead revamped to provide marketing support for Bloomingdale's retail stores and Bloomingdale's By Mail catalog. Macy's e–commerce Web site was also scaled back; its section of merchandise—especially clothing—was reduced, but increases were made to bridal, home, gifts, and jewelry, which have proven to be the most successful categories. In conjunction with the changes in the Web site, Federated also discontinued the distribution of a Macy's catalog, which has served primarily as a marketing vehicle for the e–commerce business. In a statement released by the Associated Press, Zimmerman noted, "In the current economic climate, it is important that we use our available resources in the most productive way possible." The changes eliminated 100 jobs. Analysts have speculated that Federated may have previously overcommitted to the Internet, noting that fashion items are tough to sell because the customer can't try on items to check for fit. The return rate for clothing can reach 40 percent.

Federated's outlook for the future is mixed. Assessing financial performance in fiscal year 2000, which ended January 2001, Federated's Web site states, "[T]he year 2000 was challenging and disappointing. While the department store segment performed acceptably versus our expectations—and very well compared to the retail sector as a whole—it was not enough to justify being satisfied with our overall results." Federated posted a net loss of $184 million for the 53 weeks of fiscal year 2000. Despite the tough economic conditions brought on by a recession in 2001. Federated also had some bright spots: In July 2001 it paid $200 million for Liberty House, Hawaii's largest retailer with approximately 20 stores.

Also most of the loss posted in 2000 can be attributed to one–time costs associated with the downsizing of Fingerhut and the closing of Stern's; sales actually increased in 2000 by 3.9 percent to $18.4 billion, and the company managed to post a profit in the third quarter of 2001. In 2001 Federated earned praise for holding strong in a weak economy. According to *Reuters Business Report*, "Investors ... applauded [Federated's] ability to keep inventories down in the difficult economic environment, thus limiting exposure to margin pressure from heavy mark-downs." Bill Dreher, a retail analyst for Robertson Stephens, told *Reuters*, "They have effectively cleared merchandise without giving away the store."

Social and Economic Impact

Zimmerman has his work ahead of him. Department stores have been losing ground to discount and specialty stores since the beginning of the 1990s. At the end of the 1980s, department stores accounted for 60 percent of all department and discount sales combined; by 2001, discount stores commanded 75 percent of the market. As discount stores, such as Target and Wal–Mart, began to dot the landscape and draw business from all social classes, not just the lower economic end, department stores made shifts in their inventory. They moved away from the areas where they were least able to compete: electronics, books, furniture, and toys. In place of these items, stores stocked an increasing amount of clothing, sales of which have not grown as fast as the rest of the economy. Also many discount stores offer conveniences that department stores do not, including food sections, vision centers, pharmacies, photo shops, and banking centers. Department stores such as Federated also faced stiff competition from specialty stores, such as The Gap, Abercrombie & Fitch, Circuit City, and Bed, Bath, & Beyond, that can offer a wider selection usually at lower prices.

Federated plans to face the future with new innovations and services that set it apart from its competitors. One of the first steps will be to redesign floor layouts, so the stores are more easily navigated and draw attention to certain items. Checkout will be centralized and while standing in line to pay, shoppers will be entertained with FedTV, a closed–circuit station featuring news and store promotions. Federated has already built a prototype for how the future stores may look: a Federated–owned Lazarus store in Columbus, Ohio, features a supervised children's play area, where children can be dropped off so adults can shop more easily. The store also provides mammogram screens in conjunction with a local cancer hospital.

The economic recession that dug in after the terrorist attacks on the World Trade Center and the Pentagon on September 11, 2001, has made consumers more conservative with their money. Analysts now debate whether the shift to discount stores is a temporary situation brought on by consumer insecurity or if it will result in a permanent change in the landscape of the retail industry. According to the *Boston Globe*, the jury is still out on the future of the big retailers, but there is reason to believe they will be around for some time to come: "[D]on't count out department stores just yet," remarked Chris Reidy and Kathy McCabe of the *Boston Globe*. "Federated [has] adapted to the more competitive landscape. By keeping inventories lean and costs low, a department–store chain can remain profitable...." That is exactly what Zimmerman is banking on.

Sources of Information

Contact at: Federated Department Stores, Inc.
7 W. 7th St.
Cincinnati, OH 45202
Business Phone: (513) 579–7000
URL: http://www.federated–fds.com

Bibliography

Driver, Anna. "Federated Profit Down, But Shares Rise." *Reuters Business Report*, 14 November 2001.

"Executive Business Briefing." *United Press International*, 15 August 2001.

"Federated Department Stores, Inc." *Hoover's Online*, 2001. Available at http://www.hoovers.com.

"Federated History." Federated Department Stores, Inc., 2001. Available at http://www.federated'fds.com.

"Federated Reworks Internet Businesses." *AP Online*, 29 November 2001.

"Federated Tops Wall Street Forecast." *AP Online*, 14 November 2001.

Grant, Linda. "The Broadway Deal Will Haunt Questrom: He's Making Big Bets With Other People's Money." *Fortune*, 5 February 1996.

Hobson, Katherine. "Miracle on 34th Street." *U.S. News & World Report*, 26 November 2001.

"James Zimmerman." *Forbes Online*, 2001. Available at http://www.forbes.com.

Reidy, Chris, and Kathy McCabe. "Discount Retailers Slowly Stealing Shoppers Away From Department Stores." *Boston Globe*, 4 December 2001.

Summers, Monica. "Discount Stores and Off–Price Retailers on Thursday Posted Solid October Sales as Consumers, Overwhelmed by Job Cuts and a Looming Recession, Steered Away From Department Stores." *Reuters*, 8 November 2001.

Who's Who in America: 1997. New Providence, NJ: Marquis Who's Who, 1996.

Who's Who in Finance and Industry: 1996–1997. New Providence, NJ: Marquis Who's Who, 1995.

Master Index

Master Index